D0122217

MOZART
IN VIENNA
1781–1791

MOZART
IN VIENNA
1781-1791

VOLKMAR BRAUNBEHRENS

Translated from the German by
TIMOTHY BELL

GROVE WEIDENFELD
New York

Published by Grove Weidenfeld
A division of Wheatland Corporation
841 Broadway
New York, NY 10003-4793

Published in Canada by
General Publishing Company, Ltd.

First published in German under the title *Mozart in Wien* by R. Piper, 1986

Library of Congress Cataloging-in-Publication Data

Braunbehrens, Volkmar.
[Mozart in Wien. English]
Mozart in Vienna, 1781–1791 / Volkmar Braunbehrens; translated
from the German by Timothy Bell. — 1st ed.
p.   cm.
Translation of: Mozart in Wien.
Bibliography: p.
Includes index.
ISBN 0-8021-1009-6
1. Mozart, Wolfgang Amadeus, 1756–1791.   2. Composers—Austria—
Biography.   3. Music—Austria—Vienna—18th century—History and
criticism.   I. Title.
ML410.M9B7813   1989
780'.92'4—dc19
[B]   88-13940
                                                               CIP
                                                                MN

Designed by Irving Perkins Associates

Manufactured in the United States of America

Printed on acid-free paper

First Edition 1990

1 3 5 7 9 10 8 6 4 2

CONTENTS

v

Contents

TRANSLATOR'S NOTE

The English translations of the Mozart family's correspondence are the standard versions by Emily Anderson, *The Letters of Mozart and His Family*, 3d ed. (London: Macmillan, 1989), except for a few excerpts from letters included in the complete German edition but not found in Miss Anderson's volume. Spelling and punctuation have been Americanized, and minor changes have been made in the interest of clarity or concision. I have used the monetary denomination "florins" throughout the text and in the letters, instead of the interchangeable "gulden." Grateful acknowledgment is made to Macmillan, London and Basingstoke, for permission to use Miss Anderson's translations. The translation of Mozart's poem on the death of his bird (Chapter 7) is Marcia Davenport's, from her *Mozart* (Avon, 1979). Otherwise all translations are my own.

I wish to thank Lewis and Michelle Forward, Karin Kroha, and the author, Volkmar Braunbehrens, for their invaluable assistance.

MOZART
IN VIENNA
1781-1791

PREFACE

Mozart, the wunderkind celebrated throughout Europe, a child showered with gifts by the empress, the pope, kings, and princes, was a
forgotten man when he died at thirty-five and was buried in an
unmarked pauper's grave. Thus, with many variations, has Wolfgang
Mozart's life always been presented to us: as a brilliant rise to success
followed by a single, uninterrupted period of decline. This version is
found in novels, children's books, biographical films, and even works
that claim to be scholarly. During the last 130 years of Mozart research, many details of his short life have been investigated, clarified,
and incorporated into the biographical literature. However, the key
points have remained basically the same since the publication of the
first major biography, Otto Jahn's *W. A. Mozart* (1856–59). We learn
from Jahn that Mozart's early success was followed by contempt and
humiliation in Salzburg, a short period of acclaim as a virtuoso pianist
in Vienna, failures and scheming at the Vienna Opera, the withdrawal
of support by his noble patrons, who suddenly left him in the lurch,
bitter poverty and desperate petitions for money, and finally the lonely
pauper's grave, to which not even the Freemasons accompanied him.
All this may have a certain fascination, but it does not stand up to
historical scrutiny.

The problem is partly due to the primary sources on Mozart's life.
They are numerous for the period of his youth, from which an unusu-
ally large number of the Mozart family's letters have been preserved.
After Mozart's move to Vienna (1781), the amount of surviving family

correspondence declines sharply, and after the death of Mozart's father, Leopold, this source runs completely dry. No other regular correspondence takes its place, for most of the people with whom Mozart had close personal relations lived in Vienna, and he rarely exchanged letters with them. And from nine years of marriage there are only thirty-six surviving letters to his wife, from whom he was seldom and only reluctantly separated. Half of these letters were sent to Baden near Vienna, the spa where Constanze Mozart took several cures during her husband's last years.

Everything relating to Freemasonry disappeared from the records at an early stage, probably because of fear of investigation by the secret police. And there is a further complication: we do not know of all the concerts and musical events in which Mozart took part, even in a major musical center like Vienna. The newspapers ran no public announcements, to say nothing of reviews, and publisher's advertisements have survived in greater quantities than the works they advertised. Nor can it be verified that everyone who claimed to have been Mozart's pupil actually took lessons with him; some may simply have used his name for their own advancement.

Thus we do not have nearly as much authentic source material for Mozart's adult life as we do for his early years. Since the beginning of the nineteenth century the resulting lacunae in his biography have been obscured by legends and anecdotes, all stemming from questionable sources—hearsay or oral accounts that were written down decades after the fact and elude any attempt at historical verification. These embellishments have found their way much too easily into the biographical literature on Mozart and can still be encountered today—a trusted and cherished ballast that romantically transfigures our picture of Mozart and is certainly useful for marketing purposes.

Even scholarly biographies of Mozart have contributed to this situation. For although we are indebted to them for much detailed research, they have nevertheless evaded important questions and ignored essential material, especially regarding Mozart's life in Vienna. His alleged impoverishment, his Masonic activities (and especially the lodge where he was a member), the circumstances of his personal life, his close contacts with people on the fringes of society, his strikingly friendly contacts with Jews (who at the time were still widely ostracized in Vienna), and finally his supposed pauper's burial—to name only a few of the most important points—have hardly been dealt with by musicologists; at best they have been taken up by people outside the discipline.

Musicology has obeyed the laws of the marketplace even regarding Mozart's name, and against its own better judgment still retains the romantic "Amadeus"—a blemish that marks even the recent complete edition of Mozart's works. Mozart never called himself Amadeus but always used simply Amadé (or Amadeo), in an attempt to translate his baptismal name Theophilus (Gottlieb, or "love of God"). It is therefore quite appropriate that the theater and cinema associate themselves with the name "Amadeus," thereby announcing that they want nothing to do with Mozart's actual life. "Amadeus" stands for the embellishments, legends, and fantasies about Mozart.

These have no place in this book, and no attempt will be made here to refute them individually. Even now, we know little about Mozart, and to remind the reader frequently of that fact seems to me a more thorough form of biographical investigation than pure conjecture about possibilities and probabilities. I feel it is time to remove the patina, encrustations, and later deposits from Mozart's monument—carefully, and always with the curiosity that accompanies such restoration work.

Biographers invariably try to present the most complete possible picture of their "heroes"—that is their task. Often, however, they simply overlook the gaps in their knowledge and try to give an appearance of probability to what could equally be considered improbable. They "psychologize," although the most exact knowledge of a person is necessary in order to explain his psyche; they embellish where the sources are especially meager (which is tantamount to a well-meant distortion); and they pursue lines of thought that enable them to control their heroes like marionettes. The danger with every biography is that it can fail to capture the essence of its subject by getting too close where distance is necessary. Too much distance, on the other hand, makes it impossible to explain anything.

To understand the outward circumstances of an individual's life requires a knowledge of his everyday environment as well as the historical processes that condition it. To put it plainly: what was happening outside Mozart's house while he was composing inside?

What did Mozart hear discussed in the tavern, at the salons, or at lodge meetings? To write a biography one must also write cultural history, and the theme "Mozart in Vienna" affords an excellent opportunity to do so, both at close range and from a distance.

As a Mozart biography, this book restricts itself to the last eleven years of his short life: the period of the mature artist, of the great operas following *Idomeneo,* and of his successful concert career without the aura of wunderkind, when he was finally independent and could make his own decisions. Almost ten of Mozart's first twenty-five years were spent traveling; his longest journeys were made when he was still a celebrated child prodigy. But during his Vienna years (1781–91), he took only a few short trips, usually for only six to eight weeks. His continued presence in the capital makes it appropriate to consult sources in which Mozart's name does not appear, and of which Mozart research has consequently made little use: sources on the political and social history of Vienna, the structure of the population, cultural development, contemporary political issues, and so forth. For Vienna—that unique European metropolis, heart and center of the far-flung Habsburg empire—such sources are particularly abundant.

What makes Mozart's Vienna period especially fascinating, and in fact had considerable effect on his work as a composer, is that it coincided exactly with the reign of Emperor Joseph II (1780–90). The Josephine decade was a period of unprecedented "enlightened" reform under the aegis of a centralized autocracy, an attempt to establish reason and enlightenment from above, through the power of the sovereign. The cornerstones of reform were a state church oriented toward a practical religion that would seek to control the monasteries and curtail the influence of Rome; the elimination of aristocratic privileges as part of a plan to establish a more just system of taxation; and the introduction of personal freedoms ranging from the abolition of censorship to tolerance laws for minorities. European intellectuals marveled at these internal developments in the Austrian empire. Yet during this same Josephine decade hopes of reform were gambled away, breeding a crisis that threatened to bring down the Habsburg monarchy, while in France—though under much different circumstances—the Revolution began and the people learned to take charge of their own fate.

Mozart followed these historical developments with lively interest. All of his Viennese operas contained so much politically inflammatory material that they barely conformed to the requirements of the censor and sometimes offended aristocratic sensibilities. Mozart remained committed to Freemasonry at a time when such activity was no longer opportune and was under close surveillance by the secret police, which shows that he considered it his duty to take a clear stand. And he was one of the first independent, self-employed musicians to compose for a musically educated public from *all* social levels.

This book, then, is also a biography of the Josephine decade in Vienna. It investigates the historical setting—living conditions, political conflicts, the economic and social balance of power—in which Mozart pursued his life and livelihood. The self-realization of one individual is thus seen in light of Viennese conditions and prevailing societal norms. Against this background, our knowledge of Mozart takes on a different meaning and a new interpretation.

Technical and aesthetic analysis of individual works has been deliberately avoided. It is always an awkward task to describe musical content; music must be heard. And our modern impressions of Mozart's music do not belong in a book with historical objectives. Moreover, to consider even a single work would require that many familiar listening habits be carefully laid aside; such a task would go beyond the scope of this book and pose its own problems. To give just one example, consider the case of one of Mozart's most popular piano concertos, which erroneously carries the title *Coronation* Concerto (K. 537, dated February 24, 1788). In Mozart's manuscript the second movement begins with the piano playing the eight bars shown below.

Nothing is notated for the left hand, nor are there any rests. Mozart improvised the missing line at the piano but never wrote it down.

When this work is performed in the concert hall, one usually hears the following.

One may find this accompaniment pretty, appropriate, feeble, childish, superfluous, "Mozartian," or not—it is in any case not by Mozart. The accompanying voices are missing not only here but also in most of the solo part for all three movements of the concerto. We have no idea who filled in these lines for the first edition of the printed score (1794); in any case, it was done at the instigation of the publisher Johann André. (The pianist Friedrich Wührer once dared to depart from the traditional but inauthentic version and play a different accompaniment, for which he was roundly castigated by music critics—an example of the normative power of the "tried and true.") Moreover, in Mozart's score the timpani and all the wind instruments are marked *ad libitum,* which means that the work was also conceived for string orchestra alone. As a result the wind parts are, for Mozart, unusually restrained and lacking in individuality. Would not the solo piano part, which is in any event sketchily notated, necessarily have sounded different as well? Would not Mozart have improvised differently when playing with the reduced orchestra? And does not the name *Coronation* Concerto create false expectations of a "festively brilliant" work, although the piece was not at all intended for coronation festivities but more than likely for a small and intimate setting?

This example shows that each work needs to be investigated separately. The reconstruction of historical dimensions says nothing about the interests and possibilities of modern interpretation in the concert hall, and an aesthetic discussion is itself an interpretation that cannot deny its historical remoteness from the work itself. Accordingly, this book deliberately confines itself to the portrayal of Mozart's external life in Vienna. It seeks to replace careless certainty with new perspectives.

All quotations from Mozart's letters include the date given in the complete edition, *Briefe und Aufzeichnungen,* edited by Wilhelm A. Bauer and Otto Erich Deutsch (Kassel, 1962–75). The Köchel catalogue numbers are cited from the seventh edition (Wiesbaden, 1965). When two numbers are cited for one work—for example, K. 367a/349—the first number (367a) reflects the chronological classification according to the latest historical research, while the second (349) is the original number assigned by Ludwig von Köchel, which is still used today in concert programs and radio broadcasts.

Chapter 1

ARRIVAL IN VIENNA

IN THE COACH

On March 12, 1781, Wolfgang Mozart traveled to Vienna on the orders of his employer, Count Hieronymus Colloredo, the archbishop of Salzburg, who was there visiting his sick father, Prince Rudolf Joseph Colloredo. The ecclesiastical prince was accompanied by a splendid entourage displaying all the pomp of an absolute sovereign. He had with him not only his personal servants but also a chamberlain (Count Karl Arco), the chairman of his court council, his adviser in religious matters, and his own kitchen brigade, down to the *Zuckerbäcker*, or confectioner. The entourage also included a small band of musicians. These fawning Salzburg courtiers were probably not unhappy about the journey, for Vienna provided diversion and entertainment in contrast to their restricted life in Salzburg, and offered a source of additional income for the musicians.

Mozart, however, needed a special summons, and it cannot have been a very gracious one. In early November 1780, with his employer's permission, Mozart had gone to Munich, where he composed, rehearsed, and staged his opera *Idomeneo* at the Hoftheater (electoral court theater). But he had already overstayed his leave by almost three months, and Count Colloredo's reaction to such impropriety was far less friendly than that of his predecessor, Count Sigismund Christoph Schrattenbach, whose patience the Mozart family had similarly tried on more than one occasion. Since the archbishop's journey was unforeseen, Mozart, still in Munich, had received an urgent command to leave for Vienna at once. It was not so much that Count Colloredo was keen to have his own musical entertainment; rather, he wanted to present "his" musicians to the fervently musical Viennese society. It was a matter of prestige, and in this regard Mozart was certainly his most important attraction.

Mozart's extended leave of absence was a clear provocation. The premiere of *Idomeneo* had, it is true, been postponed until January 29, but Mozart had no reason to stay in Munich beyond the beginning of February. Perhaps he thought his absence had hardly been noticed, since the archbishop had already left for Vienna at the end of January. But Colloredo had left word in Salzburg asking Mozart to follow him to Vienna immediately, and when there was no response, he had sent the necessary orders directly to Munich. By then it was already March. Meanwhile, Mozart had the support of his father, who had traveled to the premiere at the end of January, as had several Salzburg acquaintances of the Mozart family. Leopold Mozart, with his daughter Maria Anna, stayed in Munich until March 12—with one small difference: *his* presence was not required during the archbishop's absence. The understanding between father and son was not without significance for the ensuing clash with their employer. The Mozart family was united in its disapproval of the archbishop, and in his letters Wolfgang fulminates uncontrollably and sometimes unjustly against Count Colloredo. No one could be sure that these letters would not be secretly intercepted, opened, and read—as did in fact happen.

It is reasonable to assume that the sojourn in Munich with his son had also encouraged Leopold Mozart to consider plans for the future and ways to get out of Salzburg. In Salzburg the possibilities for developing a musical gift such as Mozart's were not merely limited but totally inadequate, and this problem was only partially attributable to the archbishop. Salzburg had neither a good orchestra nor an opera house, and musical activity was restricted to the small segment of society with musical interests. There was no wealthy aristocracy to provide organizational and financial support, and concerts at the court consisted mostly of chamber music. Under Colloredo even church music was reduced to a minimum, for the archbishop was an advocate of ecclesiastical reforms that called for the renunciation of all outward splendor in favor of a more practical piety.

The Mozarts reacted to this situation by making personal accusations against Colloredo, as if conditions in Salzburg were entirely the result of his dictatorial whims. Yet as far as church music was concerned, it must be noted that Mozart did not at all consider himself primarily a composer of sacred works. Significantly, he wrote almost nothing for the church after leaving Salzburg (the Mass in C Minor remained unfinished, the Requiem was a lucrative commission that could hardly be refused); and the last sacred pieces written there make a distinctly embarrassing impression, their occasional "pretty passages" notwithstanding. This is particularly true of the church sonatas, which under Colloredo could not last longer than three minutes if they were intended for ordinary services. Such external limitations usually led Mozart to a greater intensity in his composition—a concentrated and loving attention to detail—but that is missing in these church pieces. By way of comparison, the late German dances and minuets are occasional works of an entirely different caliber.

But Mozart's métier was above all opera, for which there were absolutely no possibilities in Salzburg. Wolfgang had his father's complete support in his operatic ambitions as well, and Leopold had previously made inquiries about a suitable appointment for his son. At the time news was just breaking about plans for a Nationalsingspiel (national opera) in Vienna, which was to be created under the personal supervision of the emperor. The elder Mozart had asked the advice of Franz von Heufeld, a Viennese acquaintance, and received the following answer:

> If your son will take upon himself the task of setting to music some good German comic opera, submit it to the discretion of His Majesty, and then await the decision, he might well receive the emperor's patronage if his work finds approval. In this case his presence would be necessary. Your son should have no worries regarding Benda and Schweitzer. I can assure you that neither of them will receive a commission. Their

reputation here is not so great as elsewhere. Perhaps even Wieland no longer holds these people in such high esteem since he has been in Mannheim. I have read a letter of his from the 5th of this month in which he states that Mannheim has changed all the opinions he ever had about music. (January 23, 1778)

It was certainly unusual to compose without a commission or any occasion for a performance, but in the meantime Mozart had indeed set to work and written two acts of such a German opera; he had even brought them with him to Munich. In this endeavor he most surely had his father's encouragement, for in Munich they could see if there might be a position open at the Hoftheater.

Mozart thus found himself making the break from Salzburg without knowing where he would go. The Munich *Idomeneo* was like a public audition for him, since his earlier Italian operas were hardly known north of the Alps and were in any event more or less conventional early works, limited by tradition and totally unsuitable for a major break-through as a successful opera composer. Mozart knew how to take advantage of the *Idomeneo* commission and did not reject his father's help. Since the librettist for *Idomeneo*, Giambattista Varesco, lived in Salzburg and Mozart was already in Munich, he brought his father in to negotiate the text revisions. Mozart wanted to make numerous and fundamental changes in the libretto, and it was only with great effort that his wishes could be made clear to Varesco. For Mozart had developed precise and definite ideas about opera dramaturgy and was not prepared to forgo his own involvement with the libretto. In this situation Leopold Mozart not only communicated his son's proposed revisions but also acted as a sounding-board in detailed matters of dramaturgy, composition, and instrumentation. Never before had Wolfgang's collaboration with his father been as harmonious as it was during the preparation of this opera for Munich.

Idomeneo is not an example of the new Singspiel form but rather of the courtly *opera seria*. However, what Mozart achieved within the older form was in essence entirely new, for he ignored the antiquated and well-worn traditions of the *opera seria* wherever possible. Conditions in Munich were excellent, and Mozart had enough self-confidence to take advantage of them. Above all, the orchestra was technically and musically the best he could hope for, and the musicians held him in high regard. By drawing on this wealth of orchestral possibilities, and especially by exploiting the superb wind section, he was able to compose in such a way as to establish the preeminence of music over text in opera based on the orchestral writing. For the recitatives he made highly dramatic use of this new approach, in sharp contrast to the customary tedious practice, which relied mainly on *recitativo secco*. The singers, and particularly the men, who were not up to the highest standards, were gratified by a compromise that took their needs into account without violating Mozart's firm sense of the priority of compositional considerations: he made concessions to their voices and tailored the arias to their individual capabilities, while in the choruses and ensemble numbers, which here assumed a most unusual significance, he let himself be guided purely by the musical and dramatic requirements. As a result, the dramatic construction of this opera created an impact such as *opera seria* had never known— one essentially foreign to the genre. For this reason it has rightly been said that with *Idomeneo* Mozart triumphantly brought down the curtain on the *opera seria* form.[1]

Mozart was very pleased with working conditions in Munich. Free from his irksome obligations to the despised archbishop, he was able to devote himself almost exclusively to his opera, and he was especially happy to have at his disposal one of Europe's finest orchestras, which he knew from Mannheim and in which he had good friends. (The Mannheim elector Karl Theodor became Elector of Bavaria in 1778 and moved his residence to Munich, taking almost all of the famous Mannheim orchestra with him.) After the premiere of *Idomeneo*, Mozart took in some of Munich's *Fasching* (Shrovetide carnival) and even managed a visit with his father and sister to their relatives in Augsburg. All in all, the Mozarts had made full use of the unofficially extended leave of absence. Consequently, Mozart must have had mixed feelings on receiving the archbishop's order to leave for Vienna: the lovely weeks in Munich were over (years later Mozart still considered this time the happiest of his life). On the other hand, the prospect of spending some time in Vienna was very enticing.

With *Idomeneo* Mozart had thoroughly proved himself as an opera composer, although in Vienna an entirely different kind of opera was in fashion. But that had also been provided for: the two acts of *Zaide* were in his luggage and could certainly be shown to interested parties as chance permitted. This Singspiel, however, still lacked the final scene, in which the "unexpected meeting of father, son, and daughter as slaves" was to find a happy resolution. But that would be no great amount of work. The colorless Singspiels of Anton Schweitzer, although they contained charming music, were dramatic failures and definitely not on a level with *Zaide*, in which Mozart had sought to clarify and structure the dramatic conflicts by the most novel means. He had made use principally of Georg Benda's "invention," the melodrama, a combination of musical accompaniment and spoken texts that was especially suited to moments of drama and excitement. He had with him a fair copy of the *Zaide* score, written by himself in an especially fine and delicate hand—presumably because he wished to show it to the emperor. We do not know whether Mozart was still planning to finish this score or intended the unfinished work merely as an example of his competence to take on an entirely new commission.

Mozart's high opinion of Vienna was by no means unjustified. It was based on the musical interests of the court, the high nobility, and amateur musicians, who were to be found among the nobility as well as the middle class. Yet it also betrayed a certain degree of optimism and wishful thinking, for despite the many musical opportunities, Mozart's previous experiences of Vienna had not all been encouraging. However easy it may have been to make public appearances and perform in private homes, it was still difficult to get binding commitments for bigger engagements, to compete on equal terms with local musicians, and to become established.

On the first journey to Vienna, in the autumn of 1762, the main purpose had been to present the child virtuosi at the imperial court (Mozart was not yet seven, his sister was five years older). In this respect the journey had been a complete success. Wolfgang, in his uninhibited way, had played with the cute little archduchesses and had even jumped into Empress Maria Theresa's lap. But the trip was above all an investment in the future—to make him known. (It was also overshadowed by a severe illness, a painful erysipelas, which was followed immediately after his return to Salzburg by an attack of rheumatic fever—early signs of the malady whose symptoms would appear and reappear until his final illness just over twenty-eight years later.)

The second Viennese journey (1767–69) was also marked by a life-threatening illness; at age eleven Mozart contracted smallpox during an epidemic. He survived this dangerous disease through his family's brave and judicious care and the unselfish aid of friends. But even apart from smallpox, an unlucky star seemed to rule the entire sixteen-month journey. Leopold Mozart's ambition for his highly gifted son had gone too far, for nothing less than an opera commission for the twelve-year-old child would satisfy him. He wrote back to Salzburg:

> So it is an *opera buffa*, but not a short one, for it is to last about 2½ or 3 hours. . . . What do you think? Is not the reputation of having written an opera for the Viennese theater the best way to enhance one's credit not only in Germany but also in Italy? (January 30, 1768)

Thus, not a short work in one act, like Pergolesi's *La serva padrona*, but a full-length comic opera! The idea had indeed come directly from the emperor, but there was no advantage in that. For the Vienna opera was leased by a private entrepreneur at his own risk, and this man did not have the courage to commission Mozart. So the projected opera, *La finta semplice* (to a text after Carlo Goldoni), fell victim to theater intrigues; there were plenty of composers in Vienna who did not want their "market" spoiled by a child of twelve. In any event, Mozart was definitely overtaxed by this work and could at best try to imitate the fashionable operatic models of the time—which were no guarantee against dramatic weaknesses.

A third Viennese journey, undertaken in the summer of 1773, lasted only ten weeks and again brought no results. Once more there was vague interest in an opera contract, but otherwise Mozart's reasons for making the trip (this time alone with his father) are unclear, and his letters allude to them very obscurely. The sojourn itself is described to the family in Salzburg evasively, with frequent promises to give a full report on his return, so that most of what happened remains a mystery. All we can say is that there appears to have been no contact with the nobility. But what does that imply? Why was this journey made in midsummer when the nobility left Vienna for their country estates in June at the latest and did not return until September? That made concert appearances impossible from the start. And why did the Mozarts not stay longer? What did they actually do during those weeks other than accept the many dinner invitations they received from various acquaintances? We do not know, and no clear picture can be drawn from the available information. Altogether, however, these first three journeys to Vienna cannot be considered very successful.

But now the situation was totally different. Mozart went to Vienna with no clearly defined goals, as a court musician in the employ of his archepiscopal sovereign, not voluntarily, yet not entirely against his will. In his current circumstances he had virtually nothing to lose and everything to gain. It was obvious that Mozart would give up his confining and unpromising position as court organist in Salzburg at the slightest opportunity. Doubtless there was also an agreement in principle about this with his father. And Count Colloredo himself must have been aware that he could not keep a Mozart for long. He tried to retain musicians at his court as cheaply as possible—on the one hand, because he was stingy, and on the other, because he had definite ideas about how much he was prepared to pay them. If they were not willing to accept this meager salary, they could seek their livelihood elsewhere. The archbishop was a very rational man in such matters, a fact that probably increased the Mozart family's irritation and wounded their pride, as did the frequent and often puzzling irascibility the archbishop had displayed since assuming office.

Mozart left Munich by mail coach on March 12, 1781, bound for Vienna by way of Altötting, Braunau, Lambach, Linz, and Sankt Pölten. The journey took five days. In addition to the fare, the coachman had to be tipped according to fixed rates, and there was an additional charge for extra baggage. Food and lodging cost approximately 1 florin per day. All in all one had to spend roughly 50 florins to cover a distance of 250 miles (Munich–Vienna). If we consider that Mozart received a yearly salary of 450 florins as court organist in Salzburg, we can begin to imagine how expensive it was to travel in the eighteenth century, and it becomes clear why so many travel books of the period describe journeys on foot, even all the way across the Alps to Italy. But Mozart was entitled to a travel allowance from the archbishop and regarded this journey more or less as a business trip— which in no way diminished the miseries of the mail coach. Mozart had already complained about the trip to Munich.

For I assure you that none of us managed to sleep for a moment the whole night through. Why, that carriage jolted the very souls out of our bodies! And the seats! Hard as a rock! After we left Wasserburg I really

thought I would never get my behind to Munich in one piece! It became
quite sore and no doubt was fiery red. For two whole stages I sat with my
hands dug into the upholstery and my behind suspended in the air. But
enough of this; it is all over now, though it will serve me as a warning
rather to go on foot than to drive in a mail coach. (November 8, 1780)

Mozart, however, had ample experience as a traveler and in his
twenty-five years had seen more of Europe than most young men his
age. He had spent more than a third of his life—almost ten years—
away from home, mainly on concert tours with his sister, accompanied
by the entire family and a servant. The children were displayed as
wunderkinder, and their father acted as impresario and prudent trustee
of this treasure trove of talent and precocity. They had their own
carriage, which certainly made traveling easier and more comfortable
on these long, arduous tours, and also allowed them greater independence in planning their itinerary. They did not, after all, want to go from
place to place passing the hat like wandering musicians, showmen,
peddlers, or street performers. Rather, the point was to establish an
international career, to make a name at the music-loving courts of
Europe, to obtain musical commissions for Wolfgang as he grew older,
to attract attention by giving concerts in the major cities, and to take the
measure of the greatest and most important musicians of the time.

The family's long journey to Paris and London (1763–66) had lasted
three and a half years, and they had been to Vienna three times. In
addition, Wolfgang had made three journeys to Italy with his father,
already in search of opera commissions; these lasted a total of two
years. And finally there was his first attempt to strike out on his own—
the second journey to Paris via Munich and Mannheim (1777–79),
this time in the company of his mother. Its main purpose was to seek
employment—in Munich, Mannheim, Paris, or anywhere else—or at
least to earn a respectable living as a traveling virtuoso and composer.
This trip had been a failure in every respect: it brought Mozart neither
a position nor serious prospects for one and was a financial fiasco,
leaving a debt of 700 florins. Worst of all, his mother died suddenly in
Paris after a short illness, and he had to make the burial arrangements
alone, without his family. This first attempt at an independent, autonomous existence was decidedly unsuccessful, and Mozart had every
reason to proceed much more carefully the next time.

Vienna offered very favorable conditions, and Mozart was apparently determined to make use of the opportunity without giving up the security of his unpleasant but permanent job in Salzburg. In Vienna he had numerous friends and acquaintances who could help him. And he loved the free and easy style of living associated with extravagant wealth. The many rich families that spared no expense to indulge their fondness for music, aristocrats who maintained their own orchestras and in some cases even small opera ensembles, private and public concerts that were open to any good musician and promised considerable earnings, not to mention the many amateur musicians who eagerly sought music lessons to improve their skills (especially on the fortepiano)—none of these could be found in Salzburg.

Mozart began his trip to Vienna, which was to become his new and permanent home, in obvious high spirits. After only a few miles he exchanged the hard seats of the mail coach for the soft cushions of a post-chaise.

I rode in the mail coach as far as Unterhaag—but by that time my backside and its surrounding parts were so sore that I could endure it no longer. I was intending to proceed by *ordinaire*, but Herr Escherich, a government official, had also had enough of the mail coach and gave me his company as far as Kemmelbach. (March 17, 1781)

From Kemmelbach to Vienna Mozart was alone in the coach, which meant that he had to bear the entire cost himself. Traveling "first class" in this manner was naturally much more expensive, for now, in addition to tipping the driver, he had to pay for two horses and wagon grease, the total sum easily amounting to 80 florins or more. Shortly before eight o'clock on the morning of March 16, Mozart arrived at Vienna's main customs house, where his baggage was subjected to a rigorous search; since he was coming from outside the Habsburg dominions, he was treated as a foreigner. He had quite a bit of luggage with him, including a complete wardrobe—some of which had even been sent to him in Munich—and an assortment of music and scores that added considerable weight. This time it was by no means as easy as it had been eighteen years earlier, when the six-year-old Mozart had wrapped the customs officials around his little finger. His father had described the scene:

One thing I must make a point of telling you, which is that we quickly got through the local customs and were let off the chief customs altogether. And for this we have to thank our Master Woferl. For he made friends at once with the customs officer, showed him his clavier, invited him to visit us, and played him a minuet on his little fiddle. Thus we got through. The customs officer asked most politely to be allowed to visit us and for this purpose made a note of our lodgings.

(October 16, 1762)

Tired from his long journey, Mozart finally cleared customs and was soon on his way to present himself to his employer, Archbishop Colloredo, who was lodging at the House of the Order of Teutonic Knights.

"MON TRÈS CHER AMY!"

Mozart had hardly arrived before the commotion began. He was immediately reminded just who was still paying his salary, first by his accommodations: the other Salzburg musicians who had come to Vienna with the archbishop—the concertmaster Antonio Brunetti and the castrato Francesco Ceccarelli—were staying outside the city, whereas Mozart was given "a charming room in the very same house where the archbishop is staying," which drew from him the ironic exclamation *"Che distinzione!"* This special treatment amounted to keeping Mozart under guard, so to speak, and was surely a reaction to his willfully extended leave of absence.

Equally clear in intention was the order to play a concert at 4:00 P.M. on the day of his arrival. It was evidently not a matter for discussion that Mozart had risen at two o'clock that morning to travel the last stretch from Sankt Pölten to Vienna. His fatigue was of no interest: he had to play. "Twenty persons of the highest rank" had accepted invitations to this afternoon concert—presumably because of Mozart. And on the evening of the first day there was another example of the archbishop's peculiar treatment of his employees: no evening meal was provided.

We do not meet for supper, but we each receive three ducats—which goes a long way! The archbishop is so kind as to add to his luster by his household, robs them of their chance of earning and pays them nothing. (March 17, 1781)

The growing rancor toward the archbishop is unmistakable, but the facts are another matter. Three ducats (13½ florins) for a missed meal is more than generous, since an evening meal in a tavern cost 1 or 2 florins (or was this amount intended for the whole week?). And for the concert on the day of his arrival Mozart received 4 ducats from the archbishop and another 5 ducats from the archbishop's father—in other words, an extra honorarium of 40½ florins, over and above his annual salary of 450 florins! For the moment he made no mention of this income to his father, instead expanding on his complaints about bad treatment.

We lunch at about 12 o'clock, unfortunately somewhat too early for me. Our party consists of the two valets, that is, the body and soul attendants of His Worship, the contrôleur, Herr Zetti, the confectioner, the two cooks, Ceccarelli, Brunetti, and—my insignificant self. By the way, the two valets sit at the top of the table, but at least I have the honor of being placed above the cooks. It's almost like being back in Salzburg! A good deal of silly, coarse joking goes on at table, but no one cracks jokes with me, for I never say a word, or, *if I have to speak*, I always do so with the utmost gravity; and as soon as I have finished my lunch, I get up and go off. (March 17, 1781)

Mozart is not concerned with whether a musician is more important than a valet, but exclusively with his own person. Nevertheless he sends his father greetings from the very people he has just disparaged. Once he even says of his musical colleagues, "I do not count the other two as having anything to do with me" (April 4, 1781). The arrogant stance that emerges from these letters does not present a very flattering picture of Mozart. There is also a decided undertone of propaganda against the archbishop, with which Mozart hopes to prepare his father gradually for the inevitable parting of ways. In the process he gives superb descriptions of court behavior.

What you say about the archbishop is to a certain extent perfectly true—I mean, as to the manner in which I tickle his ambition. But of what use is all this to me? I can't subsist on it. Believe me, I am right in saying that he acts as a *screen* to keep me from the notice of others.

What distinction, pray, does he confer upon me? Herr von Kleinmayr and Bönike have a separate table with the illustrious Count Arco. It would be some distinction if I sat at that table, but there is none in sitting with the valets, who, when they are not occupying the best seats at table, have to light the chandeliers, open the doors and wait in the anteroom (*when I am within*)—and with the cooks, too! Moreover, when we are summoned to a house where there is a concert, Herr Angerbauer has to watch outside until the Salzburg gentlemen arrive, when he sends a lackey to show them the way in. On hearing Brunetti tell this in the course of conversation, I thought to myself, "Just wait till I come along!" So the other day when we were to go to Prince Galitzin's, Brunetti said to me in his usual polite manner: "You must be here at seven o'clock this evening, so that we may go together to Prince Galitzin's. Angerbauer will take us there." I replied: "All right. But if I'm not here at seven o'clock sharp, just go ahead. You need not wait for me. I know where he lives and I will be sure to be there." I went there alone on purpose, because I really feel ashamed to go anywhere with them. When I got upstairs, I found Angerbauer standing there to direct the lackey to show me in. But I took no notice, either of the valet or the lackey, but walked straight on through the rooms into the music room, for all the doors were open—and went straight up to the prince, paid him my respects and stood there talking to him. I had completely forgotten my friends Ceccarelli and Brunetti, for they were not to be seen. They were leaning against the wall behind the orchestra, not daring to come forward a single step. If a lady or a gentleman speaks to Ceccarelli, he always laughs: and if anyone at all addresses Brunetti, he blushes and gives the dullest answers. Oh, I could cover whole sheets if I were to describe all the scenes which have taken place between the archbishop and the two of them since I have been here and indeed before I came. I am only surprised that he is not ashamed of Brunetti. Why, I am ashamed on his account. And how the fellow hates being here! The whole place is *far too grand* for him. I really think he spends his happiest hours at table. (March 24, 1781)

Mozart undoubtedly assumed that his father would share his animosity toward the archbishop, for the Mozarts considered themselves more than just a family of court musicians. But this feeling of superiority was definitely more pronounced in the son than in the father, who had long since resigned himself to his limited circumstances and no longer saw any chance of escaping the narrow world of Salzburg; he would be glad simply to receive a reasonable pension. Wolfgang blithely expresses his own higher self-esteem when he writes about the fees demanded by a Salzburg colleague.

> Fiala has risen a thousand times higher in my estimation by refusing to play for less than a ducat. Has not my sister been asked to play yet? I hope she will *demand* two ducats. For, as we have always been utterly different *in every way* from the other court musicians, I trust we shall be different in this respect too. If they won't pay, they can do without her—but if they want her, then, by Heaven, let them pay.
>
> (March 24, 1781)

Mozart was not prepared to compromise, and certainly not as an employee of the archbishop.

In financial matters Leopold Mozart certainly shared his son's extreme opinions, and he had admonished him on previous occasions not to sell himself too cheaply. But he certainly had mixed feelings about Wolfgang giving up his position in Salzburg. During their long journey to Mannheim and Paris, the father had tirelessly tried to find a position for his son and had prudently cultivated all possible contacts. After the failure of these plans and the death of his wife in Paris, however, he apparently felt that he had done enough for his children and that they should now be thinking of him in his declining years. As long as there were no concrete prospects and serious decisions remained at a safe distance, Leopold always offered his full support. Wolfgang had written from Munich, for example, that it would not trouble him in the least if his overextended absence resulted in dismissal by the archbishop; after all, he was only staying in Salzburg for his father's sake. Leopold responded encouragingly and was even prepared to defend his son boldly before the archbishop.

Mozart's first letter from Vienna, which begins a long series of reports on his clashes with the archbishop, opens with *"Mon très cher Amy!"*—an unusual form of address that he used here for the first and only time. One has the impression that Mozart had long since decided to make the break and was only waiting in Vienna for an opportune moment. By addressing his father thus, he was not only asking for advice but appealing to him as a friend and ally.

In the following weeks Wolfgang's letters make increasingly direct attempts to win his father's unwavering approval; the less it is forth-coming, the more he tries to obtain at least a paternal blessing for his plans. The letters finally end in justifications intended to maintain peace in the family—a difficult enough task in itself. Though father and son still had more or less the same opinion of the archbishop, Leopold was now alone in Salzburg with his daughter Maria Anna (Nannerl), who was almost thirty and still unmarried, and Wolfgang probably underestimated his father's anxiety about the future.

The situation is further dramatized by the history of the family's letters. Mozart's correspondence with his family during his stay in Munich appears to have been preserved intact, but from the Vienna period not a single one of Leopold Mozart's letters to his son has survived. The onesidedness of the extant correspondence symbolizes Wolfgang's irrevocable decision to leave home. His father's reactions can often be inferred from Mozart's letters, but never their exact wording. In this and later disagreements we have only Mozart's com-ments (and not even all of these), which is all the more regrettable in that we are dealing with a dialogue between two very different person-alities. Mozart describes all events strictly from his point of view, with no attempt to be objective. The break with the archbishop and the kick in the pants from Count Arco that sealed it have gone down in history, but we must not forget that Mozart is our only source of information for these events. He gives no account of the archbishop's accusations, a crucial element in the story; instead he concentrates on his "frenzied" hatred for the *Erzlimmel* ("arch-oaf"), as he calls his employer.

THE "ARCH-OAF"

Strangely enough, history has given us a more complete and unde-servedly flattering picture of Colloredo's predecessor, Archbishop Sigismund Christoph Schrattenbach, than of Colloredo himself. The attention focused on Schrattenbach because of the Mozart family is largely responsible for his posthumous reputation, though he is rela-tively insignificant in the history of Salzburg. He was actually a crotchety, capricious bigot who professed great piety and would have been better as a children's priest than as a bishop. He was anything but a wise and good ruler and did not always refrain from despotic behavior. In financial matters he was less wasteful than disorganized (which amounted to the same thing for his subjects). He had no wide-ranging political ambitions but instead lusted after pleasures (albeit within the bounds of Church discipline, which was somewhat unusual in an age when every second clergyman had a mistress). However, he was considered endearing and approachable, and he loved music. In all, he conforms to the picture of rococo sweetness—as long as the living conditions of his countrymen are not considered. And he treated the Mozarts well, which greatly enhanced his posthumous image. Not that they had a close or very personal relationship with him, but he was forbearing and gave them an unusual amount of freedom. That was all. He could not have had any sympathy for the intellectual, artistic, or political leanings of a man like Leopold Mozart, whose enlightened rationalism made virtually no impression on Schrattenbach. Essentially he belonged to an earlier age, and certainly not to that of "enlightened" despotism. He did rule until 1771, when the Age of Enlightenment was at its zenith, but he was hardly aware of that.

His successor, Count Hieronymus Colloredo, was cast in an entirely different mold. Born in Vienna and (like his predecessor) educated in Rome, Colloredo was a ruler steeped in Enlightenment thought and a priest influenced by Jansenism. He was descended from an old northern Italian family, and most of his male ancestors had become prominent military officers and diplomats in the imperial service; his father resided in Vienna as vice-chancellor of the Empire. The archbishop of Salzburg also thought of himself primarily as a politician. His shining example was Joseph II, whose reforms he sought to emulate as perhaps no one else had, in domestic affairs as well as in the constitution of a modern church-state. (He had portraits of Rousseau and Voltaire hanging in his study, although they were covered most of the time so as not to shock his visitors.)

Education profited most from Colloredo's views; he believed it should concentrate more on useful, practical knowledge and less on the outward trappings of piety. His concern was not only to improve secondary schools but also to develop the natural science faculty of the university and to expand agricultural knowledge. He ordered farmers to be taught better planting methods, advocated stall feeding of animals and the cultivation of fallow land, and called for improvements in cattle breeding and hygiene. The physiocratic influence on his economic policies led him to carry out a redistribution of farmland into the smallest possible divisions, to keep agriculture from becoming a secondary occupation. Payment in kind was abolished in favor of cash transactions, and the expansion of large estates was forbidden in order to protect the small farmer. Colloredo recognized that a debt-ridden agrarian system and outdated inheritance practices were major evils; but he also expected a productive agricultural economy to yield hefty tax revenues.

Health care was reformed by means of new hospitals, better training for doctors, and the introduction of vaccinations—a step greeted doubtfully by his contemporaries. (Maria Theresa had publicly announced the vaccination of her children in order to allay suspicion; once again Colloredo had learned something from Vienna.) Colloredo did little for the industrialization of his province, though he did promote mining and metallurgy. Road conditions in the province were considered exemplary, however (high praise in an age when even city streets often resembled mudbaths; one thinks of the streets in Weimar, which Goethe was responsible for improving as part of his ministerial duties).

Colloredo also made changes in the judicial system, the most noteworthy being the institution of prison reforms and limitations on the length of trials. Criminal proceedings were relatively lenient, although twenty-five executions took place between 1772 and 1791. Sentencing was especially severe in cases of poaching and other hunting violations—hardly surprising in view of the prince's passion for hunting, which, along with his love of horses, was his only expensive pleasure (he owned a stud farm with two hundred horses).

Colloredo was a skinflint devoted to frugality (perhaps because his father was regarded as a philanderer and spendthrift). He prized simplicity and economy and was constantly denouncing extravagance in food and clothing, as well as any other form of luxury. It is hard to determine how much of this austerity was political and how much an expression of his personality. Enlightened utilitarian thinking was after all, closer to Protestant puritanism than to Catholic splendor and *joie de vivre;* for Catholicism, the reform movement within the state church represented something on the order of a second Reformation. That Colloredo associated himself rather openly with such a movement is especially remarkable in a country that had brutally expelled Protestants scarcely forty years earlier.

In ecclesiastical matters Colloredo took a radically new direction that did nothing to reduce tensions with the cathedral chapter and other clerics—tensions dating back to his election as archbishop of Salzburg. Here there were also many parallels to Josephine politics. Like Joseph II, Colloredo made many enemies by reducing the number of holidays and forbidding "extravagance" in religious services, weddings, and funerals. The reduction of church music to a bare minimum was a topic of dispute for the Mozart family, who were accustomed to the exact opposite attitude from Colloredo's predecessor. (Yet Schrattenbach was much less musical than Colloredo, who had theological reasons for his musical reforms.) Colloredo's abolition of passion plays and processions likewise won him few friends, especially among the rural population. Not surprisingly, faith healing and similar religious abuses, though widely practiced, did not accord with his enlightened thinking and were suppressed. He also tried to follow the imperial example with regard to monasteries and monastic orders, although his measures were less drastic. Nevertheless, the number of monks in Salzburg decreased by a third during his rule.

His pastoral letter of 1782, in which he tried to turn on the Church in the direction of functioning as a *Volkskirche* (people's church), caused the greatest stir. He not only railed against lavish decoration but argued that the Church, instead of wasting money, should concern itself with hospitals and poorhouses. He called upon the clergy to act as teachers of the people and for that purpose to study agriculture, provincial law, health, and natural science, as well as natural law and the fine arts. In the full spirit of reform, he spoke out against the sale of indulgences and advised believers to read the Bible and the Church fathers; he also established German hymns as a regular part of the congregation's worship. The entire letter speaks of the Church's duty to disseminate reason and enlightenment; nowhere, however, does it mention heterodoxy. The era of the Protestant expulsions from Salzburg had passed, and Colloredo took a pragmatic approach to the treatment of Jews: they were tolerated but had no general freedom to conduct business; for this, permission had to be sought on a case by case basis.

In carrying out his ambitious program, this contradictory ruler tended to let his darker side dominate. Colloredo, like Joseph II, was prone to curtness and tyrannical insensitivity. Moreover, there was no reform party in Salzburg to back him. Salzburg was organized as an electoral principality, and Colloredo owed his position solely to division within the cathedral chapter; he was neither liked nor supported. His quarrels with the chapter often resulted in futile legal proceedings that did not limit his power. The citizenry, also impotent against him, expressed their disdain in satirical verses. Colloredo's predisposition to absolute dictatorship was thus reinforced by events, for he knew that no one wanted him. He considered it pointless to try to win people over to his policies under these circumstances, and he was probably right. Like Joseph II, Colloredo must be seen partially as victim of a tragic isolation that often subverted his good intentions.

The disparaging opinion of Colloredo expressed in the Mozart family's letters is thus a reflection of the general attitude in Salzburg.[2] Unfortunately, we cannot expect cool-headed judgment, which is particularly regrettable in the case of Leopold Mozart, an otherwise well-informed observer who reveals a highly sophisticated understanding of politics. (Just how far his political interests went is demonstrated by the fact that for some years he was among the subscribers to Friedrich Melchior von Grimm's *Correspondance*, an exclusive newsletter distributed to various European courts, each issue consisting of only thirty-five handwritten copies.) His rejection of Colloredo did not amount to a rejection of reform Catholicism, since he particularly welcomed a number of Joseph II's reforms, even the closing of the monasteries. Leopold Mozart not only read but owned several works by Ludovico Antonio Muratori, one of the fathers of the reform movement. But the family's prejudice against Colloredo was strong enough for Wolfgang Mozart to speculate in a letter (September 25, 1782) that the archbishop's ecclesiastical reforms were undertaken for the sole purpose of ingratiating himself with the emperor. If Leopold's aversion expressed the general opinion in Salzburg, Wolfgang's can probably be attributed to the fact that Colloredo was his employer and in his personal dealings was anything but kind—frequently he was even insultingly brusque. Objectively Colloredo did not treat the Mozarts badly, but he always managed to give them that impression. (In this respect he was the exact opposite of Joseph II, who did little for Mo-

Count Hieronymus Colloredo, elected prince archbishop of Salzburg in 1772.

zart but behaved very kindly toward him. Mozart, however, never looked upon the emperor as his employer, even when drawing a salary from the court as *Kammerkompositeur* [literally, chamber composer]; this was more an honorarium than a payment for services rendered.)

The Mozarts frequently compared Colloredo to his predecessor, in whom patriarchal affability was not accompanied by any particular intelligence; indeed, he was almost simpleminded. Colloredo, on the other hand, was unapproachable, intelligent, and crafty, and made clear to all who was prince and who subject. It was typical of him that he addressed everyone in the third person, thus showing his disdain from the outset. At the same time, though he was by no means a patron of the arts, he was much better educated and more musical than his predecessor. He liked to play the violin, and he read widely and with discrimination. He loved the theater, which his predecessor had strictly controlled for moral reasons, but even here he was unable to please the citizens of Salzburg: when he insisted on establishing a new theater in the city, the mayor resigned in protest. Colloredo always expressed himself openly and was not afraid of free expression, in private or political life. In Salzburg, Beaumarchais's comedy *Le mariage de Figaro ou La folle journée (The Marriage of Figaro)* was allowed to be performed, and the archbishop attended with his entire court; in Vienna, the emperor had personally banned the play. Overall, there was no significant censorship in Salzburg.

As a dedicated administrator (and Colloredo had indeed restored order to the crumbling Salzburg administration), the archbishop was strict regarding official duties and would not tolerate inefficiency or willfulness. In this respect the Mozarts had certainly been spoiled by Schrattenbach; Leopold Mozart had been granted every leave of absence he requested, although each was exorbitantly long. During the ten years from 1762 to 1771 his leaves totaled six years and nine months! All this vacation time not only amounted to preferential treatment over the other court employees but also meant that the Mozarts' church and court duties had to be assumed by someone else. (And Leopold almost always received his salary while on leave, either forwarded or at least paid retroactively.) Under Colloredo, such generosity was a thing of the past. After all, Leopold was assistant kapellmeister; Wolfgang was concertmaster until 1777 and became court organist in 1779. Colloredo therefore told Mozart in all candor kindly to perform his duties or seek his fortune elsewhere.[3]

Mozart biographers have generally evinced little understanding of Colloredo's stricter attitude toward job responsibilities. Joseph Heinz Eibl (1975) was the first to plead for a more just assessment of Colloredo. He rightly considered it idle to speculate as to whether the archbishop underestimated Mozart's genius in denying him extended leaves of absence. Colloredo knew Mozart primarily as a keyboard virtuoso, not as a composer. The few compositions he had heard were occasional pieces, and he was totally unaware of the important works Mozart had already composed. If a virtuoso pianist wished to make a career for himself, the Salzburg environment was indeed too limited, and to say as much was certainly no underestimation of Mozart. The situation was quite simple: the archbishop wanted in his employ (and pay) only musicians who would work for him in Salzburg. He did not want to pay honorary salaries, and he made this perfectly clear to the Mozarts. Given the archbishop's unequivocal attitude, they had only two possibilities of coming to terms with their employer. They could deceive him, as Leopold Mozart did during the third Italian journey in January 1773, when he wrote letters to Salzburg describing the sudden appearance of a painful rheumatic illness (to his wife he confided, "None of it is true"); or they could provoke him by willful behavior and see how far they could go—at the risk of being fired—as Mozart had done in Munich.

DISMISSAL OR RESIGNATION?

Mozart's decision to leave his job in Salzburg and remain in Vienna was dependent on two factors: sufficient opportunity to earn a living and his father's consent. Time was pressing; the decision had to be made in Vienna. Although the archbishop had made no preparations for departure, the musicians in his entourage received the order to return home as early as April 8. (If they wanted to stay in Vienna, it would be at their own expense—one of the archbishop's austerity measures.) At first, Mozart apparently underestimated both these difficulties. The opportunities to earn a living in Vienna existed only in ambitious dreams, and Leopold Mozart seems to have remained silent initially.

Perhaps the causes of the two problems were related. Leopold Mozart was now being forced to make decisions, whereas before only planning had been involved; and he thought his son's program for the future too uncertain, too ill considered, too impetuous. Wolfgang wrote back to Salzburg every week, full of complaints about the archbishop, who had even forbidden him to play at a charity concert benefiting the pension fund for widows and orphans of musicians; only after intervention by the nobility did he receive permission to take part.

> Well, my chief object here is to introduce myself to the emperor in some becoming way, for I am absolutely determined that he shall *get to know me*. I should love to run through my opera for him and then play a lot of fugues, for that is what he likes. (March 24, 1781)

In the next letter he writes:

> I told you in a recent letter that the archbishop is a great hindrance to me here, for he has done me out of at least 100 ducats, which I could certainly have made by giving a concert in the theater. Why, the ladies themselves offered *of their own accord* to distribute the tickets. . . . Well, how much do you suppose I should make if I were to give a concert of my own, now that the public has got to know me? But this arch-oaf of ours will not allow it. He does not want his people to have any profit—only loss. Still, he will not be able to achieve this in my case, for if I have two pupils I am better off in Vienna than in Salzburg.
> (April 4, 1781)

But these very uncertain prospects were simply not enough for the cool-headed Leopold Mozart. Mozart may have sensed his father's skepticism, yet in his next letter he was unwise enough to make even bolder promises and to press for a decision.

> I must now beg you to send me a letter as soon as possible and give me your fatherly and most friendly advice on the following matter. . . . I am thinking of asking the archbishop to allow me to remain in Vienna. Dearest father, I love you dearly! That you must realize from the fact

that for your sake I renounce all my wishes and desires. For, were it not for you, I swear to you on my honor that I would not hesitate for a moment to leave the archbishop's service. I would give a grand concert, take four pupils, and in a year I would have got on so well in Vienna that I would make at least a thousand thalers a year. I assure you that I often find it difficult to throw away my luck as I am doing. As you say, I am still young. True—but to waste one's youth in inactivity in such a beggarly place is really very sad—and it is such a loss. I would like to have your kind and fatherly advice about this, and very soon—for I must tell him what I am going to do. But do have confidence in me, for I am more prudent now. (April 8, 1781)

One thousand thalers—approximately 2,000 florins—would have been more than four times the amount of his salary in Salzburg, but there was no real mention of a position—only of teaching four pupils. Is it surprising, then, that Leopold Mozart withheld the endorsement his son requested? But Mozart would not be put off. He described conditions in Vienna more and more favorably, though the amount of possible earnings became smaller and smaller—a contradiction that surely did not escape his father. And the archbishop was always in the way, even when, in his own concerts, he let Mozart appear before the Viennese public.

But what made me almost desperate was that the very same evening we had this foul concert I was invited to Countess Thun's, but of course could not go; and who should be there but *the emperor*! Adamberger and Madame Weigl were there and received 50 ducats each! What an opportunity! I cannot, of course, arrange for the emperor to be told that if he wishes to hear me he must hurry up, as I am leaving Vienna in a few days. One has to wait for things like that. I neither can nor will remain here unless I give a concert. Still, even if I have only two pupils, I am better off here than in Salzburg. But if I had 1,000 or 1,200 florins in my pocket, I could be a little more discriminating and therefore exact better terms. That is what he will not allow, the inhuman villain. I must call him that, for he is a villain and all the nobility call him so. But enough of this. Oh, how I hope to hear by the next post whether I am to go on burying my youth and my talents in Salzburg, or whether I may make my fortune as best I can, and not wait until it is too late. It is true that I cannot make my fortune in a fortnight or three weeks, any more than I can make it in a thousand years in Salzburg.

Still, it is more pleasant to wait with a thousand florins a year than with four hundred. For if I wish to do so, I am quite certain of making that sum—I have only to say that I am staying on here—and I am not including in my calculations what I compose. Besides, think of the contrast—Vienna and Salzburg! When Bonno dies, Salieri will be kapellmeister, and then Starzer will take the place of Salieri in conducting the rehearsals; and so far no one has been mentioned to take the place of Starzer. Basta—I leave it entirely to you, my most beloved father! (April 11, 1781)

First he mentions four pupils and 1,000 thalers, now only half as many. He is concealing the fact that until autumn he had only one piano pupil, from whom he received not quite 250 florins (per year), which was nonetheless a goodly sum. Mozart is not very reliable about money; he earned 450 florins in Salzburg but reports only 400 to his father, who certainly should have known better. Furthermore, his projections about the future musical job market in Vienna are quite premature. Giuseppe Bonno remained kapellmeister until 1788, when Antonio Salieri indeed succeeded him; and Joseph Starzer retained his unofficial position as court composer until his early death in 1787. In his letters, then, Mozart is very full of himself; in reality he had no prospects, and the first year after he left Salzburg must count as his "poorest time."

Mozart was unable to convince his father that he was not spinning idle hopes for the future but was realistic, cautious, and discerning enough to make reasonable plans that would be borne out by future events. For the time being he bowed to paternal authority, obedient but unconvinced, and only on the condition that he be allowed to return to Vienna early the next year—for he had his eye on an opera libretto, *Die Entführung aus dem Serail* (*The Abduction from the Seraglio*), which might finally make his escape possible.

You are looking forward to my return with great joy, dearest father! That is the only thing that can make me decide to leave Vienna. I am writing all this in plain German, *because the whole world knows and should know that the archbishop of Salzburg has only you to thank, my most beloved father, that he did not lose me yesterday forever (I mean, as far as he himself is concerned).*

Here Mozart does not use code, as he often did; he is hoping that the archbishop will intercept the letter and perhaps fire him as a result. He continues bluntly:

If, however, anything similar should happen again, which I hope will not be the case, I can assure you that I shall lose all patience; and certainly you will forgive me for doing so. And I beg you, dearest father, to allow me to return to Vienna during Lent towards the end of the next carnival. This depends on you alone and not on the archbishop. For if he does not grant me permission, I shall go all the same; and this visit will certainly not do me any harm! Oh, if he could only read this, I should be delighted. But what I ask, you must promise me in your next letter, for it is only on this condition that I shall return to Salzburg; *but it must be a definite promise*, so that I may give my word to the ladies here. Stephanie is going to give me a German opera to compose. So I await your reply. (April 28, 1781)

Was Mozart seriously setting his father these conditions, which were really not Leopold's to negotiate? Or were they advance notice— while he was still in Vienna—that next time his patience would snap? Does this letter betoken subordination to his father's wish that he return to Salzburg, or does it indicate a hidden rebellion? In any case the "break" with the archbishop—and with Salzburg—came two weeks later. Nothing really new had happened, only one of those heated verbal exchanges that build to a point from which there is no turning back.

I was the most dissolute fellow he knew—no one served him so badly as I did—I had better leave today or else he would write home and have my salary stopped. I couldn't get a word in edgeways, for he blazed away like a fire. I listened to it all very calmly. He lied to my face that my salary was 500 florins, called me a scoundrel, a rascal, a vagabond. Oh, I really cannot tell you all he said. At last my blood began to boil, I could no longer contain myself and I said, "So Your Grace is not satisfied with me?" "What, you dare to threaten me, you scoundrel? There is the door! Look out, for I will have nothing more to do with such a miserable wretch." At last I said, "Nor I with you!" "Well, be off!" When leaving the room, I said, "This is final. Tomorrow you shall have it in writing." Tell me now, most beloved father, did I not say the word too late rather than too soon? Just listen for a moment. My honor is more precious to me than anything else, and I know that you feel the same way. (May 9, 1781)

Here the subject is wounded honor, including Leopold's, Mozart having received a paternal admonition to hold his tongue. But he had been "twice a coward" and "could never be one a third time," so he maintains that he cannot be blamed for resigning. For the archbishop did not dismiss Mozart at all, and never did sign a dismissal notice—a fact that still caused Mozart some apprehension when he visited Salzburg two years later. He even admitted candidly to having resigned "without the slightest reason," despite all warnings, but only after the archbishop had supplied him with a third pretext. Mozart had a ready response to the accusation that he had behaved rashly: his dismissal would not reflect badly on him in Vienna because everyone there already "hated" the archbishop. Mozart tried to refute his father's financial objections by promising to send money—presumably to pay off debts still left from the journey to Paris. (This remittance was delayed by at least six weeks and appears to have been very difficult for Mozart to manage.)

Finally, in the letter about his resignation Mozart mentions that he now lives at the home of Madame Weber, who "has been good enough to take me into her house." This admission is well camouflaged among references to practical matters (which are not unimportant in themselves), for Mozart must have known that his new address would arouse his father's very worst fears. Four years previously, in Mannheim, Wolfgang had not only fallen in love with one of the Weber daughters, Aloysia, but had tried to save the entire family (which included five children) from financial ruin, and had even planned a journey to Italy to improve Aloysia's singing skills and thus help support the family. Leopold must have been truly alarmed by the renewed association with this family, whose patriarch, Fridolin Weber, had died shortly after their move to Vienna. The elder Mozart probably pictured his son once more beguiled and ensnared, and soon lost in a hopeless situation now that he was living in their house.

For Leopold Mozart this letter overflowed with bad news; he answered by return post and surely did not spare harsh and drastic words. His letter is not extant, but we do have Mozart's reply (also by return post).

Mon trés cher Pére!

I could hardly have supposed otherwise than that in the heat of the moment you would write just such a letter as I have been obliged to read, for the event must have taken you by surprise (especially since you were actually expecting my arrival). . . . Believe me, most beloved father, I need all my manliness to write to you what common sense dictates. God knows how hard it is for me to leave you. But even if I had to beg, I could never serve such a master again, for I shall never forget what has happened as long as I live. I implore you, I adjure you, by all you hold dear in this world, to strengthen me in this resolution instead of trying to dissuade me from it, for if you do you will only make me unproductive. My hope and my desire is to gain honor, fame, and money, and I have every confidence that I will be more useful to you in Vienna than if I were to return to Salzburg. (May 16, 1781)

Family harmony, though, could not be restored as quickly as Mozart believed. The arguments about thoughtless behavior, ingratitude, lack of filial devotion, and so forth dragged on for months. And the Webers came in for considerable discussion as well.

Mozart wrote his letter of resignation and submitted it the following day, together with the money he had already received for travel expenses. But Count Arco, who evidently performed the duties of receptionist, would neither accept the letter nor even pass it on to the prince without the consent of Leopold Mozart. Thus began the sideshow that has received so much historical attention because of the notorious kick in the pants, which has almost completely obscured the main point: Mozart voluntarily resigned his position—without notice, we might add—and definitely not in mutual agreement with his employer.

THE "DISGUSTING AFFAIR"

Count Arco was a most suitable mediator, for he was on very close terms with the archbishop and he came from a Salzburg family with whom the Mozarts were well acquainted. The familiarity was such that Leopold Mozart wrote a letter (now lost) to Arco in Vienna, asking him to exert some friendly influence on Wolfgang and persuade him to return to Salzburg. A second discussion between Mozart and Arco was more friendly and intimate, and this time the count did not defend the archbishop's interests but simply reproached Mozart for acting rashly and thoughtlessly in anger.

Mozart had already made up his mind, as he freely admits, but he was less sure of himself after Leopold's violent reaction to his resignation. He resorted to self-justifications that became progressively more contradictory and less believable. At one point he gave the low salary as his main reason for leaving: "If I were paid such a salary that I would not be tempted to think of other places, then I would be perfectly satisfied. And if the archbishop chooses to pay me that salary—well then, I am ready to set off today" (end of May 1781). Earlier he had ascribed everything to his insulted honor: "After that insult, that threefold insult, if the archbishop personally offered me 1,200 florins I would not accept them. I am not a skunk or a rascal" (May 19, 1781).

Despite his uncertainty, it was clear that the relationship with Colloredo was strained beyond all endurance, the breach irreparable. Even Count Arco could do nothing. Mozart writes:

> He put everything before me in so friendly a manner, I could have sworn that what he said came altogether from his heart. I don't think, however, that he would be prepared to swear that the same was true of myself. In answer to his plausible speeches I told him the whole truth with all possible calmness and courtesy and in the most charming manner in the world, and he could not find a word to say against it.
>
> (End of May 1781)

Mozart was determined to remain in Vienna and try his luck, and had no intention of returning to Salzburg. The friendliest warnings and advice no longer had any effect. Count Arco then tried the argument that Leopold Mozart had probably recommended to him in his letter.

> "Believe me, you allow yourself to be far too easily dazzled in Vienna. A man's reputation here lasts a very short time. At first, it is true, you are overwhelmed with praise and make a great deal of money into the bargain—but how long does that last? After a few months the Viennese want something new." "You are right, Count," I replied. "But do you suppose that I mean to settle in Vienna? Not at all. I know where I shall

go. That this affair should have occurred in Vienna is the archbishop's fault and not mine. If he knew how to treat people of talent, it would never have happened. I am the best-tempered fellow in the world, Count Arco, provided that people are the same with me." "Well," he said, "the archbishop considers you a dreadfully conceited person." "I daresay he does," I rejoined, "and indeed I am so towards him. I treat people as they treat me. When I see that someone despises me and treats me with contempt, I can be as proud as a peacock." Among other things he asked me if I didn't think that he too often had to swallow very disagreeable words. I shrugged my shoulders and said: "You no doubt have your reasons for putting up with it, and I have my reasons for refusing to do so." All the rest you will know from my last letter. Do not doubt, dearest and most beloved father, that everything will certainly turn out for my good and consequently for yours also. It is perfectly true that the Viennese are apt to change their affections, *but only in the theater;* and my specialty is too popular not to enable me to support myself. Vienna is certainly the land of the clavier! And, even granted that they do get tired of me, they will not do so for a few years, certainly not before then. In the meantime I shall have gained both honor and money. There are many other places; and who can tell what opportunities may arise before then? (June 2, 1781)

Mozart shifts ground with every argument. First money, then insulted honor, and now it is "the land of the clavier" Vienna, and in case that doesn't sound convincing enough, he says simply, "Do you suppose that I mean to settle in Vienna?" Count Arco must surely have lost his temper at such obstinacy; Mozart's answers doubtless seemed simply frivolous. Arco could not know what Leopold at least suspected: that Mozart had a further reason, which he was embarrassed to disclose, for remaining in Vienna at all costs, a reason stemming from his renewed acquaintance with the Weber family. Clearly, Mozart did not yet have the courage to play this card. His concealed relationship with the Webers, though it became important only gradually and perhaps carried little weight at the moment of his heated exchange with Colloredo, makes all the reasons he later advanced seem less and less convincing. Mozart felt pressured to justify himself, and the more excuses he offered, the more rash and unreasonable they sounded. Thus, during a third discussion with Count Arco (again with the object

of handing in his resignation) the escalation that made a return to
Salzburg impossible finally occurred.

Well, Count Arco has made a nice mess of things! So that is the way to
persuade people and win them over! To refuse petitions out of innate
stupidity, not to say a word to your master from lack of courage and love
of toadyism, to keep a fellow dangling for four weeks, and finally, when
he is obliged to present the petition in person, instead of *at least*
granting him admittance, to throw him out of the room and give him a
kick in the behind—that is the count who, according to your last letter,
has my interest so much at heart. And that is the court where I ought to
go on serving—the place where whoever wants to make a written
application, instead of having its delivery facilitated, is treated in this
fashion! The scene took place in the antechamber. So the only thing to
do was to decamp and take to my heels—for, although Arco had
already done so, I did not wish to show disrespect to the prince's
apartments. I have written three memoranda that I have handed in five
times; and each time they have been thrown back at me. I have
carefully preserved them, and whoever wishes to read them may do so
and convince himself that they do not contain the slightest personal
remark. When at last I was handed back my memorandum in the
evening through Herr von Kleinmayr (for that is his office), I was beside
myself with rage, as the archbishop's departure was fixed for the
following day. I could not let him leave thus, and as I had heard from
Arco (or so at least he had told me) that the prince knew nothing about
it, I realized how angry he would be with me for staying on so long and
then at the very last moment appearing with a petition of this kind. I
therefore wrote another memorandum in which I explained to the
archbishop that it was now four weeks since I had drawn up my
petition, but, finding myself for some unknown reason always put off, I
was now obliged to present it to him in person, though at the very last
moment. This memorandum brought about my dismissal from his
service in the most pleasant way imaginable. For who knows if the
whole thing was not done at the command of the archbishop himself? If
Herr von Kleinmayr still wishes to maintain the character of an honest
man, he can testify, as can also the archbishop's servants, that his
command was carried out. So now I need not send in any petition, for
the affair is at an end. I do not want to write anything more on the
subject, and if the archbishop were to offer me a salary of 1,200 florins,

I would not accept it after such treatment. How easy it would have been to persuade me to remain! By kindness, not by insolence and rudeness. I sent a message to Count Arco saying *that I had nothing more to say to him.* For he went for me so rudely when I first saw him and treated me like a rogue, which he had no right to do. And, by God, as I have already told you, I would not have gone to him the last time if in his message he had not added that he had had a letter from you. Well, that will be the last time. What is it to him if I want to get my discharge? And if he was really so well disposed towards me, he ought to have reasoned quietly with me—or let things take their course—rather than throw such words about as "clown" and "knave" and toss a fellow out of the room with a kick in the ass; but I am forgetting that this was probably done by order of our worthy prince archbishop. (June 9, 1781)

Count Arco was by no means a mere mouthpiece for his employer but also represented the interests of the Mozart family and had been authorized to do so by Leopold Mozart's letter. But now he appeared to have somewhat overstepped the mark. The kick in the pants went beyond a friendly gesture and hit Mozart in a very sensitive spot. His indignation, which in the first letter is moderate and restrained, grows steadily as Mozart realizes that he now has an objective reason to consider any return to Salzburg out of the question. Again and again he expresses his conviction that the kick in the pants had been ordered by the prince archbishop himself (which shows a ridiculous misjudgment of Colloredo's personality and his use of power). For Mozart, fighting a losing battle to justify his actions to his father, the escalation of tensions was providential: he was now clearly a victim of the archepiscopal "villain."

But Leopold Mozart would not change his mind and continued to reproach his son. Now, when decisive events were taking place, there was a constant flow of letters from Salzburg; earlier, when Mozart could truly have benefited from paternal advice, his father had been silent. The reproaches were retrospective, and although Leopold's letters have not survived, their content can easily be reconstructed from Wolfgang's replies.

You say that you can never approve of my having tendered my resignation while I was in Vienna. . . . You say that the only way to save my honor is to abandon my resolve. . . . You say that I have never shown

you any affection. . . . You say that I will never sacrifice any of my
pleasures for your sake. (May 19, 1781)

After further accusations of a similar nature Mozart answers quite
plainly.

I implore you, dearest, most beloved father, to spare me such letters in
the future. I entreat you to do so, for they only irritate my mind and
disturb my heart and spirit; and I, who must now keep on composing,
need a cheerful mind and a calm disposition. (June 9, 1781)

On top of his break with the archbishop and Salzburg, Mozart now
had a rift in his family to deal with. He still wrote home every week,
but his father became less communicative and his letters rarer. The
archbishop was hardly mentioned anymore, but the ignominy of being
kicked by Count Arco remained. Mozart openly expressed thoughts of
revenge.

That arrogant jackass will certainly get a very palpable reply from me,
even if he has to wait twenty years for it. For to see him and to return his
kick will be one and the same thing, unless I am so unlucky as to meet
him first in some sacred place. (June 16, 1781)

Mozart did not see Count Arco as the archbishop's chamberlain or his
own social superior, but simply as someone who had deeply affronted
him. In his outrage over this injustice, he completely ignored the social
balance of power. It never occurred to him that he might complain to the
archbishop about his chamberlain's impossible behavior and denounce
the incident as an abuse of power toward his subject. But there would
have been little point in presenting this grievance; wounded honor does
not heal so easily. Mozart wanted to repay the humiliation in kind, and
this sentiment was no slip of the tongue in the heat of anger but was
stated several times in his letters. Mozart had enough self-control to
avoid an actual fistfight with Count Arco then and there, because the
archbishop's apartments, where the incident took place, were in his
words a "sacred place" that he must "respect." They were, after all, the
living quarters of his former employer, with whom his father still had to
contend. However, at the next opportunity, on neutral ground, nothing
would hold him back—or so he insisted repeatedly to his father, who

was almost speechless at such rebellion and insubordination. (Fortunately, Mozart and Count Arco never met again.)

DIGRESSION: THE CITYSCAPE OF JOSEPHINE VIENNA

Mozart knew Vienna from his days as a child prodigy, but that was the Vienna of Maria Theresa. Many things had changed since then. The character of a city is formed not only by its carved physiognomy— the architecture of its churches, palaces, government and residential buildings—but equally by the hustle and bustle of its streets, by its means of transportation, its markets and kiosks, its fashions, and all forms of public activity for which the architecture serves more or less as a backdrop.

Vienna's topography altered considerably after the last siege by the Turks in 1683. Medieval Vienna, which had survived unchanged until then, was largely destroyed or disfigured, and reconstruction gave the city an entirely new countenance. The foundations of the old city center (mostly within today's First District) were still intact and provided the basis for restoration, but not a single house remained standing in the suburbs outside the fortifications (which were only taken down in the nineteenth century to make way for the Ring).

During the five decades after the Turkish siege, extensive construction was undertaken (partly financed by spoils captured from the Turks), much of it still quite recognizable today, especially the contributions of the two most important families of architects during this period, the Fischer von Erlachs and the Hildebrandts, who worked for the imperial court as well as the nobility and also built many churches. Altogether nearly three hundred palaces were erected, some wedged into the crowded city center, others summer residences with spacious gardens in the sprawling suburbs. This flurry of building activity had been all but completed by Maria Theresa's time. The opportunity to create an imperial capital where baroque splendor was given free rein had not been missed. The court was the center of life; its family celebrations, entertainments, and ceremonies structured the life of the city, because these functions were the very expression of the Habsburg monarchy's will to power and sovereignty.

The situation was totally different during the reign of Joseph II

(1780–90), although no less influenced by the personality on the throne. Mozart did not find Josephine Vienna complete upon his arrival, for it developed gradually as the emperor implemented his political reforms. But his brief rule brought about such profound transformations that it is possible to see Mozart's Vienna ("the best place in the world") as a late absolutist alternative to every other European capital. Joseph II, this controversial emperor who has yet to be the subject of a comprehensive scholarly biography, also left his mark on the city's urban features, for he sought to influence everything around him with his "enlightened" ideas. He intervened personally in everything, often producing much turmoil and little benefit or satisfaction. Many of his decisions were applauded, but just as many were criticized and even despised.

The most striking feature of Joseph II's reign was the small role played by his court in Viennese social life. The emperor was widowed twice after brief marriages. Thereafter he lived as a childless bachelor, reduced his staff to a minimum, and spent half his time on inspection tours. In Vienna he was occupied almost exclusively with affairs of state; his household was spartan and devoid of all grandeur. Court ceremony virtually disappeared; Joseph II wanted to be a *Volkskaiser* (people's emperor), always approachable and responsive to his subjects. He usually wore simple, almost bourgeois clothing—a brown coat, knee breeches and a vest, sometimes a military jacket. (The paintings we have show him in official dress with the usual accoutrements and insignia, since their purpose is to portray the emperor, not the person.) He drove through the streets in a two-seated *Pirutsch*—an inconspicuous green carriage—and was often seen on foot with the populace. There were parties at court only when they were unavoidable—to entertain foreign dignitaries, for example. Otherwise, the emperor preferred to seek entertainment in the homes of various nobles. The task of keeping up appearances in the imperial capital was thus transferred from the court to the resident nobility: twenty princes and sixty counts with their numerous relatives.

Since the court did not serve as the focal point of society, it did not provide a haven for the obsequious courtiers who played such an unspeakable role in every other royal capital. There was no favoritism; the mistresses (in this case because of personal disinclination) and the many clerics who busied themselves at other courts were conspicuously absent. Even the number of soldiers at court had been reduced to a bare minimum: a total of ninety men (including the officers) made up the palace guard, which was on duty around the clock. (Today many more people are employed to guard the Vienna Hofburg, although in Joseph's time it already housed the treasure chamber and miscellaneous objects of great value that had to be protected along with the emperor.) Yet the austerity of court life had absolutely no influence on the rest of Vienna. On the contrary, the nobility filled the void completely and took charge of providing a glittering display, thereby serving the court's interests as well as their own. Since members of the great noble families also held many important government posts, their ostentation would almost have amounted to a usurpation of court functions had not Joseph II been so uninterested in the pomp of any position below his own.

His indifference to such matters only left him more time to intervene in the daily life of his people, often in the most unexpected ways. He was never motivated by mere dictatorial whim and always had enlightened educational goals in mind, but his acts were often presumptuous, even despotic invasions of his subjects' privacy. Thus, the emperor believed it his duty to forbid the wearing of such unhealthy garments as corsets; the ringing of church bells to ward off lightning was abolished; funeral banquets were censured. On the other hand, many of the steps he took in social, medical, and hygienic areas showed great foresight. He placed pharmacists under strict supervision, improved the training of physicians, increased the availability of medical care, and protected illegitimate children against discrimination.

The emperor must have seemed to the Viennese more like a mayor, personally on hand whenever possible, observing and immediately taking action—to such an extent that he was not above rushing to the scene of a fire, helping to put it out, and then rebuking the other firefighters for their tardiness. The entire city of Vienna was the emperor's private domain, whereas the Hofburg made a rather dreary and desolate impression.

Just over 200,000 people lived in Vienna, in 5,500 buildings, approximately one-quarter of them in the central district. Conditions were very crowded, with an average of almost 50 persons in each house. More than 4,000 carriages, coaches, and wagons of all kinds used the narrow streets. Although cleaned regularly, the streets were very dusty, and gusts of wind often whipped up clouds of fine dust, so that even short distances were best traveled by coach or hackney cab. It must have been rather dangerous for pedestrians to thread their way among the horse-drawn vehicles, and there were frequent accidents. In the larger squares and along the Graben (the main street) there were numerous stalls and booths selling soft drinks, ice cream, *Mandel-milch* (almond milk), and sweets; there were even a few theater stalls. Any visitor among the huge crowds must have noticed above all the colorful display of national costumes, primarily those of southeastern Europe and Turkey. The Viennese themselves always dressed in the latest fashion, though more according to English than to Parisian tastes. English fashions were lighter and more comfortable to wear, and reflected the often pronounced anglophilia of the Viennese. Great importance was attached to clothing, and the esteem a person enjoyed depended in large measure on the attention he gave to his attire.

Most houses had large, vaulted ground floors with shops, coffee-houses, workshops, or entrances to the numerous stables. These were not always easily accessible, however, for women often sat out front hawking odds and ends of every description. Next to the entrances workmen split the huge supplies of wood that every dwelling needed for fuel. On a daily basis, then, high society, in coaches drawn by as many as six horses, or sauntering through the streets showing off their finery—cosmopolitan Vienna, in short—mixed with the cramped, mundane world of merchants and street vendors in a juxtaposition almost inconceivable today. Nor do contemporary illustrations convey the effect; they either show only the world of elegance and luxury or lose the colorful activity of merchants and tradespeople in isolated representations.

Even less imaginable are the smells of this city, the street noise, the jolting of wagon wheels on cobblestones, the monotonous clatter of horses' hooves. These background disturbances were already a burden to the eighteenth-century Viennese. The most expensive lodgings were always on the third floor, where a tenant could imagine himself somewhat removed from the noise and stench of the city but did not have to carry all the necessities of life, including firewood, up too many flights of stairs. Sometimes straw was spread on the streets in front of one of the large palaces to reduce the noise from passing coaches if someone was ill within. The streets were sprayed twice a day to settle the dust. Three hundred military policemen were responsible for law and order throughout the entire city; they all wore numbered badges in case anyone wished to register a complaint about them. There were street signs at every intersection, and the street lights were not put out until 2:00 A.M.

Vienna was a pleasant and gracious city, and better organized than any other in Europe. But no visitor could fail to notice the specifically Josephine characteristics that gave the city its own unique atmosphere. The emperor's reforms left their mark on the cityscape and ensured that no one would forget where he was. For instance, among the national costumes many Jewish caftans could be seen. Although Vienna's Jewish population was still very small (about 500), many Jews who lived elsewhere came to the city on business. The caftan, however, was no longer required attire for Jews, but a traditional costume that most of Vienna's Jewish community had long since discarded. The yellow stars or bands that Jews had previously been made to wear were also abolished by the tolerance laws, along with other forms of discrimination. The transition from Maria Theresa to Joseph II was clearly visible (and for once we will leave unmentioned the truly terrible things the empress said about Jews).

The abolition of censorship was also visible on every street corner. Political questions, current events, and real or imagined problems of all kinds called forth (uncensored) brochures, booklets, leaflets, pamphlets, periodicals, and broadsides that could be bought everywhere, hot off the presses. Most were what is still known as *Wiener Schmäh* (Viennese abuse). Nothing was too slight to be attacked; the writings about the so-called Graben nymphs (prostitutes) alone are innumerable. But even highly controversial pamphlets could be freely sold, including one entitled *Warum wird Kaiser Joseph von seinem Volke nicht geliebt?* (*Why Is Emperor Joseph Not Loved by His People?*)— which became famous because it was far from unwarranted. This freedom of publication allowed an open and informal atmosphere to flourish. The Viennese could even buy translations of respected newspapers from other European cities. Books, of course, were also reprinted and sold in elegant editions (much to the detriment of the authors and original publishers). The best known of these reprinters, Johann Thomas von Trattner, became so wealthy that he was able to build by far the grandest and most luxurious house on the Graben, which was a major tourist attraction as well.

Even Joseph's legal reforms marked the cityscape. Although a modern judicial system had been introduced—one that did not exempt the nobility—deterrence was still the real purpose of every punishment. In the Hohe Markt (main square) one could still see petty criminals in the stocks or on the pillory, wearing signs that detailed their offenses. For more serious crimes, offenders had their heads shaved before being chained together with others of their kind and sent out to sweep the streets. Even the nobility could suffer such public punishments, so that counts as well as prostitutes might be seen with brooms in hand, the butt of general ridicule. After completing their four-week sentence, they lost no time in dashing to the wigmaker. Contemporary caricaturists immediately seized upon such scenes, which were unusual for an autocratic state. The emperor could not have demonstrated the abolition of aristocratic privilege more graphically.

Similarly, the consequences of Josephine church policy were everywhere in evidence. Numerous monasteries that had been closed also lost their properties, which were often located in the city center; these were subsequently developed, primarily for residential use. Joseph's Vienna, like Maria Theresa's, was a permanent construction site, but for entirely different purposes: no new palaces, castles, or government buildings were begun. Instead, middle-class entrepreneurs such as the godfathers of Mozart's children, Wetzlar von Plankenstern and Trattner, put up residential blocks. The emperor's own building projects had clearly defined functions that stemmed directly from his reform policies. They included the giant general hospital complex in the suburb of Alsergrund and the Josephinum, a medical training center that specialized in surgical techniques. These were among the most modern facilities of their kind in all of Europe.

The monastery closings and the new medical and social facilities were closely related. Joseph II only took action against the "redundant," purely contemplative monasteries, while trying to strengthen the church's charitable and pastoral role in line with his concept of a state church. The parishes were even given administrative responsibilities such as recording births, deaths, and marriages (though marriage was now a civil contract under court jurisdiction). A reorganization of the parishes resulted in many new parish churches, which naturally abjured all baroque extravagance; thus, even in appearance, they propagated a Christianity devoted to pastoral activities instead of supplication and the worship of relics. In Maria Theresa's time processions had been daily affairs that dominated the life of the city, but now only the Corpus Christi Procession remained; all others were forbidden, as were pilgrimages. People no longer had to fall reverently to their knees when the Blessed Sacrament passed by, because it was no longer carried through the streets.

Joseph's Vienna did not look like an imperial capital characterized by court ostentation and related ecclesiastical displays, but like a metropolis from which a vast empire was governed, where a bureaucracy with regular business hours produced an overwhelming crush of traffic every morning and evening, and where the bourgeois influence on daily life was becoming more pronounced. Noble and bourgeois circles were beginning to mingle at public entertainments, and attire was no longer a reliable indication of social position.

The court had given up even more of its exclusivity when Joseph II opened the Prater and the Augarten—both former royal hunting preserves—to the general public as recreation areas. Some nobles followed suit and opened their own parks. Cultural diversions had also lost their social cachet—theater, opera, concerts, and other events were open to everyone, and only the private salons retained the exclusivity of a specially selected coterie. This meant not only the opening of the Hofoper (court opera) to nonaristocratic patrons but also the reverse: the nobility began to frequent fairgrounds, watch animal baiting, and visit "suburban" theaters, even though they might have to sit on hard wooden benches.

Chapter 2

THE ABDUCTION – 1782

NEW LODGINGS

On May 1 or 2, 1781, Mozart moved out of the archbishop's erstwhile residence, the House of the Order of Teutonic Knights, and into a house called Zum Auge Gottes (The Eye of God), at 11 Petersplatz, where he rented lodgings from Cäcilia Weber. On May 9 came the interview with the archbishop that led to his resignation. His father had used unconvincing and essentially timorous arguments (as well as simply asserting his paternal authority) to get him to return to Salzburg; had the Weber family now given him courage to take this decisive step toward independence? For weeks Mozart had begged his father for support and advice, pleaded for answers to his letters, and even courted him as his closest friend (*"Mon très cher Amy!"*); yet for the most part he encountered inscrutable silence. He wrote a total of eight letters but received answers to only one or two. This was completely unprecedented, for Leopold Mozart had always taken every opportunity to write to his family, and he expected his children to do the same.

The constant exchange of information and detailed consultation on every important decision were unusually strong traditions in the Mozart family. Hardly any other family of the eighteenth century (one of abundant letter writing) maintained such a regular and extensive correspondence—in an age, incidentally, when postal rates were extremely high. His father's silence must have been a great disappointment to Mozart, but it was also clearly meant as a disciplinary measure. Leopold obviously assumed that his son would undertake nothing without his consent. At first he had not taken Wolfgang's plans to stay in Vienna very seriously; they seemed far too unrealistic, shortsighted, and financially unpromising. He had said as much to his son, and that was that! Moreover, he was still angry at him because of certain events in Munich. The excuses and denials in Mozart's letters continued throughout the entire summer. The problem apparently centered on two areas in which Leopold considered his son thoroughly immature, rash, and thoughtless: women and money.

Three years previously in Mannheim, after meeting Aloysia Weber, the second of the Weber daughters, Mozart came into direct conflict with his father for the first time. In the exuberance of his infatuation, he wanted not only to travel with Aloysia to Italy but to rehabilitate the finances of the entire Weber family. Only the hand of paternal authority put an end to this episode. In Munich the temptations had not been quite so serious. Mozart had been to balls, danced uninhibitedly, and felt free and happy for the first time. Later he confided to his wife that these had been the happiest days of his life. He had spent most of his time wandering around with members of the Munich court orchestra, though there had also been some flirting. Whatever may have happened during carnival week—and in Leopold Mozart's presence—it provoked a hail of reproaches against which Mozart defended himself like a schoolboy caught red-handed.

My only association with the person of ill repute was at the ball—and I talked to her long before I knew what she was, and solely because I wanted to be sure of having a partner for the contredanse. Afterwards I could not desert her all at once without giving her a reason; and who would say such a thing to a person's face? But in the end did I not on several occasions leave her in the lurch and dance with others? On this account too I was positively delighted when the carnival was over. Moreover, no one, unless he is a liar, can say that I ever saw her

anywhere else, or went to her house. You can rest assured that I hold to
my religion; and should I ever have the misfortune (God forbid!) to fall
into evil ways, I shall absolve you, my most beloved father, from all
responsibility. For in that case I alone would be the villain, as I have
you to thank for all good things—for both my temporal and spiritual
welfare and salvation. (June 13, 1781)

Mozart's great admiration for his father had expressed itself in
absolute subordination to his authority and molded their relationship.
Wolfgang was not intimidated by paternal severity; rather, his respect
grew from his awareness of how much he owed his father in terms of his
own development. Not only was Leopold Mozart a loving and generous
father, but he imparted to his son the artistic self-confidence without
which great works are impossible. He did not become a prodigy
through musical drills and merciless finger exercises, but through the
nurturing of his creativity as an instrumentalist. Leopold Mozart soon
left behind his role as artistic guardian and became a musical partner,
helping, criticizing, but also full of praise, even when his son pursued
his own often unconventional course. In nonmusical matters Mozart
acknowledged his father's farsighted intelligence and penetrating reason, and often sought his advice and opinions. But he was now a
twenty-five-year-old man seeking autonomy and self-sufficiency; he
had to break away from the parental home and establish an independent existence. This long-delayed step represented a difficult burden
for Leopold, an end to his life's work of providing everything necessary
to bring his son's extraordinary talents to fruition. Leopold felt himself
quite simply abandoned—an aging, increasingly embittered man with
whom the women in Mozart's life stood no chance.

When Leopold Mozart learned that his son had taken lodgings in
Cäcilia Weber's house, he was immediately concerned. Perhaps before
Wolfgang himself, Leopold sensed the connection between his son's
resignation from the archbishop's service and his renewed association
with the Weber family. In the letter describing his audience with the
archbishop Mozart had written, "My good luck is just beginning, and I
trust that my good luck will be yours also." This sentence obviously
had a double meaning. For a long time Leopold had not understood
how urgently his paternal advice was needed, and he had overlooked
many hints ("I feel that I *must* stay; indeed, I felt that when I left

Munich"). Now he sensed the danger that someone else might gain influence, and he feared his son's impulsiveness. He immediately insisted that Wolfgang leave the Weber household and withdraw his resignation. But reproaches were of no avail: for weeks Mozart continued to write bitter letters to Salzburg about the archbishop and then about the "affair" with Count Arco that irrevocably sealed his decision. Again and again he painted the rosiest picture of his financial opportunities in Vienna, though his letters were full of contradictions and inconsistencies. And he wrote innocently about the Weber family, as if living with them were the only practical option and were no cause for further speculation. To the escalating demands and admonitions from Salzburg he responded more and more irritably. He no longer wanted his every step to be calculated and determined by his father but was convinced that he himself could best judge what was right for him. His request for his father's support had met with silence; now he felt he could go his own way.

Mozart's first experiences in Vienna—his successful concerts for the nobility, the renewal of old acquaintances, easy access to the emperor (even though a meeting with him had been thwarted for the time being), the city's flourishing and welcoming musical life—all this had vindicated his decision and nourished his fondest hopes. Mozart was sure of his identity as a musician; he knew his worth as a virtuoso and still more as a composer. But above all he wanted to prove himself as an opera composer, an area in which he was virtually unknown in Vienna, but for which the city offered the best environment. In Salzburg there was no opera at all; at best Mozart could only hope that Colloredo would graciously grant him leave to accept commissions elsewhere. Vienna had not only the Italian Hofoper but also the German Singspiel with its own ensemble, which, together with the acting company, formed a true national theater; a chance to write for it must have been extremely attractive. Mozart was counting on commissions and was ready to compete with the most respected opera composers. During the unavoidable transition period he intended to earn his living from concerts and teaching, which he did not think would be difficult given the opportunities in Vienna and his wide circle of acquaintances. Later he would doubtless secure a permanent position through the emperor.

Regarding the Weber family, he wrote to his father:

I have a lovely room, and am living with people who are obliging and
who supply me with all the things which one often requires in a hurry
and which one cannot have when living alone. (May 9, 1781)

Those were in fact very important advantages, for a bachelor's life
was not easy in the eighteenth century. A servant was a necessity if
one mingled in society, since even putting on a neckcloth required
help and arranging one's hair was still more complicated. Laundry had
to be looked after; one could not simply send things out to be
dry-cleaned. Meals had to be taken in a restaurant, which was
inconvenient and expensive. When he left the Weber house, he
wrote:

Indeed I shall miss a great many comforts in my new lodging—
especially in regard to meals. For whenever I had anything urgent to
finish, the Webers always delayed the meal for me as long as I chose;
and I could go on writing *without dressing* and just go to table in the
next room, both for lunch and supper. But now, when I wish to avoid
spending money on having a meal brought to my room, I waste at least
an hour dressing (which until now I have postponed until the afternoon)
and must go out—particularly in the evening. You know that usually I
go on composing until I am hungry. Well, the kind friends with whom I
take supper sit down to table at 8 or half past 8 at the latest. At the
Webers, we never did so before 10 o'clock. (August 1, 1781)

Mozart could thus have full room and board and be treated like a
member of the family as well. That must have incensed his father, for
it meant that to all intents and purposes his son had changed families.
But conditions in the Weber house were indeed very favorable, for this
musical family placed two pianos (with entirely different mechanisms)
at Mozart's disposal. They were welcome tools for his work: "one for
galanterie playing and the other an instrument which is strung with the
low octave throughout, like the one we had in London, and consequently sounds like an organ" (June 27, 1781). Since for the time
being he had practically no income, he could not afford to buy a piano
himself, and even renting one was expensive. So at least the outward
circumstances of his start in Vienna were promising.

In his letter of May 9 Mozart had said, "Write to me (in code) that
you are pleased—and indeed you may well be so—but in public rail

at me as much as you like, so that none of the blame may fall on you."
This was, of course, a reference to his resignation and also an allusion
to the archbishop's practice of intercepting and reading letters.
Leopold Mozart was not at all inclined to adopt such tactics, because
in the same letter Wolfgang had mentioned his new address at the
Weber's house for the first time. Leopold did, however, oblige his son
by "railing" at him—but in all seriousness, and in a rage.

Three of Cäcilia Weber's daughters still lived with their mother:
Josepha, Constanze, and Sophie, all of whom Mozart had known
earlier in Mannheim. The oldest, Josepha, was already twenty-three;
Constanze was nineteen, and Sophie eighteen. (Aloysia, the second
daughter, had been married for six months to an actor, Joseph Lange,
and no longer lived in the house.) Leopold Mozart, in ordering Wolfgang to move out at once, obviously had visions of his son behaving
like a rooster in a henhouse in this all-female household. He considered it a dangerous situation, especially because he thought Cäcilia
Weber capable of anything when it came to marrying off her daughters. (But Mozart did not let himself be caught so easily, which is
something his father overlooked.) At first Mozart tried to avert suspicion by claiming that he still had feelings for Aloysia even though she
was now married.

> Indeed I loved her truly, and even now I feel that she is not a matter of
> indifference to me. It is, therefore, a good thing for me that her
> husband is a jealous fool and lets her go nowhere, so that I seldom have
> the opportunity of seeing her. (May 16, 1781)

But this diversionary tactic had only a temporary effect, for rumors
were soon circulating in Vienna and quickly reached Salzburg. At first
it was said that Mozart was staying in Vienna "only because of the
women," but soon everyone had a clear idea of whom he had chosen.
He was not one to keep a secret, so he confirmed the rumors—by
denying them. He mentioned no names. But he was certainly affected
by the gossip and had his reasons for wanting to discredit it.

> I repeat that I have long been thinking of moving to other lodgings, and
> only because people are gossiping. It is unfortunate that I am obliged
> to do this on account of silly talk, in which there is not a word of truth. I

would very much like to know what pleasure certain people find in spreading entirely groundless reports. Because I am living with them, it follows that I am going to marry the daughter. There has been no talk of our being in love. They have skipped that stage. No, I just take rooms in the house and *marry.* If ever there was a time when I thought less of getting married, it is most certainly now! For (although the last thing I want is a rich wife) even if I could now make my fortune by a marriage, I could not possibly pay court to anyone, for my mind is running on very different matters. God has not given me my talent that I might attach it to a wife and waste my youth in idleness. I am just beginning to live—am I now to embitter my own life? To be sure, I have nothing against matrimony, but at the moment it would be a misfortune for me. Well, there is no other way; although it is absolutely untrue, I must at least avoid the appearance of such a thing—even though this appearance rests on nothing but the fact that I am living here. People who have not been to the house can't even tell whether I associate with her as much as with the rest of God's creatures, for the children seldom go out; indeed they go nowhere except the theater, where I never accompany them, as I am generally not at home when the play begins. We went to the Prater a few times, but the mother came too, and, as I was in the house, I could not refuse to accompany them. Nor had I at that time heard anything of these foolish rumors. I must also tell you that I was only allowed to pay *my own share.* Moreover, when the mother heard this talk herself and also heard it from me, she, let me tell you, objected to our going out together and advised me to move to another house in order to avoid further unpleasantness. For she said that she would not like to be the innocent cause of any misfortune to me. So this is the only reason why for some little time (since people began to gossip) I have been intending to leave. So far as truth goes, I have no reason, but these chattering tongues are driving me away.

(July 25, 1781)

As a denial this was unconvincing and surely did little to pacify Leopold Mozart. Constanze Weber was certainly not a rich woman, but the general observations on marriage—that it "embitters" life, that it leads to "idleness," and so forth—are all distortions that Mozart himself did not believe. (Six months later, when he informed his father of his marriage plans and mentioned Constanze's name for the first time, Mozart admitted that he had made this decision months earlier but did not dare tell anyone.) Leopold continued to write harsh letters

about "those Weber females" until it became too much for his son, who
reacted in equally plain terms.

From the way in which you have taken my last letter—as if I were an
arch-scoundrel or a blockhead or both!—I am sorry to see that you rely
more on the gossip and scribbling of other people than you do on me—
and that in fact you have no trust in me whatever. But I assure you that
none of this disturbs me; people may write themselves blind—and you
may believe them as much as you please—but I shall not alter by a
hair's breadth; I shall remain the same honest fellow as ever. And I
swear that if you had not wanted me to move to other lodgings, I would
not have left the Webers; for I feel just like a person who has left his
own comfortable traveling carriage for a post-chaise. But not another
word on the subject. It is really no use talking about it, for the nonsense
which God knows who puts into your head always outweighs any
reasons of mine. But one thing I do beg of you. When you write to me
about something I have done, of which you disapprove or which you
think might have been done better, and in reply I send you my ideas on
the subject, please regard the whole matter as one between father and
son alone, a secret, I mean, and something which is not to be told to
others, as I myself always regard it. I entreat you to leave it at that and
not to apply to other people, for, by God, I will not give the smallest
account to others of what I do or leave undone, no, not even to the
emperor himself. Please trust me always, for indeed I deserve it. I have
trouble and worry enough here to support myself, and the last thing I
need is to read unpleasant letters. (September 5, 1781)

This is the second letter in which Mozart demands that his father
treat him as an adult and take him seriously. Like all the other letters,
it is also signed "Ever your most obedient son W. A. Mzt," but the tone
is different. Mozart goes on to say, "From the moment of my arrival I
have had to live entirely on my own resources, on what I have earned
through my own efforts," and that his father has a somewhat false
impression of his life in Vienna.

From all your letters I gather that you believe I do nothing but amuse
myself. Well, you are most dreadfully mistaken. I can truthfully say
that I have no pleasure—none whatever—save that of being away from
Salzburg. I hope all will go well in the winter; and then, most beloved
father, I shall certainly not forget you. If I see that it is to my advan-

tage, I shall remain here. If not, I am thinking of going straight to Paris.
                                              (September 5, 1781)

The overall tone of this letter is rather irritable and at the same time
more honest, more realistic. Mozart freely admits that it is difficult to
earn a living in "the land of the clavier" Vienna—the noble families,
of course, all went to their country estates in the summer. It was
possible that he might just try his luck again in Paris.

This was the first letter written from his "new room, Auf dem
Graben No. 1175, 4th floor."

A WASTED SUMMER?

It was a very hot summer. From the end of May to mid-September
there was not a single day under 68°F, and the many thunderstorms
brought no relief. The air was humid, and even at night the temperature barely dropped. Mozart was glad of the chance to spend at least a
few days in the country: Count Johann Philipp Cobenzl had invited
him to his estate on the Reisenberg. But otherwise there was little
diversion.

> The present season is, as you know, the worst for anyone who wants to
> make money. The most distinguished families are in the country. So all
> I can do is to work hard in preparation for the winter, when I will have
> less time to compose. (June 16, 1781)

There would be less time to compose in winter because he hoped to
give his own concerts then and no doubt wanted to have new compositions to perform. Yet Mozart composed precious little during this
summer. It did not suit him at all to "store up" work, as it were. He
always needed a clear motivation—a commission or a specific occasion for performance. He wrote many pieces for concerts by fellow
artists and for his own private recitals or public concerts, where he
regularly presented his new works—but that was all a long way off.
Mozart considered writing a cantata for Advent, and he was still
hoping to find a suitable opera text that would be approved by the
General-Spektakel-Direktor (literally, director of public spectacles—a
sort of general manager of the Hoftheater).

For even if I had a libretto, I would not put pen to paper, as Count Rosenberg is not here; and if at the last moment he did not approve it, I would have had the honor of composing for nothing. None of that for me, thank you! (June 16, 1781)

Although Mozart often cited payment for his compositions as the driving force behind his creative process, only deadline pressure seems to have released his artistic powers. He needed the agitation, the pressure of working against the clock, in order to gather all his forces and achieve peak concentration.

Apart from the few days on the Reisenberg, Mozart remained in Vienna, trying to find pupils (no easy task) and consoling his father (and perhaps himself as well) with letters full of overblown, almost pretentious claims—which did little to relieve his present arduous situation.

At present I have only one pupil, Countess Rumbeck, Cobenzl's cousin. I could have many more, it is true, if I chose to lower my fees, but by doing so, I would lose repute. My fees are 6 ducats for twelve lessons, and even then I make it clearly understood that I am giving them as a favor. I would rather have three pupils who pay well than six who pay badly. With this one pupil I can just make *both ends meet*, and that is enough for the present. (June 16, 1781)

Was it really a question of high fees? Could he really have had several pupils at the snap of his fingers? He certainly could not "make both ends meet." In fact, he soon discovered that Countess Maria Caroline Thiennes de Rumbeke also went to the country for several weeks, which left him with no income at all while she was away. Not until December is there any mention of a second paying pupil, Maria Theresa von Trattner, wife of the publisher and bookseller. Having learned from experience, Mozart now demanded payment for canceled lessons, but this measure was not easy to enforce. Theresa von Trattner, for example, was "too economical for that" (December 22, 1781). And what of Josepha Auernhammer, Mozart's highly gifted piano pupil who immediately fell in love with him? His letters make reference to her during the autumn of 1871, but her name is never mentioned in connection with income from teaching. Did Mozart, then, give lessons for free in certain cases? That would be difficult to imagine, considering his assured attitude toward money.

Moreover, his expenditures were considerable. He was not prepared for a lengthy stay in Vienna. Most of his clothes were still in
Salzburg and were not sent to him until summer. Thus he had no
choice but to have new clothes made; after all, Vienna was an especially elegant and fashion-conscious city, and a measure of vanity had
been bred into Mozart at an early age. During the first long journey to
Paris and London, the entire family had acquired new wardrobes;
Mozart's father was so proud of these clothes that he gave detailed
descriptions of them in his letters to Salzburg. And Mozart himself
attached great importance to his wardrobe. He considered himself a
member of the social circles that supported him as an artist, and this
conditioned his style of life. He probably tried to compensate for
his unusually small stature by dressing impressively. He thought his
presence at the bourgeois and aristocratic salons, his contact with the
court, and his public appearances as a virtuoso entitled him to
commensurate social rank that had to be reflected in his clothing.
Muzio Clementi described his appearance as indistinguishable from
that of an aristocratic courtier or chamberlain.[1] He did not believe
that as an artist he was above social convention—a view Beethoven
later presented with a certain audacious tenacity. When Mozart
speaks of his wardrobe, he is precise and unambiguous.

> I could not go about Vienna like a tramp, particularly under the
> circumstances. My clothes were a pitiful sight; no house porter in
> Vienna wore shirts of such coarse linen as mine, which in a man is
> certainly the most objectionable thing. That meant more expense.
>   (September 5, 1781)

Aside from giving piano lessons, Mozart apparently devoted most of
the summer to arranging his wardrobe, looking for new lodgings,
renting a piano, and going to the theater or the Prater. In other
words—he was in love; he probably spent most of his time with
Constanze Weber, enjoyed the summer, and waited. He waited for
"society" to return from the country, for an opera libretto that had been
promised him in April by the actor and playwright Gottlieb Stephanie
(the younger), and for commissions and other opportunities to earn
money. He still wrote nothing about Constanze, if we disregard his
constant denials of a close relationship with any of the Weber daughters. Leopold Mozart must have detected his son's idleness, just as he

detected the attraction to Constanze that made it a joy rather than a burden. Mozart was unable to convince his father that he was not simply amusing himself. But during this summer there was remarkably little discussion of music.

The Köchel catalogue, which attempts to list Mozart's works chronologically, shows that from mid-April to the beginning of October he wrote only three small sets of variations and three sonatas for piano and violin.[2] That is an unusually small yield for six months, even considering that Mozart had begun work on the first act of *Die Entführung aus dem Serail* in August. The three sonatas, along with three earlier ones, were issued in November as Opus 2 under the imprint of the Vienna publisher Artaria; they represent Mozart's entry into Viennese musical life, and he went ahead with their publication despite the fact that summer was not a good time to sell subscriptions. This debut was motivated not only by financial need but by his desire to prove himself as a composer. A review in Karl Friedrich Cramer's *Magazin der Musik* (April 4, 1783) appropriately emphasizes the originality of these six sonatas.

> These sonatas are unique; they are rich in invention, well suited to each instrument, and give evidence of the composer's great musical genius. The violin accompaniment is so skillfully united to the piano part that both instruments command constant and equal attention. As a result, these sonatas require the violinist to be as skilled as the pianist. It is not possible here to give a complete description of these original works. The connoisseur and enthusiast must first play through them himself, and he will discover that we have not exaggerated.[3]

Mozart must have chafed at his idleness, for he began to compose *Die Entführung aus dem Serail* the very day he received the libretto, July 30. Only two days later he had written three of the seven numbers in Act I, and on August 22 the entire first act was completed. It is well known that Mozart worked incredibly fast, that he worked out everything in his head, down to the last detail, before setting pen to paper, and could then write it all out in one sitting. A third of an operatic act in two days, however, surpasses all other instances of Mozart's speed at composition. He had been in a fever of impatience to write again and had waited eagerly for the text because it would provide him with the Vienna breakthrough that he hoped for.

I am so delighted at having to compose this opera that I have already
finished Cavalieri's first aria, Adamberger's aria, and the trio which
closes Act I. The time is short, it is true, for it is to be performed in the
middle of September, but the circumstances connected with the date of
performance and, in general, all my other prospects stimulate me to
such a degree that I rush to my desk with the greatest eagerness and
remain seated there with the greatest delight. (August 1, 1781)

Surprisingly, Mozart did not reflect on the quality of the libretto that
so stimulated his imagination and inspired him to musical and dramatic solutions. The important issues for him were the outward circumstances and the short time left until September, when the first
performance was to take place on the occasion of a visit from Grand
Duke Paul, crown prince of Russia, to Joseph II. The idea of having
Mozart write an opera had come from "high up," specifically, from
Count Franz Xaver Wolf Rosenberg-Orsini, director of the Hoftheater,
though the suggestion was probably first made by Joseph II himself.
They wanted to give Mozart a chance without committing themselves
to a long-term arrangement, since no permanent positions were open.
Naturally, official entertainment was required during the grand duke's
visit, and the text to be adapted had a certain piquancy given the
political background of the visit. The details of the situation may not
have been public knowledge, but the essentials were well enough
known to excite the imaginations of contemporaries. Only a year
earlier Joseph II had met with Catherine II, and they had discussed
their common interests in Turkey. The alliance with Catherine became
closer, and it was clearly necessary to be on good terms with her son
Paul as well. The grand duke was married to a Württemberg princess,
Sophia Dorothea, whose sister Elizabeth was now betrothed to Joseph
II's nephew and designated successor, Francis. So the alliance with
Russia was reinforced through family relations. At the same time that
the Russian grand duke and his wife were making their visit, Elizabeth, as Archduke Francis's bride-to-be, moved to Vienna, where she
was to be educated at a Salesian convent. A "Turkish" opera subject
was entirely germane to the political discussions with the "grand
beast," as Mozart called the future czar.

Prince Paul had grown up in the exceedingly confused, spiteful,
and loveless family environment that Catherine the Great created

around herself. She had had his father, Peter III, dethroned, had kept the prince himself from any contact with affairs of state, and had placed him under the strictest supervision; during the eighteen-month European journey that now brought him to Vienna, a courier was dispatched to St. Petersburg from every stop along the way to report on even the most insignificant occurrences. The prince was at once condemned to a life of complete idleness and held in the deepest suspicion. He sought refuge in a more or less enforced solitude and in his own unusually harmonious family life, which stood in direct contrast to his mother's frequent love affairs. He simply had to accept his inactivity and wait until he finally came to the throne.[4] In the autumn of 1781, when he visited Vienna, he was universally regarded as an enlightened and amiable gentleman. Mozart tried to raise his spirits with piano variations on Russian folksongs specially selected for the occasion.

Nothing came of the opera performance for this distinguished guest. The libretto needed extensive revision, and meanwhile the court was preparing new productions of two operas by Christoph Willibald von Gluck. Mozart had requested the revision himself and probably collaborated on every aspect of it. The glittering premiere in the presence of the ducal family of Württemberg and the Russian grand duke could not be postponed, but for Mozart it was crucial that *Die Entführung aus dem Serail* conform to his musical and dramatic standards, which required a sympathetic union of music and text. Mozart would not accept a division of responsibility and insisted categorically that he have a voice in preparing the libretto. While working on *Die Entführung,* he formulated the musical-dramatic precepts that would guide his subsequent career as an opera composer.

> I would say that in an opera the poetry must be altogether the obedient daughter of the music. Why are Italian comic operas popular everywhere—in spite of their miserable libretti—even in Paris, where I myself witnessed their success? Just because there the music reigns supreme, and when one listens to it all else is forgotten. An opera is sure of success when the plot is well worked out, the words written solely for the music and not shoved in here and there to suit some miserable rhyme (which, God knows, never enhances the value of any theatrical performance, be it what it may, but rather detracts from it)— I mean, words or even entire verses which ruin the composer's whole

idea. Verses are indeed the most indispensable element for music, but rhymes—solely for the sake of rhyming—are the most detrimental. Those high and mighty people who set to work in this pedantic fashion will always come to grief, both they and their music. The best thing of all is when a good composer, who understands the stage and is talented enough to make sound suggestions, meets an able poet, that true phoenix; in that case no fears need be entertained as to the applause— even of the ignorant. (October 13, 1781)

The collaboration with Stephanie was gratifying precisely because he was open to Mozart's theatrical ideas and saw in them no threat to his own achievement. The plot of this "Turkish" opera was not Stephanie's in any case; he had merely adapted an older play. Mozart was still somewhat new to Vienna and realized that he could easily fall victim to impenetrable theater intrigues, but Stephanie seemed to present no danger.

Everyone abuses Stephanie. It may be that in my case he is only friendly to my face. But after all he is preparing the libretto for me— and, what is more, exactly as I want it—and by Heaven, I don't ask anything more of him. (September 26, 1781)

Thorough preparation was paramount, even if it meant postponing the first performance. The Turkish subject would always appeal to the Viennese. Mozart, then, had to wait patiently until Stephanie could deliver a draft revision of the second and third acts.

Not until October do we find Mozart again at his desk, now occupied with a serenade (K. 375) for St. Theresa's Day, October 15, which he was writing for the family of the court painter Joseph Hickel: "But the main reason why I composed it was in order to let Herr von Strack, who goes there every day, hear some of my music; so I wrote it rather carefully" (November 3, 1781). Johann Kilian Strack was the valet of Joseph II, with whom the emperor played chamber music in the afternoons; Mozart hoped to make an impression on him and so reach the master through the servant. He deliberately chose to write a popular serenade, since the musical customs of the period presented many occasions for playing such a piece. Musicians in need of money could be easily engaged for a serenade, and thus on the evening of October 15 Mozart's piece was played at three different places; the six instrumentalists were paid for each performance. (Mozart soon arranged the work for eight instruments and later made a further arrangement for ten wind instruments.) Mozart in turn was given a performance of the piece at eleven o'clock on the evening of his own name day.

In November 1781 there was a small private recital at the home of the Auernhammer family. "In a rush," as Mozart says, he wrote for this program a sonata for two pianos (K. 375a/448), an ambitious work that he himself called "the grand sonata." In December we hear of Mozart's first concert earnings since his move to Vienna. Joseph II had invited him to play for his royal guests in competition with Muzio Clementi, who had recently arrived in Vienna. Clementi recounts:

> I had been in Vienna only a few days when I received an invitation from the emperor to play for him on the fortepiano. Coming into the music room, I met someone whom I held to be an imperial chamberlain due to his elegant attire. We had hardly entered into conversation when the subject turned to music and we recognized each other as fellow artists—as Mozart and Clementi—and greeted each other warmly.[5]

The emperor, who years later was still rhapsodizing about this competition, sent Mozart 50 ducats (225 florins) to express his gratitude. It goes without saying that Mozart badly needed this money. During the past six months in Vienna he had been able to bring in at most 230 florins. Although he would also have received 400 to 450 florins from the Munich *Idomeneo*, this money was presumably used to pay off debts from his Paris journey. Mozart never again lived as modestly as he did during this first summer in Vienna. Considering that he changed lodgings twice, and in view of the expenses for clothing, piano rental, and visits to the theater, we cannot entirely dismiss the possibility that Mozart was unable to survive this first summer without incurring debts, and that he turned to his aristocratic and bourgeois patrons for help.

A SPECIAL HOUSE

On December 15, 1781, when Mozart mentioned Constanze Weber's name to his father for the first time and simultaneously announced his intention to marry, he added the following comment: "One more thing

I must tell you, which is that when I resigned the archbishop's service, our love had not yet begun. It was born of her tender care and attentions when I was living in her house."

Mozart could just as well have written that the love affair with Constanze had been going on for six months and that there was some foundation to all the rumors that had reached Salzburg and worried Leopold Mozart so much. As long as Mozart was unsure of his future plans, he apparently rejected his father's demand that he move out of Frau Weber's home. But when the relationship with Constanze became so close that he (and she) began to think of marriage, Mozart too saw the necessity of finding other accommodations. For now the darker side of his future mother-in-law, Cäcilia Weber, began to show itself. Frau Weber was inclined to simpleminded plans where the fate of her daughters was concerned; she was also full of false and malicious gossip, which often made the atmosphere around her unbearable. But dealing with the man who had been Constanze's legal guardian since her father's death, and who had to be consulted about every move his ward made, was even more difficult. Moreover, this guardian, Johann Thorwart, was influential in precisely the sphere where Mozart hoped to make his fortune: the theater. Thorwart had originally been a royal servant; now, thanks to a favorable marriage and clever planning of his career, he owned several houses and had landed an important administrative position. He was "Imperial and Royal Court Theatrical Supervisor" (so he signed himself on the marriage contract)—in other words, administrator of the Hoftheater, in charge of all nonartistic matters. Not that Cäcilia Weber and Thorwart had anything against a marriage between Constanze and Mozart in principle, but their promotion of this plan was not without financial motives, and Thorwart's methods began to resemble blackmail. Mozart seems to have identified the problem early on, for he was already seeking new lodgings in July 1781. In late August or early September he moved into a small room nearby, on the fourth floor of a house at No. 1175 Auf dem Graben (today No. 17). He called it "a very prettily furnished room. . . . I purposely chose one not looking on the street in order to be quiet" (August 29, 1781). There was room for little more than a wardrobe, a table, a bed, and a (rented) piano. It had been decidedly more comfortable at Frau Weber's.

Mozart could not think seriously of marriage until he had some sort of secure income. Thorwart would never have given his consent. So Wolfgang had to wait, try as best he could to smooth out the savage conflicts that occasionally erupted in the Weber house, and remain impervious to insulting language. The atmosphere was sometimes so tense that even Constanze got fed up and temporarily fled to Baroness Martha Elizabeth Waldstätten, who frequently offered a helping hand to the young couple.

Yet life in the house on the Graben cannot have been so bad, for Mozart stayed there almost eleven months. It was a typical four-story structure on the corner of Habsburgergasse, with a view of one of the Graben's two fountains. The Graben, with its shops, coffeehouses, and soft-drink stands, was already the center of Viennese street life. Anyone seeking the hustle and bustle of city life or the company of loafers, gadabouts, or attractive women, anyone wishing to see the latest fashions, to find entertainment until the wee hours, or in general to experience the flair of a world capital, made his way to the Graben.

The house at No. 1175 was notable for the two figures of crouching lions that projected from the ledge and faced the Petersplatz and massive St. Peter's Church. The owners were Theresa Contrini, who contented herself with one room on the fourth floor as her lodgings, and Jakob Joseph Keesenberg. The ground floor was rented out to three different shopkeepers. The rest of the house—it had "nineteen rooms, ten smaller chambers, three kitchens, three garrets, two cellars, a carriage stall, a stable for six horses, and a 'hay vault' "[6]—was occupied by Imperial Court Purveyor Adam Isaac Arnstein, who paid 2,690 florins annually for rent. He lived there with his family and a large number of domestic servants, as well as office assistants and bookkeepers employed in his wholesale business. Some of them must have lived on the fourth floor, next door to Mozart and the landlady, for Arnstein's household consisted of at least thirty people.

The exceptional feature of this house can be described in a single sentence: it was the only house in Vienna that a Jew had freely selected and rented as a place of residence. Though a few Jews had residency permits, none except Arnstein had this privilege, which extended to his family and the employees whose names were included in his letters patent. This, along with the other stipulations in the letters patent, gave the Arnstein family a special status, almost on a par with baptized Jews, who enjoyed the same rights as gentile subjects.

The significance of Arnstein's position can only be appreciated in comparison with the lot of other Viennese Jews, who were forced to live under the most restrictive and oppressive conditions despite the vitally important role they played in public finance and munitions. Vienna did not even have a ghetto where the Jews could pursue their way of life as a community, with a synagogue, schools, and the security offered by separation from the rest of society. Before Joseph II's reforms, they had to pay a toll (*Leibmaut*) when entering the city gates and were subject to outrageously high taxes known as *Toleranzgelder*. They were required to wear special clothing with a yellow patch (*Judenfleck*) and could live only in designated houses. Synagogues were forbidden, and on Christian holidays Jews had to stay in their homes and could not so much as look out a window when one of the numerous Christian processions was filing past. They were positively forbidden entry to public taverns, theaters, and concerts, to say nothing of the restrictions on trade and industry. In 1782 there were some forty Jewish heads of families who held residency permits for themselves and their dependents—a total of approximately five hundred people. Maria Theresa had a bitter loathing for Jews, although she would have been forced to declare national bankruptcy without the aid of Jewish bankers and wholesalers. During audiences with Jews, she even went so far as to have a screen placed between herself and her visitors so she would not have to look at them. And Arnstein was no exception, despite the many concessions he had grudgingly been granted.

The elder Arnstein still lived strictly according to Jewish laws and customs; he wore a long flowing beard and a black coat reaching to his ankles. His son Nathan Adam Arnstein, however, was a high-spirited, fashionable man who could easily have passed for a Viennese cavalier, a *bon vivant* who made no secret of his wealth and took full advantage of his unique position. His wife, Fanny, was a daughter of the famous Berlin banker Daniel Itzig, and all the leading Jewish families in Prussia and Austria were linked through their marriage. Fanny Arnstein later founded the most important salon in Vienna, which played an outstanding role during the period of the Vienna Congress and was notable for its curious mixture of intellect, informality, and extravagant wealth. Her contacts with important artists, scientists, diplomats, and aristocrats made her salon a focal point of Viennese social life. Her rise as hostess and intermediary to the intellectual and social elite was only possible after the death of the tradition-bound family patriarch, and only when the prejudice against both practicing and assimilated Jews had begun to wane and a measure of social equality had been achieved. The process of Jewish emancipation was in its earliest stage when Mozart moved in next to the Arnsteins. Important social functions did not take place at their home until the beginning of the nineteenth century.[7]

We know nothing about Mozart's personal contact with the younger Arnstein and his wife, but they were among the subscribers to his concerts. It was very possibly through Fanny Arnstein that Mozart happened upon the book *Phaëthon, or On the Immortality of the Soul*, by Moses Mendelssohn. The fourth edition, of which Mozart owned a copy, appeared the year Fanny Arnstein moved from Berlin to Vienna. It is known that she brought copies of this important work with her and introduced it to her Viennese acquaintances.

Most of our scanty information about Mozart's social contacts has come to us by chance and concerns visits and personal associations that had little musical significance. However, we can say categorically that Mozart counted numerous Jews among his friends and acquaintances. Although many had converted and were thus viewed as equals in bourgeois circles, they too shared the experience of an oppressed minority tolerated only within narrow limits. This minority had survived periods of harsh persecution and attempts at extermination only through an awareness of its special historical role and its strong bonds of custom and tradition. In a ghetto these would have been strengthened, but in the outside world they were considerably threatened. Religion was still the great dividing line in the eighteenth century, and for many Jews baptism into the Christian faith represented a strong temptation, a definitive way to overcome centuries-old burdens, hardships, and disrespect.[8]

Not a single biography of Mozart records that he lived for almost a year in the same house as this notable Jewish family, although virtually all of them mention this address on the Graben.

Mozart was free of social prejudices and, without being aware of it, was perhaps more fascinated by outsiders—who had a heightened social awareness and a seismographic feel for the small tremors that precede great earthquakes—than by his conventional contemporaries who sought only pleasant entertainment from art and avoided anything unusual. Despite his dependence on the court and influential aristocratic circles for commissions, and his great natural self-confidence in these circles, Mozart refused to let himself be influenced or led astray in his opinions and interests.

Shortly before her death Maria Theresa issued the following statement, which suggests that anti-Semitism was still pervasive and did not stop with the empress.

> In future no Jew shall be allowed to remain here without my written permission. I know of no more evil plague upon the state than this nation, who reduce others to beggary through greed, deceit, and usury, and practice all manner of wickedness which an honest man loathes; they should therefore be prevented from coming here and their numbers decreased as far as possible.[9]

The intention here was not to set down a law of social conduct, especially not in Vienna, where a certain laissez-faire attitude had always prevailed. Elsewhere, such a statement of royal displeasure might be echoed by every subject in the land and would be sure to have an effect, but in Vienna people were more casual and spontaneous—if not in principle any more tolerant. The empress's anti-Semitism was shared primarily by the Viennese municipal authorities, representing merchants who were too inflexible to compete with Jewish businessmen. Among the educated bourgeoisie and the nobility, a great many of whom held government posts, the atmosphere was already enlightened and liberal, or at least more pragmatic and reasonable.

Thus, the uncomplicated world of Viennese society already provided growing opportunities for contact with Jewish businessmen, although complete social integration had not yet been achieved. It is hardly surprising that many elegant and charming Jewish women played a role in paving the way for such changes. With their uninhibited and self-confident poise, they helped to allay prejudices well before the so-called Jewish emancipation was introduced through reforms on the political level. And of the many bourgeois and aristocratic salons, there were apparently several that did themselves the honor of counting a Fanny Arnstein among their guests.

Mozart probably met Fanny Arnstein at a salon and thus established the contact that eventually led him to become her neighbor. We do not know when and where he first met her, nor how the lease came to be signed. However, we do have a source that offers a possible explanation and at the same time provides a noteworthy example of the social developments mentioned above. A concert at the home of Baron Gottfried Adam von Hochstetter in January 1780 is described thus by one of his guests: "A Frau von Arnstein played delightfully on the piano, and Mlle. Weberin enchanted us with her singing."[10] Did the writer of this seemingly insignificant line of reminiscence know just who these two women were who joined musical forces that evening? "Mlle. Weberin" was undoubtedly one of the Weber daughters— probably Aloysia, Mozart's beloved from his days in Mannheim, with whom he had quickly reestablished contact in Vienna. This small clue suggests that contact with the Arnsteins could have been made through the Webers. It also demonstrates the informality and lack of prejudice in this artistically active family; no fewer than three of Fridolin Weber's four daughters had become singers, and even their father showed more interest in music and the theater than in the bourgeois work ethic or the government career he had begun.

SEDUCED OR IN LOVE?

In sharp contrast to Herr Weber's liberality stood the petty, narrow-minded behavior of Cäcilia Weber and the guardian Thorwart. As soon as they were satisfied that Constanze and Mozart were firmly committed and their marriage plans definite, they used every means at their disposal to turn the entire affair into a business transaction, reducing Constanze to a commodity to be sold off at the highest price. Cäcilia Weber was certainly not doing well financially. After the sudden death of her husband she was left without an income and was entirely dependent on her daughters, three of whom still lived at home. The extra income from renting out rooms in her lodgings at Zum Auge Gottes only amounted to a small sum.

There must have been debts even before her husband's death, and Cäcilia was counting on the salary of her daughter Aloysia, who had an engagement at the Nationaloper. In any event, a loan of 900 florins was taken out upon the death of Fridolin Weber. A short time later, when Joseph Lange and Aloysia Weber announced their intention to marry, Lange promised his future mother-in-law an annuity of at least 600 florins, which was a tidy sum—about what Joseph Haydn began earning in 1761 as an assistant kapellmeister, and considerably more than Leopold Mozart's salary in Salzburg. But Cäcilia Weber, who obviously thrived on disputes, made so many demands on her future son-in-law that he finally resorted to the courts. In the end, the good-natured Lange agreed not only to raise the annuity to 700 florins but also to assume the 900-florin debt owed to the court treasury. Lange paid out the annuity punctually until Cäcilia Weber's death, even long after he himself was in straitened circumstances and was forced to go into debt.

Cäcilia Weber did not go quite so far with Mozart, but she did conceal this income from him and complained that she received no support from her daughter Aloysia. Perhaps Frau Weber's apparent drinking habit also played a role in these unpleasant confrontations over money. Even Leopold Mozart seems to have heard rumors to that effect, for Wolfgang tried to minimize Cäcilia's drinking to his father and at the same time to allay suspicions about her daughters.

> Your postscript about her mother is justified only in so far as she likes wine, and more so, I admit, than a woman ought to. Still, I have yet to see her drunk and it would be a lie if I were to say so. The children only drink water—and, although their mother almost forces wine upon them, she cannot induce them to touch it. This often leads to a lot of wrangling—can you imagine a mother quarreling with her children over such a thing? (April 10, 1782)

Mozart still visited the Webers frequently after he moved out. It was, of course, only a stone's throw from his room to the house on the Petersplatz. Cäcilia seems to have shown a certain restraint around Mozart. She knew that for the moment he was almost penniless, but she also knew that he was a highly respected musician on the brink of achieving fame throughout Europe. She had known him earlier in Mannheim, had heard of his success in Munich, and saw him as a future operatic celebrity who was composing his first work for the Nationalsingspiel. In any case, she had more respect for Mozart than for her other son-in-law. It was not difficult for her to stay out of marriage negotiations and such because Thorwart understood these matters much better. This man played his role with great single-mindedness. He probably had his own ideas about the fickleness and immorality of "theater people"—certainly including Mozart, in his opinion—and considered money a bulwark against the unreliability of artists. We must not forget, however, that such contracts concerning betrothals were not at all unusual. Constanze Weber was in a particularly awkward, embarrassing situation and tried to extricate herself as quickly as possible. She was not even consulted about the arrangements. As Mozart wrote to his father:

> Now about the marriage contract, or rather the written assurance of my honorable intentions towards the girl. You know, of course, that since the father is no longer alive (unhappily for the whole family as well as for Constanze and myself), a guardian has taken his place. Certain busybodies and impudent gentlemen like Herr Winter must have shouted in the ears of this person (who doesn't know me at all) all sorts of stories about me—that he should beware of me, for example, that I have no settled income, that I was far too intimate with her, that I would probably jilt her, the girl would be ruined, and so forth. All this made him smell a rat—for the mother, who knows me and knows that I am honorable, let things take their course and said nothing to him about the matter. For my whole association with the girl consisted in my lodging with the family and later in my going to the house every day. No one ever saw me with her outside the house. But the guardian kept on pestering the mother with his representations until she told me about them and asked me to speak to him myself, adding that he would come some day to her house. He came, and we had a talk—with the result (since I did not explain myself as clearly as he desired) that he told the mother to forbid me to associate with her daughter until I had come to a written agreement with him. The mother replied, "His whole association with her consists in his coming to my house, and I cannot forbid him my house. He is too good a friend—and one to whom I owe a great deal. I am quite satisfied. I trust him. You must settle it with him yourself." So he forbade me to have anything more to do with Constanze unless I would give him a written undertaking. What other course was open to me? I either had to give him a written contract or—to desert the girl. What man who loves sincerely and honestly can forsake his beloved? Would not the mother, would not my beloved herself place the

worst interpretation upon such conduct? That was my predicament. So I drew up a document to the effect *that I bound myself to marry Mlle. Constanze Weber within the space of 3 years and that if it should prove impossible for me to do so owing to a change in my sentiments, she should be entitled to claim from me 300 florins a year.* Nothing in the world could have been easier for me to write. For I knew that I would never have to pay these 300 florins, because I would never forsake her, and even if I were so unfortunate as to change my mind, I would be only too glad to get rid of her for 300 florins, while Constanze, if I know her, would be too proud to let herself be sold. But what did the angelic girl do when the guardian was gone? She asked her mother for the document and said to me: *"Dear Mozart! I need no written assurance from you. I believe what you say,"* and tore up the paper. This action made my dear Constanze even more precious to me, and, the document having been destroyed and the guardian having given his *parole d'honneur* to keep the matter to himself, I was somewhat relieved on your account, my most beloved father. For I had no fear but that ultimately you would give your consent to our marriage (since the girl has everything but money), because I know your sensible ideas on this subject.

(December 22, 1781)

The appeal to his father's "sensible ideas" had little effect: Leopold was incensed that Mozart had participated in such dealings. And Mozart admitted that he had foreseen such a reaction from his father. Why else would he have bound Thorwart to silence? The guardian broke his promise, however, and spread the story all over Vienna. Even Leopold, in Salzburg, learned of the written promise of marriage with a specified penalty for breach of contract, and he apparently did not mince words about it. He saw Thorwart's actions as a form of pimping, and the 300 florins as prostitution money; and he wanted the guardian to suffer the prescribed punishment (which, as stipulated by Joseph II, was sweeping the streets in chains, with shaven head, and standing in the stocks wearing a sign that proclaimed the offense). Mozart tried to appease his father without completely contradicting him.

I quite agree with you in thinking that Madame Weber and Herr von Thorwart have been to blame in showing too much regard for their own interests, though the mother is no longer her own mistress and has to leave everything, particularly matters of this kind, to the guardian, who (as he has never made my acquaintance) is by no means bound to trust me. But it is undeniable that he was too hasty in demanding a written undertaking from me, especially since I told him that as yet you knew nothing about the affair and that at the moment I could not possibly disclose it to you. I asked him to have patience for a short time until my circumstances take another turn; then I would give you a full account of everything and the whole matter would be settled. But it's all over now, and love must be my excuse. Herr von Thorwart did not behave well, but not so badly that he and Madame Weber "should be put in chains, made to sweep the streets and have boards hung round their necks with the words *seducers of youth.*" That too is an exaggeration. And even if what you say were true, that in order to catch me she opened her house, let me have the run of it, gave me every opportunity, etc.—even so, the punishment would be rather severe. But I need hardly tell you that it is not true. And it hurts me very much to think that you could believe your son would frequent a house where such things went on. Let me only say that you should believe precisely the opposite of all you have been told. But enough of this.

(January 16, 1782)

The period of Mozart's engagement was not a very happy one, for the written promise of marriage did not prevent further nastiness and malicious scandalmongering. At one point Cäcilia Weber was on the verge of calling the police to bring her daughter home (a reminder of Maria Theresa's "chastity Police," only recently abolished, who would have followed up by initiating the appropriate criminal proceedings). Another time, she refused to hand over Mozart's own manuscripts without a written receipt, lest she be accused of misappropriation. It was high time for Mozart to "save" Constanze from such a house, and "to make myself and her . . . very happy," as he wrote on December 15, 1781. But he had to wait until the beginning of August 1782, because until he was paid for *Die Entführung aus dem Serail* there was no hope of setting up a household, no chance of an "abduction" from the "Eye of God."

And the opera needed time. The early deadline of mid-August 1781 came to nothing; Mozart would have had to compose and rehearse *Die Entführung* in six weeks (which he fully believed he could do). Thereafter the performance was postponed again and again. It is unclear whether the libretto revisions were solely to blame or whether the theater was creating new obstacles. In any case, the premiere was greeted with expressions of disapproval that may have been planned. (We do not know whether they were simply attempts to stir up opinion against a newcomer to the Vienna stage who might become a dangerous rival for commissions, or whether Mozart's treatment of the subject matter irritated a Viennese public all too accustomed to the usual well-worn material.) But Mozart had put these months to good use. He attended plays and operas, reflected deeply on the musical theater, and made a thorough revision of the text with his librettist, Stephanie. He gave himself plenty of time, composing very little during this period and gathering strength for his breakthrough as an independent self-employed musician.

DIE ENTFÜHRUNG AUS DEM SERAIL

It was highly appropriate that Mozart's first work for the Viennese stage had a Turkish subject. Against the background of Grand Duke Paul's visit, at a time when the Russian-Austrian alliance against Turkey was being strengthened, the libretto for *Die Entführung* appears not only as a clever exploitation of currently relevant themes—with the added attraction of a strange and exotic atmosphere—but as a kind of political statement, a warning about concerted action against Turkey. For centuries the Turks had been something like fateful adversaries of the Habsburg monarchy. And now preparations had just begun to celebrate the hundredth anniversary of Austria's victory over the Turks in 1683. Everyone knew that the definitive boundary between Christian Europe and the Islamic empire had yet to be drawn. Whatever plans the "grand beasts" were hatching at Schönbrunn or the czar's court would have an enormous effect on the populace. They meant war or peace: higher prices, military service, human lives in danger; or stability, trade, and relative prosperity. After all, Austria had achieved a form of coexistence with Turkey, though it was not entirely without tension and small border skirmishes, and there were various trade relations on a small scale. Turkish clothing could be seen every day on the streets of Vienna.

The subject of Mozart's opera was the clash of two different cultures, but in an altered perspective: Europeans are detained against

Mozart's mother-in-law Cäcilia Weber.

their will at the court of a Turkish ruler; after a rescue attempt from outside fails, they are shown magnanimity of a higher moral order than they ever knew in their European homelands. That two other operas were chosen to be performed for the Russian visitors suggests that there was some concern about the implications of this material. A festival production of *Die Entführung* for state visitors would not have taken place without some political fireworks.

Mozart toned down and domesticated the opera's strange and exotic elements. The Pasha's country house seems more like an English manor, and the closely guarded seraglio, as a lively imagination might picture it, is only mentioned. Instead, what is actually depicted on stage resembles an open and by no means prisonlike abode along the lines of an aristocratic home with extensive parklands. But the Turkish theme was relevant in yet another sense: it corresponded to a literary tradition that had spread all over Europe since Montesquieu's *Lettres persanes* (*Persian Letters*, 1721). A foreign atmosphere provided a context in which European situations could be more sharply delineated. The Turkish setting was a literary vantage point from which the author, relatively unchallenged by the censor, could draw conclusions and portray modes of behavior that highlighted the conditions of his own time and place. The eighteenth century novel, especially, employed the literary device of a foreigner traveling in Europe, or a European traveling in foreign lands, to criticize contemporary civilization. This "view from afar" made it possible to illuminate the social situation at home more clearly. It was a sign of the times that such a cultural comparison could only be presented in the form of an adventure story.

In the theater and above all in opera (*opera seria* as well as *opera buffa*, Singspiel, or musical farce), there was an endless list of Turkish subjects, but these had less "enlightened" objectives and were more diluted and more superficial in their concentration on atmospheric effects. Such weaknesses were inherent in the genre and probably also had something to do with the audiences who patronized musical theater. In the eighteenth century opera meant almost exclusively court opera, even when the audience was no longer composed exclusively of court society; indeed, people of almost every social level had access to the opera through unrestricted ticket sales. The few independent theater troupes that traveled through Europe were not up to the demands of real musical theater; the expense of engaging properly trained singers and instrumentalists was (and is) too great, and too many concessions had to be made to the tastes of a broad and undiscriminating public.

At the personal instigation of Joseph II, part of the Hoftheater had split off to become an autonomous, German-language National-singspiel. Mozart recognized that these special conditions in Vienna would allow him to write an opera that did more than fulfill traditional operatic requirements. He could now make fuller use of the theater's true potential. He could shatter rules of form, do away with moribund patterns, and develop a contemporary music theater that was both dramatically and musically capable of portraying individuals instead of types. He could depict conflicts between characters who bore responsibility for their own actions and were not subject to laws of fate. He could take up themes that corresponded to contemporary reality or were drawn directly from it and would reflect on it.

The title *Die Entführung aus dem Serail* was a sure draw. It evoked images of adventure, abduction, and the simultaneously fascinating and terrifying aura of a Turkish harem while promising a happy ending. The initial libretto conformed entirely to the trivial models that could be found in endless variations. Stephanie had done nothing more than take an existing libretto (by Christoph Friedrich Bretzner, who promptly brought charges of plagiarism) and make slight changes and adaptations to fit the available personnel. Of course, Bretzner too had worked from existing models. Although Mozart liked Stephanie's libretto on sight, it soon proved merely a useful point of departure. Only while composing the first act and formulating a musically determined dramatic concept did he see clearly where the libretto had to be changed.

Now comes the rub! The first act was finished more than three weeks ago, as was also one aria in Act II and the drunken duet (*per i signori viennesi*) which consists entirely of *my Turkish tattoo*. But I cannot compose any more, because the whole story is being altered—and, to tell the truth, at my own request. At the beginning of Act III there is a charming quintet or rather finale, but I would prefer to have it at the end of Act II. In order to make this practicable, great changes must be made, in fact an entirely new plot must be introduced—and Stephanie

is up to his neck in other work. So we must have a little patience.
                                                    (September 26, 1781)

Mozart thus had an important part in shaping the libretto down to
the last detail, and took responsibility for all the changes. The story is
quite simple and straightforward, though it does not lack dramatic and
suspenseful scenes.

Constanze, Blonde (her maid), and Pedrillo (a servant) are captured
by marauding pirates and sold to the Turkish sultan Pasha Selim;
Belmonte, Constanze's beloved, escapes. He arms a ship in order to
free the three captives. Constanze is wooed by Pasha Selim, while
Osmin, the overseer at the Pasha's country house, pursues Blonde.
Pedrillo manages to obtain the job of tending the Pasha's gardens,
which allows him relative freedom. After Belmonte has found his way
into the gardens, he and Pedrillo work out a plan for a nocturnal
abduction; this is foiled by Osmin, despite an attempt to drug him with
a sleeping potion. Instead of ordering punishment for the attempted
abduction, the Pasha proves magnanimous after recognizing Belmonte
as the son of his enemy. The prisoners are allowed to board their ship
and sail home, abashed at the sultan's unexpected kindness.

It is proof of Mozart's dramatic gift and his feeling for stage effects
that he does not depend purely on his musical invention but plans
every detail of the theatrical development as well as the musical
devices that shape it. His statement "In an opera the poetry must be
altogether the obedient daughter of the music" is easily misunderstood
unless we read further in the same letter: "The best thing of all is when
a good composer, who understands the stage and is talented enough to
make sound suggestions, meets an able poet, that true phoenix."
Mozart considered most librettists no more than craftsmen who followed the rules of their trade and wrote mechanical sequences of vocal
numbers, using rhyme for its own sake instead of troubling over a
dramatic development that could be intensified by the music if only a
libretto presented the opportunity. He complained frequently about
bad librettists and at one point stated categorically, "If we composers
were always to stick so faithfully to our rules (which were very good at
a time when no one knew better), we would be concocting music as
unpalatable as their libretti" (October 13, 1781).

Mozart was in the process of developing a new operatic style and

was looking for librettists who shared his conception of stage charac-
terization. For Mozart it was essential to expose the logical structure of
his opera material, or even invent it, if necessary. Instead of types he
wanted to create individual characters—not puppets, but living men
and women. Mozart was a passionate theatergoer throughout his life.
He knew all the latest developments, had seen famous actors perform
Shakespeare and Lessing, and was about to revolutionize the opera
stage in the same way that Lessing had shaken up the post-Gottsched
theater. Mozart's characters are individuals who react to the world
around them according to their particular personalities and capacities. They are capable of development, and they develop only as a
result of their experiences. They do not each represent a single
character trait but are complex figures with positive and negative
sides, true to life and multifaceted.

Belmonte, the central figure of this opera, is by no means an exalted
hero. In his dealings with his servant Pedrillo he shows signs of selfish
insensitivity that serve, discreetly but with unmistakable irony, as a
criticism of the master-servant relationship itself—a relationship that
is maintained even in a risky and desperate situation of mutual
dependency. Belmonte is interested only in Constanze's fate; he never
asks about Pedrillo and Blonde and ignores all references to them. His
effusive romanticism is almost dangerous.

BELMONTE: Ah, let me collect myself! I have seen her, the dear,
faithful, wonderful girl! Oh Constanze, Constanze! What would I not do
for you, what would I not dare on your behalf?

PEDRILLO: Not so fast, my lord. You must control yourself. Subterfuge
will be much more useful to us. We are not in our country. Here
floggings and hangings are everyday affairs.

BELMONTE: Ah Pedrillo, if you knew what love is!

PEDRILLO: Hm! As if it were nothing to the likes of me! I suffer the
pangs of love as much as any one else. And do you think it doesn't turn
my stomach to see my Blonde watched over by a villain like Osmin?[11]

Belmonte can achieve nothing without Pedrillo's prudence and
resourcefulness, but this is shown more or less on the level of comic
relief. There are clearer and more serious indications of the relation-

ship in the many references to money. Belmonte, the son of a Spanish grandee, tries to save himself from an apparently hopeless situation by means of repeated allusions to his noble family and his financial resources, which impress neither Osmin nor Pasha Selim. (Here again, Belmonte offers a ransom only for himself and Constanze; the fate of his servant and Blonde does not interest him in the least.)

Just as Pedrillo has nothing but his wit, inventiveness, and self-confidence, Blonde must also depend on her own resources. Unlike Pedrillo, however, she can turn her quick-wittedness into outright combativeness. Whereas Constanze is inclined to submit wistfully to her fate, Blonde's reaction is more pragmatic. She rebels against Osmin with a sense of superiority that renders him quite helpless.

OSMIN: Aren't you forgetting that the Pasha gave you to me as my slave?

BLONDE: Pasha this, Pasha that! Girls are not goods to be given away! I'm an Englishwoman, born to freedom, and I defy anyone who would force me to do his will![12]

Later she goes so far as to advocate—albeit satirically—a world ruled by women. Here again a farcical element is perceptible, but with a serious background. It is no coincidence that Blonde mentions her English origins; this is an overt reference to civil liberty. In the literature of the period, England regularly features as an example of a nation whose citizens enjoy full personal and civil rights, in deliberate contrast to conditions under an aristocratic despotism. (The first version of Friedrich Schiller's *Kabale und Liebe* [*Love and Intrigue*], whose Lady Milford is the most famous literary example of such an Englishwoman, was completed during the same summer of 1782.)

Perhaps the most noteworthy feature of *Die Entführung aus dem Serail* is that the characters constitute a cross-section of European society, in contrast to which the Turkish Pasha and his magnanimous behavior take on added significance. Belmonte is a Spanish nobleman passed off as an Italian architect by his servant Pedrillo; Blonde is an Englishwoman, and an obviously Dutch seaman is taken along on Belmonte's ship. These representatives of "civilized" maritime nations come up against Pasha Selim, who embodies a humanity the Europeans would never have expected. He loves Constanze, but more than anything else he wants her to return his love. He gives Pedrillo a position almost equal to that of Osmin: one oversees the Pasha's house, the other his gardens. He feels deceived by Constanze and betrayed by Belmonte. At the same time he recognizes in him the son of his "worst enemy," who is characterized in a manner hardly flattering to a Spanish grandee.

> It was because of your father, that barbarian, that I was forced to leave my native land. His insatiable greed deprived me of my beloved, whom I cherished more than my own life. He robbed me of honor, property, everything—he destroyed all my happiness. [13]

But the Pasha subjects his victim to moral chastisement rather than physical punishment.

> BELMONTE: Cool your wrath on me, avenge the wrong done to you by my father. Your anger is justified and I am prepared for anything.
>
> SELIM: It must be very natural for your family to do wrong, since you assume that I am the same way. But you deceive yourself. I despise your father far too much ever to behave as he did. Have your freedom, take Constanze, sail home, and tell your father that you were in my power, and that I set you free so that you could tell him it is a far greater pleasure to repay injustice with good deeds than evil with evil.
>
> BELMONTE: My lord, you astonish me.
>
> SELIM (*with a look of contempt*): I can believe that. Now go—and if you become at least more humane than your father, my action will be rewarded. [14]

In Singspiel the plot is conveyed through dialogue while the arias and ensembles supply the reflective element. They express the moods, feelings, and passions that underline and direct the action. The vocal numbers serve to develop the characters and give voice to their emotions. The theatrical rhythm of Singspiel is established according to a carefully calculated succession of sung and spoken texts, so that two different dramatic devices—song and dialogue—blend in a harmonious unity. Mozart not only composed the musical numbers but shared responsibility for the dramatic substance. Changes or cuts in the dialogue of a Singspiel, common in opera houses today, also distort the composer's work and deprive him of the very structure that makes the musical numbers possible. It was precisely because Mozart thought of opera as musical theater that the texts were so important to him and that he insisted on collaborating on the libretti for all of his operas after *Idomeneo*. It has frequently been lamented that apart from Lorenzo Da Ponte, Mozart worked with inadequate librettists who were unworthy of him. To this we must object that Mozart himself had a hand in reworking his texts so that they corresponded to his theatrical concepts.

Mozart was especially gifted at achieving stage effects by musical means. Unconcerned with tradition, he used musical models and techniques from the Italian *opera buffa*, the strophic song, and the French *vaudevilles*, as well as the grand tragic aria. He threw them all into the melting pot to create a new kind of Singspiel, one with individualized roles, a mixture of "high" and "low" elements, and moods and passions as the motivating force behind the action. This was a Singspiel that presented quite conventional scenarios in an entirely new and surprising light.

Die Entführung aus dem Serail, then, does not live because of its contrast of the European with the "Turkish" world, but through the complexity of its characters. Although Belmonte and Constanze are a couple inclined to effusive sentiments, their "high" tone is relieved by elements of exaggeration and a paralyzing fatalism, whereas Blonde and Pedrillo, the "low" couple, are sufficiently resourceful to find opportunities for a tryst even in the most desperate circumstances. Moreover, the fine distinctions between male and female behavior had seldom been so subtly yet unmistakably drawn. The figure who most closely resembles a stock character is Osmin, a role with few nuances. He is mercilessly ridiculed as a cruel and simpleminded lackey, but the derision is not directed at Turkey, a country generally held to be a land of barbarians.

The Turkish element also offers contrasts between "high" and "low," but Pasha Selim (whose part was conceived from the outset as a speaking role) is a prince who represents an alternative to feudal despotism. His magnanimity and humanity are only to be found in foreign lands. His release of the prisoners with a letter of safe conduct comes as unexpectedly as a fairy-tale ending. Sympathy for the two couples gives way to amazement at a ruler who reveals his superior qualities by renouncing not only a display of power but also the fulfillment of his own fondest wishes. Pasha Selim does not behave like a slaveholder who has complete right of disposal over his property; he forgoes violence and respects Constanze's feelings. His enlightened humanity has no political motives, nor is it determined by family considerations. (In the original version of the libretto, Belmonte suddenly reveals himself to be a lost—illegitimate?—son of the Pasha.) Yet his magnanimity is not simply a whim, an arbitrary act with a positive result. Pasha Selim proudly places himself in enlightened opposition to the "civilized" behavior of the European nobility. He expressly refers to Belmonte's father as a barbarian. His self-respect forbids him to behave like his "worst enemy," for their enmity is so great that they cannot even avail themselves of a common language. Belmonte (and the Christian-occidental world he represents) does not escape criticism, and neither does the ruling European nobility, to whom Blonde gives a lesson in civil liberties.

Mozart clearly rejected the traditional ways of dealing with Turkish subject matter, as seen in countless plays and opera libretti, and sought instead a form of representation that would reflect primarily his own experiences. His main objective was not to achieve exotic contrasts but to analyze human behavior and to investigate how each character's fixed place in society affects his interaction with the others. He inquires into their motivations, their anxieties, and their uncertainty in love. As a result, the exotic elements recede into the background; their musical treatment is reserved only for Osmin.

Parallels between *Die Entführung aus dem Serail* and Mozart's own courtship of Constanze Weber, specifically the adversities leading up to his wedding, have been drawn repeatedly. But the difficulties of this opera go far beyond the question of how to liberate Constanze. Mozart was probably amused at the heroine's name; he was, of course, not responsible for it since it had been in the original libretto. The figures in *Die Entführung* are deliberately not made to correspond to immediate reality but are held at a critical distance and are also characterized musically from a distance. The Constanze of *Die Entführung*, with her effusive sentimentality and suffering virtue, bears less resemblance to Constanze Weber than to the famous Clarissa (in Samuel Richardson's novel of that name), even though she is spared a similarly cruel fate. And the Englishwoman Blonde does not correspond to the typical

Viennese chambermaid but could have served as an "enlightened" model for her.

In none of his operas does Mozart portray his acquaintances or use living models whose identity we can decipher. (As we will see later, even the role of Sarastro has no such model, although its original has often been sought.) On the other hand, all the operas of his Vienna period reflect contemporary social phenomena and conflicts to an unusual degree. Mozart drew such parallels more resolutely and consistently than any other opera composer of the time, to the point of courting intervention by the censor. He demonstrated again and again his ability to detect cracks in the social structure, and he was not afraid to provoke his audience. His operas offer a commentary on contemporary issues and in so doing lay the groundwork for a new type of opera. Mozart used *Die Entführung* to criticize his culture, and his keen awareness must have been stimulated by his daily life in Vienna, his own circle of acquaintances, and his observations of Viennese "society."

Looking closely at Mozart's acquaintances, we find a number of outsiders, people of unusual destiny whose very existence poses questions. Mozart's concern about the implications of his Turkish opera could certainly have been heightened by his encounter with Angelo Soliman, a black man who lived in Vienna and had himself been "abducted." His life story (up until he made Mozart's acquaintance in the early 1780s) provides a dark counterpoint to *Die Entführung aus dem Serail*. Soliman was definitely no model for this Turkish opera, but the treatment he received as a kidnapped African in Vienna reveals features of the historical background of the time, along with subtle social processes that bear upon the relevance of Mozart's successful work.

Soliman found no Pasha Selim in Vienna; here too, Mozart touched on important contemporary issues. The release of the kidnapped prisoners was a utopian dream. The abducted blacks could never return home, even if they were treated as freedmen rather than slaves, which occurred very rarely in the European colonies; their alienation from their native cultures stigmatized them irrevocably. They had no alternative but to make futile attempts to assimilate. Mozart even introduces this idea fleetingly into his opera when he has Blonde reflect, "Perhaps I would think like a Moslem (if my Pedrillo were not at my side)."[15] Mozart's *Entführung aus dem Serail* is not the pleasant, harmless fairy tale we see in opera houses today, though it appears to owe its continued success to a few "pretty" musical numbers because it is no longer staged so as to reveal its musical and dramatic relevance. A historically authentic production would have to restore and convey the political explosiveness of the material.

DIGRESSION: ANOTHER ABDUCTION

As with many African slaves in all countries, Angelo Soliman's origins are lost in the recesses of history. Forcibly removed from their native environment, where every aspect of their lives was organized according to an entirely different set of principles, they were deprived of their oral traditions. On top of all the other injustices they suffered, they were so isolated that they could barely retain a memory of their earlier existence, though because of their skin color and the fate associated with it, they could never completely forget it either. The few slaves who were lucky enough not to be viewed as objects and to be allowed some kind of human existence remained faceless outsiders like all the others—for whom they nonetheless felt no sympathy. For the few blacks who were notable enough that their stories have been preserved, a spurious romantic transfiguration often intruded: in most cases they were said to be of noble descent, and the fairy tale of the abducted prince was often invoked though such claims could never be verified.

There is biographical information of this kind about Soliman, but it gives hardly a clue to his actual existence. Tradition has it that he was born in Pangusitlong, the son of a Magui Famori prince. His real name was Mmadi Make, and his mother was named Fatuma. The year of his birth is unknown but was probably around 1726. He was stolen by an enemy tribe at the age of seven and eventually sold to Christians. Thus he came to the house of a marquise in Messina, who raised him and apparently gave him a basic education. In Messina he was noticed by Prince General Johann Georg Christian Lobkowitz, who set his heart on owning him and finally received him as a gift from the marquise.

Soliman, who in the meantime had been baptized, remained with Prince Lobkowitz for twenty years and even accompanied him on numerous campaigns, including one against the Turks. He was offered a military position but declined it. On the death of Lobkowitz in 1753, Soliman was bequeathed to Prince Joseph Wenzel Liechtenstein, another high-ranking army officer. In his house Soliman served as a valet and later as majordomo, but he was essentially the "princely blackamoor," a status symbol for his master. Soliman also accompanied Prince Liechtenstein on many of his journeys, since his master was often entrusted with diplomatic missions. When Liechtenstein was sent to Frankfurt as Austrian envoy to help secure the election of Joseph II as Holy Roman Emperor, Soliman went along, and it is not unlikely that the fourteen-year-old Goethe saw him there. As the aging poet remembers in the fifth book of *Dichtung und Wahrheit* ("Poetry and Truth"), "The dignified figure of Prince von Liechtenstein made a strong impression"; Goethe goes on to mention "the magnificent liveries" in the entourage of the imperial commissioners. Soliman was always dressed to the hilt and wore a white frock coat trimmed with gold braid, against which his black skin stood out most strikingly.

Soliman was an excellent chess player, and in Frankfurt Prince Liechtenstein encouraged him to take up faro. The stakes involved appear to have been very high, for in one evening Soliman won the enormous sum of 20,000 florins. The story goes that he risked this entire sum again and won a further 24,000 florins, which he refused to keep. He therefore manipulated the game so that his opponent was at least able to win back the 24,000 florins. Although Soliman had been "sold," "given away," and finally "bequeathed," he was a paid employee of the prince and certainly had as much freedom as any other servant. The huge winnings he brought back to Vienna apparently enabled him to establish a more independent existence. He married a Frau von Christiani, the widow of a Dutch general. This seems to have been something of a problem, for the wedding could not be publicly announced and was performed secretly by the cardinal archbishop of Vienna in St. Stephen's Cathedral. Soliman was a Catholic, and so the Church could not deny him the sacrament of marriage, but neither did it want a public discussion of mixed marriages. Soliman is said to have bought a house in the suburbs and had a happy, if clandestine, married life.

Joseph II, who had high regard for Soliman, inadvertently revealed the secret of the marriage, and thus Prince Liechtenstein also learned

of it. The prince was so incensed that he immediately dismissed
Soliman from his position and struck him from his will, in which he
had been richly provided for. Obviously Liechtenstein viewed the
private life of his "princely blackamoor" as his own property. Soliman
retired to his house and lived modestly with his wife and daughter.

Two years after Liechtenstein's death, his nephew Franz Joseph met
Soliman on the street and offered him compensation. Soliman was to
supervise the upbringing of his son Alois Joseph, Prince Liechtenstein
(founder of the family line whose seat today is Vaduz); in return he
would receive a yearly salary, to continue after his death as a pension
for his wife. Soliman moved once again into the Liechtenstein Palace
to take up his respected position.

It is reported that Soliman had a broad education, spoke perfect
German, French, and Italian, and could also express himself in
English, Czech, and even Latin. He was generally held in high esteem
and knew the most important artists and scientists in Vienna. In 1783
he became a Freemason in the lodge Zur wahren Eintracht (True
Harmony), which included mostly scholars, artists, and writers. There
he and Mozart often visited the temple together, as we know from an
extant record book. (Soliman's name does not appear in Mozart's
letters and documents, but this is not unusual: Mozart's Viennese
acquaintances are mentioned only by chance in his letters, since he
met them regularly at various functions and had direct personal
contact that made correspondence unnecessary.)

There were any number of enslaved blacks in Europe during the
eighteenth century; the unusual destinies of some were even recorded
for posterity.[16] But surely none was so vilely abused after his death as
Soliman.

At the emperor's wish, and despite vigorous protest from his family,
who had been defrauded of the body and whose case was supported by
a strong letter from the Archbishop of Vienna, Soliman was skinned
and stuffed by the sculptor Franz Thaler, then incorporated into the
imperial collection as a human specimen. There, in the company of a
capybara and various waterfowl, he was exposed to the frivolous curiosity of the public. During the bombardment of Vienna in 1848, this
shameful reminder of dynastic tastelessness went up in flames.[17]

THE BARONESS ARRANGES A WEDDING FEAST

The first performance of *Die Entführung aus dem Serail* took place on July 16, 1782; it was a great success, unsurpassed by any of Mozart's other operas. During his lifetime *Die Entführung* was given in more than forty European cities, not to mention the numerous performances in Vienna. Financially, Mozart received little more than the usual fee of 100 ducats (or 426 florins 40 crowns, at the Hoftheater box office's unfavorable exchange rate). He did manage to sell a copy of the score to the Prussian envoy in Vienna (for how much?), but that was all; because of careless supervision of the music, two pirated editions of the piano reduction soon appeared, robbing Mozart of all further income from this opera.

The first performances at the Hoftheater had been badly obstructed by the usual intrigues—the end of the first act was drowned out by hissing, according to plan—but there were also loud bravos for individual arias, and the final trio from the first act and both second-act duets were repeated. Naturally, Mozart had written to his father all about the premiere and his struggle for success in front of a packed house; he had even sent the original score so his father could read through it and share this first Viennese triumph. (Unfortunately, this letter from Mozart is lost—possibly because Leopold, full of paternal pride, passed it all around Salzburg. Toward Mozart, however, he continued to play the part of the aggrieved and wounded father who cannot bring himself to congratulate his son on his great success as long as peace in the family has not been restored. Thus Mozart was deprived of his success once again. Leopold's attitude can easily be inferred from Mozart's reply.

> I received today your letter of the 26th, but a cold, indifferent letter, such as I would never have expected in reply to the good news about the reception of my opera. I thought (judging by my own feelings) that you would hardly be able to open the parcel for excitement and eagerness to see your son's work, which, far from merely pleasing, is making such a sensation in Vienna that people refuse to hear anything else and the theater is always packed. It was given yesterday for the fourth time and will be repeated on Friday. But you—have not had the time. So the

whole world declares that with my boasting and criticizing I have made enemies of the music professors and of many others! *What* world, pray? Presumably the world of Salzburg, for everyone in Vienna can see and hear enough to be convinced of the contrary. And that must be my reply. (July 31, 1782)

So Leopold Mozart had actually said he did not have time to look at the score his son had sent him, and moreover, that he had heard nothing but what a show-off Wolfgang had become and how many enemies he had made—especially among musicians. This reaction from Salzburg represented something of a low point in this father-son relationship. There is no doubt that it was triggered by Mozart's marriage plans with Constanze Weber—perhaps Mozart had even added, after his report on the premiere, that with this success and the royalty in his pocket he could now set up his own household, and had asked for his father's consent. That his father was against this marriage was a forgone conclusion: he was simply prejudiced against the Weber family though he did not know any of them personally. He reiterated his objections constantly until the wedding and waited so long to give his consent that Mozart did not receive it until the day after the ceremony.

It was perhaps an unavoidable conflict, in part brought on by the long-overdue weaning from his parental home. But Leopold Mozart's lack of interest even in his son's musical activities, and his taking no notice of such a work as *Die Entführung* because he had "no time," indicated a deeper rift. In musical matters, in judging Mozart's works, his father had always shown ungrudging respect and admiration for his son's genius—which he had been the first to detect. He had taught Mozart everything he could and had later advised him musically in a multitude of ways; there had never been the slightest disagreement. And Mozart had always shared his thoughts on composition openly and in detail with his father. (What little we know of Mozart's ideas on the "science of composition" comes from letters to his father, often written to justify his work.) Above all, Mozart had written to Salzburg in connection with *Die Entführung*, explaining all his ideas on the theater and the task of the opera composer. He had allowed his father to share in every stage of the work (especially the first act)—and now that it was complete and had been performed to unprecedented acclaim, his father had no time to look at it, perhaps not even time enough to open the package?

One senses in Mozart's letters how strange all this seemed to him. He no longer got excited as he had the previous year regarding his resignation from the archbishop's service. In every letter he sought his father's consent to his marriage, related the most important news from Vienna, and sent music, more from a sense of duty than out of love, always closing with the formula "I kiss your hands a thousand times and am eternally your most obedient son W. A. Mozart." His letters too became cold and indifferent, shorter and less frequent.

Mozart even forgot to tell his father the exact date of his wedding. It took place on August 4, 1782, in St. Stephen's Cathedral; the marriage contract had been signed the day before. The ceremony was attended only by the witnesses, the guardian, Cäcilia Weber, and Sophie, Constanze's youngest sister. Afterward there was a dinner for even fewer guests at the home of Baroness Waldstätten, "which indeed was more princely than baronial" (August 7, 1782). None of the Mozart family's many old acquaintances were there; Mozart was in general very cautious about renewing his Salzburg relationships.

It is not known where he or Constanze was introduced to Baroness Waldstätten; in any case, their contacts with her during the first years in Vienna were very intimate, casual, and informal. The baroness, in her late thirties, was separated from her husband and appears to have led a merry social life. (It was in her house that the ladies played the game of allowing a young man to "measure their calves"; one instance, involving Constanze, has always been exaggerated in the Mozart literature, to her detriment.) Mozart says that the baroness "is inclined to be promiscuous" (April 29, 1782), but perhaps he was too. He always sought the company of lively people who paid little heed to social distinction. He loved spontaneity and high spirits and liked to be surrounded by noisy groups of people even when he was composing; indeed, he worked best under such conditions.

Baroness Waldstätten was an unconventional woman to whom her own convictions and interests were more important than superficial social conformity. She retired to the country, read, played music (on a piano Mozart chose for her), and gave up the social whirl, which she considered more a boring obligation than a form of enrichment. She was an outsider, full of vitality and obviously capable of great personal warmth. She made it her business to intercede with Leopold Mozart, and it was she who finally succeeded in coaxing cheerful, conciliatory tones from this lonely and embittered man, even though she was a stranger whose name had only been mentioned once in a letter from Vienna. Years later Leopold Mozart still referred to her as "the woman of my heart," a phrase in which irony and flattery are imperceptibly mixed. He also thanked her "for your extraordinary kindness in celebrating my son's wedding day with such liberality" (August 23, 1782). But he simply could not refrain from adding a laconic postscript that decisively confirms his grudge against the Weber family. "My son wrote to me some time ago saying that when he married, he would not live with his wife's mother. I trust that by now he has left that house. If not, he is storing up trouble for himself and his wife."

But Mozart had long ago rented his own apartment. Since the end of July he had been living at Wipplingerstrasse 19, at the corner of Färbergasse, on the third floor. He writes to his father:

I cannot understand how you got the idea that my highly honored mother-in-law is living here too. For indeed I did not marry my sweetheart in such a hurry in order to live a life of vexations and quarrels, but to enjoy peace and happiness. (August 31, 1782)

Chapter 3

AT HOME
WITH THE MOZARTS

WHO WAS CONSTANZE MOZART?

There is probably not one Mozart biography that fails to enumerate the supposed shortcomings and character flaws of Constanze, often openly and offensively, sometimes more covertly and with an undertone of contempt. These assessments are generally brief comments that boil down to one claim: Constanze Mozart was not worthy to live at her husband's side. Occasionally she is even accused of being partly responsible for his alleged impoverishment. It is clear that the theory of Mozart's social decline, which supposedly paralleled his rise to artistic perfection, has become a gauge for the low opinion of Constanze. In more balanced portrayals of her, such as the one by Erich Schenk, there are still a few potshots, explicitly stated.

Her character has always been very controversial, not least due to her sister-in-law, whose petty jealousies did not end with the death of her brother. She was surely unable to appreciate her husband's greatness. Undoubtedly she saw him first and foremost as the family provider. But he gratefully accepted the love she gave him. She was definitely not a

92

"companion" in the romantic sense. That idea was not yet current when she was young. In the crucial situations of her marriage, however, she did not fail her husband. The accusations made against her of pettiness, envy, and hard-nosed business practices are not taken as seriously today as they were from the viewpoint of smug liberalism. During her long life, which extended from the dying rococo age to the period just before the 1848 revolution, she fulfilled her principal task—that of preserving and cultivating the legacy of Mozart. [1]

Wolfgang Hildesheimer calls attention to the major difficulty we face in forming a judgment, namely the lack of source material. On the one hand he accurately asserts:

Constanze Mozart is the rare case of a key biographical figure who cannot be reconstructed from any autobiographical document whatever, at least not while she was still Constanze Mozart. Even statements by others about her are scarce. We are almost exclusively dependent on letters addressed to her and on the few, usually unfriendly references of surviving contemporaries. During her eight years as Mozart's wife she left not one single document of her own. The letters to her husband have been lost; either he lost them (he seems to have been extremely careless about looking after things) or they were destroyed by Constanze and Nissen. Why?—we do not know. Perhaps they would have revealed to posterity insufficient evidence of the love and concern she claimed to have felt for her spouse. [2]

On the other hand, one page earlier Hildesheimer cannot refrain from comments that transform the perfumed venom of his "claimed to have felt" into a foul-smelling pollutant.

Constanze had a lighthearted, instinctual nature; she granted Mozart (and perhaps not only him) erotic, or at least sexual, satisfaction, but was unable to offer him the happiness a lesser man would have needed for his self-realization. In that regard Mozart was egocentric; his standard, in all matters of human feeling, was the feeling he himself invested, not the response of a partner. He did not perceive the degree of response, or at least he perceived it only when, as in the case of Aloysia, the response was not forthcoming. His isolation was extreme, but it also protected him from wounds to his ego.

This devastating judgment implies nothing less than that Constanze Mozart could offer only sexual gratification. He even denies her the first prerequisite of being human, the capacity for mental and emotional experience: "It seems improbable that she ever suffered mental torment, and even her physical sufferings seem primarily an excuse for her visits to spas." Apparently some biographers are so enamored of their "heroes" that their jealousy extends to anyone who comes too near the object of their adoration.

Other equally damning judgments need not detain us here, with one exception: Arthur Schurig. His Mozart biography contains almost the same comments about Constanze Mozart as Hildesheimer's. "At no time in her life did she have an inkling of Mozart's profound and solitary inner life,"[3] and as far as sexuality was concerned, "the marriage robbed his artistic fertility of its intensity."[4] Nevertheless, it seems that Schurig was plagued by a bad conscience, because he subsequently had the idea of collecting all the material on Constanze Mozart, including the later correspondence with her children, publishers, etc., into a monograph that is still the only one devoted to her. However, this is only a partial advance, though it does endeavor to grasp her personality. Schurig admits that after examining the letters, he feels "obliged to change his opinion of Frau Constanze considerably in her favor." In making his revised judgment he states:

She has been dealt with unfairly. She was not a woman of importance. She certainly does not belong among the radiant figures who, in their companionship with an *homme supérieur* as a friend, lover, or wife, recognized his *calling*. During the ten years that Constanze spent at Mozart's side, her husband was not one of those people who *represent something*, according to Arthur Schopenhauer's famous classification. He had neither money, title, nor social position; in short, he made no impression on the petty bourgeois—and Constanze had no other standard of measurement. *He* did not see his life as tragic, however outwardly wretched it was. He simply could not come to terms with reality, with the *lives of other people* and the struggle against mediocrity. Thus he contented himself with simple joys. His young wife followed his example; in a word, neither of them worried about anything. But Constanze basically never changed—as Mademoiselle Weber, as Frau Musikus Mozart, or as Frau von Nissen. She always adapted herself to her circumstances, to her husband and his maxims. And when, at the age of 63, she became a widow for the second time, her increased independence clearly reveals her main characteristics, perhaps some-

what refined through her long experience of life: economy, a deep
respect for convenience, tenacity, a sense of family—and a healthy
amour propre. Her droll and excessive piety was more than likely
senility. She was without a doubt petty, narrow-minded, vain, greedy,
superstitious, and gossipy; all in all, a primitive, good-natured crea-
ture full of *joie de vivre*. One thing should not be forgotten: she was an
excellent mother to her two sons.[5]

Schurig's monograph contains the surviving letters, notes, and
documentary material on Constanze Mozart's life; and from it we can
determine how much of his judgment is based directly on the evidence
and how much he read between the lines. But virtually none of the
material actually dates from Mozart's lifetime. As far as Mozart was
concerned, he most definitely represented something. When he renewed his acquaintance with Constanze Weber, whom he had known
earlier in Mannheim, he was already esteemed throughout Europe as a
virtuoso and composer—by no means rich, but nevertheless admired
by Viennese society and thus not without financial prospects. And
Constanze Weber, *pace* Schurig, came from a family that was closer to
impoverished bohemianism than to the petty bourgeoisie; otherwise
she would never have formed an intimate relationship with Mozart,
however promising his future.

Constanze did indeed have another standard of judgment: her
affection for Mozart, her undoubtedly genuine musicality (revealed,
though not for the first time, in her correspondence with publishers),
and her willingness to live an unconventional artist's life surrounded
by musicians and theater people. It has often been said that her
business acumen and sense of economy, as documented in her letters
to publishers, were not in evidence during her marriage to Mozart, but
this accusation is totally unfounded. Even Leopold Mozart, although
suspicious and usually dissatisfied with everything concerning the
Webers, could not find fault with Constanze on a single point during
his visit to Vienna.

Nonetheless, the aversion to Constanze Mozart that continues to
this day probably originated with Leopold. But for the quarrel over his
consent to the marriage and his irrational belief that the Weber family
had been out to ensnare his son since they first knew him in Mannheim, we would probably have a different picture of Constanze. There-

fore, let us not base our opinions on the judgment of a man who was definitely biased in the matter of his daughter-in-law, a man who had been forced to release his patriarchal hold on his son. Let us rather concentrate on the little else we know of Constanze during the early years of her marriage, freely acknowledging that while this information is not sufficient to yield a complete picture of her personality, it does not offer the slightest grounds for a negative assessment.

Constanze Weber was about sixteen years old when Mozart first met her during a stopover of several weeks in Mannheim in 1777–78, on the way to Paris with his mother. From the very beginning, Mozart's comments on the Weber family were excessively optimistic and distorted out of all proportion. Leopold had a sharp eye for such things, and Mozart's effusions, contrary to his intentions, simply aggravated the conflict with his father. We cannot be sure whether Mozart believed his own descriptions of the Weber family. At the time, full of happiness over his love affair with Aloysia Weber, he wrote:

> I have become so fond of this unfortunate family that my dearest wish is to make them happy; and perhaps I may be able to do so. . . . My sister will find a friend and companion in Mlle. Weber, for, like my sister in Salzburg, she has a reputation for good behavior, her father resembles my father and the whole family resembles the Mozarts. True, there are envious people, as there are in Salzburg, but when it comes to the point, they have to speak the truth. Honesty is the best policy.
>
> (February 4, 1778)

Almost four years later, in the letter that first mentions Constanze Weber's name, Mozart expressed a very different opinion of the Weber daughters, probably in order to place special emphasis on his portrayal of Constanze.

> In no other family have I ever come across such differences of character. The eldest is a lazy, gross, perfidious woman, and as cunning as a fox. Mme. Lange [Aloysia] is a false, malicious person and a coquette. The youngest is still too young to be anything in particular—she is just a good-natured but feather-headed creature. May God protect her from seduction! But the middle one, my good, dear Constanze, is the martyr of the family and, probably for that very reason, is the kindest-hearted, cleverest, and in short—the best of them all. She takes responsibility

for the entire household, and yet in their opinion she does nothing right. Oh, my most beloved father, I could fill whole sheets with descriptions of all the scenes I have witnessed in that house. If you want to read them, I will do so in my next letter. But before I cease to plague you with my chatter, I must make you better acquainted with the character of my dear Constanze. She is not ugly, but at the same time far from beautiful. Her whole beauty consists in two little black eyes and a pretty figure. She has no wit, but she has common sense enough to enable her to fulfill her duties as wife and mother. It is a downright lie that she is inclined to extravagance. On the contrary, she is accustomed to be shabbily dressed, for the little her mother has been able to do for the children she has done for the two others, but never for Constanze. True, she would like to be neatly and cleanly dressed, but not smartly, and most things that a woman needs she is able to make for herself; and she dresses her own hair every day. Moreover she understands housekeeping and has the kindest heart in the world. I love her and she loves me with all her heart. Tell me whether I could wish myself a better wife? (December 15, 1781)

Here Mozart describes his fiancée as a true Cinderella, which amounts to another biased picture; Mozart probably assumed that he was telling his father what he wanted to hear. But Leopold remained suspicious, and his negative attitude was exacerbated by rumors and gossip. Nevertheless, Constanze Weber, now in her nineteenth year, must have been vivacious, cheerful, and sociable, and sometimes a little too lively; Mozart reproached her for her "somewhat thoughtless conduct" in allowing a young man to "measure her calves" (April 29, 1782). In the argument over this affair Constanze apparently shot back that she wanted "nothing more to do" with him. Yet there is no indication of serious ill feeling between Mozart and his wife at any time during their marriage, though later he occasionally reminded her that "a woman must always behave respectably or people will talk about her." In the same letter he said rather vaguely:

Remember that you yourself once admitted to me that you were inclined to *comply too easily.* You know the consequences of that. Remember too the promise you gave me. Oh God, please try, my love! Be merry and happy and charming to me. Do not torment yourself and me with unnecessary jealousy. Believe in my love, for surely you have proof of it, and you will see how happy we shall be. Rest assured that it is only by her prudent behavior that a wife can enchain her husband. Adieu. Tomorrow I shall kiss you tenderly. (Beginning of August 1789)

On the one hand we have the ideal wife, as depicted in the letter to his father; on the other, casual, unconventional behavior on which Mozart comments reprovingly. The personality of Constanze Mozart seems to lie somewhere between these extremes. Unfortunately, we lack the bare minimum of information that would enable us to delineate her character more sharply and form a just opinion of her nature.

But there has never been a lack of prejudice against her. It must have been unfathomable to Leopold Mozart that Constanze's father, who had begun to study law and then took up his deceased father's position as a civil servant in Zell im Wiesental, gave up this secure post (for reasons that remain unknown) to become a badly paid court musician in Mannheim. He had the almost impossible task of supporting a family of five children on an income of only 200 florins, and had to supplement his earnings through badly paid freelance work such as copying music. Yet Fridolin Weber must have been a highly cultivated man with broad interests. (He presented Mozart with an edition of Molière's works.) Such a destitute family, whose artistic inclinations could not provide a decent livelihood, aroused deep misgivings in Leopold Mozart. He undoubtedly suspected poor management of the family budget as well. Later, when the Webers had settled in Vienna, the father had died, and the family was dependent first on Aloysia's income from singing and then on renting rooms, he considered Wolfgang's move into their house an instance of flagrant procuration.

THE IMMEDIATE FAMILY

During her marriage to Mozart, which lasted slightly more than nine years, Constanze gave birth to six children. The first was born ten months after the wedding; the last, four and a half months before Mozart's death. The intervals between children were short, ranging from fourteen months to two years at most. Thus we must imagine a household full of the screaming of infants, where the days were structured around feeding, changing, bathing, and otherwise ministering to small children. Constanze was not solely responsible for these tasks; she was helped by a chambermaid and a housekeeper. Neither did she nurse her own children; in conformity with a wide-spread eighteenth-century prejudice, children were either given out to a wet nurse or fed a gruel of barley or oats ("water"). Mozart himself had a lot to say about all these matters, as evidenced by a letter to his father about the birth of his first child.

> From the condition of her breasts I am rather afraid of milk fever. And now the child has been given to a wet nurse against my will, or rather, at my wish! For I was quite determined that even if she were able to do so, my wife was never to nurse her child. Yet I was equally determined that my child was never to take the milk of a stranger. I wanted the child to be brought up on water, like my sister and myself. But the midwife, my mother-in-law, and most people here have begged and implored me not to allow it, if only for the reason that most children here who are brought up on water do not survive, because the people here don't know how to do it properly. That induced me to give in, for I should not like to have anything to reproach myself with.
>
> (June 18, 1783)

And so it must have been with the other children; the pregnancies were all apparently free of complications, and the births as well. Mozart was still inexperienced and trusted cheerfully in his wife's constitution when he made plans for a journey two months before the first child's birth.

> She is in such excellent health and has become so robust that all women should thank God if they are so fortunate in their pregnancy. As soon as my wife has sufficiently recovered from her confinement, we will be off to Salzburg at once. (April 12, 1783)

One does not know whether to admire their carefree attitude or to condemn their foolhardiness, for which Mozart was just as responsible as his wife. Under the medical and hygienic conditions prevalent in the eighteenth century, the dangers of giving birth and the risk of puerperal fever could not be dismissed. In addition, there was a very high infant mortality rate because of the many serious childhood diseases.[6]

The first child, Raimund Leopold, was just six weeks old when the Mozarts set out for Salzburg (a coach journey of two or two and a half days), leaving him in the care of a wet nurse. We do not know whether the Mozarts at least maintained postal contact with this woman; they were away for four months, after all. They probably learned only upon their return in late November that little Raimund had died of "intestinal spasms" on August 19. Although he had been described as a "fine, fat, lovely boy," he was not robust enough to survive his first illness.

The second child was Karl Thomas, born in 1784, who died a bachelor in Milan in 1858 after a career as a tax official. He seems to have been a happy, healthy child, whose education was a matter of great concern to Mozart in the summer of 1791. After Mozart's death Karl Thomas went to school in Prague and lived in the home of Franz Xaver Niemetschek, Mozart's first biographer.

The third child, Johann Thomas Leopold, was born in 1786 but died only four weeks later. The fourth, Theresa Constanza, was born in 1787 and died at the age of six months. And the fifth child, Anna Maria, survived just long enough for an emergency baptism.

Finally, in 1791, four and a half months before Mozart's death, the youngest son, Franz Xaver Wolfgang, was born. He worked as a musician, primarily in Lemberg and in the noble houses of Galicia. He enjoyed some success as a pianist but was never able to escape the burden of being the son of a famous father. Even his mother called him Wolfgang Amadeus, and he continued to use this name, thus doing his bit to keep himself in the shadow of his father, whose works also enjoyed pride of place in his repertoire. This Mozart son also remained unmarried; he died prematurely in 1844, after a life that he himself considered a failure. Thus, only two of Mozart's six children survived—almost exactly the average survival rate at the end of the eighteenth century.

The sequence of births and deaths in Mozart's family was such that there were two children in the nursery at the same time only for a total of twelve months. Mozart's everyday life was hardly touched by the children; they were not given a great deal of attention until they reached a certain age. Even the youngest child, born in 1791, was left in the care of a wet nurse when Mozart and Constanze traveled to Prague for the premiere of his opera *La clemenza di Tito*. This time, however, the journey lasted only three weeks.

Mozart made only two journeys without his wife—to Berlin and to Frankfurt am Main—each lasting six to seven weeks. Although these trips offered him diversion and many vivid travel impressions, Mozart found any separation from Constanze a painful burden. When she was taking cures in Baden, Mozart wrote her yearning letters that reveal how difficult it was for him to work without her. He visited her in Baden as often as possible, sometimes staying for weeks.

> My one wish now is to settle my affairs so I can be with you again. You cannot imagine how I have been aching for you all this long while. I can't describe what I have been feeling—a kind of emptiness, which hurts me dreadfully, a kind of longing—which is never satisfied, which never ceases, and which persists, nay rather increases daily. When I think how merry we were together at Baden—like children—and what sad, weary hours I am spending here! Even my work gives me no pleasure, because I am accustomed to stop working now and then and exchange a few words with you. Alas! this pleasure is no longer possible. If I go to the piano and sing something out of my opera, I have to stop at once, for it stirs my emotions too deeply. Basta! The very hour after I finish this business I shall be off and away from here. (July 7, 1791)

Everything points to the fact that this marriage was of crucial importance to Mozart. He needed his wife with him constantly and even let her talk to him while he composed; she was a part of his very existence. Several extant love letters from Mozart to his wife have a lighthearted, playful, and sometimes overtly sexual tone hardly intended for the eyes of prudish biographers. Though not a single letter from Constanze Mozart to her husband has been preserved, let alone a love letter, that is no reason to maintain that the marriage was one-sided. Mozart gives not the slightest hint that he ever doubted his wife, and even his "admonitions," upon closer inspection, can hardly be interpreted as serious strains in the relationship.[7]

In the years 1788 and 1789 Constanze Mozart was frequently ill; at times her condition was even dangerous. Mozart wrote to Michael Puchberg:

> Since the time when you rendered me that great and friendly service, I have been living in such *misery* that for very grief I have not only been unable to go out, but I could not even write.

At the moment she is easier, and if *she had not contracted bed sores*, which make her condition most wretched, she would be able to sleep. The only fear is that the bone may be affected. She is extraordinarily resigned and awaits recovery or death with true philosophic calm. My tears flow as I write. (July 1789)

Nothing was too expensive where her health was concerned, and the best physicians were called in. The nature of her illness, however, remains a mystery. She apparently had open sores on her feet and legs for which the prognosis was very bad. On the other hand, Constanze Mozart's general constitution seems to have been good, as confirmed by her six normal pregnancies.[8] We do not know whether she was sickly in later years, for our information about her later life remains sketchy despite the fact that she lived until 1842. She died in Salzburg, in her eightieth year.

FRAU MOZART'S APPRECIATION OF MUSIC

Constanze Mozart's services to Mozart's work were immense, and actively supported by her second husband, the Danish diplomat Georg Nikolaus von Nissen, who collected anything that had any bearing on Mozart. His work bore fruit in an exhaustive biography of the composer that appeared in 1828, after Nissen's death. Constanze has been accused of selling Mozart's manuscripts purely for financial gain, and of pettiness in her negotiations with publishers. This is all nonsense. On the contrary, we have her more than anyone to thank for the fact that so many works that were not printed during Mozart's lifetime, even fragments, have been preserved in reliable editions, and that the holographs of so many compositions have survived. In fact, by negotiating with only two publishers, both of whom were in a position to plan and begin issuing large collected editions, she prevented Mozart's vast corpus of unpublished works from being sold off. One was the house of Breitkopf & Härtel in Leipzig, with whom Leopold Mozart had earlier been in contact, and the other was Johann Anton André in Offenbach, whose family Mozart himself had known personally. Without going into the long history of how Mozart's manuscripts were located and of Constanze's correspondence with publishers, it must be emphasized that her primary objective was to have the music printed correctly; in doubtful cases she was prepared to forgo publication rather than allow something that was not indisputably authentic to appear under Mozart's name. Such scrupulousness had financial disadvantages, and these she readily accepted. Where there was the slightest question about individual notes, Constanze had the manuscripts examined again before allowing the work to be printed. She carefully preserved even the least significant pieces and fragments. Unfortunately, the same cannot be said of the letters.[9]

There is also a long story connected with the works Mozart dedicated to his wife. As far as we know, they all remained fragments. A closer inspection, however, reveals that the facts are not nearly so obvious as they appear (and are therefore less amenable to various techniques of interpretation one might apply to them). Strictly speaking, only two works appear to have been specifically dedicated to her: a fragmentary sonata movement for two pianos (K. 375c/Anh. 43) that bears Mozart's handwritten dedication "per la Sig:ra Constanza Weber ah," and two pieces from a series of solfeggios (vocal exercises) with the inscription *"per la mia cara consorta."* Yet several other works are connected with his wife, especially the Mass in C Minor, Mozart's last large church composition apart from the Requiem. Evidently Mozart had promised to write a mass for his first visit with Constanze to Salzburg; an unknown illness afflicting his beloved was also involved.

I made the promise in my heart of hearts and hope to be able to keep it. When I made it, my wife was still single; yet, as I was absolutely determined to marry her soon after her recovery, it was easy for me to make it—but, as you yourself are aware, time and other circumstances made our journey impossible. The score of half of a mass, which is still lying here waiting to be finished, is the best proof that I really made the promise. (January 4, 1783)

The soprano solo in the C Minor Mass seems to have been written for Constanze, who probably also sang it for the first time in Salzburg. She must have been a good singer, although she was perhaps not gifted with a great voice. She did come from a musical household, and two of her sisters were singers; Aloysia was evidently trained for brilliant roles and extremely high registers. Constanze undoubtedly played the piano too, for otherwise the dedication to her of a sonata for two pianos would be inexplicable. Moreover, Mozart intended to (and perhaps did) write a series of sonatas for her, in which she would have played the piano part and he the violin. Perhaps some of his violin sonatas were indeed written for her; there are also a number of fragments for violin and piano. At any rate, the numerous fugues from the "year of the fugue," 1782, are clearly connected with Constanze.

In Vienna, Mozart had immediately come into close contact with Baron Gottfried van Swieten, who was known as an aficionado of music from the time of Bach and Handel. Mozart borrowed scores from the baron and through him broadened his knowledge, of Bach's music especially. Every Sunday morning at van Swieten's house works of Bach and Handel were played, usually in arrangements for string trio, and Mozart was a regular guest at these matinees. Shortly before his marriage he wrote to his sister:

> Baron van Swieten, whom I visit every Sunday, gave me all the works of Handel and Sebastian Bach to take home with me (after I played them for him). When Constanze heard the fugues, she absolutely fell in love with them. Now she will listen to nothing but fugues, and particularly those of Handel and Bach. Since she has often heard me play fugues out of my head, she asked me if I had ever written any down, and when I said I had not, she scolded me roundly for not recording some of my compositions in this most artistic and beautiful of all musical forms, and gave me no peace until I wrote down a fugue for her. So that is its origin. I have purposely written above it *Andante Maestoso*, as it must not be played too fast. If a fugue is not played slowly, the ear cannot clearly distinguish the theme when it comes in and consequently the effect is entirely missed. In time, when I have a favorable opportunity, I intend to compose five more and present them to Baron van Swieten, whose collection of good music, though small, is great in quality. And for that very reason I beg you to keep your promise not to show this composition to a soul. Learn it by heart and play it. It is not so easy to pick up a fugue by ear. (April 20, 1782)

This letter is unusually informative about the musical taste of the period. Although interest in Bach never disappeared among musicians, we often read that his music fell into oblivion until Felix Mendelssohn's epoch-making revival of the *St. Matthew Passion*

(1829). This is a misleading oversimplification. On the one hand, musical life in Mozart's time was built around new works by contemporary composers; older works were always the exception (in contrast to our time, when most concertgoers would rather forgo new music altogether). On the other hand, fugal compositions were not peculiar to Bach's time; in church music, at least, they never really went out of fashion. In Mozart's time they appear to have been especially prized as piano pieces—which would explain why Mozart allowed his sister to play the fugues, even publicly, but asked her not to let anyone see the music, to insure that it would not be printed illegally.

Constanze Mozart loved fugues because of their "artistry," and not, as with Swieten, out of any special interest in music history. It is also known that Joseph II, an amateur musician with no unusual tastes, especially liked fugues. When the emperor was present at one of his concerts, Mozart would pay him the special compliment of playing fugues.

From Constanze Mozart's musical perspective, "most artistic" meant "most beautiful." We can certainly assume that the fugues for two pianos or piano four hands—apart from their pedagogical function—were written to be played in the Mozart home. Conceivably their fragmentary character is related to their domestic role: the manuscripts usually break off unexpectedly just before the end, which may imply that the conclusions were improvised. This pragmatic explanation may serve to refute an otherwise unanswerable accusation: that in the works written for his wife, Mozart's imagination never got past the starting point, the first breath or initial gesture, which always came to a feeble halt. Written improvisations of an entirely different kind, such as the *Bandel* Trio (K. 441), in which a domestic scene is built up into a comic interlude, reveal themselves even more clearly as pieces written for casual music making. None of these fragments were intended for publication; they stemmed directly from Constanze Mozart's musical interests or served pedagogical purposes.

The unusually scanty information we have on Constanze Mozart makes it impossible to judge what kind of sounding-board she was for the composer in musical matters. We have not a single description of the Mozart family's domestic life. However, during a visit to Salzburg in 1829, Mary Novello recorded a comment by Constanze that indicates that she and her husband regularly made music together: "She

told us that Mozart, when he finished an opera, brought it to her and
begged she would study it, after which he would play it over and sing
with her, so that not only the songs but the words she knew by
heart."[10]

In this way Mozart imparted to his wife a very thorough knowledge of
his compositions, but with no thought that she should perform them in
public. Above all, chamber music was played and discussed in numerous recitals in Mozart's home. In this genre Mozart found scope to
experiment and develop tightly woven structures through strict manip-
ulation of melodic and harmonic materials—techniques that became
increasingly strange and perplexing to his contemporaries. Thus we
read in Karl Friedrich Cramer's *Magazin der Musik* for April 23, 1787:

> It is only a pity that his artistic and truly admirable attempt to be an
> innovative creator has led him into difficulties whereby he gains little
> in feeling and sentiment. His new quartets for two violins, viola, and
> bass, which he dedicated to Haydn, are much too strongly seasoned—
> and few palates can tolerate them for very long.[11]

Constanze Mozart seems to have been very familiar with this strong
seasoning, as we learn from a certain intimate scene. The second of
these quartets (K. 421, in D minor) was written in summer 1783, just
as their first child was being born. Mozart reported to his father:

> Her pains began at half past one in the morning, so that night we both
> lost our sleep and rest. At four o'clock I sent for my mother-in-law—
> and then for the midwife. At six o'clock the child began to appear, and
> at half past six the trouble was all over. (June 18, 1783)

Almost fifty years later, Vincent Novello noted during a visit to
Salzburg:

> She confirmed the truth of his writing the Quartet in D minor while she
> was in labor with their first child: several passages indicative of her
> sufferings especially the Minuet (a part of which she sang to us).[12]

It is hard to believe that Mozart wrote the entire quartet in five hours
during the night of June 17, 1783; perhaps it was only the minuet.

Mozart must have interpreted these passages to his wife, for she knew them so well that she could still sing them for Novello in 1829.

Despite our hazy picture of Constanze Mozart's musicality, it seems clear that she was able to understand the very aspects of Mozart's music that gave contemporaries an impression of "confusion, vagueness, artificiality."[13] It was precisely her knowledge and understanding of the "difficulties" in Mozart's music—the complex formal construction, the harmonic surprises, and the contrapuntal sophistication—that allowed her to develop a healthy scrupulousness toward publishers.[14]

THE HOUSEHOLD ECONOMY

One thing Constanze Mozart apparently was not: a good little housewife who spent the whole day doing laundry, cooking, and keeping the children away from her husband so that he could have the peace to work. The Mozart house was a loud and restless one, but least of all because of the children, who played a minor role; it had more to do with music—pupils, house concerts, and rehearsals—and with Mozart's own need for constant commotion: conversation, laughter, visitors who were often houseguests, musical colleagues, and billiard games that frequently lasted into the wee hours. There were other distractions as well, as Leopold Mozart wrote during his visit to Vienna: "It is impossible to describe the rush and bustle. Since my arrival your brother's piano has been taken at least a dozen times to the theater or to some other house" (March 12, 1785)—in other words, the piano was moved every two or three days, because it was Mozart's preferred instrument.

It was in this restless atmosphere—constant running around, piano moving, music making, billiard playing, forced and overexcited activity—that Mozart preferred to compose. And instead of sitting at his desk or the piano, he liked to ponder, arrange, and connect musical ideas in his head, a process perceptible to those around him only in a slight abstraction while he was talking or playing, as his attention was claimed by inner concentration on the solution of musical problems. If Constanze had erected a barrier around him, if she had sequestered him in the peace and quiet that another composer might have required, it would probably have irritated Mozart or even interfered with his work.

Most of the evidence indicates that Constanze gave her husband just the support he needed amidst all the unrest and boisterous activity, with its sheer physical demands. The various objections to Constanze, which are unfounded and are often the product of trite fantasy, fail to take one thing into account: Mozart desired, even longed for, the presence of his wife, and it was in constant interaction with her that he created the works of his Vienna period, with their inconceivable richness and wealth of invention.

Mozart's devotion to Constanze was boundless and unquestionable; he loved her with every fiber of his physical and emotional being. It does not befit a biographer to condemn the object of his research for failing to conform to inappropriate standards; rather, he must try to discover what actually happened. It is idle to speak of Mozart's loneliness if one claims to detect it only in his music. The inner processes of composition that go beyond the purely musical handling of the material—melodic, rhythmic, and harmonic organization, as well as instrumental and vocal considerations, psychological and spiritual phenomena and the manner in which they are expressed— all these things remain a mystery. Once these elements find their way into the music they cannot be distilled out again. Only the listener can interpret them in light of the effect of the music on his own inner processes. On the one hand we have the music; and on the other, in contrast, we have the documents recording the circumstances of its creation—Mozart's daily life in the midst of a loud, confusing, and colorful environment.

The Mozart household was, "as far as eating and drinking are concerned, extremely economical," as Leopold Mozart wrote on March 19, 1785, during his visit to Vienna.[15] "Economical" undoubtedly meant comfortable without financial extravagance; and Leopold accepted invitations to dine elsewhere most of the time. Constanze would have spent as little time in the kitchen as possible; for that there were servants. In a kitchen with an open fireplace the air was often thick with smoke; utensils were extraordinarily primitive by today's standards, and every task was laborious, especially since meals were complicated and often lavish. Kitchen work was hardly compatible with an extensive social life. Constanze Mozart presided over the household but by no means had to do everything herself. Outside help was called in for certain jobs. The floors, for example, were not cleaned by domestic servants but by a special "floor scrubber" (April 2, 1785). Keeping a neat house was expensive but necessary because the demands on the Mozart lodgings went far beyond those of everyday living. Not only did Mozart's male pupils come there (he taught his female pupils in their own homes), but there were also frequent musical soirees or rehearsals to which listeners were invited. The Mozarts enjoyed going out for parties and dances; especially during the Shrovetide carnival there were frequent masked court balls that Mozart attended in disguise, in addition to offering his own entertainment in the form of theatrical sketches or word puzzles (several of which were printed in a Salzburg newspaper). But even that was not enough. The Mozarts also gave balls in their own home, which were attended by many theater people as well as friends from Salzburg and Vienna. Evidently the preparations were so thorough and the expenditure so great that Mozart requested an admission fee of at least 2 florins from his male guests. A letter to his father describes the importance of these affairs for Mozart:

And now one more request, for my wife is giving me no peace on the subject. You are doubtless aware that this is carnival time and that there is as much dancing here as in Salzburg and Munich. I would very much like to go as Harlequin (but not a soul must know about it)— because here there are so many—indeed nothing but—silly asses at the balls. So I would like you to send me your Harlequin costume. But please do so very soon, for we will not attend any balls until I have it, although they are now in full swing. We prefer private balls. Last week I gave a ball in my own rooms, but of course the *chapeaux* paid 2 florins each. We began at 6 o'clock in the evening and kept on until 7. What! Only an hour? Of course not. I meant, until 7 o'clock the next morning. You will wonder how I had so much room. That reminds me that I have always forgotten to tell you we have been living in new lodgings for the last six weeks—still on the Hohe Brücke, and only a few houses off. We are now in the small Herberstein house, no. 412, on the fourth floor. The house belongs to Herr von Wetzlar—a rich Jew. Well, I have a room there—1,000 feet long and one foot wide—a bedroom, an anteroom, and a fine large kitchen. Then there are two other fine big rooms adjoining ours, which are still empty and which I used for this

private ball. Baron Wetzlar and his wife were there, Baroness Waldstätten, Herr von Edelbach, that gasbag Gilowsky, Stephanie junior et
uxor, Adamberger and his wife, Lange and his, and so forth. It would
be impossible to name them all. (January 22, 1783)

Such descriptions do not imply a modest, homely life but a rather
lavish one with certain bohemian elements. When Leopold Mozart
described this household as "economical," he was referring not only to
the level of comfort but also to his son's success at living within his
means. One cannot escape the feeling, however, that the treatment of
the guest from Salzburg was calculated to make him revise his earlier
unfavorable opinion of a marriage to one of the Weber daughters. He
went home with a good impression of Mozart's income—and of his
expenditures. Almost every day there was a gourmet feast (even though
it was Lent), but always in other people's homes (Constanze Mozart, on
the other hand, gave her father-in-law rosehip tea for his cough). The
weeks of his only visit to his son and daughter-in-law were so crammed
with hospitality, concerts, and visits to the theater and the lodge that he
can have observed only a few details of Mozart's way of life. Thus his
letters from Vienna are a rich source of information about Mozart's
concert activity during this time, but they reveal little about his private
life and nothing specific about income and expenditures.

FREQUENT MOVES

The first striking aspect of Mozart's daily life is the fact that he moved
so frequently: in less than ten years the Mozarts occupied eleven
different dwellings (not including the two Mozart had while he was still
a bachelor). But the moves took place at irregular intervals and for
widely different reasons, and the dwellings were not all of the same
quality. It was certainly not a question of a gradual social decline
periodically obliging the Mozarts to find smaller and more modest
accommodations, but rather of a swift adjustment to each new situation, in which rent was not necessarily the primary concern. However
dearly Mozart wished to remain in Vienna and establish himself in a
secure post, he lived in a constant atmosphere of imminent departure;
he was always making travel plans and even considered relocating to
Paris, England, or another court that would offer him better financial

prospects. Mozart simply did not have the security to settle permanently in Vienna, and the picture did not change when he was named imperial *Kammerkompositeur*. These concerns began right after his marriage and remained a topic of discussion up until his death.

> The Viennese gentry, and especially the emperor, must not imagine that I am on this earth solely for the sake of Vienna. There is no monarch in the world whom I should be more glad to serve than the emperor, but I refuse to beg for any post. I believe I am capable of doing credit to any court. If Germany, my beloved fatherland—of which I am proud, as you know—will not accept me, then in God's name let France or England become the richer by another talented German, to the disgrace of the German nation. You know well that it is the Germans who have always excelled in almost all the arts. But where did they make their fortune and reputation? Certainly not in Germany! Take even the case of Gluck. Has Germany made him the great man he is? Alas no! . . . I have been practicing my French daily and have already taken three lessons in English. In three months I hope to be able to read and understand English books fairly easily. (August 17, 1782)

Thus the entire sojourn in Vienna had an air of impermanence about it, which was also reflected in the frequent changes of address.

First there were the lodgings in Wipplingerstrasse, at the corner of Färbergasse; in Arnstein's house on the Graben Mozart had had only a furnished room, and it was urgent that he get Constanze Weber out of her mother's house, but he had to wait for his earnings from *Die Entführung aus dem Serail* before he could start his own household. We have no information about the size and cost of this first dwelling. Perhaps it was only meant to be temporary, for barely four months later, in December, the Mozarts moved further down the street to Baron Wetzlar's house at Wipplingerstrasse 14, where they occupied two rooms with an anteroom and kitchen—decidedly modest quarters on the fourth floor.

In 1786 Johann Pezzl wrote the following about housing conditions in Vienna:

> A flat is one of the most important and expensive items in Vienna.
> The largest private building within the city limits is the Starhembergsches Freihaus outside the Kärntnertor, where the suburb of

Wieden begins. . . . People who know the building claim that it has
living space for three thousand people. At present this house brings its
owner 15,000 florins annually, and is therefore worth as much as many
earldoms in the Holy Roman Empire.

There are more of these stone earldoms in Vienna. It is well known
that the Trattner house, for example, brings in as much as the principality of Hechingen in Swabia. A house for a cavalier of the first or
second rank and his family costs 5,000 to 6,000 florins a year. And a
house of comparable size, not inhabited by one large family but
divided up into flats for people of the middle class, brings in still more.
For this reason, the people who buy the abolished monasteries do not
turn these buildings into glittering palaces, but make them into fifty
ordinary flats, workshops, and kiosks. . . .

The larger middle-class houses on the Graben, Kohlmarkt, Hof,
Stock-im-Eisen Platz, and Kärntnerstrasse each bring in between
6,000 and 8,000 florins per year. An ordinary grocer's shop on the
Graben or Kohlmarkt costs 700 to 900 florins. A proper dwelling for a
family with a carriage and two horses, in an ordinary street on the
second or third floor, costs 800 to 1,100 florins.

. . . In Vienna the ground floor of a house is almost never used for
living quarters; it is used for kiosks, taverns, cafés, workshops, storerooms, apothecaries, etc. Also, this floor is not counted as one of the
stories of the house; one begins counting only after the first flight of
stairs.[16]

Pezzl's figures show that even in those times a large part of one's
income was devoured by rent, and that there was already a tendency to
concentrated ownership of real estate. Mozart was personally acquainted with two wealthy property owners, both of whom became
godfathers to his children. One was Baron Raimund Wetzlar von
Plankenstern, whom Mozart must have met shortly after his arrival in
Vienna. The Wetzlars were a wealthy Jewish family from Offenbach
who had come to Vienna as court agents. After converting to Catholicism, they were granted baronial rank and, now fully assimilated,
began to acquire extensive residential property.[17] Mozart's close association with Wetzlar lasted throughout his years in Vienna, though
little is known about him and he is seldom mentioned in the letters.[18]

Nonetheless, this acquaintance was quite remarkable. It shows
Mozart's awareness of and response to people singled out by fortune,
and his interest in unusual contemporaries whose integration into

society was not a matter of course, people who had experienced isolation, even ostracism, and had surmounted these obstacles only by making drastic concessions. Hardly any Jews converted out of religious conviction; conversion was the high price paid for full civil liberties. Significantly, it was in Wetzlar's house that Mozart made the acquaintance of another Jewish convert who would come to mean a great deal to him: Lorenzo Da Ponte.

Mozart lived only three months in Wetzlar's house, then took shabby temporary quarters for another three months. This was not because of any restlessness or financial embarrassment on Mozart's part; rather, it was a favor to Wetzlar, who was apparently obliged to make major rearrangements in his houses. In return, the baron was very accommodating about the rent.

> Baron Wetzlar has taken a lady into his home; so, to oblige him, we moved before the time to a wretched lodging in the Kohlmarkt, in return for which he refused to take any rent for the three months we had lived in his house, and also paid the expenses of our removal. . . . Wetzlar paid for us too when we were in the Kohlmarkt. (May 21, 1783)

Not until April 1783 did Mozart finally obtain "good accommodation" at Judenplatz 3, in a location that had earlier been the center of the Jewish community. It was in these lodgings that Mozart's first child, Raimund Leopold, was born. The close relationship with Baron Wetzlar is evident when Mozart writes, "After my wife's safe delivery I immediately sent a message to Baron Wetzlar, who is a good and true friend of mine. He came to see us at once and offered to stand godfather" (June 18, 1783).

We know nothing about the size or quality of this dwelling on the Judenplatz, only that it was on the second floor. Mozart stayed here nine months, until he had the opportunity to move into the Trattnerhof, that prestigious house on the Graben that was surely the most famous address in all Vienna. Mozart was also well acquainted with the owner of this house, Johann Thomas von Trattner, whose wife was one of Mozart's first piano pupils. The Trattners stood as godparents for four of Mozart's children—a kindness that points to a very close friendship between the two families, even though, once again, the name Trattner is hardly ever mentioned in a letter.

The construction of the Trattnerhof on the Graben, where Mozart lived in 1784. Josephine Vienna was characterized by incessant building activity. Many public facilities (hospitals, etc.) were erected, especially after the dissolution of the monasteries.

Our sources provide no information as to whether Wetzlar and Trattner were patrons of Mozart. They never appear as creditors or as dedicatees of any of Mozart's works, nor were they among his correspondents, which is understandable since he had regular personal contact with them. Only Maria Theresa von Trattner (who was more than forty years younger than her husband and has accordingly been suspected of having an affair with Mozart) received a piano sonata with an introductory fantasie (K. 457 and 475). In any event, Trattner also gave Mozart a rent reduction of 20 florins per year.

Mozart's lodgings in the Trattnerhof must have been quite small, for the full rent was only 150 florins per year, although they were on the fourth floor. What could have prompted Mozart to move here from a "good accommodation"? It certainly was not for the sake of Frau Trattner's piano lessons. A more plausible explanation might be that Mozart planned to present a concert series of his own, for which the Trattnerhof offered the very best possibilities. The piano would not have to be moved from the house, since the building had such unusual dimensions (for the times) that it even included a concert hall; and the entire layout and appearance of the Trattnerhof made it one of the great attractions of Vienna.

Trattner was one of the most successful entrepreneurs of the eighteenth century, and the Trattnerhof, whose second floor he himself occupied, was an ostentatious display of that success. Trattner had risen in the world primarily as a publisher who specialized in reprints and pirated editions of Enlightenment literature and the so-called classics. In these activities he had the total support of the imperial court. The essential thing was to attract business to the country; that this was done at the expense of authors' royalties was at most a regrettable flaw in the system. Trattner, whose career had been especially promoted by Maria Theresa, was also the official publisher of schoolbooks for the Austrian Empire. He owned five printing plants, his own paper factory, eight bookshops, and numerous book warehouses. He was always reinvesting his profits in new projects and was adept at combining private interests and commercial success. Thus he was a landowner and peer of the realm, he entertained emperors and princes, he set up a casino in his house for the nobility and "persons of distinction," as well as a public reading room, and so forth.

On the ground floor of the Trattnerhof were businesses (among them one of Trattner's own bookshops, lavishly appointed in marble), storerooms, stalls, and outbuildings leading back to the two inner courtyards. Five separate staircases provided access to the residential quarters, which accommodated roughly 600 people. The cost of the entire edifice, with its splendidly ornate furnishings—including giant caryatids at the portal and a balustrade of sculpted figures on the balcony—was around 390,000 florins. The style of this controversial structure made no secret of Trattner's standing as a *nouveau riche* who created his own private mythology and proudly displayed what he had achieved through his business acumen. It was in total contrast to the restrained elegance of the aristocratic palaces that served as its model. Contemporaries were divided in their opinions: some were impressed by the building's dimensions and by the sheer financial boldness it represented, while others found it in poor taste.[19]

Mozart's most successful period in Vienna began in early 1784, with a series of more than twenty concerts. These were evidently so lucrative that he could contemplate renting a larger and more luxurious apartment, not on the fourth floor, but on the second, which would make transporting the piano easier. He could find nothing suitable in the Trattner house. For all the building's comforts, the Mozarts needed more space, as yet another addition to the family was expected.

On September 29, 1784 (St. Michael's Day), Mozart moved into the Camesina House on Grosse Schulerstrasse, directly behind St. Stephen's Cathedral. These rooms, which today house a Mozart museum, were richly ornamented in stucco, as one might expect in a house owned by a member of the famous Camesina family of stucco artists. The apartment consisted of four large rooms, two smaller rooms, kitchen, garret, cellar, and two areas for storing wood. During the three years he lived here (until April 1787), Mozart celebrated his greatest successes. He wrote *Le nozze di Figaro* and even had his own billiard room, a sign of his high income. He also had enough room to accommodate guests. This was the house Leopold Mozart visited (where he was impressed by the "economical" household and by his son's healthy financial situation); and musicians passing through Vienna, like Joseph Fiala and Johann André, stayed here for weeks at a time. During this period Mozart also took the young Johann Nepomuk Hummel as a live-in pupil (he remained in Mozart's home for two and a half years).

The lodgings in the Trattnerhof had been taken temporarily, out of practical considerations, but Mozart settled into the Camesina House for the long term, to enjoy his success, now that the rent was no longer a critical factor. The price of this comfortable and spacious dwelling was correspondingly high: 230 florins per half-year, more than three times the rent in the Trattnerhof.[20]

The two and a half years in the Camesina House clearly belong to Mozart's most affluent period. This was certainly the most expensive apartment he ever had. Why, then, did he give it up in April 1787? We know that a year later Mozart had considerable debts, for it was then that the famous letters to his creditor Michael Puchberg began. For this reason it has always been assumed that Mozart "moved for financial reasons from Schulerstrasse to Landstrasse 224 [today No. 75]" (Joseph Heinz Eibl in his commentary on the letter of May 10, 1787). But not a shred of evidence supports this theory. The rent in the Landstrasse was indeed considerably less, but there were other reasons for moving into this garden apartment. The move was neither precipitate nor unplanned; it took place at the end of the biannual lease period, and the Mozarts had given proper notice. Now they had a spacious house (an old photograph of which still survives) and were able to use the garden. Mozart had no pupils at this time, but he had just received an opera commission from Prague, to which he dedicated himself with utmost concentration: *Don Giovanni.*

There is no sign whatsoever of unusually large debts during this period. On the contrary, Leopold learned that his son took in 1,000 florins in Prague, and there was further talk of a visit to England. Mozart always kept his father in the dark about his living conditions. Thus Leopold could only report laconically to his daughter, "Your brother now lives at Landstrasse No. 224. But he does not say why he moved—not a word! Unfortunately, I think I can guess the reason" (May 11, 1787).[21]

Mozart, however, stayed only seven months in the Landstrasse apartment and in December 1787 moved to Unter den Tuchlauben 27, at the corner of Schultergasse in the city center. The timing of this move was very odd and cannot be accounted for. It is not unlikely that the garden house was simply unsuitable for the winter, especially since Constanze was expecting a child at the end of December; it had in fact been rather cold since mid-November. But this remains conjecture in the absence of more definite information. The lodgings in Unter den Tuchlauben seem to have been a temporary solution, for in the summer of the following year Mozart moved again, this time with longer-term plans.

From this point on, Mozart's letters to his friend and creditor Michael Puchberg must substitute for missing family correspondence. Now financial problems were discussed in connection with accommodations. Mozart asked Puchberg to "support him with one or two thousand florins, repayable over one or two years with due interest." In the same letter he wrote:

If you should find it inconvenient to part with so large a sum all at once, then I beg you to lend me until tomorrow *at least a couple of hundred florins,* as my landlord in the Landstrasse has been so importunate that in order to avoid an unpleasant incident I had to pay him on the spot, and this has made things very awkward for me! We are sleeping tonight for the first time in our new quarters, where we shall remain both summer and winter. On the whole the change is all the same to me, in fact I prefer it. As it is, I have very little to do in town, and as I am not exposed to so many visitors, I will have more time for work. If I have to go to town on business, which will certainly not be very often, any fiacre will take me there for 10 kreuzer. Moreover, the rooms are cheaper and during the spring, summer, and autumn *more pleasant,* as I have a garden too. The address is *Währingergasse, bei den 3 Sternen No. 135.* (June 17, 1788)

The information in this letter is confusing. Though Mozart had not lived in Landstrasse for six months, he evidently still owed rent. No mention is made of the flat in Unter den Tuchlauben, only of new lodgings where he can "remain both summer and winter." Had that been impossible earlier? Or never intended? And then Mozart complains about "the many visitors" who apparently disturbed him at work. He goes into the city "not very often" and only "on business"; this is another troubling sentence in that it describes a way of life entirely different from the one he had led only a short time earlier when he performed regularly at public and private concerts, moved in aristocratic circles as if in his element, attended balls (and gave them himself), and maintained a restless pace.

Whatever the reasons for moving from the Landstrasse back into the city, money problems were not yet among them, for in the autumn of 1787, after his father's death, Mozart received an inheritance of at least 1,000 florins from Salzburg. Things were different in 1788, perhaps because Mozart was living beyond his means; there may have been gambling debts as well. By 1788 the social life of Vienna had changed considerably: the mood was depressed, there were fewer concerts, and money was not so readily available for pleasure and entertainment. It was the *Türkenjahr,* the year of renewed military conflicts with Turkey, and no one knew what the outcome would be. This certainly had a decided effect on Mozart's income. Now the increasingly desperate letters to Mozart's friend and chief creditor Puchberg began.

Although Mozart had planned to settle in the lodgings at what is now Währinger Strasse 26, he gave them up after six months in exchange for a flat at Judenplatz 4—once again the reasons are unknown to us. It was his fourth move in a year and a half. The family remained at this address for almost two years, and it was here that Constanze's illness began, necessitating great financial sacrifice in addition to many other concessions to her health. Her illness may also explain the large debts to Puchberg, which accumulated until mid-1790 but were to a large extent repaid by the summer of 1791.

It appears that between 1788 and 1789 Mozart underwent a financial crisis brought on by the political circumstances of the Turkish war and the general crisis in Europe on the eve of the French Revolution, and by the personal circumstances of his wife's illness. It is equally clear that he was able to rehabilitate himself again during 1790 and 1791, and that by the end of 1791 his prospects were good enough that he could contemplate a life free of financial anxiety.

One general observation on Mozart's lodgings: during his two and a half years in the Camesina House on Schulerstrasse he had his greatest success, especially as a virtuoso pianist; at the other address where he remained for a relatively long period, Judenplatz 4, he experienced personal cares, illness, and general uncertainty.

While Mozart was traveling to Frankfurt for the coronation of Leopold II as Holy Roman Emperor, his family moved to Rauhensteingasse 8. The move took place on Michaelmas, September 29, at the end of an official rental period, indicating that in this case as well Mozart had given the required notice. His situation had already improved, and he even planned an expensive renovation of his new lodgings, as we know from a high bill from a paper hanger that has survived. The apartment in Rauhensteingasse, where he would die, was only a little smaller than that in the Camesina house; it had four large rooms, two smaller rooms, a kitchen, and side rooms, and was on the second floor. It had space for a billiard room, as well. The furnishings of this last dwelling prove that Mozart was in no way undergoing a social decline. He had certainly accumulated no riches, but he had managed to keep his debts within reasonable limits. Although his income was entirely sufficient, he spent so much that there were no reserves to carry him through an especially difficult time (as in 1788–89). However, the problem lay in his style of living and was not the result of actual poverty. If we compare Mozart's situation with that of Schubert (who died at an equally young age) or Haydn (before his retirement), Mozart emerges as a highly respected and correspondingly well-paid musician and composer.

HOUSEHOLD FURNISHINGS

Mozart's income is reflected not only in his lodgings, which were far from humble, but in their furnishings and his other possessions. The inventory of his effects, which was compiled several days after his death, provides a good idea of his household furnishings, clothes, and library (although there is some doubt as to whether the list is complete, especially with regard to books and music).[22] We can only wonder how everything fit into a flat with approximately 145 square meters of floor space: four sofas and eighteen armchairs were distributed among the four main rooms; there were five wardrobes, a secretary, a manuscript cabinet, five tables, two bookcases, four beds (one a double bed), and the large fortepiano with its specially designed pedal box and a spinet (not entered in the inventory). In addition there were kitchen furnishings—cupboards, tables, etc.—and the furnishings of the servants' quarters, not to mention the smaller items. And then there was the billiard table, which was so large that it filled an entire room.

We admittedly do not know when all this was acquired or in which flat each item was first used, nor do we know the dimensions of most of his dwellings. In any case, Mozart arrived in Vienna with nothing but his travel wardrobe and some manuscripts; he had more music, clothes, and books sent to him from Salzburg—and that was all. The furnishings, then, had all been acquired since the summer of 1782, when he moved into his own lodgings for the first time. Thus, his many relocations in no way indicate an indifference to his living conditions. His quarters had to be somewhat spacious, if only because of the large amount of furniture, which could hardly have been obtained during the financially difficult years 1788–90. Most of it was probably bought during the years in the Camesina House.

Along with the excellence of his household furnishings went another element of bourgeois prosperity: the Mozarts attached great importance to clothing, and the surviving bills from tailors are not our only evidence to that effect.[23] The inventory of Mozart's clothes at the time of his death reads as follows:

1 white frock coat with cotton vest
1 blue ditto
1 red ditto
1 nankeen ditto
1 brown satin coat and breeches, with silk embroidery
1 entire suit of black cloth
1 mouse-color greatcoat
1 ditto of lighter cloth
1 blue frock coat with fur trimming
1 blue kiria with fur trimming
4 vests and 9 pairs of breeches, various materials
2 plain hats, 3 pairs of boots, 3 pairs of shoes
9 pairs of silk stockings
9 shirts
4 white neckerchiefs, 1 nightcap, 18 handkerchiefs
8 pairs of underdrawers, 2 nightshirts
5 pairs of plain stockings

This wardrobe, unusually extensive by the standards of the time, bespeaks a sophisticated, almost conspicuously lavish taste. It could have been the red frock coat and vest in the inventory that Mozart asked for, almost impertinently, in a letter to Baroness Waldstätten. Mozart's description of the coat and associations to it provide insight into his extramusical existence, his visual sensibility, and his flamboyant vanity.

As for the beautiful red coat, which attracts me enormously, please, please let me know *where it is to be had and how much it costs*—for that I have completely forgotten, as I was so captivated by its splendor that I failed to notice the price. I must have a coat like that, for it is one that will really do justice to certain buttons which I have long been hankering after. I saw them once when I was choosing some for a suit. They are in Brandau's button factory in the Kohlmarkt, opposite the Milano. They are mother-of-pearl with a few white stones around the edge and a fine yellow stone in the center. I would like all my things to be of good quality, genuine and beautiful. Why is it, I wonder, that those who cannot afford it would like to spend a fortune on such articles, and those who can do not do so? (September 28, 1782)

A red coat served as a kind of uniform in many court orchestras, but here it is undoubtedly something more—a select garment for special occasions, the quality of which must be "good, genuine and beautiful." (By return mail Baroness Waldstätten promised Mozart the coat—for which he almost forgot to thank her). The English singer Michael Kelly remembered that at the first rehearsal for *Le nozze di Figaro* (in early 1785) Mozart stood on stage and gave the tempi wearing a red coat and gold-trimmed hat.

Mozart dressed like the nobility, the high court officials, and the wealthy idlers of the capital. For the winter he had a blue overcoat trimmed with fur and another fully lined with fur. At gala events he wore a white suit, on other occasions silk and satin. A trace of ostentation is unmistakable, though easily understandable in view of his unflattering appearance. "He was a remarkably small man, with a profusion of fine, fair hair of which he was rather vain," wrote Kelly. Another observer described him as "a small man with a large head and fleshy hands," and also as "gaunt and pale." In the course of his years in Vienna his build seems to have become more powerful; he described himself once as "fat and healthy," but that may have been one of his humorous exaggerations. We must also imagine Mozart as temperamental to the point of violence—Kelly says that he was "as touchy as gunpowder"—but also very kind, with a self-assurance that befitted his vanity. Sometimes, however, he was playful and boisterous to the point of childishness.

Mozart's carefully chosen wardrobe may have followed high-society fashions, but this should not be misunderstood as conformity to the tastes of that largely aristocratic social stratum on which he was dependent as both pianist and composer. On the contrary, Mozart had obvious bohemian traits that were not restricted to the supposed carelessness and disorder of his household and were manifested in certain behavior inconsistent with his vanity. Mozart seems to have been a pronounced individualist who claimed the total freedom of an artist's life. Yet a single short passage from one of his letters shows us a normal, everyday Mozart who has never been included in our traditional picture of the composer. He wrote to Constanze on the very day she departed for a cure at Baden:

Now for an account of my own doings. Immediately after your departure I played two games of billiards with Herr von Mozart, the fellow
who wrote the opera running at Schikaneder's theater; then I sold my
nag for fourteen ducats; then I told Joseph to get Primus to fetch me
some black coffee, with which I smoked a splendid pipe of tobacco;
and then I orchestrated almost the whole of Stadler's rondo.

(October 7, 1791)

This schedule of his morning activities shows him in a calm and
cheerful mood, as he jestingly apostrophizes Joseph Deiner, the waiter
at his favorite tavern, as Joseph the First, enjoys a relaxing game of
billiards against himself, engages in a bit of horse trading (unimagin-
able), and finally, while composing, indulges in two vices at once:
drinking black coffee and smoking a pipe. If we possessed a single
portrait of Mozart with a pipe or a horse or playing billiards, our
stereotyped picture of his supposedly wretched life would be turned on
its head. We would see a short yet striking dandy to whom the
pleasures of life are important and who will not renounce them, a man
who, undertaking some intense and (considering its quality) very
diligent work, rewards himself with extravagant pleasures that he
needs as much for stimulation as for relaxation, and that he claims for
himself without false modesty (even including smoking, which at the
time was still frowned upon in society). [24]

Mozart riding his steed through the streets of Vienna—this picture
is as strange as it is realistic. Almost every biography mentions that
Mozart's physician, Dr. Sigmund Barisani, recommended horseback
riding to him for health reasons, to counteract the effects of his
predominantly sedentary occupation. Furthermore, we have reliable
evidence that Mozart was crazy about horses and owned a horse
himself. But when did Mozart go riding, and which routes did he like
to take? Where did he keep his horse? (Many houses in the central
part of Vienna had stables that were accessible from the street and
passages leading to the cellar, where there was more room for coaches.
Other houses, especially the palatial homes of the nobility, had outbuildings or converted courtyards for keeping animals and vehicles.
Many apartments included stable space in the price of the rent.) Who
took care of his horse? We know for a fact that Mozart owned a

carriage, if only for a short time; immediately following his financial crisis he would not be denied the privilege of setting out for Frankfurt in his own carriage. During the journey he reported to his wife that his "carriage (I'd like to kiss it) is splendid" (September 28, 1790). It is uncertain what became of the carriage; perhaps it was sold right after the journey.

Billiards was also a part of his routine. Mozart already owned a valuable billiard table during his years in the Camesina House. Kelly, a very dependable witness, relates:

> He gave me a cordial invitation to his house, of which I availed myself, and passed a great part of my time there. He always received me with kindness and hospitality. He was remarkably fond of punch, of which beverage I have seen him take copious draughts. He was also fond of billiards, and had an excellent billiard table in his house. Many and many a game have I played with him, but always came off second best.[25]

They undoubtedly played for money, as was then customary. Card games for money also took place in Mozart's home. A connection to his financial problems cannot be rejected out of hand, although there is no evidence of gambling debts. On the other hand, hardly any social gathering in Vienna was without gambling. Even the court balls in the Redoutensaal or the dances in the Mehlgrube always had small rooms with gaming tables, where cards and games of chance such as faro were common.

Looking at Mozart's daily life only serves to emphasize how little we really know about him.

DIGRESSION: HOW MUCH DID MUSICIANS EARN?

When Mozart left the archbishop of Salzburg's service, he gave up a position with a secure annual income of 450 florins. We cannot enter into a discussion of whether this was an appropriate salary for a musician of Mozart's class. Its appropriateness can only be judged in relation to what other musicians earned and cannot be separated from the historical context and the social position of artists.

Musical life at the end of the eighteenth century was supported primarily by the royal courts and the nobility, and only in a rudimentary way by the bourgeoisie, to the extent that they had gained an economic and social foothold. The middle class became influential much earlier in northern Europe than in southern Germany and the Habsburg Empire. There the Church played a much greater role as a secular power, as in Salzburg with its prince archbishop. Only the courts and the often extremely wealthy nobility could afford full-time musicians and thus have their own orchestras and even private opera houses. Middle-class music societies, municipally supported concerts, and the like played a very minor role. But that did not prevent the bourgeoisie from engaging in all kinds of musical activities or occasionally even commissioning new works and organizing concerts. The orchestras for such events were mostly assembled ad hoc; the musicians were not hired permanently but were paid a small fee that gave them no security. (In Salzburg the Haffner family exemplified the extent of bourgeois enthusiasm for music, but also its organizational and financial limits.) Only now and then did a middle-class entrepreneur lease a theater (sometimes even to present opera) and put together a troupe of performers. The many traveling theater troupes that moved from city to city were only barely capable of offering even small opera productions. The private theaters of Vienna, such as Emanuel Schikaneder's Freihaustheater auf der Wieden, must be rated exceptions that were only possible in a great metropolis.

The salary a musician in a full-time post could expect was extraordinarily low by today's standards; for many it was a living wage only if one remained single and led an unimaginably frugal life. The nobility, who always tended to live beyond their means, commonly hired servants—guards, footmen, valets—who could also play an instrument. Thus, entire private orchestras could be maintained without being paid as such. Sometimes military musicians were formed into wind ensembles called *Harmoniemusiken*. The salaries of such instrumentalists, who often did not know themselves whether they had been hired as musicians or servants, cannot serve as an example of a musician's possible income. They represent, so to speak, the lowest rung of a tall ladder. The frequent combining of the instrumentalist's profession with other occupations reveals only too well their low social position. On the other hand, concertmasters and conductors often commanded very high salaries, which had more to do with the employer's desire for prestige than with any deep understanding of music.

Because only Italian musicians received such high wages, the nobility's dwindling interest in the Italian musical style can be charted economically. Whoever wished to entice Italian musicians across the Alps had to dig deep into his pockets. Thus Niccolò Jommelli, kapellmeister at the court in Stuttgart (until 1768), received a salary of 4,000 florins, had the use of a house in Stuttgart and one in Ludwigsburg, and was supplied with firewood, lamp oil, and fodder for four horses; in addition his wife was promised a pension of 2,000 florins. True, the Württemburg court was known for its wastefulness, but this salary was beyond comparison, even allowing for the fact that the Italians received an average of 50 percent more than native musicians. (The social position of Miller in Schiller's *Kabale und Liebe* is not atypical for an ordinary member of the Stuttgart court orchestra, and the social distance between him and the celebrated soloists could not be more obvious.) In principle, however, there were no fixed guidelines for wages, so regional differences among the various courts were enormous.

The Mannheim orchestra, which moved to Munich in 1778 along with Elector Karl Theodor, was certainly one of the best paid. In quality it was among the best in Europe. Kapellmeister Ignaz Holzbauer received approximately 3,000 florins, orchestra director Christian Cannabich 1,800, and concertmaster Ignaz Fränzl 1,400. A singer could get a starting salary of 400 to 600 florins. The musicians were almost all German (or Bohemian).

By comparison, salaries in Salzburg were extremely modest. Leopold Mozart received 350 florins as assistant kapellmeister; Wolfgang Mozart was engaged as concertmaster in 1772 for 150 florins; violinists in other orchestras received 300 to 400 florins. As court organist (as of 1779) Mozart received 450 florins.

Of the private orchestras, the one we are best informed about is that of Prince Nikolaus Esterházy, which Haydn directed for many years. The development of Haydn's fixed income shows how much leeway the prince allowed himself in paying his musicians. As assistant kapellmeister in 1761, Haydn drew 400 florins plus 180 for expenses; in 1764, 600 florins plus 180 for expenses. As organist, from 1779, he received an additional 180 florins in goods—altogether approximately 1,000 florins. The instrumentalists in the Esterházy orchestra received 200 to 300 florins as well as goods amounting to approximately 100 florins; they also had free (if not exactly comfortable) accommodations. Here the occasional exception was also possible: the Italian concertmaster Luigi Tomasini received not only 1,800 florins and free accommodations but also firewood and wine, which made his total salary almost twice as much as Haydn's. Life in Prince Esterházy's palace was inexpensive, and there was little opportunity to spend money. Haydn, however, did buy a house in Eisenstadt, and kept chickens, two horses, and probably a cow as well.[26]

The misery of more easily replaceable musicians can be seen in the case of Haydn's brother Johann Evangelist, who was only a tenor in the Esterházy choir and earned a mere 25 florins, finally raised in the 1780s to 60 florins plus free accommodations, goods, and the use of a green uniform jacket with red cuffs. These were starvation wages that barely allowed one to live from hand to mouth; the idea of starting a family on this income was unthinkable.

Such low salaries were not uncommon in Josephine Vienna, but musicians there had more opportunities to earn money on the side. In 1780 Mozart's brother-in-law Franz Hofer drew around 20 florins as twelfth violinist at St. Stephen's church; when he was promoted to tenth violinist in 1787, his salary was raised to 25 florins.[27] In 1788, when he entered the imperial court orchestra, he earned 150 florins more, and not until 1796 did he make a wage of 450 florins. (His wife Josepha, née Weber, who was engaged in 1790 as a singer in Schikaneder's theater, received 830 florins and 150 florins for her wardrobe.) Naturally, given his modest income, Hofer was always glad to play in private concerts, for which orchestras were usually assembled ad hoc. He could not have made ends meet without this additional money.

The artists of the Nationalsingspiel, that part of the Hoftheater devoted to German opera, enjoyed a privileged position. In this roughly thirty-piece orchestra the standard salary was 350 florins; the concertmaster received 450. But first-class wind players were hard to obtain, so the oboists, clarinetists, bassoonists, and the first two (or four) hornists each received as much as 750 florins. That made their salary almost as high as that of the kapellmeister, Ignaz Umlauf, who was paid 850 florins. [28] The members of this orchestra also took part in the many concerts given in the Burgtheater or in private homes, since they were only required to give ten to twelve performances a month (plays were given on the other days). It remains unclear how much they earned for these extra concerts; indeed, we know surprisingly little about the rich and varied concert life in Vienna at the end of the eighteenth century.

We can best estimate the social level of musicians by comparing their income with that of Viennese civil servants. [29] Here we must differentiate between court officials or councillors of state and officials of the province of Lower Austria, whose seat of government was also Vienna. As a rule, the latter earned only half as much as court officials. The highest level on the pay scale was occupied by ministers and presidents of court bodies such as the Advisory Council and the Council of State. Almost all these positions were held by members of the high nobility, and their salaries ranged from 8,000 to 20,000 florins annually. The second level included councillors, secretaries, registrars, and clerks. A court councillor could earn 4,000 to 6,000 florins, court secretaries 1,000 to 2,000, and court clerks 700 to 1,000. The registrars earned a bit more—1,000 to 1,500 florins. The majority of officials occupied the third level; they were the adjuncts, chancellery clerks, etc., either at court or in the provincial government; here again, the latter earned about half as much as the former. The salaries of these officials ranged from 200 to 1,200 florins, but the majority probably earned between 300 and 900. It should be noted that candidates for government jobs, the so-called *Praktikanten*, were not on the payroll at all and often worked for years as unpaid trainees, in hopes of a future position. There was no organized system of promotion, and it was rarely possible to advance more than two levels in the hierarchy before retirement. At the bottom of the scale, full-time servants received 60 florins per year, but a houseboy could earn as much as 144 florins. A chambermaid, however, only managed to bring in 20 or at most 30 florins annually. These low-level workers received new uniforms once a year.

At the other end of this steep social scale were the nobility, with vast incomes from their estates. The family of a prince could have an annual income of 100,000 to 500,000 florins, that of a count 20,000 to 100,000. It is not surprising that such families could hold court most lavishly and even maintain their own private orchestras. In Vienna there were probably eight or ten such orchestras, which followed their employers to the family estates in Hungary, Bohemia, Moravia, and elsewhere in the summer months. These "first" families also held the "first" posts in the government, for which, in addition to their salaries, so-called *Gratiale* were awarded by the imperial court in recognition of special services. Entire government estates were given away in this way. (On this score as well, Joseph II was the stingiest and most frugal of the Habsburg rulers; the shower of gifts that his nephew Francis II bestowed upon Count Klemens Metternich would have been unthinkable for him.)

The wages of government officials clearly show the difference between members of the nobility and the bourgeoisie. Certain posts were reserved for aristocrats, and the salaries served to maintain their lifestyle and perpetuate class differences. Thus, we should also consider the middle class and academic professions for comparison with musicians' incomes. A university professor received anywhere from 600 to 3,000 florins, but the high salaries were attained only by professors in charge of important scientific facilities—and there were very few of them. The salary paid to Friedrich Schiller, who at the beginning of his academic career was already famous and much in demand, is a typical example of the miserable wage standard. At first (1789) his chair was unpaid, and he received only students' fees; in 1790 he was given a salary equal to 400 florins, which was raised to 800 florins in 1799. Not until 1804 did this amount double. In 1789 he declared that it was possible to "live reasonably well" on an income of 1,400 florins.[30] On the other hand, a primary school teacher in Austria earned 120 to 250 florins, and a secondary school post paid 300. In other countries (e.g., Prussia) teachers' salaries were even lower. An intern at the general hospital in Josephine Vienna received 240 florins, a parish priest 300 to 800.

These figures show that orchestral musicians were paid about the same wages as servants, or at best, low-level government officials. Only if instrumentalists (such as wind players) were especially in demand were the salaries slightly higher. Most musicians occupied the lower ranks of society.

The situation was entirely different for soloists, especially singers. The enormous salaries paid to the most famous Italian castrati were not to be found in Vienna, but there too, Italian singers generally received twice the normal amount. Of the sixteen vocal soloists at the Nationalsingspiel, eight received 400 to 800 florins and six received 1,200 florins.[31] Mozart's sister-in-law Aloysia Lange was paid 1,700 florins, and the famous tenor Valentin Adamberger more than 2,000. At the Italian-language Hofoper, by contrast, Antonia Bernasconi received 2,250 florins, and that was by no means the highest salary.[32] The court did try to stay within reasonable limits. Emperor Joseph was actively involved in contract negotiations, and on his journeys he even engaged soloists for Vienna himself; the Italians were simply more expensive. The castrato Luigi Marchesi received 2,250 florins for six appearances—as much as Adamberger received in a year. The soprano Nancy Storace, who despite her name was of Italian descent and was highly esteemed by the emperor and the public alike, brought in over 4,000 florins for one concert in 1787. She declined an offer of almost 5,000 florins for the 1788 season.

Working for royalty was no guarantee of royal wages. The musicians competed with each other, which also had a detrimental effect on their fees. No other city in German-speaking Europe had such a craze for music as Vienna, but no other city had as many musicians either. The problem is illustrated by the many piano teachers who found it difficult enough to obtain students, although every self-respecting Viennese at least learned to play the piano.

Mozart gave a very vivid description of the search for a piano teacher for Princess Elizabeth Wilhelmina von Württemberg, who had come to Vienna to marry Archduke Francis. Mozart had hoped to be considered for this position himself but was happy not to have received it when he learned how much it paid.

You say that 400 florins a year as an *assured salary* are not to be despised, and that would be true if in addition I could work myself into a good position and could treat these 400 florins simply as extra money. But unfortunately that is not the case. I would have to consider the 400 florins as my chief income and everything else I could earn as a windfall, the amount of which would be very uncertain and consequently in all probability very meager. You can easily understand that one cannot act as independently towards a pupil who is a princess as towards other ladies. If a princess does not feel inclined to take a lesson, why, you have the honor of waiting until she does. She is living out with the Salesians, so that if you do not care to walk, you have the honor of paying at least 20 kreuzer to drive there and back. Thus of my pay only 304 florins would remain—that is, if I only gave three lessons a week. And if I were obliged to wait, I would in the meantime be neglecting my other pupils or other work (by which I could easily make more than 400 florins). If I wanted to come into Vienna I would have to pay double, since I would be obliged to drive out again. If I stayed out there and were giving my lesson in the morning, as I no doubt would be doing, I would have to go at lunchtime to some inn, take a wretched meal and pay extravagantly for it. Moreover, by neglecting my other pupils I might lose them altogether—for everyone considers his money just as good as that of a princess. At the same time I would lose the time and inclination to earn more money by composition. To serve a great lord (in whatever office) a man should be paid a sufficient income to enable him to *serve his patron alone*, without being obliged to seek additional earnings to avoid penury. A man must provide against want. Please do not think I am so stupid as to tell all this to anyone else. But believe me, the emperor *himself* is well aware of his own meanness and has passed me over *solely* on this account. No doubt, if I had applied for the appointment I would certainly have received it, and with more than 400 florins—though probably with less salary than would have been fair and just. I am not looking for pupils, for I can have as many as I please; and from two of them, without causing me the slightest hindrance or inconvenience, I can get as much as the princess pays her master, who has thus no better prospect than that of avoiding starvation for the rest of his life. You know well how services are generally rewarded by great lords. (October 12, 1782)

As we can see, Mozart had learned a few lessons in economics. He could now weigh a position on its financial merits. He had also discovered that a musician who sold his services too cheaply could soon be reduced to a domestic servant. Through such careful observation, Mozart avoided becoming one of these exploited musicians. A permanent position normally meant around 400 florins per year, and this was an upper limit that very few musicians exceeded—only conductors and certain virtuoso singers and instrumentalists. Mozart, however, had entirely different financial needs in mind, and he claimed that with 1,200 florins per year "a man and his wife can manage in Vienna if they live quietly and in the retired way we desire"

(January 23, 1782). In fact, starting in 1783 he earned almost twice that amount and managed to spend all of it.

Kapellmeister salaries of more than 1,000 florins a year were extremely rare, but it was possible to earn extra money by composing. Very few pensions of more than 1,000 florins were granted, usually to musicians who had already worked many years for the court and would remain loosely associated with it. Thus, Gluck received a pension of 2,000 florins; after long and difficult years of moving around Europe, without any permanent position, he achieved success entirely through his compositions and only became a rich man when he was well along in years.[33] He was sixty before the Viennese court awarded him this sinecure.

It is extremely difficult to assess the cash value this money would have today. First, we must convert all sums into a uniform currency, for in the eighteenth century there were so many different varieties of coins and bank notes that even then people found it difficult to get a clear picture of their actual worth. To avoid being deceived when changing money or engaging in business, one needed a mental conversion table and had to refuse all "bad" coins. The florin, the standard unit of currency in southern Germany and the Austrian empire, was divided into 60 kreuzer. The florin and the kreuzer, gold and silver respectively, were in use until the mid-nineteenth century; their value was based on a stable relationship between the value of the two metals.

The value of this currency must be gauged in relation to prices for goods and labor under social, industrial, and transportation conditions totally different from today's. Wages especially played a much smaller role than they do now. A journeyman received a daily wage of 1 to 1½ florins, an untrained day laborer around 15 kreuzer; these jobs neither guaranteed nor provided regular year-round employment. We do know the prices of certain goods, foodstuffs, and labor from the medieval period to the present; they are easily looked up. But the shopping list of items necessary to support an average lifestyle changed constantly, as suggested by the fact that grocery stores as we know them did not exist in the eighteenth century. Every household had to store food as best it could without modern methods of preservation. Plainly, under these circumstances, there can be no definitive conversion rate for the buying power of eighteenth-century money. To arrive at an approximation, however, we can estimate that during the

Josephine decade 1 florin was equivalent to 20 U.S. dollars (1988), a figure that represents an average of all sums previously suggested by historians for the florin's buying power.

MOZART'S INCOME

Mozart's pastimes were those of a man accustomed to the high life, and his income was correspondingly high. Yet most biographers of Mozart have portrayed an increasingly impoverished artist, without taking the trouble to inspect his income more closely. In looking at the figures, we must be aware that we are not equally well informed on all his sources of income. But we can establish the minimum income that the evidence suggests he must have had. Some earnings were never recorded, though we know of their existence. And we must also consider income about which we have no information whatsoever; Mozart was often inclined to conceal his earnings—from his wife, for instance.

Mozart's income was derived from at least four different sources: commissions for new works (e.g., operas), ticket sales from his concerts (as pianist), royalties from his publishers, and fees for piano lessons. In addition he received a salary as royal and imperial *Kammerkompositeur* beginning in 1787. These earnings, however, were not steady, and they varied substantially. A graph of Mozart's income and expenditures, which were by no means parallel, would reveal the highly changeable fortunes of his private life, which helped to create the legend of "abject poverty." Mozart was indeed unable to cope with the alternation of good and bad times, and the problem was aggravated by a lack of thrift.

There were, of course, no "fixed rates" for composers (any more than there are today), but fees for the different compositional genres were not entirely arbitrary; certain guidelines had evolved. The Nationaloper, for example, normally paid 100 ducats, or about 450 florins, for a full-length work—for *Così fan tutte* (1790), Mozart received twice that amount. Payment for other types of composition was also greatly dependent on a composer's public esteem—Mozart was certainly more "expensive" than his rival Leopold Koželuch, his senior by eight years. And it is likely that the significance of a work was reflected in the composer's asking price: for example, Mozart asked the unusually high sum of 50 louis d'or from his publisher for the six string quartets dedicated to Haydn. We must keep in mind that an artist gave up all rights to a work when he sold it for a flat fee to a publisher or to a private individual for his own use. If, however, a composer offered his work for sale by subscription, he was taking the entrepreneurial risk of coming up short after paying his expenses. The same was true for works that were distributed only in handwritten copies.

Nor did concerts pay any set fees arranged ahead of time with the promoter. Artists usually appeared in concerts they had organized themselves, and their financial success was based on the surplus that remained after expenses. The audience, and especially members of the nobility, often voluntarily paid more than the ticket price, thus extending the artist a measure of patronage. When Emperor Joseph attended a concert, for instance, he usually sent a contribution ahead of time. That could be as much as 25 ducats (112 florins 30 kreuzer), as in the case of Mozart's concert in the Burgtheater on March 23, 1783. (Those permitted to use the Burgtheater as a concert hall did not have to pay rent for it.) Concerts were often billed as benefits to indicate certain financial expectations. It was different with private concerts in the wealthier homes, particularly those of the nobility, where the artist was remunerated by a single—often lavish—gift from the host. It is known that Mozart played many private concerts in aristocratic homes. As early as December 1782 he was engaged by Prince Dmitri Galitzin "for all his concerts" and was given the royal treatment. As Mozart indicated in a letter to his father, "I am always fetched in his coach and brought to his house, where I am treated most magnificently" (December 21, 1782).

Soloists naturally performed free of charge in concerts given by their colleagues, whereas most orchestra musicians had to be paid; their income was in any case so small that they were very dependent on such extra earnings. Benefit concerts for singers took place at the Nationaloper and often brought enormous receipts because of the public's craze for certain star performers.

Mozart was undoubtedly among the best-paid soloists in Vienna. Based on our knowledge of his concert receipts, after deducting the

EINLASS - KARTE
z u m
CONCERT
von
W. A. Mozart.

The only surviving ticket to one of Mozart's own concerts. The date of this concert cannot be reconstructed.

costs of the concert hall and orchestra, he netted, at a very conservative estimate, 300 florins on average. In the case of subscription concerts, which were given in series of three to six performances, a conservative estimate suggests a surplus of at least 100 florins. And for concerts in the homes of nobles, princes or counts such as Galitzin, Esterházy, Zichy, Pálffy, etc., he typically received gifts of 50 florins and often probably more. We know that he received 50 ducats (225 florins) for his contest with Muzio Clementi in the presence of Joseph II at Christmas 1781.

The story of Mozart's publication fees remains a very obscure chapter in his biography. If we add up all the works that were printed during his years in Vienna, we arrive at the considerable total of 110 numbers from the Köchel catalogue (the sixth edition of which contains around 790 numbers). Approximately one-fifth of these works printed between 1781 and 1791 were composed before Mozart moved to Vienna, and almost one-sixth of the works written in Vienna were printed during his lifetime. With music publishing still in its infancy, this is an unusually high number that very few of his musical colleagues were able to match; there was no one as productive as Mozart. Of these 110 numbers 65 are large works; the others are smaller pieces, including dances and songs. Most of them were published by

Artaria in Vienna, a few by Hoffmeister, and the rest by smaller houses in Vienna, Paris, and elsewhere. Mozart undoubtedly derived some income from most of these printed works, although it was rarely such a princely sum as he received for the *Haydn* Quartets. But some of the fees Mozart requested leave us with an unclear picture. He asked 135 florins for six violin sonatas, or more than 20 florins for each piece, yet he asked 30 to 100 florins for a piano concerto. We do not know if he actually received this much (from Artaria, for example). The evidence does reveal that most of the works appeared between 1785 and 1788, with noticeably fewer publications in the other years. Here too the beginning of the Turkish war in 1788 proved a heavy burden. Cultural life appears to have suffered a sharp setback, and the death soon afterward of Joseph II at a time of political uncertainty in Europe (the French Revolution) also had a paralyzing effect on public life.

During the early Vienna years, before Mozart began receiving larger fees from his publishers, his fees as a piano teacher played an important role in his finances. Mozart charged his pupils 6 ducats (27 florins) per month, for which he was prepared to give twelve lessons. Three pupils provided him with almost 1,000 florins per year. He restricted his teaching schedule as he began to appear more often in public concerts, but he always had pupils who came occasionally and thus did not guarantee him a regular income. Between 1785 and 1787 he was doing so well financially that he could often dispense with these comparatively small earnings. By 1790, however, he again had pupils, although each had lessons for only a short period.

If we add up all of Mozart's recorded earnings, we arrive at the following picture of his minimum income (loans to Mozart appear in italics):

YEAR	SOURCE OF INCOME	FLORINS
1781	*Idomeneo*	450
	Quarterly salary from Salzburg	112
	Fees (concerts, pupils)	400
1782	*Die Entführung aus dem Serail*	426
	Fees (concerts, pupils, publishers)	1,100
1783	Concert in the Burgtheater (March 23)	1,600
	Fees (pupils)	650
	Fees (other concerts, publishers)	?
1784	Subscription concerts in the Trattnerhof	1,000
	Fees (pupils)	650

	Fees (other concerts, publishers)	?
1785	Concert in the Burgtheater (March 10)	559
	Fees (publishers)	720
	Fees (other concerts, pupils)	?
1786	*Der Schauspieldirektor*	225
	Le nozze di Figaro	450
	Three piano concertos for Donaueschingen	81
	Fees (concerts, pupils, publishers)	?
1787	*Don Giovanni* (Prague)	450
	Don Giovanni (benefit performance)	700
	Concert in Prague	1,000
	Fees (concerts, pupils, publishers)	?
	Inheritance	1,000
	Salary (as of December)	66
1788	*Don Giovanni* in Vienna	225
	Fees (concerts, pupils, publishers)	?
	Benefit performance of Handel's *Pastorale*	?
	Salary	800
	Borrowed from Puchberg	*300*
1789	Journey to Berlin:	
	2 gold boxes, filled with money	1,285
	Fees (concerts, pupils, publishers)	?
	Salary	800
	"From abroad" (?)	450
	Borrowed from Puchberg	*450*
	Borrowed from Hofdemel	*100*
1790	*Così fan tutte*	900
	Journey to Frankfurt	165
	Salary	800
	Borrowed from Puchberg	*610*
1791	*La clemenza di Tito*	900
	Die Zauberflöte	?
	Requiem (first installment)	225
	Fees (pupils, publishers)	?
	Salary (paid until his death)	600
	Unexplained sum (letter of June 25, 1791)	2,000
	Borrowed from Puchberg	55

These figures have been known for over a hundred years, since Otto Jahn's first extensive biography of Mozart (1856–59). Since then they have not been further clarified, nor have we been able to amplify them.

They represent exclusively earnings that can be verified by letters or documentary material. The yearly totals are as follows:

1781	962 florins	1787	3,216 florins
1782	1,526 florins	1788	1,025 florins
1783	2,250 florins	1789	2,535 florins
1784	1,650 florins	1790	1,865 florins
1785	1,279 florins	1791	3,725 florins
1786	756 florins		

The many question marks make it immediately clear that Mozart's income was much higher, but the figures are lacking to establish the actual amounts. We know almost nothing about his concert receipts, with very few exceptions. As for instruction fees, Mozart's approximate earnings during the first three years can be inferred from his own statements, but for the period beginning in 1784, we are not even sure who his pupils were or how long they studied with him. And we are still completely in the dark about income he received from the publication and sale of his works.

The list of Mozart's definite earnings also has some strange entries. During the first three years his actual income from fees was indeed higher, but not significantly so. If only because of the frequent concerts, the years 1784–86 were one of his most successful periods and certainly must have brought financial rewards, yet our list documents a sharp drop in income at this time. This means only that we are especially ignorant about his earnings for those years. All other Mozart biographies also describe this period as his most successful and maintain that his impoverishment came only later. But he must have had a large income in these later years as well. Even discounting the inheritance from Leopold Mozart in 1787, a balance of more than 2,200 florins remains for that year. In 1790 Mozart's financial situation began to stabilize—at a relatively high level. (The mysterious 2,000 florins might well be explained by the offers of pensions he received from Amsterdam and the Hungarian nobility.)

The income represented by these documented earnings must be considered above average for musicians and certainly disproves the theory of his impoverishment. Compared to the salaries of civil servants, Mozart's income corresponds to that of a court secretary—a rather high position. His earnings were obviously increasing at the end of his life and were no doubt unusual for a man his age. Haydn, who as we know received high royalties from his publishers, had his first works printed at an age Mozart never reached. Haydn's actual rise to success—including financial success—did not begin until he was in his mid-forties.

The question of how large Mozart's income really was is best left in the realm of conservative speculation. Uwe Krämer, in a study provocatively titled "Wer hat Mozart verhungern lassen?" ("Who Let Mozart Starve?," 1976), has made some superficial calculations that reverse all previous conclusions on this subject. Suddenly Mozart is supposed to have been a Croesus who gambled away all his money. According to Krämer, "Mozart must have drawn around 10,000 florins per year as a concert pianist. In addition there were 900 florins in instruction fees and considerable earnings from his compositions."[34]

Carl Bär makes more serious calculations and tries to balance the verifiable income against the supposed expenditures, which he derives from careful estimates of wages, rent, and other living costs. For the years 1785 to 1791 he arrives at the following result:

As we can see, earnings of approximately 11,000 florins are matched by expenditures in the same range. They would seem to balance each other out. But 1,000 florins of the income are actually loans. Strictly speaking, then, there is a deficit. Furthermore, there are imponderables on both sides, which only appear to affect the income more than the expenditures. We can thus assume that during these six years the Mozart family spent 12,000 florins—an average of 2,000 florins per year.[35]

Bär, however, does not take into account the other earnings Mozart must have had according to the number of documented concerts and publications. Mozart, after all, did not regularly play concerts free of charge, nor did he hand his works over to publishers for nothing. He certainly did not always bring in 1,600 florins for a concert, as in March 1783, and neither could he always demand a fee as high as the one he received for the *Haydn* Quartets. But by estimating conservatively we can suggest minimum earnings for each concert and each published work, averages that might exceed or fall short of the actual amount. These can then be used in making our own calculations.

Let us assume that Mozart received 300 florins for one of his own concerts, 100 florins for subscription concerts, and gifts equivalent to 50 florins at private concerts for aristocrats; and let us further assume that his publishers paid him an average fee of 20 florins for longer works and 5 florins for smaller works. Adding these amounts to his recorded earnings, we can guess that Mozart's average income between 1782 and 1791 was 3,000 to 4,000 florins, at a very conservative estimate. In 1781 Mozart could not have made more than 1,500 florins; he had to establish contacts, since he had come to Vienna without any preparation. For 1786 we arrive at a sum of only 2,000 florins, while our estimate for the following year approaches 4,000; in other words, there was no striking decrease in receipts.

The year 1788, in which the first letters requesting loans from Michael Puchberg were written, was somewhat exceptional.[36] That year the Turkish war reached its height, and social life in the capital came to a standstill; much of the male nobility had gone off to military service, and the rest had withdrawn to their estates, which were more difficult to manage in wartime and thus required more attention. The emperor himself spent the entire year with the army, and the mood in Vienna was one of dejection; it was undoubtedly an especially difficult time for artists.

Obviously, Mozart tried to maintain his standard of living by running up debts. We can well assume that he periodically asked for short-term loans to compensate for the irregularity of his income: he realized most of his earnings from concerts, which he usually had to present during the short periods around Lent and Advent. But in the eighteenth century private debts were at least as common as personal loans and overdrawn bank accounts are today. The crux of Mozart's financial difficulties between 1788 and 1790 seems to have been that he was for the first time unable to pay off his short-term obligations from 1788. The sole cause of this was his wife's expensive illness, which began in the early summer of 1789, required several spa sojourns, and lasted well into 1790. Mozart apparently earned considerably more than 3,000 florins in 1789, but he was not in a position to discharge his debts. His situation did not really stabilize until 1791, a year that brought him well over 4,000 florins (perhaps even as much as 5,000). Now he had sufficient resources to pay off the loans from Puchberg and at the same time to finance two further health cures for his wife, although her illness was no longer a medical emergency. He was also able to place his son in an expensive boarding school.

Not only was Mozart's income exceptionally high in comparison with the earnings of most of his musical colleagues, but it showed every sign of being on the increase. Shortly before his death, Mozart began to enjoy some of the international fame he had sought—not as a wunderkind, but as a serious and admired composer—and with this recognition came financial rewards. Invitations from England and Russia mounted up—we know from Haydn's experience what such journeys could mean financially. Moreover, patrons came forward who were prepared to offer Mozart a measure of financial security so that he could maintain his expensive lifestyle and work without being dependent on fees and honoraria. Independently of each other, a group of Amsterdam merchants and several Hungarian magnates offered him honorary pensions.

Joseph Haydn's basic income at this time was much lower, since he received virtually no fees for concerts or from pupils. Nevertheless, until 1790 he performed daily the taxing duties of court kapellmeister and occasionally those of organist as well. His journeys to England, the first of which was in 1790, enabled him to accumulate a fortune that amounted to approximately 35,000 florins at the time of his death. Mozart's prospects for success were even better just before he died, especially since he was twenty-four years younger than Haydn. But Mozart was not one to live frugally, setting aside part of his income against emergencies, sickness, and old age. Haydn had made private interest-bearing loans to individuals and had invested in public securities; his fortune was totally wiped out by the high inflation of the Napoleonic period. Mozart, on the other hand, spent his money as soon as he got it and put nothing away in banks, which offered little security. In a sense he was acting quite reasonably considering the unreliable financial structure at the end of the eighteenth century. In any event, Mozart was far from poor.

Chapter 4

ARISTOCRATIC
AND BOURGEOIS SALONS

"FOR MY MÉTIER
THE BEST PLACE IN THE WORLD"

Mozart's decision to settle in Vienna after leaving the archbishop's service against the express advice of his father was a self-confident resolution to stake everything on one opportunity. It was not at all a blind or ill-considered step. Except for Paris, Vienna was the only real metropolis on the continent and certainly the most attractive one for musicians. Perhaps in Paris money was spent more ostentatiously, the court was more magnificent, the nobility more numerous and more wildly extravagant; but only in Vienna did music play such an important role. No other city had so many musicians and such a pronounced love of music, which was no mere social affectation. Certain courts indeed spent enormous sums, especially on opera, as was the case in Stuttgart; and some, such as the court that moved from Mannheim to Munich, could afford the very best orchestras. But in Vienna, court was held not only by the emperor but also by the many aristocratic families who practically competed with each other in expenditures on their own resident musicians, orchestras, and sometimes even opera ensembles.

Every seat of royalty naturally attracted the local nobility, who sought to protect their influence through their presence at court; many wished to be considered for high government posts and had an economic interest in attaining a share of political power. But the imperial court was certainly more attractive and important than the Prussian court, for instance, even apart from the fact that the resident nobility in Austria was much wealthier than the Prussian Junkers.[1] The importance of the Viennese court did not lie exclusively in the emperor's title, for coronations took place in Frankfurt am Main, the imperial insignia were in Nürnberg, and the parliament sat in Regensburg; rather, it lay in the size of the empire itself, which extended from Bohemia to Romania, and from the Netherlands to Italy.

Mozart, of course, knew these things; he had already been to Vienna three times in his youth. Furthermore, his upbringing had stressed the importance of assessing power relations in autocratic states and of using powerful connections sensibly to further one's artistic endeavors. He was not simply looking for a permanent position that would pay him more than he earned in Salzburg; he also sought a milieu in which he could make the greatest impact, win the most fame, and ensure the widest dissemination of his works. Mozart's career had been planned along international lines from his early youth—hence the long journeys to Paris and London and the three journeys to Italy.

From his seventh to his twenty-third year, Mozart was away from home more than half the time; he was educated privately at the same time he was displaying his talent as a virtuoso and a composer. There was hardly another musician who at such a young age had so much experience concertizing, fulfilling commissions, and reaping the financial rewards to be had wherever there was a passion for music. In fact, Mozart was spoiled by success, but he did occasionally have to swallow defeat. He had experienced both intrigue and aristocratic arrogance, and despite the craze for music it was by no means easy to become a successful musician in Vienna. The city had a vast number of musicians courting public favor, trying to obtain opera commissions, and competing for the patronage of wealthy nobles.

Anyone who claimed for himself and his family the right to participate in court and government activities, whether in the civil service, the military, or any of the numerous administrative branches—in short, anyone who wished to have influence at court—had to maintain a residence in the capital. All important positions in the empire were allocated to members of the same few noble families, from the seventeenth to the nineteenth centuries, and this ensured a continuity in government service that gave it a distinct social character. Accordingly, the many palaces in Vienna were not built solely for reasons of prestige but also to guarantee that the owners' descendants would occupy similarly high positions in politics and society, for which they would need an appropriate residence within sight of the court. The close intermarriage of these aristocratic families meant that there were only a few influential clans. The amount of money spent to maintain prestige revealed on the one hand an ambition for power, and on the other, the ability to manage numerous properties and preside over a household that was a microcosm of the court itself.

The assets available to this aristocracy, which included proceeds from vast estates as well as from other sources, were extraordinarily large. Even families of the so-called lesser nobility (knights, barons, etc.,) generally had 10,000 to 20,000 florins at their disposal. Such sums were also within reach of a few merchants, court agents, purveyors, and money changers who had proved their worth by organizing munitions supplies for Empress Maria Theresa's army. They were often rewarded with ennoblement, which added to their healthy incomes. The financial resources of people at these levels of society, who together accounted for only 2 or 3 percent of the population, were the basis for an unprecedented flowering of culture—with the disadvantage that over 90 percent of the population remained in poverty.[2]

An important feature of all musical activity among the nobility was the fact that it was open to everyone. The Viennese aristocrats at the end of the eighteenth century were not yet so bigoted as to shut their doors to anyone of lower social rank—a common practice during the sixty years after the French Revolution. It was relatively easy to be admitted to a performance, even if a wide public was not actively sought, as is clearly demonstrated by the many open-air concerts in public squares or parks. During the Josephine period most of these were open to everyone. The emperor himself started the process by opening the Augarten to the public; the inscription over the main entrance read, "Place of recreation, dedicated to all my people, from their admirer." The Hoftheater, which was open for concerts on all free days, was just as accessible. Joseph II had not only taken on the supervision of the opera but had put himself at the head of a reform movement when, in 1778, he created a German Nationalsingspiel alongside the Italian court opera.

We have very scanty information about the size of the nobility's private orchestras or the nature of their musical activities. Only the orchestra of Prince Nikolaus Joseph Esterházy has received some attention and is well documented, as a result of Joseph Haydn's long tenure as its conductor. However, between 1770 and 1790 there were many other private orchestras about which little or nothing is known. This is all the more surprising in that these ensembles are fundamental to the music history of this period: much music would never have been written without them. [3] All we know about most orchestras comes from biographies of instrumentalists who played with one ensemble for a while, then moved to another, and so forth. No concert programs or printed announcements are extant, but certain archives of noble families in Bohemia and Hungary are still maintained today. Thus far they have hardly been touched, though they may contain valuable material such as account books.

Those who could not afford their own orchestras nevertheless presented concerts on a regular basis, assembling the necessary orchestras from the large pool of amateur and professional musicians who were always willing to participate. The professionals, especially, earned so little money that they depended on this type of work to augment their income. The members of the imperial court orchestra had express permission to play in other concerts. Church musicians needed these extra wages most of all, simply to eke out an existence. For his concerts Mozart always had an ad hoc orchestra at his disposal, regardless of who was organizing the event, and the quality of these ensembles was not necessarily below that of the full-time orchestras. Groups of this kind were quite common even well into Beethoven's time. The relative ease of finding musicians meant that the middle class was also very active in organizing musical events. Concerts were not a special privilege of the nobility, for there were plenty of willing instrumentalists as well as appropriate concert venues. Many of these had a café or restaurant attached and were thus suitable for balls and dances. In Mozart's time there was no clear demarcation between popular music and "serious" music (this distinction was established only in the mid-nineteenth century), and concertgoers could often find gaming tables and refreshment stands in adjoining rooms.

Today we are still very poorly informed about concert life in Vienna.[4] Public announcements in newspapers were rare, and concerts were not regularly reviewed. The best records, though still insufficient, are personal documents such as letters and diaries. Such sources give evidence of frequent concert activity that was not confined to aristocratic circles, though the details are unknown to us. We know, for instance, of at least four locations for outdoor concerts: the Augarten, the Belvedere park, the Liechtenstein palace gardens, and the Bastei "by the refreshment stands." Then there were the concerts in the Mehlgrube house and in the Jahn rooms in Himmelpfortgasse. In addition to regular amateur performances, mention must be made of the four annual concerts of the Tonkünstlersozietät, a support group for widows and orphans of musicians, made up entirely of professionals. These concerts usually featured large oratorios for which it was possible to assemble huge orchestras, since every musician willingly donated his services to this organization.[5] Traveling musicians, who visited the musical metropolis Vienna in large numbers, could perform in the Burgtheater on evenings when it was free. In this way Vienna came to hear almost every famous virtuoso, and Mozart also gave concerts of his own in the Burgtheater, often with considerable financial success.

It was decisive for Viennese musical life that neither the aristocracy nor the bourgeoisie played a passive role as enthusiastic onlookers; domestic music making took place on all social levels, starting with the emperor, who retired to play chamber music for an hour each afternoon (almost all the Habsburgs played an instrument). In the aristocratic salons there were excellent musicians, some of whom are mentioned in Johann Ferdinand von Schönfeld's *Jahrbuch der Tonkunst* (1796). There was music making in all middle-class homes as well, and owning a piano was considered a sine qua non.

This constant activity among amateurs had one important effect on musical life: it created an insatiable demand for new compositions. The nobility needed new works for their private orchestras; public concerts consisted almost exclusively of new music; and in domestic circles there was always a need for piano pieces and chamber works.

The result was a booming market for sheet music, in which the latest operas circulated very quickly in the form of piano reductions or instrumental arrangements of the most popular excerpts. Only the newest pieces were wanted; no one bothered with "old" works. Almost all the music to be heard was contemporary in the most literal sense. In order to appreciate fully what that means, one must imagine what it would be like if all the music performed today—in concert halls and opera houses, in broadcasts and on recordings—had been written within the last ten years. With such widespread musical activity, the demand for new compositions of all kinds must have been inexhaustible, especially since each new work was performed immediately upon completion. Most pieces, of course, were written on request or with a specific performance in mind, if not for the composer's own use. Mozart frequently emphasized that he would never consider writing something for which there was no such occasion. Indeed, hardly a single work of his was not written for a particular occasion, or at least for use in his own concerts. The drawback of this practice was the waste of the composer's efforts: how many compositions were played only once and then disappeared into the music collections of those who commissioned them? Haydn is a clear example of this extravagance: countless occasional works, such as more than one hundred baryton trios he wrote for Prince Esterházy, were each intended for only a single performance. The same holds for all the other composers who also served as instrumentalists in their employers' orchestras. Thousands of compositions by so-called minor masters probably have yet to be heard a second time.

How many musicians lived in Vienna during the Josephine period cannot be established. The *Jahrbuch der Tonkunst* of 1796 mentions over two hundred "virtuosi and dilettanti" by name. There must have been hundreds of professional musicians, especially if we include the members of church orchestras and dance ensembles, to say nothing of military musicians. And the number of amateurs can hardly be overestimated, for in his *Jahrbuch* Schönfeld mentions only those who appeared in public at least occasionally, not necessarily in advertised concerts, but before a public drawn from musical circles.

For this purpose there was the salon, an institution supported by noble and bourgeois alike. The Viennese salon of the Josephine period was clearly distinguishable from its famous Parisian model in that it made no claim to a leading role in the literary and philosophical process of forming public opinion. This may have been due to the lifting of censorship, the Enlightenment-inspired goals of Joseph II, the relative intellectual backwardness of Vienna, or the existence of several different cultural centers within the empire. Whatever the reason, the Viennese salons could never attain a politically effective role in society. Nevertheless, they were important in all facets of social life, open to any interested parties, and most significantly, not closed to people of lower social status. People of all social levels mingled freely, and nowhere else were class differences so little in evidence. Even the emperor, who abstained from social life at court as much as he possibly could, visited salons as a replacement for other diversions. (Since he had neither a mistress nor a real family life and loathed court ceremony—an attitude also reflected in his simple, almost bourgeois clothing—the court was for him primarily a workplace. For entertainment he went to people's homes, where he found congenial company.) He did not, of course, pay house calls on the bourgeoisie. But neither did he restrict himself to the homes of princes, those nearest to him on the social ladder. For example, he was a regular guest at the salon of Countess Maria Wilhelmine Thun, whose family could claim no social proximity to the emperor through important court positions; it was the personality of the countess herself that lent distinction to her house.

In Viennese musical life the frequent private concerts in aristocratic and bourgeois salons were not an attempt to defend the isolation of aristocratic culture against the public concert as the first expression of bourgeois culture. (In the bourgeois salons the newly forming middle class often aped aristocratic lifestyles, albeit without the requisite self-confidence.) Private concerts were more a way of satisfying an overflowing passion for music by expanding domestic musicales into semi-public events. And amateur musicians deserved to be heard in public; many of them were equal in skill to the professionals. At that time the term "dilettante" (amateur) had no negative connotations but simply referred to the nonprofessional practice of an art. Most public concerts were also "*Dilettantenkonzerte.*" On the other hand, professional musicians were invited to perform at private concerts, "private" meaning simply the more intimate setting of a house, which did not in itself rule out the presentation of orchestral music.

Mozart was well acquainted with all forms of Viennese musical life when he arrived in 1781. Most of all, he knew that the casual atmosphere of the salon offered many possibilities, before or after concerts, for conversations that could lead to future engagements. Nowhere else was there such a good opportunity to display one's skill and be invited to give further demonstrations of it. He describes in drastic terms an opportunity he missed during his first weeks in Vienna, when he was still in the archbishop's service.

> But what made me almost desperate was that the very same evening we had this foul concert I was invited to Countess Thun's, but of course could not go; and who should be there but—*the emperor!* Adamberger and Madame Weigl were there and received 50 ducats each! And what an opportunity! I cannot, of course, arrange for the emperor to be told that if he wishes to hear me he must hurry up, as I am leaving Vienna in a few days. One has to wait for things like that.[6] (April 11, 1781)

Mozart thus clearly expressed the character of the salon as a semi-public concert hall where good money could be made, as well as a meeting place for different levels of the social hierarchy. In this respect the salon of Countess Thun assumed particular importance.

AT THE SALON OF COUNTESS THUN

On their many journeys the Mozarts had often met members of the Thun family, several of whom were clergymen in Salzburg. Most of the Thuns' property was in Bohemia. The family patriarch, Count Johann Joseph Thun, resided in Prague and Linz. He was a music lover and maintained his own theater and orchestra in Prague. In Linz he owned a palace on Minoritenplatz. When Mozart was returning to Vienna from his visit to Salzburg in 1783, he was waylaid in Linz by Count Thun.

> Young Count Thun (brother of the Thun in Vienna) called on me immediately, saying his father had been expecting me for two weeks and would I please drive to his house at once, for I was to stay with him. I told him that I could easily put up at an inn. But when we reached the

gates of Linz on the following day, we found a servant waiting there to drive us to old Count Thun's, at whose house we are now staying. I really cannot tell you what kindnesses the family are showering on us.

(October 31, 1783)

This stopover immediately provided another opportunity to play a public concert, for which Mozart, "at breakneck speed," wrote a new symphony, known as the *Linz* (K. 425). He also visited "old" Count Thun when the latter was taking a cure at Baden in June 1784, a sign of the very cordial relations between the two men. During his first journey to Prague in January 1787, Mozart was once again the Thuns' guest at their palace on the Kleinseite. Count Thun even had "an excellent pianoforte" put in his room, and Mozart did not leave the instrument "unused and untouched."

Relations were equally cordial at the Thuns' Viennese palace, where the count's son, Franz Joseph Thun, lived with his family. Mozart was already frequenting their house during his first days in Vienna in 1781. He had known the younger Count Thun for some time and called him "the same peculiar but well-meaning and honorable gentleman" (March 24, 1781). Franz Joseph was a Freemason, like his father, and belonged to the Viennese lodge Zur wahren Eintracht, whose members were interested in Enlightenment philosophy and natural science, and with which Mozart also had close connections. The count was branded a "dreamer"; his penchant for speculative and pseudomystical secret societies was frowned upon by the lodge. Count Thun had dabbled in experiments with so-called animal magnetism under the influence of the Viennese physician and scientist Franz Anton Mesmer, who had made important contributions to the field of physiotherapy but occasionally went beyond the bounds of natural science and employed speculative methods. Later the count attracted some attention with miracle cures effected through the laying on of hands, and he even made what became a notorious tour giving demonstrations of the technique. He claimed that he could cure gout and paralyzed limbs simply by the touch of his right hand. Mozart was probably thinking of such experiments when he termed the count as "peculiar."

The main attraction of the house was undoubtedly his wife, Countess Maria Wilhelmine Thun, whose salon was hospitably open to

A.G. Rämel pinx.　　　　　　　　　C. kohl sc.

Count Franz Joseph Thun, according to Mozart a "peculiar but well-meaning and honorable gentleman." A Freemason with an interest in alchemy, he was married to Countess Maria Wilhelmine Thun.

everyone. For a newcomer to Vienna, her house was the first place to
be introduced into society and casually make the acquaintance of
artists and scientists, who could not mingle in such a lively way with
the aristocracy anywhere else. The countess particularly cultivated
connections with England, which on the Continent served as a political model of a free and democratic land and was no less influential in
scientific and literary affairs. Countess Thun possessed all the qualities of a versatile go-between. One of her English visitors described
her succinctly:

> The Countess has more ability to entertain her guests, and to make
> them entertain each other, than anyone I have ever known. She has
> great humor, a thorough knowledge of the world, and a most unselfish
> heart. She is the first to discover the good qualities of her friends, and
> the last to notice their weaknesses. One of her greatest pleasures is to
> remove prejudices from among her acquaintances and to establish and
> promote friendships. She has an invincible army of high spirits, which
> she can so skillfully utilize that she delights her cheerful guests
> without offending her despondent ones. I have never known anyone
> who had such a multitude of friends and was able to lavish so much
> magnanimity and friendship on each one of them. She has created a
> little system for happiness in her own house and is herself the enticing
> focal point from which everything radiates.[7]

Mozart had her to thank not only for much good advice and several
very significant aquaintances, but above all for constant encouragement during the preparations for his Vienna debut as a mature opera
composer—*Die Entführung aus dem Serail*. Countess Thun was a
sounding-board in musical matters; she was a superb pianist and as a
young girl had probably been a pupil of Joseph Haydn. Music also
played a great role in the education of her three daughters, two of
whom are mentioned in Schönfeld's catalogue *Virtuosen und Dilet-
tanten von Wien*.[8]

If Mozart received any financial support from the Thun family, no
records of it survive. He must have received honoraria on some
occasions, such as for the *Linz* Symphony; otherwise he would certainly have noted the omission in one of his candid assessments. But
the countess's indirect support was actually much more important to
him. Not only did she lend him her "beautiful Stein pianoforte" for

such important concerts as the contest with Clementi in the presence of the emperor; she obviously considered him a protégé who would receive suitable commissions if she brought him together with the right people. As an unobtrusive mediator she was an expert. She saw to it that Mozart's most recent success, *Idomeneo*, quickly became known in Vienna, preferably as played by the composer himself. While Mozart was still bickering with the archbishop (Count Arco had not yet become violent), Countess Thun arranged a gathering at her house where Mozart played through *Idomeneo* for Baron Gottfried van Swieten and Count Franz Xaver Wolf Rosenberg-Orsini, general manager of the Hoftheater. Mozart knew both men from his childhood visits to Vienna, but now the situation was very different: an opera commission would depend on Count Rosenberg-Orsini. When Countess Thun left for the country weeks later, the score remained in her house, presumably because she wished to show it to other people. She kept a copy of the libretto for months until it was lost while the family was moving.

Mozart was in close contact with Countess Thun while composing *Die Entführung aus dem Serail*. He played each act for her as he finished it. He wrote to his father:

> I lunched yesterday with Countess Thun and will do so again tomorrow. I played to her what I have finished composing and she told me afterwards she would venture her life that what I have written so far cannot fail to please. But on this point I pay no attention whatever to *anybody's praise or blame*—I mean, until people have heard and seen the work *as a whole*. I simply follow *my own feelings*. All the same you may judge from this how pleased she must have been to express herself so emphatically. (August 8, 1781)

On May 7 Mozart played her the second act, "which pleases her no less than the first" (May 8, 1782), and on May 30, the third act.

Mozart played frequently in Countess Thun's salon, and the countess went to Mozart's concerts whenever she had the opportunity. Strangely enough, very little information about his contact with the Thun family has survived, and that rather haphazardly. Thus, only a reference in the diary of Count Karl Zinzendorf informs us that Mozart performed at the countess's salon on December 14, 1782. Likewise, other dates are often recorded in a single insignificant reference that survives almost by accident. After 1782 the name of Countess Thun hardly ever surfaces in Mozart's letters, but there is not the slightest reason to assume that his relationship to the Thun family had cooled or even broken off. Mozart's letters to his father simply became less frequent after his first year in Vienna, and their information about his everyday life is sketchy and disjointed. Countess Thun's name appears only when her presence at a concert is mentioned. If Mozart had not gone with her husband to visit the elder Count Thun, and if the latter had not invited him to stay at the Thuns' palace in Prague, it would be difficult to resist the unwarranted assumption, which still surfaces from time to time, that a rift had taken place. But one must not simply paint in a blank spot on a map; one must leave it blank pending further investigation.

Take, for example, a small episode during Mozart's journey to Berlin in the spring of 1789, in the company of Prince Karl Lichnowsky. Mozart had to lend the prince 100 florins, "as his purse was getting empty. I couldn't very well refuse him—you will know why" (May 23, 1789, to Constanze). The remark "you will know why" is rather obscure, but at the time Lichnowsky was just about to marry the second daughter of Countess Thun, Maria Christina. Does this comment refer to the close and beneficial relationship with the Thun family, which he could not ignore when confronted with the prince's peculiar habit of running up debts? And how did Mozart know Lichnowsky, who is never even mentioned in the earlier letters? One thing is certain in any case: Lichnowsky was already a familiar face in the countess's home by the time Mozart and Count Thun paid a visit to the latter's father in 1784.

During his first weeks in Vienna, when he was introducing himself to Countess Thun's salon, Mozart wrote to his father, "She is the most charming and most lovable lady I have ever met, and I am very high in her favor" (March 24, 1781). Other visitors to her home have also described—sometimes effusively—the deep impression she made. The countess knew how to captivate all those around her and at the same time show personal esteem—unbiased, generous, and without a hint of coquettishness—for each individual.

In a brief digression we shall see what another of the countess's guests, Georg Forster, had to say about her, her salon, and the daily happenings in this house. Almost everyone Forster met there was closely acquainted with Mozart; he and the composer generally moved in the same circles. The total absence of Mozart's name from Forster's journal and letters can only be explained by the fact that this traveler had no special interest in music. But the two of them probably met often or were at least together in the same room. Their ignorance of each other does not diminish the importance of the fact that they moved in the same milieu, and the following descriptions serve as unwitting testimony—a view from within.

DIGRESSION: GEORG FORSTER VISITS COUNTESS THUN

On a journey from Kassel to Vilna, where he was to assume a professorship, Georg Forster arrived in Vienna in July 1784. He stayed a total of seven weeks, deeply impressed by the city and its reception of him. He was virtually passed around Viennese society—among nobility, in the intellectual community that admired him as a natural scientist who had circumnavigated the globe, and at the bourgeois salons of merchants and civil servants who also honored him in the Masonic lodges. One of the first people he encountered, at a lodge, was Prince Karl Lichnowsky, whom Forster knew from his student days in Göttingen and whom he called "my old friend from Göttingen." Together they attended the opera, and afterwards Lichnowsky took him to the Thuns' home for the first time. On this visit only the countess's three daughters were present, and they are described in glowing terms in Forster's journal. He met Countess Thun several nights later at a masked ball, where he remained in animated conversation with the her until 2:00 A.M. In the first two weeks of his sojourn Forster moved primarily in circles connected with Freemasonry; he met Baron Gemmingen, Sonnenfels, Blumauer, Gebler, and Hunczovsky, and visited the homes of Prince Kaunitz, Franz von Greiner (where he met Alxinger and Rautenstrauch), and others. But he found time for regular visits to the Thun family, sometimes even daily. He came with Gemmingen, Lichnowsky, or Born, and usually stayed until late at night—once until 4:00 A.M. In his journal Forster describes an afternoon in the countess's garden in the Landstrasse.

To Born. With him and Blumauer to Countess Thun. There dined with
Gemmingen, Stütz, Werthes. Afterward played ballon with Countess
Elizabeth. Showed the engravings, with Countess Bassewitz and her
daughter present. Afterward saw Count and Countess Cziczi ??, who
departed for Hungary. Wonderful afternoon spent playing word games
and reciting all manner of poetry. Conversed alone with the Countess in
her room. Have been invited to visit whenever and as often as I please.[9]

(August 18, 1784)

This invitation was meant literally. The house was always open, and
some member of the family was always there to receive guests, if not
the count or countess, then one of the three daughters, who ranged
from seventeen to twenty years of age. Evidently no caller could
disturb the free and easy atmosphere; instead, an attempt was made to
engage each visitor in conversation and make him feel thoroughly at
home. There were no formalities, no strict visiting hours, just hospitality at any time of the day or night. One could chat, look at
pictures, play parlor games, dance, make music, recite—whatever
struck the fancy of those present.

On another occasion Forster brought fresh figs from Sonnenfels'
garden. That evening he wrote: "Beer soup—afterward they danced a
quadrille and I had to join in nolens volens. Christiane was my
partner. Then Frau von Puffendorf sang like an angel, until 12"[10]
(August 19, 1784).

Forster felt more and more at home in the Thun salon. After an
audience with the emperor he hurried "at 4 o'clock to Countess
Thun's" and later wrote:

Am on very intimate terms with her. I am very fond of her, and I am
beginning to shed my awkwardness and my apprehension, which stems
from either exaggerated humility or over-sensitive pride—and there is
such a fine line between the two! The entire evening I recited English
poems to her: Gray's Elegy in a Churchyard, Eton College; Pope's
Eloisa to Abelard; Shenstone's Pastoral, etc. Finally went home at 10,
but not before receiving an invitation to come Thursday at noon and
promising to be there. (August 24, 1784)

But in the meantime he met the Thun family again on Sunday, at a
gathering in the home of Count Johann Philipp Cobenzl, where he took

a long walk with the countess. He was at the Thuns' house again on Tuesday, Wednesday, and Thursday. After lunch "a game of volante was played," followed by an outing with the countess, "who rides with me in my carriage to the Prater, the 3 Contessas and Mariana follow in another carriage. We walk in the Prater—I alone with the Countess. The conversation revolves around the education of children: what one should keep from them, etc., Afterward talked of religion, faith, reunion after death, etc." (September 2, 1784). Almost every day Forster was at the countess's home or on an outing in her company. On one occasion Baron Otto von Gemmingen recited Lessing's *Nathan der Weise* (*Nathan the Wise*) and on another "we walked, jumped, and ran in the garden, which has completely tired me out. Later there was some hectic singing" (September 13, 1784). Lichnowsky was present at almost all these gatherings, and often Gemmingen or Councillor Born. Forster encountered virtually all Mozart's acquaintances during his seven weeks in Vienna, but he never once mentions Mozart's name. However, Mozart had been confined to his bed with a bad cold ever since the premiere of Giovanni Paisiello's *Il re Teodoro* on August 23.

In his journal Forster describes—in more detail than the impetuous Mozart—the social life in which the composer took part. Mozart himself mentions only those events that were connected with his musical appearances, while Forster depicts the social environment of those activities, in which Mozart must have figured significantly.

Looking back on his Viennese sojourn, Forster wrote to the countess from Warsaw:

Everything I experienced there now seems like a wonderful dream. Is it really true that I lived there among human beings—the kind of human beings about whom Nathan says *it is enough for them to be human.* Is it true that I have seen the happiest days of my life pass, days when I was among people who did not ask me if I was learned and wise, but only if I was happy, and if I knew what was necessary for happiness! Pity me my disbelief, dear Countess, and give me some tangible proof that I did not dream it all. One line from your hand will suffice for me to become reconciled with my memory. How happy I would be if I could convince myself that your family still holds me somehow in remembrance!
(October 12, 1784)

Forster was by no means forgotten. Countess Thun wrote several letters to him in Warsaw (none seem to have survived), and in his long, effusive answers Forster continued the conversations begun in Vienna. What impressed him most of all was the total absence of aristocratic pride and the enlightened intellectual atmosphere.

> The great noblemen here benefit immensely from a comparison with even petty servants of petty noblemen elsewhere. You would not believe how cordial and unpretentious everyone is. One is hardly aware of being among titled people, and might any moment forget oneself and treat them as friends of equal status—I would say "handle gently" instead of "treat" when I am with the Countess—the best woman in the world—and her three beautiful daughters.
> (September 3, 1784, to Therese Heyne)

Like Mozart, Forster came to think of Vienna as the most pleasant place in the world—not least under the influence of the Thun family. Here in the Catholic south, which was considered somewhat backward and unreceptive to Enlightenment thought, with an aristocracy oriented toward prestige and ostentation, Forster observed the gradual emergence of the bourgeois influence, which added cheerful vitality to the more ascetic attitudes of the Protestant north, and to which Forster was very susceptible.

> Hers is the finest conversation, totally honest yet carried on with the greatest delicacy; her reading is very wide, well thought out and assimilated; a pure, sincere religion, free of all superstition, rests in her heart, which is gentle, innocent, and at peace with nature and creation. (September 3, 1784, to Therese Heyne)

That was Forster's impression of Countess Thun.

FREELANCE MUSICIAN OR MUSICAL FUNCTIONARY?

The description of daily activities in this house affords insight into Viennese life during the Josephine period. Aside from the guests who casually stopped by every day, there were also invitations to special soirees where ambitious concerts with first-rate soloists were presented. These events, which took place regularly, were doubtless attended by Emperor Joseph with some frequency. Some sources even record that he made weekly visits to the Thun home when he was not away on one of his numerous journeys.

Countess Thun undoubtedly created her own unique and attractive style, but there were many other houses that presented musical soirees and private concerts, sometimes even with full orchestras. Although few hosts organized these events with such regularity as the countess, they were no less discriminating. They were not high nobles who maintained their own orchestras, at least on a temporary basis, but people who put varying amounts of money and effort into private musicales and concerts, not for reasons of prestige, but solely out of a love for music, often demonstrated by the active participation of the hosts. We are still very poorly informed about the many distinctive musical salons of Vienna, particularly since our only source material is pieced together from diaries and letters in which the accuracy and authenticity of the descriptions are infinitely more important than the names and social positions of their authors. We owe this insufficiency to past historical scholarship, which attached almost no importance to everyday life and considered such sources worthless unless they concerned "famous" personalities. Today's broader historical perspective recognizes everyday life as a source very much worthy of research but is faced with a submerged rubble heap of material that will not easily yield up its treasures.

There are, for example, numerous indications that Countess Thun's famous salon was virtually vying with that of Countess Pergen for pride of place in Viennese society, yet there is no surviving report of any significance on the activities of Countess Philippine Gabriele Pergen. Her house, too, was frequented by Joseph II; Count Johann Anton Pergen was president of the provincial government of Lower Austria, with responsibility for overseeing the Vienna police, among other duties.

We are no better informed about other salons, such as that of the Greiner family. Caroline Pichler, the daughter of Court Councillor Franz Sales von Greiner, did provide detailed descriptions of Viennese society in her *Denkwürdigkeiten aus meinem Leben* ("Memorabilia from My Life"), published in Vienna in 1844, but she said very little about her childhood home near the Neuer Markt. She wrote:

"According to my father's wish, our house was filled with music. The great Mozart, although he was not my teacher, gave me many lessons free of charge, and I had ample opportunity to hear him play and to perfect my playing under his tutelage." All contemporary references indicate that Councillor Greiner's salon was the most important and influential of all the bourgeois salons. There were musical soirees in this house every Tuesday during Advent and Lent, as well as larger-scale concerts on important family occasions. Greiner, who had been a political adviser to Maria Theresa, is best characterized as a dedicated Josephinian who furthered the Enlightenment reforms in numerous ways. He belonged to the Masonic lodge Zur wahren Eintracht and was considered a friend of science and the arts. His daughter was required to learn Latin in addition to the European languages and was taught by three private tutors (Johann Baptist von Alxinger, Gottlieb Leon, and Lorenz Leopold Haschka), all Freemasons. (All three wrote lyrics or libretti for Mozart.) Any person of standing in science and the arts frequented the Greiner home, which was a nerve center of the Enlightenment. The style cultivated here was dictated less by aristocratic models than by an enthusiasm for new music and literature.

Mozart certainly played for many bourgeois hosts, including Auernhammer, Councillors Braun and Spielmann, Ployer, Trattner, and Wetzlar, to name only those for which evidence of his concerts has survived. The list of aristocratic homes in which he played is much longer, which is perhaps explained by the better preservation of information dealing with the nobility. Thus, we can verify his appearances before Joseph II and Archduke Maximilian, Princes Galitzin and Auersperg, Counts Esterházy, Hadik, Pálffy, and Zichy, his pupil Countess Rumbeke, and Baron van Swieten. But it is highly unlikely that he omitted the salons of Prince Liechtenstein, Count Czernin, or Countess Pergen, all of whom had established private concerts as a tradition in their homes.

Mozart's entire manner—his conspicuously well-groomed appearance, his self-confidence in dealing with the nobility, an air that presumed equality by virtue of his status as an exceptional artist—made it plain that he did not see himself as an underling. When he learned of the low salary offered by the princess of Württemberg, he realized that only a high and more or less independent position at the imperial court would be suitable for him—court composer or court kapellmeister, for instance. Otherwise he would simply make a career for himself as a freelance composer and virtuoso pianist, and live on his fees for commissions and concert appearances, supplementing his income by giving lessons (at rates commensurate with his standing as a musician, of course).

The many aristocratic and bourgeois salons in Vienna, the prestigious musical life of the high nobility, the Nationaloper, and the general enthusiasm for music that made frequent public concerts possible all represented clear alternatives to a career as a musical functionary, especially for so self-assured a musician as Mozart.

Being a freelance musician meant something fundamentally new in Mozart's case: it initiated a kind of artistic existence that later became a matter of course in bourgeois society, at least for composers. There had always been performing artists—singers and instrumentalists—who lived as traveling virtuosi, but they never quite managed to shed the image of the vagabond, the minstrel who performed at fairs and other public entertainments and usually had to pass the hat for donations. (Leopold Mozart was well aware of this danger on the long journeys with his wunderkinder, and attempted to dissociate himself from the socially denigrated caste of itinerant musicians through skillful presentation.) Instrumentalist and composer were not yet separate musical professions in the sense they are today. Any self-respecting virtuoso also composed, especially for his own use on his own instrument. Mozart, however, proved himself in public as a composer at a very early age, with compositions whose melodic invention and technical mastery gave him every reason to be proud. Traveling, as well as the practical experience and international success connected with it, had always appealed to Leopold Mozart, yet he insisted that his son seek the security of a permanent position.

Wolfgang Mozart did seek this security—but always with the stipulation that such employment must never tie him down or in any way prevent him from realizing his artistic goals. He took the risk of waiting for the ideal position, and until he found it, he preferred to live without a permanent commitment; one must admire him for this unusual and courageous decision. Had he found no livelihood in Vienna, he was prepared to go abroad again. He began learning English as soon as he decided to try his luck as a freelance musician in Vienna. He drew up and frequently discussed travel plans (especially for England) but delayed and postponed them as long as this life buoy was not needed.

Mozart gradually cast off the role of traveling virtuoso, exchanging it for that of a resident composer who competed for commissions and concert patronage in a free market at his own risk. There was no precedent for this. He was not consciously trying to become a new kind of composer, of course; this development represented a process of reaction, adjustment, and growing self-confidence, not a judicious professional and rational assessment. But Mozart was aware of his special situation, especially since it was the result of deliberate decisions. And we must repeat that Vienna was the best place to find work and an adequate livelihood as a resident freelance musician.

Vienna's musical salons as well as its concert audiences demanded not only exceptional virtuosi but also new compositions. The concert-going public wanted new music as much as it sought new forms of musical entertainment. The private orchestras of the nobility were largely self-sufficient institutions with full-time musicians who also delivered most of the required new compositions. But domestic music and amateur recitals, salons, and public concerts organized by music societies (another early example of musical entrepreneurship among the bourgeoisie) all had a need for compositions, and this need created the conditions for a new type of freelance composer. The change was brought about by people unwilling or unable to maintain their own ensembles: certain aristocrats with small incomes or with no desire for ostentation, but also, increasingly, middle-class entrepreneurs. Bankers, businessmen, wholesalers, and civil servants often performed as amateurs themselves, now and then assembling entire orchestras from the ranks of low-income musicians. This emergence of the bourgeoisie in musical life was soon accompanied by the disbanding of the high nobility's private orchestras, a development in which the Josephine state's fading interest in pomp and prestige must have played a decisive role. The nobility's conflicts with Emperor Joseph II, which reached a high point at the end of the 1780s, were probably just as important as the Turkish war in bringing about their temporary withdrawal from Vienna, which further impoverished musical life.

But that was only a brief test of endurance. A change in the entire musical structure was more crucial: more and more musicians were discharged from their permanent positions with the nobility; composers no longer wrote exclusively for their employers; and earnings from public concerts and publishers' fees played an increasingly large role in a musician's livelihood. A new form of patronage developed, making financial support available to composers and thus allowing them to work freely and independently. Mozart was beginning to receive such patronage at the end of his life, although his illness and early death prevented him from ever enjoying it. Significantly, the offers of honorary pensions that would have guaranteed his financial independence came from two different sides: one from a group of Dutch merchants, another from Hungarian aristocrats. Nobility and bourgeoisie no longer differed in their relationship to artists, and they had become more alike economically as well.

"TO INTRODUCE MYSELF TO THE EMPEROR IN SOME BECOMING WAY"

Being a freelance composer and working independently for an ever larger circle of musical patrons from all ranks of society did not represent an ideal situation for Mozart, accustomed as he was to success. He may have accepted such a role temporarily, but only because Vienna offered enough opportunities to prove himself while earning his living as a teacher and virtuoso pianist. The only permanent employment he would consider, however, was a position somehow connected to the imperial court. All positions there were filled for the time being, but Mozart, convinced he would not be passed over, was more than willing to wait his turn. Gluck, the *Hofkomponist*, and Bonno, the kapellmeister, were both old and ailing, and even if their logical successors, Salieri and Starzer, were given first consideration, there was still one door open.

In the event, the game of musical chairs turned out somewhat differently in 1787, although in one sense Mozart had been exactly right. There were other positions at the court and the Burgtheater, but they did not coincide at all with his artistic plans. Mozart wanted to be *Hofkomponist* rather than kapellmeister or *Kammermusikdirektor* (director of chamber music), which would have required his daily presence for rehearsals or performances, leaving hardly any time for composing—quite apart from the fact that they were badly paid.

(Small wonder that Mozart never once cast a covetous eye on these two posts when discussing employment prospects in his letters.)

That Joseph II was a "scrooge" is the tenor of many letters. His petty stinginess was almost proverbial. Yet this judgment is certainly colored by contrast with the opulent extravagance of the reign of Empress Maria Theresa. Many people found fault with Joseph II's austerity, but no one could fail to respect a monarch who, on becoming regent during the empress's lifetime, handed over his paternal inheritance of 22,000,000 florins to the state treasury and demanded a similar sacrifice from his brother Leopold, much to the latter's disgust. Under Joseph II the almost indiscriminate allocation of positions and the granting of generous pensions became things of the past. Only useful and necessary positions were maintained, a well-organized civil service was established with official pensions according to length of service, and social life at court was reduced to a minimum. Joseph himself resided most of the time in a small pavilion in the Augarten. Only certain parts of the Hofburg were in use; the others were boarded up to avoid the expense of guarding them. The same went for Schönbrunn Palace, the favorite residence of his mother the empress: everything there was nailed shut, with the exception of the Orangerie, which was occasionally used for the inevitable large functions when other royalty paid a visit to Vienna.

Artists, of course, received fair remuneration from Joseph II, but as soon as the subject of permanent employment came up, he made sure that the salary was kept within limits and was no higher than absolutely necessary to keep the desired artist in Vienna. The effects of this austerity campaign were most evident at the Hoftheater, whose management Joseph personally oversaw. His own instructions to the theater director, as well as the reports he made while "shopping" for singers on his journeys (usually in Italy) always dealt with the relationship of salary to ability. Yet the emperor, who often attended public concerts or private performances in salons, always gave the participating artists generous honoraria: normally 25 ducats (approximately 112 florins), but sometimes twice as much. Thus it would seem that he was not personally stingy; his economies only affected his court payroll and had nothing to do with a lack of appreciation for music.

Nevertheless, the emperor's understanding of music has often been disparaged. Joseph was certainly not among the Habsburgs who could claim a role in music history as a musician, but to characterize him as unmusical is not only unfair but patently false. This judgment can generally be traced back to some pointed but suspect anecdotes, almost all concerning Mozart. They convey the impression that Viennese society, and above all Joseph II, were to blame for Mozart's lack of recognition, slow demise, and interment in a pauper's grave, for his cruel abandonment by a society that did not acknowledge his genius and even prevented him from earning a living (every word of which is demonstrably false). Thus it is related that Joseph II said to Mozart regarding *Die Entführung aus dem Serail*, "Too beautiful for our ears, and an awful lot of notes, dear Mozart." (Mozart is supposed to have made the quick-witted reply, "No more notes than necessary, Your Majesty!") A more extreme example of the emperor's alleged inability to understand Mozart is the negative judgment he is rumored to have pronounced on *Don Giovanni*, although he had not even seen the opera: "Mozart's music is too difficult to be sung." This remark was in fact prompted by embarrassing difficulties in finding new young singers who were equal to the demands of Mozart's opera roles. The modest success of the *Don Giovanni* premiere prompted the following comment from the emperor, who was away on a journey: "I am not at all surprised that the opera met with a disappointing response. In Vienna only the newest things have value, and if the Viennese were deprived of all opera for a year's time, they would simply develop a taste for something much more ordinary."[11] The emperor was actually defending Mozart against the taste of the Viennese public. It is possible that he already knew the opera from the score; he enjoyed playing through new opera arias in his afternoon chamber music sessions.

In truth, Mozart is partly to blame for creating a contradictory picture of the emperor's musical interests. His letters contain remarks that his biased defenders have perverted into a truly one-sided picture, such as the statement that the emperor appreciated "no one but Salieri" (December 15, 1781). The conflict between Mozart and the director of the Hoftheater is mostly the product of wild speculation and has been so exaggerated as to include even the preposterous notion that Salieri poisoned his rival. Joseph II did have a general preference for Italian opera, but that would hardly explain his efforts on behalf of a German Nationalsingspiel. Indeed, not a single recorded opinion of the emperor's shows a preference for an opera by Salieri over one by Mozart. Salieri was simply the representative of "welsch," or Italian, opera, while Mozart was a composer without official connection to the court. Actually, the evidence tends to suggest that they admired each other greatly and maintained cordial relations, except for occasional misunderstandings that were always aggravated by Salieri's advantageous position as director of the theater. Joseph II welcomed the friendly rivalry between the two composers, and proved it by commissioning both of them to write short operas for the entertainment of visiting royalty: thus, Mozart's *Schauspieldirektor* and Salieri's *Prima la musica e poi le parole* were performed in Schönbrunn on the same evening.

There is a further point that calls into question or even refutes the emperor's preference for Salieri (beyond mere recognition of his official capacity at court): Salieri was exclusively an opera composer and wrote hardly anything else, least of all instrumental works. Mozart, on the other hand, was known primarily as an instrumental composer and virtuoso pianist; before 1786 his only stage success in Josephine Vienna had been *Die Entführung*. It was in fact his piano music that brought him the unqualified admiration of the emperor, who was full of praise for Mozart's salon performances. Characteristic of the emperor's taste was the special pleasure he derived from hearing fugues; on certain occasions where the monarch was present, Mozart would play fugues as a special compliment. But even without such flattery the emperor admired Mozart's instrumental style, which utilized varied and unusual tone colors to achieve highly dramatic effects. In this respect Mozart was unique among his contemporaries. After one concert in the emperor's presence, the following little scene took place, which Leopold Mozart described as an eyewitness: "When your brother left the platform the emperor waved his hat and called out 'Bravo, Mozart!' " (February 16, 1785).

This vignette points to an informal acquaintance, free of ceremony, and by no means restricted to musical matters; Joseph II learned of Mozart's marriage plans almost as soon as the composer's father did. By the time of the keyboard contest with Clementi on Christmas Day 1781, there was already enough familiarity for Mozart to confide in the emperor: "The emperor . . . said a great deal to me privately, and even mentioned my marriage" (January 16, 1782). In the same letter

Mozart describes the favoritism shown him during the contest, which could almost be considered overt bias.

> The funny thing was that although I had borrowed Countess Thun's pianoforte, I only played on it when I played alone; such was the emperor's desire—and by the way, the other instrument was out of tune and three of the keys were stuck. "Never mind," said the emperor. Well, I put the best construction on it I could, that is, that the emperor, already knowing my skill and my knowledge of music, merely wanted to show special courtesy to a foreigner.

(Joseph II made an ironic remark when he invited Clementi to begin: " '*La santa chiesa Catholica*' [The holy Catholic Church], he said— because Clementi is a Roman.")

Mozart's letters do not lack for acerbic comments on his milieu, and he was even inclined to uncontrolled fits of temper that he could hardly have indulged publicly. Yet there is not a word against Joseph II, apart from frequent complaints about his ubiquitous austerity measures. Instead, the letters indicate a secret admiration, which is openly expressed in Leopold Mozart's letters with their political "*tours d'horizon*." Mozart himself very seldom commented on political events, but he did describe personalities in great detail, including those of the imperial family. For example, he writes of the emperor's brother Archduke Maximilian, who had just been named coadjutor to the archbishop of Cologne:

> When God gives a man a sacred office, he generally gives him understanding; and so it is, I trust, in the case of the archduke. But before he became a priest he was far more witty and intelligent, and he talked less but more sensibly. You should see him now! Stupidity oozes out of his eyes. He talks and holds forth incessantly, always in falsetto—and he has started a goiter. In short, the fellow seems to have changed completely. (November 17, 1781)

An objective look at Mozart's criticisms of Joseph II clearly reveals that they all refer to his economic measures and never reflect a lack of musical respect, let alone personal differences. Mozart accuses the emperor of doing too little for the arts but never of showing unjust favoritism to the Italians. A detailed letter on this subject shows that

Mozart was prepared to see his own destiny in relation to the emperor's entire cultural policy (and those of absolute rulers all over German-speaking Europe). Mozart is not demanding a special position for himself but a change in attitude. It is with good reason that Mozart calls for such a change from Emperor Joseph, on whom the hopes of numerous German intellectuals rested.

The Viennese gentry, and in particular the emperor, must not imagine that I am on this earth solely for the sake of Vienna. There is no monarch in the world whom I would more gladly serve than the emperor, but I refuse to beg for any post. I believe I am capable of doing credit to any court. If Germany, my beloved fatherland, of which I am proud, as you know, will not accept me, then in God's name let France or England become the richer by another talented German, to the disgrace of the German nation. You know well that it is the Germans who have always excelled in almost all the arts. But where did they make their fortune and their reputation? Certainly not in Germany! Take even the case of Gluck. Has Germany made him the great man he is? Alas no! Countess Thun, Count Zichy, Baron van Swieten, and even Prince Kaunitz are all very much displeased with the emperor because he does not value men of talent more, and allows them to leave his dominions. Kaunitz said the other day to Archduke Maximilian, when the conversation turned on myself, *"Such people only come into the world once in a hundred years and must not be driven out of Germany, particularly when we are fortunate enough to have them in the capital."* You cannot imagine how kind and courteous Prince Kaunitz was to me when I visited him. When I took my leave, he said, *"I am much obliged to you, my dear Mozart, for having taken the trouble to visit me."* You would scarcely believe what efforts Countess Thun, Baron van Swieten and other eminent people are making to keep me here. But I cannot afford to wait indefinitely, and indeed I refuse to remain hanging on here at their mercy. Moreover, I think that even though he *is* the emperor, I am not so desperately in need of his favor.

(August 17, 1782)

Joseph II certainly wanted to bring the best artists to Vienna, but at the lowest possible price. As we learn from his numerous letters to Count Rosenberg-Orsini, he was always prepared to haggle over a salary, even at the risk of losing an engagement. Such was his policy when personally intervening in opera administration, and it held for other matters as well. The emperor undoubtedly wished to keep Mozart in Vienna; but as long as it could be done at no cost, so much the better. Mozart was well aware of this attitude, which did not indicate any lack of personal regard. Interestingly, he did not compare Joseph II to lesser German potentates such as those in Stuttgart and Munich, whose musical extravagance was at least as great as that of the imperial court. If not Vienna, then France or England; those were the alternatives. Mozart was not experiencing a sudden surge of nationalistic feeling. His viewpoint was strongly influenced by the Josephine model of an "enlightened" state program that sought to combine centralization with popular education. Thus, Mozart showed himself to be among those who had placed their hopes for public enlightenment in the young emperor but were now somewhat disillusioned. In this he was in very good company, along with such German poets and thinkers as Klopstock, Lessing, Herder, and others, some of whom had heartily welcomed Joseph's assumption of power.

Their hope was that Joseph II would make the Catholic southern areas of German-speaking Europe accessible to Enlightenment philosophy, but above all that he would himself become the protector of a German national culture, and that the parochial interests of the smaller states would thereby be overcome, at least in the cultural sphere. (They could expect no cooperation from the Prussian king, who had a bias toward French culture and made contemptuous remarks about German writers in his essay *De la littérature allemande* ("On German Literature," 1781.) They were encouraged by efforts to raise funds for the University of Vienna and by a project to form a Vienna Academy of Fine Arts, which had been discussed in the early 1770s. Another good sign was the attention Emperor Joseph gave to the theater—for example, by engaging important actors like Friedrich Ludwig Schröder and Franz Brockmann for his court ensemble, which he had christened the Deutsches Nationaltheater (German National Theater) in 1776. Joseph even sent a representative to northern Germany with instructions to find actors suitable for this promising institution. He also visited Lessing, who at the end of his *Hamburgische Dramaturgie* (*Hamburg Dramaturgy*, 1769) had written about the "kindhearted idea of providing the Germans with a national theater—since we Germans are not even a nation!" Elsewhere Lessing is less resigned, and he tells the imperial representative:

I honor your emperor; he is a great man! He will undoubtedly be the
first monarch to give the Germans a national theater, since the king in
Berlin has little use for our native theater and does not support it as
your sovereign does. [12]

Nothing came of the attempt to establish a national theater, and
Lessing's remark about the nonexistent nation was still valid. The
Viennese public retained all its old predilections for light comedy and
was only slowly coming to terms with the French theatrical tradition.
There were still many obstacles to creating a modern national theater
in the spirit of Lessing's reforms.

The outlook was no better for the German Nationalsingspiel, which
also owed its existence to the emperor's personal initiative and had to
struggle against similar obstacles. It had to hold its ground against the
Italian *opera buffa* but was handicapped by a lack of competent
librettists and composers. The project probably suffered additionally
from the halfhearted way it was established. There was an orchestra of
more than thirty pieces as well as a group of good and in some cases
excellent singers (at least after the first few seasons). But a resident
composer or poet and a new approach to opera dramaturgy were not
envisaged, presumably for reasons of economy. In this division of the
Nationaltheater there was no position of *Hofkomponist*, though it was
totally dependent on local talent, for the North German Singspiel
movement was completely ignored. In the context of music history, the
Viennese Nationalsingspiel was unable to realize its potential, since it
improvised in "splendid isolation" instead of taking on a potentially
avant-garde role in the reform of German opera. Perhaps there was
some truth in Lessing's resigned observation that the time was not yet
ripe.

Mozart was undoubtedly thinking of this Nationalsingspiel when he
considered how to "introduce myself to the emperor in some becoming
way." His half-finished opera *Zaide* was in his luggage when he came
to Vienna. The commission for *Die Entführung aus dem Serail* was
probably intended as a test of his talent. When *Die Entführung* finally
reached the Nationalsingspiel stage after a nine-month delay, it enjoyed an unprecedented success, but that alone could no longer save
the institution. The next season was the last for the Nationalsingspiel;
it closed on March 4, 1783. Of all the works it had presented, *Die*

Entführung was the only one to survive and enter the (Italian) operatic repertoire of the Burgtheater, before it began its triumphal procession through Europe.

The dissolution of the Nationalsingspiel did not spoil Mozart's operatic prospects. His wish to make a favorable impression on the emperor was now perhaps even more likely to be fulfilled—not because Joseph II was generally more fond of Italian opera, but because opera at the Burgtheater had a wider circle of high-society patrons, consisting primarily of the high nobility.[13]

The nobility, accustomed as it was to the courtly style cultivated in Maria Theresa's time, had an exclusive taste for music in the Italian style, however much Joseph II may have experimented with German Singspiel, which spoke clearly to, and perhaps even represented, bourgeois taste. But as we have noted, Joseph II was decidedly indifferent to "courtly" matters, and a great many Mozart admirers were among those who wanted to see him write for the Italian court opera.

Mozart himself had no special allegiance to the German Singspiel; it was a relatively new genre in which he was sure he could achieve success. With *Die Entführung* he had claimed his place, but he had much more experience in the Italian opera tradition and was very interested in the stylistic mixture represented by the new *opera buffa*. For Mozart there was little difference between Singspiel and Italian opera; he was at home in both genres and always eager for commissions. And perhaps it was actually better to refine opera dramaturgy first in a form with a long tradition that had already undergone many stages of development. The Singspiel was a new idea still in the experimental stage. And Mozart had discovered for himself how difficult it was to find suitable librettists, to say nothing of the entirely different sound structure of the German language, which was much more difficult to bend, stretch, or spin as the music required.

The Nationalsingspiel showed a final flicker of life, so to speak, when Mozart was commissioned to write another Singspiel, ironically, one with a text concerning theatrical life—*Der Schauspieldirektor*. That work, however, immediately preceded the commission for *Le nozze di Figaro*, the opera that really did bring him "becomingly" to the emperor's notice.

To summarize Joseph II's conduct toward Mozart in the simplest terms, we can say that the emperor tried to deal fairly with him. Mozart had come to Vienna without official encouragement, and there were no positions open. At no time did the emperor make promises to Mozart that he could not have kept; on many occasions he showed his unbounded admiration for Mozart and rewarded him accordingly. Mozart received opera commissions almost regularly every three years, sometimes at twice the normal fee. As soon as positions were vacated (through the deaths of Bonno and Gluck), Mozart was given an entirely new position, without significant duties but carrying a sort of honorary stipend that corresponded roughly to the salary of the music director at the Nationalsingspiel. The personal relations between the two men were characterized by deep mutual respect and were not at all strained by Mozart's openly acknowledged Freemasonry, his politically provocative opera libretti, or his plans to emigrate, of which the emperor doubtless knew. Neither was their relationship marred by the imperial austerity campaign, which, without granting Mozart special treatment, accommodated him just enough to keep him in Vienna.

Chapter 5

VIENNA
1782–1785

THE EVENT OF THE CENTURY

Mozart's letters, unlike his father's, contain very few observations and descriptions of daily occurrences or noteworthy events unless they were directly connected with his musical interests. Nor do they contain any details of his conversations with important personalities, although he had frequent opportunities to meet and talk with such people. It was very important to Mozart that he be treated as an equal even in the highest aristocratic circles; he did not believe that his function as a musician was simply to provide social entertainment, and he successfully resisted being placed on the level of a lackey. All extramusical aspects of his life in society remain unknown to us, yet we cannot deny or underestimate this side of his personality just because we think of him almost as a spirit from another world who could only live and think in musical terms. On the contrary, everything about Mozart was very much of this world (and even his music, however inspired, shows a carefully considered, note-for-note process of composition). Though we can easily imagine Mozart moving in society, often high society, we have no idea what his conversations

were like—the everyday chitchat that would also reflect the personalities, interests, and professional activities of the people with whom
he associated, particularly the highest aristocrats and government
officials. But he was apparently accepted without reservation, as an
active participant in the exchange of ideas—which, incidentally,
suggests his considerable adaptability and informal, unobtrusive
manner.

An example of such casual dealings is his acquaintance with Count
Johann Philipp Cobenzl, vice-chancellor to Joseph II and one of the
emperor's closest associates. Mozart knew the count, as he did so
many members of Viennese society, from one of his journeys as a
wunderkind. Several times during his first summer in Vienna he was a
guest at the count's country seat, the Reisenberg. The Palais Cobenzl
had not yet been built (it was razed around 1896 to make way for a
hotel), and the count had only a small estate, whose surroundings he
had turned into an impressive artificial park. Here wild, romantic
mountain landscapes presented unexpected vistas, and pavilions appeared from nowhere, offering relaxation. There was even a man-
made grotto that especially delighted Mozart. (There are marvelous
descriptions of this park in the letters of Georg Forster, who took long
walks here with Countess Thun.) But the accommodations must have
been rather simple, as Mozart writes:

> The little house is nothing much, but the country—the forest—where
> my host has built a grotto that looks just as if Nature herself had
> fashioned it! Indeed the surroundings are magnificent and very de-
> lightful. (July 13, 1781)

An invitation there presumed an interest in long conversations, walks,
and communing with nature; it had very little to do with music and the
salon. And Mozart was there more than once.

The count's government position naturally meant that there was
much discussion of political affairs, so it is not surprising that Mozart
learned the news of the day from the count and gained insight into the
workings of imperial politics. Quite unexpectedly, the pope himself
had announced that he would make a visit to Vienna, and almost
everyone realized the significance of this. Mozart knew that his father,
as a supporter of enlightened thinking, followed world politics with

great interest, and uncharacteristically he hurried to inform Leopold of the sensational news. On January 9, 1782, he wrote: "Meanwhile I must inform you that the pope is supposed to be coming to Vienna. The whole city is talking about it."

When the pope embarked on a journey, it could only mean that the Church was in trouble; such a trip was highly unusual. Indeed, the emperor's policy toward the Church had gone so far that the pope had to use the entire weight of his personal authority to save what could still be saved. The controversy centered on nothing less than the primacy of church or state.

Even under Maria Theresa—a pious and dedicated Catholic if there ever was one—imperial policy had begun to curtail the Church's influence. The most obvious measure was the dissolution of the Jesuit orders; more drastic, if less apparent, was the endeavor to "nationalize" the Church and render clergymen also subject to the state, thus undermining the influence of Rome. We must not forget that some monasteries had been closed even during the empress's reign. Joseph II merely radicalized a policy already in existence, with the goal of making the Church serve national interests, so that it would become, in effect, a state church. This had nothing to do with matters of faith— Joseph II was himself a devout Catholic—but rather with the control of Church power, the eradication of parasitical elements, and the principle of tolerance for heterodoxy, all of which were in the interests of an "enlightened" state and a modern economic policy.

The measures taken by Joseph II were certainly alarming to the Roman Church, for they amounted to a recognition of the pope only as regent of a church-state, not as political leader of Catholic Christendom or even of his own clerical legions. The struggle was centuries old, but no one had gone as far as Joseph II with his "enlightened" reforms. He attempted to push through a plan that required diocesan districts to correspond to secular political districts, making them easier to control. Papal proclamations (bulls, briefs, etc.) could only be published after they were approved by the emperor. The monasteries were placed under the control of bishops; contemplative or "idle" monasteries were closed, the property confiscated and put up for auction; the proceeds were used to fund the many newly organized parishes and to pay pensions to former monks. The parishes were intended as a network for social reform as well as propaganda centers for the state's educational measures. The priests' function was not merely pastoral; they were also educators and charity workers employed by the state in an administrative capacity. The seminaries were nationalized, and the education of young clerics was no longer the province of monasteries. Joseph II even intervened in the observance of age-old religious traditions: he restricted the ringing of church bells, banned many processions, abolished private chapels, forbade the display of offerings in the church, and would not allow figures of saints to be adorned with real garments. Such measures may have been in keeping with enlightened thinking and abhorrence of waste, but many saw them simply as despotism and an affront to the Church. But his dissolution of the "idle" monasteries and the action he took against Church mendicancy encountered wider acceptance, if not general approval.

These Church reforms, which extended over a number of years, began as early as 1780 with the edict on the dissolution of the monasteries. The outline of the emperor's reforms and their goals was already clear when Pius VI decided to travel to Vienna personally, hoping to avoid the worst and persuade the emperor to reverse his policies. The Viennese were stunned and momentarily unsure whether they even wanted a visit from this uninvited guest. Joseph II must have considered ways to prevent observers from misinterpreting the expected hordes of onlookers as a sign of Viennese support for papal authority—or whether it might be better not to allow the journey in the first place.

Count Cobenzl kept Mozart well abreast of these deliberations, which suggests that Mozart had at least a basic idea of the purposes behind the pope's journey. Not that he was privy to government secrets, but neither was he excluded from the political calculations of the count, who, along with Joseph's other advisers, carefully analyzed the advantages and disadvantages of a papal visit, and in the end undoubtedly saw it as a possible incitement against the emperor. The pope's appearance would attract a vast number of visitors, and the spectacle might give rise to internal political pressures that would be difficult to handle. Mozart wrote his father that he did not believe the pope would come, "for Count Cobenzl told me that the emperor will decline his visit" (January 9, 1782). Here Mozart was passing on the count's opinion and was probably as surprised as Cobenzl when, two

Pope Pius VI visited Vienna in 1782 to induce the emperor to alter his Church policy. The journey was a political failure but brought huge crowds of on-lookers to Vienna.

days later, the emperor suddenly decided to approve the visit after all. It was a bold decision that could only have been made after careful consideration of every item on the pope's agenda. Joseph II met the challenge with inflexibility and extravagant courtesy in equal measure. Count Cobenzl himself was sent to the Austrian border to receive the pope, who was even more surprised when the emperor rode a day's journey to meet him along the way. Mozart wrote to his father on March 23: "I must tell you that the pope arrived in Vienna yesterday afternoon at half past three—a pleasant bit of news."

A crowd of 200,000 onlookers had already assembled for the pope's arrival, and it is reported that 30,000 visitors, to say nothing of the city's residents, swarmed into Vienna for his Easter blessing. An extensive sightseeing schedule was drawn up for the pontiff, doubtless to allow as little time as possible for political negotiations. And the emperor had a brilliant excuse to be seen only infrequently with his guest: he suffered from an unpleasant eye problem and had to spend most of his time in darkened rooms, so that even political discussions had to take place in semidarkness. The emperor was not prepared to make any political concessions; on the contrary, while the pope was in Vienna, three Viennese monasteries were closed almost as a deliberate demonstration, and the first set of Josephine burial regulations (not as offensive as those to come) was promulgated. At the same time, the pope was treated kindly and with a meticulous observance of protocol that avoided any appearance of an affront. Joseph II came through this visit brilliantly, without letting himself be swayed in his Church policy. Moreover, this pope did not have the type of personality that went very far with a ruler like Joseph II; the pope's vanity and desire for lavish display were weak points that the emperor skillfully manipulated. He could easily parry any vigorous negotiation on the pontiff's part. On the whole, sympathy for the pope seemed to dwindle as a result of this visit. (His lucrative business of selling posts had made him so despised in the papal states that there were even attempts on his life.)

If Mozart used only the word "amusing" to describe the papal visit, he must have been referring primarily to its splendor and elaborate ceremony, which took on the character of a public entertainment; his comment hardly indicates any respect for the pope's spiritual authority. (Although his predecessor, Clemens XIV, had conferred the Order of the Golden Spur on Mozart, he made no use of this title, unlike Gluck.) His one-word description suggests that Mozart viewed the whole affair with a positively Josephine smile. He was not impressed, nor did he voice the slightest opposition to the emperor's Church reforms. Mozart was clearly a devout Christian but a halfhearted Catholic, increasingly influenced by Enlightenment thought and the Christian-humanistic views of Freemasonry rather than by Church tradition. (If Mozart had any explicit theological views in any particular direction—reform Catholicism, for example—they are unknown to us.)

Interestingly, Mozart did not write a single religious composition in honor of the pope's visit. This is perhaps significant considering that Mozart's reputation was partly based on his religious music, which made up a quarter of all his works written before the move to Vienna. It is true that as court organist in Salzburg he had been required to produce music for the church, but it is striking nevertheless that he composed virtually no religious music during the Vienna years and that the little he did write was almost exclusively for Masonic functions after he became a Freemason in 1784. The paucity of Mozart's religious output can hardly be explained by a lack of commissions, though this would explain why he wrote nothing for the pope's visit. By contrast, on the occasion of a rather informal visit from the governor-general of the Netherlands, Duke Albert Kasimir of Sachsen-Teschen, and his wife, Archduchess Maria Christine (a sister of the emperor), both Mozart and Salieri were commissioned to write short operas (1786); and the premiere of *Die Entführung* was supposed to have taken place in honor of a visit from Grand Duke Paul of Russia, who was almost traveling incognito (1782). Yet on such an unusual occasion as a papal state visit, not a single work was commissioned to honor the illustrious guest. The real significance of protocol seems to lie in the political signals it sends.

Mozart had already been confronted with the Church reform movement in Salzburg: Archbishop Colloredo was an overzealous advocate of the Josephine reforms, one of which involved the reduction of church music to a minimum (thus limiting Mozart to church sonatas lasting only three minutes). But Mozart's polemics against these measures were directed solely at the person of the hated archbishop and must not be equated with a rejection of church reform as a whole. Mozart emphasized again and again that the emperor "despised" the Salzburg archbishop, however much Colloredo emulated imperial policy. More than once Mozart revealed his sympathy for Joseph's goals.

> It was news to me to hear that the paintings in the churches which serve no useful purpose, the many votive tablets, the instrumental music, and so forth, which are to be done away with in Vienna, have already been abolished in Salzburg. No doubt the archbishop hopes *by doing this* to ingratiate himself with the emperor, but I can hardly believe that this policy will be of much service to him. (September 25, 1782)

Leopold Mozart, a pious man who inquired after his son's regular church attendance (and who also became a Freemason, which betrayed no inconsistency), also expressed himself about the closing of monasteries, clearly in complete agreement with the emperor.

The purely contemplative orders are anathema to true Christianity. . . .
It is and always will be a good thing to close down the nunneries. They
represent neither a real profession, a calling from above, true spiritual
zeal, nor a school of true worship and mortification of the passions; but
rather servitude, dissimulation, pretense, hypocrisy, and no end of
childishness; in reality they are malevolence in disguise.

(October 14, 1785)

It would seem that Leopold Mozart was very critical of religious
institutions, and that his piety had more of a Protestant ring to it. Nor
was his son among those who lined up to kiss the pope's slippers,
which were considered so precious that they were carried into aristocratic homes—surely one of the more tasteless phenomena of the
pope's visit. Mozart was undoubtedly anticipating such symptoms of
misguided piety when he termed the pontiff's arrival merely "amusing." He did not entirely ignore the papal visit, but he seems to have
invested it with no more political significance than it actually had.

ORIENTATION IN SOCIETY

Mozart used his first weeks in Vienna to make extensive contacts; he
was anything but shy or apprehensive in society and openly approached people without being intimidated by class differences or
other social considerations. Thus he quickly established personal
contact with the Russian ambassador, Count Galitzin, Countess Thun,
numerous families whose homes were frequented by important people, and eventually the emperor himself. But only with the long-
delayed premiere of *Die Entführung aus dem Serail* on July 16, 1782,
was he able to demonstrate his ability in his favorite genre. At the time
he was still searching for a permanent position.

Every Sunday Mozart could be found at the home of Gottfried van
Swieten, where a small group of enthusiasts with a special interest in
older music met from 12:00 to 2:00 P.M. Swieten had lived for a time as
an envoy in Berlin, and had become acquainted there with the music
of Johann Sebastian Bach and his contemporaries, who were remembered primarily for their church music (though before the "rediscov-
ery" of Bach in the nineteenth century, there were always groups of

connoisseurs who preserved an awareness of music written prior to 1750, and especially of Bach and Handel; Swieten was only the Viennese sponsor of these efforts). Swieten collected old sheet music and manuscripts, and Mozart eagerly made use of these valuable resources. It was also here (if not at Countess Thun's) that Mozart met Prince Lichnowsky, who had himself brought copies of Bach's works to Vienna.[1]

Mozart always made an effort to contribute something unusual to these Sunday matinees. From his hand came works like the Fugue in C Minor for two pianos (K. 426) or arrangements of Bach fugues for string quartet. Mozart even invited his father to send some of his own early compositions and tried to talk him out of his reservations about the antiquated style of this music.

> When the weather gets warmer, please make a search in the attic under the roof and send us some of your own church music. You have no reason whatever to be ashamed of it. Baron van Swieten and Starzer know as well as you and I that musical taste is continually changing— and, *what is more*, that this extends even to church music, which ought not to be the case. Hence it is that true church music is to be found *only* in attics, and in a worm-eaten condition. (April 12, 1783)

These men did not have merely an archival interest in such music but were concerned to preserve an inheritance that did not deserve to be forgotten, even for the sake of new music. And Swieten himself did not compose in the "old" style any more than Mozart did, apart from stylistic exercises that Mozart found very helpful in the composition of *Die Zauberflöte*.

Gottfried van Swieten was one of the most significant politicians of his time and, as president of the Court Commission on Education, one of the most important reformers in Joseph II's government. This circle also included Court Councillor Anton von Spielmann, whose position as assistant to Prince Wenzel Anton Kaunitz made him responsible for foreign policy. It is always fascinating to observe that the most influential personalities in political life were also the most enthusiastic patrons of the arts. In most cases, active interest seems to have been more compelling than the social aspect; the Swieten circle was restricted to real connoisseurs and enthusiasts—an exclusive private salon—though Spielmann's salon was more concerned with social pleasures. (His daughter Franziska, a piano pupil of Haydn's, played there, and Mozart apparently performed there as well.)

With all this stimulating activity, however, Mozart did not lose contact with professional musicians. Throughout his years in Vienna, for instance, he maintained close relations with the hornist Joseph Leutgeb, who had been employed earlier in Salzburg but moved to Vienna and took a position in the private orchestra of Prince Grassalkovics. Here Mozart did not have to maintain appearances but could give free rein to his effervescent temperament. Thus one of the horn concertos he wrote for Leutgeb is graced with annotations (in several different colors of ink) that practically turn the work into a theater piece.[2]

The same exuberance, albeit of a less unruly nature, characterizes a pantomime Mozart performed with friends at a public masked ball in the Hofburg. Unfortunately the music for this event has survived only in fragments. The idea came from Mozart; the text in rhymed couplets was written for him by an actor. The five characters were Colombine, Harlequin (Mozart), Pierrot, Pantaloon, and a Doctor. A few days earlier, a ball that lasted until the early morning hours had taken place in Mozart's home. And although he had moved three times during that winter and spring and had played a number of concerts—not to mention teaching his piano pupils—he still found time for a day's outing in the Prater.

> I simply cannot make up my mind to drive back into town so early. The weather is far too lovely and it is far too delightful in the Prater today. We have taken our lunch out of doors and will stay on until eight or nine in the evening. My whole company consists of my little wife who is pregnant, and hers consists of her little husband, who is not pregnant, but fat and flourishing. (May 3, 1783)

Six weeks later Mozart's first child, Raimund Leopold, was born.

In addition to enjoying himself, Mozart had worked very hard during this first year of his marriage, though without the strain of the coming years and the many obligations that frequent concerts later entailed. He left unfinished many projects that nevertheless played a significant role in his musical development. He completed the Serenade for Winds (K. 384a/388), the *Haffner* Symphony, three piano concertos, one horn concerto, the Horn Quintet, three of the six *Haydn* Quartets, six concert arias, and several fugues. Among the unfinished works were several movements of violin sonatas, a piano fantasy, an oboe concerto, and the Mass in C Minor. Other fragments were probably intended as sketches. He also made plans for three operas, two of which were actually begun (they will be discussed shortly). This immense corpus must have required an amazing degree of discipline, yet we never find Mozart complaining about too much work during this period. On the contrary, he sought new concert possibilities, and the three new piano concertos were intended for the first available opportunities. Two weeks before *Die Entführung*, the first Augarten concert took place, at which Mozart performed the Concerto for Two Pianos (K. 316a/365) with Josepha Auernhammer. There were, of course, several private performances, but he wanted public exposure in the form of his own concert in the Burgtheater, which he was not able to arrange until March 23; it was evidently a glittering success. Mozart wrote to his father:

> I need not tell you much about the success of my concert, for no doubt you have already heard of it. Suffice it to say that the theater could not have been more crowded and that every box was full. But what pleased me most of all was that His Majesty the Emperor was present and, goodness!—how delighted he was and how he applauded me! . . . his delight was beyond all bounds. (March 29, 1783)

If the report in Karl Friedrich Cramer's *Magazin der Musik* (May 1783) is accurate, this concert brought Mozart 1,600 florins, the highest receipts of his career. Eleven works were on the program, among them the *Haffner* Symphony, two piano concertos, and six concert arias and scenes. On March 11, Mozart had already performed a piano concerto (K. 387b/415) at a concert given by his sister-in-law Aloysia, and at the end of March he played another of the new concertos in his Burgtheater concert. The enthusiasm was boundless. Gluck spontaneously invited Mozart to dinner, and in exchange Mozart played at his next concert an improvised set of variations on a theme by Gluck (K. 455). These successes in Vienna following *Die Entführung* made it possible for Mozart to settle in properly and assured him of many invitations to salons during the next season.

Besides frequenting the homes of Baron van Swieten, Councillor von Spielmann, and musical colleagues, Mozart was also a familiar face in the salon of Countess Thun, who had just as many bourgeois as high aristocrats among her guests. Mozart in turn brought members of this circle into the home of Finance Councillor Johann Michael Auernhammer, whose daughter Josepha perfected her piano playing under Mozart's tutelage and developed such a crush on Mozart that he reacted quite indignantly. Apparently unrelated to these circles was his close friendship with Baroness Waldstätten, a solitary figure whose life history remains obscure to this day. Mozart introduced her to some of his old Salzburg acquaintances, to new friends from the theater (the singer Valentin Adamberger, Aloysia and Joseph Lange), and to Raimund Wetzlar von Plankenstern, who was becoming more and more involved in real estate speculation. At Plankenstern's home Mozart made the acquaintance of the Italian abbé Lorenzo Da Ponte, whom he regarded initially with skepticism. They gradually developed a close friendship, and Da Ponte became Mozart's most important librettist.

A motley and colorful society was beckoning Mozart. There was continual give and take, a free exchange of ideas, and a constant receptivity to new ones. Mozart did not give up all thoughts of moving to Paris or London (he took French and English lessons), but at the same time Vienna had become for him "the nicest place in the world," and he would not leave unless he had to. Mozart was captivated by Vienna's liberal atmosphere and lack of social complications, his encounters with unconventional people, and the unlimited passion for music shared by all Viennese. He met hardly anyone who was not somehow involved in musical activities. Baroness Waldstätten herself played the piano and asked Mozart to select a new instrument for her. Even his friend Wetzlar von Plankenstern, despite all his complicated business dealings, was a great music lover and held frequent musical soirees at his home; he was, incidentally, an excellent performer on the guitar, an instrument which was coming back into fashion.

A TOUCH OF TREASON

It cannot be emphasized strongly enough that our knowledge of Mozart's circle of friends and acquaintances is woefully inadequate.

Strangely, Mozart scholarship has shown scant interest in this subject beyond its obligatory preoccupation with all members of the composer's family. Although biographers have paid close attention to Mozart's musical colleagues, they have been less interested in the list of his pupils and have largely ignored anyone outside the musical sphere. This is particularly regrettable since Mozart by no means associated only with musicians and guests of the musical salons but had a decidedly broad and heterogeneous circle of acquaintances. A further problem with source material is that Mozart had no need to correspond with his Viennese friends; some are mentioned by chance in letters (mostly those to his father), but descriptions of his daily social intercourse are anything but complete. As a result, certain acquaintances are virtually never mentioned (regardless of how frequently he saw them), and we find no clues to them in the Mozart literature, although they were very important to him. We might mention in this connection Fanny Arnstein, Baroness Waldstätten, Michael Puchberg, and Baron Wetzlar, to say nothing of Mozart's lodge brothers. It is notable that Mozart had various contacts with Jews, who were practically ostracized in Vienna, and that he did not belong to one of the "prestigious" Masonic lodges but to one with a primarily bourgeois membership. It would be particularly informative to draw up a genealogy of his acquaintances that might tell us where and when he established his first contacts.

It was possibly in the Arnstein house that Mozart met one of the emperor's closest aides, Johann Valentin Günther, who was a kind of private secretary to Joseph II. In this capacity he traveled with the emperor in 1780 to meet with Catherine II. At the time the empress was still an ally of Prussia, and the sensitive mission of this journey was to make her a partner of the Habsburgs. Only the most trusted associates could help carry out such a difficult assignment. We know hardly anything about Günther—too little, in any case, to help us discover the reason for Mozart's acquaintance with him. Perhaps he hoped that Günther would recommend him to Joseph II, but that was something he wanted from everyone who was in close contact with the emperor. And Mozart called Günther a "very good friend," by which he was surely implying more than just "connections."

Günther was unmarried but had lived for a number of years with Eleonore Eskeles, who was born to Jewish parents in Vienna, grew up

in Amsterdam, married in Berlin, then separated from her husband
(Moises Fliess) and moved to the home of her brother, Bernhard
Eskeles, in Vienna. Her story suggests the cosmopolitanism of those
who, as Jews, could never really settle down anywhere and were
always barely tolerated. Bernhard Eskeles was a banker and merchant
in Vienna, and together with Arnstein he later opened a banking and
retail business; thanks to lucrative international connections, it soon
became one of the largest and most important firms in Vienna. Fanny
Arnstein was a distant relative of Eleonore Eskeles and became her
closest friend.

Mozart dined with Günther on June 27, 1782; the next morning
Günther was arrested on suspicion of spying for Prussia. This affair
created quite a sensation, which is hardly surprising in view of
Günther's position of trust with the emperor. Günther had easy access
to important state secrets, such as those dealing with the attempt to
woo Russia away from Prussia, as well as current treaty negotiations
with the Habsburgs. Even the *Frankfurter Zeitung* published detailed
reports on all new developments in the affair. Mozart must have been
quite shocked, not just because of his friendship with Günther, but
even more because of the consequences the charges might have if they
were proved. The circumstances of this case were drastic even for the
eighteenth century, when treason and breach of trust were quite
common. Mozart was so troubled that he did not write to Salzburg
about the matter until his father, who had read the newspaper accounts, asked for more information. Fortunately, suspicions had not
hardened against Günther, although there were certain loose ends
concerning the involvement of Eleonore Eskeles, as Mozart recognized. He accepted the emperor's hotly disputed version of events,
whereby Günther was rehabilitated but Eleonore Eskeles became a
victim of the emperor's remaining doubts. Mozart wrote:

> The Jewess *Eskeles* has no doubt proved a very good and useful tool for
> breaking up the friendship between the emperor and the Russian
> court—the day before yesterday *she was taken to Berlin* so that the
> King might have the pleasure of her company. She is indeed a sow of
> the first order. Moreover, she was the whole cause of Günther's misfor-
> tune, if indeed it be a misfortune to be imprisoned for two months in a
> beautiful room (with permission to have all his books, his pianoforte,

and so forth) and to lose his former post, but to be appointed to another
at a salary of 1,200 florins; yesterday he left for Hermannstadt. Yet an
experience of that kind always injures an honest man and nothing in
the world can compensate him for it. I just want you to realize that he
has not committed any great crime. His conduct was due entirely to
étourderie, or thoughtlessness, and consequently lack of discretion,
which in a privy councillor is certainly a serious fault. Although he
never divulged anything of importance, his enemies—chief of whom is
the former stadtholder Count von Herberstein—managed to play their
cards so cleverly that the emperor, who formerly had such immense
confidence in Günther that he would walk up and down the room arm in
arm with him for hours, now began to distrust him with an equal
intensity. To make matters worse, who should appear on the scene but
that sow *Eskeles* (a former mistress of Günther's), who accused him in
the most violent terms. But when the matter was investigated, these
gentlemen cut a very poor figure. However, the affair had already
caused terrific commotion, and great people never like to admit that
they have been in the wrong. Hence the fate of poor Günther, whom I
pity with all my heart, as he was a very good friend of mine and, if
things had remained as they were, might have rendered me good
service with the emperor. You can imagine what a shock and how
unexpected it was to me and how very upset I was; for Stephanie,
Adamberger, and I had supper with him one evening and the next day
he was arrested. (September 11, 1782)

Events did not transpire exactly as Mozart related them, however.[3]
The idea that Günther was incriminated by Eleonore Eskeles is nonsense; the accusation was probably another attempt to justify her
deportation, at least belatedly. According to Mozart's version, which
was widely accepted, there was no proof of treason, though Eleonore
Eskeles did pass on confidential information—mostly gossip about
the emperor's love life—according to other contemporary reports. But
that was another falsehood.

What actually happened was that two Viennese Jews had made a
plan to swindle the Prussian court by selling information they had
obtained in Prussia as intelligence from an imaginary informant in
Vienna. The scheme was brilliantly planned but badly executed; a
third party had been initiated who exposed the pretended espionage
hoping for personal gain. For his own reasons and also, perhaps, to

inflate the value of his information, he brought up the names of Günther and Eskeles. The entire situation was cleared up rather quickly, especially since the two real culprits confessed their guilt; they were severely punished. A further consequence, however, was that this affair was linked to the Jewish community, which was why Eleonore Eskeles was expelled from the country.[4]

This turn of events seemed highly unjust even to contemporaries, since all charges against both Eleonore Eskeles and Günther proved to be totally unfounded. It is thus all the more surprising that Mozart, even when writing to his father, still claimed to believe the version of the story circulated by the imperial court. Perhaps this was a precautionary measure, for the Mozarts had experience with intercepted letters. The worst possible thing that could happen to Mozart would have been for the emperor to hear his name in even the remotest connection with such an affair. Günther, despite his total innocence, was forced to accept a position that almost amounted to banishment; Mozart's prospects for an imperial post would have been, at the least, greatly jeopardized.

"BUT PRIMARILY BECAUSE OF THE OPERA"

Die Entführung aus dem Serail appears to have been the most successful of all the German Nationalsingspiel's productions. Eighteen performances were given within seven months. But it was too late to save this halfhearted theater project. During the last two seasons only three of the nine productions were performed more than three times, and the others were translations of French Singspiels or Italian *opera buffa*. In other words, the German-language Singspiel—a new idea in need of promotion and development—was being played off against the very competition it had been intended to supplant. Moreover, according to Mozart, some of the new German Singspiels were so "execrable" that they threatened to ruin the reputation of the entire theater. He commented on these developments in no uncertain terms: "The German opera will no longer exist after Easter, but it seems they want to kill it off even before then. And Germans themselves are doing this—it's disgusting!" (February 5, 1783).

Indeed, the Nationalsingpiel had great difficulty reaching the end of that season. For the next season Italian singers were engaged once again. We must avoid seeing the fate of this project through the eyes of the Italian-oriented nobility, as a failed bourgeois undertaking. Although it may be easy to establish that partisans of the Singspiel came mostly from the bourgeoisie and those of the Italian *opera buffa* from the nobility, the fact remains that the Singspiel never had a real chance in this theater because it made no attempt to engage the services of the most competent composers and librettists. In this respect Mozart's bitter comment is entirely justified. He was equally justified in not writing off the Singspiel entirely. True, he could just as easily have concentrated on Italian opera and was prepared to do so as long as he received commissions, but he refused to give up on the Nationalsingpiel—not purely out of patriotic sentiment, but mainly because he saw possibilities for future development.

> I don't believe that the Italian opera will keep going for long, and besides, I hold with the Germans. I prefer German opera, even though it means more trouble for me. Every nation has its own opera—why not Germany? Is not German as singable as French and English? Is it not more so than Russian? Very well then! I am now writing a German opera for myself. I have chosen Goldoni's comedy *Il servitore di due padroni*, and the whole of the first act has now been translated. Baron Binder is the translator. But we are keeping it a secret until it is completely finished. Well, what do you think of this scheme? Don't you agree that I can make something good of it?
>
> (February 5, 1783, to his father)

This plan was not carried out, however. Mozart may have underestimated the problems of setting Goldoni's fast-paced comedy of mistaken identities to music. But his interest was so great that he was prepared to undertake the project with no prospects of an actual performance. His choice also casts light on the difficulties of finding suitable libretti and librettists, especially in Vienna. (The Italian original was already more than thirty years old but had enjoyed continued theatrical success in the commedia dell'arte tradition.)

The experience with *Die Entführung aus dem Serail* confirmed Mozart's claim that opera was his true métier. Had he not achieved the only financial and popular success of the entire final season? And for it he received only a flat fee that might be equaled by the receipts from one performance! He was too confident of future triumphs to be satisfied with this arrangement, especially since elsewhere (e.g., in Paris) royalties were paid for a work that enjoyed lasting success. Mozart developed a bold plan—a little too bold, considering his chances of carrying it through.

> I am willing to write an opera, but not to look on with a hundred ducats in my pocket and watch the theater make four times that much in only two weeks. I intend to produce my opera at my own expense, I will clear at least 1,200 florins after three performances and then the management may have it for 50 ducats. If they refuse to take it, I will have made some money and can produce the opera anywhere. I hope that so far you have not detected the least inclination on my part to act shabbily. No man should be mean, but neither should he be such a simpleton as to let other people take the profits from his work, which has cost him so much study and labor, by renouncing all further claims upon it. (October 5, 1782)

There are undertones of a bad conscience here, for Mozart had secretly had *Die Entführung aus dem Serail* copied so that he could sell it again to the court in Berlin. (Given the strained relations between the Berlin and Viennese courts, it was a clear provocation for the Prussian envoy to approach Mozart about the opera; Mozart had the copying done in Salzburg to avoid premature exposure of his plan.) But his worries were unnecessary, for the Viennese theater management always proved to be generous in such matters.

It is unclear whether the work Mozart thought of producing at his own expense was a German Singspiel or an Italian opera; in any event, he was now occupied with two more Italian libretti. Both operas remained fragments.

The first of these, *L'oca del Cairo* ("The Goose of Cairo"), is a variation on the abduction theme, in which a rich young man is promised the daughter of an evil marquis if he can reach her in the fortified tower where she is held prisoner. The highlight of the opera is a fake goose in which the hero hides, and which is smuggled into the compound like the Trojan horse. By means of intricate subplots, three couples are happily united at the end. This story capitalized on the general fascination with mechanical marvels, but its comic element was especially weak. Mozart was far more willing to rely on the dramatic element, and he worked with the librettist Giambattista Varesco (who also wrote the libretto for *Idomeneo*) to devise simplifications that would allow enough leeway for a more dramatic musical treatment. (Mozart was fully aware that the hero would need some trick besides the goose in order to reach his goal.) In any case, a large part of the first act of this three-act work was completed, but the librettist himself apparently made no headway with the rest of the text.

The other projected opera was *Lo sposo deluso ossia La rivalità di tre donne per un solo amante* ("The Dejected Bridegroom, or The Rivalry of Three Women for a Single Man"). Here the title gives everything away. A somewhat older wealthy man is engaged to a young woman; a rival for the young woman appears and is soon besieged by two other women. The intrigues among the five central characters constitute the action, which combines comic and tragic elements and shows affinities with *Don Giovanni* in its device of a rival loved by three women. (The librettist is unknown, but Alfred Einstein's conjecture that it may have been Lorenzo Da Ponte is not implausible.) The interest of this opera for Mozart lay not just in the intricate plot but also in the opportunity to characterize individuals musically—as he did so brilliantly in his next three operas, *Le nozze di Figaro*, *Don Giovanni*, and *Così fan tutte*. The music depicts the characters' feelings while caricaturing, exaggerating, and commenting on the stage action and the protagonists. Evidently the problem with this opera did not lie with the librettist, nor did Mozart lose interest in the material; it would seem that a total absence of performance prospects caused him to lay the score aside temporarily. In his copy of the text Mozart had already written the names of certain singers from the Nationaltheater; so he apparently wrote each part for a specific performer.

Perhaps Mozart thought it would be easier to gain access to the Nationaltheater than it proved. It was out of the question as long as he had no commission, especially since first consideration was given to composers who had permanent positions at the theater or the court. But there is no indication that Mozart suffered any actual discrimination.[5]

During this period Mozart not only worked on opera drafts and sketches for other compositions but also attempted to formulate his ideas on opera dramaturgy. Opera is not merely theater set to music; it adds to spoken language the element of musical language, which can be combined with words and the special physical language of the theater in myriad ways. The text can be given musical form, either sung or spoken over orchestral accompaniment. And the music can also be an independent partner in the dialogue; it is by no means simply "reinforcement." Furthermore, the presence of the musical element in the theater means that events on stage are subject to an entirely different time structure, aside from the fact that music has its own formal structure that must be subordinated to the "speaking" of the protagonists without dispelling the illusion of reality. Opera is thus one of the most complex art forms and demands careful consideration of its artistic possibilities.[6] Composition is not simply the result of divine inspiration; it requires above all an intellectual grasp of musical ideas. In opera this is visible as well as audible, and it is just in that respect that Mozart's superiority to the endless ranks of minor masters is confirmed.

The relationship between text and music is always an artificial one, and Mozart tried to formulate his ideas on the subject while working on a small commission that nevertheless proved to be quite a problem.

> At the same time I am engaged in a very difficult task, the music for a bard's song by Denis about Gibraltar. But this is a secret, for a Hungarian lady wishes to pay this compliment to Denis. The ode is sublime, beautiful, anything you like, but too exaggerated and pompous for my fastidious ears. But what is to be done? The golden mean of truth in all things is no longer either known or appreciated. In order to win applause one must write stuff which is so inane that a coachman could sing it, or so unintelligible that it pleases precisely because no sensible man can understand it. (December 28, 1782)

Opera called for similar reflection, and Mozart, who was struggling simultaneously with the projected Singspiel after Goldoni and the plan for an Italian *opera buffa*, "would like to write a book—a short critical work with musical examples—but not under my name," as he said in the same letter to his father.

Mozart never wrote this book, which offers more cause for regret than many of his fragmentary or projected musical works. If he had, we might now possess his approach to the aesthetics of music, perhaps even a book on compositional theory—in any case a polemical work on his craft that would have been of great significance. (Such a book would most certainly have had considerable influence on later portrayals of Mozart; it might even have thrown a few salutary wrenches into the romantically tinged Mozart biography.)

JOURNEY TO SALZBURG

His head full of opera plans, Mozart traveled to Salzburg with his wife at the end of July 1783 for their first (and last) visit to his father and sister. The journey had been in the works for a year and was to have taken place just after the wedding but was postponed again and again for any number of reasons. First Mozart had to stay in Vienna to give a concert with his pupil Josepha Auernhammer; then their departure date proved unsuitable because the nobility was returning from summer vacation and the new concert season was beginning; after that came a spate of "nasty weather" with heavy snowfall, and finally, Constanze's pregnancy in the spring. Through all this Wolfgang and Constanze proclaimed that they were very anxious to see his father and sister. When, after the birth of Raimund, there was no longer anything to prevent them from going, a new problem occurred to Mozart: What would the archbishop have to say?

I feel sure we will be able to set out in September; and indeed you can well imagine that our most ardent longing is to embrace you both. Yet I cannot conceal from you but must confess quite frankly that many people here are alarming me to such an extent that I cannot describe it. *You already know what it is all about.* However much I protest I am told: *"Well, you'll see, you will never get away again. You have no idea what that wicked malevolent prince is capable of! And you cannot conceive what low tricks he resorts to in affairs of this kind. Take my advice and meet your father in some third place."* This, you see, is what has been worrying my wife and me and what continues to perturb us. I often say to myself, "Nonsense, it's quite impossible!" But the next moment it occurs to me that it might be possible after all, and that it would not be the first injustice he has committed. Basta! In this matter no one can comfort me but you, my most beloved father! And as far as I am concerned, whatever happened would not worry me very much, for I can now adapt myself to any circumstances. But when I think of my

wife and my little Raimund, then my indifference ceases. Think it
over. If you can assure me that I will be running no risk, we will both be
overjoyed. If not, then we must hit on some plan, and there is one
which I would prefer above all others! I will tell you about it as soon as I
receive your reply. I am convinced that if one is to enjoy a great
pleasure, one must forgo something. Why! In the greatest happiness
there is always something lacking. (July 5, 1783)

Admittedly, it is difficult to take this letter very seriously. Despotism
was indeed the order of the day, and there was no guarantee of civil
liberties in Salzburg. Might the archbishop, who had never signed a
certificate of discharge, still hold that Mozart left his service illegally
and have him forcibly detained and incarcerated? Such measures were
only taken against ordinary servants, if at all. There were cases like
that of Christian Friedrich Daniel Schubart, a journalist who had been
kidnapped on foreign territory because he had expressed himself
much too frankly (he was imprisoned without trial for more than ten
years in Hohenasperg Castle), but it was a bit farfetched for Mozart to
think a similar fate might overtake him. There may well have been
people in Vienna who warned him about the archbishop, who was very
unpopular there, but it all sounded like an excuse to Leopold Mozart,
who was by no means a rash man. He must have found the reference to
his son's family quite histrionic and sentimental. His answer was
evidently forceful, and Mozart not only had to defend himself but also
to make up his mind. He wrote back:

If you insist on calling real obstacles mere humbug, I cannot prevent
you from doing so. Anyone may call a thing by a wrong name if he
pleases, but whether it is right to do so is a very different matter. Have I
ever given you the impression that I had no desire or longing to see
you? Most certainly never! But assuredly you will have observed that I
have no desire whatever to see Salzburg or the archbishop. So, if we
were to meet in a third place, who would then be humbugged? Why, the
archbishop, and not you. I suppose I need not repeat that I care very
little for Salzburg and not at all for the archbishop, that I shit on both of
them and that it would never enter my head to go there voluntarily were
it not for you and my sister. So the whole business was due solely to the
well-meant caution of my good friends, who surely are not devoid of
sound common sense. And I did not think I was acting unreasonably

when I asked your opinion on the subject and then followed your advice. My friends' anxiety was simply that the archbishop might have me arrested, as I have never been discharged. But you have now set my mind completely at rest and we shall come in August, or certainly in September at the latest. (July 12, 1783)

This letter reveals a note of discord, a certain tension expressed in his total rejection of Salzburg. Mozart leaves no doubt that he wants nothing to do with his birthplace—and not only because of the archbishop. He had an aversion to the entire limited milieu of this city, and Leopold Mozart felt personally included in his son's judgment. The actual purpose of the journey, however, was to introduce Constanze and have her accepted into the family, and no one has ever proved that it failed in this respect. It would seem that the notorious rejection of Constanze Mozart enshrined by later generations has once again reversed all the facts. There is nothing in the family records about such a rejection, and the following story, though often repeated, is merely an example of how the blank pages of Mozart's biography are continually filled in with fanciful psychologizing.

Mozart had hoped that his wife would receive some of the precious objects presented to him in his youth. The father, however, true to his principles, declared that his son's family could expect nothing more from him, and locked up his cabinets. Naturally Constanze was most highly indignant over this reception, and never forgave her father-in-law and sister-in-law. But Wolfgang was also disappointed and upset when he bade farewell to the city of his birth.[7]

We know precious little about the visit to Salzburg; only the diary entries of Mozart's sister tell us of the daily visits, excursions, parties, theater performances, and open-air bathing. All this was noted down simply as events of the day, without comment. Naturally, there are also many references to family music making. The only striking thing is that Mozart seems often to have gone his own way—in any event, he was not present at every visit paid to Salzburg acquaintances. He also appears not to have gone to church every morning at seven o'clock, as his sister did. Her notations are so meager that they do not even confirm whether the Mass in C Minor was actually performed in Salzburg—it could have been another of his masses. All we know is that Constanze sang the soprano solo and that the entire court orchestra was involved.

The Mass in C Minor (K. 427) was probably written for Salzburg, but it remained unfinished. It was the result of an oath taken by Mozart while Constanze was suffering an illness (before the wedding; it was not written to celebrate either his first child or the long hoped-for marriage itself, as is often maintained). Mozart had to be reminded of his oath by Leopold, who often admonished his son about his duties and regularly inquired about his religious observance.

> I forgot to tell you last time that on the Day of Portiuncula my wife and I performed our devotions together at the Theatine Chapel. Even if a sense of piety had not moved us to do so, we would have had to do it on account of the banns, without which we could not have been married.
>   (August 17, 1782)

Mozart may have realized that such explanations were a great disappointment to his father, for he immediately added the following (without making himself more believable):

> Indeed for a considerable time before we were married we had always attended mass, gone to confession, and received communion together; and I found that I never prayed so fervently or confessed and received communion so devoutly as by her side, and she felt the same. In short, we are made for each other, and God who orders all things and consequently has ordained this also, will not forsake us. We both thank you most submissively for your fatherly blessing.

Such statements reveal a certain alienation independent of the connection to Constanze Mozart. Religious laxity was only one of several symptoms of this alienation, which apparently had more to do with Mozart's migration to the metropolis and the keenly felt contrast with Salzburg provincialism. He was now accustomed to Viennese liberality and, nourished by the favorable atmosphere of Josephine Vienna, had become in his own way an independent freethinker. He now had other interests, other topics of discussion, other friends— and the work plans he had brought with him to Salzburg concerned three different opera projects.

During the three months Mozart spent in Salzburg, he seems to have composed nothing but the two duets for violin and viola (K. 423 and 424), which were written to help Michael Haydn out of an awkward situation; nonetheless, they are lovely pieces. Not even the Mass in C Minor was completed, although he had brought it with him and indeed had a mass performed in St. Peter's shortly before his departure.[8] What Mozart really did in these three months remains obscure. Perhaps the extent of this gap in the biography becomes clear when we remember that while stopping over in Linz on the return trip, Mozart wrote an entire symphony in four days, "because I have not a single symphony with me" (October 31, 1783).

Though Mozart never again saw the birthplace he had so bitterly reviled, his wife actually ended her life there (in immediate proximity to Mozart's sister, with whom she maintained cordial but not close relations). Constanze helped the detested city become a permanent attraction, and the names Mozart and Salzburg became almost synonymous, while Vienna, where Mozart chose to settle, is saddled with the reputation of having basely relegated a genius to obscurity, even oblivion. But in the autumn of 1783 the situation was just the reverse. The family trip to Salzburg had no far-reaching artistic success, brought no successful concerts, offered no stimulus for important compositions—nothing of consequence occurred. In Vienna, however, Mozart's most successful years were beginning. His schedule was to be so packed with concert dates and new compositions (as a tribute to his success) that we can hardly conceive how he managed even to write everything down, quite apart from the actual work of composing, the artistic communion with the imagination. It is almost reassuring to learn that Mozart's keyboard facility could apparently be maintained without practice.

WORKING UNDER PRESSURE

At the beginning of February 1784, Mozart opened a blank manuscript book and wrote on the first page, "Catalogue of all my works from the Month of Febrario 1784 to the Month . . . Wolfgang Amadé Mozart." Most of the entries were made very carefully, usually on the day a work was completed, always with the first measures notated to identify the piece. The exact instrumentation is also noted, and there are frequent references to the occasions for which the works were written. Thanks to this catalogue we are very well informed about the dates of compositions from 1784 on; only in a few cases were belated entries made in summary fashion.

For the year 1784, six piano concertos, one piano quintet (with winds), one string quartet, and two sonatas and two sets of variations for piano are listed, as well as a few smaller compositions. This enormous output was not the work of a composer writing in undisturbed peace and seclusion, but of one whose schedule included teaching obligations, subscription concerts, private concerts, houseguests, and two changes of residence, as well as all kinds of other distractions, any one of which would have been enough to make an ordinary person nervous. Altogether, twenty-six concert appearances are recorded for that year, among them four of his own and twenty in fashionable salons. Most of the compositions were written under even greater pressure, however, for between April 21 and September 30 only one work was entered in the catalogue: the piano variations on a theme by Gluck, which Mozart had improvised in Gluck's honor at an earlier concert (March 23, 1783).

Such gaps in creativity were not unusual for Mozart, although it is surprising to find one lasting at least four months.[9] On the other hand, they indicate that the creative phases were so intense that they must have been an excessive strain on his energies. Between February 9 and April 12, 1784, he produced three piano concertos and the Quintet for Piano and Winds. Mozart writes that this work "called forth the very greatest applause: I myself consider it to be the best work I have ever composed. How I wish you could have heard it! And how beautifully it was performed!" He then adds, "To tell the truth, I was really worn out at the end after playing so much—and it is greatly to my credit that my listeners never got tired" (April 10, 1784). During these nine weeks, in addition to composing, Mozart had given no fewer than twenty-four concerts.

The list of concerts and compositions is almost as long for 1785, when there were twenty concert appearances, as well as at least three house concerts and two performances at Masonic lodge functions. (Mozart organized ten of these concerts himself.) That year he composed three piano concertos, two string quartets, one piano quartet, a sonata and the Fantasy in C Minor for piano, the *Maurerische*

Trauermusik ("Masonic Funeral Music"), one operatic scene each for vocal trio and quartet, several songs, and the arrangement of music from the Mass in C Minor as part of the cantata *Davidde penitente.* Also during 1785 Leopold Mozart spent ten weeks in Vienna, and Wolfgang paid many visits to the lodge, some in the company of his father.

Leopold Mozart had the satisfaction of observing his son engaged in frenetic activity and enjoying a well-ordered domestic and financial situation. But he did find his stay in Vienna a little too long and became homesick for humble Salzburg. Even the outward circumstances of his visit were arduous enough. Just after his arrival on February 11, Vienna suffered a cold spell that lasted until the beginning of March, with heavy snowfall and temperatures so low that several people froze to death. Despite the weather, Mozart's piano had to be taken out of the house to a concert every other day. There was constant uproar in the house, and a concert or a visit to Mozart's friends and acquaintances every evening—at times the calendar was so full that Herr and Frau Mozart each had to accept a different invitation or attend a different concert. In late March and early April there was again heavy snowfall, and Leopold Mozart contracted a severe cold. Yet attendance at the opera, theater, and lodge functions continued, all in miserable weather. The elder Mozart was naturally quite impressed with Viennese life and his son's success, and the descriptions he included in letters to his daughter offer much more insight into Mozart's daily life than we can glean from any Viennese source. (Many missing details were probably communicated personally upon his return.)

He was overwhelmed by the music in Vienna, especially the quality of the orchestras: "I was sitting only two boxes away from the very beautiful Princess of Württemberg and had the great pleasure of hearing so clearly all the interplay of the instruments that for sheer delight tears came into my eyes" (February 16, 1785). He gave the highest praise to his son's new piano concertos, which he had not heard or seen before. Most important for him, however, was the opinion of Joseph Haydn, whom he met at a chamber music soiree in Mozart's home, where three of the *Haydn* Quartets were performed: "Haydn said to me: 'Before God and as an honest man I tell you that your son is the greatest composer known to me either in person or by name. He has taste and, what is more, the most profound knowledge of composition" (February 16, 1785).

Leopold Mozart also checked secretly into his son's finances and compared his concert receipts with those of other musicians. Here again, the results put his mind at ease: "If my son has no debts, I think he could now put 2,000 florins in the bank; the money is there, and the household—as far as eating and drinking are concerned—is very economical" (March 19, 1785). This judgment is especially significant as Leopold Mozart was outraged at the high prices in Vienna, particularly rents. The Mozarts usually dined with friends, but even there Leopold was astounded at the expense involved.

> On Thursday the 17th we lunched with your brother's mother-in-law, Frau Weber. There were just the four of us, Frau Weber and her daughter Sophie, since the eldest daughter is in Graz. I must tell you that the meal was neither too lavish nor too stingy, and was cooked to perfection. The roast was a fine plump pheasant; and everything was splendidly prepared. On Friday the 18th we lunched with Stephanie junior, just the four of us and Herr Le Brun, his wife, Karl Cannabich, and a priest. Let me tell you at once that there was no thought of a fast-day. We were only offered meat dishes. As an extra dish there was a pheasant with cabbage, and the rest was fit for a prince. Finally we had oysters, most delicious glacé fruits, and (I must not forget to mention this) several bottles of champagne. I need hardly add that coffee is served everywhere. (February 21, 1785)

Despite the very full schedule during his father's visit, Mozart wrote one piano concerto (K. 467), the cantata *Davidde penitente*, an andante for violin and orchestra, and two Masonic compositions during these ten weeks. One has the impression that Mozart preferred to work under pressure, against the clock, pressed by deadlines, yet without omitting a single one of the many visits and dinner invitations, as if what would have distracted anyone else were necessary for him to crystallize his musical ideas.

During the following summer Mozart also allowed himself a break of several months—from May 20, when he entered the Fantasy in C Minor (K. 475) in his catalogue, until October, when he composed the first piano quartet (K. 478). Even the letters to his father are few and

Nachricht.

Donnerstag den 10ten März 1785. wird Hr. Kapellmeister Mozart die Ehre haben in dem

k. k. National-Hof-Theater

eine

grosse musikalische Akademie

zu seinem Vortheile

zu geben, wobey er nicht nur ein neues erst verfertigtes Forte piano - Konzert spielen, sondern auch ein besonders grosses Forte piano Pedal beym Phantasieren gebrauchen wird. Die übrigen Stücke wird der grosse Anschlagzettel am Tage selbst zeigen.

In February and March of 1785, Mozart gave seven concerts and appeared in at least seven more. In the handbills, attention is drawn to a pedal mechanism built especially for Mozart and housed in a large box underneath the piano. No example of the device has survived.

far between during this period. A single short but well-loved work, dated June 8, 1785, is the only item entered in the catalogue that summer: the song "Das Veilchen," on a text by Goethe.[10] We do not know where Mozart was during all this time; his father, who seldom heard from him, assumed he was "in the country." Only on August 12 is a visit to the Masonic lodge recorded, then nothing more until a concert on October 20 (also in the lodge). This entire summer is one of the blank areas on our biographical map; we cannot be sure he composed, but one thing seems certain: sometime in early summer Mozart must have read Beaumarchais's comedy *Le mariage de Figaro*, which must have fired his imagination and sent him out looking for a suitable librettist.

Since May 1783 Mozart had been in contact with the Italian poet Abbé Da Ponte, whom he had met at the home of his friend Baron Wetzlar. Da Ponte had had intermittent successes as an opera librettist and had worked with Antonio Salieri, the director of the Hofoper and Mozart's principal rival. Da Ponte was enough of an intriguer to work simultaneously for three composers who were all competing with each other. His best working relationship was with Mozart, however, probably because Mozart was the only composer who took an interest in the libretto, making changes and suggestions, rejecting what did not suit him, and refusing to be swayed in his conception of dramatic and musical development. Other composers, adhering to the traditional division of labor, waited for the complete libretto and then set to music whatever the poet delivered, but Mozart considered his participation on the text a prerequisite for success. Either Da Ponte had so much respect for Mozart's dramatic genius that he let himself be persuaded, or they just worked well together. In his occasionally long-winded memoirs, Da Ponte is silent about the details of his collaboration with Mozart. Sometime during the summer, work was begun on the libretto for *Le nozze di Figaro*, and it must have been soon thereafter that Mozart started composing this large score. This marked the beginning of his five-year working relationship with Da Ponte—a most fruitful collaboration that brought both of them lasting fame. It gave both artists the opportunity to realize their creative possibilities fully, and for Mozart it was a congenial partnership such as he had always hoped for.

DIGRESSION: LORENZO DA PONTE

Da Ponte (originally Emanuele Conegliano) was born in 1749 in the ghetto of Ceneda, a small town in the Venetian Republic. Although Da Ponte never denied his origins, he mentioned them only vaguely in his memoirs. As a Jew, he was confronted with a choice that would determine the course of his life: he could stay in Ceneda and become a craftsman and merchant like his father, remaining within the narrow confines and (relative) protection of an isolated and threatened Jewish community; or he could become something totally different, depart from the old beliefs and traditions and be reborn into a second life, as it were, without the stigma of an oppressed and persecuted religious group. Of course Da Ponte was not free to make such decisions himself; they were made for him when he was fourteen years old. His mother died early, and after remaining a widower for ten years, his father decided to remarry—this time, a Christian woman; he thus renounced Judaism for himself and his entire family. The bishop of Ceneda, Lorenzo Da Ponte, stood as godfather at the baptism, thereby passing his name on to the Conegliano family. Thus Emanuele Conegliano became Lorenzo Da Ponte, who now had a sixteen-year-old stepmother with whom he did not get along.

The bishop proved to be generous, and for five years he paid the costs of educating Lorenzo and his two brothers. Perhaps for this reason, their father promised the bishop that all three boys would study for the priesthood; in any event, Da Ponte took minor orders in 1770 and became a priest in 1773. In his memoirs he holds this against his father, since the priesthood was a contradiction of "my true calling and my character." His father must have had a dominating influence, for by that time Da Ponte was an adult but still did not dare to show any opposition. Later he described his becoming a priest as the only embarrassing incident of his life. Looking at his later life, we must concede that he was right: any other profession would have suited him better.

On the other hand, it was only by virtue of his education as a priest that he was able to employ his talents. Immediately after taking minor orders, he was made a professor of rhetoric at the seminary, and upon his ordination he became professor of fine arts at the seminary in Treviso. During this period Da Ponte acquired an extraordinary knowledge of Italian literature as well as the ancient classics, developed a subtle feeling for language, and began to test his poetic abilities. The results were humorous, elegant, and slightly sophistic, rebellious, malicious, and sometimes thoughtless. A speech he had written as an exercise in declamation for his students occasioned his first serious controversy. It posed the question whether mankind would be happier in a state of nature than in human society. Equally offensive was a Latin elegy called "The American in Europe"—a title with many associations for his later life; he was charged with inciting young people to heresy and rebellion, and an official court in Venice banned him from teaching within the Venetian Republic for the rest of his life.

Da Ponte was neither a rebel nor a heretic, but he was impertinent; he had sharpened his satirical knife and made people laugh. That was enough to outrage the authorities. But he was not intimidated by his severe punishment, for he had attained popular success and was admired. Further difficulties resulted from the permissive life he led despite his holy orders—he lived with a woman and fathered a child by her. Da Ponte's personal life was "indecent," and that was almost worse than the intellectual corruption of his students. Once again he was prosecuted, this time as a renegade priest, on charges of adultery and concubinage. The sentence for these offenses was fifteen years' banishment from the republic, but Da Ponte fled to Austria before being convicted.

Da Ponte's experiences were similar to those of his older friend Giacomo Casanova, yet there was an essential difference. Da Ponte did not seek adventure for its own sake; rather, an adventurous life was forced upon him. He found no focal point for his life, although he constantly searched for one. He sought domestic happiness with a woman, whereas Casanova was in love with being in love. Da Ponte believed that his true calling was as a poet and patron of Italian literature, and he always returned to this fundamental concern, which brought him his greatest success. Again and again, however, he involved himself in relationships, scandals, intrigues, and business dealings that sidetracked him and almost led to disaster. His memoirs, which purport to be totally honest, nonetheless suffer from one serious flaw: the frustrations, failures, and disappointments of his long life are almost melodramatically emphasized, and he frequently depicts himself as the victim of intrigue and deceit, and occasionally of his tempestuous love affairs; the high points of his life, his successes, the wealth he always managed to regain, and his many years of happiness are less thoroughly described. In his old age Da Ponte must have seen himself as a man dogged by misfortune, but in fact he seems to have been the type who always bounced back, who never let himself be caught in a desperate situation, who could always find new and often unusual ways to muddle through and promptly scale new heights. One has the impression that throughout his life Da Ponte profited from the abilities that an oppressed and persecuted people develop early on: self-assertiveness, the fortitude to start again from scratch periodically, and the inventiveness to cope with a humiliating outsider's existence, drawing strength from the knowledge of being special.

After his banishment from Venice, Da Ponte came to Vienna by a rather circuitous route. Again and again he found friends who paid his travel expenses and provided him with necessities, and each time he expressed his gratitude with a sample of his poetic ability. He was virtually unknown in Vienna, but he had a letter of recommendation to the opera director, Salieri, and also gained an introduction to Pietro Metastasio, the doyen of Italian dramatic poets, who shortly before his death (1782) praised Da Ponte publicly. When the German Nationalsingspiel was closed in 1783 and Italian opera was once again installed at the Nationaltheater, Da Ponte applied for a position as dramatist, having been encouraged by Salieri and probably recommended by him to the emperor. Da Ponte himself described the decisive audience with Joseph II:

I had never spoken with a monarch before. Although everyone told me that Joseph was the kindest and most benevolent prince in the world, I appeared before him not without some timidity and a shudder of apprehension. But his smiling face, his pleasant voice, and above all the great simplicity of his dress and manners—none of which I had ever associated with a sovereign—not only gave me courage but practically made me forget that I was standing before an emperor. I had heard that he very often judged people by their facial features. It appeared that mine did not displease him, for he showed immense grace and kindness during the first audience I was granted. He was eager for knowledge and asked me many questions about my country and my education, as well as the circumstances which led me to Vienna. I answered them all briefly, which seemed to satisfy him. At the end he asked me how many opera texts I had written, to which I answered, "None, sire." "Fine," he answered with a smile, "then we will have a virgin muse."[11]

Da Ponte must indeed have had powerful advocates for Joseph II to take a chance on such an inexperienced writer. His salary was 1,200 florins, as well as the profits from the sale of libretti in book form—a supplementary income tied to his success. At about this time Da Ponte met Mozart for the first time, in the home of Baron Wetzlar, who was likewise a convert to Christianity. Mozart's first reference to Da Ponte is guarded and rather skeptical, concerned only with his potential authorship of an opera libretto.

> The Italian *opera buffa* has started again here and is very popular. The *buffo* is particularly good—his name is Benucci. I have looked through at least a hundred libretti and more, but I have hardly found a single one which satisfies me; that is to say, so many alterations would have to be made here and there that even if-a poet would undertake to make them, it would be easier for him to write a completely new text—which indeed it is always best to do. Our poet here is now a certain Abbate da Ponte. He has an enormous amount to do in revising pieces for the theater, and he has to write *per obbligo* an entirely new libretto for Salieri, which will take him two months. He has promised after that to write a new libretto for me. But who knows if he will be able to keep his word—or will want to? For, as you are aware, these Italian gentlemen are very civil to your face. Enough, we know them! If he is in league with Salieri, I will never get anything out of him. But indeed I would dearly love to show what I can do in an Italian opera. (May 7, 1783)

Did Mozart know how inexperienced Da Ponte was, that he had to read twenty libretti to learn how an opera text is made? But Da Ponte would not be discouraged. He wrote for Salieri, Vicente Martín y Soler, Gazzaniga, Storace, and others, as well as for Mozart, and he achieved enormous success with the Mozart operas and Martín y Soler's *Una cosa rara*. But he was soon so entangled in the intrigues

and petty jealousies of the theater that he was practically surrounded
by enemies and envious rivals. He himself showed not a trace of self-
restraint but joined actively in the fray, always full of snide humor and
spiteful remarks. Nevertheless, he had a powerful supporter in Joseph
II. After the emperor's death, Da Ponte could stay in Vienna no longer.
Leopold II, who at first had more important things on his mind than the
theater, took little interest in the guilt or innocence of individuals
involved in theater scandals. He wanted peace on this front, and Da
Ponte was now nothing but trouble. Da Ponte was given no more
audiences, and that created further intrigue; he was finally asked to
leave Vienna. He made one last attempt and waylaid the emperor in
Trieste, where an emotional and histrionic meeting ensued, but
Leopold II refused to engage him further. Da Ponte seemed to create
turmoil and "accidents"; most of the singers opposed him, and he had
no supporters left.

Da Ponte had to make a completely new start, and he did it in two
ways. He married a young Englishwoman whom he had known only
briefly, and in 1792 went with her—again with many detours—to
London. His wife, Nancy Grahl, was twenty years younger than he and
was the daughter of a prosperous Jewish merchant. He hardly knew
her, but he was not after her father's wealth, which he refused to
touch—boastfully commenting that he was well provided for, though
at this point he was actually destitute. Banished from his homeland,
living unemployed in a country whose language he had yet to learn,
and at once a married Catholic priest and the author of Mozart's great
operas—a bizarre fate. But in London he found no peace either. He
soon became assistant to the opera manager William Taylor, functioned as an administrator at the theater, wrote further opera libretti,
and ran the theater café with his wife. Later he owned a printing works
and a publishing house that issued his own libretti in book form. He
also founded an antiquarian book business and an Italian bookshop,
and later became part owner of a piano factory and a music publishing
house. All these activities were overshadowed by numerous business
dealings (often in the interests of his theater management) that drove
him to the wall again and again; several times he barely escaped
debtors' prison. In London, too, he was constantly involved in theater
intrigues. He vacillated constantly between the heights and the
depths, success and failure, wealth and poverty. On the other hand,

he had a very happy marriage, in a way the only point of stability amid the wild fluctuations of his life. Perhaps he felt reconciled to his Jewish background, at home in exile.

But his days in London were also numbered. In 1805 Da Ponte went to America, having sent his wife and children ahead of him. Here he experienced the same changeable fortunes—now rich, now poor, sometimes involved in business ventures and living in luxury, yet overtaken again and again by sudden adversity. In America his failures were outnumbered by his successes, which generally involved Italian language and literature and the opera. Da Ponte lectured on Italy, gave Italian lessons, published articles, and eventually became the first professor of Italian language and literature at Columbia College in New York. He also arranged the first visit of an Italian opera troupe to New York, which resulted in the first performance of *Don Giovanni* in that city. His success as an impresario encouraged him to collect funds for New York's first opera house, which was erected in 1832—one of the high points of his life. He died six years later, when he was almost ninety.

Da Ponte spent most of his life abroad, yet he was always concerned with the dissemination of Italian literature. He had a wide variety of professional occupations but always thought of himself as an Italian poet. He had become a Catholic priest against his will and spent his entire life at the side of the women he loved, usually in long-standing relationships. His love life culminated in forty years with his wife, Nancy, a marriage in which constancy and devotion were curiously mingled with restlessness and agitation. (His memoirs, clearly modeled on those of his friend Casanova, generally reveal a character who was the opposite of that carefree adventurer. Their fates had many points in common, however, despite their essentially different natures.)

The events of Da Ponte's brilliant life did not take place behind a curtain of mystery. Everyone knew that he was a priest, nor were his love affairs a secret. In Vienna he was the protector of a woman and child who shared his lodgings for ten years, and his mistress was an Italian opera singer famous for her escapades. But in a sense Da Ponte was unusually faithful, always in search of an idyllic family life, a refuge in his exile, which only Nancy was able to provide. He was equally constant in his friendships, often with people of very different persuasions, and these friendships survived considerable strain, ill feeling, and many stormy episodes. When he made promises, however boastful and unrealistic, he did not behave like a gambler or con man but simply tried to keep his word. Perhaps this was part of the reason why he always managed to win friends: he knew how to convince people of his exceptional human qualities and allay suspicions that he was simply an adventurer.

Mozart's initial skepticism soon proved unfounded. For although Da Ponte worked with Salieri, he nevertheless kept his promise to Mozart. That was quite unusual and gave evidence of a strong character. On the other hand, there was no enmity between Mozart and Salieri, as is frequently maintained. Salieri was in a powerful position, and not even a Mozart could displace him. He sincerely admired Mozart, which did not prevent him from scheming against him when his own interests were involved. Da Ponte usually stood behind Mozart in such conflicts, although he was somewhat dependent on Salieri, who had, after all, recommended him to the emperor. Da Ponte's relations with Mozart must have been close and very friendly, and this is not disproved by the fact that their intimacy is nowhere confirmed in letters. Why would they have corresponded when they regularly met and worked together in Vienna?

Da Ponte belonged to Mozart's close circle of friends, all of whom were connected in various ways. And Da Ponte was also one of those exceptional people with whom Mozart preferred to associate— outsiders, nonconformists, those under threat or pursued by fate, whose place in society was not already established at birth.

THE EMPEROR FORBIDS/THE EMPEROR COMMANDS

Lorenzo Da Ponte's memoirs indicate that Mozart himself selected Beaumarchais's comedy *Le mariage de Figaro* as an opera subject and asked Da Ponte to work it up into a suitable libretto. However unreliable Da Ponte may be (especially with dates), he would hardly have let someone else take credit if he had really been the originator of this bold idea. And although his narrative is often highly embellished, certain details have historical credibility. The idea for this opera was bold in three ways: first, the work had not been commissioned and thus had to be accepted by the opera management; second, the play had already been banned from public performance, and an operatic version would undoubtedly meet with considerable difficulties; and third, the adaptation of such a lengthy play built on fast, lively dialogue into a singable libretto posed serious dramaturgical problems. Moreover, Da Ponte was not an experienced librettist but a beginner.

Although Da Ponte met with skepticism everywhere, he had plenty of confidence and was eager to grapple with these difficulties. Mozart believed it would be impossible to get a commission because he was familiar with the theater and its intrigues. Baron Wetzlar had doubts because the play had already been banned, but he was prepared to offer his patronage. Da Ponte wrote:

> Baron Wetzlar offered me a very respectable fee for the text. He would then have the opera performed in London or France if it was forbidden in Vienna. But I declined his offer and suggested that we write the text and music without letting anyone know about it, then wait for an opportune moment to offer it to the management or the emperor himself, and I courageously volunteered to carry out this project. . . . Thus we set to work side by side; each part of the text was set to music by Mozart as soon as I had written it, and in six weeks the work was finished.[12]

It cannot have been quite that simple . . .

We can believe that Da Ponte was a suitable diplomat and negotiator for this project even without knowing the details of his interview with the emperor. It is also possible that the opera was more or less "finished" when he began trying to arrange a performance—especially since both composer and librettist thought it necessary to prove (especially to the emperor) that they had "toned down" the play. For Joseph II had recently issued a directive to the minister of police, Count Pergen, in which he expressed himself quite clearly:

> I have learned that a German translation of the well-known comedy *Le mariage de Figaro* is being considered for the Kärntertor theater. Since this play contains much that is offensive, I order the censor to either reject it entirely, or to have changes made that would enable him to take

responsibility for the performance of this work and the impression it might create.[13]

Emanuel Schikaneder, who planned to perform the play with his troupe three days later, on February 3, 1785, learned of the emperor's directive from placards announcing that the play was "approved for publication but not for performance." Thereupon the text was immediately printed, and the translator, Johann Rautenstrauch, would not be deterred from dedicating the edition "to the memory of 200 ducats"—the fee he lost as a result of the ban.[14]

The emperor was not disturbed by such jibes. He was undoubtedly well informed about the varied history of this comedy up to its Paris premiere the previous year. At first it had been banned there as well, but it had circulated among the frivolous nobility, who celebrated what was aimed against them. Even a private performance at the home of Count d'Artois was banned, but the play only became more and more famous, until finally a premiere at the Comédie Française could be avoided no longer. The performance began in turmoil and commotion—an unmistakable fanfare for the play's subsequent triumph. Later the royal couple tactlessly appeared at the theater. Joseph II was understandably concerned to avoid a sensation and doubtless proceeded more judiciously than his royal sister Marie Antoinette. His note to the minister of police did not institute a direct ban but simply demanded precautions that would keep the situation under control.

Beaumarchais's text indeed contains some strong passages. The intent is especially clear in Figaro's monologue in act V, scene 3, where Figaro lashes out in opposition to the count and his plan to rape Susanna—for the feudal *droit du seigneur* cannot be described otherwise. He expresses himself with such force that the entire social system is unmistakably called into question. Here the prerevolutionary undertone is clearly perceptible.

No, my lord count, you shan't have her, you shall not have her! Do you think you are a great intellect just because you are a great nobleman? Do nobility, wealth, and rank make you so proud? What have you done to deserve such advantages? You took the trouble to be born, nothing

more. Otherwise you are a very ordinary man. Whereas I, lost in the
obscure crowd, have had to utilize more knowledge and ingenuity to
survive and work my way up than was necessary to rule all of Spain for
a century! And you want to measure yourself against me . . .

Count Almaviva's valet then describes his life so far as a vain attempt
to make use of his intelligence, which always results in his being
maltreated, persecuted, and thrown in prison because of repeated
clashes with his superiors.

> Locally there was much debate about economic surplus, and since one
> doesn't have to own something to talk about it, I wrote a treatise on the
> significance of money, in which I lost myself in long-winded considera-
> tions of its purpose—with the result that I again landed in prison. Oh,
> how I would like to get my hands on one of the powers that be, who are
> so quick to condemn the evil they themselves have created, when his
> pride has been broken by disgrace! I would tell him that the freedom to
> criticize only makes praise more valuable, and that only small minds
> are irritated by the scribblings of small people.[15]

Da Ponte very wisely omitted this and similar passages from his
version, but it is not only such individual statements that give the play
its highly political character. More important, it presents a drastic and
ruthless picture of domestic conditions among the nobility—the reverse side, more or less, of their social exterior—and this picture
surely applied to a large majority of Austrian aristocrats. Yet Da Ponte
made no changes in the dramatic structure of the text. In fact, by
cutting and telescoping the dialogue, he created an even more intense
presentation of the material, doing away with comic stereotypes and
pointing up the individuality of the characters. The result was a
libretto of such richness that a dramatically sensitive composer like
Mozart was able to underscore and comment ironically on even the
smallest details, or interpret them through musical associations, by
means of orchestral color and every technical trick at his disposal
(which makes *Figaro* harder to appreciate fully than even *Don Giovanni*).

Da Ponte claimed he was able to win approval for the opera by
convincing the emperor to hear a few sample numbers with Mozart at
the piano, whereupon the emperor, supposedly satisfied that there was

*Mozart at the piano; unfinished oil painting by Mozart's
brother-in-law Joseph Lange.*

Constanze Mozart.

Mozart's two surviving sons, Karl Thomas and Franz Xaver Wolfgang (later called Wolfgang Amadeus the Younger).

Leopold Mozart.

Joseph II at the harpsichord. The emperor—pictured here in a private salon—was extremely musical and played chamber music almost daily.

Emperor Leopold II. *Emperor Joseph II.*

The Graben, in Mozart's time the most fashionable promenade of Vienna; at right is the Trattnerhof, with sculpted figures on the cornice.

The Michaelerplatz, with the Michaelerkirche and the Burgtheater (far right).

Countess Maria Wilhelmine Thun.

Prince Karl Lichnowsky.

Fanny Arnstein.

Initiation ceremony at a Masonic lodge. The blindfold is removed from the seeker's eyes only after completion of the journey. A bishop is among those present (middle of wall at right). The first figure in right foreground is said to be Mozart.

Angelo Soliman, a lodge brother of Mozart's. Brought from Africa
as a slave, he eventually entered the service of Prince
Liechtenstein and was later freed. After his death, at the behest of
Emperor Francis II, he was stuffed like an animal and put on
display at the museum.

Certificate of membership from Mozart's lodge, Zur gekrönten Hoffnung (Crowned Hope).

Fellow Craft apron (of white deerskin) from the lodge Zur gekrönten Hoffnung; the degree is indicated by the number of silk rosettes.

Contemporary illustrations for Die Zauberflöte. *Act I, Scene 15: Tamino tames wild animals—here a horde of apes—with his flute playing. The three temples in the background are clearly inscribed:* Vernunft (Reason), Weisheit (Wisdom), Natur (Nature).

Sarastro makes his first entrance in imperial splendor on a wagon pulled by six lions, in stark contrast to the idealizations common today.

Tamino — Hier sind die Schreckensforten
Achtundzwanzigster Auftritt. II Act

*In the trial scene, the waterfall (left) and the fire (right) are
clearly to be seen. In addition to the two Men in Armor, two
priests are pictured, but it is unclear whether they are men
or women; the final chorus (known as the "Priests' Chorus")
is also scored for women's voices.*

In 1791 François Blanchard's attempts to fly created a sensation in Vienna. After several failures he made a short balloon flight on July 6. Mozart took up this theme immediately in Die Zauberflöte.

The beginning of the "Lacrymosa" from the Requiem, presumably the last notes written by Mozart. The last two bars are in the hand of Mozart's pupil Joseph Eybler.

Die Metropolitankirche zum Hal. Stephan in Wien.

L'Eglise cathédrale de Saint Etienne à Vienne.

Wien und Mainz bey Artaria Compf.

St. Stephen's Cathedral. Mozart's funeral service was held in a small chapel to the left of the main entrance (at far right of picture under the small "Heidenturm," or Tower of Pagans). Afterward the coffin was placed on a bier in the Crucifix Chapel (entrance to the crypt).

nothing "offensive" in the work, personally instructed the theater management to produce it. Be that as it may, it must be emphasized that *Figaro* represented an absolute novelty on the opera stage. It was a true-to-life music drama set entirely in social reality, undiluted by traditional genre characteristics, unencumbered by rules governing the portrayal of "high" and "low" characters on the stage. Although its descriptions of the social milieu are unvarnished, it is free of harmful or inflammatory invective (much more so than Beaumarchais's text); its social criticism is actually more consistent than that of the original play. The music avoids trivialization and gives each detail crucial dramatic significance. In short, it was a work that reflected its times in a way never before seen on the operatic stage (its effect was unequaled even by Offenbach's operettas); that was the most shocking thing about this opera, and Joseph II had a special interest in bringing it to the stage.[16]

Le nozze di Figaro is a political opera not only in the sense of being immediately relevant to its times but also because it was a contribution to Josephine domestic policy. It may be that when they first set out on this hazardous venture, Mozart and Da Ponte were thinking only of what a sensation the play was in France and of the fact that it had been banned in Vienna, which guaranteed that it would attract attention. Nevertheless, they must have had some interest in its content and its political implications. There was certainly no danger that their explosive subject would harm them or make them social outcasts. Even Leopold Mozart, although clearly apprehensive by nature, expressed no such concern when he heard about the opera. He saw only musical-dramatic problems, not political ones.

> I know the play. It is very long-winded, and the translation from the French will surely have to be reworked to make an effective opera. God grant that the project turns out well. I have no doubts about the music, but it will cost him much effort and disputation before the libretto finally achieves a form that will suit his purposes.
>
> (November 11, 1785)

The nature of this work made it perfect for the emperor's plans, and his order that the opera be performed in Vienna was not a concession, an accommodation, or a reconsideration of his doubts about the original play—it was a political calculation. (The first performances of Mozart's opera in Italy, in Monza and Florence, came about at the personal suggestion of Joseph II.)

The Viennese theater appealed to a broad public, especially the bourgeoisie; with its low admission fees, it was among the few pleasures almost everyone could afford. To present the "follies of a day" to such audiences might easily lead to "follies of the night"—riots, vandalism, and incitement to insubordination. The people might understand it as an invitation to reconsider their situation and not to let the behavior of the aristocracy go unanswered. Since it was generally known that the emperor wished to abolish the legal privileges of the nobility and make its members subject to the same laws as the common man, a performance at the imperial Burgtheater, before a broad public, would seem like an official inducement to interpret the emperor's abrogation of aristocratic privilege as approbation of universal equality. Yet the emperor was not a revolutionary but an autocratic monarch (though the two are still often confused today[17]).

A performance by the Italian company of the Hofoper would send entirely different messages. The high admission prices alone insured a different class of patron, and the Hofoper embodied old court traditions, notably retention of the Italian language, which ordinary audiences did not understand. Most boxes were permanently reserved by the various noble families, who thus had guaranteed seats even if they arrived late. Especially now that social affairs rarely took place at the imperial court, the opera became a center of entertainment. With *Le nozze di Figaro*, the clear social distinction between theater and opera audiences also meant two equally distinct perspectives on the story: the theater public would have seen a somewhat degenerate, unsympathetic nobility through Figaro's eyes, while at the opera the nobility would be confronted with a representative of their own class and with servants who would not silently tolerate whatever befell them. By expressly ordering this subject matter to be presented at the Hofoper, the emperor was creating a political issue, regardless of whether the work succeeded or failed. From this viewpoint, the servant who defends his rights was only of minor interest; it was far more important to hold a mirror up to the nobility. There could be no misunderstanding on this score, and as far as imperial policy was concerned there was no danger of "offensiveness."

This opera secretly advocated a basic element of Josephine domestic policy: the elimination of aristocratic privilege, and judicial equality for all subjects. Within the framework of Josephine reforms the text was hardly revolutionary; it would have been so only if the emperor had been preserving and defending the conditions it described. Rather, *Figaro* served as a signal, a convenient form of propaganda that furthered the goals of Josephinism. Thus, Mozart took up a frontline position in defense of Josephine policy, which surely corresponded to his own political views, at least insofar as they are expressed in this opera.

JOSEPHINISM

If we were to describe in a few words the fundamental ideas behind Josephine reform policy—what could be called its national goal—we could say that Joseph II wanted a modern, economically stable, "enlightened" state, militarily unassailable and governed by a sovereign whose chief interest was the overall well-being of the polity and its inhabitants. Although this objective may sound reasonable and unproblematic, its realization entailed a reform program that changed the very structure of the traditional state. The emperor endeavored to stimulate the economy through freedom of trade and new ways of fostering industry and manufacturing; he sought to improve roads, increase the return on agricultural production through better methods of cultivation and livestock breeding, promote public health, and encourage population growth. He reorganized the judicial system and introduced a civil code of law, made improvements in education, and liberalized censorship. At the same time, he limited the rights of the governing estates, gradually did away with aristocratic privileges, and reduced the power of the Church. Yet Joseph II was neither a freethinker nor a democrat. On the contrary, he wished to strengthen centralized autocratic power, to bolster his position in a pyramidal system of government so that the sovereign would not be answerable to any other institution, be it the estates of the realm, which still had some financial and political authority, or the Church, whose many claims made it a very powerful factor.

It was a bold program, because it was prepared to break with all inherited laws and traditions, and it was progressive, because it did not reflect the tyranny of a wasteful, complacent autocrat but was meant to enhance the well-being of the entire population. However, it was also despotic, because the emperor was uninterested in his subjects' opinions of his plans; he ruthlessly pursued whatever course he considered reasonable and single-mindedly ignored even well-meaning criticism.

Many of the Josephine reforms had already begun under Maria Theresa, and to a certain extent Joseph II represented continuity in the Habsburg regime. With the beginning of his reign in December 1780, however, policies were introduced more swiftly and carried out more consistently, thus increasing the rate at which their dynamic consequences were felt. Joseph II was carried along on a wave of sympathy so great that even those who had to relinquish some of their hereditary claims of ownership did not deny the emperor their respect, or were at least very restrained in their public criticism. Many clergymen, especially, understood and approved Joseph's program, which did not spring from anti-Catholic sentiment but was part of a widespread movement for ecclesiastical reform that sought to emphasize the pastoral and social responsibilities of the Church, and to do away with contemplative monastic orders, superstitious customs, and lavish ceremonies that had little to do with true faith.

Joseph's reign began with several thunderbolts that received great attention all over Europe. The Patent of Tolerance (1781) proclaimed total religious freedom and forbade curtailment of civil liberties on religious grounds. For Jews especially, this was a decided improvement, even though it did not bring about an end to all discrimination. A separate decree detailed the special regulations pertaining to Jews: freedom of movement was still restricted; a special tax had to be paid; and German was the required language for all official communication. On the other hand, many discriminatory rules were abolished: beards and special clothing were no longer obligatory; Jews could now visit theaters and public entertainments; complete freedom of trade was guaranteed; the *Leibmaut* was abolished; and Jewish dignitaries were even allowed to wear rapiers. This law made clear, however, that the new regulations were purely a result of economic considerations; an increase in the Jewish population was by no means desired.

None of the Josephine reforms caused such a stir as the dissolution of the contemplative monasteries and the sale of Church property to finance salaries and pensions for former monks and nuns. More than 700 monasteries and convents were closed, and as a result, approximately 3,000 new parishes and pastorates were established. It is clear from this restructuring alone that the emperor was not opposed to the Church as such, but he was determined to curtail its economic power, cancel its special privileges, and bring about its integration into the state, which had a greater interest in public education and spiritual welfare than in perpetuating sinecures and parasitism. Also at issue was the Church's allegiance to papal authority as a state within a state; many reformers, even within the Church itself, advocated reorganization along the lines of a state church. The bishops' competence was questioned, along with matters dealing with the education of priests. Naturally, the Church also had a conservative faction opposed to reforms, grouped largely around the archbishop of Vienna, Christoph Bartholomäus Anton Migazzi. After Pope Pius VI's unsuccessful visit to Vienna, however, Migazzi's influence waned. Further plans for an "enlightened" state church could not be realized because of the Turkish war and the emperor's premature death.

But church policy was only one aspect of Josephine reform, which left no stone unturned when the emperor saw need for improvement. He banned the wearing of corsets (because it was unhealthy), the ringing of bells during thunderstorms (a harmless superstition), the baking of honeycakes (because they were supposedly bad for the digestion)—Joseph was not above wanting to control everything himself. Of course many of these regulations led to bitterness and anger among the population, but none was detested as much as the so-called Burial Decree. Its original objective was to place cemeteries outside the city limits for hygienic reasons, which drew no objections. But then the emperor decided that he should ban coffins in order to save wood, and that bodies should be buried in linen sacks to allow faster decomposition. The protests against this "enlightened" ordinance were so strong that it had to be rescinded after a few months, and Joseph II was heard to comment resignedly on widespread public foolishness in the guise of piety. Although his reforms had clear objectives, he was blind to the unreasonableness of his demands and did not understand the necessity for adequate preparation and proper timing.

Joseph was most consistent about his two most cherished issues: Church reform and the elimination of aristocratic privileges. At first he found support among some members of the nobility. The abolition of serfdom met with almost no opposition, although it drastically affected the organization and profits of the large estates. The elimination of the nobility's special status in the criminal code was accepted unwillingly, however, because it was now possible to see a count subjected to the degrading punishment of sweeping the streets with shaven head if he had committed a criminal offense. These were bitter pills for the nobility to swallow. There were many ways in which the emperor served notice that the old privileges were a thing of the past. Court etiquette was reduced to a minimum, and more and more members of the bourgeoisie came into high government positions; many later received titles themselves. But Joseph II made it clear enough that such ennoblements meant nothing to him, however fanciful some recipients may have been in the creation of coats of arms and other heraldic devices. He considered everyone equally as subjects and thus demanded their total equality, especially before the law.

Joseph II was so convinced of the justice and effectiveness of his policies that he saw no reason for strict censorship in his empire. He did not renounce censorship entirely, but he wanted to moderate its effect on all publication, which in a sense included the theater. This is best illustrated by the example of *Figaro*. Despite the ban on theater productions, the operatic version was approved, and the emperor saw no danger in allowing the text of the original play to be published. Rautenstrauch was thus free to print and sell his translation of Beaumarchais's comedy. On the title page he quoted a passage that expressed quite accurately the emperor's opinion of censorship: "Stupidities that appear in print are only important where their free circulation is restricted. Fifth act, third scene."[18]

The emperor's ideas on censorship are crucial to his concept of the state. They show that Joseph II had learned his lesson about natural rights, individual freedom, and public welfare, and they exemplify his implementation of Enlightenment thought and his perception of himself as an educator and benefactor. Under Maria Theresa the responsibility for censorship lay first in the hands of the Jesuits. After the Jesuit orders were banned, attempts were made to transfer censorship duties to government commissions, but they failed because of the

MONUMENT IOSEPHS II.

Memorial leaflet on the death of Joseph II. The stones of the pyramid are inscribed with his achievements, among which are "elimination of religious abuses," "introduction of tolerance," "abolition of serfdom," "freedom of the press," and "abolition of burials in cities."

empress's halfheartedness in all matters pertaining to the Church. Among the first reforms of Joseph's reign were those dealing with censorship, which was entirely taken over by the government and centralized for the whole empire. The connection with Church reform is obvious and may even have prompted this move. For the censor proved to be a very effective instrument in furthering the emperor's goal of a state church and in trimming the power of the Curia Romana, which meddled in the affairs of all Church institutions.

According to the new principles, which went hand in hand with the tolerance laws, everything "systematically" directed against religion was forbidden, as well as any writings that subjected religion to "public mockery and ridicule." On the other hand, there was nothing to prevent reform Catholicism from trying to reconcile the Church with reason and rationalism; superstition and miracle working had no place here. In keeping with the idea of state control, clergymen were not allowed to participate in the censorship process, even when religious writings were involved. On the contrary, censorship was nowhere stricter than with the Church, especially when it tried to question the primacy of state power. Thus, the distribution of at least four papal bulls was prohibited. When a prayer book was published without being submitted to the censor, the authorities handed down a harsh punishment that was then increased by the emperor himself. Where the Church was concerned, censorship truly deserved its name; it was the emperor's most important means of propagating reform Catholicism and freeing his subjects from the spiritual domination of Rome.

The basic principle of the new censorship regulations was simply to forbid only what was harmful to the state. Yet everything depended on the practical interpretation of this none too reassuring formulation. Joseph II was so deeply committed to the Enlightenment, by nature as well as education, that he would never have understood the words *"L'état c'est moi!"* (which he too believed) as condoning self-righteous tyranny. Rather, he endeavored to guarantee the rights of all his subjects. To that end he initiated a comprehensive judicial reform that was binding on everyone, from the lowest to the highest, and applied to criminal law, civil law, and legal procedure. He believed in the basic equality of all men and recognized the individual's right to the greatest possible freedom. Even as a young man he had written in a memorandum to his mother:

All men are equal from birth: we inherit only animal life from our parents and in that there is not the slightest difference between king, count, burgher, and peasant. I believe that no divine or natural law opposes this equality.[19]

The duty of the state (i.e., of the absolute monarch) as the emperor understood it was to serve the public welfare, which itself could only be realized through the state. Such a definition carries with it the danger that even a well-meaning ruler may use despotic means to impose what he considers worthy objectives, and Joseph II was not immune to this temptation. In the matter of censorship, however, the system he established was one of the most liberal in Europe. For instance, entire publications were not rejected merely because a few isolated passages were deemed offensive. Moreover, "works dealing with science and the arts" were not subject to censorship at all—except for those dealing with the state, which had to be submitted for approval. Anything that promoted reason and enlightenment was to be approved—a broad guideline that led to occasional misunderstandings and inconsistencies, which on the whole should not be taken too seriously; Goethe's *Die Leiden des Jungen Werthers* (*The Sorrows of Young Werther*), for example, was banned for a time because of fears that it might encourage wild behavior.

An especially important development that clearly demonstrates the enlightened goals of the entire censorship policy was the general freedom of criticism, which expressly included criticism of the sovereign. This was not just empty talk for the sake of appearance, as is shown by a flood of pamphlets that began to appear in 1782, mostly in Vienna. They addressed every theme of current interest, sparing nothing and no one. (At first they were evidently more useful than damaging to the emperor.) In his censorship policy Joseph II did not emphasize a powerful state, but rather a moderate and liberal one, more disposed to trust its subjects than to control and supervise them. He even put an end to the overly strict inspection of travelers' luggage at the borders; personal possessions were not to be confiscated, even if forbidden publications were found, as long as there were not multiple copies obviously intended for distribution. Josephine censorship was thus acclaimed at home and abroad as "freedom of the press." Only a few critics, mostly from the Church, called for more stringent measures, while a few Enlightenment radicals found that the reforms did not go far enough. The emperor's practical application of censorship won valuable support for his reforms; it was especially beneficial to his Church policy and more or less fulfilled his expectations, for in general he found wide acceptance for all his actions regarding the Church. The relaxation of censorship proved that the emperor was seriously dedicated to enlightenment and rationalism.

His idea of human dignity and equality gives further proof that his commitment to reform was genuine. The state clearly recognized its duty to help those who could not provide for themselves, and the Church shared this duty through its ministry to the poor. The idea of removing geriatric care from medical institutions, however, was entirely new. For centuries the old, sick, and infirm had been packed together in charitable establishments. Now hospitals were made a separate category, and special attention was given to the promotion of medical science. In Vienna Joseph II founded the general hospital (1784), the military medical college (Josephinium, 1785), a maternity hospital, a children's clinic, and finally a mental hospital. Surgery was removed from its traditional classification as a manual trade and taught at the university, which, as of 1784, even granted surgical doctorates; thus the field was finally accorded the same importance as internal medicine. Hygiene was also taught as a discipline, for Joseph II was well aware that in wartime, for instance, more soldiers died in epidemics than in battle. Smallpox vaccinations were introduced, and great importance was attached to improvements in obstetrics and ophthalmology. The emperor was also personally involved in organizational details. He ordered that no woman be forced to give her name in the maternity hospital and that unwanted children be sent directly to the orphanage. This anonymity was a practical attempt to combat prejudice against unmarried mothers; their privacy was protected by the state. The children from the orphanage were placed with foster parents in the country; these parents received financial support from the state until the children were eight years old.

The entire school and university system was thoroughly reorganized. Joseph II tried to introduce compulsory school attendance for all children and to improve instruction comprehensively. Nor was he afraid to introduce compulsory school fees, though unlike the Prussians, he exempted the poor; moreover, instruction remained free in the primary schools. A new school was always established when a village had more than ninety children of school age. School supervision was strict and textbooks were prescribed, but the intention, at least, was that students should be taught to think and judge for themselves.

The university reforms were less successful. Church influence (especially that of the Jesuits) was indeed broken, but at the same time the universities lost their autonomy and came entirely under state control. Higher education began to resemble primary schooling: textbooks were prescribed, a student's progress was monitored through regular examinations, and the period of study was considerably shortened.[20] As a result, the university lost its status as a center of research; the professors themselves no longer engaged in research activities and indeed were prevented from doing so. The university was no longer a part of the intellectual community; its independence gone, it became a state-controlled training institute. Study abroad was forbidden, and this naturally discouraged foreigners from studying at Austrian universities. The result was a self-perpetuating isolation worsened by the absence of free scientific academies (although there were many plans for such institutions). State control may have been beneficial in other areas, but for the universities it was devastating.

Practical considerations were supremely important in the emperor's reforms. Strangely enough, this led to liberality—that is, government restraint and trust in private initiative—where one would least have expected it. In the area of economics, monopolies and guild privileges (which were especially important to the governing estates and the nobility) were so severely curtailed that they became almost superfluous. This reform led to genuine freedom of trade among the various nations of the Habsburg Empire, which were joined as an economic unit. It was hoped that private initiative as well as competition would stimulate and increase production. In trade with countries outside the empire, however, heavy tariffs were introduced, making the importation of goods extremely difficult, if not impossible.

An example of a man who profited enormously under this system was the bookseller Johann Thomas von Trattner, a notorious publisher of pirated editions who was hated by German intellectuals. His reprints hindered the importation of original editions, and his business prospered as never before. Trattner owned two paper factories, thirty-seven printing presses, and a type foundry, so that he could print in more than a hundred different typefaces; he employed over two hundred people. (The goodwill of the court, which was a necessity for such phenomenal success, can be partially explained by the fact that Joseph II himself had learned the art of printing from Trattner.)

Josephine trade policy had considerable significance in a nation whose population was steadily growing, but the empire's economy was still mostly agrarian. Food production and tax revenues were two fundamental issues that made agricultural development the government's most important domestic concern. The main goal was an increased return on agricultural output, which could hardly be achieved within the traditional system of large estates worked by peasant farmers. Apparently the abolition of serfdom was undertaken mainly for economic reasons. The peasants had to be motivated, introduced to new agrarian methods, and allowed to share in the profits; that was the central idea. Education for peasants was improved; the *Robot* (feudal tenure of land in return for agricultural services) was replaced with simple monetary payments, and the traditional tithing system was abolished in favor of a uniform profit tax. A prerequisite for these reforms and for extensive tax adjustments was an up-to-date land register, without which the calculation of payments was impossible. This land register alone took years to complete and was compiled very inadequately. For the nobility, with their vast estates, the delay meant that they were unable to obtain a broad picture of their finances in terms of income and tax liability. Perhaps they considered the entire reform package unworkable and decided to wait it out (even the land surveyors had to be trained before they could begin work). The whole plan was aimed at nothing less than a complete transformation of the established tax system, which would now have a basic property tax as its foundation, thus superseding the old system of voluntary and unreliable tax collection by the governing estates. Essentially a modified version of physiocratic models, the plan was also the first step toward abolishing the power of the governing estates in favor of a centralized autocracy. (The land survey began in 1785 and lasted until 1789; the fate of the tax reforms thus belongs to the second half of Joseph's reign and will be dealt with later.)

Joseph II pursued his reforms largely on his own initiative—he observed conditions on his frequent journeys throughout the empire and was always contemplating possible improvements. Yet he also had at his disposal a large number of well-qualified advisers and officials from both bourgeois and aristocratic circles. Many of them were "enlightened" thinkers who advocated Josephine reforms in principle, with the support of the educated bourgeoisie, scientists, and writers, and with the moral encouragement of all those who subscribed to the European Enlightenment. Small wonder that most of them were members of Viennese Masonic lodges, which were among the intellectual centers of the capital. One could even say that the most important Masonic lodges in the empire were dominated by progressive men of the Enlightenment who can more or less be described as dedicated Josephinians.

Chapter 6

MOZART AND FREEMASONRY

MOZART JOINS THE LODGE

Shortly after six one evening, Mozart walked across the Bauernmarkt toward Landskrongasse. Normally the lodge opened "at half past six o'clock," which was also the usual curtain time for opera, theater, concerts, and other evening functions; afterward people went to the salons to converse, make music, or dance, usually not before nine and often until long after midnight. Between six and six-thirty there must have been a terrible crush, since most people came in their own carriages or in hackney cabs and the streets were too narrow to accommodate so many vehicles. Attendance at lodge meetings was usually between fifty and a hundred. The Freemasons had occupied premises at the house of Baron Moser in the Landskrongasse since 1782. They rented the entire second floor for the sum of 850 florins per year. This meeting place was used by several lodges, each paying a share of the rent, heating costs, and wages for the servants, who were lodge brothers themselves. Today the house is no longer standing, but a very informative document has survived, namely, a "catalogue of all effects found in the headquarters of the honorable lodge Zur gekrönten Hoffnung in Baron Moser's house."[1]

Just inside the entrance was a small room "painted to resemble a charnel house," obviously the "dark chamber" that was the first room entered by a Seeker wishing to be initiated into the order. This room was a place for self-examination and contemplation, in this case probably appointed in black and decorated with paintings of skeletons. The Masonic rituals describe in numerous ways the journey from darkness into light, which does not omit the terrors of death but strives to overcome them. Mozart took up such thoughts in his last letter to his father. The ideas were certainly not unfamiliar to Leopold Mozart, who was himself a Freemason.

> As death, when we come to consider it closely, is the true goal of our existence, I have formed during the last few years such close relations with this best and truest friend of mankind, that his image is not only no longer terrifying to me, but is indeed very soothing and consoling! And I thank my God for graciously granting me the opportunity (you know what I mean) of learning that death is the *key* which unlocks the door to our true happiness. I never lie down at night without reflecting that—young as I am—I may not live to see another day. Yet no one of all my acquaintances could say that in company I am morose or disgruntled. For this blessing I daily thank my Creator and wish with all my heart that each one of my fellow creatures could enjoy it.
>
> (April 4, 1787)

Mozart earnestly wanted to become a Mason. He was not among the social opportunists who joined for their own personal advantage, because friends and acquaintances had joined or because it was fashionable. He was motivated by inner conviction and a personal belief in the "improvement of the human race" through self-perfection. Freemasonry meant the training of the self, practical humanity, and tolerance. In Vienna, not without reason, it represented an alliance of all who worked in the spirit of the Enlightenment—scientists, artists, writers, and physicians, as well as government officials, even those in the highest offices. They usually met once a week in their various lodges, where they occupied themselves with the initiation of new members and heard scholarly lectures. There were also more festive gatherings and concerts as the situation required.

The meeting place was large and suitably furnished for all occasions. At the entrance, in addition to the "dark chamber," were "two smaller rooms decorated with paintings à l'antique," then a third room, also "with paintings à l'antique," that served as a library. Here one could find Masonic books and periodicals, of which there were a large number in Vienna, though not always recognizable as such; some were written or edited by Freemasons to promote "enlightened" objectives among the public at large. The library also contained political magazines and scientific and literary publications for the use of the Masonic brothers. Immediately adjacent was a fourth room, again "painted in antique style," and containing among other things "three music desks." Music played a not inconsiderable role in lodge meetings, and today it is assumed with good reason that many of Mozart's numerous compositions for winds (especially those for clarinets and basset horns) were written for "Masonic ceremony" (see K. 484a/411, note). A fifth room, diagonally opposite, was "likewise painted in antique style."

In the middle was a large room. Upon entering it everyone was required to sign the *Präsenzbuch* (attendance book) held ready by the Brother Doorkeeper; to protect the secret that formed the core of the ceremonies, no outsider, or Profaner, was allowed to take part in the meeting. Any Seeker coming to the lodge for the first time had already signed a declaration that read:

> I, the undersigned, hereby give my word of honor that no one has tempted me to seek initiation into the Order of Freemasons with promises of extraordinary discoveries or worldly advantage, but rather, I take this step on my own initiative. Having been assured that in this Order nothing is undertaken against state, sovereign, religion, or public decency, I give my word as an honest man that I will divulge to no one, clergymen included, anything of what is revealed to me or of what I otherwise experience, even if I should not be accepted for initiation.[2]

Mozart was also required to sign this statement. One did not need a guarantor or sponsor in order to become a lodge member. In the extant correspondence from the lodge Zur wahren Eintracht (True Harmony), there are many letters of application such as this one:

> Honorable friend! It has always been one of my fondest wishes to come together with people who have made it their laudable goal to work

toward the enlightenment and well-being of their fellow men. I believe that in Freemasonry I have found people of this quality; for a number of reasons I am not disinclined to believe that you are one of those.[3]

Upon entering the lodge's actual meeting hall, or "middle chamber," the first thing one noticed was its size. Along the walls were 105 white chairs with iron fittings. On the east side were three steps leading to a platform on which stood two covered tables, each holding a three-armed candlestick. There were also a number of symbolic objects there, among them the gavel belonging to the Master of the Lodge. The windows were covered. This room is described in the catalogue of effects as "painted in the Corinthian manner, with figures and hieroglyphs." (From this description, we can surmise that a painting in the Historisches Museum der Stadt Wien, *Initiation in a Viennese Lodge*, represents the meeting hall at Baron Moser's house in the Landkrongasse.[4]) When a member was to be promoted to Master, the lodge temple, including the altar, was hung with black cloth. "Death's heads are affixed to the north and south walls and behind the altar. Three skeletons appear instead of candlesticks at the corners of the Master's table."

Before the meeting opened, the lodge brothers donned their garments and insignia: a stonemason's apron of white leather; white gloves symbolic of purity; a small ivory key on a leather band as a sign of secrecy; a small trowel, its three corners representing wisdom, beauty, and strength; and a shining five-pointed star representing the sun, which illuminates the earth with its rays. Mozart's lodge paraphernalia have disappeared, as has the parchment certificate confirming his membership, a document richly adorned with symbols and representations.

> The candidate's insignia are on the treasurer's table, in the blue-lined apron adorned with three blue triangles. A sufficient number of black cloaks must be made available. The brothers don their garments in the lodge and do not let themselves be seen outside the hall. The aprons are tied on over the cloaks. The Master of Ceremonies remains without a cloak until he no longer needs to leave the hall. The candidate may not leave the dressing room.

When it is established that the lodge has been sealed to prevent eavesdropping by outsiders, "the Master of the Lodge strikes the altar

Lodges issued such insignia as a trowel (for an Entered Apprentice), a square (for a Master), and in some cases a key (as a symbol of secrecy).

three times: these strokes are then repeated by the two Wardens with the pommels of their rapiers." After the session is opened, "everyone speaks in a somewhat quieter voice."

> MASTER OF THE LODGE: Worthy brothers. What is the Sign of the Master?
>
> *(All brothers make the Sign once.)*
>
> FIRST WARDEN: Worthy brothers, help the venerable Master to open the lodge.
>
> *(All brothers make the Sign of the Master two more times. They take their seats and sing the Song of the Master. During the first journey:)*
>
> SECOND WARDEN *(by the southern death's head)*: Our whole life is only a journey toward death.
>
> MASTER OF THE LODGE *(during a pause behind the altar, striking sharply with his gavel)*: Be mindful of death!
>
> SECOND WARDEN *(by the northern death's head)*: Only the fool arms

himself with obliviousness against the terrors of death. It is more terrible if unforeseen.

(During the second journey:)

SECOND WARDEN *(in the south)*: Early acquaintance with death is the best schooling in life.

MASTER OF THE LODGE *(as above)*: Be mindful of death, it is inevitable.

SECOND WARDEN *(in the north)*: Mindfulness of death is a consolation for the despondent, a profitable warning for the cheerful.

(During the third journey:)

SECOND WARDEN *(in the south)*: The journey toward death is the journey toward our goal of perfection.

MASTER OF THE LODGE: Be mindful of death, perhaps it is near at hand.

SECOND WARDEN *(in the north)*: The gloating misanthropist may tremble before death, which for him is the henchman who carries him off to his execution. To the friend of suffering humanity he is a bearer of glad tidings, who invites him to enjoy forever the fruits of his magnanimity.

(After the journeys are completed, the two wardens suddenly turn the candidate so that coffin and altar are directly before his eyes.)

MASTER OF THE LODGE *(after a pause)*: The mourning in which our temple is shrouded might displease you. Hear the reason. . . .[5]

This opening of a Master ritual helps clarify what Mozart wrote in his last letter to his father. Mozart first experienced this ritual when he himself was promoted to Master in the spring of 1785, and then many times after that.

Lodge membership was not a replacement for religious belief but a form of practical Christian faith that was not understood to be in any way opposed to the Church. A long list of Catholic priests were members of Viennese lodges during the Josephine period.[6] Two papal bulls (1738 and 1751) condemned Freemasons as heretics, but papal opinion was not valued very highly at a time when the pope's influence was diminishing and the Church was the object of a reform movement. In the Habsburg lands there were even bishops who had joined the order. But the religious question is less important for the Josephine period than the political character of the lodges, which enjoyed a surge of popularity in connection with imperial reforms under the banner of the Enlightenment, yet quickly collapsed when the emperor sought to bring them under his control with the Freemasonry Act.

On December 5, 1784, Mozart was put up for membership in the lodge Zur Wohltätigkeit (Beneficence), and he was initiated on December 14. Mention of his lodge membership of almost seven years to the day is all but nonexistent in his surviving correspondence. Only his letters to Michael Puchberg, treasurer of the lodge Zur Wahrheit (Truth), contain references to Freemasonry, in the salutation "Most honorable friend and brother member!"; but even here he uses the abbreviation "O. B." (*Ordensbruder*) common in lodge circles. Nor are there any direct Masonic references in his letters to Leopold Mozart; Mozart's sister reported that her father destroyed all letters referring to the subject, but this has always been doubted by Mozart scholars. It is conceivable, however, that the traces were later obliterated. We know of at least one letter from Mozart to Puchberg that did not survive, written from Leipzig on the way to Berlin (April 28, 1789); it contained no request for money and was probably not preserved for that reason. Possibly it described a visit to a lodge in Leipzig.

This intentional (so we must assume) disappearance of letters does not seem so unforgivable when we consider that beneath the Biedermeier veneer of Francis II's reign as Austrian emperor (1792–1835), a systematic persecution and denunciation of all secret societies and "enlightened" or liberal movements was carried out. Nevertheless, much extant material from the confidential records of the Kabinettskanzlei (in the Haus-, Hof- und Staatsarchiv in Vienna) provides information on the diversity of the Viennese lodges. (This is a fine example of the double character of state intervention for purposes of suppressing opposition movements: incriminating evidence is confiscated, thus ensuring that it will be reliably documented and preserved for posterity.)

DIGRESSION: FREEMASONRY IN JOSEPHINE VIENNA

The first Masonic lodge in Vienna was founded as early as 1742. One of its members was supposedly Franz von Lothringen, father of Joseph II. Until the 1770s the Viennese lodges were of little consequence, which is not surprising in view of Maria Theresa's vehement hostility to Freemasonry. But new lodges continued to spring up, mostly under the aegis of Masonic groups in Regensburg, Breslau, and Dresden. All were dependent, however, on the Grand National Mother Lodge in Berlin, a difficult situation because of the political tensions between Prussia and the Habsburg Empire. In 1776 the Viennese lodges united to form an Austrian provincial lodge. In 1780 there were said to be approximately two hundred Freemasons in Vienna, distributed among six lodges. The reign of Joseph II definitely encouraged the immense surge of interest in Freemasonry during the following years, for the emperor's reform program had clear affinities to the humane and "enlightened" philosophy of the Freemasons.

A number of Rosicrucian elements began to spread through the lodges, which quickly led to heated factionalism. The Rosicrucians saw Freemasonry only as the preliminary stage of an esoteric science in which magic, alchemy, cabalism, and theosophy combined with chemistry and physics in the quest for the Philosopher's Stone. The Asiatic Brethren, on the other hand, were entirely devoted to their leader, Baron Heinrich von Ecker und Eckhoffen, and differed from the Rosicrucians above all in their acceptance of Jews, a practice otherwise unheard of. (Baron Otto von Gemmingen, who supposedly introduced Mozart to the lodge, was associated with the Asiatic Brethren.) The Illuminati also exerted influence in a number of lodges, especially Zur wahren Eintracht, founded in 1781. This became the most famous lodge in Vienna and is still erroneously considered the lodge most typical of Viennese Freemasonry. Its leading figure was the eminent scientist Ignaz von Born, who had made outstanding contributions to the fields of geology and metallurgy. He was highly respected among Viennese intellectuals and maintained contacts with the leading salons of the nobility; thus he had excellent connections in all circles of society. Born was also the author of several sharply satirical writings—particularly on monastic life—that showed him to be an avowed supporter of Josephine reforms.

The founding in 1784 of an Austrian national lodge brought total independence from Berlin, and several provincial lodges were established in Austria. This development paved the way for important accomplishments by Viennese Freemasons, especially since the highest government officials and the most devoted advocates of the emperor's reform policy were active in the lodges by the early 1780s. An attempt to win Joseph II over to Freemasonry ended in failure, however. The emperor was too much the rationalist to associate himself with an order that approached its praiseworthy objectives of free thought, tolerance, and practical enlightenment by way of symbolic ritual, and bound its members to secrecy, however carelessly preserved.

In the autocracies of the eighteenth century—the ancien régime as well as the Josephine reform monarchy—any secret kept from the public eye was a matter of grave political concern, for all social behavior came under the scrutiny of the reigning monarch as supreme sovereign. The pyramidal structure of the state dictated that there could not (and must not) be any horizontal or lateral power relationships. All power must originate in the sovereign, who could therefore tolerate no secrets, no special interests seeking to evade the illuminating rays of his omnipotence. The welfare (or misfortune) of each individual was entirely dependent on the autocratic ruler, and surely none was so convinced that he was serving the public welfare as Joseph II.

We should not be surprised that so many secret societies flourished in the eighteenth century. It was not simply a matter of amusement and camaraderie; the independent interests of small unorthodox groups could only be nurtured in secrecy. The authorities were not just concerned about conspiratorial groups; even a reading circle, a religious society, or a students' club could pose a threat to autocratic power. Freemasonry in its different varieties was only the most familiar and widespread secret organization, which in addition had an international network and attracted most of the freethinkers and critical minds of the age by virtue of its humanistic philosophy. The lodges provided an opportunity for their members to act as a free society of equals, protected by their isolation from the outside world. In the lodge, the only laws were imposed by the members themselves. The brothers enjoyed the right to free speech, and care was taken that nothing said in the lodge could reach the ears of the uninitiated. A general feeling of brotherhood prevailed among the different lodges; when a member was traveling, a visit to the local lodge always offered a chance to meet people of similar interests in a confidential atmosphere. The motto of the French Revolution, "Liberty, Equality, Fraternity," was anticipated here (with no actual revolutionary intent) in a type of extraterritorial society within the larger society of the autocratic state, which recognized only ruler and subject. At no time did Freemasonry have such an emancipatory character as in these years before the French Revolution.

The lodge secrets, of course, had nothing to do with the state or the supreme sovereign. They were concerned only with preserving and handing down Masonic ritual, and the only means of doing so was the oath of silence taken by the members. Different Masonic groups approached the secrets in different ways. Lodges with as many as ninety grades of membership attached more importance to the secrets than did those recognizing only the three degrees of the St. John ritual, Entered Apprentice, Fellow Craft, and Master. However, it has always been easy (and is particularly so today) to find out whatever one wishes to know. And there have always been "traitors" who revealed lodge secrets to the public. Shortly before Mozart's initiation, a short-lived Viennese magazine called *Der Spion von Wien* ("The Spy of Vienna") carried a report that disclosed certain aspects of the rituals for all three degrees. The publisher of this magazine was Thomas von Trattner, himself a Freemason, who at the time happened to be Mozart's landlord. Mozart did not have to look far for information about the brotherhood.

The vow of secrecy alone gave Freemasonry the character of a state within a state, and with it a reputation for subversiveness, even though Freemasons were supposed to refrain from any interference in affairs of state. The makeup of the membership played a significant role in this connection. In his book *Kritik und Krise* ("Critique and Crisis"), Reinhart Koselleck describes the political structure of secret societies in the autocratic state and emphasizes the many things their members had in common despite their different social backgrounds. With only a few modifications his remarks would apply to France as well as Austria.

There were the nobility, socially prestigious but without political influence; the financiers, who had economic power but were branded socially as *homines novi*; and the philosophers, who enjoyed great intellectual prestige. Out of all these different groups a new category was formed. These people had divergent, even opposite interests, but their common fate was to find no adequate place in the existing institutions of the autocratic state. The autocratic ruler kept his hand on all elements of the state's power structure—legislation, the police, and the military—and waged a bitter struggle against what was left of the governing estates, through which the new elite, at least partly represented, was able to protect its interests. This new elite had absolutely no influence on foreign policy or decisions about war and peace. . . . Thus, under the protection of the autocratic state, the new society created its own institutions, whose tasks—whether approved or merely tolerated by the state—were "social." This led to a behind-the-scenes institutionalization that could not develop its political power openly—i.e., along the lines dictated by royal legislation or within the weakened framework of the governing estates. The representatives of this society could only exercise political influence indirectly, if at all. Hence all the institutions of this new social stratum acquired a political character, and insofar as they already influenced politics and national legislation, they became instruments of indirect political power. [7]

This character of a state within a state was especially emphasized by the complete equality of all Masonic brothers, the absence of distinctions of background and social status, whether one was a prince or a prince's servant, a rich banker or a poor artist, a philosopher or a soldier, a scientist or a craftsman. (A letter dated January 14, 1776, from Mozart to Count Wenzel Johann Joseph Paar, in which he excuses himself from "our first ceremony today," begins "Dear Brother" and closes with "I remain always your most sincere br. Mozart—your most honorable—oh yes, certainly . . ." Here we observe Mozart's growing awareness of the social significance of the word "brother": he first uses it as an adopted commonplace, then as a less familiar term of respect with different applications inside and outside the lodge.)

In the "enlightened" lodges less emphasis was placed on symbols and more on the search for illumination through Enlightenment philosophy and practical reason. The work of these lodges became more and more concerned with political and social life. A major issue was the practical application of such concepts as humanity, tolerance, and charity. In the Viennese lodges, especially where (as in Zur wahren Eintracht) the latest developments in natural science and technology were discussed, we see a clear example of the paradox that enlightenment, intended for the benefit of the public, had to function under cover of secrecy. On the other hand, political self-awareness was so highly developed that the community of lodges explicitly defined itself as a state, in terms that were wisely concealed from the public and the government. In a surviving handwritten copy of the *Gesetzbuch der Provinz Österreich. Für die sehr ehrwürdige Johannis-Loge zur Wahrheit in Wien* ("Statute Book of the Province of Austria. For the very honorable lodge Zur Wahrheit in Vienna"), dated "Austria in the Orient, at Vienna, on John the Baptist's Day in the year 5786" (June 24, 1786), the first principle reads, "Freemasonry is constitutionally *democratic*, and each lodge is a *democracy.*"[8] This formulation was surely not intended to reflect a revolutionary tendency in the lodges, but it does reveal how political ideas found their way into Freemasonry.

A report by Georg Forster,[9] who visited several lodges during his stay in Vienna in 1784, characterizes the Viennese lodges as follows:

> Freemasonry is thriving. All lodges in the empire are united under one leader, Count von Dietrichstein, as National Grand Master (this includes lodges in Austria, Bohemia, Hungary, and Italy). Count Dietrichstein is said to be a Rosicrucian, but he has no power to spread Rosicrucianism or to gain the slightest advantage for it in the lodge organization. On the contrary, all Masons are working so aggressively in the spirit of enlightenment that Freemasonry might have brought about the suppression of the monasteries and many important reforms during the late empress's lifetime (for these were her objectives as well) had it not been for her untimely death. The lodge Zur wahren Eintracht is the one working most actively for enlightenment. It publishes a Freemason's journal in which everything—faith, the oath and ceremonies, and even fanaticism—is more openly discussed than at home in Saxony. The best scholars and poets are members of this lodge. They make light of the whole idea of secrecy and have transformed the entire thing into a society of rational, unprejudiced men dedicated to enlightenment. Born is Master of the Lodge there.

This description confirms that "fanaticism"—Forster's term for Rosicrucianism and other mystical elements—was also a tendency in the "enlightened" lodges. Moreover, Forster knew what he was talking about, for he had recently been ignominiously deceived at a Rosicrucian lodge in Kassel and thus had a number of reservations about Freemasonry in general. But he was impressed by the Masonic activities of several "enlightened" men whom he highly respected, most notably Ignaz von Born. With him Forster openly discussed whether

Freemasonry and the Enlightenment were not contradictory and whether there was not a danger of exploitation. But Born answered him so frankly that Forster was even prepared to join Born's lodge.

> I did it for a number of reasons. (1) Out of respect for Born. (2) Because it entails no obligations whatsoever. (3) As a political move, because I have a secure following there. All the brothers are very fond of me and would do anything to have me join them. If any good can be accomplished by Freemasonry, it will be done along the path this lodge is following in the effort to restore reason to its rightful place. The brothers are completely free of any fanaticism.

Born was obviously seeking to surround himself with like-minded men in order to strengthen his "enlightened" influence. Indeed, he made efforts to convert the lodge Zur wahren Eintracht into a Masonic academy of arts and sciences, as a prototype of or substitute for the imperial academy that had been planned but never built. To a certain extent Born was successful in this venture. At its founding in 1781 Zur wahren Eintracht had 15 members; two years later it already had 96, and in 1785 it reached its peak of 197 brothers. They maintained the collection of natural history specimens begun by Born, as well as a library of 1,900 volumes devoted primarily to natural science, and even issued a scientific magazine in addition to the *Journal für Freymaurer* ("Journal of Freemasonry"), which sought to spread this lodge's interests among the other Austrian lodges. Forster even hoped that through the influence of the scholars assembled here, he himself might be appointed to an academic chair in Vienna.

It is also interesting to see how Born responded to Forster's doubts about Freemasonry.

> I told him my objection to Freemasonry, namely that it could so easily be exploited. If he were to die or move away, all his work might be destroyed if the lodge fell into the wrong hands and became an instrument of evil. He admitted this possibility, but said that it seemed wrong to him to think about what might happen in his absence; if he is sure that he can accomplish something good during his lifetime, then he must do it. One cannot assume responsibility for the possible misuse of any human endeavor, whatever it may be. Should he abandon his efforts because of this? We would be wrong to look so far ahead, for today we must work.

Forster's report gives no indication of whether Born went into detail about the organizational methods by which he sought to link Freemasonry with support for the Josephine reform policy. Born was not only Master of his own lodge but was also secretary of the national lodge, which gave him influence over Masonic activities in all the provincial lodges of the empire. He used every means at his disposal to insure that leading positions in lodges throughout the Habsburg lands were filled with Freemasons who supported the emperor's political reforms. In some cases governors and other political leaders were made provincial Grand Masters or lodge Masters. However, since there were not enough Masons among these influential people, Born made it his task to approach new government officials before they departed to take up their provincial assignments; they were quickly initiated and promoted to Master in a crash course sometimes lasting only a week. Similar procedures were followed with travelers who paid short visits to Vienna. If they were likely to hold influential positions and were looked upon as "enlightened" men, they were also initiated and promoted as swiftly as possible. Forster is only one example; another is Leopold Mozart, who was initiated and promoted to Master within a period of sixteen days.

Born's "personnel policy" was explicitly directed against fanatical elements among the lodge brothers and was the result of very clear ideas about the mission of Freemasonry. He apparently commanded so much respect among the brothers that he managed to avoid becoming the object of discord within the lodges and retained his leading position for a long time. Although we may wonder whether Born always proceeded in the true spirit of Masonic ideals, he nevertheless led a great number of important thinkers to Freemasonry and gave it a better public reputation than it had ever had.[10]

MOZART'S WORK IN THE LODGE

We do not know the details of Mozart's entry into the lodge, only the date: December 14, 1784. There were Freemasons of all persuasions among Mozart's acquaintances. Count Franz Joseph Thun, for example, belonged to the Asiatic Brethren; Mozart had long known of the count's interest in alchemy and described him as a "peculiar but well-meaning and honorable gentleman" (March 24, 1781). But Born, spokesman for the opposing ideology, was a frequent guest at the Thun home as well. There were also many musicians among the lodge members. It would indeed seem that Freemasonry was openly discussed everywhere, as Forster confirms. At this time there were 600 to 800 Masons in the lodges of Vienna, and they were all nobles or well-to-do bourgeois. Mozart was virtually surrounded by Freemasons. To mention just one example: at least one in four of the subscribers to Mozart's concerts in the Trattnerhof in March 1784 was a documented lodge member, a ratio that is probably fairly typical of the society Mozart moved in. The only surprise is that he waited so long to join himself.

When we consider that the lodge Zur wahren Eintracht counted many "VIPs" among its members, along with scholars and writers, and even attracted a man like Joseph Haydn, it is not surprising that Mozart found his way to the lodge Zur Wohltätigkeit, whose membership was much "simpler." It was founded in 1783, and like Zur wahren Eintracht, it had its origins in the lodge Zur gekrönten Hoffnung (Crowned Hope). In 1784 it had 32 members. Naturally, there were many connections between the different lodges; two or more often shared the same meeting place, for instance. It happened that Mozart's promotion to Fellow Craft took place in Zur wahren Eintracht, which would indicate a particularly close cooperation between these lodges. Of Zur Wohltätigkeit's 32 members, only Baron von Gemmingen and Count von Lichnowsky were from the nobility; both were among the most frequent guests at Countess Thun's salon. The lodge brought honor to its name in the spring of 1784 by taking up a collection for flood victims that brought in the considerable sum of 4,184 florins—the equivalent of more than $80,000 today. This relief project was the talk of all Vienna. Was Mozart moved by such examples of practical humanity to join this lodge and no other?[11]

Mozart's first activity on behalf of the lodge was of an entirely different sort, however: he brought his father in as a member during Leopold's visit to Vienna in March 1785. We do not know what prompted this step. There was a lodge in Salzburg, Zur Fürsicht (Prosperity), founded no later than 1783 and closely connected to the Munich lodges. In addition there were said to be two Illuminati lodges in Salzburg, Apollo and Wissenschaft (Science). The Mozarts knew several members of these lodges, including some Illuminati. The elector of Bavaria had banned the Illuminati in 1784, partly because they were thought to be associated with plans to exchange the Netherlands for Bavaria, thus delivering the latter over to Habsburg domination. But it could not have been the Illuminati issue that dissuaded Leopold Mozart from joining a lodge in Salzburg, for they played an even greater role in Vienna's "enlightened" lodges. Leading lodge members in Vienna—Born, for example—were themselves Illuminati. These matters were discussed rather openly, and Leopold followed the story of the ban on the Illuminati with lively interest. After the elector issued the ban a third time, in August 1785, a harsh persecution of these groups began, and in his letters Leopold passed on to his daughter everything he heard about these events.[12] The Vienna *Journal für Freymaurer* gave detailed reports on all developments in Bavaria, including the texts of original documents and statements by Born.

However little it may conform to our traditional but questionable picture of Mozart, we must emphasize that we find him close to important political events again and again. Although his father's political views are well documented, we have no definite political statement from Mozart. At best we have hints about his convictions: once he refers to himself as an "arch-Englishman." However, we can still see Mozart as an alert and informed observer who had a lively interest in political events and ventured to address the most pressing issues of his day in his operas, with no attempt at "timelessness" or "universal relevance." That presupposes a sharp social instinct, close observation, and critical judgment.

Mozart also gave evidence of a sure instinct with regard to Freemasonry when he joined Zur Wohltätigkeit rather than Zur wahren Eintracht. The two had begun as sister lodges and both had an "enlightened" orientation, yet their later development was very different: only Wohltätigkeit, not Eintracht, would survive the chaotic period initiated by the emperor's Freemasonry Act.

Mozart frequently rendered musical services to the lodge. Music played an important role in lodge meetings; the rituals were often accompanied by ceremonial songs, and instrumental pieces were presented as well. Sometimes there were even full-length cantatas with demanding solo parts and orchestral accompaniment, in small yet colorful instrumentations. His first effort was a song (K. 468) for the *Gesellenreise* (Fellow Craft Journey). It was followed shortly by a cantata in honor of Born, *Die Maurerfreude* ("Masonic Joy," K. 471), which was performed at a festive lodge dinner attended by 84 people (including Leopold Mozart). Typically, the occasion was a new scientific development: Born had invented an "amalgamation method for separating metals" that drastically cut costs in mining and ore processing. Joseph II immediately introduced it throughout the empire, and Born was given a generous share of the profits. This lodge celebration was a clear protest against the speculative or alchemical preoccupation with metals.[13]

Mozart quickly became a kind of resident composer in his lodge. Before the end of 1785 came more songs and, in the fall, the *Mauerisches Trauermusik* (K. 477/479a), written on the deaths of two brothers and performed at their memorial service in the lodge. This is a demanding work with a large and highly varied instrumentation. Another example of Mozart's work in the lodge has come down to us purely by chance, which suggests that there were many lodge activities—especially during the next few years—of which no records have survived. In the Vienna police files are printed invitations to a concert (December 15, 1785) for the benefit of two Freemason musicians in financial difficulties. On this varied program Mozart played a piano concerto and ended with a series of free improvisations. Other works connected with Freemasonry probably include a series of songs written during this period to benefit the "new children's library" at Vienna's institute for deaf-mutes. This was a government establishment, but apparently the Freemasons supported it with gifts to be sold for cash.

THE FREEMASONRY ACT AND SIGNS OF DECLINE

The surge of prosperity that Freemasonry had enjoyed in Vienna since 1783 ended abruptly with the proclamation of the Freemasonry Act in mid-December 1785. It came like a bolt of lightning and sent the fearful running in all directions. Obviously no one had imagined that the emperor, who until now had shown no particular interest in the movement, would strike deep into its organizational structure with one blow. His choice of words was especially alarming.

> The so-called Freemason societies, whose secrets are unknown to me and whose chicanery I have until now not taken seriously, continue to multiply and are now spreading to smaller cities. Their assemblies, if unsupervised and left entirely to themselves, can be a haven for profiteers and can have a corrupting effect on law and order, religion and morals, especially in cases where people holding positions of authority fanatically band together and show grave injustice toward their subordinates who are not members of these societies.
>
> Previously in other lands the Freemasons have been punished or forbidden, and their lodges broken up, simply because they would not reveal their secrets. Although I am also ignorant of them, it is enough for me to know that these Masonic societies have engaged in some good work for their fellowmen—for charity and education; more, indeed, than in any other land. Accordingly, I herewith ordain that although I know nothing of their laws and practices, they shall be taken under the protection of the State—as long as their good work continues—and their assemblies shall be officially sanctioned.

The ordinances that followed, dealing with police supervision of the lodges, were not very drastic. At least they were not intended to destroy any essential feature of Freemasonry; they had to do exclusively with the right of assembly. The use of the term "chicanery" makes it immediately clear what the emperor thought of the Freemasons, although he did not wish to deny that they "have engaged in some good work for their fellowmen—for charity and education."

The reason for this decree is still puzzling today. Some speculate that "enlightened" brothers like Ignaz von Born had a hand in drawing it up—except for the unfriendly choice of words. Others believe that the Freemasons (and through them the Illuminati) were of use to the emperor as long as he pursued his goal of exchanging the Austrian Netherlands for Bavaria; when his plan failed, he turned his back on these supporters. However, Helmut Reinalter points to what was probably the basic reason: a secret organization is incompatible with the concept of an autocratic state and was totally unacceptable to a man as uncompromising as Joseph II. Neither must we forget that following in the wake of Freemasonry was a host of other secret societies, not all of them harmless. Obviously Joseph II knew all too well which lodges supported his reform policy or were primarily engaged in humanitarian activities and which ones had other main objectives. The word "chicanery" referred for the most part to the Rosicrucians, the Asiatic Brethren, alchemists, etc.[14]

Some secret societies were in fact quite dangerous, for example, the Fratres de Cruce. A fraternity of Rumanians from Transylvania, it was not confined to Vienna. Its Viennese membership included many supporters of the so-called Horia Uprising, which had broken out against the Hungarian nobles and landed gentry in 1784, in what is today Rumania. The rebels killed more than 100 nobles and destroyed 62 villages and 132 estates. It required a full-scale military effort to crush the rebellion, an operation that cost 4,000 lives. The unrest was touched off by the continued existence of serfdom in Hungary, an unjust tax system, and the outrageous conduct of the nobility—in other words, by the fact that Josephine reforms had not been carried out fast enough in some parts of the empire because of resistance from the nobility and the still powerful governing estates. This uprising, which received much attention throughout Europe, was a reflection on Joseph II himself and showed that he was in danger from two directions: on the one side, from members of the nobility and the governing estates who were not prepared to relinquish any of their privileges; and on the other, from those who supported the emperor but became impatient or demanded more radical measures.

It was no great problem to keep an eye on the Masonic societies in Vienna, but in the outlying Habsburg dominions they were seen as an uncontrolled menace. The problem was even reflected in the composition of their membership. In the "enlightened" lodges were the Josephinians (who, however, were not always uncritical of the emperor; their ranks would later furnish many defendants in the Jacobin trials). In other lodges, especially those with Rosicrucian leanings, most members came from the nobility and also occupied important government posts. Under existing domestic conditions, it must have been a matter of some urgency to place tighter controls on the lodges, especially since the political character of certain provincial lodges was becoming more and more obvious.

The Freemasonry Act required the lodges to comply with the following regulations: lodges could be established only in cities where the government was represented, and not in rural areas or on estates; local authorities had to be given a schedule of all meetings; a list of members and the names of officeholders had to be submitted annually (it was not necessary to give the Masonic degree of each member). Once these conditions were met, further investigation would cease. All "spurious" lodges and similar organizations were forbidden. It was decided that no more than three lodges, with a maximum of 180 members each, could be established in any one location.

Some Viennese lodges responded to this edict with a series of mergers: Zur wahren Eintracht, Zum Palmbaum (Palm Tree), and Zu den drei Adlern (Three Eagles) were incorporated into the lodge Zur Wahrheit, while Zur Wohltätigkeit, Zu den drei Feuern (Three Fires), and Zur gekrönten Hoffnung merged into Zur neugekrönten Hoffnung (New-Crowned Hope). Other lodges disbanded completely. It seems that Baron Moser's house on Landskrongasse now became the principal lodge temple in Vienna. Its 105 chairs were sufficient, for many Freemasons used the reorganization as an opportunity to leave the movement—perhaps because they sensed the emperor's obvious displeasure from the wording of the Freemasonry Act, perhaps because of increasing internal bickering among the lodge brothers. Before the edict there had been at least 600 to 800 Freemasons; thereafter a maximum of 400 members remained, whose numbers decreased again by half within another year.

In the *Journal für Freymaurer* there was at first no sense of resignation; rather, the "enlightened" wing used its pages to continue working toward specific goals. In the fall of 1786 this periodical, which was intended to provide direction and leadership for Freemasons throughout the empire, published "news" about the "scientific institutes of the two very honorable lodges Zur neugekrönten Hoffnung and Zur Wahrheit" that almost sounds like an agenda.

The lodge Zur neugekrönten Hoffnung, which will eagerly sieze any opportunity to prove itself worthy of the protection afforded it by the state, considers its main objective to be the promotion of learning and human welfare. It believes it can contribute something in this direction if it offers all brother Freemasons the opportunity to increase, maintain, and amend their knowledge in the sphere of activity where they can best serve the public good. With this intention, the lodge asked a number of its brothers for suggestions as to how such a useful plan could be materialized, and it was decided to erect a museum for the use of all brother Freemasons.[15]

The museum was to include scientific instruments and collections on natural history, as well as "technological collections on manufacturing and production." As we can see, the work is now clearly characterized by the bourgeois interest in the union of science and industrial technology. The institute was to be supplemented by a library of books and periodicals, to be open "daily from eight o'clock in the morning until nine o'clock in the evening." The collection would also include specialized literature, so that each user could "learn of each new development in his science, because a knowledge of the newest literature is indispensable to each in his discipline." Moreover, "gradually the best classical authors of all nations" were to be acquired, and "because no one can remain indifferent to the events of his own time, . . . the best political newspapers and journals." It also appears that a separate room was to hold a special lodge library, with an impressive array of publications, records, and rituals from almost all degrees and all known systems of Freemasonry. The use of all these collections was to be free of charge; they were to be financed with "regular contributions from the lodges' operating funds."

The report ends with a pledge to continue working in the same spirit as before: the lodge,

> by spreading the riches of nature before the brothers' eyes, wishes also to portray something of its generosity, which, ever industrious, is constantly producing something useful—even where no human hand tills and sows. All these preparations, which have been underway for years, had in the beginning and still have no other goal than self-perfection and the dissemination of useful knowledge to our fellowmen. . . . To this end a committee made up of lodge brothers shall investigate and consider what is still lacking in the arts and sciences, but above all in the area of technology, and how new discoveries can be made for the benefit of production and manufacturing. . . . We felt it necessary to present our honorable fellow brothers with this outline of our future activity so as to convince them that the imperial protection granted to Freemasonry will not result in our lassitude.[16]

It is very unlikely that such an ambitious plan was more than partially carried out. We do not know whether the library, the natural history specimens, or the periodical collection—all of which were extensions of previously established facilities—even existed after 1786, much less whether they were accessible on a daily basis, which would have meant an enormous organizational and financial obligation. All lodge activity after the Freemasonry Act is very scantily documented (with the exception of the new lodge Zur Wahrheit, to which we will return shortly). Obviously the remaining lodges considered it wiser to keep their files, correspondence, and other documents under lock and key, so that even later almost nothing fell into the hands of Francis II's secret police. But when historians lack source material for reasons of this kind, it does not mean that the subject of their research ceased to exist.

The original library and the natural history collection were based on extensive material that Born had made available to the lodge. As a result of the Freemasonry Act, however, Born had also "covered himself"—that is, given up Freemasonry—taking his collections with him. Thus, it is even more doubtful that the proposed facilities were established. But the plan was instructive if only as an announcement of the direction to be taken in subsequent lodge work— particularly because it was offered in the name of Zur neugekrönten Hoffnung (thus, not in the name of Born's lodge but of Mozart's).

The lodge Zur Wahrheit, in which Born still acted as Master for a time, was reestablished in January 1786 with 100 members in attendance. This lodge saw itself as the epitome of "enlightened" Freemasonry and included most of Vienna's best minds among its membership, yet it was here that quarrels quickly erupted, eventually rendering all Masonic activities untenable. The first altercation involved several brothers who had left the order as a result of the edict. Leopold Alois Hoffman, who had belonged to Zur Wohltätigkeit and was secretary to Baron von Gemmingen before receiving an academic chair in Pest, began by publishing a pamphlet against Freemasonry in general. Later his anti-Masonic activities proved him to be a malicious renegade and informer. As revealed in police records, it took him only a week to latch on to the emperor's term "chicanery" and use it to attack his former Masonic brothers. Opportunism was obviously one of this man's particular strengths. Another critic, Franz Kratter, only spoke out against Freemasonry's connection with the Illuminati: Born, especially, must have felt himself to be the target of this criticism, and he was not above intercepting letters in order to expose his detractor. What is more, he invited the unsuspecting Kratter to a meeting for the purpose of unmasking him publicly; the scene almost erupted in physical violence. Born was fully prepared to protect his position by dubious means. But the bickering grew to such proportions that after six months he left the lodge, thus precipitating its total decline. Withdrawals increased: there were 6 in the second quarter of 1786, with just a single new member (revealingly, one of the lodge servants). Henceforth there were only withdrawals: 5 in the third quarter, 30 in the fourth quarter, and another 7 at the beginning of 1787. The lodge meetings became less frequent—there were only seven between June 1786 and June 1787, the last of which was attended by a mere 24 brothers. Then activities ceased altogether, until the lodge was formally disbanded in April 1789. The last treasurer, Michael Puchberg, administered funds of over 3,000 florins at the end. [17]

The decline of this lodge has all too often been equated with the general decline of Freemasonry in Vienna. Since Born was seen as the leading figure who commanded respect from all sides, he was identified with the entire brotherhood of lodges. What effect this had outside Vienna is demonstrated by a letter from Georg Forster, in Vilna, describing a visit from a Count Gallenberg, who informed him of the situation.

> I learned from the count that the reform of Freemasonry in Austria was initially provoked by secret assemblies among the Hungarians, who are working against the emperor's new institutions. These men had used Masonic meetings as a subterfuge in order to plan their resistance. That gave rise to the ordinance that lodges may only be established in cities that have courts and tribunals, and the local authorities must be advised of each meeting. These developments have led to much divisiveness among the Freemasons in Vienna. Born and Sonnenfels have completely parted company over the matter. Born is very disturbed and frustrated, and Freemasonry has lost its good reputation. It seems to me, insofar as I am qualified to judge, that this blow has come at the right time, for the mystery cults were gaining too much influence. [18]

Forster's mistrust of Freemasonry as a force that could be exploited—by the Hungarian nobility against the emperor, in this case—and his suspicions about secret mystery cults had thus been confirmed. He could not have known, of course, that Born was partly responsible for the internal strife. Born had tried to make "enlightenment" and support for imperial reforms an integral part of lodge work. When it became clear what the emperor thought of the lodges, he was placed in an awkward position. He, who had used lodge work as a political instrument, now saw himself confronted by critics who were pressing for greater political independence. Born repelled these attacks by means inimical to the spirit of Freemasonry. This problem lay at the heart of the infamous "auto-da-fé" against Kratter, which triggered a veritable flood of pamphlets.

Mozart definitely took no part in this memorable meeting of March 10, 1786, which almost amounted to a secret trial of Kratter. On that day he was composing two new arias for a private performance of *Idomeneo* in the Palais Auersperg. But he was undoubtedly informed later about these events, which caused such a sensation among Viennese Freemasons.[19]

MOZART DOES (NOT) LEAVE THE LODGE

Mozart's lodge, Zur neugekrönten Hoffnung, did not entirely escape the symptoms of decline. It had been reestablished in January 1786 with 116 members. Here as well, there seem to have been withdrawals, probably in large numbers. But in 1786 and 1787 there were numerous initiations and promotions, and later there was even an increase in membership: from 1789 to 1790 the number of lodge brothers rose from 79 to 89. Obviously this lodge, after a period of reorganization was able to rethink its Masonic goals and find a new identity. It would seem that it dealt much more cautiously with political issues and adopted a goal expressed in the name of one of its predecessors, centering its activities around charity (*Wohltätigkeit*). But it was still a secret society, albeit one sanctioned by the emperor—as long as it abided by the restrictions of the Freemasonry Act. This it apparently did, as demonstrated by the surviving annual membership lists, in which Mozart's name regularly appears. However, the lodge's complete internal correspondence, letters to and from other lodges, financial records, and minutes were so carefully guarded and hidden away that later even the secret police came away empty-handed—and we, accordingly, know little about its activities. Its sister lodge Zur Wahrheit, on the other hand, seems to have taken no precautionary measures, so that all its records are to be found today in the "confidential files" of the state archives. Curiously, we are better informed about the decline of Zur Wahrheit than about the rise of Zur neugekrönten Hoffnung. Even its many unused certificates for new members have been preserved, ornately printed sheets of parchment with pictorial and symbolic representations and a pompous text, to which only the new brother's name had to be added—futile preparations, for no new brothers were to be found. No such unused documents from Zur neugekrönten Hoffnung are extant.

The membership structure of the surviving lodge seems to have changed drastically. The largest of its predecessors, Zur gekrönten Hoffnung (1785, 195 members), was made up mostly of aristocrats. Now the aristocracy was hardly represented—a mere 7 members. Notable in comparison was the large number of apothecaries (10) and doctors (of both medicine and pharmacology), as well as manufacturers and merchants. The lodge had become a bourgeois organization. The number of influential political officeholders had similarly declined; undoubtedly these people no longer considered it opportune to belong to a lodge. Thus it seems especially noteworthy that Mozart apparently gave no thought to denying his Freemasonry. On the contrary, he continued to acknowledge it publicly, although he was heavily dependent on the emperor's patronage; Joseph II did, after all, look after the interests of his Nationaltheater personally. Either Mozart was aware that he was risking imperial disfavor and was prepared to take his chances, or he believed he could overcome this handicap by virtue of his reputation and the emperor's basic goodwill toward him. Indeed, *Don Giovanni* and *Così fan tutte* were performed in Vienna thanks to Joseph II, who made the arrangements himself. Mozart, who evidently never held a Masonic office, and the printer Christian Friedrich Wappler were the only brothers from this lodge who remained members for the entire period 1784–91. Mozart's loyalty at a time when most members were fleeing the order testifies to his unshakable optimism and his devotion to the work of the lodge. He must have been determined to stand firm against the claim that Freemasonry was nothing but "chicanery." As a Josephinian, he wanted to prove the unfairness of the emperor's judgment through patient and consistent work, without relying on the protection of the nobility.

Mozart even ventured to outline and develop in writing his own plan for a secret society. Unfortunately, this unique document has been lost, and our information about it is very sketchy. In a letter from Constanze Mozart to the publisher Breitkopf & Härtel in Leipzig, dated July 21, 1800, we read:

> I am sending you herewith some items for use in the biography, which I ask you to return to me postpaid at your convenience. 1. An essay, mostly in my husband's hand, describing an order or society called Grotta which he wished to establish. The court clarinetist here, the elder Stadler, who wrote the last part, could help me in this, but hesitates to admit his involvement because secret orders and societies are now so despised.

Further correspondence with the publisher gives no reason to suppose that the enclosures might not have arrived in Leipzig, which means that this essay by Mozart still existed in 1800 and was lost some time afterward. Neither can any clues as to the fate of this document be obtained by way of Anton Stadler, who was Mozart's lodge brother and was often with the composer during his last years.

The Mozart literature has usually mentioned this Grotta society as a typical Mozart joke. It has been suggested that he drew up a plan for a drinking club or even an "epicurean society." Yet there is not a shred of evidence to support these confident assertions (except that this secret club would otherwise not correspond to our questionable but entrenched view of Mozart). Moreover, regardless of how seriously we take this society, Mozart was clearly treading on thin ice by proposing it, for it was just such obscure secret organizations that the emperor and his newly reactivated police force found most suspicious—which was why they had been banned expressly and without exception by the Freemasonry Act. Not only was Mozart all too well acquainted with the edict through his regular lodge attendance, but he had seen evidence that the new regulations were not to be taken lightly.[20] If we decide to assume that the plan for the Grotta was serious and that Mozart was not a total fool, we will have to consider one further possibility: it could have been nothing less than a plan for the reorganization or reestablishment of a Masonic lodge, perhaps a subsidiary of his own lodge. (The history of Freemasonry is to a large degree the history of dissatisfied lodge brothers who constantly strove to improve, reform, or alter their lodge systems; as a result, many members separated from their mother lodges and founded new ones. This type of productive restlessness seems to be a distinguishing feature of Masonic activity; the brothers were already looking to the next task while still completing the previous one.) The collaboration with Stadler on this secret plan would support this theory, as would the references to a rejuvenation of Masonic activity found in Mozart's last work for the lodge, the *Kleine Freimaurerkantate* ("Little Masonic Cantata," K. 623).

Elsewhere in the empire the Freemasonry Act brought about a reorganization, but not a discontinuation, of Masonic activity. In Prague the merger of several lodges created a new one, Wahrheit und Einigkeit zu den drei Säulen (Truth and Unity at the Three Pillars). Mozart was a frequent visitor there during his sojourns in Prague and was personally acquainted with several of its members. During his last visit to this lodge in September 1791, his cantata *Die Maurerfreude* was performed in his honor. Presumably he also visited lodges on his other travels, especially during his stay in Berlin in April and May 1789. Mozart identified himself as a brother Freemason when he wrote a dedication for the *Kleine Gigue* ("Little Gigue," K. 574) in the guest book of the Saxon court organist Karl Immanuel Engel, who was also acting as music director for the Guardasoni troupe, then appearing in Leipzig. In Dresden he met with Johann Gottlieb Naumann, a very active Freemason who had himself written an opera, *Osiride (Osiris)* in 1781.[21] Mozart also traveled with his lodge brother Prince Karl von Lichnowsky; they may have visited a lodge together in Berlin. Virtually no records of these contacts have survived, so they are important only as indications of Mozart's unwavering affiliation with Freemasonry.

Soon the Freemasons were afflicted with new burdens. The outbreak of the French Revolution was immediately portrayed as a great Masonic conspiracy—partly because some people actually believed this, and partly because it was a convenient excuse to propagandize against those who made philanthropy, justice, equality, brotherhood, enlightenment, and free thought the subjects of their secret assemblies. The French Revolution indeed had many ideological points of contact with Freemasonry, at least at the beginning. However, many of the reforms demanded during the early phase of the Revolution had already been or were about to be carried out under Joseph II. As long as an oath on the constitution was demanded of the French king—that is, as long as a constitutional monarchy was retained—there was even a certain sympathy in Vienna for the goals of the Revolution, more pronounced under Leopold II than under his brother and predecessor Joseph II. The Austrian rulers shared a critical view of the moral depravity of the clergy and the nobility in France—their corruption, tyranny, injustice, arrogance, and overall incompetence at guiding the fortunes of the state. According to these Habsburgs, the primary interest of the state was the general welfare of the people. Yet the Habsburg Empire was also threatened by a spirit of revolt and separatism welling up on its periphery (particularly in Hungary and the Netherlands), although its main cause was the governing estates' refusal to surrender their traditional rights and privileges, not the revolutionary goal of a new political and social structure. The French Revolution was a beacon to the rebellious Habsburg dominions, and thus a challenge to the stability of the empire. Moreover, there had recently been social unrest in Vienna itself, brought on by the Turkish war of 1788–90 and the resulting economic slump. And there had always been periodic local rebellions and peasant uprisings against the manorial system; here, as well, the example of France offered dangerous encouragement.

Actually, there was very little risk that a revolution on the French model would take place in the Austrian monarchy—less, in fact, than in any other German state. Yet widely disparate movements in Austria (often with conflicting objectives) were influenced and stimulated by events in France. This situation allowed the opponents of Freemasonry to carry out their denunciations most effectively. The opposition included aristocrats who wished to restore the old feudal system, acting through the minister of police, Count Johann Anton Pergen; the clergy, led by Vienna's archbishop, Count Christoph Migazzi; and former Masons like Hoffmann who for various reasons had become bitter enemies. Some, Pergen and the Church among them, tried to blame Freemasonry for the Revolution; others developed plans to infiltrate the lodges in order to observe them more closely, establish new lodges loyal to the emperor, or even make them instruments of imperial policy.

Mozart's lodge, the most important in Vienna after the dissolution of Zur Wahrheit, must have been deeply concerned about such developments. Pergen was referring specifically to this lodge in a memorandum to the emperor that called for more direct action against secret organizations.

> The mania to establish such secret and deceptive organizations has never been greater than in our own time. We know for a fact that many of these secret societies, which are known under various names, are not, as they claim, dedicated solely to rational enlightenment and practical humanity. Rather, their intention is nothing less than to undermine the power and prestige of the monarchs, encourage liberation movements, and sway the people's opinion by means of a secret ruling elite. The loss of the English colonies in America was the first operation of this secret ruling elite; from there they sought to spread their influence further, and it is beyond doubt that the fall of the French monarchy was the work of such a secret society. And France was not to be the only scene of anarchy, as proved by the emissaries sent into all countries and the incendiary literature they distribute. The French Masonic lodges, especially, seek to produce similar attitudes among their brothers in other lands. A noteworthy example is a publication from the lodge in Bordeaux, which states: The wise principles of the new French constitution correspond so closely to the Masonic principles of freedom, equality, justice, tolerance, philosophy, charity, and social order that their success seems assured. Indeed, from this point on every good French citizen is worthy of being a Mason—because he is free.[22]

This letter from Bordeaux was addressed to Mozart's lodge, which found itself in grave danger as a result. If any such correspondence fell into the hands of the secret police, it could lead to a detailed investigation and a ban on the lodge. Since the lodge was in any event the focus of many private and even public accusations, it decided after thorough consultation to go on the offensive and avoid all unnecessary risks. Count Pergen had begun to wonder why no answer from Mozart's lodge had been intercepted by the secret police, but then he himself received a letter from the lodge, on which he reported to the emperor.

> I presume that the officers of the local lodge Zur gekrönten Hoffnung have become suspicious; and in the apprehension that their continued silence could result in trouble from the police, because the letter contains inflammatory statements, they have sent me the original letter along with their comment that they had no intention of responding to it.[23]

The correspondence clearly shows that the Freemasons reacted to danger by beating an open retreat. They did not go so far as to consider abandoning their activities, but they avoided anything that could be misinterpreted as opposition to the state or as sympathy with the goals of the French Revolution.

DIE ZAUBERFLÖTE: A MASONIC WORK?

In the summer of 1791, Mozart was occupied with Freemasonry in an entirely different way, which did not preclude his attendance at the meetings where a response to Count Pergen was being discussed. It is easy to understand why Countess Pergen's salon is never mentioned in connection with Mozart, while that of her rival Countess Thun plays such an important role: the attitude toward Freemasonry was something of a dividing line, as proved by the guest lists insofar as they can be reconstructed. One might object that Freemasonry was in principle closed to women and therefore could hardly be a major topic of conversation in a salon presided over by the mistress of the house. But it must not be overlooked that the lodges had become an eminently political question, that their political character was at issue; and Countess Pergen represented the conservative but influential high nobility, which controlled many important government posts. By then this social stratum was hardly to be found in the lodges. Countess Thun, however, represented the informal socializing of the "enlightened" nobility with the educated and self-confident bourgeoisie that belonged to the "enlightened" lodges. Neither should it be forgotten that Freemasonry was discussed in the presence of women and that the

subject was not a mystery to them. Women were excluded only from
the Masonic rituals themselves; they were admitted to all festive
gatherings and functions, and even wore jewelry with Masonic symbols, received white gloves as gifts from lodge brothers, and in turn
presented them with embroidered Masonic emblems. Moreover, the
character of Freemasonry as a men's club was often discussed and
called into question, as contemporary periodical literature attests.

During this summer Mozart worked on *Die Zauberflöte* (*The Magic
Flute*), his contribution to the debate about Freemasonry, and a work
that takes on special significance against the background of events in
1791. In this opera the goals and procedures of a secret society of
"initiates" are presented to a "secular" public, while for lodge members and others familiar with Masonic matters the portrayal contains
an unmistakable critique of Freemasonry. The opera is directed to a
public different from that of all previous Mozart operas: the exclusively bourgeois public of the suburban theaters, the "little people"
whose expectations of the theater were vastly different from those of
the Hoftheater patrons. Bourgeois audiences still loved buffoons and
Punch and Judy shows, and cheered the use of the latest theatrical
machinery and stage effects; theirs was a theater that still had the air
of a circus. And the expert at handling this public was Emanuel
Schikaneder, director of the Theater auf der Wieden and librettist for
Die Zauberflöte. (At this point we will not explore the question of
whether Schikaneder wrote the libretto alone or Mozart had a hand in
it. For the present, it is enough to say that Schikaneder composed this
text and was partially responsible for its content, especially where it
touches on Freemasonry.)

We shall consider in this connection only the Masonic elements of
the plot. A prince wishes to belong to the circle of initiates; he must
undergo a series of tests, and at the end of the opera he can count
himself among the priests of the Isis and Osiris cult. The rituals of his
initiation and many of the accompanying symbols belong to Freemasonry. As such they represent no secret; the only secret is the experience of purification achieved through use of these symbols. Thus,
neither Mozart nor Schikaneder "betrayed" anything. Their portrayal
of the initiation by no means duplicates the ritual practiced in any of
the Viennese lodges but takes up some elements of Masonic ritual and
combines them with elements from the ancient Egyptian mysteries,

novels about secret societies, and other sources. (The ancient Egyptian material came from the *Journal für Freymaurer*, the organ published by the lodge Zur wahren Eintracht, which claimed to be an instrument of "enlightened" influence and was obviously read carefully by both Mozart and Schikaneder.)

Does Prince Tamino really want to be initiated? At no point does he say so clearly and unequivocally. He is more intent on freeing Pamina from the hands of the "monster" and "tyrant" Sarastro, who has abducted her from her mother's garden. Tamino's transition from Sarastro's accuser to an admirer of his "wisdom" is not shown. Tamino and Pamina comment on the end of their trials merely with the exclamation "Ye gods! What a joyous moment! We are granted the joy of Isis."[24] They appear again only in the final scene, standing "in priestly dress" with "Egyptian priests on both sides." (We will return to this scene later.)

Tamino first learns that Sarastro is a "tyrant," an "evil demon," and a "villain" from the three ladies who serve the Queen of the Night. It sounds plausible, since he really did abduct Pamina, and since no one, not even the priests, will provide an explanation, for "the tongue is bound by oath and duty!" Sarastro's only attempt to explain is his remark to Pamina about her mother: "It would destroy your happiness forever if I delivered you into her hands." To the end Pamina never utters a word of gratitude to Sarastro, whose wisdom can only be asserted through violence and abduction. And Sarastro's behavior toward Tamino is not that of a sympathetic mentor, but of a despotic tutor who predetermines the path to enlightenment according to his own whim. (He never refers to the voluntary nature of initiation or to the initiate's oath that no one has tempted or induced him to join the order.) Yet Sarastro's power over the priests is limited, since they represent a democratic fraternity. He must put Tamino's initiation to a vote.[25]

In purity of heart I declare unto you that our assembly today is one of the most important in our history. Tamino, the son of a king, twenty years of age, waits at the north door of our temple. His virtuous heart longs for that which we all must achieve through diligence and effort. In short, this youth wants to tear the veil of night from himself and gaze into the shrine of supreme light. One of our most important duties today shall be to watch over him and offer him the hand of friendship.

Tamino enjoys no special advantage simply because his father is a king, although Sarastro's presentation might seem to indicate otherwise. Only the possession of three virtues—virtue, discretion, and charity—entitles him to be initiated. And still one priest has doubts.

> Noble Sarastro, we know and admire your wise proclamations; yet will Tamino withstand the severe trials that await him? Forgive me expressing my doubt so openly. I am afraid for the youth. What if, overcome with grief, he should lose heart and prove unequal to the struggle? He is a prince.

Whereupon Sarastro can only answer, "Still more—he is a man!" In a sense, Sarastro must take back his reference to Tamino's lineage, for there are no exalted positions among the initiated; there is only equality among peers, and only "men" can be equals.

Sarastro's weak point is that the wise pronouncements made in his sonorous bass voice often have little to do with his conduct. If his abduction of Pamina was questionable, his entrance is even more so. He "enters in a triumphal coach pulled by six lions" and thus appears to be a ruler who revels in outward displays of his power. He is constantly surrounded by slaves, a point that is obscured in most productions, often by indiscriminate cutting of the spoken dialogue. The slaves even have several scenes of their own that are almost always omitted.[26] (The playbill for the first performance, which is pictured in many program booklets today, lists the roles of First, Second, and Third Slaves, whereas the Three Boys are not listed at all!) Both Sarastro's slaves and his despotism are clearly presented. Monostatos, the black overseer, succeeds in recapturing Papageno and Pamina after their escape, yet instead of gratitude for his vigilance he receives the following response:

> MONOSTATOS: You know me, my vigilance—
>
> SARASTRO: Deserves a path of laurel leaves.
> Ho, give this worthy man—
>
> MONOSTATOS: Your favor alone makes me rich!

SARASTRO: —seventy-seven lashes!

MONOSTATOS: Oh sir, I had not hoped for such payment!

SARASTRO: Do not thank me! It is my duty![27]

This cynicism of a ruler toward his subordinate—in this case one already despised and disadvantaged because of his color—was not introduced without a purpose. Sarastro may belong to the initiated, but he is far from being a model of virtue and wisdom; he needs to apply his teachings to himself. Sarastro's famous aria is to the above scene as ideal is to reality. He is spouting pure ideology, for his behavior does not correspond to his solemn utterances.

> Within these sacred halls,
> Revenge is unknown.
> And when a man has fallen
> Love shows him his duty.
> A friend's hand then guides him,
> Happy and satisfied, to a better land.
>
> Within these sacred walls,
> Where mankind lives by love,
> There can lurk no betrayer,
> For we forgive our enemies.
> Whoever is not gladdened by such
>   teaching
> Is unworthy to be called man.[28]

Implicit in this text is a further aspect of the opera—a decided element of misogyny. Here again, this negative trait is most visible in Sarastro. His reason for abducting Pamina is expressed in abstract terms: "A man must guide your hearts, for without him, every woman tends to overstep her natural bounds."[29] More concretely,

Pamina, that gentle virtuous maiden, is destined by the gods for this fair youth. It was for this reason that I took her from her proud mother. That woman, believing herself to be important, hopes to enchant the people through deception and superstition, and destroy the solid structure of our temple. But she shall not succeed.[30]

Sarastro's misogyny is founded on the traditional philosophy of ruler-
ship, however, not on any misogynous tradition among the initiates. In
this he resembles Pamina's father, who bequeathed him his power, as
we learn from a dialogue between Pamina and her mother, the Queen
of the Night.

> QUEEN: Dear child, your mother can no longer protect you. My power
> went to the grave with your father.
>
> PAMINA: My father—
>
> QUEEN: —voluntarily bequeathed the seven-pointed solar orb to the
> initiates. Sarastro wears this powerful amulet on his breast. When I
> spoke of it to your father, he said to me with knitted brow, "Wife, my
> final hour has come. All the wealth which was mine alone now belongs
> to you and your daughter." "And the all-powerful solar orb?" I quickly
> asked. "Is bequeathed to the initiates," he answered. "Sarastro will
> administer it as honestly as I have. And now not another word. Do
> not seek knowledge that is beyond a woman's comprehension. Your
> duty is to entrust yourself and your daughter to the guidance of
> wise men."

The Queen of the Night is thus a sworn enemy of Sarastro and the
initiates; Tamino must decide between them and Pamina, who tries to
analyze her mother's enmity.

> Dear mother, if the youth were initiated, could I not still love him as
> tenderly as I do now? My father was himself associated with these wise
> men. He always spoke of them with respect, and praised their good-
> ness, their knowledge, their virtue.[31]

Her mother answers only by referring to Sarastro as her mortal enemy,
and in the following "revenge aria" she even swears to lay a curse on
her daughter unless the girl kills Sarastro with her own hands.

Tamino's trials are administered by the priests or the two Men in
Armor, who are undoubtedly initiates as well. One test, however, is
administered by Sarastro himself. Significantly, it is the one in which
Tamino must bid farewell to Pamina before facing "mortal dangers"—

23

Tamino, Papageno.

Drey Knäbchen jung, schön, hold und weise,
Umschweben uns auf unsrer Reise.

Alle Fünf.

So lebet wohl! wir wollen gehen,
Lebt wohl! lebt wohl! auf Wiedersehen.

(Alle ab.)

Neunter Auftritt.

Zwey Sclaven tragen, so bald das Theater in ein prächtiges ägyptisches Zimmer
verwandelt ist, schöne Pölster nebst einem
prächtigen türkischen Tisch heraus, breiten
Teppiche auf, sodann kommt **der dritte
Sclav.**

Dritter Sclav. Ha, ha, ha!
Erster Sclav. Pst, Pst!
Zweyter Sclav. Was soll denn das
Lachen? —
Dritter Sclav. Unser Peiniger, der
alles belauschende Mohr, wird morgen si-
cherlich gehangen oder gespießt. — Pami-
na! — Ha, ha, ha!
Erster Sclav. Nun?

One of the scenes most frequently cut from Die Zauberflöte. *Sarastro is not only an embodiment of humanity; he is also depicted as a slave owner.*

24

Dritter Sclav. Das reizende Mädchen! — Ha, ha, ha!

Zweyter Sclav. Nun?

Dritter Sclav. Ist entsprungen.

Erster und zweyter Sclav. Entsprungen? — —

Erster Sclav. Und sie entkam?

Dritter Sclav. Unfehlbar! — We-
nigstens ist's mein wahrer Wunsch.

Erster Sclav. O Dank euch ihr guten
Götter! ihr habt meine Bitte erhört.

Dritter Sclav. Sagt ich euch nicht
immer, es wird doch ein Tag für uns schei-
nen, wo wir gerochen, und der schwarze
Monostatos bestraft werden wird.

Zweyter Sclav. Was spricht nun der
Mohr zu der Geschichte?

Erster Sclav. Er weiß doch davon?

Dritter Sclav. Natürlich! Sie ent-
lief vor seinen Augen. — Wie mir einige
Brüder erzählten, die im Garten arbeiteten,
und von weitem sahen und hörten, so ist
der Mohr nicht mehr zu retten; auch wenn
Pamina von Sarastros Gefolge wieder ein-
gebracht würde.

Erster und zweyter Sclav. Wie so?

Dritter Sclav. Du kennst ja den üppi-
gen Wanst und seine Weise; das Mädchen aber
war klüger als ich dachte. — In dem Au-

25

genblicke, da er zu siegen glaubte, rief sie Sarastros Namen: das erschütterte den Mohren; er blieb stumm und unbeweglich stehen — indeß lief Pamina nach dem Kanal, und schiffte von selbst in einer Gondel dem Palmwäldchen zu.

Erster Sclav. O wie wird das schüchterne Reh mit Todesangst dem Pallaste ihrer zärtlichen Mutter zueilen.

Zehnter Auftritt.

Vorige, Monostatos (von innen.)

Monost. He Sclaven!

Erster Sclav. Monostatos Stimme!

Monost. He Sclaven! Schaft Fesseln herbey. —

Die drey Sclaven. Fesseln?

Erster Sclav. (lauft zur Seitenthüre) Doch nicht für Pamina? O ihr Götter! da seht Brüder, das Mädchen ist gefangen.

Zweyter und dritter Sclav. Pamina? — Schrecklicher Anblick!

Erster Sclav. Seht, wie der unbarmherzige Teufel sie bey ihren zarten Händchen faßt. — Das halt ich nicht aus. (geht auf die andere Seite ab.)

a clear admonishment to abstain from women, given by Sarastro alone. And it seems as if the Men in Armor are secretly rectifying Sarastro's decision when they suddenly allow Pamina to enter the temple with Tamino because she has also remained steadfast in the face of death: "What joy it will be to meet again, happily, hand in hand, to enter the temple! A woman who fears not darkness and death is worthy to be initiated."[32]

Sarastro's decision is overtly countermanded by the priests, who have abolished differences between the sexes in their circle. (The question arises as to whether some of the priests might not be women; in any event, the Chorus of Priests is certainly scored for soprano, alto, tenor, and bass.)

Against the background of Viennese Freemasonry, *Die Zauberflöte*'s initiates appear not as a monolithic bloc but as a group full of contradictions, without any claim to infallibility. Mozart underlines this questioning attitude musically. The priests' duet, for example ("Beware the wiles of women; this is the first duty of our order! Many a wise man has been deceived, . . . death and despair were his reward."[33]) is set to such parodistic music that it is unclear whether the priests are making fun (of Sarastro, for example) or Mozart is caricaturing the priests. (There were, incidentally, a number of "adoption lodges" in Vienna where men and women worked together—a historically unexplored subject that research on Freemasonry has ignored or played down until recently.)

The music, in fact, often works *against* the ostensible meaning of the story and invites us to a closer reading of the text that invalidates the idea that Sarastro is the embodiment of Good and the Queen of the Night the embodiment of Evil (though the reception of *Die Zauberflöte* has always been characterized by this dualism, which itself has thus become historical fact). Unbridled passion to the point of instigating murder (Queen of the Night); grandiose display, lust for power, and crass injustice (Sarastro); suicidal self-pity (Papageno and Pamina); garrulousness and lack of self-control (Papageno); contempt for women (Sarastro and the two priests)—these weaknesses are distributed among many of the opera's characters, who all need purification. Yet one could also draw up a list of their estimable qualities. It is deeply significant that the three temples are not inscribed with the Masonic ideals—"Beauty, Strength, Wisdom"—but with "Nature,

Reason, Wisdom." The Masonic message of this opera is not one of confidence in Sarastro's limited wisdom; it is that one must learn to find one's way in this field of conflict, to find a path of wisdom between Nature and Reason. It is as if Mozart and Schikaneder wrote a private memorandum to Freemasons, admonishing them to replace self-righteousness with modesty, fight authoritarianism in their own ranks, pursue freedom, equality, and brotherhood, and maintain their goal of "enlightenment," which brings with it reason, justice, and humanity.

On the other hand, *Die Zauberflöte* represents not only a declaration of belief in Freemasonry but also an attempt to dispel the myths that had sprung up around it—at a time in history when the order was suspected of subversion and under threat of banishment (in connection with the French Revolution). Rather than present a spruced-up picture of Freemasonry, the opera achieves its ends through a wide variety of theatrical techniques, even extending to farce and echoes of the Punch and Judy characters so popular with "suburban" audiences. As the historical reception of this opera makes clear, the histrionic, parodistic, and magical-farcical elements have not detracted from its overall seriousness.

The *Kleine Freimaurerkantate* (K. 623) offers further evidence of Mozart's earnest commitment to Masonic reform in the summer and fall of 1791. This work, the last he entered in his catalogue, seems almost a legacy intended exclusively for internal use by Masons—a supplement, more or less, to *Die Zauberflöte*. The text of the cantata was also by Schikaneder, who had been a Freemason since 1788. It was written for the consecration of a new temple for Mozart's lodge, Zur neugekrönten Hoffnung, and was conducted by the composer himself on that occasion, November 18, 1791. This was his last appearance before his sudden death two weeks later. A tenor aria from the cantata contains words that almost seem a commentary on the splendor of Sarastro's world.

> The omnipotence of this Godhead rests
> Not upon noise and splendor;
> In quiet reflection it confers
> Its blessing upon mankind.
> Silent Godhead, the Freemason's breast

> Swears allegiance to your image,
> For your warmth falls upon his heart
> Like sweet and gentle sunlight.

The work directly addresses the turbulence and dissension that followed the Freemasonry Act of 1785 and had such a damaging effect on the order. The brothers are called upon to cease their infighting and, upon dedicating the new temple, to rededicate themselves to Masonic work.

> Come, brethren, give yourselves over completely to your joyous feelings, that you may never forget you are Freemasons. Let our celebration today be a monument to the steadfast renewal of our covenant. Let envy, greed, and slander be banished forever from the Mason's breast, and may harmony tighten the precious bonds that pure brotherly love has woven.

The reference to "harmony" (*Eintracht*) is no accident. Masonic work is a continuous process that knows no final stage of perfection.

> Begin the work joyfully, and you who have begun already, begin anew today. If in this place we have completely dedicated our hearts and words to virtue, then envy is silenced and the wish that crowns our hope completely fulfilled.

There was no hope of saving Freemasonry, however. After the sudden death of Leopold II (1792), he was succeeded on the Habsburg throne by his son Francis, who destroyed once and for all the achievements of the Josephine period. He saw seeds of rebellion and revolution everywhere. His regime persecuted freethinkers and suppressed "enlightened," progressive ideas. Zur neugekrönten Hoffnung ceased activities on December 2, 1793, with a letter to the emperor; their mission could no longer be fulfilled because it was "questioned, misunderstood, and hindered."

> It has become more and more difficult to pursue the noble aims of Freemasonry with that unclouded serenity of mind which is essential for beneficent work, and to the extent necessary for our work to benefit the state and humanity as well as provide satisfaction for our members.[34]

Chapter 7

❦

VIENNA
1786–1790

HOW PLEASANT TO BE INNOCENT

The period when Mozart worked on *Le nozze de Figaro* (late October 1785 to the end of April 1786) was the most productive of his life. The intense concentration on musical solutions for the complicated dramaturgy of this opera not only resulted in new approaches to difficult ensemble problems but also unleashed a flood of creativity that found expression in a series of works written during this same time, each a unique masterpiece. The most astounding thing about the compositions of these six months (at least those that can be reliably dated) is the wealth of different genres. We must keep in mind that Mozart did not sit and wait for the *Figaro* libretto to be delivered but undoubtedly took an active and critical role in its creation, and sought to realize his own musical and dramatic ideas. That meant reading through and discussing each line with Da Ponte from the viewpoint of an opera practitioner, which took time and made further demands on imaginative powers already strained by the work of composition.

Even apart from writing *Figaro* and the other works, Mozart's daily schedule was varied and overcrowded. He still had pupils (including

Thomas Attwood, one of whose exercise books, containing very demanding assignments, has survived). There were guests who stayed in Mozart's home for weeks at a time (the oboist Joseph Fiala with his pupil André—a friendly act of solidarity with a musician who, like Mozart, had fled his post in Salzburg and was seeking better opportunities). During this period Mozart also paid frequent visits to the lodge (which was in the midst of a total reorganization following the Freemasonry Act) and was in heavy demand as a performer. In these six months alone he played or appeared as conductor (for example, at a private performance of *Idomeneo* for members of the nobility at the Palais Auersperg) in at least seven concerts. In addition to all this, he completed the following compositions, most of which are anything but minor works: three piano concertos (K. 482, 488, 491); the *Maurerische Trauermusik* (K. 477); a violin sonata (K. 481); two Masonic songs for chorus and organ (K. 483 and 484); several insert numbers for operas—a vocal quartet (K. 479), a trio (K. 480), a duet (K. 489), and a scene with solo violin (K. 490); numerous small pieces for winds; a rondo for piano (K. 485); the comedy with music *Der Schauspieldirektor;* and, of course, *Le nozze di Figaro,* an *opera buffa* in four acts. The purely mechanical task of writing it all down—again, quite apart from the creative work of composition—required that he fill an average of six pages per day in the twelve-stave format he used almost exclusively throughout his years in Vienna. (By comparison, in 1791—which, with *Die Zauberflöte, La clemenza de Tito,* the Requiem, the Clarinet Concerto, and other works, also counts as one of Mozart's most productive years—his daily average was three pages in this same format.)

During these six months Mozart pursued all his interests simultaneously. He performed in a concert of the Tonkünstlersozietät (the insurance organization for musicians) and at the Masonic lodges, played concerts for charity and in the salons of the nobility, and gave his own concert in the Burgtheater as well as three subscription concerts. He conducted private performances for the nobility and for the emperor, and wrote music for his own concerts, the lodges, the emperor, the singers of the Hoftheater, private salons, a large social function at court, and so on. He also found time to attend a masked ball at the Redoutensaal and to distribute leaflets containing riddles of his own devising. Mozart here, Mozart there; he was riding a wave

of sympathetic support from all social circles. It was no coincidence
that the resourceful Viennese publisher and engraver Hieronymus
Löschenkohl included a silhouette of Mozart in his calendar for the
year 1786. Mozart was a celebrity in Vienna.

It is hardly surprising that Mozart found no time to write letters
amid such frenetic activity. We do not know the full extent of his
correspondence and can only go by letters that have survived or whose
contents can be reconstructed. His father received only a brief newsletter every six weeks; even the birthday greeting for November 14
reached Salzburg more than a week late. Did the excessive activity
make Mozart oblivious to what was happening around him? Was he
still able to register the highly important developments taking place in
both domestic and foreign affairs? Or did Mozart have nothing but
music and performances on his mind? Surely not. The Freemasonry
Act had just been issued, necessitating drastic changes in lodge
structure. Mozart had just contributed a musical work to a ceremony of
rededication, and he visited the lodge frequently during these months.
And then there was *Figaro*, a work that touched closely on conditions
in the aristocracy yet owed its first production to a particular aspect of
imperial policy. Its composition required a keen sensitivity to the
society on which its success or failure depended, a seismograph
capable of measuring the public's tolerance for provocation and its
ability to assimilate Mozart's subtle and complex portrayal of individual characters. Added to this was the strain caused by continual
theater intrigues, which called for great prudence as well as aggressive self-assertion. Minute attention to every detail was important. A
musician who enjoyed such favor in society could not rely solely on
creativity and dazzling piano technique. The most cherished plans
were often ruined by the clouds of intrigue.

The *Figaro* period was a time of fermentation and also represented
Josephine politics at precisely the halfway point in the emperor's
reign. Leopold Mozart, who was now writing to his daughter almost
twice a week, related current events in detail and provided a remarkably farsighted commentary that she found most impressive and
praised. He replied:

It may well be that I could have made a good journalist. It is not
difficult for a man who has seen the world, who knows it and has

studied it, and then has time to think and write in tranquility before presenting his thoughts to the public. What I wrote to you were merely reflections jotted down in haste. (November 11, 1785)

Leopold Mozart had the time for extensive correspondence, and his commentary was undoubtedly based on a thorough reading of the newspapers. This cosmopolitanism and curiosity about the latest political developments (in which subjects of an autocratic state had little chance to participate) were imparted to his children and characterized a self-assured family life in which "enlightenment" was not merely rationalist humbug but the foundation of bourgeois self-esteem. The bourgeois individual felt himself to be equal, if not superior, to the nobility, which, although still in power, was widely considered superfluous. Wolfgang Mozart had acquired this self-esteem as well as a pronounced curiosity that went well beyond his musical interests. His Masonic membership was not primarily for the purpose of establishing contacts that might benefit his career; it was rather the expression of a social ideal that anticipated the motto "Liberty, Equality, Fraternity."

What were the political themes that Leopold Mozart found so interesting during this winter of 1785–86? First there were matters of foreign policy connected with the plan to exchange the Austrian Netherlands for Bavaria. Then came domestic affairs, such as the peasant uprisings in Transylvania, complaints about the nobility in the parliament at Regensburg and subsequent reprisals against the complainants, and such local occurrences as the case of a soldier from the Salzburg garrison who was made to run the gauntlet. Did Leopold Mozart include such lengthy reflections in his less numerous letters to his son? We cannot know, for these letters have not survived; but it is highly probable, since he was also curious to know what people thought in Vienna.[1]

Although Joseph II was indeed an enlightened monarch, the brusqueness of his manner became more and more irritating, as did the ruthlessness with which he undertook to push through every step he deemed reasonable and useful. He saw himself as an educator, bringing light to his nation, and as far as his power allowed, he was merciless toward traditional behavior, customs, and ideas of morality. Often enough the emperor overestimated his power. He was able to abrogate the nobility's privileges and thus establish equality before the law as a major step toward civil justice, but he was unable to abolish all the privileges enjoyed by the governing estates or to put through his tax reforms, which would have placed a heavier burden on the nobility. He tried to rob the Hungarians of their crown as a symbol of national identity but was forced to restore it. He succeeded in curtailing Church privileges and in closing redundant monasteries, but he could not tell the populace how to bury their dead and had to rescind his burial ordinances. Joseph II was completely blind to the fact that not everything he considered reasonable was necessarily feasible. He made no attempt to gain public approval for his measures but was concerned only that obedient subjects follow his commands—they could think whatever they wished. Joseph II was a rational despot whose behavior antagonized even his supporters, with the result that they maintained a critical distance. The Freemasonry Act, with its curt and insensitive reference to "chicanery," cost him much sympathy, not because he placed the lodges under state supervision, but because of his contemptuous phraseology. The recurring criticism of the emperor was that he should be less miserly and more forbearing toward the mistakes and weaknesses of others, avoid making rash decisions, and give more support to science and the arts. Criticism also increased within the ranks of his supporters, indicating general dissatisfaction. His policies were simply too inconsistent for his contemporaries to comprehend. One drastic example was the Zahlheim case, in which the achievements of the "enlightened" state came into conflict with its despotic ruler. In this instance Joseph II intervened in the judicial process to such an extent that he nullified his own reforms and passed a harsh sentence for no other reason than its supposed deterrent effect.

DIGRESSION: THE ZAHLHEIM CASE

Franz Zaglauer von Zahlheim, a nobleman and government official, had a relationship with an older woman whom he had promised to marry. He led an unsettled and dissolute life, however, and had debts of approximately 16,000 florins. His immoderate ways finally led him to rob and murder his fiancée, who had approximately 1,000 florins in cash. It was a reprehensible crime but a fairly ordinary case from a criminological standpoint; neither the circumstances nor the deed itself indicated that it would make judicial history. In Vienna at the end of the eighteenth century there were one or two murders a year among a population of roughly 200,000. Some were certainly more shocking and had a more terrifying effect than this one. Yet the public responded sympathetically in this case as in no other—not because of the crime, but because of the punishment inflicted on the criminal.

After the de facto abolition of the death penalty in 1776 (known to the courts but not to the public), offenders were normally given a harsh or even cruel sentence for purposes of deterrence, which was then commuted to a much lighter punishment. The practice of torture, to extract confessions or for other reasons, had already been abolished by Joseph II in January 1776; it was one of his first reforms. (Torture had been common under Maria Theresa and was provided for in detail in the *Constitutio Criminalis Theresiana* of 1769.[2]) It must be said of his criminal law reforms that Joseph II also viewed deterrence as the main objective of punishment, but he rejected the death penalty as ineffective, preferring lifelong hard labor—a state of permanent hopelessness with no chance of probation. The worst punishment in this category was pulling boats: prisoners were given only one meal a day and had to work in irons, often waist-deep in mire, racked with fever and epidemics, until they collapsed. These prisoners, from all parts of the empire, assembled in Vienna before being sent on to Hungary or Trieste. Virtually none survived their life sentences longer than one year. They were also subjected to flogging with birch rods.

In the area of criminal justice, then, the "enlightened" Joseph II had hardly progressed beyond the Middle Ages and was plainly no tolerant philanthropist. Perhaps the emperor's supporters, who celebrated the abolition of torture and the death penalty as an act of goodwill, overlooked the dark thoughts that led him to these reforms.[3]

Joseph favored extremely severe punishments, as established in the Josephine criminal justice code of 1787. But the courts generally imposed the minimum sentence, which the appeal courts then reduced by a third. If appeal was made to the highest court, the sentence was usually reduced further. This practice undoubtedly signaled the opposition of the law courts to the emperor's ideas.

The execution of the murderer Franz Zahlheim was seen as a break with the emperor's reform policy and provoked heated debate. It was carried out in medieval fashion before 30,000 spectators.

It may be that such leniency annoyed Joseph, for in the Zahlheim case he intervened personally and made his own disposition, violating his principle of noninterference in judicial matters and invalidating his guarantee of equal justice. Upon conviction Zahlheim was sentenced to death while the court of appeals considered several milder punishments. But in a personally signed rescript, Joseph II insisted that "in accordance with the regulations of the *Nemesis Theresiana,* the death penalty described therein shall be administered without mercy to the delinquent at the usual place of execution." This meant that

the nobleman Franz Zaglauer von Zahlheim, convicted of murder, shall be taken to the Hoher Markt, where after the public reading of his sentence, glowing hot pincers shall be applied to the left and right sides of his chest. He shall then be led to the usual place of execution, where his body shall be broken on the wheel from the feet upward and then displayed on a gibbet.[4]

Vienna had not witnessed such a gruesome execution for many years. Four hours passed between the reading of the sentence and the final display of the corpse on the gibbet. In accordance with the deterrence theory, an execution was a public event, and contemporary reports indicate that Zahlheim's sentence was carried out before 30,000 spectators. It is true that public gallows were still not unusual at this time and that travelers frequently saw places of execution when passing through larger villages; the public nature of this punishment was no more inhumane than the secrecy so common today. Nevertheless, the execution of Zahlheim was a relapse into barbarism, and contemporaries were well aware of its unique significance as a sign of the limits of progress in a self-proclaimed "Age of Enlightenment"— especially in Vienna, that stronghold of secular life, whose sophistication and progressiveness had long since given it precedence over the other center of the Enlightenment, Berlin. The Zahlheim case shattered confidence in Joseph II's reform policies for a number of years and became the most widely discussed event of its time. It was debated in every tavern, salon, and Masonic lodge. There was concern that this case might herald an end to reform, a reversion to a harsh regime, and a revocation of imperial "acts of goodwill," as the reform laws were called. For the first time people began to ask themselves whether Joseph II was not turning back the wheel of history.

MOZART COMPOSES

Zahlheim's execution took place on the morning of March 10, 1786. Mozart was in Vienna, but we do not know if he witnessed the execution, the first stage of which began a few hundred yards from his home. The bustle in the streets and the shouting of such a large crowd could certainly have been heard from his lodgings.[5]

On the afternoon of that same day, the Masonic meeting that became known as "Kratter's auto-da-fé" took place in the Leopoldstadt quarter of Vienna. Whatever Mozart's reaction to the events taking place on his doorstep, or to those of more personal significance, we know that on March 10 he wrote two arias intended as inserts for a performance of *Idomeneo* in the Palais Auersperg. Their content does not in any way reflect the tempestuous events of the day. One might expect an unsettled mood to find its way into the music. That no such distress is evident in these arias, however, has a musical explanation and is not a sign of heartlessness or apathy.

Perhaps a nonmusical example will illustrate this point further. A painter working on a portrait or landscape has a specific idea of his picture in mind, nourished by actual observation. But his idea also includes the composition of objects and the distribution of colors and surfaces so as to create a field of tension between elements of varying significance. Personal consternation and external events that occur while the artist works on the picture usually have nothing to do with what is represented there. He will complete his portrait or landscape according to his intentions, formulating and solving the problems involved.

The situation is similar for a musician. His composition represents the solution of musical problems within a specific context—in this instance, the interpolation of new material into the action of *Idomeneo*. It was a mostly technical task of rewriting two numbers to suit the specific vocal and instrumental demands of a particular performance. Creative work always entails solving problems dictated by the musical materials the composer has selected. The day's events should not be related to Idamante's aria—that is, unless they hindered its success-ful completion. We are tempted to make such a connection, however, because the new text for the aria—which, of course, Mozart had had for some time—calls up misleading associations: Idamante, accom-panied by solo violin, sings, "Fear not, my love, my heart beats always for you. Cruel, merciless stars, have you no pity? Lovely souls, you who see how I am suffering now, tell me if a faithful heart can stand such misery."

Whether the Concerto in C Minor (K. 491), which Mozart wrote over the next fourteen days, represented a musical reaction to, perhaps even something of a commentary on, a tense and oppressive situation is another question. (The concerto was written for a concert Mozart gave in the Burgtheater on April 7; the rest of the program cannot be determined.) Practically every musicologist who has written on this work refers to its "tragic" or "demonic" elements (Abert, Einstein). Alfred Einstein even speaks of "dark eruptions," an "explosion of dark, tragic, passionate emotions." However, Wolfgang Hildesheimer states, "I, too, hear in [the first] movement a gloomy agitation, but strangely enough I hear in it (even aside from the E-flat major passages) a major mood, violent and energetic, to be sure, but not 'tragic.' "[6]

The main theme of this opening movement is constructed of two very concise motivic cells: a slow and heavy succession of intervals imbued with great harmonic interest, followed by an abrupt, sharply accented leap. This type of thematic construction was taken up and further developed by Beethoven, whose compositions generally reveal less interest in melodic invention and greater preoccupation with scraps of thematic material. In "processing" of this material, too, Mozart departs from all traditional generic patterns, even those he developed himself in earlier concertos. The obstinate originality of this music, extending even to its instrumentation in the almost soloistic treatment of the wind instruments, does indeed lend the concerto a unique quality, but it has nothing to do with "tragic elements." "Tragic" rather describes the mood or effect created by the music— which, however, is subject to historical variation. As far as we know, Mozart's contemporaries who heard him play the concerto did not describe the music as "tragic" or "demonic"; these words were first applied much later, in the nineteenth century, and today they again seem inappropriate. In Mozart's time a much clearer distinction was made between musical phenomena and the feelings they arouse.

Not one of his contemporaries recorded his impressions of Mozart's C Minor Concerto; or rather, no such recorded impressions have survived. We are thus unable to reconstruct the effect created by this work, especially since we do not discuss music in the same terms Mozart's contemporaries used. For this reason I urge extreme caution in the interpretation of historical reactions, to say nothing of Mozart's own impressions during the composition of such an arresting work. Yet it is certainly clear that this music represents an uncompromising attitude, a refusal to employ conventional formulas or indulge in gratuitous virtuosity. This piano concerto was not intended for the salon, where there was often chatter or card playing during concerts and the piano, in a manner of speaking, "socialized" with the other guests, taking part in the brilliant conversation and commanding attention through wit, elaborate artistry, and scintillating invention. Rather, the C Minor Concerto is like a speech that silences a crowd through sheer earnestness and gravity of expression. There is something unrelenting and defiant about the music. It shows no traces of frivolity and does not seek shallow approval; it is neither questioning nor diffident, but powerful and declarative. In this respect, it does express the tense mood of these few days, which in the eyes of many people marked a turning point after years of encouraging improvements. Mozart was not one of the disappointed or fainthearted people who gave up and withdrew from the struggle. He expressed his reaction in his own language, music (though he also retained his lodge membership, against the current of the times). His compositions became more demanding and uncompromising, less "entertaining," yet far from being removed from the events and conditions of the time, they stood in progressively clearer and more palpable relation to them, as the operas clearly demonstrate.

Mozart had no cause for a retreat of any kind. He had already undertaken a daring venture with *Figaro*, which was probably completed during the winter of 1785–86, though the first performance was delayed until May 1786. Everything depended on its success, which would be a good indication of his possibilities for remaining in Vienna. Since his existence there was not assured by contracts or permanent employment, he was entirely dependent on public acceptance of works written for the artistic "free market."

THE FOLLIES OF A DAY: *LE NOZZE DI FIGARO*

Even before the premiere there were "follies" enough. The theater was riddled with intrigues motivated by professional rivalry, several operas were awaiting performance, and each composer wanted his to be produced first. Mozart must have been quite nervous, since he personally supervised every detail of the production. Lorenzo Da Ponte wrote that Mozart was "in despair" over plans to omit the ballet at the end of Act I; he wanted to punish those who were scheming against him physically and even to withdraw the entire opera. (As a result of Da Ponte's intervention, however, the emperor instructed the theater to perform the work in its entirety.[7]) Mozart's friend, the singer Michael Kelly, also reported, "Mozart was as touchy as gunpowder, and swore he would put the score of his opera into the fire if it was not produced first."[8] Mozart had good reason to risk everything on this one chance, especially since he was sure of the emperor's support for the work. On the other hand, everything about the opera was so entirely new, and it was such a drastic break with everything that had previously been seen on the opera stage, that difficulties were to be expected. This was more than a matter of internal problems at the theater.

Never had the everyday social conflicts of contemporary life been made the subject of a comic opera. It was neither a grand spectacle nor an ordinary comedy with stereotyped roles. Rather, in a clear act of rebellion, bourgeois sensibilities and moral ideals were compared favorably with aristocratic frivolity and misuse of power. Mozart and Da Ponte had departed from the well-worn path of *opera buffa* and created a new form of the *commedia per musica*. The play on which their opera is based was considerably shortened, but its structure was retained to a large degree, so that the opera takes about four hours to perform—not because the musical numbers are overlong, but because, despite the cuts, the plot contains a wealth of incidental action that is nevertheless germane to the central conflict. Especially noteworthy is the theatrical immediacy of the fast verbal exchanges in the excited recitatives, which one must almost imagine as spoken dialogue. Indeed, *Figaro* is primarily a "play with music" in which everything is conceived in terms of theatrical effect. The music interprets every word, every gesture and stir of emotion, with a subtlety never before known on the operatic stage, commenting sincerely or ironically, paraphrasing, supporting, or exaggerating, and utilizing elements of "tone painting" as well as forms of absolute music. The score is composed with such delicacy and attention to detail that one discovers something new on each listening. (Not until Alban Berg's *Lulu* did opera again achieve such a versatile treatment of dialogue and such an exact musical reflection of the text.)

In his preface to the published libretto Da Ponte makes specific reference to the novelty of the work, after apologizing for its unusual length.

We hope that ample recompense will be offered by the variety of themes woven into the action of this play, as well as its originality and large dimensions. The musical numbers are of the widest possible variety, so as not to leave any performers unoccupied for long periods, to avoid the tedium and monotony of long recitatives, and to lend expression to the many different passions which the characters experience. We wanted to present our most gracious and honorable public with a virtually new kind of play.[9]

Da Ponte deliberately uses the term "play," never "opera"; he did not wish to associate the new work with this genre and its well-known traditions.

Although *Figaro* contrasts bourgeois morality with hedonism, there is no simple dichotomy of good and evil. It is not a work of political agitation, but neither is it a timeless opera on universal themes, on the "aberrations of human life" (Anna Amalie Abert).[10] Class conflict is clearly depicted here, but the people involved in it are also individuals, distinctive personalities, down to the smallest incidental roles. None of them embodies a social type; each is a responsible individual. Every character must endure some humiliation—Susanna least of all, perhaps, Count Almaviva most—and each has a lesson to learn; there is no attempt to establish universal theorems. Thus there is no "happy ending" in which all conflicts are resolved. Even the "marriage," which by the end is possible again, is hardly touched on and is emphasized less than in Beaumarchais's original. When the count, who is completely unforgiving himself, finally asks the countess for her forgiveness (and receives it), every one sings, "So let us all be happy." The final chorus that follows is directed to the public and is no longer a part of the stage action.

> This day of torments,
> Of caprices and folly,
> Only love can end
> In contentment and joy.
> Lovers and friends, come and celebrate
> With dancing and fireworks.
> And to the sound of a cheerful march,
> Let's hasten to the festivities.

Count Almaviva must learn above all that he has no power to fulfill his frivolous desires, whether through money, his *droit du seigneur*, or intrigues. Regardless of the means he employs, he always suffers defeat. This dismantling of aristocratic power is particularly impressive in that the count does not change or repent his actions in any way but simply blunders headlong into the trap. The revolt against him begins with Figaro, who only learns of his employer's intentions from Susanna. Later, Susanna determines the course of events, until the countess herself takes control of the plot against her husband. What begins for her as mere sympathy for the pair of servants later becomes an attempt to put an end to the count's unfaithfulness (and it remains an open question whether she will ever succeed).

When even the countess begins to intrigue against the count, the hopeless isolation of a nobility that insists on its feudal rights is revealed. For the countess, who comes from a bourgeois background, makes it increasingly clear that she too subscribes to the bourgeois moral concepts of love and fidelity, and that she is prepared to defend them, even in partnership with the servants Figaro and Susanna. The servants' revolt against the despotic count is transformed into a struggle of bourgeois values against feudal rights—a struggle in which the servants no longer find themselves alone. Count Almaviva, then, does not personify the nobility as such, but the feudal-patriarchal nobles who refuse to recognize the emancipation of the bourgeoisie until they are forced to do so by their loss of power. He is no insignificant, laughable representative of the rural nobility who is not taken seriously by the "enlightened" members of his class (the aristocratic Freemasons, for example). This count holds a number of high posts and belongs to the political and military leadership of the nation. He is described as a minister, is given a diplomatic post in London, and even commands a regiment.

Josephine reforms gave full scope to bourgeois moral concepts (as long as they did not call the autocratic ruler himself into question), strongly encouraged bourgeois productive forces, and stressed the equality of all subjects in the social and legal spheres. Against this background, *Le nozze di Figaro* decidedly took the emperor's side, along with the Freemasons and other "enlightened" elements of society. Joseph II could be content with the opera's criticism of the nobility; it fitted beautifully into his program. The "enlightened" autocratic ruler drew his authority from the responsibility he claimed for the general welfare of his subjects. To a certain extent he himself had adopted bourgeois values and could not accept the nobility's insistence on special rights and privileges, particularly when these interfered with the public weal. In the emperor's eyes, it was a case of legitimate versus illegitimate power.

But how did Nationaltheater audiences react to an opera that broke with all accepted traditions and carried a distinct political message? On the one hand, the opera had its source in French comedy, a genre favored by the nobility, and it joined that tradition with courtly Italian opera, maintaining a distance from the bourgeois Singspiel and especially from *Volkstheater*. On the other hand, its ideology derived from the theater of bourgeois enlightenment, and it conveyed this ideology through aesthetic means entirely new to the operatic stage. A report in the *Wiener Realzeitung* from July 11, 1786, shows a mixed reaction undoubtedly attributable to the opera's provocative subject matter.

"In our times, we sing what we are not allowed to say," we could proclaim along with Figaro. This play was banned in Paris and was not allowed to be performed here—in either a good or a bad translation. Now we have the good fortune to see it as an opera. It is clear that we are better off than the French. Even in the first performance, Herr Mozart's music found enthusiastic approval, except among those whose pride and vanity prevent them from finding anything good which they did not write themselves.

The public, however, did not really know what to think. It heard many bravos from impartial patrons, but there were impetuous rowdies in the gallery who burst their hired lungs in order to distract both the singers and the audience with their noise. Consequently, opinions were mixed at the end of the performance.

Furthermore, it is true that the first performance was somewhat inept, because of the difficulty of the work.

Now, however, after repeated performances, it would show either partisanship or lack of taste to deny that Herr Mozart's music is an artistic masterpiece. Its beauty and wealth of invention could only have come from a born genius.

Some critics have written that Herr Mozart's opera met with no approval at all. One can guess what kind of journalists would continue to write such obvious lies. At the third performance of this opera, the audience demanded constant repetitions of musical numbers, and I believe it is well known that this was the reason why, several days later, the emperor himself ordered that in future only solo arias may be repeated during opera performances.[11]

There was obviously enthusiastic approval as well as (prearranged) disapproval, this also from musical colleagues (Salieri, perhaps?), and both were openly demonstrated. Then public approval seems to have increased; in the second performance five arias had to be repeated, in the third as many as seven, "one of which, a short duetto, had to be sung three times" (Leopold Mozart, May 20, 1786); we do not know which one. The ensuing ban on multiple encores was an attempt to avoid a deliberately planned sensation. After all, most of the patrons were aristocrats, and there was no cause to provoke them unnecessarily. In his *Reminiscences*, Michael Kelly says the emperor told the singers, somewhat hypocritically, that the da capos must have been " 'a great fatigue, and very distressing to you,' " whereupon several of them agreed. Kelly, always an ardent defender of Mozart, replied, " 'Do not believe them, Sire, they all like to be encored, at least I am sure I always do.' His Majesty laughed, and I believe he thought there was more truth in my assertion than in theirs. I am sure there was."[12]

A good example of how the nobility reacted to *Figaro* is found in a diary entry by Count Karl von Zinzendorf, who, as director of the court accounting office and the commission on tax adjustment, was one of the most influential officials in the government. His judgment is laconic: "The opera bored me." After a later performance he noted smugly, "Mozart's music shows great dexterity but has no ideas." Even this man recognized Mozart's skill, but apparently the subject of the opera left him completely indifferent.

The emperor, however, invited the cast to give a special performance at his summer residence, Laxenburg Castle—a clear indication of his esteem. Evidently he also considered *Figaro* a successful means of getting his opinions across to the nobility. The first Italian performances, in Monza and Florence, were undertaken at his suggestion, as was the performance in Prague to celebrate the marriage of his niece, Archduchess Maria Theresa, to Anton Klemens, the future king of Saxony. There was strong resistance from the nobility, as Mozart wrote to Gottfried von Jacquin in the fall of 1787, on the occasion of the Prague performance.

So yesterday my *Figaro* was performed in a fully lighted theater and I myself conducted. In this connection I have a good joke to tell you. A few of the leading ladies here, and in particular one very high and mighty one, were kind enough to find it very ridiculous, unsuitable, and Heaven knows what else that the princess should be entertained with a performance of *Figaro*, the "Crazy Day," as the management were pleased to call it. It never occurred to them that no opera in the world, unless it is written especially for it, can be exactly suitable for such an occasion and that therefore it was of absolutely no consequence whether this or that opera were given, provided that it was a good opera and one which the princess did not know; and *Figaro* at least fulfilled this last condition. In short, by her persuasive tongue the ringleader brought things to such a pitch that the government forbade the impresario [Pasquale Bondini] to produce this opera on that night. So she was triumphant! "*Ho vinto*," she called out one evening from her box. No doubt she never suspected that the *ho* might be changed to a *sono*. But the following day Le Noble appeared, bearing a command from His Majesty to the effect that if the new opera [*Don Giovanni*, which was not yet finished] could not be given, *Figaro* was to be performed! My friend, if only you had seen the handsome, magnificent nose of this lady! Oh, it would have amused you as much as it did me! (October 15, 1787)

Although the emperor personally supervised the Nationaltheater, he was not to blame that *Figaro* only ran for nine performances and was not produced again in Vienna until August 1789, after the first news of the French Revolution had reached the city; this time it ran for twenty-eight performances. The opera was obviously boycotted by the Viennese nobility and could only establish itself later under different political conditions. The performances outside Vienna confirm that the work only enjoyed success during and immediately after the Revolution; later productions were sporadic compared with those of Mozart's other operas. When serious interest in *Figaro* finally revived in the 1830s, its highly political content was often diluted and it was reduced to a simple *opera buffa* about love entanglements, which for Mozart and Da Ponte had only been the theatrical medium for their political argument.

Only in Prague was *Figaro* a resounding success from the first performance, for special reasons that will be discussed in connection with *Don Giovanni* and Mozart's journeys to Prague.

NO JOURNEY TO ENGLAND

Around the time Mozart began work on *Le nozze di Figaro* a new pupil
came to him for composition lessons: Thomas Attwood, who was then
roughly twenty years old, and who stayed in Vienna from the fall of
1785 to the beginning of 1787. During this same period Mozart had
become friends with the singer Michael Kelly, who had two small roles
in *Figaro*; he also had close contact with Nancy Storace, who sang the
first Susanna, and with her brother, the composer Stephen Storace,
who was in Vienna until early 1787. Mozart found some of his old
desires reawakened by this small English colony.

Mozart had made his first travel plans as early as August 1782,
when he had been married only two weeks and his future in Vienna
was still uncertain. In a letter to his father he wrote that Paris would
probably be his first stop since he had no contacts in England. And he
could not resist a sideswipe at the emperor, who did not do enough to
encourage "people with talent."

> My idea is to go to Paris next Lent, but of course not simply on chance.
> I have already written to Le Gros about this and am awaiting his reply. I
> have mentioned it here too—particularly *to people of position*—just in
> the course of conversation. For you know that often in conversation you
> can throw out a hint and that this is more effective than if the same
> thing were announced in the tones of a dictator. (August 17, 1782)

But it seems that this plan was not very serious, for after ruminating on
possibilities for earning money in Paris, he unexpectedly indicated his
preferred choice: "I have been practicing my French daily and have
already taken three lessons in English. In three months I hope to be
able to read and understand English books fairly easily."

Was Paris, then, only tossed out as a threat to influential Viennese,
in hopes of getting better offers? Or did Mozart want to read English
literature in search of opera subjects—Shakespeare, perhaps? In any
event, English literature was often read at Countess Thun's salon,
where Mozart was a frequent guest during this period, and where
Vienna's rampant anglophilia was especially cultivated. At the theater, which Mozart attended regularly, the actors Friedrich Ludwig

Schröder and Franz Brockmann often performed English plays, especially Shakespeare, and in Salzburg the Mozarts had had frequent opportunities to see *Hamlet* and other popular works. Leopold Mozart clearly understood the reference to language lessons and characteristically admonished his son to make no hasty decisions. Such foreign adventures could not be undertaken without definite prospects and help from one's contacts abroad. Mozart agreed.

> You are perfectly right about France and England! It is a step which I can always take, and it is better for me to remain in Vienna a little longer. Besides, times may change too in those countries. (August 24, 1782)

Leopold Mozart, still disgruntled that his son had left him alone in Salzburg, did not consider the matter settled and wrote to Baroness Waldstätten:

> After receiving my letter, my son to some extent abandoned his resolve to leave Vienna; and as he is coming to visit me in Salzburg, I will make further very necessary and weighty representations to him. (September 13, 1782)

A short time before, Mozart had described himself to his father as an "arch-Englishman" and had specifically referred to the English victory over the French fleet after the three-year siege of Gibraltar. This indicates that Paris was not his first choice for a relocation; nor did memories of earlier sojourns there offer much encouragement, financial or otherwise.

Plans to visit England were not mentioned in the following years, but they were not forgotten. When Attwood came to Vienna as a protégé of the prince of Wales (the future King George IV of England), Mozart perhaps saw his chance to arrange a journey. Naturally Constanze would come with him, since Mozart found it unbearable to be separated from her for more than four weeks. The two children were a problem, however; they would have to be boarded somewhere. Just at this point Mozart accidentally learned something that had been deliberately concealed from him: his sister's son was now living with Leopold Mozart in Salzburg. Did that not offer a solution?

Mozart's sister Maria Anna had married a much older man, Johann Baptist von Berchtold zu Sonnenburg, who had already been widowed twice and had five children. After his third wife delivered a child in her father's house in July 1785, she left the baby with its delighted grandfather and devoted herself to caring for her five stepchildren. Since Leopold Mozart had at least two servants to help look after his grandson, could he not look after two more children for a while?

But the elder Mozart grew indignant at this suggestion and felt he was being used. He also made a distinction between his son and his daughter. He wrote to her:

> I had to reply today to a letter from your brother, and this took me considerable time. So I cannot write very much to you. Moreover it is late and I want to go to the play today, as I have a free pass, and have only just finished that letter to Vienna. You can easily imagine that I had to express myself very emphatically, as your brother actually suggested that I should take charge of his two children, because he was proposing to undertake a journey through Germany to England in the middle of next carnival. I wrote therefore very fully and added that I would send him the continuation of my letter by the next post. Herr Müller, that good and honest maker of silhouettes, had said a lot of nice things about little Leopold to your brother, who heard in this way that the child is living with me. I had never told your brother. So that is how the brilliant idea occurred to him or perhaps to his wife. Not at all a bad arrangement! They could go off and travel—they might even die—or remain in England—and I would have to run off after them with the children. As for the payment which he offers me for the children and for maids to look after them—Basta! If he cares to do so, he will find my excuse very clear and instructive. (November 17, 1786)

His concern was justified, for Mozart did not rule out the possibility of remaining in England permanently.

Apparently Mozart was not much bothered by this rejection, especially since he had meanwhile been invited to attend the Prague production of *Figaro*. He may originally have intended to leave for England at the end of February 1787, with Kelly, Nancy and Stephen Storace, and Attwood, but the plan was postponed so that Attwood could first arrange concerts or an opera commission for him in London.

Attwood was the perfect go-between in such matters. The prince of Wales had financed his education in Italy and Vienna, and upon his return he became a chamber musician to the prince, who led a life of unbelievable extravagance. He gambled, owned expensive race-horses, and assumed the role of "first gentleman of Europe." This dandy was actively involved in creating a wave of admiration for Mozart in England. Attwood was primarily engaged in securing com-missions for operas and drawing up contracts with theater directors and impresarios. Nowhere outside London was there such a flourish-ing concert life; it was entirely in the hands of the bourgeoisie and was not only viable but fully commercialized. Nowhere else did artists receive such high fees for concerts. The entrepreneurs found them-selves in fierce competition, which was only possible in a city with a population of almost a million—several times that of Paris or Vienna.

The celebrated singer Nancy Storace could also smooth the way for Mozart. For her farewell concert in Vienna he wrote a *scena con rondo* with a part for solo piano (K. 505)—an odd combination of vocal aria and piano concerto. Mozart himself performed it with her at that memorable concert, which brought in more than 4,000 florins. It was a highly personal remembrance and expression of gratitude for the *Figaro* premiere.

Mozart had not given up his plans to visit England. Despite the lack of encouragement from Salzburg, the journey was still under serious consideration, as shown in a letter he wrote from Prague to his Viennese friend Gottfried von Jacquin.

I must frankly admit that, although I meet with all possible courtesies and honors here and although Prague is indeed a very beautiful and pleasant place, I long most ardently to be back in Vienna; and believe me, the chief cause of this homesickness is certainly *your* family. When I remember that after my return I will enjoy only for a short while the pleasure of your valued society and will then have to forgo this happiness for such a long time, perhaps forever, then indeed I realize the extent of the friendship and regard I cherish for your whole family.

(January 15, 1787)

Mozart now spread the word that he was going to leave Vienna, so that even the newspapers reported it. Or was this, too, only a tactic meant to persuade "the powers that be"—i.e., the emperor and the influential nobility—to offer him commissions and thus make it more attractive for him to stay? For in Prague he had just accepted the commission to write *Don Giovanni,* which would have to be completed before he could undertake any journey.

Meanwhile, Nancy Storace and her family, along with Kelly, Attwood, and numerous companions, stopped in Salzburg on their way to England and brought with them a letter from Mozart to his father. Leopold Mozart acted as tour guide for a day.

> In the evening she sang three arias, and they left for Munich at midnight. They had two carriages, each with four post-horses. A servant rode in advance as courier to arrange for the changing of eight horses. Goodness, what luggage they had! This journey must have cost them a fortune. (March 1, 1787)

Leopold was undoubtedly relieved that his son and daughter-in-law had not come along.

> I sent him a fatherly letter, saying that he would gain nothing by a journey in summer, as he would arrive in England at the wrong time, that he ought to have at least 2,000 florins in his pocket before undertaking such an expedition, and finally that, unless he had procured in advance some definite engagement in London, he would have to be prepared, no matter how clever he was, to be hard up—at first, anyway. So he has probably lost courage, particularly as Madame Storace's brother will of course write the opera for the next season.
> (March 2, 1787)

It is not known what Attwood and Nancy Storace were able to do for Mozart in London, but for the time being he had other priorities, whether offers came from England or not; they remained the ultima ratio.

When the London publisher John Bland came to Vienna in the fall of 1789, Mozart was at work on *Così fan tutte.* Bland probably made contact with Mozart before going on to visit Haydn at Esterháza. Amidst so much contact with the English, it is fitting that Mozart should have written an English phrase in the guest book of a Viennese English teacher from whom he himself may have had lessons (and who was also a brother Freemason in the lodge Zur Neugekrönten Hoffnung): "Patience and tranquillity of mind contribute more to cure our distempers as the whole art of medecine."[13]

Somehow every offer came at the wrong time. When Mozart was in Frankfurt (September–November 1790), a letter arrived for him in Vienna from the English concert manager Robert May O'Reilly, who proposed the following: Mozart would come to London and stay from December 1790 until the end of June 1791, during which time he would write at least two operas, comic or dramatic, as decided by the opera management, for which he would receive 300 pounds sterling (roughly 2,400 florins). In addition, he could write for other impresarios, but not for other theaters. In making this offer O'Reilly specifically referred to "a person closely associated with the Prince of Wales," from whom he had learned of Mozart's plans to visit England, and who can only have been Attwood. This time it seems Mozart was detained by the ill health of his wife, who was suffering from an ulcerated leg, but he still considered traveling the next summer (1791). He wrote to his wife from Munich:

> I am looking forward to seeing you, for I have a great deal to discuss with you. I am thinking of taking this very same journey with you, my love, at the end of next summer, so that you may try some other waters. At the same time the company, the exercise, and the change of air will do you good, for it has agreed very well with me. I am greatly looking forward to this, and so are all my friends. (Before November 4, 1790)

He was apparently thinking of a journey in the Munich area.

Just after his return there was a farewell dinner for Joseph Haydn, who was leaving the next day for London with the impresario Johann Peter Salomon. Mozart also received an offer from Salomon, who had been a celebrated violinist in Bonn and later Berlin, then went to London in 1781 and became one of the city's most successful impresarios. Haydn earned a fortune in England through contracts negotiated by Salomon. But Mozart could not bring himself to make binding commitments. He was not willing to make a long journey without his wife, and he would only leave Vienna if he received an extended and more lucrative engagement elsewhere.

After an absence of only two weeks, Mozart wrote Constanze from Frankfurt:

If only you could look into my heart. There a struggle is going on between my yearning and longing to see and embrace you once more and my desire to bring home a large sum of money. I have often thought of traveling *farther afield*, but whenever I tried to make the decision, the thought always came to me, how bitterly I would regret it if I were to separate myself from my beloved wife for *such an uncertain prospect, perhaps even to no purpose whatever.* I feel as if I had left you years ago. Believe me, my love, if you were with me I might perhaps decide more easily, but I am too much accustomed to you and I love you too dearly to endure being separated from you for long. . . . If I work very hard in Vienna and take pupils, we can live very happily; and nothing but a *good engagement at some court* can make me abandon this plan.

(October 8, 1790)

(Haydn had it much easier; he and his wife got along so poorly that he never even entertained the idea of taking her along on one of his journeys. The money he earned during the two years he spent in England—about 24,000 florins—would have made a court position unnecessary even for Mozart.)

Nothing came of Mozart's plans to visit England. Two Englishmen "who refused to leave Vienna without making my acquaintance" (July 2, 1791) called on Mozart during the last summer of his life and spent several enjoyable hours with him in his favorite tavern, Zur ungarischen Krone (Hungarian Crown). The next English visitors tried unsuccessfully to find his grave, thereby helping to start another legend—about which more later.

HIS FATHER'S DEATH

"Little Leopold is healthy." Leopold Mozart used this phrase to begin almost every letter he wrote to his daughter in Sankt Gilgen after October 1785. He was referring to his grandson, who had been born in Salzburg the previous July, and who remained there until his grandfather's death. There was an active correspondence between Salzburg and Sankt Gilgen—at least one letter a week, often more. The grandchild was naturally the main subject, but Leopold Mozart also reported and commented on events in Salzburg as well as on the international political scene. His letters, which relate in detail all the daily happenings in his household, form a more thorough and comprehensive picture of everyday life than we have from any other contemporary.

We learn very little about Mozart, however. The correspondence between Salzburg and Vienna was apparently restricted to an occasional and fragmentary exchange of news. Leopold Mozart often complained about this, but it seems that he too neglected the correspondence, maintaining closer ties with his daughter. Mozart was very surprised one day to hear that his father was gravely ill. He wrote immediately to Salzburg:

> I hope and trust that as I write this you are feeling better. But if, contrary to all expectation, you are not recovering, I implore you by . . . not to hide it from me, but to tell me the whole truth or get someone to write it to me, so that I may come to your arms as quickly as is humanly possible. I entreat you by all that is sacred—to both of us. Nevertheless I trust that I shall soon have a reassuring letter from you.
>
> (April 4, 1787)

Mozart was seriously worried, for he had just been deeply affected by the sudden death of his friend Count August Clemens Hatzfeld, which had moved him to write to his father regarding his Masonically oriented ideas about death. And now, since that letter had been lost, he again mentioned his concept of death as the "true goal of our existence, . . . this best and truest friend of mankind." Through Freemasonry he had the good fortune "of learning that death is the key which unlocks the door of our true happiness."

But Leopold Mozart's condition did not seem terribly serious as yet. He had been sickly for a long time without having any clearly identifiable illness. He had written earlier to his daughter:

> You always want to hear that I am in excellent health. You are not allowing for the difference between an old and a young man. I don't have time to write a long letter, suffice it to say that for an old man there is no such thing as excellent health. There is always something wrong, and an old man declines just as youth grows and prospers. In short, one must mend as long as there is something to mend. I hope for improvement as better and warmer weather gradually sets in. You will, of

course, find me much thinner, but that in itself is no cause for concern. (February 24, 1787)

He had indeed become weaker and more delicate; apparently he had heart trouble and suffered from an accumulation of fluid. On May 10, 1787, he wrote: "I am no worse, thank God, and I hope for prolonged good weather so that I might take the fresh air." But a short time later he wrote that he hardly expected to survive the summer. He died suddenly on May 28.

The only record we have of Mozart's reaction to his father's death is an inconsequential postscript in a letter to Gottfried von Jacquin, to whom he was sending the great piano sonata for four hands (K. 521), which he had finished a few days earlier: "I inform you that on returning home today I received the sad news of my most beloved father's death. You can imagine the state I am in." (End of May 1787). We know nothing more on this subject.[14]

Although Mozart's activities during this time are known to us, we cannot draw any conclusions from them. We have no idea what went on in his mind; the individual events of this period lie scattered about like erratic boulders, and any attempt to establish a continuity between them would be fraudulent. We simply do not have the data necessary for a psychological explanation—least of all in the case of a historical personality who cannot respond to questioning.

Several days later there was another death: Mozart's pet bird, which he had bought three years earlier for 34 kreuzer. The bird must have been clever and quick to learn, for it could whistle the rondo theme from the piano concerto written for Barbara Ployer (K. 453). Its death prompted Mozart to write the following poem on June 4, 1787:

> A little fool lies here
> Whom I held dear—
> A starling in the prime
> Of his brief time,
> Whose doom it was to drain
> Death's bitter pain.
> Thinking of this, my heart
> Is riven apart.
> Oh, reader, shed a tear,

You also, here.
He was not naughty, quite,
But gay and bright,
And under all his brag
A foolish wag.
This no one can gainsay
And I will lay
That he is now on high,
And from the sky,
Praises me without pay
In his friendly way.
Yet unaware that death
Has choked his breath,
And thoughtless of the one
Whose rhyme is thus well done.

At this same time Mozart was composing a symphonic parody that he entered in his catalogue under the title *Ein musikalischer Spass* ("A Musical Joke," K. 522). It is certainly a bitter joke, a merciless derision of musical dilettantism. It was also during this period that he wrote his "musical dice game"—a kind of musical-mathematical puzzle in which the participants cast dice to create aleatory sequences of minuets, polonaises, and contredanses—and began working on his commission from Prague, the opera *Don Giovanni*.

CONDITIONS IN PRAGUE

Mozart's astounding successes in Prague—first with *Le nozze di Figaro*, then with *Don Giovanni*—cannot be fully explained by the Bohemians' renowned love and enthusiasm for music, which yielded such a large number of Bohemian musicians in European orchestras. Nor can we attribute them purely to Mozart's many friends and patrons in Prague, for he also had friends and patrons in Vienna, where the reaction to these works was somewhat different. It appears that Mozart's triumph in Prague was to a large extent a product of Bohemia's relationship to the Viennese court—a relationship that had been strained since the Thirty Years' War and had led to Bohemia's unusual position within the Habsburg empire.

It must be remembered that Prague was a seat of the Holy Roman Empire until 1612. The "family quarrel in the house of Habsburg" ended with the Battle of the White Mountain and led to the total subjugation of the Bohemians, who had refused to recognize the emperor. Subsequent trials resulted in expulsions of rebellious bourgeois and aristocrats. Almost half the nobility's property fell into the hands of the emperor's supporters in the military aristocracy of Italy, Spain, and Germany, or was handed over to Catholic feudal lords in Bohemia itself. A ruthless counter-reformation led by the Jesuits held sway over culture and education, while Germanization relegated the Czech population to insignificance. Not until almost a century later (1709) did Vienna relax its control, which had turned a self-assured nation into a politically marginal province. The Bohemian governing estates had practically no authority except to collect huge taxes, and the Bohemian nobility had a more or less insignificant position at the Viennese court until well into the eighteenth century. Throughout Bohemia national, social, and religious repression was evident in all areas of life.

As a result of this situation, eighteenth-century Bohemia was plagued by war more often than other nations—in particular, the Silesian Wars of 1740 to 1763. Yet the Bohemian estates were unable to regain their former privileges; the nation was governed from Vienna with the help of the Bohemian court chancellery, and with little consideration for national origin or traditional customs. The governing estates united Czech elements, including members of the aristocracy, with the German Bohemians under the banner of a Bohemian patriotism in which, as usual, the aristocracy played a leading role. Nobles already had economic leadership, and they used their capital to build up a significant manufacturing industry—much of it on the feudal manors themselves—including textile weaving (largely a cottage industry), glass production, and later, iron and paper mills. Such feudal institutions as serfdom made it easier for the nobility to develop manufacturing alongside agricultural production and gave them a sure advantage over bourgeois entrepreneurs, who were hardly able to compete.

The Josephine reforms aggravated tensions in all areas. Joseph II's attempt to establish a centralized state under firm autocratic rule, with a strictly organized administration, only incited the Bohemian patriots, who did not want to see the historical individuality of their nation suppressed by foreign domination. This foreign ruler had not even thought it necessary to have himself crowned king of Bohemia. Moreover, the preference for the German language—required in higher education, for example—showed disdain for Bohemia's historic bilingualism.

As far as agriculture was concerned, high taxes, crop failure, and high rates of land tenure led to tensions in a population forced to live at the subsistence level. Peasant revolts were the result. An edict of 1774 attempted to limit the demands made on serfs, but the peasants were disappointed with this reform because it did not go far enough, while the feudal overlords sought to prevent the new regulations from being enforced. The abolition of serfdom (1781) caused a migration to the cities as well as a modernization of agriculture. A further relaxation of the guild system encouraged a shift to industrial production among the bourgeoisie.

The Bohemian aristocrats, only a few of whom occupied military or administrative positions in Vienna, were more or less obliged to remain on their rural estates or in their sumptuous urban palaces. Yet it was just this development that contributed to a flowering of culture in the region. Many nobles established their own orchestras, and in a few significant cases, private theaters intended mainly for opera. The aristocrats had learned well how to economize and only engaged domestic personnel who could also play an instrument; by combining the functions of musician and liveried servant, they could simultaneously reduce their payrolls and increase the size of their ensembles. The other economic foundation of Bohemian life was the Church, which placed great emphasis on religious music. Most church musicians came from rural areas, where they were in almost perpetual supply thanks to the Bohemian school system.

In the true spirit of the counter-reformation, church music was one of the highest priorities of village schoolmasters, and they themselves had to serve as organists. This meant that every teacher had to have a good musical education, and musical training of schoolchildren was of utmost importance. Every schoolmaster was expected to compose, rehearse, and perform at least one mass each year. It is hardly surprising, then, that school lessons consisted mostly of musical instruction and that there were so many skilled instrumentalists from whom the nobility and the Church could take their pick. In the second half of the eighteenth century, with population pressure aggravating social tensions and unemployment, many saw a musical career as their only chance to earn a living. Thus, the emigration of Bohemian musicians had its roots in the unusual features of the school system; their training made them highly esteemed in other countries.

After 1774, educational reforms prohibited teachers from serving as organists; the general level of education rose considerably, and music occupied a much less significant place in the curriculum. But the musical tradition, preserved to a large extent in the home, remained unbroken. Many nobles reduced their private orchestras to wind ensembles as a way of saving money; the abolition of serfdom also brought about the dissolution of private ensembles and overall personnel reductions in aristocratic homes. The emigration of Bohemian musicians continued unabated.

In the wake of the reforms, village musicians migrated in greater numbers to the cities, where musical life—apart from Church institutions—gradually moved out of the taverns, establishing itself in public theaters and finally in concert halls. These developments were echoed everywhere. Only in the capital did private salons play a larger intermediary role (if comparable private institutions existed at all outside the capital). Every traveling virtuoso who came to Prague was greeted with enthusiasm and given a chance to perform, although he might have to make do with a large room in a tavern. Nonetheless, the public was musically very sophisticated.

The absence of a court meant that opera could only exist on a private basis; large-scale productions only took place during grandiose coronation festivities. There was great interest in opera, however. An opera house was founded by Count Franz Anton Sporck as early as 1724, and a smaller theater was built by Count Thun in 1735. Now, in addition to Jesuit school dramas and large oratorio performances, there was Italian opera, including examples of both *opera buffa* and *opera seria*. The reliance on independent entrepreneurs with their own ensembles produced much closer contacts with Leipzig and Dresden than with Vienna. Leipzig was the home of the Pasquale Bondini opera troupe, which gave the first performances of *Figaro* and *Don Giovanni* in Prague. In addition there was the Prague Nationaltheater, founded on the Viennese model by Count Franz Anton Nostitz-Rieneck in 1783. *Die Entführung aus dem Serail* had already been given there that year, and its success was largely due to Mozart's brilliant orchestral writing, especially for the wind instruments. Unlike Vienna, Prague saw performances of both the North German Singspiel (by way of Leipzig) and the Viennese Singspiel, which lasted only a short time at Vienna's Nationaltheater.

Among Mozart's musical friends in Prague was the influential couple Josepha and Franz Xaver Duschek, who spread the news of the intrigues preceding the *Figaro* premiere in Vienna. And he had long been acquainted with the Thun family, whose patriarch lived in Prague, maintained his own theater, and presented concerts in his home. But even without these personal connections, conditions in Prague were extremely favorable for Mozart. Bondini, whose theatrical venture needed a spectacular success, decided to make *Figaro* his first production—the work that had aroused curiosity both for its politically provocative subject matter and for its musical language, which made it very advanced, if not avant-garde. In Prague there was no jaded court society to stand in the way of success, and audiences were musically receptive enough to appreciate at first hearing a work that in Vienna had to struggle against popular tradition. *Figaro* was immediately understood in Prague as a contrast to the well-worn traditions of Italian opera (although there too it was sung first in Italian). It was precisely this turning away from Italian operatic models that triggered Prague's enthusiasm for Mozart, who became a rallying point for Bohemian patriotism at all social levels.

In a poem by the Prague physician Anton Daniel Breicha, which was distributed as a pamphlet at the *Figaro* performances, Mozart is not only-praised as a "melodic thinker" but celebrated in histrionic terms as the "German Apollo," while the courtly Italian opera is said to suffer from "envy that feeds upon itself." The fifth and last stanza of this homage, which Mozart triumphantly sent on to Salzburg, reads as follows:

> Behold! Germany, your fatherland, offers you its hand
> In the German custom, dissolves your ties
> Of friendship with strangers, honors

In you the German Apollo, thus
To gratify Germania's muses, and to scorn
Purblind envy that feeds upon itself. [15]

In light of Bohemian nationalism, the anecdote about the well-known Prague harpist Joseph Häusler is even more revealing. Häusler performed regularly in the Neues Wirtshaus and was constantly requested by patrons to play the most famous tune from *Figaro*, "*Non più andrai farfallone amoroso . . .*" ("No more, amorous butterfly, will you flutter around day and night"): he steadfastly maintained that Mozart was a native Bohemian.

It was an unusual honor for Mozart to be invited by a "company of distinguished connoisseurs and lovers of music" (January 12, 1787) to hear a performance of *Figaro* in Prague. After all, it was a journey of three and a half days that no one could be expected to make without some financial compensation—concert earnings, at the least. Moreover, the invitation came from the orchestra as well, a clear sign that he need fear no cabals among the musicians and that, on the contrary, they admired and honored his musical achievements. These were all obvious gibes at the musical scene in Vienna, where success was more a function of connections and intrigue than of talent and ability.

We do not know who made up this society of musicians and connoisseurs; it may not have been an official organization at all. Probably an invitation was drawn up and circulated among both aristocratic and bourgeois music lovers for signature. It is also possible that the Prague Freemasons, with whom Mozart made contact as soon as he arrived, arranged the invitation. Freemasonry played an important role in Prague, and many of Mozart's friends and acquaintances there, including the elder Count Thun, were lodge brothers.

JOURNEY TO PRAGUE

"This journey must have cost them a fortune!" exclaimed Leopold Mozart when Nancy Storace, Michael Kelly, Thomas Attwood, and five other people came through Salzburg in two coaches each drawn by four horses. He did not know that a short time earlier his son and daughter-in-law had undertaken their first journey to Prague under scarcely less luxurious circumstances. Wolfgang liked to travel in style, but he certainly had less luggage than the Salzburg visitors, since he would only be away for five weeks. The Mozarts also had a party of eight, for they were accompanied by Constanze's future brother-in-law Franz Hofer (who would also accompany Mozart to Frankfurt in 1789), the clarinetist Anton Stadler, the young violinist Marianne Crux with her aunt, Elizabeth Barbara Quallenberg, the violinist Kaspar Ramlo, Mozart's servant Joseph (who worked for the family for many years), and even Mozart's dog Gauckerl. This entourage traveled in two coaches and so was required by law to have two coachmen and at least six horses. Mozart probably paid for everything himself, for the musicians were poor (only the connection to Marianne Crux and her aunt remains unclear; perhaps they were traveling on their own and simply joined Mozart's party). Hofer, for example, was engaged as a violinist at St. Stephen's Cathedral, with a yearly salary of 25 florins (not even enough to pay the one-way fare), and Stadler already owed Mozart money. Everyone was in good spirits during the journey, and at the end they were calling each other by nicknames—Mozart was Punkititi, Constanze was Schabla Pumfa, and so on.

The Mozarts stayed in Count Thun's palace; the others, presumably at an inn. In Prague they were instantly overwhelmed with hospitality.

Immediately after our arrival at noon on Thursday, the 11th, we had a dreadful rush to get ready for lunch at one o'clock. After the meal old Count Thun entertained us with some music, performed by his own people, which lasted about an hour and a half. This kind of *real entertainment* I could enjoy every day. At six o'clock I drove with Count Canal to the so-called Breitfeld ball, where the cream of the beauties of Prague is wont to gather. (January 15, 1787)

Things continued in this fashion for the duration of their visit. If Mozart ever made a pleasure trip for its own sake, this was it. He apparently composed nothing in Prague except six German dances (K. 509) written shortly before his departure. Yet the city offered many opportunities to present his works, either by giving his own concerts or by writing something for any of the numerous private orchestras of the nobility. He did bring with him a three-movement symphony (K. 504), which was first performed in Prague and later became known as

the *Prague* Symphony. But as far as we know, he did not play a single
piano concerto there; it is only recorded that he played fantasies on the
piano, more than likely improvisations. Naturally Mozart's music was
a prominent feature of Count Thun's house concerts and was undoubtedly played on other occasions as well, but this generated no new
compositions. Mozart had really come for no other reason than to
enjoy his success with *Figaro*. He wrote about one of the balls he
attended:

> I neither danced nor flirted, . . . the former, because I was too tired,
> and the latter owing to my natural bashfulness. I looked on, however,
> with the greatest pleasure while all these people flew about in sheer
> delight to the music of my *Figaro*, arranged as quadrilles and waltzes.
> For here they talk about nothing but *Figaro*. Nothing is played, sung, or
> whistled but *Figaro*. No opera is drawing like *Figaro*. Nothing, nothing
> but *Figaro*. Certainly a great honor for me! (January 15, 1787)

Mozart and Constanze took in all the sights of Prague like real
tourists. He was given a tour of the famous Clementinum by Father
Karl Raphael Ungar, the librarian of this former Jesuit seminary, and a
member of the Prague lodge Zur Wahrheit und Einigkeit (Truth and
Unity). He was invited to dine with Count Emanuel Joseph Canal von
Malabaila, a member of the same lodge. The Mozarts spent their
evenings at the opera and slept late every morning. His musical
obligations were few; he gave one concert at the theater that brought in
1,000 florins, and three days later he conducted a performance of
Figaro, as he may also have done on one other occasion.

Pasquale Bondini, the lessee and director of the theater, had every
reason to be satisfied with Mozart's visit. *Figaro*'s triumph emboldened
him to commission a new opera from Mozart, at the same fee he might
expect to command in Vienna. Bondini undoubtedly discussed the
character of the opera with the composer, who had to take the singers
and theatrical capabilities of the troupe into consideration. But at this
point there was certainly no librettist and no idea for a libretto.
Bondini left that matter entirely to Mozart. For an independent opera
impresario, success was measured differently than at Vienna's Nationaltheater, which was under imperial supervision and shared the funds
of the Hoftheater (i.e., it was subsidized by the emperor). At the

Nationaltheater in Vienna, some operas were performed only three or four times and then disappeared from the program. Bondini could not afford such a loss, especially when he had to pay the composer a fee. But *Figaro* had proved that Mozart's music could be a great popular success despite its extraordinary demands on both singers and instrumentalists. Bondini took the precaution of asking Mozart, the experienced man of the theater, to return to Prague and attend the last few rehearsals of the new opera, which was to be introduced at the beginning of the next season so that there would be enough time for it to make a healthy profit.

When Mozart arrived in Prague again seven months later, at the end of September 1787, he had *Don Giovanni* with him. Not all of it was in final form, of course; many details had to be worked out during rehearsals with the singers. The overture, as usual, was not written down until the last minute (it is dated the evening before the premiere). [16]

This second visit to Prague was definitely a working vacation; Mozart was accompanied only by his wife, from whom he was rarely separated. The premiere had to be postponed from October 14 to October 29, and the entire time was occupied with rehearsals, for

> the stage personnel here are not as smart as those in Vienna, when it comes to mastering an opera of this kind in a very short time. Secondly, I found on my arrival that so few preparations and arrangements had been made that it would have been absolutely impossible to produce it on the 14th, that is, yesterday. (October 15, 1787)

To make matters worse, one of the singers was taken ill.

> As the company is so small, the impresario is in a perpetual state of anxiety and has to spare his people as much as possible, lest some unexpected indisposition should plunge him into the most awkward of all situations—that of not being able to produce any show at all! So everything dawdles along here because the singers, who are lazy, refuse to rehearse on opera days and the manager, who is anxious and timid, will not force them. (October 21, 1787)

But Mozart did not betray his impatience. He conducted *Figaro* again in place of the canceled premiere, certainly a sign of goodwill toward Bondini and his ensemble.

That *Don Giovanni* still needed a lot of work is clear from the fact that Lorenzo Da Ponte, the librettist, arrived in Prague several days before the date originally scheduled for the premiere, which he was unable to see because of the postponement.[17] Mozart complained that he hardly even had time to write letters. His problems were no longer compositional but lay in adapting his material to prevailing conditions, so that "I am far too much at the disposal of other people and far too little at my own. I need hardly tell you, as we are such old friends, that this is not the kind of life I prefer" (October 25, 1787). His efforts were repaid: the premiere was a brilliant success, "received with thundering applause," as Mozart proudly reported to Vienna on November 4.

Mozart, who conducted the premiere himself, had found a public that acclaimed him, apart from musical considerations, simply because he had written an opera especially for Prague and had come from the capital to perform in the provinces. When Mozart "entered the orchestra pit, he had to bow three times before the applause stopped, and the same thing happened when he left the pit," as the *Prager Oberpostamtszeitung* reported. The article continued:

> In view of the opera's many difficulties, it is admirable that such a good performance was achieved with so few rehearsals. Everyone—singers and orchestra—gave everything they had to gratify Herr Mozart and show their esteem for him. Great expense was incurred by the need for extra singers in the chorus and by the scenery, beautifully designed by Herr Guardasoni. The unusually large audience guaranteed an enthusiastic reception.[18]

Bondini gave Mozart the receipts from the fourth performance, which must have totaled 700 to 1,000 florins, in addition to his fee.

Mozart stayed in Prague for two weeks after the premiere, conducting several more performances and finally finding some time for his friends. For Josepha Duschek he wrote a dramatic vocal scene associated with a certain anecdote that the piece itself does nothing to discredit. It seems that Mozart had long promised to write this aria, and the singer finally forced him to do so by locking him in his room until he finished. Mozart then agreed to give her the aria only if she could sing it flawlessly at sight. One passage in the text has a double meaning and can be translated, "What breathlessness, what a terrible place for me!" Mozart gave these words such unexpected harmonic twists that they might have given even the most experienced singer pause. Josepha Duschek lived in a charming garden villa (still standing today) in a suburb of Prague. This house has also been the focus of several Mozart anecdotes (about which the local experts are extremely well informed, as visitors to Prague soon discover).

On November 4, Mozart wrote to Gottfried von Jacquin:

> How I wish that my good friends, particularly you and Bridi, were here just for one evening in order to share my pleasure! But perhaps my opera will be performed in Vienna after all! I hope so. People here are doing their best to persuade me to remain on for a couple of months and write another one. But I cannot accept this proposal, however flattering it may be.

Why not? In Vienna Mozart had no obligations or commissions; Constanze was with him in Prague, and the three-year-old Karl Thomas was being well looked after in a private institution. There is no clear reason why Mozart should have turned down an opera contract, for opera commissions were what he wanted most. Erich Schenk speculates that Mozart had received news of Christoph Willibald von Gluck's imminent death.[19] Gluck, who had been ill for years and had already suffered two strokes, died quite unexpectedly of a third stroke while taking a drive.[20]

Mozart began his return journey no earlier than November 13. He may have reached Vienna just in time for Gluck's lavish funeral, which took place on November 17 and was attended by vast numbers of Viennese. Gluck's death may have had something to do with Mozart's receiving the position of *Kammerkompositeur* shortly thereafter. According to official records, the position was given to Mozart so that "such a rare musical genius may not be compelled to seek his livelihood abroad."[21] Mozart's plans to visit England had been announced in the newspapers, and along with his recent successes in Prague, they underlined the fact that he was highly esteemed elsewhere. (It is likely that Countess Thun also urged the emperor to make this appointment.) In any event, the Prague newspaper reports on *Don Giovanni* were subsequently reprinted in the Viennese papers.

IL DISSOLUTO PUNITO: DON GIOVANNI

Mozart was naturally very anxious for *Don Giovanni* to be performed in Vienna. If we can believe Lorenzo Da Ponte, the reports from Prague had the desired effect and the emperor himself wanted the opera produced as soon as possible (but was not able to see it until the end of the year because he was off fighting the Turkish War). To accommodate the singers, Mozart had to make a few changes that were somewhat damaging dramatically—he added a duet between Zerlina and Leporello, for instance, which is gratuitous and can only be understood as a concession to the public. The changes in the score point to a certain apprehension, perhaps resulting from the risks of working with some new, inexperienced singers.

A triumph in Prague—a flop in Vienna? Was the nobility, the Nationaltheater's most important opera audience, once again to blame? After attending the premiere, Count Zinzendorf wrote that he found the music agreeable and full of variety; he attended six of the fifteen performances and only once complained of boredom, possibly because of the quality of that particular performance.

The reservations about *Don Giovanni* are not reservations about Mozart. Joseph II was probably right when he pointed out that the opera contained nothing new and that the story (not Mozart's music, of course) was well-known to the Viennese and did not really reflect prevailing tastes, especially those of educated, "enlightened" people among both the nobility and the bourgeoisie.

The Don Juan theme had long been a subject for the crude humor of the popular theater; its "demonic" side and its potential as a character drama were discovered only in the nineteenth century and need not detain us here. (We are interested specifically in the world of Mozart and his contemporaries, not in later opinions of Mozart.) Tirso de Molina's *Burlador de Sevilla y convidado de piedra* ("The Gallant of Seville and the Stone Guest"), the original model for all adaptations of this theme, combined comic and fantastic elements with a Christian call to repentance. His "gallant" is not entirely unsympathetic, but he ignores all admonitions to repent his sins until it is too late and he is dragged down to Hell. All themes found in later adaptations of this material are present to some degree in Tirso de Molina; in most subsequent versions the emphasis is merely shifted. During the next century and a half, the story was taken up by such major dramatists as Molière, Corneille, and Goldoni, but it achieved wider circulation in popular theatrical forms: *commedia dell'arte*, puppet shows, improvisational theater, farces, and vaudeville. These versions were rife with fake pathos and irrational comic-burlesque elements; the relationship between master and servant became an important ingredient in the story because it allowed the character of Leporello to be transformed into a harlequin, a buffoon—a figure so popular that it alone could hold the audience's interest. The play had become a piece of folk theater through a process that had been resisted by every theater reformer since Johann Christoph Gottsched. Attempts were made to salvage the theme and introduce it into serious, sophisticated theater. Molière's adaptation can be understood as rationalist moral criticism, and Gluck's *Don Juan* ballet raises the play to an almost mythic level solidly based in the *opera seria* tradition, without any comic element whatsoever. But none of these attempts could make any real headway against the other Don Juan tradition. The popular theater generally ignored the objections of zealous reformers, heedlessly combining crude jokes with grand passions before an audience that wanted to be dazzled and mystified by mechanical effects. This was a theater that stubbornly resisted the precepts of rationalist enlightenment.

Far from being relegated to ad hoc performances on temporary stages, the popular theater was very much at home in Vienna. The Leopoldstadt Theater, especially, nurtured this tradition, which eventually spawned Ferdinand Raimund's *Zauberpossen* (magic farces) and flourished in Vienna more than anywhere else. Mozart, with his highly developed theatrical sense and feeling for dramatic effects, had always had a certain affinity for this type of theater; was not *Die Zauberflöte* an example? He often visited such theaters and was even motivated to write (or at least begin) a play for the popular stage, *Die Liebesprobe* ("The Test of Love").[22] And it was in the Leopoldstadt Theater that a local celebrity, Karl von Marinelli, first presented his *commedia dell'arte* versions of the Don Juan story in 1783. The Viennese, then, were well acquainted with the theme.

People in other cities were equally familiar with the play about the "stone guest"—an important point, because the comments of theater critics outside Vienna can help us understand contemporary reservations about Mozart's opera. In Vienna the criticism was actually quite restrained and was more or less concealed in journalistic reports on the performances. Elsewhere, however, a clear distinction was drawn between the action and the music, and serious doubts were expressed about the discrepancy between "low" theater and Mozart's "high" artistic achievement.

One of the clearest and most detailed contemporary discussions of *Don Giovanni*, Johann Friedrich Schink's review[23] of a Hamburg performance in 1789, points to these problems. He praises Mozart's music as

> thoughtful, deeply felt, and well suited to the situations and feelings of his characters. . . . He never composes runs and trills on awkward syllables, and avoids ornamenting his vocal line with empty and unnecessary coloratura. Such superfluity is the enemy of true expression in music, for expression does not lie in individual words, but in the natural, intelligent combination of tones, through which true feeling is communicated. Mozart has completely mastered this kind of expression. . . . He is a real virtuoso, whose intellect is never crippled by his powers of imagination. His enthusiasm is guided by reason, his portrayals by careful consideration.

Schink is obviously not a musician, but the music, at least, meets with his approval. The figure of Don Giovanni is another matter entirely: for Schink he is the ultimate lecher, the very embodiment of evil and immorality. Schink is incapable of perceiving the other elements of Don Giovanni's personality—his charm, for instance, which is characterized musically in the duet with Zerlina and elsewhere. The supernatural appearance of the Commendatore is worse still because it flouts all the rules of reason.

> Don Juan combines in himself all that is irrational, bizarre, unnatural, and contradictory, and only poetic nonsense from a human hand could raise him to the level of an operatic hero. . . . A most vile, miserable, and dastardly fellow, whose life is an unbroken chain of infamies, seductions, and murderous deeds. . . . He coldheartedly commits the worst atrocities with as much equanimity as if he were drinking a glass of water; cuts down another person as if he were going to a dance; seduces and deceives virtuous women as if he were taking a pinch of

snuff. And he is amused by these abominations, and finds great diversion in his bestialities. . . . A stone statue sings, is invited to dinner, accepts the invitation, climbs down from its horse, and arrives safely at the appointed hour. How charming! What a shame it does not eat as well—then the fun would be complete.

Schink criticizes the opera as representing a theater of the unnatural, the inauthentic, and the irrational, which does not live up to "enlightened" standards and offers only low entertainment.

How can reason on the operatic stage be amusing to people who hear only singing, who only want their eardrums shattered, who only wish to digest their oysters in comfort and while away a few mindless hours? What could be more welcome under these circumstances than the kind of fatuous nonsense perpetrated here?

This argument could equally have come from Joseph von Sonnenfels, who liked to think of himself as the high priest of Viennese critics. But *Don Giovanni* could not be written off so easily, and Schink may have sensed this. He therefore drew up a strange catalogue of objections that on the one hand accused Mozart of providing inadequate music for this "fatuous" operatic material—music too complicated for the low intellect of the average opera enthusiast—and on the other hand accused opera audiences of having no sensibility.

What induced him to adorn such a typically Italian opera subject with such beautiful, noble, unoperatic music? Is this splendid, majestic, powerful singing perhaps wasted on ordinary opera patrons, who bring only their ears to the theater and leave their hearts at home? And would not the heart be unnecessary for a play in which only seeing and hearing are important? The first prerequisite of a successful play is that the poet write with his heart as well as his head. Herr Mozart may be an excellent composer, but he will never be so for our ordinary opera patrons, for he would first have to instill in them a quality that they understand as poorly as a blind man understands color—sensibility.

Despite his strictly rationalist objections, Schink clearly demonstrates that Mozart has created a new type of opera, totally outside the traditional forms of Singspiel and *opera buffa*. Mozart deliberately took his impetus from the spoken theater, whether a topical play like *Figaro* or, as in this case, a popular folk comedy. And he experimented with an entirely new musical language, most evident in the ensemble numbers and large-scale finales—through-composed sequences that lend a totally new temporal structure to the stage action. In *Don Giovanni* Mozart even went so far as to abandon the conventional opera aria: Don Giovanni himself is not given a single aria in the traditional sense. The closest thing to such an aria is the famous number in which Leporello reels off the daunting list of Don Giovanni's conquests—to, of all people, his employer's abandoned mistress, Donna Elvira. If Mozart wished to make a story associated with popular burlesque viable in the opera house, he had to utilize operatic means. His contemporaries, who were accustomed to innocuous Singspiels, and who applauded Karl Ditters von Dittersdorf's *Doktor und Apotheker* ("Doctor and Apothecary"), suddenly found themselves confronted with the techniques of heroic grand opera and an orchestra including trumpets and trombones, all in order to depict the life of a philanderer realistically and without moralizing. Their dismay is clearly expressed in a review of a performance in Berlin on December 20, 1790.

> With his *Don Juan* Mozart wanted to write something extraordinary, something inimitably great; that much is certain. It is indeed extraordinary, inimitably great it is not! Whims, caprices, and pride, rather than the heart, created *Don Juan*, and we would rather admire the high achievements of this composer's art in an oratorio or other religious music than in his *Don Juan*—whose ending is more or less analogous to a depiction of the Last Judgment, where graves burst open like soap bubbles, mountains explode, and the Angel of Death blows the signal on his trumpet. Nevertheless, this opera is bringing the management good returns, and the gallery, boxes, and stalls will not soon be empty, for a ghost in armor and fire-breathing furies are great attractions— "Oh, these wise men of Gotham!"[24]

A Weimar newspaper reported on the same performance:

> The music of this Singspiel is quite beautiful, but here and there rather artificial and too heavily orchestrated. The story is old and well known, and finds favor with the masses only through the burlesque humor of

Leporello—a latter-day Harlequin—and the stone Commendatore on his horse.[25]

The criticisms alternate between a disapproval clearly stemming from North German Protestantism and—as in Weimar—a snootiness about the bad taste of "the masses." The debate about the opera attracted more and more attention and spread steadily. A Berlin reviewer wrote, "I went full of high expectations and heard an opera which, in my opinion, satisfies the eye, charms the ear, offends reason, insults morality, and treads wickedly upon virtue and feeling."[26] This reviewer also draws a clear distinction between Mozart's music and the play.

> There is very little dialogue; most of the text is sung. And if ever a nation could take pride in one of her sons, so Germany must be proud of Mozart, the composer of this opera. Never, indeed never before, was the greatness of the human spirit so tangible, and never has the art of composition been raised to such heights! Melodies that an angel might have invented are here accompanied by celestial harmonies, and anyone whose soul is the least bit receptive to the truly beautiful will surely pardon my saying *our ears are enchanted.*

The critic rightly gives Mozart a share of the blame for the choice of libretto (though his comments demonstrate a total lack of understanding).

> Your music and your harmony would penetrate infinitely deeper into the souls of your listeners if they were not held back by the baseness of the text! No, dear man! In future do not be so cruel to your kind and generous muse. Seek to build the permanent structure of your fame on pillars of virtue that will not make honest maidens blush for shame. What does it avail you if your name is written in diamond letters on a golden plaque, if this plaque hangs on a pillory?

All these reviews have one common tendency: they praise Mozart's music as beautiful but difficult (for both performers and listeners) while more or less condemning the libretto as tasteless. The triumph in Prague, then, was the product of enthusiasm for Mozart's music on the part of a sophisticated audience always eager to understand the new, the unusual, and the complex; it demonstrated open-mindedness toward an avant-garde musical language. In Vienna and elsewhere Mozart's music was often considered too complicated and ornate, and in this instance wasted on a text that would not find acceptance among educated society.[27] But for Mozart *Figaro* was no "accident" or isolated experiment; he continued along the same lines in *Così fan tutte* and *Die Zauberflöte*. Mozart was developing a type of opera that eluded all attempts at genre classification. It cannot be described with invented terms like "heroico-*buffo*" or "tragico-*buffo*" because both the *buffo* and the serious elements arise naturally from the realistic character portrayal, the careful observation of all the qualities that make up a character's personality. And at the opera's conclusion there is no naive reconciliation, no restoration of an ideal world where everything is as it should be. Questions remain, breaches have become visible, and Mozart's music creates enough objective distance so that the listener is unable to ignore the problems.

THE EMPEROR AT WAR—WITH EVERYONE

When *Don Giovanni* was given for the first time, in Prague on October 29, 1787, the Habsburg monarchy had already been at war with Turkey for two months, though war had not yet been declared. When the opera was first performed in Vienna, the imperial forces had been sitting idle for months in an ill-fated campaign near Belgrade. There the emperor ruled the entire monarchy from his tent; he directed the war council, wrote letters, and even sent instructions to the management of the Nationaltheater in Vienna. Within a very short time, the political situation had deteriorated drastically. Joseph II suffered one defeat after another—militarily, at the hands of the Turks, and domestically, in his relations with the Habsburg dominions.

The change had begun in the Austrian Netherlands. As of January 1, 1787, as part of his plan for centralization, Joseph II had reorganized the administrative structure and the judicial system of the Netherlands, without consulting the governing estates and despite the fact that he had earlier sworn to uphold their constitution. Opposition was so violent that the governors were forced to reinstate the old system after only a few months. Instead of pacifying the Flemish, this action only advertised the emperor's weakness. The opposition managed to join forces with clerics opposed to imperial reforms in Church administration, and a revolt was launched. The Austrian authorities fearfully gave way, and all new measures were annulled—without the consent of the emperor, who replaced the officials with new ones and sent additional troops to the region.

At the same time Turkey had declared war on Russia, undoubtedly in answer to the expansionist policies of Catherine II, who had long wanted to possess Constantinople. Joseph II's alliance with the czarina committed him to providing an army of 30,000, but in fact he deployed more than 280,000 men along the Turkish border. After all, he also wished to profit from military conquest. It soon turned out that Catherine was letting the emperor wage war against the Turks alone (especially since Russia was now under attack from King Gustav III of Sweden). Joseph's army was in excellent condition, but his military leadership was miserable. No offensive was launched because the Russian troops never arrived; instead, there were minor skirmishes with the Turks. Worst of all were the epidemics: the lazarettos were filled to capacity, half the army was sick, and thousands of soldiers died. In 1788 the emperor himself fell ill; he would not recover.

Now everything happened at once. In Hungary discontent reached a high point, with open talk of secession; there too Joseph II had exceeded the limits of tolerance. First, refusing to be crowned king of Hungary, he had carried the crown off to Vienna and moved the Hungarian capital from Pressburg (Bratislava) to Ofen (Buda). Then he had proceeded with his plans for centralization, introduced a new administrative structure in Hungary, and made German the compulsory official language. Opposition increased within the self-assured Hungarian aristocracy, only a small percentage of whom were Josephinians, and the situation grew still worse in 1785 when serfdom was abolished. The Hungarian nobles, who would not relinquish their tax exemption, soon found themselves under economic pressure: Austrian products entered Hungary tax-free, while Hungarian goods were subject to customs duties in Austria. This disparity was to remain until equal taxation of all subjects was introduced in Hungary. The Hungarian governing estates still considered their country an autonomous nation and were no longer willing to be systematically deprived of power. Some even considered deposing Joseph II as Hungarian monarch and choosing a new king (a likely candidate was Duke Karl August of Sachsen-Weimar, who had acted as secretary-general of the *Fürstenbund*).

Joseph II had already tasted defeat several times. In the so-called Schelde Conflict of 1785, he was unable to gain access to the Schelde for shipping to and from the Austrian Netherlands. His plan to exchange the Netherlands for Bavaria had failed. He had only managed to suppress the peasant uprisings in Walachia and Bohemia by dint of military force. Now that he was at war with the Turks, he was faced with revolt in the Netherlands and separatism in Hungary. To make matters worse, trouble was brewing in Vienna itself. There was open opposition to the Turkish war, fueled by the enormous economic burden it placed on the population. Food prices had risen drastically and in some cases doubled; bakeries had been looted for the first time in Vienna's history. The nobility spent less and less time in the capital. The tax reforms scheduled to go into effect in 1789 had apparently been blocked, and finally Count Rudolph Chotek, president of the court commission on taxation, resigned in protest. This signal was completely misread by the emperor, who wrote Chotek saying he was accustomed to ingratitude but was astonished that a man like the count would take such a quixotic step out of pure obstinacy. The nobility, however, heartily endorsed Chotek's action.

Vehement criticism also emerged from bourgeois circles that had supported imperial reforms. A famous pamphlet by Joseph Richter— *Warum wird Kaiser Joseph von seinem Volke nicht geliebt?*, published in 1787—examined both the praise and criticism of the emperor. Under Joseph II, according to Richter, there was freedom of thought and of the press; he had shattered the chains of serfdom, legislated religious tolerance, reduced the number of monks, made bishops imperial subjects, and stopped the flow of money to Rome; he had introduced widespread legal and economic reforms and improved medical care. Special mention is made of the emperor's personal modesty, his accessibility to all his subjects, and his industrious nature: *Joseph wacht, wenn die Nation schläft* ("Joseph watches while the nation sleeps"). Yet Richter also pointed out that Joseph had made many enemies: priests, aristocrats (whose power he curtailed) and their dependents, government officials suddenly forced to do their

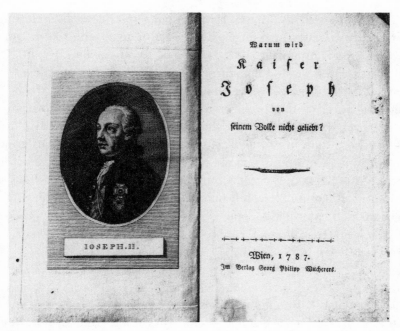

Title page of a pamphlet (Why Is Emperor Joseph Not Loved by His
People?) *written by a disillusioned follower of the emperor. Vienna was
flooded almost daily with new pamphlets and leaflets on current events,
which were published without interference from the censor.*

jobs, people who lost their industrial and trade privileges, and many
others who had reason to be disgruntled at his reforms. But all his
"honorable subjects" had legitimate grievances, which was why he
was not loved by the people. The emperor should raise the pensions of
government officials, grant more exemptions from military service,
introduce milder punishments for offenders, be more tolerant of burial
customs and other traditions, and show more consideration for birth
and social position (to which the common people also attached great
importance). He should be more lenient toward the mistakes of his
subjects (especially government officials), less frugal, and more generous to science and the arts. Finally, he should not be so rash in his
decisions or heed informers. This peculiar catalogue of complaints
shows that although the emperor had many achievements to his credit,
he had forfeited public approval through arrogant behavior and deci-

sions he made without thought for their consequences. The reference to the many enemies of reform was a warning to Joseph that he must not alienate his supporters or he would be totally isolated.

But the emperor would not learn. He acted alone, against the advice of ministers, advisers, and well-meaning friends, often making decisions that were politically unsound. He believed he could prevail in the Netherlands through military might but succeeded for only a brief time before rebellion erupted again, eventually becoming an armed revolt of such proportions that the insurgents were able to drive out the imperial troops and the Habsburg administration, spurred on by the French Revolution, which had broken out in the meantime. The Austrians fled so quickly (some even on foot) that they were forced to leave behind the national archives and the national treasury of 3,000,000 florins.

Nor was there any real success in the Turkish war. The military situation began to improve somewhat only after General Gideon von Laudon became supreme commander in August 1789. Belgrade was captured in October, Bucharest in November. But these events brought no ultimate victory, and Joseph II did not live to see the war's unsuccessful conclusion. (An armistice was signed in September 1790; peace came a year later. The Austrians came away with nothing; the conquered territory, including Belgrade, was given back.)

On his deathbed, the emperor was forced to revoke all the ordinances that had made Hungary little more than an Austrian province. Even the crown of St. Stephen had to be returned, an event greeted with great jubilation. Of all the emperor's measures only the abolition of serfdom and the tolerance laws were retained—the Hungarians would accept no more.

Dissatisfaction with Joseph II's policies had become widespread at all levels of society. The Turkish war was very unpopular: no one understood its objective, but everyone suffered because of the heavy war taxes. Developments in the Netherlands were of little relevance in Vienna, for the Viennese nobility and officials had few personal or family connections with that distant corner of the empire. The unrest in Hungary had a much greater effect on life in the capital, since many Hungarian aristocrats spent most of their time there and played an important role in society.

The oppressive atmosphere had a dampening effect on the city's cultural life, which was supported mainly by the nobility and the higher levels of officialdom, and only to a small extent by the bourgeoisie, which gained economic—and thus cultural—influence later in Austria than elsewhere. The opera and theaters remained open and continued to offer their usual fare, but even the richest families now had tighter budgets and were less inclined to spend large sums on private concerts and recitals. It must not be forgotten that all male members of the high nobility who held military rank were on the battlefield. Many others had withdrawn to their estates, either out of bitterness or because their economic interests required much more attention during periods of unrest. It is not surprising to read in historical documents that aristocrats had to dismiss many of their servants and even sell some of their horses.[28]

It goes without saying that more and more aristocrats disbanded their private orchestras as a result of political events. The evidence clearly indicates a decrease in concert activity, though we lack statistical data and have very scanty information about the particulars of concert life. There is still much research to be done on this subject, much important information to be gleaned by consulting the archives of noble families and the autobiographies of musicians. Almost all Mozart biographies claim that Mozart lost the support of the nobility during these years, could not get his works performed or give concerts himself, and died in obscure penury as a result. The grounds for this arbitrary assessment are never identified, but it has been so tirelessly repeated that it has given rise to a stream of legends that are now part of our historical baggage. Yet the contention that Mozart lost aristocratic patronage is certainly false.

All other reasons aside, it is false because it reduces the problem of wartime economic structure to a personal level. Mozart did not have a harder time than any other musician in Vienna during the Turkish war. They all suffered from the decline in performance opportunities and the resulting drop in income. (Individual examples of this phenomenon still need to be verified historically.) That the war affected the salon as well as public concert life is hardly astonishing in view of the political situation. Mozart himself, however, received numerous signs of good faith from patrons between 1788 and 1791, including commissions for new works from the court (Nationaltheater), wealthy aristocrats (Baron van Swieten and his circle), and even well-to-do bourgeois (loans from fellow Freemasons). The year 1791 was actually one of his most productive; most of the works he wrote then were commissioned. But it was also a year of recovery for Austria, thanks to Leopold II's efforts to maintain peace (1788 and 1789 had been overshadowed by the Turkish War, then came the turmoil caused by the French Revolution, and in 1790 the death of Joseph II brought further instability to domestic and foreign affairs).

Everyone had to suffer during wartime, and there is no reason to believe that musicians were an exception. Mozart too had his share of professional hardship between 1788 and 1790. (His wife's illness undoubtedly caused him great concern, and he spared no expense for her with medical treatment.) All in all it must be emphasized that in times of crisis Mozart could still rely on dedicated friends and was even able to make new ones. The emperor himself, returning from the battlefield deathly ill, gave Mozart yet another opera contract—even though in August 1788 he had made preparations to suspend performances of Italian opera at the Nationaltheater temporarily, primarily because of the operating expenses; the 1787–88 season alone had required an additional subsidy of 80,000 florins. Joseph II did not carry out this plan, but he doubtless took no more pleasure in the Nationaltheater. He came back to Vienna on December 5, 1788. On December 15 he attended a performance of *Don Giovanni*, which he had not yet seen. It was his first public appearance since returning from the war, and the audience gave him such an insultingly cold and indifferent reception that he left long before the end of the opera. Even in "his" Nationaltheater, the ailing emperor was made to realize that he had almost no friends left and had become at best an object of pity.[29] Mozart probably witnessed this scene, but no record of his reaction has survived.

AN ARISTOCRATIC PATRON: BARON VAN SWIETEN

The disbanding of private aristocratic orchestras may have increased as a direct result of the war, but it was also a product of changing forms of aristocratic display. These developments had drastic consequences for musicians, even though the nobility was not known for paying high salaries and sometimes even hired musicians as servants in order to save money. But Mozart had nothing to do with such musical service after leaving Salzburg. In Vienna he could earn as much for one concert as he had earned for the entire year in Salzburg (450 florins), and in December 1787 he began receiving an annual salary of 800 florins from the imperial court, with no specific obligations beyond the composition of dance numbers for the carnival balls. (This sinecure was only the foundation of his income, yet it was more than most other musicians earned through daily drudgery.) Vienna was finding new ways of cultivating music, which could be characterized as an appropriation of cultural life by the bourgeoisie, though the nobility retained its dominant economic influence for some time. The new kind of public concert did not serve feudal prestige or the private indulgence of aristocrats, to which music had formerly been subordinate; rather, it sought to present the individual work of art as a manifestation of the creative spirit. Against this background, phenonema such as the Society of Associated Cavaliers deserve special attention. This group was made up of aristocratic "connoisseurs and lovers of music" who originally sought to maintain their exclusivity by accepting only noblemen into their circle. Their main interest, however, was the presentation of unusual large-scale works that went beyond the means of the (very wealthy) individual members, especially since they were determined to have only first-rate performances. The initiator of this enterprise was Baron van Swieten, who became a patron of Mozart just at the time when the war's restrictive effect on musical life was giving him cause for concern.

Gottfried van Swieten was the son of Empress Maria Theresa's personal physician, Gerhard van Swieten. The elder Swieten had also served as prefect of the court library and was succeeded by his son. This extraordinarily learned and multilingual government official began his career as a diplomat and was especially adept at securing an unusually high income from the state. He also inherited a considerable estate from his father (his total income was ten times Mozart's). In addition to his legal training, he had a thorough knowledge of music, which later enabled him to assume the undisputed role of high priest in matters of musical taste. From 1770 to 1777 Swieten was imperial envoy at the Berlin court, where he was always a welcome guest of Frederick II. In Berlin he came into contact with the pupils of Carl Philipp Emanuel Bach (who had left in 1768 to take a position in

Hamburg) and thereby discovered the music of Johann Sebastian Bach and George Frideric Handel. Swieten's close association with these circles is attested by the fact that he is the dedicatee of Johann Nikolaus Forkel's Bach biography and of Carl Philipp Emanuel Bach's third collection of sonatas and rondos. Swieten's musical interests were by no means restricted to older music, however energetically he later sought to save it from obscurity, but encompassed contemporary music as well. He even composed himself; several of his symphonies and Singspiels have survived. He actively solicited subscriptions for C. P. E. Bach, arranged for his works to be brought out by the Viennese publisher Artaria, and even commissioned six string symphonies from him.

When Joseph II began his reign, Swieten was appointed president of the court commission on education and censorship in addition to his directorship of the court library. This made him something like a minister of culture for the Josephine era, entrusted with the supervision of schools, the university, and scientific facilities. He played an important role in the disposition of monastic properties, and his influence over censorship gave him a crucial role in the Josephine Enlightenment.[30] Swieten had the full confidence of Joseph II and was one of the collaborators on his reform program. He was also a Freemason, as were many other high government officials. It is small wonder that in the post-Josephine period, when the government and its somewhat muddled bureaucracy were once again being reorganized, he quickly lost his influence and eventually his important posts.[31]

Shortly after his move to Vienna Mozart began a close musical association with Swieten. He belonged to the small circle of connoisseurs who met each Sunday at Swieten's home to play works by earlier masters. Through Swieten's immense private music library Mozart became acquainted with the keyboard works of Bach and the music of Handel, and was moved to write his own extensive fugal studies (1782)—with additional incentive from the supposedly unmusical Constanze Mozart.

At these Sunday matinees, entire Handel oratorios were often presented, with Mozart at the piano playing from the score. But playing through such works in this unsatisfactory manner only emphasized the need for a complete performance with full chorus and orchestra and professional soloists. To this end Swieten founded the

GODEFR. L. B. de SWIETEN.
Stud. Cens. Libr. et Bibl. Cæs. Præfect.

I. C. de Lakner del.   Mansfeld sc.

Gottfried van Swieten, diplomat and musician, who in 1782 became president
of the Court Commission on Education and Censorship (equivalent to minister
of culture) under Joseph II. He furthered the study of "older" music but
supported contemporary music as well.

Society of Associated Cavaliers, which besides himself included Princes Schwarzenberg, Lobkowitz, and Dietrichstein, and Counts Apponyi, Batthyány, and Johann Esterházy. (The membership was by no means random; these were all wealthy aristocrats with strong musical interests, and many maintained their own orchestras.) The society was founded in 1786, and each year it organized at least one large oratorio performance, usually in premises provided by Count Esterházy (who then lived in the Palais Pálffy) or Prince Schwarzenberg, or in the large hall of the court library. A public performance would then follow in the Nationaltheater or the Jahn Rooms. Mozart's other obligations prevented him from taking part in these performances until 1788, when he began serving as conductor. A chorus and an orchestra of more than eighty musicians were engaged from the Nationaltheater and were well paid for their services; the soloists were the best that could be found. Exemplary performances were achieved through many intensive rehearsals—an unusual practice at the time. The participants were certainly among the most distinguished performers who could be assembled north of the Alps. It should not be forgotten that by this time Mozart's fame in Europe was equal to that of Haydn and C. P. E. Bach.

Mozart was also commissioned to make arrangements of the choral works by Handel that were performed with the support of the Cavalier Society between 1788 and 1791. (We do not know the dates of all the performances, but it is certain that Mozart conducted a public performance of *Acis and Galatea* for his own benefit in 1788.) Swieten himself made the German translations, and Mozart carefully modernized the instrumentation, for historically authentic performances were unheard of. He fundamentally changed the instrumentation in some numbers by discarding the simple juxtaposition of obbligato lines with basso continuo and substituting full orchestral accompaniments. Unlike other Handel arrangers, Mozart made no attempt to "improve" or "spruce up" the compositions but merely adapted them according to late eighteenth-century practice, thus rendering them more comprehensible to the audiences of his day.[32]

Mozart arranged and conducted four of Handel's works between 1788 and 1790: *Acis and Galatea* (1788), *Messiah* (1789), *Alexander's Feast* (1790), and the *Ode to St. Cecilia* (1790). He was undoubtedly paid for this work, since Swieten and the Society of Associated

Cavaliers saw themselves as patrons of Viennese musical life. Haydn, for example, reported that Swieten "helped me out occasionally with a few ducats and presented me with a comfortable carriage for my second journey to England."[33] Unlike Haydn, Mozart was at times in dire financial straits, and Swieten probably offered him support as well, though no evidence to this effect has survived.[34]

PUCHBERG: BOURGEOIS PATRON?

We have little definite information about Mozart and his creditors during the last years of his life, but some of his letters to Michael Puchberg have survived (probably only those that record debts), many with Puchberg's notations of the amount he sent to Mozart. The loans add up to roughly 1,450 florins between 1788 and 1791; approximately 1,000 florins were outstanding at Mozart's death.

We do not know how Mozart met Puchberg, but they were probably introduced in Masonic circles, for Mozart usually addressed him as "Dearest friend and Brother of the Order." Puchberg had been manager of a large textile concern; he married his employer's widow and seems to have become a wealthy man who lent considerable sums to people besides Mozart. But as Mozart's letters to Constanze suggest, his contact with Puchberg was apparently personal and friendly, not merely a business association. In June 1788 Mozart asked Puchberg for a long-term loan.

Most honorable Brother of the Order,
dearest, most beloved Friend!

The conviction that you are *indeed my friend* and that you know me to be a *man of honor* encourages me to open my heart to you completely and to make the following request. In accordance with my natural frankness I shall go straight to the point without affectation.

If you have sufficient regard and friendship for me to assist me for a year or two with one or two thousand florins, at a suitable rate of interest, you will help me enormously! You yourself will certainly admit *the sense and truth* of my statement when I say that it is difficult, nay impossible, to live when one has to wait for various odd sums. If one does not have at least *a minimum of capital*, it is impossible to keep one's affairs in order. *Nothing* can be done with nothing. If you will do me this kindness then, *primo*, as I shall have some money to go on with, I can meet necessary expenses *whenever they occur,* and therefore *more easily,* whereas now I have to *postpone* payments and then often *at the most awkward time* have to spend *all I receive at once; secondo,* I can work with a mind *more free* from care and *with a lighter heart,* and thus *earn more.* As to security I do not suppose you will have any doubts. You know more or less how I stand and you know *my principles.* (Before June 17, 1788)

Puchberg sent "only" 200 florins, which was apparently just enough to pay the back rent on Mozart's long since abandoned lodgings in the Landstrasse. Only ten days later Mozart found it necessary to ask for another, longer-term loan—this time more insistently.

I have been expecting to go into town myself one of these days and to be able to thank you in person for the kindness you have shown me. But now I would not even have the courage to appear before you, as I am obliged to tell you frankly that it is impossible for me to pay back so soon the money you have lent me and that I must beg you to be patient! I am very much distressed that your circumstances at the moment prevent you from assisting me as much as I could wish, for my position is so serious that I am unavoidably obliged to raise money somehow. But good God, in whom can I confide? In no one but you, my best friend! If you would only be so kind as to get the money for me through some other channel! I shall willingly pay the interest and whoever lends it to me will, I believe, have sufficient security in my character and my income. I am only grieved to be in such an extremity; but that is the very reason why I would like a *fairly substantial sum* for a *somewhat longer period,* so that I can prevent a recurrence of this state of affairs. If you, my most worthy brother, do not help me in this predicament, I will lose my honor and my *credit,* which of all things I wish to preserve. I rely entirely on your genuine friendship and brotherly love, and confidently expect that you will stand by me in word and deed. If my wish is fulfilled, I can breathe freely again, because I will be able to put my affairs in order and *keep them so.* (June 27, 1788)

The obvious gist of this letter is that Mozart had accumulated debts (apart from the back rent, which he had since paid) and found himself temporarily in an embarrassing situation that could ruin his "honor and credit." For Mozart it was doubtless an unusual situation that could have had any number of causes. Gambling debts are one possible explanation, but it would be idle to speculate further. Puchberg, in any case, was not ready to lend a larger sum, and Mozart appears to have gone to a pawnbroker for help.

Owing to great difficulties and complications my affairs have become so involved that it is of the utmost importance to raise some money on these two pawn tickets. In the name of our friendship I implore you to do me this favor; but you must do it immediately. Forgive my importunity, but you know my situation. Ah! If only you had done what I asked you! Do it even now—then everything will be as I desire.

(Beginning of July, 1788)

During this time Mozart wrote his last three symphonies,[35] two piano trios, and two piano sonatas for beginners, as well as several smaller works—all within eight to ten weeks. He had also moved again, on June 17. He must have been under enormous pressure, or he would hardly have written three substantial symphonic works in such a short time. The "difficulties and complications" he mentions probably refer to this hectic pace of work and also to his six-month-old daughter Theresa's sudden death from an intestinal disorder at the end of June.

At least one of the two piano trios was written for Puchberg, whether on commission or as a friendly gift is not clear. The symphonies were clearly intended for the concerts Mozart planned to give in the Casino. It is generally assumed that these concerts never took place—but why? Mozart sent Puchberg two complimentary tickets, so tickets must have been printed and distributed, probably for a series of three subscription concerts. The letters do not indicate when they were to be presented—presumably in the fall of 1788, since Mozart is not likely to have given concerts in the summer, when most of his audience would be out of town.

Why is there so much skepticism about these concerts? Mozart referred to them quite explicitly in his letters. He wrote to Puchberg:

Your true friendship and brotherly love embolden me to ask a great favor of you. I still owe you 8 ducats. Apart from the fact that at the moment I am not in a position to pay you back this sum, my confidence in you is so boundless that I dare to implore you to help me out with 100 florins until next week, when my concerts in the Casino are to begin. By that time I certainly will have received my subscription money and will then be able quite easily to pay you back 136 florins with my warmest thanks.

I take the liberty of sending you two tickets which, as a brother, I beg you to accept without payment, seeing that, as it is, I will never be able to adequately return the friendship you have shown me.

The original of this letter appears to have been lost. In the complete edition of Mozart's correspondence it is reprinted chronologically as the first extant letter to Puchberg (no. 1,076) and dated June 1788. It was first given this date by Philip Spitta in 1880, but he was surely in error. The above-mentioned "subscription money" has always been mistakenly associated with the three string quintets offered for subscription in the *Wiener Zeitung* on April 2.[36] Yet in the letter Mozart clearly states that he should receive his subscription money by the time his concert series begins, "next week," and thus he can only be referring to concert subscriptions. Accordingly, the letter quoted above could not have been written earlier than August and may even date from the autumn. Is there sufficient evidence that the concerts in question did not take place? Why did he write the last three symphonies—to file away in a drawer, perhaps? That would be a first, since Mozart never wrote purely for his own enjoyment; it is well known that he composed exclusively on commission or for a specific occasion.

The original dating of the letter and the resulting interpretations, however, conform more easily to the cliché of Mozart as forlorn and destitute artist. The letters to Puchberg, with their constant petitions for money, have always been read as a drama of ever increasing poverty and depression, culminating in the legend of the pauper's grave as the final humiliation of unrecognized genius—a legend that has stubbornly persisted in the face of all historical information. Once the existence of the Casino concerts is denied, one can draw the following conclusion.

Mozart's letters to Puchberg begin at a time when the composer's sources of income had almost run dry, for reasons still unclear to-

day. The last of his own concerts is recorded on April 7, 1786; . . .
from then on he only performed occasionally in concerts given by other
musicians. . . . After 1784 he no longer mentions playing in private
concerts at the homes of aristocrats; "the most pleasant and useful
acquaintanceships on earth," as he described them to his father in
1781, were no longer the basis for his remaining in Vienna.[37]

Although Mozart urgently requested loans from Puchberg between the middle of June and the end of July 1788, his situation
must have improved beginning in August, for no further petitions
were made (or at least, none have survived) until well into the next
year. Apparently Mozart brought his income and expenditures back
into balance, and the Casino concerts may have contributed to
this recovery just as much as the commissions from Swieten and
the Cavalier Society.

One fact is noteworthy: Mozart was frequently in debt, but always to
bourgeois patrons. We never hear of gifts from his bourgeois friends,
some of whom were extremely wealthy—one need only think of Raimund Wetzlar von Plankenstern, then the most active building spec-
ulator in Vienna (the Plankengasse is named after him). The nobility,
on the other hand, never loaned money; they bestowed gifts (as with
Haydn and Beethoven as well as Mozart). Even for their private
concerts, aristocrats paid the musicians at their own discretion; the
honorarium was usually high, but might occasionally be somewhat
"meager" (letter of October 23, 1790). Bourgeois concertgoers, however, seem to have paid only the ticket price; the bourgeois knew his
arithmetic. Thus Mozart specified that Puchberg should accept the
tickets "without any payment." For his part, Puchberg recorded even
the smallest sums he loaned Mozart.

Active bourgeois patronage of the arts really got under way about
this time, but Mozart received no such patronage in Vienna. The
Hungarian nobility had just promised him a yearly pension of
1,000 florins when he received "from Amsterdam the offer of an
even higher annual sum, which only obliged him to compose a few
pieces exclusively for the subscribers."[38] This offer undoubtedly
came from the merchants' guild of the United Provinces of the
Netherlands.

ROUND TRIP: VIENNA-BERLIN

Mozart's journey to Berlin from April 8 to June 4, 1789, is a particularly obscure chapter in his biography. We do possess eight letters to Constanze that provide some data about the circumstances of the trip, but four letters are lost (as are all seven of hers). The lack of firsthand information has given rise to a series of anecdotes and long-held theories that have little claim to credibility but have remained in circulation to this day. Among biographers of famous personalities there is something like a *horror vacui*—a fear of gaps or empty spaces. Many writers seize on doubtful anecdotes or undoubtedly spurious legends rather than admit that they have no historically reliable information. However, we need not resort to a dry point-by-point refutation of what is obviously false; suffice it to say that there is seldom a grain of verifiable truth to be found in the profusion of anecdotes, and this is especially true of Mozart's journey to Berlin.

Our first problem is that we do not know why he made the journey in the first place. Mozart would never have taken such a trip—especially not without his wife—unless he had some prospect of benefit in the form of concerts, commissions, or future engagements. But in this case no concerts had been arranged; there had been virtually no correspondence with anyone in Berlin, and there were no opera contracts or engagements in sight. We know nothing of any plans to move to Berlin. The entire journey appears to have been unpremeditated, perhaps even ill-considered. We know only that Mozart traveled in the company of Prince Lichnowsky, who lived in Vienna but had strong contacts with the Berlin court through his estates. Mozart had known Lichnowsky for years. Since the early 1780s the prince had been a regular visitor to the home of Countess Thun, whose daughter Maria Christina he married in the fall of 1789. Lichnowsky was also a regular guest at Baron van Swieten's Sunday matinees. The association went even further: the prince's brother, Moritz Lichnowsky, was for some time Mozart's piano pupil, and there was also a Masonic connection, for the prince belonged to the lodge Zur wahren Eintracht. These personal ties probably had something to do with the journey, for it is known that Lichnowsky invited Mozart to travel with him.

On the way to Berlin they stopped in Prague but only stayed one day, and Mozart was unable to meet with any of his acquaintances there except Domenico Guardasoni, a member of the Bondini opera troop who now served as its director. He promised Mozart a contract for a new opera, on very favorable terms: a fee of 200 ducats plus 50 ducats for travel expenses, more than 1,100 florins in all. The opera was ordered "for the coming autumn," but the contract was not signed then and there, probably because Guardasoni was in the midst of negotiating a contract for himself in Warsaw (it eventually materialized, rendering Mozart's contract invalid since Guardasoni did not return from Warsaw until 1791). We do not know what Mozart may have had in mind for a libretto, but it was probably not a version of *La clemenza di Tito*, whose subject was totally unsuited to the type of opera with which Mozart had been so successful in Prague.

From Prague they proceeded over bad roads to Dresden, where they remained longer than they had intended. Here Mozart was reunited with numerous acquaintances and played a concert before the electoral princess of Saxony, for which he received "a very handsome snuff-box" ("handsome" no doubt referring to its contents of 100 ducats, which he failed to mention). There was naturally a lot of music making with colleagues in Dresden, especially with Johann Wilhelm Hässler, an organist from Erfurt, on the Silbermann organ in the court chapel. (Hässler had long wished to play in competition against Mozart, an indication of the esteem Mozart enjoyed as a virtuoso even in northern and central Germany, where he had never performed.)

Next came a three-day sojourn in Leipzig. On April 22, Mozart played the organ at the Thomaskirche, where Bach was cantor for the last twenty-seven years of his life. On April 25, after almost two weeks, they finally arrived in Potsdam, where a court official announced him to the Prussian King Frederick William II in the following manner:

The gentleman named Motzart (who declares himself to be a kapellmeister from Vienna) announces that he has arrived in the company of Prince Lichnowsky, and humbly wishes to display his talents to His Royal Majesty. He awaits His Royal Majesty's command, whether he may be allowed to appear before Him.[39]

We can almost hear the pen scratching on the paper—the paper has survived. In the margin the king has written, "Directeur du Port." Mozart was to report to Jean-Pierre Duport, who had for many years been concertmaster of the court orchestra and director of royal chamber music, in which the king frequently took part. Mozart was, so to speak, sent through official channels, but this does not imply lack of interest. Earlier, Mozart had written to his wife from Prague:

> Only a week ago Ramm [oboist and friend of Mozart] left Prague to return home. He came from Berlin and said that the king had frequently and insistently inquired whether it was certain that I was coming to Berlin, and as I had not yet appeared he said a second time: "I fear that he will not come at all." Ramm became very uneasy and tried to convince him that I really was coming. Judging from this, my affairs ought to be fairly successful. (April 10, 1789)

Does this single remark imply more than the hope of an appearance before the king, or at best a commission? Unlikely. And we know nothing about the ten to twelve days spent in Potsdam—not even if a meeting with the king took place. All we can verify is that Mozart used a theme by Duport—which omniscient legend tells us was the king's favorite piece—for a set of piano variations (K. 573). The king did commission Mozart to write six string quartets and six piano sonatas for Princess Friederike, and gave him an honorarium of 100 friedrichs d'or (about 785 florins), probably for a concert at the court.[40] Of the money he received, Mozart was obliged to lend 100 florins to his traveling companion, the prince, who then left him on his own, so that Mozart himself "had to pay for my keep in Potsdam, which is an expensive place." It is still unclear why Mozart, before going from Potsdam to Berlin, made another detour through Leipzig, where he gave a concert on May 12.

Perhaps Lichnowsky wanted to introduce Mozart personally in North Germany, for he also made the second trip to Leipzig. The concert, in the old Gewandhaus, had a mammoth program. Mozart played two piano concertos, the Fantasy in C Minor, and a set of variations; Josepha Duschek sang two arias, and two symphonies were played as well. The concert "was absolutely magnificent as far as applause and glory are concerned, but the profits were wretchedly meager" (May 16, 1789); Georg Nikolaus von Nissen later wrote that the hall was almost empty—but the price of admission was unusually high, and moreover, on the same evening *Le nozze di Figaro* was given at the opera.

After eight days in Leipzig, Mozart went to Berlin for ten days; what he did there remains obscure. On the day of his arrival he supposedly witnessed a performance of *Die Entführung aus dem Serail*, where he met the sixteen-year-old Ludwig Tieck. He played once for the queen at court, but no public concert could be arranged. He wrote to his wife on May 23, 1789:

> (1) If I gave a concert here, I would not make much out of it, and (2) the king would not care for me to give one. So you must simply be satisfied *as I am with this*, that I am fortunate enough to be enjoying the king's favor.

It is totally incomprehensible why the king "would not care" for Mozart to give a public concert. Possibly he wanted to avoid creating competition for Johann Friedrich Reichardt's *concerts spirituels*, but at the time Reichardt was away in Weimar. If the king and Mozart had wished to draw up an employment contract, nothing would have stood in their way. The king was generous toward musicians (even Luigi Boccherini in Madrid received a pension from him), and there would have been a position for Mozart: a short time later Felice Alessandri, a composer of minor significance, was engaged as assistant director of the court opera at a salary of 3,000 talers. Neither the king nor Mozart ever expressed any interest in such a contract; thus Mozart could hardly have turned it down as he is supposed to have done, refusing to leave Vienna and Joseph II. The persistence of this legend can only be explained as wishful thinking—on the part of the Prussians, who claim that their king made Mozart an offer worthy of his talents, one that would have spared him the alleged ignominy of a pauper's grave; and on the part of the Viennese, who fancy themselves rewarded by Mozart's loyalty—he really was one of them after all. But all Mozart brought home with him from Berlin were two commissions and a bag of money (even after deducting travel expenses, he must have had close to 1,000 florins left).

Naturally, several affairs with singers have been imputed to Mozart in connection with his Berlin journey, for reasons known only to the

purveyors of such tales. Mozart's letters fulfill the romantic expectations of posterity much better than any biographical theorizing, except
that his erotic missives were addressed exclusively to his wife in terms
that have long been a source of discomfort to the composer's more
prudish admirers. Mozart wrote Constanze from Berlin (May 23):

> You see that there is a gap between April 13th and 24th. So one of your
> letters must have gone astray and thus I was without a letter for
> seventeen days. If you too had to spend seventeen days in the same
> condition, one of my letters must have been lost. Thank God these
> mischances will soon be behind us. *In your arms* I will be able to tell
> you all, all that I felt at that time. But you know how I love you. Well,
> where do you think I am writing this letter? In my room at the inn? Not
> at all. In a restaurant at the Tiergarten (in a summer house with a lovely
> view) where I lunched today *all by myself,* in order to devote myself
> entirely to you. . . . On Thursday, the 28th, I shall leave for Dresden,
> where I shall spend the night. On June 1st I intend to sleep in Prague,
> and on the 4th—the 4th—with my darling little wife. Arrange your
> dear sweet nest very daintily, for my little fellow deserves it indeed, he
> has really behaved himself very well and is only longing to possess your
> sweetest [word deleted]. Just picture to yourself that rascal: as I write,
> he crawls onto the table and looks at me questioningly. I, however, box
> his ears properly—but the rogue is simply [word deleted]. Now the
> knave burns even more fiercely and can hardly be restrained. Surely
> you will drive out to the first post-stage to meet me? I will get there at
> noon on the 4th. I hope that Hofer, whom I embrace a thousand times,
> will be with you. If Herr and Frau von Puchberg drive out with you too,
> then all the friends I want to see will be together. Don't forget to bring
> our Karl. But the most important thing of all is that you bring with you
> someone you can rely on (Satmann or someone else) who can drive off
> to the customs in my carriage with the luggage, so that *I* won't have to
> face that unnecessary seccatura, but can drive home with all you dear
> people. Now remember this.
>
> Well, adieu, I kiss you a million times and am ever your most faithful
> husband.
>
> W. A. Mozart

Mozart was in such a hurry that he even wanted someone else to take
his bags through customs for him (a request he repeated in his next

letter) so that he could avoid the tedious and time-consuming inspection—anything to expedite the reunion with his wife.

DEBTS

Mozart did not return from Berlin empty-handed. He brought a considerable sum of money with him, although he underestimated its equivalent in Viennese currency when he wrote Constanze.

> When I return, my darling little wife, you must be more delighted with having me back than with the money I shall bring. A hundred friedrichs d'or are not 900 florins but 700—at least that is what they tell me here. (May 23, 1789)

Actually the sum was worth 785 florins, almost as much as his annual salary; he told her nothing about other income from the journey. In addition he brought two important commissions, one for a set of six string quartets and another for six piano sonatas. Nevertheless, only a few weeks later began a phase of Mozart's life filled with deep distress and misery such as his letters had never revealed before and never revealed again. Constanze became dangerously ill; apparently she suffered from an ulcerated leg, and it was feared that "the bone may be affected" (second half of July 1789)—a very serious condition considering the state of medical knowledge and the therapeutic possibilities of the time. The cost of treatment and medicine was staggering, for there was no insurance system and Mozart spared no expense to save his wife. After the acute phase of the illness came an urgent follow-up treatment with sulphur baths, which necessitated a cure at Baden, an expensive spa. Mozart suffered along with his wife and was so preoccupied with caring for her that he was unable to work, "hovering between hope and fear" (July 17, 1789).

We do not know, of course, how much Constanze's medical care cost, but it appears to have put Mozart in desperate need of money, as reflected in his letters to Michael Puchberg. These were no longer requests for loans to help him out in moments of financial embarrassment, but heartfelt entreaties from a man who saw almost no way out of his distress, financial or otherwise.

July 12th, 1789

Dearest, most beloved Friend and
most honorable Brother of the Order,

Great God! I would not wish my worst enemy to be in my present position. And if you, most beloved friend and brother, forsake me, we are altogether lost, *both my unfortunate and blameless self* and my poor sick wife and child. Only the other day when I was with you I was longing to open my heart to you, but I did not have the courage to do so, and indeed I would still not have the courage—for, as it is, I only dare to write and I tremble as I do so—and I would not even dare to write, were I not certain that you know me, that you are aware of my circumstances, and that you are wholly convinced of my *innocence* so far as my unfortunate and most distressing situation is concerned. Good God! I am coming to you not with thanks but with fresh entreaties! Instead of paying my debts I am asking for more money! If you really know me, you must sympathize with my anguish at having to do so. I need not tell you once more that owing to my unfortunate illness I have been prevented from earning anything. But I must mention that in spite of my wretched condition I decided to give subscription concerts at home in order to be able to meet at least my present great and frequent expenses, for I was absolutely convinced of your friendly assistance. But even this has failed. Unfortunately Fate is so much against me, *though only in Vienna*, that even when I want to I cannot make any money. Two weeks ago I circulated a list for subscribers and so far the only name on it is that of Baron van Swieten! Now (on the 13th) that my dear little wife seems to be improving every day, I should be able to set to work again, if this blow, this heavy blow, had not come. At any rate, people are consoling me by saying she is better—although the night before last she was suffering so much—and I on her account—that I was stunned and despairing. But last night (the 14th) she slept so well and has felt so much easier all morning that I am very hopeful; and at last I am beginning to feel inclined for work. But I am now faced with misfortunes of another kind—though, it is true, only for the moment. Dearest, most beloved friend and brother—you know *my present circumstances*, but you also know *my prospects*. So let things remain as we arranged; that is, *thus or thus*, you understand what I mean. Meanwhile I am composing six easy clavier sonatas for Princess Friederike and six quartets for the king, all of which Kozeluch is engraving at my expense. At the same time the two dedications will bring me something. In a month or two my fate must be decided *in every detail*. Therefore, most beloved friend, you will not be risking anything so far as I am concerned. So it all depends, my only friend, on whether you will or can lend me another 500 florins. Until my affairs are settled, I undertake to pay back 10 florins a month; and then, as this is bound to happen in a few months, I shall pay back the whole sum with whatever interest you may demand, and at the same time acknowledge myself to be your debtor for life. That, alas, I will have to remain, for I will never be able to thank you sufficiently for your friendship and affection. Thank God, that is over. Now you know all. Do not be offended by my confiding in you and remember that unless you help me, the honor, the peace of mind, and perhaps the very life of your friend and brother Mason will be ruined.

Ever your most grateful servant, true friend and brother

W. A. Mozart

At home, July 14th, 1789

O God, I can hardly bring myself to dispatch this letter!—and yet I must! If this illness had not befallen me, I would not have been obliged to beg so shamelessly from my only friend. Yet I hope for your forgiveness, for you know both the good *and the bad prospects of my situation.* The bad is temporary; the good will certainly persist, once the momentary evil has been alleviated. Adieu. For God's sake forgive me, only forgive me!—and—adieu!

This dramatic call for help raises a number of questions. Mozart repeatedly emphasizes his "innocence" in his "unfortunate situation" and asks Puchberg for his forgiveness. Undoubtedly he still had outstanding debts to Puchberg and was embarrassed to be asking for more money instead of settling accounts. Had Puchberg been sending Mozart reminders or even reprimands? What is meant by the sentence "So let things remain as we arranged; that is, *thus or thus,* you understand what I mean"? Equally unclear are the "prospects" Mozart mentions, the "affairs" that have yet to be settled. He cannot be referring to his hopes for a position at the Viennese court (evidenced the following year by the draft of a letter to Archduke Francis), because Joseph II was still alive and there was no prospect of a new position or a change in personnel. More likely he was referring to a possible opera contract, which he indeed received in the course of the summer or fall. [41]

This time Puchberg was more cautious; he finally sent Mozart 150 florins after a second call for help. Perhaps he had the impression that Mozart's need for money was a bottomless pit. In this letter, however, Mozart added a clarification:

> (1) I would not require such a considerable sum if I did not anticipate very heavy expenses in connection with the cure my wife may have to take, particularly if she has to go to Baden. (2) As I am positive that in a short time I will be in better circumstances, the amount of the sum I will have to repay is a matter of indifference to me. Nevertheless at the present moment I would prefer it to be a large sum, which would make me feel safer. (July 17, 1789)

The wording here is notably optimistic for someone in such bad straits: Mozart expresses himself plainly, with no diplomatic circumlocution. A few days later he gives a brief report on his wife's condition, the most precise description of her illness that we have. The terseness of the letter also reveals Mozart's own distraction.

> Dearest Friend and Brother!
> Since the time when you rendered me that great and friendly service, I have been living in such *misery* that for very grief I have not only been unable to go out, but I could not even write.
> At the moment she is easier, and if *she had not contracted bed sores*, which make her condition most wretched, she would be able to sleep. The only fear is that the bone may be affected. She is extraordinarily resigned and awaits recovery or death with true philosophic calm. My tears flow as I write. Come and see us, most beloved friend, if you can; and, *if you can*, give me your advice and help *in the matter you know of.*

The "matter you know of" remains obscure.

At the beginning of August, Constanze was able to go to Baden. Wolfgang Hildesheimer writes:

> Rather untouched by it all, Constanze continued taking the waters in Baden, more or less fulfilling her objective in these extended visits, vague as it seems to us. But diseases at the time were ill-defined, chronic illnesses even more so, and imaginary complaints were not defined at all.

And elsewhere: "It seems improbable that she ever suffered mental torment, and even her physical sufferings seem primarily to be an excuse for her visits to spas."[42]

After a close reading of the surviving letters, we have no reason to doubt the truth of their contents, even though they are full of vague allusions that can never be fully understood. We know from Mozart's earlier letters that he was apt to exaggerate, to place everything in a favorable light and overestimate his possibilities. His portrayal of the events that led him to resign his position in Salzburg clearly revealed these tendencies. But it is unlikely that Mozart blew his wife's illness out of proportion to make Puchberg more receptive to his petitions— that would have been too audacious, even insolent.

> Unfortunately Fate is so much against me, *though only in Vienna,* that even when I want to I cannot make any money. Two weeks ago I circulated a list for subscribers and so far the only name on it is that of Baron van Swieten!

Here we have a more plausible example of Mozartian exaggeration. Puchberg seems to have been good at figures, and he would hardly have continued to lend Mozart money if the odds of getting it back had not been reasonable. That is why Mozart spends so much time describing his "prospects"—that is, possibilities for earning money. It was of little consequence that a subscription list sent out in June came back with only Swieten's name on it, because as Mozart well knew, virtually no concerts took place in the summer months from June to September when the nobility were staying at their country estates.[43]

The "prospects" mentioned to Puchberg probably referred not only to an opera commission in Vienna (*Così fan tutte*) but to the negotiations with Domenico Guardasoni in Dresden, "who has practically arranged to give me 200 ducats next autumn for the opera and 50 ducats for traveling expenses" (April 10, 1789). In the end this lucrative project failed to materialize, but at the time Mozart was still counting on it.

The next extant letter to Puchberg is dated December 1789. Once again the requests for money are justified by medical bills, which must be settled by the first of the year "unless I wish to lose my good name."

This time Mozart asked for 400 florins, and the ever careful Puchberg sent 300, although Mozart announced:

> According to the present arrangement I am to receive from the management next month 200 ducats for my opera. . . . Beloved friend and brother! I know only too well how much I owe you! I beg you to be patient a little longer in regard to my old debts. I will certainly repay you, that I promise on my honor. Once more I beg you, rescue me just this time from my horrible situation. As soon as I get the money for my opera, you will have the 400 florins back for certain. And this summer, thanks to my work for the King of Prussia, I hope to be able to convince you completely of my honesty.

But events took a different turn. Mozart constantly interrupted his progress on Frederick William's commission to take up other work; he wrote only three of the six Prussian quartets and only one of the six piano sonatas (K. 576).

COSÌ FAN TUTTE

Mozart often complained that Joseph II was stingy, but he could never say that the emperor had left him in the lurch. After all, Mozart held no official post; they were all occupied long before he came to Vienna. Neither had he been "overlooked." Mozart had received just enough inducements to keep him in Vienna: occasional opera commissions and eventually the honorary position of *Kammerkompositeur*. And precisely when he found himself in deep financial embarrassment, a new opera commission came along, for which he was offered the unusually high fee of 900 florins. (Viennese society was so "confined" that the emperor must have known about Mozart's problems.)

We know less about the origins of *Così fan tutte* than about those of any other Mozart opera. Legend has it that the story is based on an actual occurrence in Vienna, which the emperor, in his typically derisive manner, wished to make the subject of an opera, and that he commissioned the work himself. In September and October 1789, Mozart composed three arias as inserts for opera productions at the Burgtheater. This could not have happened without the knowledge of the theater management. Were these arias officially paid commissions? Was Mozart trying to curry favor with the singers? Did he already have the *Così* commission, or were the arias meant to prepare the ground for it? We do not even know when the new opera was written; the entry in his catalogue, "January 1790," appears to have been made before the first performance (January 26, 1790), yet he had already noted in December, "An aria intended for the opera *Così fan tutte*," which was eventually replaced by another. He invited Puchberg to a rehearsal of the opera on December 31.

> I invite you, you alone, to come along on Thursday at 10 o'clock in the morning to hear a short rehearsal of my opera. I am only inviting Haydn and yourself. When we meet I will tell you about Salieri's plots, which, however, have completely failed already. Adieu.
>
> (December 1789)

We must not make too much of "Salieri's plots," for only a week earlier Salieri had arranged the first performance of the Clarinet Quintet (K. 581) at a concert presented by the Tonkünstlersozietät, of which he was president. There was no real dislike between Mozart and Salieri; indeed, they had a friendly relationship characterized by mutual respect. The "plots" were probably ordinary professional differences such as one might expect to develop in an opera house between composer and management, especially during preparations for a new production.

If any sustained intrigues surrounded this opera, Mozart did not live to witness them. Indeed, no other work of his was so distorted, perverted, and badly adapted as was *Così fan tutte* throughout the nineteenth century. The target of all the criticism was Lorenzo Da Ponte's libretto. "A miserable thing, debasing to all women. It cannot be a success, for no woman in the audience will like it," the famous actor Friedrich Ludwig Schröder wrote in his journal on April 28, 1791, after reading the libretto.[44] And a review of a 1792 Berlin performance in the *Journal des Luxus und der Moden* declares, "It is much to be regretted that our best composers waste their time and talent on deplorable subjects. The present opera is the silliest rubbish in the world, and it draws an audience only because of the splendid music."[45] No one expressed his reservations more clearly than Arthur Schurig.

The libretto ridicules not only women's love but the idea of passionate love itself. Love has often been dragged through the dirt in literature— think of the great satirists Aretino, Boccaccio, Machiavelli, Rabelais, Fischart—but no one has done it so unimaginatively as Da Ponte. And Mozart is surely one of the very few great artists who have devoted their energies indiscriminately to a piece of mediocre hackwork like the text of *Così fan tutte*. Through his collaboration he has ridiculed the very thing he has tirelessly idolized and transfigured in his other works— earthly love. It is beyond question that this ridicule did not reflect his true feelings. For him the story was mere buffoonery, nothing else. It remains for posterity to interpret and quibble over the works of the great masters. A man who respected women as Mozart did would not become their detractor overnight under the influence of an opera text. Yet one thing is very strange. In *Die Entführung* Mozart glorified sentimental German love, in *Figaro* gallant love or *amour goût* (according to Stendhal's famous classification), in *Don Juan* demonic sensual love, and in *Die Zauberflöte* the upward impulse of a man who seeks the highest ideals but who is eternally fated to be held down by worldly attachments. There remained only one phenomenon to which Mozart could apply his art: *Venus vulgivaga,* who gives herself to whichever man happens to please her at the moment. Thus the cycle was completed.[46]

This judgment is ludicrously exaggerated, but it has retained its power. Today almost all productions of *Così fan tutte* are based on the idea that the opera deals with an almost mathematical experiment to which the lovers' fidelity is sacrificed. The result is the decidedly puppetlike behavior of the protagonists, calculated symmetrical portrayals (however inconsistent with the music), and a dull presentation of stock figures where Mozart and Da Ponte endeavored to create individuals with distinct traits. In place of the lively realism with which this opera abounds, we are offered a faceless monotony that is apparently supposed to create the illusion of universal relevance. Why, for example, are the two sisters always presented as wealthy and refined ladies, sometimes in evening dress, and their house as a virtual rococo palace? Why is the wedding scene set in a festive banquet hall when the libretto only calls for a "pretty room"?

It is quite obvious that this opera is about bourgeois people. The two male leads do threaten to draw their rapiers in the first scene, but they are soldiers, after all, and their language is anything but courtly and sophisticated; in fact, it often borders on vulgarity.[47] Every detail of the libretto was important to Mozart, and one cannot tamper with his and Da Ponte's instructions without damaging the text. Although the cast of characters appears to be a series of ordinary *buffo* figures, the action soon proves to be a *dramma giocoso* involving six living personalities who come to know themselves through their relations with each other. At the end they are confused and full of ambivalent feelings, their inflated self-assurance has been shattered, but they are not disheartened and are prepared to begin the search for true self-knowledge, happiness, and wisdom—by no means a conventional happy ending. A bourgeois drama—and a comedy as well. It takes place in our society, without the distance created by wealth, refinement, and aristocratic rank.

The opening scene shows the "old philosopher" Don Alfonso in conversation with the two "lovers" on the subject of women's fidelity. The setting is a café—not a private salon but a place frequented by the bourgeoisie. Don Alfonso expatiates in quite general terms on the subject of women: do they represent an ideal or are they human beings, "goddesses or women"? The theme of disillusionment is introduced. When Don Alfonso expresses doubt and asks "what kind of animal these beautiful creatures of yours are, whether they have flesh, bones, and skin like us," the two lovers already feel that their honor has been offended. This public café is a place for the gallant defense of bourgeois values as well as for deliberation. The two lovers demand immediate proof of their sweethearts' infidelity—as if Don Alfonso had made any specific accusations—or a duel. The philosopher does not believe in the purifying effect of bloodshed and retorts, "What proof do you have that your sweethearts are always faithful to you? What makes you so sure that their hearts are constant?" And after several overenthusiastic assurances of their uniqueness: "And what if I were to prove to you that they are like all the others?" To avoid a duel Don Alfonso strikes a bet and for the time being manages to escape a collision with the bourgeois sense of honor. But it turns out that Don Alfonso is by no means a skilled puppeteer who can pull strings to make everyone dance to his tune. When the time comes to act, he leaves everything to Despina. Wisdom and the ability to take intelligent action do not always go together. "Leave the whole business to me," Despina says. "I'll handle everything. When Despina plans something, it can't go wrong. . . . But you must do everything I tell you."[48]

Only toward the end, when the confusion of feelings and the dizzying view into the heart's inner recesses have unearthed some startling truths, can Don Alfonso again make a contribution with his (entirely dubious) proposals for minimizing the damage and his (successful) application of reason as "peaceful serenity amid the storms of life." In disillusioning the two young men, Don Alfonso is attempting to expose not so much feminine infidelity as a stereotyped picture of women that allows for nothing inconsistent with masculine ideas.

> Take them as they are; Nature couldn't make an exception or grant you a privilege by creating two women of different clay just for your handsome faces. You must see everything philosophically. . . . All men accuse women, but I excuse them—even if they change their affections a thousand times each day. Some call it a vice, others a habit, but I believe it to be a necessity of the heart. The lover who is disillusioned at the end should not condemn the folly of others, but his own.[49]

At this point in Da Ponte's libretto Mozart has added, "Repeat with me: All women behave that way [così fan tutte]." This insertion, although very effective musically, throws the serious exhortation to the men somewhat out of focus.

To an extent Mozart debases the character of Don Alfonso by underlining his acerbic and skeptical rationality with dry string accompaniments and denying him support from the wind instruments. He is definitely no longer capable of tempestuous feelings and does not even respond to Despina's lewd jokes. He is primarily a catalyst who rouses the two irascible lovers to action but later reunites and reconciles the other characters when they are overcome by shame and embarrassment.

The fact that the two ladies have a chambermaid is no indication of wealth or of an especially privileged position. Domestic servants were paid so little that almost everyone could afford them (the Mozarts employed as many as three). Despina's first line is: "How abominable is a chambermaid's life. From morning till night, sweating, toiling, working, and when all is done we get nothing out of it for ourselves."

Yet her behavior toward the two ladies shows no trace of obsequious-
ness; rather, it is blunt to the point of rudeness and impudence,
without ever being taken amiss. "Deal with love *en bagatelle*" is her
motto, and she does not need Don Alfonso to teach her this philosophy.
She knows the ways of the world, having had to learn at an early age
how to defend herself and safeguard her own interests. Her principle
is self-determination—not because she is emancipated but as a result
of experience. (This was not the first time Mozart portrayed a chambermaid who clearly has more courage, practical wisdom, and ability
to think and act independently than her mistress: Blonde and Susanna
immediately come to mind, however different their origins, circumstances, and significance as characters.)

> A woman of fifteen must have all her wits about her, she must know all
> the devil's wiles, what's good and what's bad, how to turn a man's head,
> how to feign laughter and tears and to invent good excuses.[50]

The two ladies are somewhat bewildered by such opinions, but they
are also fascinated by them. Dorabella is soon convinced: "If we
amuse ourselves a little so as not to die of melancholy, we're not being
unfaithful"; and Fiordiligi concedes, "That's true."[51] But there is a
crucial difference between the two sisters: Dorabella, who is more
active and full of *joie de vivre*, always tries to find excuses and talk her
way out of any difficulty, whereas Fiordiligi always struggles with her
conscience. Thus, in the seduction scenes, Dorabella and Guglielmo
can approach each other with relative ease because neither has more
than an amorous flirtation in mind, whether to win a bet or for
amusement—both equally frivolous motivations. At first Fiordiligi is
more aware of her self-imposed limitations and can only act within the
bounds of convention. Nor is Ferrando much of a lady-killer in his
behavior toward her. We can even surmise that he invites failure by
carrying out his task of seducing her in a very clumsy and aggressive
fashion. Fiordiligi remains the epitome of modesty, which is hardly
surprising in view of an attack she describes clearly enough, though
the audience does not witness it.

FIORDILIGI: I've seen a viper, a hydra, a basilisk!

FERRANDO: Oh, cruel woman. I understand! The viper, the hydra, the basilisk, and all the wild creatures of the Libyan desert you see in me alone.

FIORDILIGI: That's true, that's true! You want to destroy my peace of mind.[52]

But then Fiordiligi gets caught up in the growing conflict between her feelings for Guglielmo and her awakening interest in Ferrando; while Ferrando, disappointed and wounded by Dorabella's unfaithfulness, also experiences a growing emotional conflict to which no solution seems possible.

Suddenly, what Don Alfonso initiated with his bet is no longer a game in which all the participants return to their starting positions at the end. It has become a serious love entanglement, with both couples experiencing equal shares of joy, pain, and disillusionment. Everything is left unresolved at the end of the opera. Dorabella and Fiordiligi promise to be faithful in the future, but this promise is not put to the test. Fidelity is presented as a dam against a flood of ambivalent, irrepressible feelings and passions whose explosive force is as indisputable as their existence.

This is not a pleasant little comedy of intrigue but great theater, forthright and provocative, diametrically opposed to all the little *buffo* operas that present the illusion of an ideal world where everything returns to normal at the end, where love promises only happiness and once begun lasts forever. To be sure, Mozart and Da Ponte fall back on the traditional characters of *opera buffa*, but they invest them with individual personalities that carry them far beyond the well-known *buffo* figures. The plot, too, transcends all generic conventions, even if the bet made at the beginning is quite in keeping with tradition. The public did not reward Mozart and Da Ponte for their efforts to transform an innocuous operatic genre into serious theater. *Così fan tutte* was not very successful at the Nationaltheater; there were only ten performances during all of 1790, while the new production of *Le nozze di Figaro* had twenty-nine performances during the same period.

This opera was the only one of Mozart's works to jeopardize his posthumous fame. The unflinching realism was misunderstood as amorality and taken amiss. The frequent adaptations and even "translations" of the text, which can still be seen today (Devrient, Niese, Levi/Possart, Schünemann), represent gross distortions for the very reason that they try to "save" the opera by depriving it of its message. We have yet to become fully acquainted with this work, despite gratifying new approaches from such directors as Dieter Dorn and Karl Ernst Herrmann, among others.

Così fan tutte shows how consistently Mozart sought to break away from the traditions of the court opera, even though he was still largely dependent on it for commissions. In this connection the circumstances in Vienna were very much against him. Had not the emperor himself, with his Nationalsingspiel experiment, tried to free the opera from its stultifying conventions? With *Die Entführung aus dem Serail* Mozart had not simply written the most successful of all Singspiels; and in each work that followed, without actually establishing a new genre of bourgeois music drama, he had created more new examples of a realistic musical theater directed at audiences from all levels of society. With *Die Zauberflöte* Mozart took another step forward by bringing elements of popular theater—better represented in Vienna than anywhere else—into the opera house. The use of magical and fairy-tale subjects reveals Mozart's broad concept of realism, which he had already demonstrated in the finale of *Don Giovanni*.

Every aspect of Mozart's operas is provocative; they all call into question unwritten aesthetic, social, and political laws. *Figaro* portrays a bigoted, degenerate aristocracy through the eyes of a servant and attacks it mercilessly. *Don Giovanni* resurrects an old "baroque" stage piece that had deteriorated into popular farce and transforms it into great theater. *Così fan tutte* insistently portrays the ambivalence of human emotions at the risk of appearing amoral. And *Die Zauberflöte* deals with Freemasonry, which had become politically suspect; moreover, its staging was so rich in imagery that many contemporaries saw it as an allegory of the French Revolution.

Mozart took great risks with all his operas, which reflected social conditions and contemporary opinions with such an unerring political sense that the libretti sometimes barely got past the censor. At the same time, Mozart used an attractive musical language that was very persuasive despite the complexity some contemporaries complained about. Mozart's musical-rhetorical abilities did not obscure his operas' provocative points, but they went far to palliate the controversial elements in the eyes of those who harshly and unjustly condemned his subject matter. Nowhere is this effect seen so clearly as in the contemporary (and subsequent) criticism of *Così fan tutte*.

THE EMPEROR DIES

Emperor Joseph II did not live to see a performance of *Così fan tutte*. The premiere was on January 26, 1790, at the climax of Vienna's carnival, which as usual was celebrated with wild abandon. Four more performances were given during the following two weeks, and then the Burgtheater was closed for a period of official mourning: Princess Elizabeth, wife of Archduke Francis, had died in childbirth on February 17. Joseph II was especially saddened by her death, for he was very fond of his niece by marriage. He suffered from tuberculosis, and his health had so deteriorated that he was hastening toward death himself, but whenever he had the strength he kept busy writing letters, dictating ordinances, and holding audiences. On the day of the princess's death he remarked that her body could only lie in state in the court chapel for three days, because the chapel would then be needed for his own lying in state.

The emperor's condition was known to everyone. There was scant evidence of grief or sympathy except in his immediate circle, among his few personal friends and trusted advisers, whom he personally bade farewell in numerous letters and conversations. (Among these was Countess Thun, at whose salon he had been a frequent guest.) Most other people spoke of the emperor in a detached and sometimes disrespectful manner. There seemed to be general satisfaction that most of his reforms had fallen through and that he had failed to achieve his military and political goals. Viennese morale was at a low point, which made the carnival celebrations all the wilder. The spirit of rebellion, encouraged by news of the French Revolution, spread like morning fog. Some people went so far as to circulate satirical verses about the dying monarch. Someone fastened a note to the Hofburg that read:

Whom peasants adore
And townsmen abhor
And noblemen scoff at
Will soon be no more.

The emperor died on February 19, 1790, the Friday after Ash Wednesday. He had done all he could to insure that at least his coffin would be simple and unadorned, but the funeral had to follow Habsburg protocol. Even in death the emperor had trouble maintaining his dignity: Count Zinzendorf noted in his diary how carelessly the body had been laid out. This was the ruler who personified the hope for a humane, "enlightened" state, still autocratic, yet devoted to justice and tolerance. He had abolished serfdom in his dominions, established a modern state church, and created a carefully structured centralized government. This emperor who fascinated all of Europe had died at only forty-eight years of age, an object of ridicule and hatred in many quarters. He left an empire on the brink of disintegration, shattered by unrest, rebellion, and separatism. Austria's situation was in no way comparable to that of France, but it was explosive enough to threaten the continued existence of the Habsburg monarchy.

Through his reforms Joseph II had brought the bourgeois enlightenment to his court and made it serve his own ends. It was just this process that heightened political consciousness among the peasants and the bourgeoisie, who accordingly increased their political demands. The peasants, for example, rejoiced at the abolition of serfdom, but they also expected further economic concessions, which inevitably brought them into serious conflict with the landed gentry. The aristocracy, for its part, was irritated at the loss of its privileges (e.g., special legal status), and would not accept the emperor's tax reforms. Then there was the radical curtailment of the power wielded by the governing estates in the various crown lands, which created further dissension and even encouraged short-lived nationalist coalitions (as in the Netherlands, for instance). Joseph II was forced to rescind many of his reforms and, because of widespread opposition, to organize a secret police force. During the last months of his life the emperor saw many of his "enlightened" officials lose their influence. These were the true Josephinians, most of them also Freemasons, who

had helped him draft many of the reforms. At the same time, representatives of the landed gentry (e.g., Count Pergen) were gaining ascen-
dancy. This was the beginning of a restoration that would develop into
full-scale reaction two years later, under Francis II.

The emperor's police officials kept him fully informed about the
general mood in Vienna while he was on his deathbed. In one report
we read:

> Your Majesty is not unaware how much the mood of the capital city has
> changed in recent years. Our citizens are no longer the good-natured
> folk they once were—who blindly and unthinkingly submitted to the
> rule of law, looked upon their leaders with respect, and, proud of the
> honor of being a subject of the German Emperor, would not have traded
> their happiness for that of any other nation on earth. In vain does one
> seek these honest, genial, contented people in our capital today.[53]

If the satirical verse found on the Hofburg was passed on to the
emperor, he must have known that this report was in fact restrained.
Nor did the news from France calm the situation. The Viennese were
well informed about events in Paris. Even the *Wiener Zeitung* reported
extensively on the meetings of the National Assembly and published
the first draft of the Declaration of the Rights of Man word for word.
One could also read drafts of a constitution, along with reports on the
most important lines of argument. (French newspapers were also read
in Vienna—at least the higher government officials had access to
them.) All these developments were openly debated in the cafés. The
demands for a constitution met with general approval, and malcon-
tents drew angry parallels with France that reached the ears of police
informers. There were probably no organized conspiracies in Vienna
at this time, but it is worth noting that virtually all the members of the
so-called Jacobin Conspiracy (1794) were Freemasons—the lodges,
then, had apparently functioned as political clubs.

We know that during this period Mozart's lodge Zur neugekrönten
Hoffnung maintained a correspondence with French lodges that was
intercepted by the police. These were the first signs of the conflict
between former Josephinians—as most of the Freemasons can be
characterized—and the reactionary movement favoring the abrogation of reforms, the introduction of police surveillance, and the resto-

ration of the old ruling elite. Mozart's lodge obviously considered itself politically oriented. Small wonder that unlike most others, it was adept at guarding its secrets, especially from the police.

Mozart, who was among these Josephinians, must have been very disappointed at the new course of events. His Viennese operas, particularly *Le nozze di Figaro*, had clearly shown where his sympathies lay. No other composer of his time had written such overtly radical operas. It seems that his personal relations with the emperor also cooled. His earlier letters indicate respect and admiration for Joseph, despite his complaints about "stinginess." Now Mozart had just received a lucrative opera contract—welcome imperial assistance at a time of great financial difficulty—yet he went on with business as usual. While the emperor lay dying, Mozart wrote sets of dances for the carnival balls, as he did every year. The next morning as the church bells announced the death of Joseph II, he wrote humorously to Michael Puchberg:

> If I had known that your supply of beer was almost gone, I would never have ventured to rob you of it. I therefore take the liberty of returning herewith the second measure, as today I am already provided with wine. I thank you heartily for the first one, and the next time you have a supply of beer, pray send me a little of it. You know how much I like it. I beg you, most beloved friend, to lend me a few ducats just for a few days. (February 20, 1790)

Mozart composed no music on the death of Joseph II (unlike Beethoven, who wrote a cantata); no one commissioned such a work, and he never wrote anything on his own initiative. The emperor was dead, and Mozart's thoughts were already on his successor. Apparently with the encouragement of Baron van Swieten, Mozart petitioned the new monarch to create a second kapellmeister post just for him.

LONG LIVE THE EMPEROR!

Mozart's petition has not survived, but we do have the unfinished draft of a letter in which he asked Archduke Francis for support:

Your Royal Highness

I make so bold as to beg your Royal Highness very respectfully to use
your most gracious influence with His Majesty the King with regard to
my most humble petition to His Majesty. Prompted by a desire for
fame, by love of work and by a conviction of my wide knowledge, I
venture to apply for the post of second kapellmeister, particularly as
Salieri, that very gifted kapellmeister, has never devoted himself to
church music, whereas from my youth on I have made myself completely familiar with this style. The slight reputation which I have
acquired in the world by my pianoforte playing has encouraged me to
ask His Majesty for the favor of being entrusted with the musical
education of the Royal Family. In the sure conviction that I have
applied to the most worthy mediators who, moreover, are particularly
gracious to me, I have the utmost confidence and shall . . . [manuscript
breaks off here] (First half of May 1790)[54]

We have no reason to believe that Mozart wished to abandon opera
and devote himself to church music; he had not composed a religious
work for ten years (apart from the unfinished C Minor Mass). Under
Joseph II church music had played a minor if not negligible role. But
Mozart was well acquainted with the political situation, and he realized that a change in church policy was inevitable. No doubt the
reference to Salieri was purely tactical, for his tenure as court kapellmeister appeared to be unshakable. Mozart was probably hoping
to be entrusted with the musical instruction of the imperial family, for
Leopold II had sixteen children. To guard against an offer of some
miserable fee (such as the 400 florins for the instruction of Princess
Elizabeth in 1782), Mozart conceived the idea of a second kapellmeister position that would have guaranteed him roughly 2,000 florins
a year.

Mozart's entire imagination was focused on this project, which he
pursued by every means at his disposal. Naturally he had to protect
his reputation and make sure that the new ruler had no reason to
consider him a debt-ridden spendthrift. He expressed this concern in
an informative letter to Michael Puchberg.

I now stand at the threshold of my fortune; but the opportunity will be
lost forever if this time I cannot make use of it. My present circumstances, however, are such that in spite of my excellent prospects I

must abandon all hope of furthering my fortunes unless I can count on the help of a staunch friend. For some time you must have noticed my constant sadness—and only the very many kindnesses you have already rendered me have prevented me from speaking out. Now, however—once more, but for the last time—I call upon you to stand by me to the utmost of your power in this most urgent matter which will determine my whole happiness. You know how my present circumstances, were they to become known, would damage the chances of my application to the court, and how necessary it is that they remain a secret. For unfortunately at court they do not judge by circumstances, but solely by appearances. You know, and I am sure you are convinced that if, as I may now confidently hope, my application is successful, you will certainly lose nothing. How delighted I will be to discharge my debts to you! How glad I will be to thank you and, in addition, to confess myself eternally your debtor! What a pleasant sensation it is to reach one's goal at last—and what a blessed feeling it is when one has helped another to do so! Tears prevent me from completing the picture! In short—my whole future happiness is in your hands. Act according to the dictates of your noble heart! Do what you can and remember that you are dealing with a right-minded and eternally grateful man, whose situation pains him even more on your account than on his own.

(Late March or early April 1790)[55]

In fact, between December 1789 and May 1790 Mozart borrowed the enormous sum of 875 florins from Puchberg, over and above his other earnings of at least 1,300 florins. This seems even more astonishing when we consider that in the fall of 1790 Mozart could plan an almost luxurious journey to the emperor's coronation in Frankfurt without incurring new debts as a result of this unusual expenditure. His evident concern for his reputation in the letters to Puchberg may suggest gambling debts or bad investments, but nothing is conclusive.

Mozart was somewhat unsure of the new emperor. He had known Leopold II in Italy as Pietro Leopoldino, grand duke of Tuscany, with a seat in Florence. But twenty years had passed since then, and their acquaintance was no longer a personal one.

There was also uncertainty among the Viennese about the new emperor. They knew that he had tried to found a model state in Tuscany, and they were familiar with his policies there. But how would he handle the situation in Vienna? How would he deal with the bureaucracy; what dismissals and reorganizations would he implement; and what aspects of the administration would he change? Most of all, what would he do to take control of foreign policy (the war with Turkey was still in progress) and to pacify the restless crown lands? Would he seek to placate the nobility by restoring its former privileges? Would he propose new tax reforms? There was general apprehension about all these crucial matters, for the emperor's decisions would affect each and every citizen of Vienna in one way or another.

Many people wondered whether Leopold's experience in governing the small grand duchy of Tuscany was adequate preparation for ruling the vast and complex Habsburg Empire. During his thirty years in Florence, Leopold had made Tuscany one of Europe's most modern states: the feudal rights of the landowners were eliminated, and the rights of the peasants were recognized and extended; improved trade, economic freedoms, and the construction of new roads created a basis for relative prosperity; and education underwent a thorough reform. Leopold also brought the modern state church to Tuscany: the Inquisition was abolished, bishops won greater independence from the pope, the number of monasteries was reduced, and better provision was made for individual parishes. Leopold had called in Cesare Beccaria, a dedicated Enlightenment thinker, to draw up the Tuscan criminal code, which was widely translated and became famous throughout Europe. Two points best illustrate the spirit of this document: first, Beccaria asserted that punishment should serve to rehabilitate the criminal; and second, the category of "crimes against the crown" was done away with, thus clearing the way for a future constitution.

It was plain that Leopold's reforms had been much more consistent than those of his brother Joseph, though conditions in Tuscany were admittedly more favorable and more easily controlled than in the vast Habsburg dominions. The goals of their reforms were essentially the same, but their methods differed greatly. Unlike his brother, Leopold knew how to proceed at a moderate pace and avoid unnecessary provocations. He could compromise without losing sight of his objectives and was seen as a conciliator because he tried to persuade his opponents rather than push his reforms through despotically. Leopold was also free of the pettiness that led Joseph to interfere in even the least important and most personal matters.

Vienna had to wait some time for Leopold's arrival. Since the beginning of January, his brother had written numerous letters imploring him to come so that he might see him once more before his death and brief him on the most important developments. But Leopold had no intention of coming and continually made excuses. His reluctance was understandable to a certain extent; he had no desire to sit idly in Vienna and await his brother's death, powerless to intervene in affairs of state, which seemed thoroughly muddled to him. Not until three weeks after Joseph's death did Leopold arrive in Vienna, whereupon he plunged into restless activity. The people, however, saw little evidence of his labors, and their uncertainty remained. He was there, but he rarely appeared in public. He never went to concerts or the theater, which would have been the least demanding way to make public appearances; Joseph II had made frequent use of such opportunities. Suddenly everything seemed different, but people were not yet sure what the difference was.

At first Mozart remained optimistic, though his optimism was based on rather nebulous prospects. He wrote to Puchberg:

> I now have great hopes of an appointment at court, for I have reliable information that the emperor has not sent back my petition with a favorable or damning remark as he has the others, but has retained it. That is a good sign. (On or before May 17, 1790)

Or did he already suspect that nothing would come of his petition? His postscript to this letter reads, "I now have two pupils and I would like to raise the number to eight. Do your best to spread the news that I am giving lessons."

Did Mozart find himself in the same situation as nine years before, when he first arrived in Vienna? The postscript was intended mainly to reassure Puchberg, who had often urged Mozart to stabilize his income by taking pupils. Shortly thereafter—Puchberg would have received the news as soon as Mozart—the court made its decision: an additional kapellmeister post was out of the question; the royal children were to be instructed by Ignaz Umlauf, theater kapellmeister and assistant to Salieri. It was the simplest possible solution, involving no new positions and no changes in personnel. During these first months Leopold II had more important things to worry about than the organization of Viennese musical life. The Vienna correspondent for *Bosslers Musikalischer Korrespondenz* filed the following report on June 5:

The new monarch has not yet been to the theater; he has no music at his court and shows no sign of any interest in music. *Malum signum*, cry our false prophets. Yet I believe that when the mountain of state business facing him has been reduced to a mere hill of sand, and when he has restored golden peace to his dominions, another golden age of music will begin for us. At least Leopold has arranged for the musical instruction of his five princes, whom we have already seen several times at the opera in the company of the queen. She appears to have an understanding of music, but we do not notice that she takes any particular pleasure from our music in Vienna. Her reactions have perhaps a simple explanation: if one's ear is attuned to the fiery execution of the Italian masters, he will at first have little taste for the German's phlegmatic interpretations. I could support my contention with statements from numerous musicians and music lovers who have spent time beyond the Alps—but I will not be the one to judge.[56]

Malum signum—a bad sign: six months passed before the not very musical emperor found his way to the opera. Only his conservative and moralistic wife had the opportunity, in early summer, to see Mozart's operas; *Le nozze di Figaro* and *Così fan tutte* were given frequently. Doubtless she found them both distasteful, and we can assume that she did not want her children taught by such a freethinking musician as Mozart.

Mozart must have realized that his chances were not good at the new imperial court; indeed, he would be lucky to retain his position as *Kammerkompositeur*. Thus he was faced with a fundamentally new situation: he had to search for fresh opportunities because all his previous hopes had suddenly been dashed at a time when he was burdened with a mountain of debts and was obliged to finance expensive cures for his sick wife. Joseph II, "stingy" though he was, had nevertheless had an active interest in the Nationaltheater and had arranged several commissions for Mozart. Nothing of this kind could be expected from his successor, certainly not a permanent post as *Hofopernkomponist* (court opera composer).

This painful realization meant an end to his long-cherished dreams. Mozart's own health began to fail at about this time, and it is clear that his physical condition was influenced by his circumstances. The surviving letters from this period are almost all to Michael Puchberg.

In addition to their constant requests for money, they point to a crisis affecting both body and soul.

As early as April 8, 1790, Mozart wrote: "I would have gone to see you myself in order to have a chat with you, but my head is covered with bandages due to rheumatic pains, which make me feel my situation still more keenly." At the beginning of May: "I am very sorry that I cannot go out and have a talk with you myself, but my toothache and headache are still too painful and altogether I still feel very unwell." And on August 14:

Whereas I felt tolerably well yesterday, I am absolutely wretched today. I could not sleep all night for pain. I must have got overheated yesterday from walking so much and then caught a chill without knowing it. Picture to yourself my condition—ill and consumed by worries and anxieties. Such a state quite definitely prevents me from recovering. In a week or two I will be better off—certainly—but at present I am in want!

Mozart still had outstanding commissions—six string quartets for the king of Prussia and six piano sonatas for the Prussian princess. He began work on these pieces very reluctantly, driven more by necessity than by musical conviction: "I have now been obliged to give away my quartets (those very difficult works) for a mere song, simply in order to have cash in hand to meet my present difficulties. And for the same reason I am now composing some clavier sonatas" (June 12 [?], 1790).

But Mozart had already begun to make new resolutions and had even taken a more suitable apartment, which would not be free until the end of September and would probably have to be renovated first. (How else can we explain the paperhanger's bill for 208 florins found among his effects?) Mozart wrote to Puchberg about his plans:

I share your view about getting some good pupils, but I thought of waiting until I should be in our new quarters, as I intended to give lessons at home. In the meantime I beg you to tell people about this plan of mine. I am also thinking of giving subscription concerts at home during the months of June, July, and August. So it is only my present situation which oppresses me. When I move out of these quarters, I will have to pay 275 florins towards my new home. But I must have something to live on until I have arranged my concerts and until the quartets I am working on have been sent to be engraved. So if only I had at least 600 florins in hand I would be able to compose with a fairly easy mind. Ah! I must have peace of mind.

(Beginning of May 1790)

Indeed, the musical harvest of this summer was unusually small. Mozart entered *Così fan tutte* in his catalogue in January 1790, and the only other works entered before December of that year are two string quartets (K. 589 and K. 590), one string quintet (K. 593), and "in July Handel's *Caecilia* and *Alexander's Feast* arranged for B. Swieten."[57]

In early summer Mozart stayed for a time with Constanze in Baden and was only in Vienna to conduct performances of *Così fan tutte*. During one of these brief trips he wrote to his wife about an intrigue that reveals how much the wind had changed.

N.N. (you know whom I mean) is a cad. He is very pleasant to my face, but he runs down *Figaro* in public—and has treated me most abominably in the matters you know of—*I know it for certain*. (June 2 [?], 1790)

The "matters you know of" is a mystery to us, but it was something Mozart would not refer to directly or even by a coded nickname. He often took such precautions in his letters, but in this case he was especially careful and withheld the name of the hypocrite as well. It is surprising, however, that someone who was "pleasant" to Mozart would attack *Figaro* in public at a time when it was one of the most successful operas in the repertoire (it was given five times in May alone). This would only make sense if the well-known political objections to *Figaro* were being dragged out again—the old suspicions about its revolutionary import, which must now have seemed like an enthusiastic commentary on events in Paris. Mozart was obviously the victim of political defamation, no doubt an especially hard blow for him after his loss of standing at court.

Did Mozart actually present the summer series of subscription concerts mentioned in his letters to Puchberg? He probably meant chamber music concerts at his home, to include the string quartets for the king of Prussia; he had invited Puchberg to such a performance on May 22. But who were the other guests? If we had a list of the subscribers, we would know much more about the society in which Mozart moved during this period. Did Baron Wetzlar still belong to his circle of friends? Countess Thun? Baron van Swieten? Who else?

FRANKFURT—A POINTLESS JOURNEY?

Mozart's plan to search out new projects included traveling to Frankfurt am Main for the coronation of Leopold II as Holy Roman Emperor in the fall of 1790. Was this a renewed effort to gain a foothold outside Vienna? Or was Mozart only seeking new commissions while using the journey as an opportunity to give concerts and earn extra income? In any event, he was not part of the emperor's official entourage, which consisted of 1,493 cavalrymen and 1,336 foot soldiers[58]; the civilian music corps consisted of a mere 15 men under the direction of Antonio Salieri and Ignaz Umlauf. Mozart had no official function and traveled at his own expense in the company of his brother-in-law Franz Hofer and at least one servant, who also drove Mozart's private carriage. (Or did they travel in a carriage provided by Baron van Swieten, as Haydn did on his second journey to England in 1794?[59]) It was in any case a costly undertaking, because they had to rent two post-horses at every stop. To pay for the trip Mozart had to pawn his silver—whatever that may have included—at the Dorotheum, the state auction house (which still exists today).[60]

Frankfurt was always a very expensive city at coronation time. Apart from the giant entourages of the various electors and ambassadors, there were said to be 60,000 to 80,000 visitors, who were shamelessly fleeced by business-minded citizens full of pride in their "Free City of the Holy Roman Empire." Goethe's mother estimated that "a single room will certainly cost one carolin [11 florins] per day, and meals not less than one laubthaler [2 florins] per day."[61]

A visitor who witnessed the emperor's entry into Frankfurt on October 4 wrote, "To be present on this day is worth 100 florins. I have not been here long, and it has already cost that much. But I will stay for the coronation [on October 9], even if it costs me 100 more."[62] On the Römerplatz people were even selling spaces at their windows. The wealthy patricians of Frankfurt, however, demonstrated all their bourgeois pride.

Three days ago a very important person offered 12,000 florins to rent a house for himself and his family for a month. The merchant who owned the house declined, saying he needed it for his own *plaisir*. That shows you the kind of wealthy cranks they have here. And niggardly as the devil! They don't bother themselves with noblemen—not even counts. These merchants have their own little groups, like gossiping housewives, and have nothing to do with aristocrats.[63]

The free cities had the reputation of being immensely wealthy, but Mozart's experiences reveal the other side of the coin: "Besides, all this talk about the imperial towns is mere misleading chatter. True, I am famous, admired, and popular here; on the other hand, the Frankfurt people are even more stingy than the Viennese" (October 8, 1790). He at least had the luck to find accommodation with an acquaintance, the theater manager Johann Heinrich Böhm, at Kalbächergasse 10: "We pay 30 florins a month, which is wonderfully cheap" (September 30, 1790).

Five letters to Constanze have survived from the three weeks Mozart spent in Frankfurt. It is notable that they do not mention any of the highly impressive events surrounding the coronation. Only once, in a postscript, Mozart writes, "The state entry takes place on Monday (tomorrow), and the coronation a week later" (October 3, 1790). Regarding his concert:

My concert took place at 11 o'clock this morning. It was a splendid success from the point of view of honor and glory, but a failure as far as money was concerned. Unfortunately some prince was giving a big *déjeuner* and the Hessian troops were holding a grand maneuver. But in any case, some obstacle has arisen every day during my stay here.
(October 15, 1790)

Constanze, of course, could read detailed descriptions of the Frankfurt festivities every day in the *Wiener Zeitung*, but we sense in Mozart's omission a certain bitterness toward the emperor that is never articulated. This is a change from previous years, when his letters contained frequent references to Joseph II.

His bitterness was probably fueled by all the fuss and court ceremonial, which also seemed ridiculous and unnecessary to many contemporaries. Mozart, however, met everywhere with respect and admiration. "I am as excited as a child at the thought of seeing you again," he wrote to his wife. "If people could see into my heart, I would almost feel ashamed. To me everything is cold—cold as ice. Perhaps if you were with me I might take more pleasure in the kindness of those I meet here. But, as it is, everything seems so empty" (September 30, 1790). Although the separation frequently lamented in these letters lasted only seven weeks, it intensified his sense of aversion—the "coldness," the alienation, and the desire for a peaceful life without financial worries. "If I work very hard in Vienna and take pupils, we can live very happily; and nothing but a *good engagement at some court* can make me abandon this plan" (October 8, 1790).

Were those the alternatives? Give lessons or find employment at a court? Did Mozart travel to Frankfurt in order to find such a "good engagement"? Perhaps, yet we can detect a certain reluctance.

> Up to the present I have been living here altogether in retirement. Every morning I stay indoors in my hole of a bedroom and compose. My sole recreation is the theater, where I meet several acquaintances from Vienna, Munich, Mannheim, and even Salzburg. . . . This is the way I would like best of all to go on living—but I fear it will soon come to an end and that I am in for a restless life. Already I am being invited everywhere, and however tiresome it may be to put myself on view, I see nevertheless how necessary it is. So in God's name I submit to it.
> (October 3, 1790)

This does not at all sound like the familiar, lively Mozart who thrived on the hustle and bustle of society. He had apparently set out on this journey with no inner conviction—perhaps with his creditors in mind—and thought of it rather as a tiresome responsibility. On September 30, 1790, he wrote to his wife:

> My love, there is no doubt whatever that I shall make something in this place, but certainly not as much as you and some of my friends expect. That I am both known and respected here is undeniable. Well, we shall see.

Mozart seems to have kept his distance from the many aristocrats who were in Frankfurt, and from the numerous coronation festivities as well. He never mentions any contacts that might lead to a court appointment, and even his own concert seems not to have amounted to much.

> If my concert is at all successful, it will be thanks to *my name*, to Countess Hatzfeldt and the Schweitzer family who are working hard on my behalf. But I shall be glad when it's over. (October 8, 1790)

This concert did not take place under the patronage of a prince but was sponsored by private acquaintances and the wealthy Frankfurt banker Franz Maria Schweitzer, who also invited Mozart to dine with him. As with all other prices during coronation time, admission to the concert was very high—2 florins 45 crowns—though it did last three hours. Among other works, Mozart played two piano concertos, including the one in D major known as the *Coronation* Concerto (K. 537).[64] Mozart's entire attitude to the coronation hubbub is succinctly expressed in one sentence: "Tschiri-tschitschi—seek safety in flight!" (October 8, 1790).

Up to this point the journey had not been worth the expense, and the following weeks were hardly more encouraging. Mozart went first to Mainz, as he had probably planned to do while still in Frankfurt. He received 165 florins for a concert at the elector's palace—and was disappointed. (He does not say whether the other noble guests gave him anything, as they normally would have. Nothing definite is known about further concerts in Mainz.) A few days later he was in Mannheim, where he met old friends who were busy rehearsing *Figaro* in German translation at the theater. Reviews of their performance called it a mutilation, but Mozart was silent. After an excursion to Schwetzingen, he proceeded via Augsburg to Munich, where the better part of the Mannheim theater was then employed. Mozart planned a short stay, just long enough for a reunion with old friends, including kapellmeister Christian Cannabich. Another dignitary who happened to be in Munich was the king of Naples, who was married to the sister of Leopold II. The royal couple had been to the coronation in Frankfurt and were now making a stopover on their way to Vienna, where they planned to stay several months. The elector of Bavaria wanted to offer his guests some entertainment and invited Mozart to play a concert in the Kaisersaal of the Residenz. Mozart thought it ironic that the

Viennese guests could only hear him in Munich: "It is greatly to the credit of the Viennese court that the king has to hear me in a foreign country." Mozart was back in Vienna around November 10.

What was the real goal of this journey, and what did it achieve? It must have been strenuous, for Mozart spent almost a third of his time on the road. Although he did have his own carriage and could thus avoid the uncomfortable mail coach, it could hardly have been enjoyable to travel for such long periods. He had been reunited with many old acquaintances in Frankfurt, Mannheim, and Munich. He had given a few concerts, from which he had earned only slightly more than the cost of the entire trip. And he never had enough time in any one place.

During these weeks important things were transpiring in Vienna, and Constanze Mozart had to deal with them in her husband's absence. There were important financial transactions, which Mozart mentioned in all his letters to Vienna, and there was also the family's move to the Rauhensteingasse, which had been planned the previous summer.

He wrote to his wife from Munich:

I look forward to seeing you, for we have a great deal to discuss. I am thinking of making this same journey with you, my love, at the end of next summer, so that you may try some other waters. At the same time the company, the exercise, and the change of air will do you good, for it has agreed very well with me. I am greatly looking forward to this, and so are all my friends. (November 4, 1790)

It almost sounds as if he promised to take Constanze to Bavaria as a reward for her skillful handling of his business affairs while he was away.

Constanze had been involved in loan negotiations. Mozart wanted to arrange a two-year loan of 2,000 florins, half of which would be used immediately to pay off existing debts; he was willing to put up all his household furnishings as security. He intended to repay the loan with fees from his main publisher, Franz Anton Hoffmeister, and was confident that he could earn the necessary amount with new compositions. The situation was complicated, because Mozart had been offered a loan of 1,000 florins in cash and the other half in cloth. He also wanted Hoffmeister to be his cosignatory on the loan contract. Mozart must have had a high opinion of his wife's business acumen, for he embarked on a journey with doubtful prospects and left her to make the final arrangements. Naturally, this theme dominated their entire correspondence during the trip. Mozart especially did not want it known that he was simply covering his short-term debts.

> But you will have to give some other reason; say, for example, that I am involved in some speculation which you know nothing about. . . . But as in every case I prefer to play it safe, so I would like to make that deal with H[offmeister], because then I will obtain money and not have to pay anything. All I have to do is work, and that I shall willingly do for the sake of my dear little wife. (September 30, 1790)

It is not clear how this matter was concluded. The only surviving record is a promissory note for 1,000 florins to Heinrich Lackenbacher, a Viennese merchant. Here Mozart's household furnishings are offered as security, but Hoffmeister's signature is not on the document. Nevertheless, the promissory note was probably supplemented by an agreement with Hoffmeister (for an unknown sum), because the balance sheet drawn up just after Mozart's death shows that this loan had already been repaid. No outstanding debts to Hoffmeister are listed, but in his letter of October 8, 1790, Mozart urges Constanze to "settle the affair with Hoffmeister" and notes, "I need never repay the sum, *as I am composing* for Hoffmeister."

There are several reasons why this episode is particularly interesting and informative. First, it shows that Mozart was endeavoring to replace Michael Puchberg with other creditors. We do not know if Puchberg had limited Mozart's credit and was now pressing for at least partial repayment; in any case, the loan was used to pay off debts to him, and from then on Puchberg was approached only twice more for small loans (April 13, 1791, 30 florins; June 25, 25 florins). There is no evidence of a falling-out with Puchberg, however. Second, the letter to Constanze throws some light on the financial practices of the time: it was apparently more respectable to need money for speculation than to have debts—a common enough idea among businessmen, but also Mozart's personal opinion. We can even assume that Mozart

often engaged in speculation—successfully or not—as long as he had
no unusual expenses.

A third revealing facet of this affair is that it demonstrates Mozart's
readiness to establish a bourgeois existence for himself; in other
words, he had finally abandoned his hopes for a position at court
(either at the Hoftheater or at the court itself). He retained his sinecure as royal and imperial *Kammerkompositeur*, without specific duties. Mozart was obviously making long-term plans to earn his
livelihood primarily from two sources—instruction fees and income
from publications. In addition, he applied to the Viennese municipal
authorities for a position as cathedral kapellmeister at St. Stephen's,
which alone would have brought in 2,000 florins and considerable
supplementary income. Since the current kapellmeister was old and
sickly, Mozart asked "to be attached for the time being as an unpaid
assistant" so that he would "have the opportunity of helping this
worthy man in his office, thus gaining the approbation of our learned
municipal council by the actual performance of services which I may
justly consider myself especially fitted to render on account of my
thorough knowledge of both the secular and ecclesiastic styles of
music" (petition to the municipal council, May 1791). Thus it is clear
that Mozart, though he might still contemplate extended journeys—to
England, for example—preferred to remain settled in Vienna as long
as he could support himself there. All references to "a good engagement at some court" constitute nothing more than a last resort, in case
there was no alternative.

Chapter 8

THE LAST YEAR

REORGANIZATION

When Mozart returned from Frankfurt, he found a letter from London containing an attractive offer—presumably arranged by Thomas Attwood, the protégé of the Prince of Wales. Mozart was invited to come to London at the end of 1790 and remain for six months; there he would compose at least two operas, *"sérieux ou comiques"* as desired by the opera management, for which he would receive 300 pounds sterling (2,400 florins). It would be an exclusive contract as far as opera was concerned, but he was guaranteed the opportunity of giving his own concerts. These were splendid financial terms, yet Mozart hesitated. His answer to the impresario Robert May O'Reilly is unknown, but he probably suggested a postponement because he did not want to travel without Constanze, who was ill at the time. Several weeks later there was a farewell dinner in Vienna for Joseph Haydn, who was embarking on his first journey to England with the impresario Johann Peter Salomon. Salomon probably proposed a similar tour to Mozart that evening.

All at once Mozart's prospects were considerably brighter, inaugurating a year that was generally happy and successful, but sadly was also his last. His works were on sale in all the leading Viennese music shops—Artaria, Traeg, and Lausch, as well as Hoffmeister. His operas were being performed everywhere. During this last year, *Don Giovanni* was performed in Berlin, Augsburg, Hanover, Bonn, Kassel, Bad Pyrmont, Munich, Prague, and Cologne; *Die Entführung aus dem Serail* in Amsterdam, Erfurt, and Pest; *Le nozze di Figaro* in Bonn and Hamburg; and *Così fan tutte* in Frankfurt, Mainz, Leipzig, and Dresden. Most of the performances were in German, an indication of the importance attached to comprehension of text *and* music, although the German versions were often based on indescribably bad translations. In the absence of copyright laws, Mozart had no financial share in any of these productions, but his fame grew daily and led to contractual agreements with publishers and impresarios. New piano and composition pupils also presented themselves at his door. Their names tell us little or nothing, for only a few can be proved to have studied with Mozart; it is highly unlikely that he actually gave lessons to all those who later called themselves his pupils.

When we consider the compositions of these last years, we are astounded not only by the number of pieces he wrote but by the diversity of musical genres. We also notice that Mozart's preference for certain types of composition changes, which may reflect a change in public tastes. For example, after 1787 he wrote no more serenades, cassations, or divertimenti and instead began the series of dances for the *Fasching* balls—minuets, German dances, *Ländler*, and contredanses. For the long season 1790–91 he wrote more of these than ever before, since Ash Wednesday was not until March 9. Unlike the serenades and divertimenti, these new dances often appeared in print immediately, so anyone could play them on the piano. Many new works of this kind were advertised in the *Wiener Zeitung* during Mozart's last years, bringing him substantial fees from publishers.

Between 1782 and 1786 Mozart had appeared frequently in concerts and had written for concerts given by other musicians, but over the next few years he virtually stopped writing solo concertos; a single one, for piano (K. 537), dates from 1788. Now, in 1791, he wrote not only another piano concerto (K. 595) but also the Clarinet Concerto (K. 622); he obviously wanted to maintain a presence in the concert hall. He performed the piano concerto at a concert given by the

Viennese clarinetist Joseph Beer—not in the imperial Burgtheater, however, but in the bourgeois Jahn Rooms. For the annual concert of the Tonkünstlersozietät, Mozart added two clarinet parts to his Symphony in G Minor (K. 550), which was conducted by Antonio Salieri. Does this indicate a renewed interest in large symphonic works? Since the mid-1780s Mozart had turned increasingly to demanding chamber works—trios, quartets, and quintets for various combinations— sometimes containing writing of soloistic brilliance; on the other hand, the commission for a set of six string quartets remained only half completed.

During his years in Vienna, Mozart wrote scenes and arias only in connection with opera projects—in some cases probably to flatter the individual singers, for most of these compositions are extremely virtuosic. A typical example is the bass aria *"Per questa bella mano"* (K. 612), written for Franz Gerl, the first Sarastro. In 1791, however, Mozart had no reason to curry favor or fear theater intrigues, for *La clemenza di Tito* was written for Prague, where he always enjoyed great popularity at the theater, and *Die Zauberflöte* was written not for the Hoftheater but for Emanuel Schikaneder's popular Freihaustheater.

Despite the effort of writing two large operas during this last year, Mozart also turned to religious music for the first time in eight years. The Requiem (K. 626) was a commission, but Mozart could have had many opportunities to write church music in Vienna, especially given the "thorough knowledge" of liturgic styles mentioned in his petition to the municipal council. *Ave verum corpus* (K. 618), written for the schoolmaster and choir director Anton Stoll in Baden, was an important indication of his renewed interest in church music. He also began to play frequently on the organ of the former Jesuit church at court.

It is especially worthy of note that *Die Zauberflöte* is not the only work of this last year in which Mozart professes (albeit critically) his Masonic beliefs; for lodge membership had long since become unpopular and was anything but opportune. The *Kleine Freimaurerkantate* (K. 623), the last piece that Mozart completed and performed himself, is programmatic in nature, calling for the renewal and intensification of Masonic work. Nor should we overlook the setting of Franz Heinrich Ziegenhagen's hymn *"Die ihr des unermesslichen Weltalls Schöpfer ehrt,"* for it takes up Masonic ideas, and Mozart knew its author at least by name. This work was intended as a supplement to Ziegen-

hagen's essay "Lehre vom richtigen Verhältnisse zu den Schöpfungs-
werken" ("Theory of the Proper Relationship to Works of Creation"),
whose social-utopian character was probably unknown to Mozart.

Looking at the compositions of this last year, we notice that none of
them was written for the aristocratic salon, which had been an important proving ground for Mozart's music during the *Figaro* period. He
had also turned his back on the court opera. It is true that *La clemenza
di Tito* was written for the coronation of Leopold II as king of Bohemia,
yet the commission came not from the court but from the (usually
dissident) Bohemian estates. Nor did Mozart make any attempt to
improve his relationship with the court, but instead sought a new
opportunity from the bourgeois municipal council of Vienna. He was
no longer waiting for a position at the Nationaltheater, as he had under
Joseph II, but was striving for greater independence. Obviously he
made the right decision, for his financial situation appeared to be
improving steadily and he did not lack for commissions. Indeed, his
last year became his most productive. As the year drew to a close his
prospects were even brighter: he was offered pensions by organizations in Amsterdam and Hungary and was invited to visit England and
Russia. In this light, Mozart's premature and sudden death may seem
less tragic (or more so?); at least he lived long enough to witness this
change in his fortunes.

When Leopold II arrived in Vienna three weeks after the death of
Joseph II, he found both domestic and foreign affairs in a shambles. It
is hardly surprising that he did not want to let Joseph's officials remain
in their posts without a review of their competence—especially since
he had not been very impressed by them on his previous visits to
Vienna. He also thought he detected a fair amount of inefficiency. He
would not retain a single one of his brother's clerks and secretaries
because he had no confidence in them. The use of inexperienced
personnel meant that during the first few weeks not even the *Hand-
billette* announcing his decisions were properly drawn. The higher
government officials, however, could not simply be replaced, for there
was no one to fill their positions. The situation thus called for great
circumspection. Unrest and irritation at the new ruler were inevitable
at first—not least because his political course appeared to be a
complete rejection of Josephine policy: restoration of privileges to the
estates and the nobility, a conciliatory stance toward the Church,

preparations for a sweeping reorganization of the educational system, and so forth. Leopold proceeded very discreetly; he somehow had to pacify all sides while remaining in control. The opposition movement (especially in Hungary and the Netherlands) was openly supported by Prussia, which wanted to take advantage of Austria's weakness (also a result of the continuing war with Turkey). Leopold II was willing to make all necessary concessions, but he wanted to grant them of his own accord and would not submit to extortion. The ultimate success of his brilliant imperial policy justifies the memorable phrase that has been applied to it by scholars Ernst Wangermann and Adam Wandruszka: "One step back, two steps forward."

Contemporaries must have found it difficult to discern a clear and consistent course behind this policy. Furthermore, the Viennese considered the emperor sly, deceitful, and unapproachable; though he was apparently willing to hear any complaint in person, a cordial relationship could never be established.

Mozart's aversion to the new court, which had begun with the refusal to create a second kapellmeister position, was reinforced by many changes in policy and personnel that affected his own circles. In the early summer of 1790 it became apparent that Gottfried van Swieten was beginning to lose his influence. He still headed the court commission on education, but at the same time he had to tolerate the formation of another commission, under the leadership of Karl Anton von Martini, which was preparing a complete reorganization of the school system. Swieten's exit was thus only a matter of time; it was finally formalized in October 1791 and was announced the day after Mozart's death. Since Swieten was perceived as one of the most dedicated Josephinians, his gradual demotion signaled a new course.

There were drastic changes at the Nationaltheater as well. Count Franz Xaver Wolf Rosenberg-Orsini was replaced as director by Count Johann Wenzel Ugarte. It was also at this time that the controversy surrounding Lorenzo Da Ponte came to a head. Da Ponte's contract as court librettist ran until 1792, but he had become increasingly embroiled in intrigues stirred up by his cohabitation with the famous singer Adriana del Bene.[1] Her capriciousness and violent temper had made her highly unpopular with the rest of the ensemble at the Nationaltheater, yet Da Ponte favored her above all the others. The entire scandal, with its endless complaints, accusations, and slander, was brought before the emperor; Da Ponte was obliged to justify himself and wrote a somewhat presumptuous letter to Leopold II. The emperor had other problems, however, and his interest in the Nationaltheater was not great enough for him to intervene in the matter. He ungraciously informed Da Ponte that he no longer required his services as librettist and requested him to leave Vienna before Easter 1791. (Da Ponte, though, was not one to give in easily. For an entire year, even after he had fled to Italy, he struggled to rehabilitate himself, but to no avail.)

Theater intrigues and disappointment at the emperor's lack of interest must have increased significantly in 1791, for Salieri gave up his post at the Nationaltheater during that season, and his pupil Joseph Weigl was named his successor. This was the very position Mozart had dreamed of while Joseph II was alive. Now he did not even bother to apply for it; he could not imagine himself working at the court of Leopold II.[2]

No statement by Mozart regarding any of these events has survived. He no longer had a correspondent like his father—curious, attentive, and always ready to give an opinion. Most of his acquaintances were in Vienna, where everything could be discussed in person. Nor do later reminiscences provide much additional information. We know a multitude of details about the second half of 1791 because during those months Mozart wrote numerous letters to his wife, who was taking the waters at Baden. Yet we know very little about the period from November 1790 to April 1791, and the handwritten catalogue of his works contains few entries.[3] In view of the enormous workload of the next six months, it would seem that Mozart took a break from composing. Even if we assume that he had a number of pupils at this time and that he began work on *Die Zauberflöte* as early as March 1791, the output is very small compared with other periods, and we seem to have reached another blank spot in his biography.

MOZART'S SON IN BOARDING SCHOOL

There are no letters from this period in which Mozart bewails his money problems. A few such letters may have been lost, but Mozart's financial situation had apparently stabilized to the point where he felt he could afford to send his son to a relatively expensive boarding school in Perchtoldsdorf near Vienna.[4] The annual cost of board and tuition at this institution came to 400 florins—more than Leopold Mozart had earned in a year as assistant kapellmeister in Salzburg (350 florins). Despite its prohibitive cost, the school does not seem to have had an especially high reputation, for in August 1790 the following notice appeared in the *Wiener Zeitung:*

> *Education.* For some time I have been surprised and dismayed to hear the question: Does my institution in Perchtoldsdorf still exist? I have also had to tolerate the many know-it-alls who assert that it no longer exists. I thus find myself obliged to publicly assert: (1) that this institution not only never ceased operations, but is in fact flourishing, as any visitor will attest; (2) that one may obtain detailed information by sending written inquiries to the Heegersches Erziehungshaus in Perchtoldsdorf near Vienna; and (3) that the enrollment period has been extended until the end of September. Perchtoldsdorf, August 21, 1790. W. B. Heeger, owner and headmaster.

Mozart was very concerned about his son's education and was apparently unimpressed by Wenzel Bernhard Heeger's methods and results. In a letter to Constanze he describes a visit there, when he went to fetch Karl and take him to a performance of *Die Zauberflöte*.

> Karl was absolutely delighted at being taken to the opera. He is looking splendid. As far as health is concerned he could not be in a better place, but everything else there is wretched, alas! All they can do is turn out a good peasant into the world. But enough of this. As his serious studies (God help them!) don't begin until Monday, I have arranged to keep him until after lunch on Sunday. I told them that you would like to see him. So tomorrow, Saturday, he and I will drive out to see you. You can then keep him, or I will take him back to Heeger's after lunch. Think it over. A month can hardly do him much harm. . . . On the whole, Karl is no worse; but at the same time he is not one whit better than he was. He still has his old bad manners. He never stops chattering just as he used to do in the past, and he is, if anything, *less inclined to learn than before*, for out there [at Perchtoldsdorf] all he does is wander about in the garden for five hours in the morning and five hours in the afternoon, as he himself

Antonio Salieri came to Vienna in 1766; he became Hofkomponist (court composer) in 1774 and court kapellmeister in 1788.

confessed. In short, the children do nothing but eat, drink, sleep and go for walks. (October 14, 1791)

Karl, then, was not receiving a thorough education—something Mozart took very seriously. He even owned a large number of instructional books for teaching young children.

Heeger, of course, wanted to squelch any rumors that his institution was nothing more than a day nursery. Emperor Leopold, who had a strong interest in education, sent Archduke Francis on an inspection of the school, and Heeger managed to exploit this visit for publicity purposes. He had an article printed in the *Wiener Zeitung* that read in part:

Whoever is acquainted with Father Leopold's broad and penetrating wisdom—and who does not admire it!—will easily recognize the effectiveness of the training and instructional methods so favored by His Majesty and which have been introduced into this institution. Accordingly, those who would be inclined to have their young offspring brought up, so to speak, directly under the eye of the wise Leopold, are herewith requested to secure enrollment by October 8 of this year. . . . The fee of 400 florins per annum covers all possible expenses, including clothes; no visitors are allowed before 5 o'clock except on Thursdays and Sundays; students are required to remain on the school premises except during the semiannual vacations, and may not be prematurely withdrawn from school without three months' notice. The curriculum is already well known.[5]

But Mozart was not swayed by such exhortations and shortly thereafter removed his son from Heeger's institution. Karl was to have a sound primary education, and for this the Piarist Institute in Josephstadt was the best choice. Apparently it was no easy task to have his child accepted there. In order to make a good impression, Mozart felt called upon to "join the procession to the Josephstadt, holding a candle in my hand," as he amusedly wrote to Constanze (June 25, 1791). The "Löwenburgisches Erziehungshaus der P. P. Piaristen" was undoubtedly the most distinguished institution of its kind in Vienna although it was considerably cheaper than the school in Perchtoldsdorf; not only well-to-do bourgeois families but also the nobility had their children educated there. A detailed prospectus described the impressive facilities:

Training and instruction are carried out by ecclesiastics who maintain constant supervision of the students. They are taught in the public *Gymnasium* and in addition receive extra instruction from our own clerical teachers—most importantly in true Christianity and moral discipline. Other subjects are reading, writing, arithmetic, in general and in particular, as well as literature, geography, and all other subjects required by either the German or the Latin grammar schools. Secular instructors are employed by the school to teach the French language, drawing, and dancing. Boys of the same age live together, supervised by ecclesiastics, in a number of large rooms; these student quarters are heated, cleaned, lit, and provided with servants at the school's expense. Meals consists of porridge at breakfast, four courses at lunch, and two courses at supper, as well as fruit or salad according to season; also a suitable portion of wine, if the parents or guardian so desires. Extra courses are provided on holidays and special occasions.

In summer our private garden is used for recreation, in winter a special room is available. The total cost is 250 florins per year, payable quarterly to the headmaster in advance so long as the current rise in prices persists. An extra charge of 10 florins is made for use of the school's laundry service. Students who do not remain on the premises during vacations pay 25 florins less. A boarding student wishing to withdraw from the school must give three months' notice. The Löwenburgisches Erziehungshaus recognizes all types of grants and scholarships, as all students by court decree must attend the local public gymnasium. No uniform or special clothing of any kind is required. Pupils may dress as they please but are asked to maintain a plentiful supply of clean garments. Additional expenses include books, the imperial school fees, and in case of illness—for which a separate infirmary is provided—all fees for physicians, nurses, and medicine. In addition, arriving pupils are required to bring their own bed linen, silverware, toilet articles, and other personal necessities; a list of these items must be made in duplicate—one copy for the parents or guardians, the other for the headmaster. Be advised: Any student wishing to have a private room, his own clergyman, his own servant, or only one of these, must pay in addition to the above fees 50 florins for a private room, 200 florins for his own clergyman, and 130 florins for a servant and his livery.[6]

Mozart considered this arrangement appropriate for his son's education—naturally, the question of a private servant or cleric would never have come up. His decision is the more noteworthy in that he himself had no formal schooling, only private instruction during his wunderkind years. Fortunately he received a broad and comprehensive education this way, primarily because his father was a man of unusually wide intellectual interests and a gifted pedagogue. Mozart undoubtedly realized that he himself led a very different, less structured life and that the education of his children could never be the focus of attention it had been for Leopold Mozart, even when he and Wolfgang were away from home for years at a time. And Mozart made no attempt to force Karl into an early musical development or to raise him as a wunderkind, although the child showed a definite musical gift. Apparently Mozart took his son to the opera for the first time on October 13, 1791, when they saw *Die Zauberflöte*, and the seven-year-old thoroughly enjoyed himself.

Karl did not get to see his father very often, but he did accompany his mother when she went to Baden in June and July of 1791, and Mozart came out three or four times to visit them for several days. During this period he was composing *Die Zauberflöte*, and Karl probably had his first real opportunity to observe his father at work. He may have known some of the songs already when he saw Papageno, the merry bird catcher, on stage for the first time, as played by Schikaneder, the librettist of *Die Zauberflöte*.

DIGRESSION: EMANUEL SCHIKANEDER

Mozart's acquaintance with Emanuel Schikaneder dated back to his Salzburg days. At the time (1780) Schikaneder was a frequent visitor to the Mozart home and was among the small circle of friends who met regularly for *Bölzlschiessen*, an earthy outdoor amusement in which participants competed for cash prizes by shooting at wooden targets often adorned with suggestive erotic scenes. Schikaneder was almost part of the family, and he reciprocated by providing the Mozarts with complimentary theater tickets for the entire season, of which they made ample use. When Wolfgang left for Munich on November 5, 1780, to handle the preparations for *Idomeneo,* his sister Maria Anna had to promise that she would write him all about Schikaneder's theater productions in Salzburg. Schikaneder, for his part, commissioned Mozart to write an insert aria for one of his musical plays. Their mutual interests were thus the foundation of a close relationship.

Schikaneder was born in Straubing in 1751, the son of domestic servants. He lost his father very early, and his mother supported the family by selling devotional objects at the cathedral in Regensburg. She earned enough for Schikaneder to attend the Jesuit school for several years, but he soon began to travel about as a street musician and singer, and at the age of eighteen became an actor with an itinerant theater troupe. His versatility was immediately put to the test, for he not only had to act but to compose, direct, and even dance in the ballet sequences that were then part of almost every theater performance. Nevertheless, the theater troupes with which Schikaneder worked had serious artistic goals, though for financial reasons frequent concessions were made to the taste of a far from discriminating public. Schikaneder soon learned the classics of modern German drama and performed Lessing, Goethe, and a great many *Sturm und Drang* plays. His specialty, however, was Shakespeare: Hamlet was his most famous role, and he also appeared in *Macbeth, King Lear,* and *Othello,* and as Richard III.

In 1778 he took over the direction of the Moser troupe and went on the road with his own ensemble and at his own expense. He stayed in Salzburg almost six months during 1780–81. Here Mozart saw him as Hamlet and in numerous other plays including Lessing's *Emilia Galotti.* But he also offered Singspiels, at the time an entirely new genre that was as different from opera as the operetta is from the musical today. It seems that Schikaneder presented Singspiels more frequently than usual, so that Mozart was able to hear the following works before he left for Munich: *Die Lyranten oder das Lustige Elend* (by Schikaneder), *Die pucefarbenen Schuhe* (Ignaz Umlauf), *Ariadne auf Naxos* (a melodrama by Georg Benda), *Der Barbier von Sevilla* (after Beaumarchais, by Friedrich Ludwig Benda), and *Der Seefahrer oder Die schöne Sklavin* (Niccolò Piccini). Schikaneder's troupe had nine other Singspiels in its repertoire, five of which were given in Salzburg. The quality of the performances cannot have been very high, of course, but they were nonetheless of great importance because they made these works known in areas where there was no resident theater.

Schikaneder had a superb theatrical instinct. Everything he did was calculated for maximum effect on the public, and he himself was always ready to participate, even to extemporize if necessary. Schikaneder's resourcefulness was unlimited: Goethe's *Götz von Berlichingen*, Schiller's *Die Räuber*, and Törring's *Agnes Bernauer* were given giant open-air productions, utilizing the natural landscape as a set, with whole companies of soldiers as supernumeraries for the battle scenes. An actual bridge across a river served as the set for Agnes Bernauer's death by drowning; the scene was so effective that members of the audience intervened, saved the heroine, and pursued the "culprit."

Schikaneder had a decided preference for theatrical opulence. His was a theater of imposing sets and the latest stage technology— elevators, flight machines, and movable light sources for special effects; his specialty was fires and waterfalls. To implement his innovations fully he needed his own theater, but that required a stroke of luck, for Schikaneder had no income other than his receipts, and all his profits were immediately squandered on new stage effects. As if in a fairy tale, Emperor Joseph II happened to see him in Pressburg, summoned him to an audience, and spontaneously offered him the Kärntnertortheater in Vienna for his productions. The emperor was probably hoping to revive the Nationalsingspiel, which had recently folded, by having Schikaneder carry on its activities as a private theater. And it was certainly no coincidence that on November 5, 1784, *Die Entführung aus dem Serail* was the opening production in the first theater Schikaneder had leased exclusively for his own use.

He now had a chance to prove himself, but he was soon brought down by his almost compulsive womanizing. This time his wife Eleonore, one of the most important members of his ensemble, had had enough; she left him, precipitating the breakup of his entire troupe. During the last week of this brief theater episode, the emperor personally intervened in the repertoire by summarily forbidding Beaumarchais's *Mariage de Figaro*.[7] Schikaneder, however, did not fall into disfavor as a result. Since he had to give up his lease on the Kärntnertortheater for purely personal reasons (not because of the censor's ban), he was taken on by the ensemble at the Burgtheater, though only for supporting roles. There is no evidence that Schikaneder renewed his friendly relations with Mozart during his first years in Vienna, but from the involvement of both men with Beaumarchais's scandalous play, we know that they had certain intellectual and theatrical interests in common.

The subsidiary roles at the Burgtheater naturally did not satisfy Schikaneder's broad ambitions. After another period of wandering, he once again managed to assemble a troupe of his own and even to find a powerful sponsor. In Regensburg, subsidized by Prince Carl Anselm von Thurn und Taxis, Schikaneder was again able to mount his huge open-air spectacles. Schiller's *Die Räuber* was performed by several hundred participants. Schikaneder also joined the influential Regensburg Masonic lodge Zu den drei Schlüsseln (The Three Keys), but shortly thereafter his membership was suspended for six months due to a "highly sensational incident." It is unlikely that his suspension was the result of financial problems, for Schikaneder's existence was fairly secure despite the enormous costs of his productions; Prince von Thurn und Taxis held a group subscription for his entire household—a total of 100 tickets for each performance. However, there is ample evidence that Schikaneder's many love affairs were causing considerable trouble; they must have created quite a stir in the provincial atmosphere of Regensburg.

Schikaneder was now at the height of his success thanks to good luck and his ability to exploit sudden advantages. His wife had separated from him in 1785 and lived with the actor Johann Friedel, who had leased the Theater im Freihaus auf der Wieden in Vienna. After Friedel died suddenly in 1789 and bequeathed the management of the theater to Eleonore Schikaneder, she reconciled with her husband, who left Regensburg and assumed joint management with her.

Theater auf der Wieden was a "suburban" theater, one of many in Vienna, but lay within easy reach of the city and was part of a large residential complex owned by Prince Starhemberg that encompassed roughly 225 dwellings. The entire acting company could live there cheaply among the laborers, craftsmen, and servants who made up much of the theater's audience, though it was also patronized by members of Viennese "high society." In the stalls one had to sit on simple wooden benches, but there were also two circles with boxes of four and eight chairs; the entire theater could accommodate around eight hundred people. The basic orchestra consisted of twenty-three musicians but could be expanded as necessary. As a theater manager, Schikaneder showed careful judgment and an eye for organization; he was also dedicated to artistic quality. The wages he paid were not high—by no means comparable to the enormous salaries at the Nationaltheater—but they were generous enough to attract good talent. For example, Josepha Hofer, Mozart's sister-in-law and the first Queen of the Night, received a yearly salary of 830 florins plus 150 florins for her wardrobe. But since the theater did not employ a hairdresser, she had to pay for her own coiffure. Her contract, one of the few extant theater contracts from that time, reveals that Schikaneder was very interested in maintaining a good public image and attached great importance to the reputation of his theater. One passage commits the artist to helping the directors make ends meet by accepting less attractive roles. The relevant articles read as follows:

II. *Madame Josepha Hofer* commits herself for the duration of her engagement to perform, unquestioningly and to the best of her ability, all roles which the directors feel are suited to her capabilities. Naturally the artist will be allowed as much time as necessary for the preparation of her roles. She will accordingly be required to perform only one major role or two supporting roles each week. Exceptions will be made for leading roles of unusual difficulty.

III. Since the directors of the theater are interested not only in the artistic achievement of their personnel but also in their moral deportment, *Madame Hofer* thus commits herself by this contract to abide by the following regulations which apply to the entire ensemble: she must (a) lead a respectable home life; (b) avoid indebtedness; (c) avoid scandals; (d) refrain from disorderly conduct—quarreling, brawling, nocturnal dissipations, envious squabbling over roles—in short, anything which, through the actions of a few mischiefmakers, could in any way harm the directors and the ensemble as a whole. Any party receiving three warnings about such offenses will be subject to immediate dismissal. . . .

VII. It is impossible for such a private organization to employ suitable performers for every theatrical style, and neither is it possible to have so many performers that the best actors and actresses can appear only in important roles. Accordingly, *Madame Hofer* also commits herself to accept secondary roles; i.e., to take on minor roles in plays that have no important parts suitable for *her*, and walk-on roles in plays that are already in the repertoire. Most importantly, she and all other members must leave the casting entirely to the directors—who in any case follow the practice of placing each performer in the most favorable light, because it is to their advantage when each member of the company makes the best possible impression before the public.[8]

Schikaneder was too much a man of the theater not to learn from experience; hence the precise formulation of each item of the contract. He was no less aware that his theater could only fulfill its potential if he found investors willing to support the enterprise without meddling in artistic matters, and he almost always succeeded in finding such sponsorship. First there was Joseph von Bauernfeld, who functioned as associate manager—until he went bankrupt. In 1799 Schikaneder got together with Bartholomäus Zitterbarth, who immediately assumed some of the theater's debts. In 1802 Schikaneder gave up his managerial position and regular salary, and instead drew a fee for each of his own performances. He was particularly adept in financial matters. At the height of his career he was even able to build his own house, which was so resplendent that it became known as the "Schikanederschlössl" (Schikaneder's little castle). It was magnificently decorated inside and out, and one large room was painted with allegorical motifs from *Die Zauberflöte*.

In the long run, however, the Theater auf der Wieden proved much too small and modest for Schikaneder. He succeeded in persuading Zitterbarth to help him fulfill his old dream of a theater built to his own specifications. The work was completed in 1801, and Schikaneder established the Theater an der Wien, the largest in Vienna, with a capacity of 2,200. Two-thirds of this space was standing room, but that was not considered a serious limitation at the beginning of the nineteenth century. Boxes and galleries were arranged in a series of five circles; on the main floor were double rows of stalls and an orchestra pit.

Schikaneder was not only a successful theater manager, director, and actor, but also the author of plays for "his" theater. During his most successful period, between 1790 and 1802, he presented on average five of his own plays each year—all with leading roles written expressly for himself. His works included comedies, Singspiels, historical dramas—any genre that might appeal to his audience. Naturally he was spurred on by competition with the other Viennese "suburban" theaters, especially the Leopoldstadt, but he owed his success primarily to his deft handling of contemporary issues, trends, and fashions. Through the characters he invented (and portrayed himself), he was able to deliver social commentary of a more or less direct nature. Schikaneder's theater was a mixture of cabaret, farce, revue, and clown show that utilized every possible comic form and theatrical cliché. It parodied itself and satirized everything else, but it was always relevant to the times and never lost sight of the Enlightenment maxim that theater should edify as well as entertain.

Schikaneder, however, was not self-critical enough to notice the first small signs that audiences were growing tired of what he had to offer, and he was soon faced with a sudden shift in public taste. He had ridden all his popular warhorses to death, and his humor had become stale; he had cooked and recooked the same recipe until it was thin and watery. Schikaneder suffered the tragic fate of a man spoiled by success because he has no understanding of his own limitations. He experienced an unprecedented artistic decline that ended in total failure within five years. At first he was only hissed, but eventually he was unable to make a living even playing the provinces. The old thespian had lost his standards and his sense of perspective; he died in 1812, lonely, impoverished, and allegedly insane—but perhaps only "lost to the world," unable to understand how or why.

Despite his bitter end, the events of Schikaneder's life show that *Die Zauberflöte* was not a product of chance and that he was the perfect librettist for this material. It is especially important to emphasize this point in view of the customary yet fully unjustified condemnation of Schikaneder at the hands of musicologists and Mozart biographers. Hermann Abert, for example, subjects him to malicious ridicule:

> He barely had the education to read, write, and do sums. He had all the qualities of a born vagabond—good-naturedness, a sharp, natural wit, braggadocio, and an unbelievable lack of scruples that he was very adept at concealing beneath his charm and humor.[9]

Abert is nonetheless unable to dispute Schikaneder's authorship of the *Zauberflöte* libretto; one wonders why it was ever doubted in the first place. In a work by Julius Cornet entitled *Die Oper in Deutschland* ("Opera in Germany"), which appeared some sixty years after the premiere of *Die Zauberflöte*, we read, "At a tavern in Vienna, during the summer of 1818, we were joined at our table by an elegant old gentleman wearing a white neckerchief and a decoration on his blue frock coat."[10] It was Karl Ludwig Gieseke, who had sung in the chorus at Schikaneder's theater in 1791. He was a member of the lodge Zur neugekrönten Hoffnung and had no doubt been acquainted with Mozart. At the first performance of *Die Zauberflöte* he had played the role of the First Slave. At the tavern Gieseke, who had since become a botanist and held a professorship in Dublin, let drop the remark that he was actually the author of the *Zauberflöte* libretto. This bit of barroom claptrap is the foundation for the entire controversy over the authorship of the text. Gieseke used the opportunity to utter several similar falsehoods. For example:

> Schikaneder's personal acquaintance with *Mozart*, as well as his later acquaintance with *Zitterbarth*, began in a Masonic lodge—not the famous *Born* lodge, which counted Vienna's highest dignitaries and most distinguished men of literature among its members, but rather one of the "spurious" lodges, whose members met once a week in the evening to enjoy music, games, and the many pleasures of a well-laden table.[11]

The men in question were indeed not members of Born's Zur wahren Eintracht but of Zur neugekrönten Hoffnung (although there is some doubt about Schikaneder's membership); this organization was anything but a "spurious" lodge.

We can concede that Gieseke did in fact write plays and Singspiels. It is debatable whether they can stand comparison with those of Schikaneder. In any event, Schikaneder's authorship went unchallenged during his lifetime, and his name appeared on all playbills and published copies of the libretto. As long as the doubt has no foundation beyond a comment made in a tavern and written down imprecisely some twenty to thirty years after the fact, Schikaneder's authorship should not be questioned.

THE ORIGIN OF *DIE ZAUBERFLÖTE*

Innumerable legends have grown up around *Die Zauberflöte*. The work
purportedly had its origins in Schikaneder's financial difficulties,
which prompted a reluctant Mozart to offer help in the form of a new
opera for his suburban theater. As the story goes, Schikaneder tried to
keep Mozart happy with orgies of food and drink, and gave him the use
of his garden house so that he could compose undisturbed. Schikaneder is said to have shamelessly exploited the composer by denying
him a share of the opera's profits. A building alleged to be the garden
house has even been preserved as a museum piece by the Mozarteum
in Salzburg, though the nagging question remains as to whether the
wood used in its construction actually dates back to the eighteenth
century. And "garden house" suggests a pleasant garden in the suburbs, but if this hut existed at all it stood in one of the numerous inner
courtyards of the Freihaus auf der Wieden; at the time Schikaneder
did not yet have a garden of his own.

The only garden mentioned in Mozart's letters of the early summer
of 1791 is one belonging to the hornist Joseph Leutgeb.

> J'écris cette lettre dans la petite Chambre au Jardin chez Leitgeb [*sic*]
> ou j'ai couché cette Nuit excellement—et J'espère que ma chere
> Epose aura passé cette Nuit aussi bien que moi, j'y passerai cette Nuit
> aussi, puisque J'ai congedié Leonore, et je serais tout seul à la maison,
> ce qui n'est pas agreable.[12]

The other chambermaid (besides Leonore) was with Constanze and
Karl in Baden. Whenever possible, Mozart went to Baden for a few
days; otherwise he wrote to his wife daily. These letters afford much
insight into his everyday life, revealing names of people he saw on a
daily basis and recounting numerous visits to suburban theaters—but
Die Zauberflöte is mentioned rather seldom. Mozart was invited to
dine with Schikaneder several times, but these were probably working
visits to discuss details of their joint project—at least Mozart never
mentioned having feasted or engaged in revelry. He hated to eat alone
and took every opportunity to be with friends or acquaintances at
mealtimes.

There appear to have been no significant changes in the libretto for *Die Zauberflöte* after June; the theory that later changes were made because a rival theater was preparing a similar opera is untenable.[13] Mozart must have completed the first two acts around this time and brought them with him to Baden on June 13 so that Franz Xaver Süssmayr could transcribe the short score. The second act (except for the March of the Priests and the overture) was ready by the end of July, when Mozart entered this "German Opera in two Acts by Eman. Schikaneder, consisting of 22 numbers" in the catalogue of his works.

Everything we know about this period indicates that the origin of *Die Zauberflöte* was decidedly undramatic. There were no theater intrigues, Mozart was not working under pressure, and no one was complaining about the financial arrangements. No information about Mozart's fee has survived, which would suggest an agreement along the usual lines. Mozart had known Schikaneder for some years, and they had much in common regarding the theater, though a close personal friendship between the two men cannot be verified. The Theater auf der Wieden was a quite normal, in fact flourishing, business venture, with Schikaneder as one of the two "Directeurs." Schikaneder was undoubtedly aware of Mozart's more or less established fees for commissioned works. Mozart received 900 florins each for *Così fan tutte* and *La clemenza di Tito*, and the Prague commission also included travel expenses. There was no difference, then, between the fees he received at the Nationaltheater in Vienna and those he obtained from a private entrepreneur (Domenico Guardasoni, for whom Mozart had written *Tito*, was a private theater director in charge of his own finances). Accordingly, we must take Mozart's customary fees as our standard—or are we in all seriousness to believe that he received no money for this successful opera merely because the amount has not been preserved in any surviving record books? Would that not be a grave underestimation of Mozart's sense of his own artistic worth? When was Mozart ever prepared to write a large work without receiving appropriate payment? It would seem that the admittedly touching tale of Mozart's impoverishment is the only thing that denies him his rightful fee in this case, since it is already difficult enough to make the recorded income from Mozart's last year resemble poverty: he brought in roughly 2,000 florins even apart from *Die Zauberflöte* and his publisher's fees.

Biographical curiosity should rather occupy itself with an entirely different question: Why did Mozart not stay with Constanze in Baden, given that he visited her there as often as possible, almost every week and usually for several days at a time? Did he think he would be unable to compose there undisturbed? Once he visited with a large group of acquaintances, as he announced in a letter.

> At five o'clock tomorrow morning, we are all driving out, three carriagefuls of us, and so between nine and ten I expect to find in your arms all the joy which only a man can feel who loves his wife as I do! It is only a pity that I can't take with me either the clavier or the bird! That is why I would rather have gone out alone; but, as it is, I can't get out of the arrangement without offending the company. (June 7, 1791)

If he had gone alone he would have taken the clavier—not the large piano—and the bird with him. Why, then, this self-imposed isolation in Vienna, where there was not really anyone to look after him?[14]

A frankly malicious legend has it that Constanze Mozart was amusing herself in Baden with a lover, allegedly Süssmayr, of all people— which is said to be why his first two names were given to the son Constanze bore on July 26, 1791. But Süssmayr lived somewhere else altogether and was thoroughly occupied with the transcription of the short score for *Die Zauberflöte*. Mozart occasionally made caustic jokes at Süssmayr's expense, but they are more a sign of exuberant spirits than of ill feeling, much less jealous sarcasm: "I can never resist making a fool of someone—if it is not Leutgeb, then it must be Süssmayr"[15] (June 25, 1791).

The actual reason Mozart remained alone in Vienna, and even "from sheer boredom" composed an aria for the opera (June 11, 1791), was that his presence was required by a certain business affair. Unfortunately its nature remains totally obscure, although it is discussed in all the letters from June and the first part of July. It is an open question what kind of "speculation" Mozart was involved in; perhaps he was trying to sell something, although it is difficult to guess what it might have been. A letter to Michael Puchberg from June 25, 1791, requesting a small sum of money, sheds no light on the matter, for he did not refer to this "business" and was already hinting about payments he had been promised from the Hungarian nobles or the Amsterdam merchants. In any case, he wrote the following with regard to repayment of this small loan:

> If you, most beloved friend, can assist me with a small sum which I can send to her [Constanze] at once, you will oblige me exceedingly. I require the loan only for a few days, when you will receive 2,000 florins in my name, from which you can then refund yourself.

Puchberg sent 25 florins intended to defray unforeseen costs of Constanze's health cure.

Two things emerge clearly from the letters: first, Mozart had dealings with a man whom he referred to only as "N.N."—he was constantly running after this man and was constantly worried about whether he could successfully conclude his "business"; and second, his wife expressed a strong wish to return to Vienna because she also found the separation difficult. Mozart wrote to her on July 5, 1791:

> Do not be melancholy, I beg you! I hope you received the money. It is surely better for your foot if you stay on at Baden, for there you can go out more easily. I hope to hold you in my arms on Saturday, perhaps sooner. As soon as my business here is over, I shall be with you, for I mean to take a long rest in your arms; and indeed I shall need it, for this mental worry and anxiety and all the running around connected with it is really exhausting me. I received the last parcel safely and thank you for it. I can't express how delighted I am that you aren't taking any more baths. In a word, all I need now is your presence. Sometimes I think I cannot wait for it any longer. True, when my business is over I could have you back for good—but I would like to spend a few more delightful days with you at Baden.

The next day he alluded to the balloon flights that François Blanchard attempted in public demonstrations in the Prater.

> This very moment Blanchard is either going up in his balloon—or else will fool the Viennese for the third time. That this should be taking place today is most inconvenient for me, as it prevents me from settling my business. N.N. promised to come and see me before going out there, but he hasn't turned up. Perhaps he will when the fun is over. I shall wait until two o'clock, then I shall stuff down a little food and go

off to hunt him up. Our life is not at all a pleasant one. But patience! Things are bound to improve. And then I shall rest in your arms!

I thank you for your advice not to rely entirely on N.N. But in such cases *you are obliged to deal with only one person.* If you turn to two or three, and the affair becomes common property, others with whom you cannot deal regard you as a fool or an unreliable fellow. (July 6, 1791)

It was on this day that Blanchard managed his first ascent in Vienna. He had made previous attempts in March and May, and the Viennese, who for years had followed the development of the captive and free balloons with great interest, were anxious for a demonstration by the most famous aeronaut of his time, who six years earlier had become the first man to fly across the English Channel. So far all they had been able to do was pay out money—just to catch a glimpse of the famous balloon, which was on display in a large hall at the Mehlgrube. The prices had already aroused considerable anger. In the Prater, on the site where Johann Georg Stuwer mounted his famous fireworks displays, barriers and grandstands were erected and several thousand spectators waited to see the show (again the admission prices were high). Archduke Francis himself cut the rope; the airship ascended slowly and floated away out of sight. Blanchard landed in Gross-Enzersdorf, where he was received with great jubilation and escorted back to Vienna. Mozart wrote to his wife in Baden:

I did not go to see the balloon, for it is the sort of thing that one can imagine. Besides, I thought that this time too nothing would come of it. But goodness! How the Viennese are rejoicing! They are as full of his praises now as they have been up to the present of abuses.

There is something in your letter which I can't read and something I can't understand. You say: "I am certain that my . . . little husband will be in the Prater today in numerous com." etc. I cannot read the adjective before "little husband". I presume that "com." stands for "company"—but I can't think what you mean by "numerous company." (July 7, 1791)

Could this be a reference to Schikaneder, who with his brilliant theatrical instinct had taken up the idea of Blanchard's balloon flights—successful or not—for an aerial demonstration in *Die Zauberflöte*?[16] He would first have to build a complicated apparatus, along with the machinery for all the other stage effects in *Die Zauberflöte*. But just then, when Mozart was almost finished with the opera, he received two new and very important commissions.

AN URGENT COMMISSION

In mid-July Mozart brought his family home from Baden. Constanze was in the last month of her pregnancy and was expected to go into labor any day. But there was no time to make calm preparations for the birth. On July 14 the Prague impresario Domenico Guardasoni arrived in Vienna to discuss with Mozart an opera to be commissioned for the festivities surrounding the coronation of Leopold II as king of Bohemia. It was a very urgent matter, for the coronation was to take place at the beginning of September and only eight weeks remained. Mozart already knew Guardasoni; in April 1789 they had "practically arranged" an opera contract that had failed to materialize because Guardasoni had accepted an engagement in Warsaw.[17] There was not much time left for adapting a libretto, but Guardasoni must have pulled a few strings. The commission for this "festival opera" came from the Bohemian governing estates, the "estates of the realm," who had difficulty agreeing among themselves on the nature of the festival program. Guardasoni had signed a contract only a week before he came to Vienna and had received two drafts for libretti. At his request, however, the contract included the provision that Pietro Metastasio's *La clemenza di Tito* should be adapted if the two other libretti proved unsuitable. He had probably already retained the Saxon court poet Caterino Mazzolà to make the adaptation of *Tito*. The commission would not have come as a complete surprise to Mozart, for Mazzolà had been in Vienna since the middle of May. But Guardasoni was only now able to obtain firm commitments from Mozart and Mazzolà, and then he had to proceed immediately to Italy in order to "shop" for singers. Thus he was not even able to give Mozart a final cast list. Mazzolà, at least, remained in Vienna, if only for two weeks.

Would Mozart be able to revise the text completely with Mazzolà in this short time? It is certain that he collaborated with the poet. The libretto was over fifty years old and was cast in the antiquated *opera seria* format that tediously alternated recitatives and arias, with the former carrying the action while the latter served as reflective pauses. This text had to be brought into conformity with Mozart's idea of opera dramaturgy: clear delineation of character, large-scale ensemble numbers, and dramatization by purely musical means instead of the monotonous sequence of recitatives and arias. Mozart and Mazzolà may have begun work before Guardasoni's arrival: in any event, composer and poet must have developed a good understanding in the brief time available to them, for when he entered the work in his catalogue, Mozart expressly noted, *"Ridotta à vera opera dal Sig: re Mazzolà. Poeta di Sua A:S: l'Ettore di Sassonia"* ("rewritten as a real opera by Signore Mazzolà . . ."), whereas with the Da Ponte operas the librettist is never mentioned.

Only after Guardasoni's return from Italy in mid-August did Mozart learn which singers would make up the cast. That is the only element of truth in the legend that Mozart wrote this opera in eighteen days. Aside from the fact that composition amounts to more than writing notes and requires creative preparation—which in this case also included the production of a suitable text—there exist drafts and sketches for the opera that were undoubtedly written *before* Guardasoni's return from Italy. They assign the role of Sesto to a tenor, whereas in the final version this role is sung by a castrato.[18] The use of castrati was already dying out by the end of the eighteenth century, since they were only required for *opera seria,* which was going out of fashion. Mozart could not have been pleased to discover that Guardasoni had engaged a castrato (Domenico Bedini) to sing Sesto and had even cast a woman (Carolina Perini) in the role of Annio. This arrangement was not in keeping with his realistic approach to music-drama. He complied, however, as he had no other choice, and he would not have given up the entire commission over this grievance, for his fee was 200 ducats plus 50 ducats for traveling expenses—a total of 1,125 florins.

At the end of August Mozart set out for Prague, where he planned to write the last few numbers and supervise the rehearsals. He was accompanied by his friend Anton Stadler, the clarinetist, who was to be part of the orchestra and play the difficult solos, and by his pupil and assistant Franz Xaver Süssmayr. Constanze Mozart, who had given birth to her sixth child only six weeks earlier, also went along.[19] Naturally, the pressure to meet the deadline was enormous. It is not surprising that Mozart could not write the recitatives himself (except for the *accompagnati*); they were presumably written by Süssmayr. Further difficulties arose when Mozart became ill shortly before the premiere.[20]

All in all it was an ill-fated performance. It took place in the Nationaltheater on the evening after the coronation, and everyone of any importance in Prague was there. But the newly crowned king and his entourage arrived an hour late. Count Karl Zinzendorf remarked in his journal, "We were regaled with the very tedious opera *La clemenza di Tito*." The official libretto available at the performance did not mention Mazzolà's name; he enjoyed no popularity with Leopold II.[21]

Even if the omission of Mazzolà's name can be considered accidental, there is indisputable evidence that Mozart had long been in disfavor with Leopold II. The empress, who had probably thwarted Mozart's engagement as second kapellmeister, is supposed to have called out from her box, "*Una porcheria tedesca!*" ("German hogwash!"), which undoubtedly referred to the whole opera. We may question the authenticity of this story, though it was recounted by contemporaries; but there is also an official document that tells us something about the opera's reception. The hour's delay in beginning the performance was itself an affront—also to Guardasoni, who had put a lot of money into the production, especially for new scenery. In fact, he applied to the Bohemian estates for compensation. A report by Count Heinrich Rottenhan recognized the legitimacy of Guardasoni's petition.

Compensation for the expenses incurred by the opera would be purely an act of grace, as the legal obligations are all set forth in a formal contract. It is well known, however, that both entrepreneurs drew very small crowds as a result of the many festivities at court and the parties and balls given in private homes. Also, the court displayed a preconceived aversion to Mozart's composition, so that attendance was very poor after the premiere on Coronation Day. The entrepreneurs' entire speculation that the receipts from ticket sales would considerably augment the donation from the honorable estates has proved to be totally mistaken."[22]

As Rottenhan says, the court's notorious aversion to Mozart's opera meant that it played to very poor houses for the duration of the coronation festivities, which was why Guardasoni applied for reimbursement. He did not mention, however, that "in Prague the opera gained in popularity as its public changed. Later performances played to audiences also drawn from local bourgeois circles, among whom it enjoyed considerable success, as attested by Mozart's letter to his wife of October 7, 1791."[23] In this letter he says that the last performance of *Tito* in Prague received

> tremendous applause. Bedini sang better than ever. The little duet in A major for the two maidens was repeated; and if the audience had not wished to spare Madame Marchetti, a repetition of the rondo would have been very welcome. Cries of "bravo" were shouted at Stodla [Stadler] from the parterre and even from the orchestra—"What a miracle for Bohemia!" [Stadler] writes, "indeed I did my very best."

Tito, then, could achieve no success during the coronation festivities, but it did find favor afterward with a "normal" public. Such audiences were much different from those at court functions, where tickets were distributed according to the social standing of the guests and irrespective of their musical interests. Moreover, there had not been a coronation in Prague for decades, and the number of visitors in the city on official missions, along with their retinues, must have been in the thousands. As a result, there were events of every description in Prague—from magic shows and street theater to operas, plays, concerts, banquets, fireworks, and so forth. Some sources maintain that the plethora of events led to poor attendance at the plays and operas. Thus it is all the more astonishing that Guardasoni, who was hoping to profit from all this activity along with his company, spent most of his time performing Mozart. During these weeks in Prague he gave three of Mozart's operas: *Don Giovanni, Tito,* and *Così fan tutte. Don Giovanni,* for example, was given "by highest request" four days before the coronation, in the presence of the imperial couple and the princes. As yet they had had no opportunity to see this famous work in Vienna, which in the event did not suit the ascetic taste of the empress.[24] *Don Giovanni,* at least, gave Guardasoni no cause for complaint about attendance. The *Prager Oberpostamtszeitung* noted, "The large theater, which can accommodate several thousand people, was jammed to capacity, and the aisle down which his majesty strode was overcrowded with spectators."[25]

As in Frankfurt, Mozart seems to have avoided official court circles for the most part. Instead he got together with old friends, including some members of the high nobility, and paid several visits to the Masonic lodge Zur Wahrheit und Einigkeit, where his cantata *Die Maurerfreude* (K. 471) was performed in his honor.

LA CLEMENZA DI TITO

La clemenza di Tito, by the revered court poet Pietro Metastasio, was one of the most popular opera texts of the eighteenth century, though less because of its poetic qualities than because of its content, which gave the composer a unique opportunity to combine praise for a sovereign with the depiction of exemplary rule under humane conditions—all in the context of ancient Roman grandeur. Titus (Tito) was the first post-Augustan emperor who did not degenerate into a cruel and depraved despot but believed in moderation and leniency. His brief reign saw two major disasters: the eruption of Mount Vesuvius, which buried Pompeii and Herculaneum in A.D. 79, and the burning of Rome in A.D. 80, which lasted three days, and during which Titus did his best to aid his subjects. He sacrificed all private interests to his imperial office. Any day on which he did not do something for his fellow man was wasted, he declared. The historians competed with each other in depicting his kindness, mercy, and sense of justice. If any Roman emperor seemed an appropriate example for future generations, it was Titus—almost more so than the illustrious Augustus. His life, however, provided little in the way of dramatic action. For this reason Metastasio concocted a love intrigue leading to an attempt on the emperor's life, with his subsequent clemency preparing the way for a happy ending.

As adapted for Mozart by Caterino Mazzolà, the libretto unfolds in two acts (Metastasio rather long-windedly held forth for three, as required by the rules of his genre). In the first act, Tito has just returned from Syria (where he ended his campaign against the insur-

gent Jews by destroying Jerusalem) and has brought his beloved
Berenice with him, which greatly displeases the Romans. Even more
outraged is Vitellia, daughter of the former emperor Vitellius, whom
Tito has deposed. Vitellia had hoped to marry Tito and thus become
the emperor's wife. Tito's best friend, Sesto, loves Vitellia, although
she does not return his affection, and he is so blinded by his love that
he plans Tito's murder on her instructions. Tito, however, bows to the
will of the people and renounces Berenice, which gives Vitellia new
hope; the murder is called off. Annio, a friend of Sesto's, wishes to
marry Sesto's sister Servilia and asks Sesto to secure the emperor's
permission for the marriage. But now Tito suddenly wishes to marry
Servilia. Vitellia once again sees her hopes dashed and orders Sesto to
carry out the murder. Then Servilia informs Tito that she is already
promised to Annio. For the second time Tito renounces a woman; he is
now prepared to marry Vitellia. Upon learning of his decision Vitellia
tries to prevent Sesto from carrying out the murder, but she is unable
to find him. Sesto, tortured by the conflict between his blind love for
Vitellia and his respect for Tito, carries out the attack. The act ends
with the burning of the Capitol.

In the second act Annio encounters Sesto in the midst of the
confusion and tells him that Tito is still alive. It is soon revealed that
only a mix-up saved Tito's life. Sesto is arrested and condemned to
death. Tito can hardly believe he has been betrayed by such a good
friend and goes to speak with him one last time before the execution.
No appeal to their earlier friendship can bring Sesto out of his silence:
he wishes to protect Vitellia. Tito confirms the execution but is determined to prevent it at the last minute. Vitellia is so moved by Sesto's
silence that she goes to Tito and confesses her guilt. In the end Tito
bestows his forgiveness on everyone.

Mazzolà's libretto was well suited to a coronation, for it expressed
the expectation that a good ruler would subordinate his personal
inclinations to the interests of the state, exercise moderation, and let
reason and justice prevail as the highest virtues of a sovereign. Very
admirable, one might say, but somewhat stale in its rationalist
serenity—theater of the Gottsched period. Only one character is
capable of passionate development—the insulted, vindictive, uncontrolled Vitellia. All the other figures are bloodless "puppets," as
Alfred Einstein called them. Sesto is putty in Vitellia's hands, but his

love for her remains only an assertion, and we almost feel that he can only convince himself of it by becoming her instrument of revenge. He is given no opportunity to express the violent inner tension between his blind love and his guilt at betraying his best friend; like the other characters, he is depicted as a type and restricted to one function in the drama. This is even more true of Tito, who is frozen into an embodiment of good, a lifeless statue with no possibility of showing any human characteristics, such as emotion, shock, or doubt. He is denied passions by the author's enlightened rationalist conception of the story. And so he must renounce first his beloved and then another woman of his choice without showing the least personal distress. Even the attempt on his life by his best friend hardly fazes him; it only gives him an opportunity to prove his extraordinary mercy, whose boundlessness has no motive and cannot be explained by Tito's character. There is simply no element of the plot that serves to portray his personality.

The weakness of the dramaturgy, stemming from Metastasio, was clearly revealed by Mazzolà's attempt to eliminate the alternation of recitatives (to further the action) with arias (to provide reflection or express feelings) and replace it with a theatrical version composed of animated scenes and dramatically structured ensemble numbers. Mozart considered the revision indispensable before he could even begin to work with such material. He expressed gratitude that the text was "rewritten as a real opera by Signore Mazzolà." In other words, Metastasio's libretto did not correspond to Mozart's idea of an opera, which is not surprising in view of the dramatic concept behind *Le nozze di Figaro, Don Giovanni,* and *Così fan tutte.*

The question naturally arises as to whether Mozart noticed the inherent weakness in the libretto even after the revision, on which he certainly collaborated. A partial answer is that Mazzolà was not able to write a new text; he had to adhere to Metastasio's plot and wanted to make whatever improvements he could in the short time available. And it must be admitted that he achieved a skillful condensation of the material with dramatically effective climaxes that inspired Mozart to some of his best music—or rather, best individual *numbers,* for the opera as a whole remains unsatisfactory.

Part of the problem may be that Mozart had no opportunity to reflect any element of the zeitgeist in this opera. Compared with the other

operas of his Vienna period, *La clemenza di Tito* remains an
anachronism—not only because of the archaic *opera seria* format
resurrected for this ceremonial event (when did Mozart ever let himself be tied down by genre rules?), but also because the subject matter
could not be related to the person of the newly crowned king or
the circumstances of the coronation. Leopold II was not a young
and inexperienced man who had to be ushered into his reign with
pleas for fair, lenient government; he had spent twenty-five years
ruling Tuscany and had made it into a model state admired
throughout Europe. The Roman Titus could not serve as an example
for Leopold II. The Tuscan criminal code and its legal implications
alone carried more weight than the *clemenza* of Titus. One might
hold this Roman emperor up as a model to an absolute monarch full
of dictatorial pride, but not to a prince who, as a result of his own intellectual insight (and not pressure from below), was preparing the way
for a constitutional state. Leopold II was a highly realistic personality with a clear awareness of political necessities. It was a rather
tactless move to present him with this otherworldly ideal in the figure of Titus.

Domenico Guardasoni, who was under great pressure to meet the
coronation deadline, may have said to himself, "This book by Metastasio has long been successful and has been set to music about sixty
times; it may also suit my purposes, especially if Mozart writes the
music." But as a method of praising and admonishing a ruler, the text
was simply inappropriate at a time of revolution in France, renewed
insurrection in the Austrian Netherlands, and open separatism in
Hungary. When the opera was finally acclaimed in Prague, at the end
of its run and no longer as part of the coronation festivities, the
enthusiastic reception came from musical connoisseurs and admirers
of Mozart; they were undoubtedly applauding the music and not the
opera as a whole (as had also been the case with *Figaro* and *Don
Giovanni*), though the libretto drew very little criticism.

Interestingly enough, *Tito* was the most successful of all Mozart's
operas at the beginning of the nineteenth century and was probably
among the most frequently performed operas of the time. In the second
half of the century, however, there was a sharp decline in the number
of productions, until *Tito* became one of Mozart's most neglected

works. Only now are we witnessing a revival, which began in the 1970s.[26]

"BUT WHAT PLEASES ME MOST IS THE SILENT APPROVAL"

Mozart could not stay long in Prague, and in mid-September he and his wife returned to Vienna, where preparations were underway for the first performance of *Die Zauberflöte*. Emanuel Schikaneder had been concentrating on the construction of lavish sets that are said to have cost 5,000 florins. Mozart still had to compose the overture and the March of the Priests as well as supervise the rehearsals. He conducted the premiere on September 30, and Constanze's sister Josepha Hofer sang the Queen of the Night—a role she portrayed for more than ten years at Schikaneder's theater. The opera was an immediate success and was already being performed almost daily before the end of October. A notice in the Berlin *Musikalisches Wochenblatt* apparently ignored the facts.

> A new comedy with mechanical effects: *Die Zauberflöte*, with music by our kapellmeister *Mozard*, being produced at great expense and with lavish sets, has not received the hoped-for reception because the content and the language of the play are very bad.[27]

Obviously this comment reflects the personal opinion of the author, who was not versed in the tradition of Viennese *Volkstheater*. Mozart, however, expressed great satisfaction at his success. He wrote of the premiere, "My new opera was performed for the first time with such success," and on October 7:

> I have this moment returned from the opera, which was as full as ever. As usual the duet "Mann und Weib" and Papageno's glockenspiel in Act I had to be repeated, and also the boys' trio in Act II. But what pleases me most is the *silent approval*. You can see how this opera is becoming more and more esteemed.

The next day he wrote, "Although Saturday, being post-day, is always a bad night, the opera was performed to a full house with the usual applause and repetition of numbers." Yet Mozart must have had his suspicions that the main attraction was Schikaneder's garish production and that there was too little real understanding of content *and* music. Thus the reference to "the silent approval" of music lovers and cognoscenti, who could appreciate the subtle details over and above the grand spectacle. The musical understanding of an opera requires that the text be comprehensible—something overlooked often enough in today's performance practice. In describing his own visits to the opera, Mozart revealed how important he considered the spoken dialogue. He wrote regarding an unidentifiable visitor:

> But he, the know-it-all, showed himself to be such a thorough *Bavarian* that I could not remain or I would have had to call him an ass. Unfortunately I was there just when the second act began, that is, at the solemn scene. He laughed at everything. At first I was patient enough to draw his attention to a few passages—still he laughed at everything. Well, I could stand it no longer. I called him a Papageno and cleared out. But I don't think that the idiot understood my remark.
>
> (October 8, 1791)

During the first two weeks of *Die Zauberflöte* Mozart went to the opera almost every day, often accompanied by friends and musical colleagues. Antonio Salieri was driven to one performance by Mozart personally and took pleasure in the work's overwhelming success.

> At 6 o'clock I called in the carriage for Salieri and Madame Cavalieri and drove them to my box. Then I drove back quickly to fetch Mamma and Karl, whom I had left at Hofer's. You can hardly imagine how charming they were and how much they liked not only my music, but the libretto and everything. They both said it was an *operone* [grand opera], worthy to be performed at the grandest festival and before the greatest monarch, and that they would often go to see it, as they had never seen a more beautiful or delightful show. Salieri listened and watched most attentively, and from the overture to the last chorus there was not a single number that did not call forth from him a *bravo!* or *bello!* It seemed as if they could not thank me enough for my kindness. They had intended in any case to go to the opera yesterday. But they

would have had to be in their places by 4 o'clock. As it was, they saw
and heard everything in comfort from my box. When it was over I drove
them home and then had supper at Hofer's with Karl.

(October 14, 1791)

That one had to show up three hours before curtain time to obtain
even relatively good seats is proof of the opera's unprecedented
success.

Unfortunately, the age of regular press reviews had not yet begun,
so we have almost no information about the contemporary reception of
Die Zauberflöte, an opera that unites the most heterogeneous elements, draws upon the most diverse sources, and even today gives rise
to the most contrasting interpretations. In performances up to the
nineteenth century, literal compliance with the stage directions seems
to have been the rule, and this approach worked against an idealistic
interpretation. Thus Sarastro actually made his entrance in a wagon
pulled by lions, and the wild beasts were there in the flesh. Goethe's
mother wrote to her son about a production in Frankfurt:

Nothing new here, except that *Die Zauberflöte* has been given 18 times,
and the house has always been packed. No one wants it said of him that
he hasn't seen it. All the workers, gardeners, even the *Sachsenhäuser*
whose boys play the lions and apes go to see it—such a spectacle has
never been seen here before. The theater must be opened before 4
o'clock on the day of each performance, and still many people are sent
away without seats. The money they're making! When the King was last
here, he saw the opera 3 times, and paid 100 carolins [1,100 florins]
for Willmer's little box at the theater.[28]

The complexity of the work was actually emphasized when the
scenes were arranged exactly as instructed in the text—which also
made it possible to interpret *Die Zauberflöte* as an allegory on the
French Revolution. The decisive factor here was not so much whether
Mozart and Schikaneder themselves wanted to convey a political
message (for or against the Jacobins) but that it could easily be read as
such by contemporaries. In 1794 a Jacobin interpretation was first
circulated in print; it attributed the following symbolism to the opera's
principal figures:

THE QUEEN OF THE NIGHT	The ancien régime
PAMINA, HER DAUGHTER	Freedom, which is always a daughter of despotism
TAMINO	The people
THE THREE NYMPHS OF THE QUEEN OF THE NIGHT	The deputies of the three estates
SARASTRO	The wisdom of better legislation
THE PRIESTS OF SARASTRO	The National Assembly
PAPAGENO	The wealthy
AN OLD WOMAN	Equality
MONOSTATOS THE MOOR	The emigrés
SLAVES	Servants and mercenaries of the emigrés
THREE BOYS	Intelligence, justice, and patriotism, which guide Tamino

The basic idea of this opera is: the liberation of the French people from the hands of the old despotism through the wisdom of better legislation.[29]

If *Die Zauberflöte* had not achieved such enormous popularity within only a few years, it would never have had such a hidden agenda foisted upon it. The above interpretation, which can also be understood as a form of propaganda, was no isolated phenomenon: favorite melodies from the opera were even provided with new lyrics. Friedrich Lehne, a Jacobin from Mainz, wrote the following text for Papageno's famous aria *"Der Vogelfänger bin ich ja"*:

> I am a loyal underling
> with no use for freedom and justice!
> I esteem the noble dog;
> his master beats him black and blue,
> yet still he wags his tail and comes
> to lick the hand of his tormentor.
> Happy the man who can say:
> I am a loyal underling! . . .

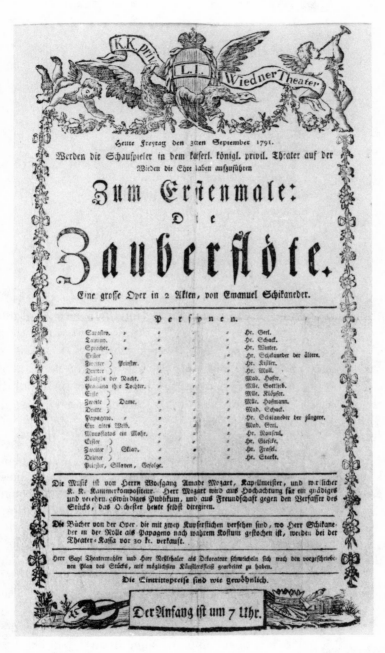

Playbill for the premiere of Die Zauberflöte *(1791). The Three Slaves are listed individually in the cast of characters, but the Three Boys are absent.*

The noble feasts upon my bread;
yet even if I die of hunger,
I'll gladly give the worthy lord
the last morsel I have left;
for he wears the star and ribbon
of our beloved fatherland.
    Happy the man, etc.

I do not know the prince at all,
they say he is the poorest wretch—
he lives in luxury like a sultan
and amuses himself with harlots.
If he hunts me down with his dogs,
it must be the will of God.
    Happy the man, etc.[30]

There was, of course, an anti-Jacobin faction that saw a revolutionary conspiracy behind every dissenting opinion and reflected the
anxious mood of Leopold's successor, Emperor Francis II. This group
did not wait long to set about promulgating its own interpretation of
Die Zauberflöte. One such explication, by Johann Valentin Eibel, has
scarcely anything to do with Mozart or Schikaneder, and sounds quite
labored and implausible.

The basic plot is as follows: The Night—that is, the Jacobin
philosophy—bore a daughter, namely the Republic, whom she wishes
to raise in the Kingdom of Night. She then intends to arrange a Jacobin
marriage for her daughter and thus link herself to the revolutionaries.
In the first scene, Tamino represents the prince whom France will
receive and who will put an end to her unmarried status as a republic.
At the very outset, however, the Jacobin serpent threatens him with
destruction. The three ladies who kill the serpent are among those who
live in the Kingdom of Night but who hold with the royalists. The
second scene introduces Papageno, the Jacobin bird catcher, whose
task it is to lure people into the Jacobin circle, lock them in the
national cage, and deliver them up to the Night in this condition.

And so it continues for pages on end. Sarastro is said to represent
"the forces united against Jacobinism. . . . The initiates would appear to be essentially the anointed ones, the kings of other lands and

A drawing of Papageno, from the libretto printed for the premiere; it presumably shows the original bird costume used for this character.

all those who have dedicated themselves to the service of these kings."[31]

Oddly enough, the Masonic interpretation of *Die Zauberflöte* was hardly in evidence during these first years—not that the connection was overlooked. On the contrary, there was nothing mysterious about Freemasonry, which was quite common in both bourgeois and aristocratic circles. Lodge insignia were worn in public, and Masonic symbols adorned jewelry, were embroidered on handkerchiefs, and served as decorative ornaments. Freemasonry had such a high profile that no one could construe anything in *Die Zauberflöte* as a betrayal of lodge secrets. (And indeed there *are* no secrets revealed to an "unauthorized" public in this opera.) Nor was it a secret that Freemasonry worked for human rights—that is, Liberty, Equality, Fraternity. Yet the Masons were anything but revolutionaries, and they were not perceived as such, although many who subscribed to the goals of the French Revolution—as even many aristocrats did—were also lodge members. In this respect it was more reasonable to interpret *Die Zauberflöte* as an allegory on the French Revolution than as an attempt to disclose Masonic symbols. The latter interpretation belongs to a subsequent period when in the wake of political reaction and restoration Freemasonry disappeared from the public consciousness, banned, persecuted, and in most places eradicated.

AN ANONYMOUS COMMISSION

After the premiere of *Die Zauberflöte*, Constanze Mozart spent another ten days in Baden, apparently at Mozart's insistence, although he was suffering from her absence after only one day. He would rather have gone with her, but he found it inconvenient to work in Baden. Mozart had been inundated with commissions at least since March. Besides the two operas, he had written a series of shorter occasional pieces and the Clarinet Concerto. Now he was occupied with yet another commission, for which he had already received a large initial payment: the Requiem.

No detail of Mozart's life has been discussed and embellished as often as this commission from an unknown figure. Here the story itself is not a matter of legend; everything may well have transpired as

Mozart's first biographer, Franz Xaver Niemetschek, related it. Only the costume is an added ingredient, the long cloak and the now automatic reference to the bearer of the commission as "the grim messenger." But Niemetschek's account is generally free of just such romantic accessories.

> Shortly before the coronation of Emperor Leopold, even before Mozart received the commission to go to Prague, an unknown messenger presented him with an unsigned letter full of flattering phrases, inquiring if Mozart would undertake to write a mass for the dead, also what fee he would ask and how long it would take.
>
> Mozart, who never acted without consulting his wife, told her about the strange commission, and expressed his desire to also try his hand at this genre, especially since his genius was always ideally suited to the lofty and dramatic style of church music. She advised him to accept the commission. He wrote back to the unknown patron, saying he would compose the Requiem for a certain fee. He could say nothing definite about the date of completion, but he did wish to know where he should deliver the work when he had finished it. Shortly thereafter the same messenger appeared, bringing not only the stipulated fee, but also, in view of his moderate price, the promise of a considerable bonus upon receipt of the work. He was free to write as his moods and inclinations dictated, but should make no attempt to discover the identity of his patron, as his efforts would surely be in vain.
>
> In the meantime Mozart received the noble and lucrative commission to write an *opera seria* for the coronation of Emperor Leopold in Prague. How could he decline the delightful opportunity to visit Prague again and write for his beloved Bohemians?
>
> Just as Mozart and his wife were entering the carriage to embark on their journey, the messenger appeared like a ghost, tugged at Frau Mozart's skirt, and asked, "What will now become of the Requiem?"
>
> Mozart offered his apologies, saying that the suddenness of the journey and his patron's unknown identity had made it impossible to notify him of his departure. He would take up the Requiem immediately upon his return, if the unknown gentleman was prepared to wait. The messenger expressed no objections.[32]

Niemetschek had heard the story from Constanze Mozart and had himself seen "one of the letters written by the unknown patron." But secrets often become public knowledge more readily than things that actually take place in public. Information is almost totally lacking about many of Mozart's concerts, performed in the presence of several hundred listeners. In this case, the unknown patron did everything to conceal his identity, yet it appears to have been discovered after only a few months.

The patron was Count Franz Walsegg-Stuppach, who resided at Stuppach Castle in the Semmering region. The count was a music lover who played both flute and cello and gave chamber music soirees at his home twice a week. He is also supposed to have asked Mozart's price for string quartets. It is said that he had the peculiar habit of asking his guests to guess who had written the music they had just heard; when they flattered him with the suggestion that he might be the composer, he gave a meaningful smile and made no denial. That, however, is conjecture—which has nonetheless become common property. In any event, he ordered the Requiem as a memorial to his wife, Anna, who had died prematurely in February 1791. Count Walsegg owned the house on the Hoher Markt in Vienna where Puchberg lived, and it has been surmised that Puchberg served as intermediary since he was better informed than anyone else about Mozart's financial distress. A name has also been put forth for the count's messenger: his steward Franz Anton Leitgeb, who could be said to have a "sinister" appearance in his one surviving portrait. It should be noted that Abbé Maximilian Stadler, an acquaintance of Mozart's who later helped his widow organize his unpublished manuscripts, claimed to have known the patron's identity early on.

> I learned just after Mozart's death that Count Walsegg had ordered the Requiem. I also knew all along about the count's plans and everything else that was kept secret. . . . But as it is improper and forbidden to reveal secrets, I never once permitted myself to reveal the patron's name.[33]

Other people also claimed to have known about Count Walsegg. Constanze Mozart, in any case, had good reason not to reveal his identity even if she was aware of it. Her objective was to deliver the Requiem to the man who had commissioned it, especially as he had already paid for it. The fact that Mozart was not able to finish it only made the situation more difficult. She wanted it to be completed by

Mozart's pupil Joseph Eybler, who, like Franz Xaver Süssmayr, had discussed the progress of the work in detail with Mozart. When Eybler abandoned the effort after a short time, she entrusted the Requiem to Süssmayr, who composed the remaining movements and filled in the instrumentation. The work was then delivered to the count after copies of the score had been made. In December 1793 Count Walsegg conducted the Requiem in Wiener Neustadt, doubtless in the belief that it was all Mozart's work. Are we to suppose he did not know that Gottfried van Swieten had had the work performed in Vienna eleven months earlier? This performance was even described in the newspapers.

> Mozart, who achieved an immortal name in the art of music, left a widow and two orphans in poverty. Many noble benefactors are helping this unfortunate woman. Two days ago Baron Swieten presented a public concert with a sung Requiem as a memorial to Mozart. The widow received proceeds of over 300 gold ducats.[34]

Constanze's attempt to have the Requiem printed almost resulted in a lawsuit. Through his attorney Count Walsegg claimed sole ownership of the work and could only be pacified with a financial settlement.

THE FINAL ILLNESS

On November 18, Mozart conducted the *Kleine Freimaurerkantate* (K. 623), which he had completed three days earlier, at the ceremony marking the dedication of a new temple for his lodge. This work was the last to be entered in his catalogue. Two days later he took to his bed. Between November 18 and November 20 came the first violent autumn storms, with a relatively warm south wind and temperatures of 54° F to 57° F, and then the barometer rose again. After a few days Mozart appears to have felt somewhat better, but it was only a short remission. Georg Nikolaus von Nissen, who got his information from Constanze, wrote, "His mortal illness, during which he was bedridden, lasted 15 days. It began with swelling in his hands and feet, which he was soon unable to move."[35] This rheumatic phase must have been extremely painful. Sophie Haibel (née Weber), Mozart's

sister-in-law, described a "night-jacket which he could put on front-
ways, since on account of his swollen condition he was unable to turn
in bed," and a "quilted dressing gown (his dear wife, my sister, had
given us the material for both garments), so that when he got up he
would have everything he needed. We often visited him, and he
seemed to be really looking forward to wearing his dressing gown. I
used to go into town every day to see him."[36]

It is very doubtful whether Mozart ever left his bed again; there is no
mention of any such improvement. It is even doubtful whether he
could actually compose on his own once he was confined to his bed.
His pupils Eybler and Süssmayr were probably there much of the
time, and they also collaborated on the Requiem, as his sister-in-law
confirmed. Mozart's ability to work unaided might be judged from his
signature, especially since inflammatory swelling and stiffening of the
joints would probably have resulted in shaky handwriting, but there is
no evidence of such weakness. Composition, however, is not simply
drawing notes on a staff, and Süssmayr himself tells of the precise
instructions he received for carrying on the work. We must also
consider that the treatment of Mozart's illness with venesection,
emetics, and cold compresses would have allowed him very little time
for productive work on the Requiem. The actual progress of the illness
during these last fifteen days cannot be reconstructed with certainty.
Mozart's personal physician, Dr. Thomas Franz Closset, would have
looked in frequently, and his colleague at the general hospital, Dr.
Matthias von Sallaba, may have paid an occasional visit as well. The
two discussed Mozart's illness; whether they held a formal consultation, as stated in a highly doubtful source,[37] is open to debate.

The most authentic source of information about Mozart's death
would appear to be the testimony of Sophie Haibel, which she sent to
Nissen in 1825 when he was preparing his biography. This woman is
all the more reliable in that she was the only eyewitness who wrote
down her own recollections.

Alas, how frightened I was when my sister, who was almost despairing
yet still trying to keep calm, came out to me, saying: "Thank God you
have come, dear Sophie. Last night he was so ill that I did not think he
would be alive this morning. Do stay with me today, for if he has
another bad turn he will not survive the night. Go in to him for a while

and see how he is." I tried to control myself and went to his bedside. He immediately called me to him and said: "Ah, dear Sophie, how glad I am that you have come. You must stay here tonight and see me die." I tried hard to be brave and to persuade him of the contrary. But to all my attempts he only replied: "Why, I already have the taste of death on my tongue. And if you do not stay, who will help my dearest Constanze when I am gone?" "Yes, yes, dear Mozart," I assured him, "but I must first go back to our mother and tell her that you would like me to stay with you today. Otherwise, she will think that some misfortune has befallen you." "Yes, do so," said Mozart, "but be sure and come back soon." Good God, how distressed I felt! My poor sister followed me to the door and begged me for Heaven's sake to go to St. Peter's and implore one of the priests to come to Mozart—a chance call, as it were. I did so, but for a long time they refused to come, and I had a great deal of trouble persuading one of those clerical brutes to go to him. Then I ran off to my mother, who was anxiously awaiting me. It was already dark. Poor soul, how shocked she was! I persuaded her to go and spend the night with her eldest daughter, the late Josepha Hofer. I then ran back as fast as I could to my distracted sister. Süssmayr was at Mozart's bedside. The well-known Requiem lay on the quilt and Mozart was explaining to him how, in his opinion, he ought to finish it when he was gone. He also urged his wife to keep his death a secret until she informed Albrechtsberger, who was in charge of all the services at the cathedral. A long search was made for Dr. Closset, who was found at the opera but who had to wait for the end of the performance. He came and ordered cold compresses to be placed on Mozart's burning head, which, however, affected him to such an extent that he became unconscious and remained so until he died. His last movement was an attempt to express with his mouth the drum passage in the Requiem. That I can still hear. Müller from the art gallery came and took a cast of his pale, dead face. Words fail me, dearest brother, to describe how his devoted wife in her utter misery threw herself on her knees and implored the Almighty for His aid. She simply could not tear herself away from Mozart, however much I begged her to do so. If it was possible to increase her sorrow, this was done on the day after that dreadful night, when crowds of people walked past his corpse, weeping and wailing for him.[38]

The Requiem rehearsal at Mozart's bedside on the last day of his life is apparently a romantic embellishment derived from an oral source that has been preserved only indirectly. Every Mozart biography

includes this anecdote, although it is clearly inconsistent with Sophie
Haibel's testimony. If it contains any truth at all, it must refer to an
earlier point in his illness when the symptoms were not yet so advanced.

> Even on the eve of his death he had the score of the Requiem brought to
> his bed (it was two o'clock in the afternoon). He sang the alto part; his
> friend Schack sang the soprano part, as he had often done before; Hofer,
> his brother-in-law, sang tenor; and Gerl, later a singer at the Mannheim
> theater, sang bass. They were at the opening measures of the Lacrymosa
> when Mozart began to weep uncontrollably and laid the score to one
> side. Eleven hours later, at one o'clock in the morning, he expired.[39]

Constanze Mozart was so desperate and distraught at this sudden
loss that she and her two children soon left the apartment and went to
stay with friends. The elder son was seven years old, the younger not
yet six months. She did not have the strength to attend the funeral
service at St. Stephen's—she may have been urged not to go. Posterity
has never forgiven her for this—as if people had a right to observe a
widow's bereavement at a public funeral.[40] The following notice appeared in the *Wiener Zeitung* on the day of Mozart's burial:

> The Royal and Imperial *Kammerkompositeur* Wolfgang Mozart died
> during the night of December 4–5. From childhood on he was known
> throughout Europe for his most exceptional musical talent. Through
> the successful development and diligent application of his extraordi-
> nary natural gifts, he scaled the heights of the greatest masters. His
> works, which are loved and admired everywhere, are proof of his
> greatness—and they reveal the irreplaceable loss which the noble art
> of music has suffered through his death.[41]

Mozart's death was announced in many European newspapers—
hardly an indication that he was a forgotten man at the end of his life.

THE CAUSE OF DEATH

Posterity has occupied itself with Mozart's death and burial more than
with any other element of his biography. The "investigations" have
turned up increasingly theatrical incidents to satisfy the discriminat-

ing palate of a public with little taste for simple historical fact. Any number of medical conditions have been advanced as the cause of death. Poison theories, especially, have been bandied about in numerous variations, since they offer a wide field for speculation: if Mozart was poisoned, who was the murderer and what was the motive? This interesting question can lead to very strange notions, as shown by a newspaper report from May 18, 1983.

London, May 17 (AFP). Wolfgang Amadeus Mozart was poisoned in Vienna on December 5, 1791, aged 35. This conclusion was reached by a British "investigative committee" after a "court of inquiry" at the music festival in Brighton. The investigation was carried out on the stage by two professional judges and three lawyers. After the interrogation of the five chief suspects, including Mozart's wife, Constanze, the majority of the "jurors"—about 250 spectators—were convinced that the composer was murdered.

Although the identity of the murderer could not be established beyond doubt, the "court" was inclined to the opinion that the culprit was Franz Hofdemel, the jealous husband of one of Mozart's pupils. He committed suicide right after the master's death. Suspicion of murder was raised primarily by Mozart's secret burial; his wife, who later married a diplomat, is said never to have visited his grave. Judge Michael Hutchinson, who chaired the proceedings, said that in the "Mozart case" a "charge of homicide against a person or persons unknown" should be considered. [42]

There is almost no supporting documentation for the poisoning theory, which essentially stems from only three sources. The first, a report from Prague by a correspondent for the *Musikalisches Wochenblatt*, appeared in Berlin at the end of December 1791.

Mozart is—dead. He returned from Prague feeling sickly, and his condition became steadily worse; it was thought he had dropsy, and he died in Vienna at the end of last week. Because his body swelled up after death, some people even thought he had been poisoned. [43]

As far as can be verified, virtually nothing in this short notice is true, not even the vague time of death (Mozart died on a Monday). It is surely false that Mozart's "condition became steadily worse" after his return from Prague, as is obvious from the letters written in September to his wife in Baden. The correspondent's medical observations are not confirmed by the physicians or anyone else who was present during Mozart's illness.

The second source for the poison theory is Franz Xaver Niemetschek's biography, first published in Prague in 1798. It is based on statements by Constanze and friends of Mozart but shows a tendency toward embellishment that carries seeds of distortion. The passage in question reads as follows:

> Upon his return to Vienna he at once took up the Requiem and worked with great diligence and lively interest; but his illness became visibly worse and put him in a dark and melancholy mood. His wife was greatly distressed by his condition. Once she drove with him to the Prater to divert his mind and liven his spirits. When they were sitting alone Mozart began to speak of death, and maintained that he was writing the Requiem for himself. Tears welled up in the sensitive man's eyes. "I feel it too strongly," he said, "I won't last much longer— someone has surely poisoned me! I cannot free myself from this thought." These words fell very heavily on his wife's heart. She was hardly able to console him and prove that his dark suspicions were groundless.[44]

Niemetschek's source for this anecdote is unknown, but it provides no proof of poisoning, especially as we have no reliable evidence that Constanze Mozart herself ever suspected murder.

The third reference to poisoning is the one connected with Antonio Salieri; this tale, the most dubious of all, begins more than thirty years after Mozart's death. A correspondent's report from Vienna in the Leipzig *Allgemeine Musikalische Zeitung* for May 25, 1825, stated:

> Our worthy Salieri *just won't die*—as the popular expression goes. His body suffers all the infirmities of old age, and his mind is gone. In his distorted fantasies he actually claims to be partially responsible for Mozart's death—a bit of lunacy which surely no one but the poor, delirious old man believes.[45]

At no time did Salieri confess to having poisoned Mozart, though he certainly denied the rumor to that effect, which was already circulating. Ignaz Moscheles, one of his pupils, described a visit to the sick old man in October 1823:

> It was a sad reunion, for his appearance was ghastly, and he spoke to me in broken phrases of his swiftly approaching death. At the end he said, "Although I am mortally ill, I assure you in good faith that there is no truth to that absurd rumor. Mozart, you know—I am supposed to have poisoned him. But no, it's malice, nothing but malice. Tell the world, dear Moscheles; old Salieri, who is about to die, told you so himself."[46]

This denial did nothing to help Salieri. As early as 1830 Pushkin wrote a play about the murderer Salieri, which was later made into a short opera by Rimsky-Korsakov. Several years ago Peter Shaffer recognized and brilliantly exploited the great stage possibilities of this material, which are not diminished by its lack of authenticity. His *Amadeus* has enjoyed worldwide success. Even if no one makes the mistake of accepting its theatrical fiction as historical fact, Miloš Forman's film version of the play is an even greater deception, especially in its claim to have been shot "on location." Anyone who has seen this film must admit, however reluctantly, that not a single word, scene, or location, to say nothing of the behavior and appearance displayed by the film's characters, has anything at all to do with historical reality.

The rumors accusing Salieri of murder prompted his friends to defend the dying old man. Their efforts resulted in a report on Mozart's death that provides thorough and reliable information from the two attending physicians. One of them, Dr. Sallaba, was actually a specialist in toxicology and six months before Mozart's death had called for the recognition of forensic medicine by the judicial system; thus, he was certainly familiar with poisoning and its legal implications. And Mozart's personal physician, Dr. Closset, had made a special study of mercury overdoses. That two of the most competent physicians in Vienna did not even consider the possibility of poisoning deprives this already shaky argument of legitimacy.

Advocates of the poisoning theory face an even greater difficulty in identifying the murder suspects and their motives. Here there is nothing but conjecture, speculation, and sensationalism. At the

"court of inquiry" in Brighton, for example, it was proposed that
Mozart

> was killed by his lodger and pupil Franz Xaver Süssmayr. Süssmayr
> was the lover of Mozart's wife Constanze and often spent his holidays
> with her. On the day of Mozart's death Süssmayr left the house and
> never saw Constanze again, and she struck his name from every
> document.[47]

Süssmayr was Mozart's pupil and assistant, and often copied music for
him, but he never lived in his home. When Constanze, eight months
pregnant, was taking the waters at Baden in the summer of 1791,
Süssmayr was also there and received new assignments from Mozart
every few days. Puritanical historians who have always been eager to
find fault with Mozart's wife have suggested that her son Franz Xaver
Wolfgang, born on July 26, 1791, was actually fathered by Süssmayr,
who gave his first two names to the child. This assertion is not even
worth refuting. And in any event, Constanze did see Süssmayr again
on several occasions. His name was struck from Mozart's letters by
Constanze's second husband, probably because Mozart frequently
made fun of Süssmayr and made crude jokes at his expense.

And what of Hofdemel, who is also mentioned as the possible
culprit? He was a Freemason and lent Mozart money on at least one
occasion (April 1789). The wife of this chancery official was possibly
one of Mozart's piano pupils. On the day after Mozart's death there was
a violent quarrel in the Hofdemel home, probably caused by the
husband's jealousy. The scene ended tragically in a bloodbath:
Hofdemel went after his wife with a razor and cut her face and upper
torso savagely. He then committed suicide with the same razor. Maria
Magdalena Hofdemel survived, but she defended her husband and
refused to divulge what had provoked the assault. That is all we know
about this affair, but its "proximity" to Mozart's death obviously
invites speculation. However, there is no evidence to support the
rumors that Frau Hofdemel was romantically involved with Mozart,
much less that Hofdemel was Mozart's murderer.

But there are still other "culprits"—and here the speculation becomes even more adventurous. In the nineteenth century it was already being suggested that Mozart had been poisoned by the

Freemasons, and not only because he supposedly revealed details of lodge ritual in *Die Zauberflöte*. Mathilde Ludendorff was the most prominent exponent of this theory in our century, and part of her argument has even been cited by reputable scholars. She wrote:

> Because the composer was a Mason, the goal of the brotherhood was obviously to suppress and humiliate the unsuspecting, openhearted, world-famous Mozart. He was much too consciously German for them, and he frankly expressed his conviction.[48]

Ludendorff, one of the most fanatic racists of her time, tried to show

> how well the lodges, in which Rome and Judah jointly pursued their anti-German activities, managed to suppress German cultural achievements. . . . Thus we know that Mozart had already of necessity incurred the bitter hatred of Rome and Judah at a time when he was aware only of the Masons' anti-Germanness, and not of their murderous crimes.[49]

This is Ludendorff's real argument, though it is not quoted by those who subscribe to her thesis of Masonic execution. Neither do they cite the following entirely serious conclusion:

> Now, of course, the illustrious brotherhood of the lodge Zur Wohltätigkeit in Vienna sought to ensure that Mozart remained in poverty and misery. They had enormous influence at court and vast sums of money at their disposal, as well as authority over Mozart's lodge Zur neugegründeten [!] Hoffnung. It was much more difficult to keep the famous Mozart in penury than to facilitate a brilliant career for him in Vienna.[50]

The poisoning theory is clearly untenable, especially as there is no evidence of the physical manifestations that inevitably appear in such cases. The history of Mozart's illness has often been investigated by medical historians, who have researched a number of different possibilities. Some have defended the poisoning theory and have attempted to support it with evidence from Mozart's medical history, while others—particularly Aloys Greiner—have maintained that Mozart died of kidney disease—a thesis that does not entirely contradict the

poisoning theory. Uremia, which is treated by dialysis today, constitutes internal poisoning through kidney failure, and a "poisonous"
taste can often arise in the patient's mouth. Now, however, this diag-
nosis can also be firmly rejected.

The cause of Mozart's death can now be viewed as substantially
clarified, not as a result of any newly discovered documents, but
through careful analysis of source material that was already known in
the mid-nineteenth century and that Otto Jahn, for example, could
have consulted for his Mozart biography (1856–59). In view of the
strange fascination exerted by Mozart's death and burial (on which
source material also existed in Jahn's time), it is indeed astonishing
that the well-loved saga of a mysterious death and pauper's grave held
sway for such a long time.

Carl Bär has published a thorough and exemplary study that dis-
cusses all the available sources and scrutinizes them both medically
and historically. His extensive research need not be examined here in
detail; a summary of his results will suffice. Bär concludes that Mozart
suffered an attack of rheumatic fever—as he did several times in his
youth—and died from the effects of this illness and the treatment
prescribed for it.

> The symptoms may be summarized as follows: *an acute febrile condi-*
> *tion with inflammatory swelling in the extremities, impaired mobility*
> *resulting from severe pain, rash, vomiting (?), sweating (?), headache.*[51]

After a detailed discussion of the official cause of death, "acute
miliary fever," and how it should be understood in light of eighteenth-
century medical knowledge, Bär reaches the following conclusion:

> *On the strength of the criteria based on Jones, with two primary symp-*
> *toms and at least two secondary symptoms, and taking all contemporary*
> *sources into consideration, it has been possible to substantiate the diag-*
> *nosis of Mozart's mortal illness as "rheumatic fever," with the proof of*
> *early rheumatic illness being a deciding factor.*[52]

Bär explains that physicians of the time usually treated this condition with venesection, saline beverages, and then emetics and
sudorifics. In Mozart's case we know of venesection, vomiting (pre-

sumably induced by emetics), and sweating (which can be inferred from the fact that he frequently changed his shirt). Based on his examination of prevailing procedures, Bär concludes regarding venesection, "Even a conservative estimate indicates that Mozart in all probability lost roughly two liters of blood."[53] This obviously led to a further weakening of his already debilitated and febrile body. Moreover, at the end of the eighteenth century there was no knowledge of the coronary effects of rheumatic fever.

It has hitherto been overlooked that venesection could have contributed directly to Mozart's death, but this possibility is worthy of serious consideration. Nothing, however, can be proven in this regard. In addition, it must remain open whether acute heart failure was caused by the illness itself or by a staphylococcal or streptococcal infection. The investigation of Mozart's death must end here. Any further attempts to reach a more precise explanation would go beyond the demands that—even for a hypothesis—we can make on the sources.[54]

JOSEPHINE BURIAL PRACTICES

It is not historical events that change over the course of time, but our knowledge and interpretation of them. This becomes especially clear when we ponder the legends that have grown up around Mozart's burial. Contemporary reports conflict even regarding the date, which was not clearly established until recently. We read again and again that Mozart was buried in a pauper's grave; this received opinion has almost become part of our education. The burial, in a communal grave, took place during a rainstorm with only the gravediggers present—Mozart was interred without a single witness. No one paid for a gravestone, which meant that within a short time no one knew where the grave was located. At his death Mozart was a more or less forgotten musician (although the recently premiered *Zauberflöte* was playing nightly to a full house at the "Imperial Royal Priv. Theater auf der Wieden"). For more than 170 years Mozart's many biographers have spun this touching tale, and in the process most of them have cast bitter accusations at Constanze Mozart—having decided, for exam-

ple, that she had "at no time in her life an inkling of Mozart's profound
and solitary inner life" (Arthur Schurig), and so forth. One can almost
believe that the biographers pieced together the picture of Mozart
desired by their readers: a lonely, unrecognized genius who died
young but "perfect," interred in a communal grave because no one
understood his importance. The reader of such melodrama feels elevated because he appreciates Mozart and loves his music (if he knows
it), and because he sympathizes with the lonely hero. Constanze
Mozart is sometimes envied because she was allowed to live at the side
of this genius, sometimes despised because she was not able "to
comprehend her husband's greatness" (Erich Schenk). Anyone who
judges bereavement by the loudness of the widow's lamentation and
the cost of the burial will indeed have to condemn Mozart's wife. But to
do so displays total ignorance of the customs of the time, the Josephine
regulations concerning death and burial.

Among the most controversial reforms of Emperor Joseph II was
undoubtedly the burial ordinance issued on August 23, 1784. As with
his other reforms, his motives are easily appreciated, whether or not
one agrees with his means. The reforms were simply too "reasonable,"
and too obvious an affront to traditional customs, opinions, and
feelings, all of which found clear expression in existing burial practices. Joseph's ordinance was part of an overall public health policy,
but its goal of improved hygiene was combined to an exaggerated
extent with his economic puritanism, which he, as guide to the nation,
tried to impose on all his subjects. His ideas on the wastefulness of
burial procedures came not only from political economy but from
considerations of public welfare; he wanted to eliminate the heavy
financial strain of burials among a generally poor population. (The
burial ordinance naturally did not apply to the nobility, who needed no
writ of exemption to prove it. They, as well as some wealthy bourgeois,
already had their own family vaults.)

Although Joseph II was less isolated and closer to his people than
any other Austrian ruler, he was absolutely deaf and blind to their
ordinary thoughts and feelings. They had no place in his conception of
reason as a guiding principle. He was certainly no tyrant, unlike a
number of his fellow rulers on European thrones, but as an "enlightened" despot he surely surpassed the no less rationalist King Frederick II of Prussia.

On August 23, 1784, Joseph II issued his "court decree on religious and police matters," which reads as follows:

... All vaults, churchyards, and so-called God's acres located within the city limits shall henceforth be closed, and only those located at a suitable distance outside the cities may be used.

2. As hitherto customary, so in future shall each and every corpse, as arranged by the deceased or his family in accordance with the regulations pertaining to funeral processions, be carried or driven to the church and blessed with the usual prayers and music. Thereupon, however, it shall be conveyed by the priest without ceremony to an outlying cemetery for interment.

3. For these cemeteries a sufficiently large plot of ground is to be chosen which is not exposed to any water source and does not contain any variety of soil which would prevent decomposition. When the ground has been selected it is to be marked with a cross.

4. The only objective in burial is to promote decomposition as soon as possible, and there is no greater hindrance to this process than the burial of bodies in coffins. Thus it is recommended for the present that all bodies be sewn unclothed into linen sacks, placed in coffins, and so brought to the cemetery.

5. In the cemetery a grave six feet deep and four feet wide shall be prepared, and each body removed from the coffin and placed in the grave still sewn into its linen sack. It shall then be strewn with unslaked lime and immediately covered with earth. If several bodies arrive at one time, they may all be placed in the same grave; it is, however, imperative that each grave in which dead bodies are placed be immediately filled in with earth and that a distance of four feet must be left between graves.

6. To save unnecessary costs each parish shall acquire a suitable number of well-made coffins in different sizes, which shall be provided free of charge to parishioners. No one shall be prevented from acquiring his own coffin for a deceased relative if he so desires, but the body must never be buried in the coffin. All coffins must be reused for other burials.

7. If survivors wish to erect a memorial to the deceased as a demonstration of love, respect, or gratitude, they shall be permitted to do so. Any such memorials must, however, be erected along the walls and not in the cemetery itself, in order to save space.

8. Lastly, all vaults and graves in the numerous monasteries, as well as the so-called shafts and lime pits of the hospitals, the Brothers of Mercy, and the Sisters of St. Elizabeth, shall henceforth be closed, and all deceased persons buried in the cemeteries of their respective parishes. Accordingly, these monasteries and hospitals shall give all gravediggers a satisfactory remuneration for their increased labors, and the parish cemeteries in whose precincts the hospitals and monasteries are located shall be enlarged as required.[55]

The relocation of cemeteries outside the city gates—which Joseph II had first observed in France in 1777—was understandable and certainly a wise step according to prevailing medical opinion. The call to refrain from burying bodies in coffins was an altogether different matter, even if it did save large amounts of wood and have the desired effect of reducing costs (which was also the reason cremation was not suggested, although it was certainly the most hygienic method). Burial in a sack, especially to promote faster decomposition, was felt to be undignified. It must have seemed especially irreverent that people who did not wish to forgo a coffin were given the opportunity to borrow one for the funeral and transportation of the body to the cemetery. The protest against these new regulations was vehement and widespread. After only six months Joseph II was forced to alter his decision; a "circular on religious matters" dated January 27, 1785, reads, "Burial in linen sacks will not be forced upon anyone; however, its recommendation as set forth in the ordinance of August 23, 1784, will remain unchanged."

In a circular to his administration Joseph II revealed how difficult it was for him to make this concession.

Every day I see—unfortunately—how living people think in such material terms. They go to great lengths to insure their bodies will decay slowly after death, and thus remain stinking carrion for as long as possible. So I no longer care how they want to be buried. And you must explain to them that after I have demonstrated how practical and reasonable this method of burial is, I have no desire to force reason upon anyone who is not convinced. As far as coffins are concerned, each person may freely do in advance what he considers appropriate for his dead body.

In practice the moderation of Joseph II's burial ordinance meant that although burial in sacks was still provided for and still desirable, it was not forced upon anyone.

The question arises as to whether Mozart, who supposedly received "the cheapest burial available" (Michael Levey), was given a Josephine "sack burial." This possibility has thus far remained unexplored. According to the regulations, Mozart would have been strewn with unslaked lime and covered with earth until the grave was filled in, generally after five or six bodies had arrived. (From the death register it would be easy to reconstruct a list of Mozart's companions in the grave.) Though this form of burial in a communal grave may strike us as unusual, it was entirely normal at the time. We must also keep in mind that the entombment of bodies in large church vaults or charnel houses was widely practiced well into the nineteenth century. In rural Austria especially, one can still see many charnel houses, known as *Karner,* in which skeletons are neatly stacked one on top of the other; for the burial plots were emptied and reused every six to eight years.

The Josephine burial regulations express a certain puritanism, which in church services took the form of an unadorned, "enlightened" piety. They corresponded in every way to the emperor's Church reform policy and are by no means evidence of cynicism, as is often mistakenly suggested. Joseph II regarded unnecessary grandeur as a sign of false piety. Lavish display had been a fact of life in the Vienna of Maria Theresa; the expenditure for the funeral of the singer Anna Maria Schindler, for example, was 341 florins 24 kreuzer—38 times the cost of Mozart's "modest Josephine" burial. Looking at the itemization of expenses, we can appreciate why Joseph II tried to encourage frugality in just this area. Constanze Mozart would have had to spend almost half a year's imperial salary for the following *pomps funèbres:*[56]

Burial costs	59 fl. 9 kr.
Funeral mass	25 fl. 3 kr.
Candles	53 fl. 21 kr.
Funeral knell (Minorities)	3 fl. 3 kr.
Funeral knell (Lichtenstein Chapel)	1 fl. 30 kr.
3 lay brothers	3 fl.
Funeral escutcheon	18 fl. 39 kr.
Trauerflöre (black cloth)	148 fl. 33 kr.
Funeral oration	29 fl. 33 kr.

Joseph II forbade such things outright and did not even hesitate to order "a complete halt to the eulogies which have hitherto been customarily presented at funerals." The funereal splendor that reached its peak in Vienna after 1800 during the reign of Francis II is a completely different story.[57]

NO PAUPER'S BURIAL

How did Mozart's burial actually proceed? There are no firsthand reports from participants or eyewitnesses, and the secondhand information we have is mostly vague, contradictory, or of doubtful authenticity. We can nonetheless form a fairly clear picture by comparing the few references to Mozart's burial with the normal burial procedures so precisely stipulated in the official regulations—in a manner similar to Carl Bär's painstaking method.

A corpse could not be buried until forty-eight hours after death. Exceptions were made only in case of epidemics, and with a certificate signed by a physician. Accordingly, Mozart's interment could not have taken place before December 7. The entry in the register of deaths under "date and location of burial" reads December 6 and is presumably a slip of the pen. Moreover, four sources record "unfavorable" or "inclement" weather[58] on the evening of the day of burial, and these descriptions only apply to December 7.

Sometime before three o'clock in the afternoon, the body was taken from the apartment and brought to St. Stephen's Cathedral for the funeral service. To the tolling of one bell, a crossbearer walked at the head of the procession, followed by a priest. The coffin, covered in a pall, was borne by four men in long cloaks, flanked by four boys in habits, each carrying a lantern. We have no information about which relatives—all from the Weber family—and which friends and acquaintances followed the coffin. The service took place in a small chapel just inside the cathedral's main entrance. It is not known whether any music was performed; if so, it was presented without charge, for it is not listed in the burial costs. It is entirely possible that Mozart, having been an assistant kapellmeister of the cathedral, was given a musical tribute by colleagues, perhaps by his successor in this post, Johann Georg Albrechtsberger. It is also conceivable that other musical colleagues took part, some of whom may have attended the funeral service. We do not know how many mourners were present. The names of about ten friends and six family members appear in the recollections of a few participants. No conclusions should be drawn from these figures, however, and it would be especially rash to assume that there was general indifference to Mozart. The number of mourners may have been much greater; on the other hand, it may not have been a common practice to attend such ceremonies in what was still the period of Josephine convention, which discouraged extravagance in burial services. But Mozart's death did not go unnoticed; his Masonic lodge held a "Lodge of Sorrows" in his memory, and a memorial service in Prague drew over 4,000 mourners.

After the service, the coffin was carried out of the cathedral and into the Crucifix Chapel, which forms the entrance to the crypt and is accessible only from the outside. There it was placed on a bier, and the formal obsequies were concluded. Only after six o'clock in the evening (in summer only after nine) could the coffin be transported to the cemetery. There were no ceremonies at the gravesite, and no priest was in attendance—only the gravedigger and his assistants. A few of Mozart's friends are said to have assembled with the intention of following the coffin to the cemetery, but they were forced to turn back at the Stubentor because of the bad weather and the speed of the hearse. This anecdote appears in every Mozart biography, usually followed by the comment that not even Constanze Mozart accompanied the coffin to the cemetery. Even the judicious Carl Bär makes a somewhat reproachful remark: "The hearse arrived unaccompanied at the cemetery gate in St. Marx. There the story of Mozart's pitiful end reached its conclusion"[59]—despite having informed us on the previous page that "although accompanying the coffin to the gravesite was unusual at the time, no one was barred from following the hearse."

This small detail would be insignificant if it had not been inflated into a justification for the view that Mozart was neglected in death, only two of his pupils (Franz Jakob Freystädtler and Otto Hartwig) having enough reverence at least to try to accompany the coffin.

> But they, too, had to abandon their effort, because the coachman, who had no need to show consideration for any miscellaneous mourners who might be following, drove the horse at top speed and they were unable to keep pace.[60]

"Any miscellaneous mourners" would have had to take a coach themselves, however, for the distance was too far to walk. The cemetery of

St. Marx was laid out in 1787, after the cemetery on what is now the Stephansplatz had been closed and leveled off and the small houses along the cemetery wall torn down. It was approximately three miles from the cathedral in the Landstrasse district. The area around St. Marx was almost completely undeveloped and was approached by a simple country road leading beyond the city limits—a good hour's walk. But the hearse could not depart until evening, and after six o'clock it was already dark at that time of year. The gravediggers, then, would not have carried out the actual burial until the next morning, and the coffin would have been kept overnight in a small mortuary (which had to be left open, since cases where death was only apparent were not unknown). For these reasons, it was no longer common practice to accompany the body to the gravesite after the relocation of cemeteries outside city limits. Moreover, the interment itself usually had little to do with reverence for the dead, since communal graves were the rule (four adults and two children to a grave, buried in the order of their arrival at the cemetery), individual graves the exception. The nobility and the wealthy bourgeoisie sometimes had family vaults marked by a monument. Otherwise gravestones were permitted only along the cemetery walls, for reasons of space. The tending of individual graves, let alone planned landscaping in cemeteries, was entirely unknown. At most a few trees or bushes were planted between the burial plots. The cemeteries outside the city limits, especially, were anything but attractive parks. This simple form of interment in rather bleak surroundings meant that regular visits to gravesites were hardly customary.

What, then, of Mozart's so-called pauper's burial? How did this legend ever originate? What distinguished a pauper's burial from a normal burial? Perhaps we should be asking whether Mozart was buried in a linen sack rather than in a coffin. For even in the case of a so-called sack burial, a coffin was used for the funeral in the church and to transport the body to the cemetery. The coffin was emptied into the open grave and sent back in the hearse to be reused. Every parish church maintained a supply of reusable coffins.[61] The amendment to the burial ordinance did not mean that sack burials were abolished; it merely stated that individual coffins were no longer forbidden. Sack burials occurred into the first years of the nineteenth century. Anyone who died in a hospital, for instance, was usually transported to the church in a reusable coffin. And since the bier was covered with a pall during the funeral, the mourners had no way of knowing what kind of coffin it was.

In Mozart's case this question can be answered unequivocally. In the death register of his parish, the following information appears under his name: "8 fl. 56 kr." for a third-class burial, and "wagon 3 fl." The latter entry refers to the cost of a hearse, which was only paid if the deceased had his own coffin; there was no charge for the hearse in the case of a sack burial—obviously one of Joseph II's financial incentives. Mozart's coffin is not included in the burial costs, so it must have been ordered from a carpenter and was probably paid for on delivery. Since Gottfried van Swieten handled all the formalities for the family, he must have arranged for the coffin and paid for the burial immediately, for in the "Inventory and Appraisal" of Mozart's estate these costs are not listed separately; there is only this general remark: "After his decease there remained the sum of 60 fl. in ready cash, out of which the burial and other costs were defrayed."[62]

It is difficult to reconstruct just when a "pauper's burial" for Mozart was first mentioned. In any event, the term does not appear in the recollections of those who were present, family members in particular. But succeeding generations, unfamiliar with Josephine burial customs, were unable to avoid this misunderstanding, especially after the appearance in 1828 of the Mozart biography by Georg Nikolaus von Nissen, Constanze Mozart's second husband, who offered the following vague formulation:

> Mozart's mortal remains were buried in the cemetery of St. Marx just outside Vienna. [Because Swieten] took into consideration the greatest possible economy for the family, the coffin was deposited in a common grave and every other expense avoided.[63]

This description gives no clue that the same circumstances applied to 85 percent of the bourgeois population. By the time it was written, a "common" grave had become a rare form of interment and was naturally misunderstood as a sign of callousness or extreme poverty. In the Josephine period a communal grave was an expression neither of shabbiness nor of thoughtlessness, but rather a reflection of the sober rationalism that promoted—not without reason—what were then the most advanced ideas about hygiene.

In fact, we must concede that the burial customs of that age showed a high degree of human sensitivity, reflected in a solicitousness hardly apparent today. There was no actual "pauper's burial," and everyone was entitled to the usual third-class arrangements. When the deceased had no money, the fees were waived and the word "gratis" was entered under the appropriate heading in the register of deaths, though the character of the ceremonies did not change in the least.[64] In this way it was ensured that the poor would be buried with the same consideration shown to all other citizens, and—a matter of particular concern to Joseph II—that the financial expenditure for a burial did not become a questionable demonstration of the extent to which the deceased was mourned and respected. In the burial ceremony the outward appearance of equality was reestablished, which undoubtedly corresponded to the emperor's ideas on theological reform. In contrast to all his predecessors, he himself insisted on a totally plain coffin.

The idea of a pauper's burial certainly gained credence from the fact that soon after Mozart's death his grave could no longer be located. Even this cannot be considered so unusual, for the communal graves held four to six bodies and were generally unmarked. Monuments such as gravestones were erected, if at all, not on the grave but along the cemetery wall where space permitted. One could only determine the general burial area, which was emptied and used again after eight years at most. The gravedigger could usually provide information, because he could tell from the burial records when each row was used.

This neglect of individual graves was diametrically opposed to later Viennese customs and soon met with total bewilderment. As early as 1799, just when Mozart's grave was presumably reused, an "Inquiry concerning Mozart" appeared in Christoph Martin Wieland's *Der Neue teutsche Merkur*,[65] in which we read:

> What follows is the literal translation of a passage from a letter written by an Englishman in Vienna: "The Briton, in the happy knowledge that he can appreciate true merit, points to the German Handel's gravestone in Westminster Abbey. Here no one knows where Mozart's mortal frame (perhaps shed by force) lies in its grave." This is a grievous accusation, although not new in the history of our worthies. Is it justified? Dear Mozart! You erected a monument to your favorite bird in the garden of your rented house, and wrote the inscription yourself. When will someone honor you as you honored your bird?

This reproachful article was plainly intended as an invitation for someone who might know the exact location of Mozart's grave to come forward, but even more important, it was a call for the erection of a monument on that spot. The remarks on the pet bird and the possibility that Mozart died "by force" were founded on the recently published first edition of Franz Xaver Niemetschek's biography (1798); the writer was not referring to the rumor of poisoning by Antonio Salieri, which first circulated in 1825. But no one made a move, and the article was reprinted nine years later in a Viennese periodical. This time, Georg August Griesinger came forward with an approximate description of the gravesite. Griesinger, who made a name for himself by writing the first biography of Joseph Haydn, later described the effect of this "reprimand that no one knows where Mozart is buried, although he himself composed a song on the death of a parrot."

> I read this passage to Mozart's widow, whom I often saw on my visits to her second husband, the royal Danish chargé d'affaires v. Nissen. I then asked her if she would be willing to drive with me to the St. Marx cemetery in order to seek Mozart's gravesite. She agreed to accompany me and we drove there with her son Wolfgang, who passed away this last summer (1844). Well do I remember the widow's comment that if it were the custom here as it is in some places to collect and display the bones of the decomposed bodies, she would recognize her husband's skull among the many thousands.
>
> At the cemetery we discovered that the gravedigger who was responsible for this work in 1791 was long dead, that the graves from that year had already been dug up and reused, and that the bones which came to the surface were not set out in public but were buried again in the earth. There was nothing we could do but inquire which rows served as the final resting place for those who died in 1791. The gravedigger could only tell us that it was the third and fourth rows down from the monumental cross which stands in the middle of the cemetery. No more information could be obtained.[66]

The search for Mozart's grave continued, but with no result— fortunately, we are tempted to say. For, as Griesinger's report indicates, respect for the dead was bound up with a curious interest in skulls in the Biedermeier period. Goethe, for example, retrieved Schiller's skull from the charnel house in Weimar and for a time kept it in his home. Joseph Haydn's skull was stolen from his grave as early as 1809 (the year he died) and remained in the possession of the Gesellschaft der Musikfreunde in Vienna from 1895 to 1954. It was reinterred in his grave at Eisenstadt in a solemn ceremony on June 5, 1954. Mozart's dead body was at least spared such a fate. Yet indignation over the shameful neglect of his grave continues unabated to this day. Let the reader form his or her own opinion.

APPRAISAL

Mozart died without means—that is, with no financial reserves. He had always lived from hand to mouth and had spent his often considerable earnings as soon as he got them, which meant that he was sometimes deeply in debt for short periods because of the general irregularity of his income. Since his financial prospects were greatly improved at the time of his death, it is hardly surprising that he left a number of unpaid bills, fastidiously recorded in the inventory of his estate.

Record of bills paid after the decease
of my husband Wolfgang A. Mozart

No.		fl.	kr.
1.	To Herr Georg Dümmer, Tailor	282	7
2.	To Anton Reiz, Paperhanger	208	3
3.	To the Royal and Imperial Court Apothecary	139	30
4.	To Herr Johann Heydegger, Merchant	87	22
5.	To Herr Friedrich Purker, Tradesman	59	–
6.	To Frau Regina Haselin, Apothecary	40	53
7.	To the same, making a total of 74 fl. 53 kr.	34	–
8.	To Michael Anhamer, Shoemaker	31	46
9.	To Herr Georg Mayer, Tailor	13	41
10.	To the merchant Reuter	12	54
11.	To Herr Andre Igl, Barber-Surgeon	9	–
	Total	918	16

Constanze Mozart, widow

Not listed here is the outstanding debt to Michael Puchberg of approximately 1,000 florins, which was eventually repaid in full.

It is unclear where Constanze got the money to pay these debts. She may have had help from Gottfried van Swieten, who proved himself a devoted friend of the Mozart family, for she herself had only small sums at her disposal.[67]

		fl.	kr.
After his decease there remained in ready cash the sum of out of which the burial and other costs were defrayed.		60	–
Collectable debts (remaining salary from the court)		133	20
Uncollectable debts			
Owed to the deceased by Herr Franz Gilowsky	300 fl.		
Owed without recourse by Herr Anton Stadler, Royal and Imperial *Hofmusikus*	500 fl.		
Total	800 fl.		
		Latus 193	20

Mozart, it seems, was himself prepared to lend considerable and, as it turned out, irrecoverable sums to unreliable debtors. His carelessness is also reflected in the fact that he simply "forgot" to subscribe to the pension fund for widows and orphans of musicians maintained by the Tonkünstlersozietät, although he appeared often enough in their annual benefit concerts.

Under these circumstances Constanze Mozart was not provided for and had nothing but her husband's unpublished manuscripts. She was not yet eligible for a pension based on Mozart's income as *Kammerkompositeur*. After her difficult situation became known, however, an exception was made and she was eventually granted a small pension.

In the ensuing years Mozart's widow encountered considerable generosity. Swieten financed the children's education for many years, and Countess Maria Wilhelmine Thun may have helped as well. During the first years after Mozart's death numerous collections and

benefit performances testified to the very high esteem in which
Mozart, and by extension his family, was held. It is said that Emanuel
Schikaneder gave a benefit performance of *Die Zauberflöte* for Mozart's
widow as early as December 1791; on December 28 there was a
concert for her benefit at the Nationaltheater in Prague; the elector of
Cologne sent her 100 gold ducats; and a memorial concert at Vienna's
Nationaltheater raised 1,500 florins for Mozart's children, 675 from
the Viennese court alone. There was also organized support from the
Freemasons, including the publication of the *Kleine Freimaurerkantate* (K. 623) "for sale by subscription, to benefit his needy wife and
orphans"; six months later they took up a collection for Constanze. In
February 1792 King Frederick William II of Prussia bought eight of
Mozart's unpublished works for 3,600 florins, which amounted to a
generous donation. In June 1792 there was another memorial service
for Mozart in Prague at which donations were collected for his survivors, and in Vienna Baron van Swieten arranged the first performance of the Requiem on January 2, 1793—before the performance
organized by the commissioner of the work, Count Walsegg-Stuppach.
Swieten's endeavor brought in more than 300 ducats (1,350 florins) for
Constanze Mozart.

There was great consternation everywhere at Mozart's sudden and
premature death, but nowhere did it find such eloquent expression as
in the solemn requiem celebrated in Prague on December 14, 1791. A
report on that event appeared in the *Wiener Zeitung* on December 24,
and reads as follows:

> On the 14th of this month the friends of music in *Prague* held solemn
> exequies for the late *Kapellmeister* and Royal and Imperial *Hofkompo-
> nist* Wolfgang Gottlieb *Mozart*, who died here on December 5th. This
> ceremony, held in the parish church of St. Niklas, was organized by the
> orchestra of Prague's Nationaltheater under the direction of Herr Jo-
> seph *Strohbach*, and all the city's famous musicians took part. On that
> day all the bells of the church were rung for half an hour; almost the
> entire city turned out, so that the square in front of the church could
> not accommodate all the coaches, and neither could the church ac-
> commodate all the admirers of the departed composer, although it has
> room for almost 4,000 people. The Requiem was by the *Kapellmeister*
> Rössler, and was superbly performed by 120 leading musicians, at the
> head of whom was the beloved singer Madame *Duscheck*. In the middle

MAURERREDE
AUF
MOZARTS TOD.

VORGELESEN

BEY EINER

MEISTERAUFNAHME

IN DER

SEHR EHRW. ST. JOH. ☐

ZUR

GEKRÖNTEN HOFFNUNG

IM ORIENT VON WIEN

VOM

Bᵈʳ· H . . . . r.

WIEN,

GEDRUCKT BEYM BR. IGNAZ ALBERTI.

1792.

Mozart's lodge brothers held a "Lodge of Sorrows" in his memory, and Karl Friedrich Hensler gave the eulogy, which was subsequently printed. Hensler praised Mozart's charitable work for the poor and for widows and orphans.

of the church stood a magnificently illuminated catafalque; three choirs of trumpets and drums sounded mournful strains; the requiem mass was celebrated by Father Rudolf *Fischer;* 12 students from the local grammar school carried torches, with black crepe over their shoulders and white cloths in their hands. A solemn stillness prevailed, and countless tears flowed in painful remembrance of that artist whose harmonies had so often moved our hearts to joy.[68]

NOTES

ABBREVIATIONS

Dokumente   Mozart, Wolfgang Amadeus. *Die Dokumente seines Lebens.* Collected and annotated by Otto Erich Deutsch. Kassel, etc., 1961 (NAW vol. 10, Supplement, Werkgruppe 34).

ISM   Internationale Stiftung Mozarteum

MBA   Mozart, Wolfgang Amadeus. *Briefe und Aufzeichnungen.* Complete edition, published by the Internationale Stiftung Mozarteum, Salzburg, collected and annotated by Wilhelm A. Bauer and Otto Erich Deutsch. 7 vols. Vols. 1–4, text; vols. 5–6, commentary, edited by Joseph Heinz Eibl; vol. 7, index, compiled by Joseph Heinz Eibl. Kassel, etc., 1962–75.

NAW   Mozart, Wolfgang Amadeus. *Neue Ausgabe Samtlicher Werke.* Published by the Internationale Stiftung Mozarteum in cooperation with the Mozart cities Augsburg, Salzburg, and Vienna. Kassel, etc., 1955– .

VA   Vertrauliche Akten des Haus-, Hof-, und Staatsarchivs, Vienna.

1. ARRIVAL IN VIENNA

1. This view, first advanced by Otto Jahn, still has many advocates today; even Alfred Einstein (*Mozart: Sein Charakter, Sein Werk*, Frankfurt a. M., 1968, pp. 420–22 shares it. The exact opposite viewpoint does have its supporters, however, the most vocal being Hermann Abert, who says of *Idomeneo:* "Anyone who claims that it marks a new epoch in the history of the genre or represents its crowning achievement shows inadequate knowledge of both the contemporary and the immediately preceding generation of Italian opera composers" (*W. A. Mozart: Neubearbeitete und erweiterte Ausgabe von Otto Jahns Mozart*, 9th ed., Leipzig, 1978, part 1, p. 695). The conflict is between two types of musicology, one oriented toward cultural history, the other concerned with the history of forms and genres.

2. Later Colloredo made his subjects pay dearly for the rejection and contempt he experienced as archbishop of Salzburg. Events in the wake of the French Revolution taught him that his political isolation was not without its dangers and that the days of his kind of autocracy were numbered, however devoted he may have been to the goals of reason and "enlightenment." He had no real friends or allies in other countries, and he could only expect hatred from his own subjects. Suddenly he was mortally afraid. When French troops eventually threatened Salzburg, Colloredo's only thought was to save himself. He attempted to flee with as much money from the state treasury as he could carry, and after several almost tragicomic episodes he succeeded. In 1799, after he had reached safety, he had the nerve to demand (successfully) reimbursement of the expenses incurred during his escape (36,000 florins). Naturally, he was then obliged to abdicate as prince archbishop. It is unlikely that anyone in Salzburg shed a tear for him. He even had an annual pension of 80,000 florins sent to him in Vienna, where he retired to private life. The decline of this intriguing political figure, who had tried so earnestly to follow the example of the Josephine reforms, was more sensational and humiliating than anyone could have imagined. Leopold and Wolfgang Mozart did not live to see his fall. But perhaps they were justified in their aversion to Colloredo, although he treated them no worse (or better) than numerous other minor potentates treated their court employees. Only Mozart's sister Maria Anna witnessed the bizarre end of Colloredo's reign in Salzburg; unfortunately we have no record of her reaction to it.

3. Colloredo "could not tolerate people going about the world begging" (August 31, 1778), as he once admitted to Leopold Mozart. Apparently he did not differentiate between a respected artist making a concert tour and itinerant musicians playing in the streets, which was something he did not want to encourage in his province. Mozart considered the archbishop's attitude disrespectful and condescending. He was especially sensitive in this regard because his father had always told him that his journeys throughout Europe were not just for the purpose of earning money; the main objectives were to gain a musical reputation, to be paid as an artist and not as a showman, to display musical genius as opposed to empty virtuosity, and to astound the public. The Mozarts did occasionally violate these self-imposed limitations when trying to impress people of influence: then Wolfgang had to perform silly tricks

such as playing the clavier with a cloth spread over the keyboard. By the time he arrived in Vienna, however, he no longer needed such tricks.

2. THE ABDUCTION—1782

1. Abert, op. cit., part 1, p. 727.

2. The variations K. 374a/359, 374b/360, and 374c/352, and the violin and piano sonatas K. 374d/376, 374e/377, and 374f/380. That the great serenade for winds (K. 370a/361) known as the "Gran partita" was also completed during this summer is disputed by recent Mozart research; see *NAW,* series 7, Werkgruppe 17, vol. 2, p. xii.

3. *Dokumente,* p. 190.

4. When the grand duke ascended the throne and became Czar Paul I in 1796, it turned out that he was not fit to rule. He had been isolated, neglected by his mother, and subjected to harsh treatment, including an attempt on his life. These vicissitudes now exacted a heavy toll. His policies were so muddled that people began to doubt his sanity. A powerful opposition developed, and he was finally murdered in 1801.

5. Quoted in Abert, op. cit., part 1, p. 727.

6. Hilde Spiel, *Fanny von Arnstein oder Die Emanzipation: Ein Frauenleben an der Zeitenwende 1758–1818* (Frankfurt, 1962), pp. 54f.

7. Further insight into this milieu is provided by two interesting family connections: Fanny Arnstein was the great-aunt of Felix Mendelssohn-Bartholdy, and Constanze Weber, Mozart's future wife, was a cousin of Carl Maria von Weber.

8. This denial of the old religion and the cultural-historical cohesion it provided initially gave Jews some measure of social equality. But it is among the bitter lessons of history that in the end they gained nothing by their sacrifice: the persecutions of Jews in the twentieth century, which were entirely racist in nature and had nothing to do with religion, made no exceptions for those who believed they had long since shed their historical uniqueness.

9. Quoted in Spiel, op. cit., p. 75.

10. Johann Baptist Fuchs, *Erinnerungen aus dem Leben eines Kölner Juristen* (Cologne, 1912); quoted in Spiel, op. cit, p. 80.

11. Act I, scene 9.

12. Act II, scene 1.

13. Act III, scene 6.

14. Act III, scene 9.

15. Act II, scene 5.

16. One of them, Anton Wilhelm Amo from Guinea, studied at the university in Halle and wrote a dissertation on the rights of blacks in Europe (*De jure Maurorum in Europa,* 1729). He had been a freedman for some time and had even managed to obtain a professorship in philosophy. He was not able to avoid racial hostility,

however, as he discovered when he tried to marry. At one point (around 1747?) he decided to return to his African homeland, where his trail disappears. His grave can still be seen today in Shama, Ghana. Another "princely blackamoor," Ibrahim Hannibal, became a lackey at the court of the Russian czar and was then sent to study naval engineering in Holland. He subsequently returned to the court of Peter the Great and attained the rank of grand admiral in the navy. After the czar's death he was banished to Siberia, where his trail likewise disappears. He was the great-grandfather of Alexander Pushkin.

17. Quoted in Eugen Lennhof and Oskar Posner, *Internationales Freimaurerlexikon* (unabridged reprint of the 1932 edition, Vienna and Munich, 1980), col. 1476. Georg Forster wrote to Samuel Thomas von Sömmering about Joseph II (August 14–16, 1784): "The emperor cannot bear to see a stuffed animal. The entire imperial family has this idiosyncrasy" (Forster, *Werke, Samtliche Schriften, Tagebücher, Briefe*, Berlin, 1978, vol. 14, p. 160). At the time it was not yet clear that the emperor's nephew and eventual successor, Francis II, would be the opposite of his uncle in every respect.

3. AT HOME WITH THE MOZARTS

1. Erich Schenk, *Mozart: Eine Biographie*, (Munich and Mainz, 1977), p. 584.

2. Wolfgang Hildesheimer, *Mozart* (Frankfurt a.M., 1977), pp. 253f.

3. Arthur Schurig, *Wolfgang Amadé Mozart: Sein Leben, seine Persönlichkeit, sein Werk*, 2d ed. (Leipzig, 1923), vol. 2, p. 379.

4. Ibid., p. 131.

5. Constanze Mozart, *Briefe/Aufzeichnungen/Dokumente*, ed. Arthur Schurig (Dresden, 1922), pp. x–xi.

6. Almost one child in four died within twelve months of birth; only one in three survived until its third birthday. Only after this age did the mortality rate drop substantially. The problem was a general helplessness in the face of nutritional disorders and febrile (inflammatory) conditions in infants and small children. Even teething represented a serious danger. And in any event the mother's quick recovery was considered more important than the child's well-being. Most people saw the death of children as an inevitable stroke of fate for which they had to be prepared. Frequent births in quick succession undoubtedly contributed to attitudes that seem alien and perplexing to us.

7. It is indeed peculiar that Constanze Mozart's letters were either deemed unimportant or were deliberately suppressed (by whom?), but that does not allow us to draw conclusions about their content. Nevertheless, the loss of her letters has left room for indignant and spiteful assumptions, character judgments, and distortions untenable in a scholarly context. Constanze has been defamed in most Mozart biographies up to and including Hildesheimer, and the question of how this disparaging picture came about is itself worth investigating.

8. The cures at Baden in 1791 were apparently not due to a new outbreak of her illness but were taken in the course of her pregnancy as a precautionary measure. In

the fall, she went to the spa to convalesce after giving birth to her sixth child. She seems to have gone at Mozart's express wish, and he wanted to take a holiday himself and accompany her.

9. It seems that many of the letters have disappeared. Both the extent of the lost correspondence and the reason for its disappearance remain unclear. Anything having to do with Freemasonry seems to have been censored for political reasons. During the reign of Emperor Francis II (beginning in 1792), Freemasonry was almost a political crime. It is possible that all letters containing specific references to lodge membership were destroyed. We do not know whether Nissen had a hand in this operation. We do know that despite his passion for collecting Mozartiana, he played havoc with Mozart's letters, rendering certain words—especially names— illegible, and was thus not a very trustworthy administrator of the estate.

10. *A Mozart Pilgrimage. Being the Travel Diaries of Vincent and Mary Novello in the Year 1829*, ed. Nerina Medici di Marignano and Rosemary Hughes (London, 1955), p. 94.

11. *Dokumente*, pp. 255f.

12. *A Mozart Pilgrimage*, op. cit., p. 112. The part she sang can only be the chromatic passage in the minuet, a strange harmonic progression above a pedal point in the cello (marked "piano," incidentally). Later commentators have unanimously described it as "gloomy" and an expression of "psychological torment," and ruled out any connection to the birth on those grounds. Mozart's contemporaries did not hear "psychological torment" or "inner pain" in this quartet; at worst they found it "too strongly seasoned"—that is, overladen with contrived, artificial, erudite passages, which were difficult to comprehend because they broke the rules. Those who did not take the "unobliging" critics seriously but tried to meet the challenge of Mozart's music came to admire his wealth of invention and the bold simplicity of his ideas. Still, some critics who found this music incomprehensible made the mistake of trying to prove its "defectiveness," and their failure to do so is manifest in the numerous "improvements" made during the nineteenth century—especially to the last of the *Haydn* Quartets (K. 465). Constanze Mozart, however, knew this music so well that she could sing the most complicated passages. Yet Wolfgang Hildesheimer is so convinced of her lack of musicality that he even has her confuse a minuet (allegretto) with an andante. He finds the idea of her cries being written into the quartet "so farfetched . . . that we believe it. Not even a Constanze could invent something like that. The statement changes neither the way she wanted to be seen nor the way she really saw herself. It neither increases nor decreases her importance. Why, then, should this particular detail of memory have stuck so strongly? Constanze even sang the labor-pains passage to the Novellos. Unfortunately, Vincent did not take it down. But we are probably right in assuming that it was the sudden forte of the two octave leaps and the following minor tenth (bars 31–32 of the andante)." (op. cit., pp. 164f.)

13. Abert, op. cit., part 2, p. 140.

14. Most of the letters to publishers are in the hand of her second husband, Nissen,

but he seems to have acted only as a business and legal adviser. The musical understanding revealed in these letters undoubtedly came from Constanze Mozart, who insisted on reliable editions and urged that even the fragments be published.

15. Strangely enough, this is the only letter from Leopold Mozart to his daughter that is preserved only in a quotation in another source; could it have contained further—critical—comments about Constanze that were deemed best withheld from posterity? In any event, the loss of the original letter creates a conspicuous gap in the family correspondence.

16. Johann Pezzl, *Skizze von Wien: Ein Kultur- und Sittenbild aus der josefinischen Zeit*, ed. Gustav Gugitz and Anton Schlossar (Graz, 1923), pp. 63–66.

17. The father, Karl Abraham Wetzlar, had been in Vienna since the 1760s. He must have received special permission to live and conduct business there, and was probably involved in banking. His conversion took place in 1777, while his wife retained her Judaism—the only member of this large family to do so, as it soon turned out. For in the following years all nine of their children converted to Catholicism. Almost all of them eventually married into the Austro-Hungarian nobility—another sign that conversion did away with any kind of ostracism of former Jews. The family must have been extremely wealthy; among their jewels was a $13^3/_4$-carat diamond solitaire. Only after their conversion could the Wetzlars buy residential property. When the Dorothean Cloister was closed by Joseph II and its grounds sold for development, Wetzlar bought the property and erected large residential blocks. In 1778 he was granted hereditary nobility for himself and his descendents and was henceforth known as Baron Wetzlar von Plankenstern. Accordingly, his son also became a baron, though he did not convert until 1779. The Plankengasse in Vienna, on the site formerly occupied by the gardens of the Dorothean Cloister, owes its name to Wetzlar von Plankenstern's building projects.

18. Several of Raimund von Wetzlar's siblings also knew Mozart, but they are rarely mentioned in his letters. A visit at Easter 1785 and a chamber music soiree featuring the six "Haydn" string quartets (April 1785) may have taken place at Baron Wetzlar's house: in his letters Leopold Mozart writes simply "at the banker's" to describe both occasions. It is also possible that he was referring to the Jewish banker Adam Albert Hönig von Henikstein, who later boasted of his friendship with Mozart.

19. It was probably an early and impressive example of kitsch, which makes it all the more regrettable that this building was demolished in 1911 and replaced by two very ordinary ones.

20. Since Leopold Mozart found this household "economical," and since he obviously knew how high the rent was, his judgment reflects the enormous price differences between Salzburg and Vienna. Leopold Mozart paid only 45 florins for his giant apartment in Salzburg, which had eight rooms including a *Tanzmeistersaal* (dancing master's room). His pupils paid only 12 crowns per lesson, whereas his son charged ten times that much. In other words, Leopold would have had to give 450 lessons to pay his annual rent, his son in Vienna only 205, although his apartment was five times more expensive.

21. This was Leopold Mozart's last letter. He had been ill for some time, and he died not quite three weeks later. His death brought the family correspondence to a virtual standstill, for Mozart seldom wrote to his sister; only a few letters to his wife provide information on personal and family matters after 1787.

22. The values listed for the individual items cannot be considered very accurate. Normally only half the estimated value was given, in an attempt to minimize the inheritance tax. The inventory of Mozart's effects was drawn up by one of his lodge brothers, who undoubtedly helped Constanze keep the estimates down. However, his arithmetic was often wrong—sometimes even slightly to the widow's disadvantage. The entire catalogue of effects and the records pertaining to it are reproduced in *Dokumente*, pp. 493–511. See also Carl Bär, "Er war kein guter Wirth: Eine Studie uber Mozart's Verhältnis zum Geld," in *Acta Mozartiana*, no. 1 (1978): 37ff.

23. According to the inventory of effects, Mozart's clothes and linen were worth three times as much as his books and music together. To put it another way, all his household furnishings—the dinnerware, silver, furniture, etc. (except for the piano and the billiard table)—were worth only twice as much as his wardrobe. (These calculations, of course, do not take Constanze Mozart's clothes into account.)

24. In the eighteenth century smoking was forbidden in public, partly because of the danger of fire. Some cafés and reading rooms had special smoking areas, which required a license from the police. Smoking at social functions was considered highly ill-mannered because of the smell, especially in the presence of women. At home one usually wore a special smoking jacket to prevent the odor from collecting in one's clothes: these garments often appear in illustrations from the Biedermeier period. Smoking did not become widespread until the second half of the nineteenth century.

25. Michael Kelly, *Reminiscences*, reprint (London, 1975), p. 113.

26. When Prince Nikolaus Esterházy died in 1790 and the orchestra was disbanded, Haydn received—without further obligation—an annual pension of 1,000 florins in addition to his salary of 400 florins, which was raised to 700 in 1797, probably as a cost-of-living increase. As of 1806 he received a total of 2,300 florins a year from Esterházy; his income had thus quadrupled in forty-five years. See also Ulrich Tank, *Studien zur Esterhazyschen Hofmusik von etwa 1620 bis 1790* (Regensburg, 1981), and other documents in Chris Stadtlaender, *Joseph Haydns Sinfonia domestica: Eine Dokumentation* (Munich, 1963).

27. Emil Karl Blümml, *Aus Mozarts Freundes- und Familienkreis* (Vienna, Prague, and Leipzig, 1923), pp. 26ff.

28. These figures are from Robert Haas's introduction to Ignaz Umlauf, *Die Bergknappen*, DTÖ, vol. 36, pp. xviif.

29. See Joseph Karl Mayr, *Wien im Zeitalter Napoleons* (Vienna, 1940), pp. 186ff.

30. As a comparison, we may take the not unhealthy salary Goethe received as a government official in Sachsen-Weimar. As a privy councillor in 1776 he earned the equivalent of 2,400 florins. In 1788, when he had been entrusted with numerous

responsibilities and had just spent two years traveling through Italy, his salary was raised to 3,600 florins. Meanwhile he had been made a nobleman. Later in his career he had "supervision over the scientific and artistic facilities in Weimar and Jena," with the title of *Staatsminister* (minister of state) and a salary of 6,000 florins. This was somewhat reduced, in actual value, however, by the drastic currency depreciation of the 1790s.

31. See Haas, introduction to Umlauf, op. cit.

32. Interesting details are given in *Joseph II als Theaterdirektor: Ungedrückte Briefe und Aktenstücke aus den Kinderjahren des Burgtheaters*, ed. Rudolph Payer von Thurn (Vienna and Leipzig, 1920).

33. Only at the Paris Opera were composers guaranteed royalties by contractual agreement. This arrangement meant that under certain circumstances composers could even claim a pension: Gluck's agreement with the Paris Opera brought him a pension of 1,200 florins. See Rudolph Angermüller, *Antonio Salieri, sein Leben und seine weltlichen Werke unter besonderer Berücksichtigung seiner grossen Opern*, parts 1, 2/1, and 3, Munich, 1971–74 (*Schriften zur Musik*, vols. 16, 17, 19), especially part 2/1, p. 87, note 1.

34. Uwe Krämer, "Wer hat Mozart verhungern lassen?" in *Musica* (1976): 206.

35. Bär, op. cit., p. 52.

36. The Puchberg letters are always given too much importance; Mozart repaid some of the debts they mention before he died. The repayment is not confirmed in any documents but can clearly be inferred from the list of outstanding debts drawn up at Mozart's death. Constanze later discharged these as well. Although the letters provide insight into Mozart's occasionally serious financial problems, they give a far from complete picture of his circumstances. We can also assume that there were other short-term liabilities—in addition to the two further promissory notes that have been recorded. Mozart himself, however, also lent money to a number of his friends. In two of these cases the outstanding sums were designated "lost"—i.e., uncollectable—in the financial record compiled after Mozart's death (*Dokumente*, p. 494).

4. Aristocratic and Bourgeois Salons

1. The relative insignificance of Prussian court life is illustrated by the fact that the Prussian kings, if they were crowned at all, had to travel to Königsberg—which was outside the Holy Roman Empire, along with most Prussian territory—for the coronation. The Habsburgs, on the other hand, could boast three crowns in addition to the imperial title: those of Bohemia (in Prague), Hungary (in Pressburg), and the Austrian Crown Lands (in Vienna).

2. Among the Viennese population (206,000 in 1782) there were approximately 2,600 nobles, 2,000 clergymen, 5,900 city burghers, just over 3,000 civil servants, and roughly 500 Jews. The number of military personnel came to 12,500. There were 30,000 domestic servants (not counting chambermaids), of whom 4,000 were

lackeys. The number of foreigners living in Vienna was unusually high—about 25,000. These figures are from Pezzl, op. cit.

3. Private music ensembles were maintained at least on a temporary basis by Princes Batthyány, Esterházy, Grassalkovics, Liechtenstein, and Schwarzenberg, as well as several Counts Erdödy and Counts Batthyány, Chotek, and Harrach. We could also mention in this context the *Harmoniemusik* of Court Councillor Johann Gottlieb von Braun. Even after most of these groups had probably ceased to exist, Prince Lobkowitz founded a new ensemble and Prince Lichnowsky formed the famous string quartet led by Ignaz Schuppanzigh. It is probably safe to assume that new ensembles were established even as others were being disbanded, especially before 1800. These ensembles have not been thoroughly researched, so the list is surely not complete. The question naturally arises as to why Mozart never sought permanent employment among the Viennese nobility—a position similar to the one Haydn occupied in the household of Prince Esterházy. The opportunity was undoubtedly open to him. But Mozart had conditions for such employment that were not easily met. He expressed himself quite clearly on the matter in a letter to his father: "Now I'll tell you what I think about my prospects for a small permanent income. I have my eye here on three sources. The first is not certain, and even if it were, it would probably not be much; the second would be the best, but God knows whether it will ever come to pass; and the third is not to be despised, but the pity is that it concerns the future and not the present. The first is young Prince Liechtenstein, who would like to collect a wind instrument band (though he does not yet want it to be known), for which I would write the music. This would not bring in very much, it is true, but at least it would be something certain, and I would not sign the contract unless it were to be for life. The second (but in my estimation the first) is the emperor himself. Who knows? I intend to talk to Herr von Strack about it and I am certain he will do all he can, for he has proved to be a very good friend of mine— though indeed these court flunkeys are never to be trusted. The manner in which the emperor has spoken to me has given me some hope. Great lords do not like to hear these speeches, and, needless to say, they themselves do not make them; for they must always expect a stab in the back and are great adepts in avoiding it. The third is Archduke Maximilian. Of him I can say that he thinks the world of me. He shoves me forward on every occasion, and I could almost say with certainty that if at this moment he were elector of Cologne, I would be his kapellmeister. It is indeed a pity that these great gentlemen refuse to make arrangements beforehand. I could easily manage to extract a simple promise from him, but what use would that be to me now? Cash would be more acceptable" (January 23, 1782). A contract with Prince Liechtenstein never materialized, but Mozart probably received commissions from him; the emperor had no positions open, and it would be some time before Archduke Maximilian became elector of Cologne. It is intriguing to speculate what might have become of Mozart if he, instead of Joseph Reicha, had become music director at the Bonn court, which maintained one of the largest orchestras in German-speaking Europe. But Mozart thought of himself primarily as a piano virtuoso as far as performance was concerned, and he would have had to exchange this role for that of

a violinist-conductor. As a composer, he wanted most of all to find an opera house where he could realize his concept of music theater. The question is whether he would have accepted a contract like the one Haydn had with Prince Esterházy. For aside from the not overly generous financial arrangements, this contract contained a few stipulations that Mozart would have found difficult to tolerate. Haydn was considered a *Haus-Officier,* which meant that he was required to appear "always in uniform . . . in white stockings, white shirt, with hair powdered and either in a pigtail or otherwise bound, but always with a uniform appearance." Most important, he had to compose what was required of him and could not show his compositions to others, "much less have them copied, but rather compose exclusively for His Highness, and write nothing for anyone else without His Highness's prior knowledge and gracious consent." Especially unacceptable to Mozart, although perhaps less strenuously enforced, was the stipulation that Haydn "appear every morning and afternoon in the antechamber, have himself announced, and inquire whether there is to be any music." If music was required, it was Haydn's task to see that the musicians appeared on time. He also had administrative responsibilities, such as the purchase of instruments, music copying, filling vacant positions, even book-keeping. In the revised contract of 1779, Haydn was no longer entrusted with the duties of a subaltern, and his compositions were no longer designated the exclusive property of the prince. Still, Mozart would hardly have been gratified. With a salary of roughly 1,000 florins including emoluments (produce, firewood, etc.), Haydn was now entrusted with the organist's post in Eisenstadt, and was required to pay for a substitute in the event of his absence. See also chapter 3, note 26.

4. Still relevant in this regard is the monograph by Eduard Hanslick, *Geschichte des Concertwesens in Wien* (Vienna, 1869; reprint Farnborough, U.K., 1971). A good survey is *Musikgeschichte Österreichs,* ed. Rudolph Flotzinger and Gernot Gruber (Graz, Vienna, and Cologne, 1979), vol. 2: *Vom Barock zur Gegenwart,* Chapter 13.

5. The orchestras for these concerts often had 150 to 180 musicians. Since large-scale oratorios were often performed, there would have been a chorus of adequate dimensions in addition to the soloists.

6. This would not have been his first appearance before the emperor, for Joseph II had heard Mozart play a piano concerto four days earlier at a concert of the Tonkünstlersozietät. Mozart wanted to meet the emperor in the casual atmosphere of a salon, where the musicians had the opportunity to converse with the guests after the musical presentation.

7. Quoted in Alfred Orel, "Grafin Wilhelmine Thun," in *Mozart-Jahrbuch* (1954): 92f.

8. More significantly for music history, the eldest daughter, Elizabeth, later married the Russian ambassador in Vienna, Count Andreas Razumovsky, and her sister Christina married Prince Karl Lichnowsky, whom Mozart accompanied on a journey to Berlin. On these two marriages, see the excerpts from Count Zinzendorf's diary in *Wien von Maria Theresa bis zur Franzosenzeit,* selections from the diary of Count Karl Zinzendorf trans. and ed. Hans Wagner (Vienna, 1972), pp. 88f. Both

Razumovsky and Lichnowsky later played important roles as patrons of Beethoven, who was often a guest of Countess Thun and dedicated his Clarinet Trio op. 11 to her.

9. Forster's letters are found in Forster, op. cit.

10. Anna von Pufendorf, the wife of an imperial court commissioner, was an excellent singer. She sang the role of Ilia in an amateur performance of *Idomeneo* that Mozart conducted at the Palais Auersperg in March 1786. Her husband began his association with Mozart even earlier. In 1762, on the occasion of a concert in Vienna, he circulated copies of his poem "Auf den kleinen sechsjährigen Clavieristen aus Salzburg" ("On the Little Six-year-old Clavier Player from Salzburg").

11. Letter of May 13, 1788, to Count Orsini-Rosenberg, quoted in *Joseph II als Theaterdirektor*, op. cit., p. 74. The date given there—May 3—cannot be correct; perhaps it is the emperor's mistake. The *Don Giovanni* premiere reported on by Count Rosenberg was on May 7, so the emperor's reply could not have been written before May 13.

12. Quoted in ibid., p. 1.

13. There was also a financial side to this. Tickets to the Nationalsingspiel were no more expensive than ordinary theater tickets (for plays); in other words, prices were kept down by imperial subsidies. Admission to the Italian Hofoper was considerably higher. These differences had a pronounced effect on the social makeup of the audiences and were undoubtedly so intended.

5. VIENNA 1782–85

1. The Counts (later Princes) Lichnowsky were a noble family with estates on the Austrian-Prussian frontier and strong connections to the Berlin court. They had acquired their titles in Berlin, not at the Viennese court.

2. K. 386b/412 (and 514). Unfortunately this concerto is never played in accordance with Mozart's "stage directions," so we make note of them here. The Rondo is marked "allegro" for the orchestra and "adagio" for the soloist. Mozart wrote the following comments in the solo part: "A lei signor Asino—Animo—presto—sù via—da bravo—Coraggio—e finisci già—bestia—oh che stonatura—chi—oimè—bravo poveretto!—oh seccatura di coglioni!—ah che mi fai ridere!—ajuto—respira un poco!—avanti, avanti!—questo poi va al meglio—e non finici nemmeno?—ah porco infame!—oh come sei grazioso!—Carino! Asino!—ha ha ha—respira!—Ma intoni almeno una, pazzo—bravo evviva! e vieni a seccarmi per la quarta, e Dio sia benedetto per l'ultima volta—ah termina, ti prego!—ah maledetto—anche bravura? bravo—ah trillo di pecore—finisci? grazie al ciel! basta, basta!" These are jokes for Leutgeb: "Bravo, you poor thing!—how you make me laugh!—breathe a while—have you finished?—thank Heaven!" etc.

3. The following account is based on the only archival investigation into this matter, by Gustav Guglitz: "Zu einer Briefstelle Mozarts (Die Affaire Günther-Eskeles)," in *Mozarteums-Mitteilungen* (1921): 41ff. A biased and distorted synopsis is found in the commentary to letter no. 691 in *MBA* vol. 6, p. 118, where we read, "She ingratiated herself with Günther, became his . . . mistress, and bore him two

children. From Günther she managed to finagle political information that her contacts then sold to Berlin." The writer cites the essay by Guglitz yet somehow reaches exactly the opposite conclusion!

4. In Berlin Eleonore Eskeles sought rehabilitation, which was finally granted by Leopold II—who leveled harsh criticism at the judicial system in the process. It was only in 1802 that she returned to Vienna, where she founded one of the more intellectual salons. Later, in Karlsbad, she met Goethe, for whom, ironically, she obtained Mozart autographs from the composer's widow. Presumably she knew Constanze from those days in the Arnstein home more than thirty years before. She also seems to have had numerous contacts with Mozart's circle. For instance, she rented a box at the Nationaltheater with Baron Wetzlar von Plankenstern (Otto G. Schindler, "Das Publikum der josefinischen Ära," in *Das Burgtheater und sein Publikum: Festgabe zur 200-Jahr-Feier der Erhebung des Burgtheaters zum National-altheater*, ed. Margret Dietrich, Vienna, 1976, p. 79). Günther, for his part, had been a Freemason since 1779 and was designated no. 33 in the "Verzeichnis Sämmtlichen Brüdern und Mitgliedern der . . . Loge zur gekrönten Hofnung" for 1781 (VA 72, folios 265ff.).

5. The schedule for the "Italian" period from 1783 to Mozart's death shows that apart from the director of the theater, Antonio Salieri, only Vicente Martín y Soler had three premieres. Salieri naturally enjoyed pride of place in the repertoire because he was engaged to write for this opera house; he was represented by seven commissioned works. Besides Mozart, only two other composers with two commissions each appear on the schedule, while five composers received only one commission each during those nine years. Of the nine new productions each year, an average of two or three were new operas. It is also worth noting that Mozart received half again as much as the usual fee for *Don Giovanni*—although it was not a "world premiere"—and twice the usual fee for *Così fan tutte*.

6. Most of the many thousands of operas produced during the second half of the eighteenth century were so formulaic, boring, and uninspired that they could hardly be performed today, and this is surely due to the lack of reflection on relationships between theatrical and musical techniques.

7. Abert, op. cit., part 2, p. 34.

8. We know only that Constanze Mozart sang the soprano solo, which makes it conceivable that the work in question is the fragment of the Mass in C Minor. With a new text and several added movements, this fragment was transformed into the cantata *Davidde penitente* (K. 469)—a unique case that violated Mozart's entire conception of the relationship between text and music.

9. There appears to have been an equally long break after *Così fan tutte* (1790).

10. The weather conditions during this spring and summer are of interest in this connection. After a very cold winter there was heavy snowfall at the beginning and end of April, which caused floods. Then in mid-June it rained so much that the rivers overflowed their banks and did serious damage.

11. Lorenzo Da Ponte, *Geschichte meines Lebens: Memoiren eines Venezianers*, trans. and ed. Charlotte Birnbaum, foreword by Hermann Kesten (Tübingen, 1969), p. 102.

12. Lorenzo Da Ponte, *Memoiren des Mozart-Librettisten, galanten Liebhabers und Abenteurers* (Berlin, 1970), p. 125.

13. *Dokumente*, p. 208.

14. *Dokumente*, p. 209.

15. German translation by Josef Kainz, in Jürgen Petersen, *Die Hochzeit des Figaro. Deutung und Dokumentation* (Frankfurt and Berlin, 1965).

16. This had nothing to do with an imperial judgment on the success of the composition; if Joseph II ever did say, "Too beautiful for our ears, and an awful lot of notes, dear Mozart!" he was probably referring to *Figaro*, not *Die Entführung*.

17. Saul K. Padover's biography, for instance, is entitled *Joseph II: Ein Revolutionär auf dem Kaiserthron* (published in English as *The Revolutionary Emperor: Joseph II*); numerous other examples could be found.

18. The censoring of plays continued, however, because the theater had "such a strong influence on morals," though this does not mean that the theater would have been subjected to unusually rigid censorship. But the Burgtheater was something of a benchmark for the whole empire; any play performed there was deemed to have been "recommended," which necessitated special supervision by the censor.

19. "Nous n'héritons en naissant de nos parents que la vie animal, ainsi, roi, comte, bourgeois, paysan, il n'a pas la moindre différence. Ces dons de l'âme et de l'esprit, nous les tenons du créateur, les vices ou les qualités nous viennent par le bonne ou mauvaise éducation, et par les exemples que nous voyons." Memorandum by Joseph II on the state of the Austrian monarchy (late 1765), in *Maria Theresia und Joseph II: Ihre Correspondenz samt Briefen Joseph's an seinen Bruder Leopold*, ed. Alfred Ritter von Arneth (Vienna 1867–68), vol. 3, p. 353. Figaro did not express himself any more clearly in his diatribe against Count Almaviva.

20. Two centuries later, much university reform seems doomed to repeat the mistakes of those years.

6. MOZART AND FREEMASONRY

1. VA 71.

2. VA 68.

3. VA 68. Many such letters of application from well-known contemporaries like the writer Johann Pezzl have survived, along with written requests for promotion to a higher degree. No such documents from Mozart are to be found, however. In the secondary literature we read again and again that Mozart was introduced to Freemasonry by Baron Otto von Gemmingen, but there is no proof for this assertion; it is, in fact, most unlikely. Gemmingen was among the founders of the lodge Zur Wohltätigkeit but soon became dissatisfied with its activities, and he appears to have left Vienna in 1785.

4. Historisches Museum der Stadt Wien, inventory no. 47,927. Another oral source—no longer verifiable today—maintains that the lodge premises depicted here were located in the "Haus zu den 7 Schwertern" (House of the 7 Swords) at Schwertgasse 3. There have been many attempts to identify the men in this picture. Naturally, some claim to recognize Vienna's "most famous" Freemason, Wolfgang Mozart, in the right foreground. This suggestion is no more convincing than the very extensive cryptanalysis by H. C. Robbins Landon published in the catalogue for the exhibition *Zirkel und Winkelmass—200 Jahre Grosse Landesloge der Freimaurer* at the Historisches Museum (Vienna, 1984), pp. 25ff.; its historical premises are too easily called into question. As of 1787 the lodge premises in the Landskrongasse probably housed the lodges Zur Wahrheit (which absorbed Zur wahren Eintracht) and Zur neugekrönten Hoffnung (which emerged from Zur Wohltätigkeit).

5. VA 41, folios 299–318. This Master Ritual comes from the lodge Zu den drei gekrönten Säulen (Three Crowned Pillars) in Prague, which Mozart often visited. It is doubtless very similar to the ritual followed in his Viennese lodge.

6. In the lodge Zur neugekrönten Hoffnung alone there were five priests and canons. A systematic examination of all membership lists reveals that there were 45 churchmen (priests, monks, canons, etc.) in Viennese lodges during the Josephine decade. However, the documentary material is insufficient, and the lists are probably not complete. Moreover, churchmen may have occasionally concealed their membership to avoid conflicts with the Church authorities. See Franz Wehrl, "Der 'Neue Geist': Eine Untersuchung des Klerus in Wien von 1750–1790," in *Mitteilungen des österreichischen Staatsarchivs* 20 (Vienna, 1967): 55ff.

7. Reinhart Koselleck, *Kritik und Krise: Eine Studie zur Parthenogenese der bürgerlichen Welt*, 3d ed. (Frankfurt, 1979), pp. 52f.

8. VA 65, folios 1ff.

9. Forster, op. cit., letter of August 14, 1784.

10. When the Freemasonry Act (December 1785) threw the lodges into a state of crisis, everything—especially Born's efforts—collapsed like a house of cards. Perhaps the undertone of criticism was also aimed at Born; the secretary of the lodge in which he was Master spoke of a "democratic coexistence" among the lodges. Born's procedures are more reminiscent of a self-assured politician adept at pulling strings in secret than of a democratic-minded leader and educator.

11. At the "Lodge of Sorrows" held after Mozart's death, special mention was made of his charitable activities.

12. As, for example, in the letter of October 14, 1785.

13. The score of Mozart's cantata soon appeared in a lavish edition, the proceeds of which were intended "to benefit the poor." Only Mozart's name is given in full; everything else appears in abbreviations understood only by the initiated. The title reads, "*Die Maurerfreude*. A cantata sung on April 24, 1785, in honor of Hw. Br. B..n of the B. B. of the lodge zur G. H. at Vienna in the O....t. The text by B. P..n, the music by B. W. A. Mozart" (in deciphered form: ". . . in honor of our worthy

Brother Born, of the Brothers of the lodge Zur gekrönten Hoffnung at Vienna in the Orient. The text by Brother Petran . . ."). Franz Petran, incidentally, was a secular priest and Freemason.

14. There were also numerous societies, seemingly similar to lodges, that were pure shams, such as the Steinert lodge, or nothing more than drinking clubs, such as Zu den drei Schwarzen Katern (Three Black Cats). In other groups money was extracted from the members through various forms of mystification. The emperor undoubtedly knew of Count Thun's involvement with the Gablidonische Gesellschaft. There is even said to have been a very liberal women's lodge headed by a confidante of the emperor. So far we know very little about these "spurious" lodges, for historical research into Freemasonry has always been too restricted. The best source on this complex subject is still the rare and not easily accessible work by Gustav Brabbé, *Sub Rosa: Vertrauliche Mittheilungen aus dem maurerischen Leben unserer Grossväter* (Vienna, 1879). Here (p. 176) the number of Freemasons in Josephine Vienna is given as 10,000, but this is surely a misprint, with one zero too many; otherwise this work is extremely reliable.

15. *Journal für Freymaurer* 3 (1786): 204.

16. Ibid., pp. 212ff.

17. Lodge membership was rather expensive. In addition to the monthly fee of 1 florin there was an initiation fee of 50 florins, while promotion to the degrees of Fellow Craft and Master cost 20 and 35 florins respectively.

18. Forster, op. cit., letter of October 12, 1786.

19. Those who consider Born the model for Mozart's Sarastro, as many do, should consider Born's role in the dissolution of Zur Wahrheit at the infamous Kratter "auto-da-fé." See also chapter 6, n. 10.

20. Or did this Grotta plan perhaps originate after Joseph II's death? That would have been even more dangerous for Mozart, because one of Leopold II's major priorities was the reorganization of his secret police; the Habsburg empire was, after all, in shambles and threatening to fall apart when he came to power. In addition, the events of the French Revolution were setting a dangerous example.

21. The text is by Caterino Mazzolà (the librettist of Mozart's *La clemenza di Tito*), with help from his friend Lorenzo Da Ponte.

22. VA 41.

23. VA 41.

24. Act II, scene 28.

25. Act II, scene 1.

26. Act I, scenes 9 and 10.

27. Act I, scene 19.

28. Act II, scene 12. Those who see Ignaz von Born as the model for Sarastro would have to understand this aria as a critical allusion to "Kratter's auto-da-fé." Mozart's fellow Freemasons, at least, would have noticed the deep irony of this text.

29. Act I, scene 18.

30. Act II, scene 1.

31. Act II, scene 8.

32. Act II, scene 28.

33. Act II, scene 3.

34. Quoted in Brabbée, op. cit., p. 117f.

7. VIENNA 1786–1790

1. Especially regarding Joseph II's plans for centralization. One of the emperor's objectives was to persuade the elector of Bavaria—who had come from Mannheim and felt thoroughly out of place in Munich—to cede Bavaria to Austria in exchange for the Austrian Netherlands. For this plan to work, the duke of Pfalz-Zweibrücken, who was deeply in debt, also had to be won over, and the intention was to bribe him with an appropriate sum. Such an exchange would have given Joseph II enormous advantages, even in a purely geographical sense. He would no longer have to administer rebellious provinces remote from the rest of the empire, and at the same time he could expand his contiguous dominions to the west with the acquisition of Bavaria—a most favorable arrangement that must have alarmed a number of other European powers. In connection with such a South German–Austro-Hungarian empire, the *Fürstenbund* gained considerable importance. The *Fürstenbund* was a group of small, increasingly insignificant principalities that had formed a bulwark against two giant powers (Frederick II in Prussia and Joseph II in the south). It brought together the minor states that were eager for reform because of their poverty, such as the margravate of Baden, Sachsen-Weimar-Eisenach, and Sachsen-Coburg-Gotha. The duke of Weimar, whose most important minister was Goethe, functioned as something like executive secretary of this alliance. Goethe had a falling-out with the duke over this question and resigned from active service as privy councillor after his return from Italy in 1788. He correctly foresaw that the principalities were helpless against the great powers and that the *Fürstenbund* would only be a distraction from reforms necessary within the individual small states. When Joseph II acted on his plan to acquire Bavaria, the *Fürstenbund* saw an alliance with Prussia as its only hope. In the end, of course, the Austrian initiative came to nothing. On the other hand, many bourgeois intellectuals were prepared to trust Joseph II and thought a gradual introduction of his reforms would lead to a steady improvement in living conditions, social justice, and the end of aristocratic tyranny. Even the plan to acquire Bavaria found supporters, especially in the somewhat backward South German areas where the power of the Church was still unbroken. Plainly Leopold Mozart did not concern himself with trifling matters, but with the most important political questions of the time.

2. In printed copies of the *Constitutio Criminalis Theresiana* techniques of torture are graphically illustrated in thirty oversized fold-out engravings. Among the methods pictured are thumbscrews, the iron boot, fire, the rack, and treadmills.

3. His brother Leopold, grand duke of Tuscany, proved that other paths were being

pursued in the application of criminal law. In making his reforms Leopold consulted the most advanced jurists of his time. Under the influence of Cesare Beccaria, he not only abolished all crimes against the crown (which remained crimes in the rest of Europe until 1918) but also established the principle that punishment should be administered for purposes of rehabilitation, not as a deterrent or—worst of all—in retribution. (Although this idea has been introduced into most criminal codes today, it is by no means always implemented by the penal system.) Upon succeeding Joseph II as emperor (1790), Leopold abolished pulling boats and public flogging, but both, along with the death penalty, were reinstated by his son Francis and remained on the books in Austria until 1867. The "seventy-seven lashes" with which Sarastro punishes the Moor Monostatos in *Die Zauberflöte* (1791) are in keeping with the mixture of despotism, tyranny, and severity that Joseph II embodied, and they are symbolic of the penal system during *his* reign, not that of his successor.

4. Being broken "from the legs upward" meant that the bones were gradually broken from the feet to the head until death occurred; "from the head downward" was a form of mercy, since death occurred immediately.

5. Mozart witnessed several executions himself. And Leopold Mozart wrote laconically in a letter from Munich on February 22, not quite two weeks earlier, "This morning hundreds of people assembled outside the city gates to see the execution— a soldier was hanged for burglary, armed robbery, etc., etc."

6. Alfred Einstein, op. cit., p. 328; Hildesheimer, op. cit., p. 171.

7. Da Ponte, *Memoiren*, op. cit., pp. 126ff.

8. Kelly, op. cit., p. 130.

9. *Dokumente*, p. 240.

10. Anna Amalie Abert, *Die Opern Mozarts* (Wolfenbüttel and Zürich, 1970), p. 93.

11. *Dokumente*, pp. 243f.

12. Kelly, op. cit., p. 133.

13. *Dokumente*, p. 253.

14. Mozart has been accused of being so hardhearted that he did not even attend his father's funeral. This charge has only been made in the twentieth century, however, and ignores the fact that mail from Salzburg took at least three days. Leopold Mozart was already buried by the time his son learned of his death. Mozart could not have arrived in Salzburg for at least six or seven days. The funeral was attended by whatever friends and family were in town at the time.

15. *Dokumente*, p. 248.

16. The genesis of *Don Giovanni*, especially the overture, is surrounded by an impenetrable wall of legend, not a word of which has been substantiated, and which only contributes to a way of presenting Mozart that paints attractive scenes in spaces that should be left blank. Romantic retouchings and completions have already created more distortions than precise biographical research can put straight.

17. Da Ponte was called back to Vienna for the preparation of a Salieri opera—such

an unusual occurrence that we might easily imagine intrigue in Vienna. On the other hand, the delayed premiere was an inconvenience for everyone. Is it possible that Da Ponte's friend Giacomo Casanova stepped in as dramaturge? In any event, Casanova's literary remains contain the draft of a scene for *Don Giovanni*, and he himself was in Prague for the premiere.

18. *Dokumente*, p. 267.

19. "The delivery of [Gluck's] *De profundis* to Salieri for the emperor's collections corresponded to his wish, uttered in a premonition of death and indeed fulfilled, that the work should be performed as his requiem. This was general knowledge in both Vienna and Prague, and may, with Da Ponte's urging, have been the reason for Mozart's early return" (Schenk, op. cit., p. 513).

20. However, the return to Vienna may also have been due to the fact that Constanze Mozart was expecting another child, who was born on December 17. The Mozarts would naturally have wanted the child to be born at home.

21. *Dokumente*, p. 378.

22. An outline for another comedy by Mozart exists; it was to be called *Der salzburger Lump in Wien* ("A Salzburg Rogue in Vienna"). Both fragments appear in MBA, vol. 4.

23. *Dokumente*, pp. 310–13.

24. *Dokumente*, pp. 334f.

25. *Dokumente*, p. 335.

26. *Dokumente*, pp. 343f.

27. Significantly, the same objections have been raised against Alban Berg's *Lulu:* that it combines the salon, the circus ring, and the gutter with the highest artistic technique in a sacrilege against art.

28. Saul K. Padover, *Joseph II: Ein Revolutionär auf dem Kaiserthron* (Düsseldorf and Köln, 1969), p. 270.

29. Paul von Mitrofanow, *Joseph II: Seine politische und kulturelle Tätigkeit* (Vienna and Leipzig, 1910), p. 222.

30. The most heavily censored institution was the Church, which brought out a steady stream of anti-Enlightenment tracts, prayer booklets, and devotional writings. Baron van Swieten undertook a comprehensive reform of higher education, introducing more "academic" procedures and regular examinations—in total contrast to the somewhat later university reforms of Baron von Humboldt. Swieten did not have in mind the liberally educated university graduate but rather one who had been intensively trained in a single practical discipline. Accordingly, academic freedom for professors and students was not a primary objective for this "enlightened" rationalist.

31. Swieten was completely staggered by his loss of power and withdrew into embittered private life. He continued to play a part in musical affairs, however. He prepared the libretti for Joseph Haydn's *Die Schöpfung (The Creation)* and *Die*

Jahreszeiten (The Seasons), and exercised considerable influence over the musical form of these two very successful oratorios.

32. The adaptations included small cuts and omissions. Mozart's arrangements have been much abused, but it must be remembered that today hardly any of Mozart's operas are performed complete with all spoken and sung texts and with no adaptations, that no play of Goethe's time would be successful with today's audiences in its original form, and that not even Rembrandt's paintings are preserved in their original luminosity but are darkened by centuries-old varnish; even the Greek temples were once painted in bright colors. In view of our casual attitude toward historical authenticity, we have no reason to cavil at Mozart's attempt to make these works approachable for his contemporaries, who found such music outmoded.

33. Georg August Griesinger, *Biographische Notiz über Joseph Haydn* (reprint, Leipzig, 1975), p. 51.

34. Mozart research has tended to blame Swieten for abandoning Constanze after Mozart's sudden death. This accusation is refuted by the fact that Swieten and his Society of Associated Cavaliers mounted the first performance of the Requiem (K. 626), which brought in 1,300 florins for the widow and her children. The aristocratic circle that later financed Haydn's *Die Schöpfung* and *Die Jahreszeiten* (1798ff.) was partly a continuation of the Cavaliers Society. It is also possible that some of the Hungarian nobles who offered Mozart a pension of 1,000 florins shortly before his death (*Dokumente*, p. 372) were among the members of this society. Later, Beethoven lived on such a life annuity from members of the nobility.

35. K. 543, dated June 26, 1788; K. 550, July 25; and K. 551, August 10.

36. "Subscriptions can be purchased daily from Herr Puchberg at the Sallinzische Niederlagshandlung on the Hoher Markt, where the work itself will be available as of July 1st" (*Dokumente*, p. 274). There was apparently little response, for on June 23 Mozart put another notice in the *Wiener Zeitung:* "As the number of subscribers is still very small, I am compelled to delay the publication of my 3 quintets until January 1st, 1789" (*Dokumente*, p. 280). It is not known if this edition ever appeared; in any event, no copy has yet been found.

37. Joseph Heinz Eibl, *MBA*, commentary to letter no. 1,076.

38. *Dokumente*, p. 372.

39. *Dokumente*, p. 298.

40. The fee for the commissioned works, which Mozart planned to have printed at his own expense, would be paid on receipt of the dedicatory copies, as indicated in a letter to Puchberg (July 14, 1789).

41. The opera was *Così fan tutte*. The requested loan of 500 florins is thus easy to explain, for the usual opera fee was 100 ducats (450 florins), paid after the premiere. Until then, according to Mozart's plan, he would pay 10 florins on the debt each month. Puchberg had indeed nothing to lose.

42. Hildesheimer, op. cit., pp. 271, 253.

43. Every Mozart biography concludes from this remark that the composer had lost

his public in Vienna; this seems to me a very arbitrary interpretation. No other city in Europe—except Paris and London—had such an active musical life. In some cases, however, one could earn more money in Paris or London. Mozart must surely have known that Salieri, for example, had earned almost 5,000 florins in Paris for a single opera (*Les Danaïdes*, 1784)—a sum totally unheard-of in Vienna.

44. *Dokumente*, p. 346.

45. Quoted in Schurig, op. cit., p. 302.

46. Ibid., p. 296.

47. In a linguistic sense virtually all the German translations are indescribably bad. They utilize an affected operatic language that reduces the jarring clarity of the Italian original to incomprehensible nonsense—especially when applied to the opera's many sexual innuendos.

48. Act I, scene 13.

49. Act II, scene 13.

50. Act II, scene 1.

51. Act II, scene 2.

52. Act II, scene 6.

53. Quoted in Ernst Wangermann, *Von Joseph II zu den Jakobinerprozessen* (Vienna, 1966), p. 47f.

54. The manuscript is full of canceled passages, and the conclusion is illegible.

55. It remains unclear why Mozart had to incur further debts so soon after receiving his fee for *Così fan tutte* (900 florins) and his quarterly salary (200 florins).

56. July 28, 1790, quoted in Angermüller, op. cit., part 3, p. 58.

57. Mozart research has been able to add very little to his own list of works composed during these months: a few small piano pieces and a comic duet (K. 592a/625).

58. Joseph Heinz Eibl, *Wolfgang Amadeus Mozart: Chronik seines Lebens*, 2d ed. (Munich, 1977), p. 106.

59. Griesinger, op. cit., p. 51.

60. Georg Nikolaus Nissen, *Biographie W. A. Mozarts* (reprint, Hildesheim and New York, 1972), p. 683.

61. *MBA*, vol. 6, p. 399.

62. *Wahl and Krönung Leopolds II, 1790: Brieftagebuch des Feldschers der kursächsischen Schweizergarde*, ed. Erna Berger and Konrad Bund (Frankfurt, 1981), p. 63.

63. Ibid., p. 55.

64. The name *Coronation* Concerto is indeed inappropriate. The work was not written for this occasion but was completed as early as February 1788, and the performance had little to do with the coronation beyond temporal proximity.

8. THE LAST YEAR

1. She was called "La Ferrarese"; in *Cosi fan tutte* she sang the role of Fiordiligi, one of the "ladies of Ferrara."

2. If Peter Shaffer had taken Salieri's voluntary resignation into account, it would have demolished the entire dramatic structure of his play—which is in any case based on pure fantasy. Why would a fatal rivalry between Mozart and Salieri develop during the very year in which they both succumbed before the new emperor?

3. Since July 1790: a string quintet (K. 593, December 1790), the last piano concerto (K. 595, January 5, 1791), the last string quintet (K. 614, April 12, 1791); and three short occasional pieces, a bass aria (K. 612), numerous dances for the *Fasching* balls, and three songs.

4. It cannot be firmly established when Karl Mozart was enrolled in boarding school. In the commentary to Mozart's letters the year 1787 is frequently given, but that is probably too early: the letters indicate that Karl was still at home in the spring of 1789 while his father was in Berlin, but apparently was no longer there at the time of Mozart's journey to Frankfurt in September 1790.

5. *Wiener Zeitung*, September 14, 1791.

6. *Wiener Zeitung*, June 6, 1789.

7. Fifteen months later Mozart brought out his *Figaro*, this time with the emperor's active interest. The publication of Johann Rautenstrauch's translation was not forbidden.

8. Quoted in Blümml, op. cit., pp. 128f.

9. Abert, op. cit., part 2, pp. 582f.

10. *Dokumente*, 475.

11. *Dokumente*, 471.

12. "I am writing this letter in a small room in Leitgeb's garden, where I slept very well last night. And I hope that my dear wife slept as well as I did. I will stay here tonight as well, for I sent Leonore home and would be completely alone in the house, which is not pleasant" (June 6, 1791; original in French).

13. The play that is always cited in support of this theory is *Kaspar, der Fagottist, oder Die Zauberzither* by Wenzel Müller (text by Joachim Perinet), first performed on June 8 at the Leopoldstadt Theater. Mozart attended a performance three days later and wrote to his wife, "To cheer myself up I went to the Kasperle Theatre to see the new opera *Der Fagottist*, which is making such a sensation, but which is shoddy stuff" (June 12, 1791). Mozart would certainly have had more to say if this opera had necessitated changes in *Die Zauberflöte*.

14. "Madame Leutgeb has laundered my necktie today, but you should see it— good God! I kept telling her, *'Do let me show you how my wife does them!'*—but it was no use (June 6, 1791). He had, after all, sent the maid home.

15. The two names can only be surmised, for Georg von Nissen later rendered them

illegible. Most commentators, however, consider Leutgeb and Süssmayer the most likely targets of this Mozartian derision.

16. Just after Sarastro's aria "*In diesen heil'gen Hallen*" the stage is "transformed into a hall where a balloon can ascend. The balloon is decorated with roses and other flowers" (*Zauberflöte* libretto, scene change for act II, scene 13).

17. It is frequently assumed that this contract was for a version of *Tito*, an assertion neither verifiable nor probable. Guardasoni worked at his own risk and sought crowd-pleasers rather than the formal *seria* operas with their pronounced courtly character. The success of *Don Giovanni* in Prague would point to an *opera buffa* in the broadest sense.

18. Castrati were a common feature of the courtly *opera seria*, though by the end of the eighteenth century this theatrical absurdity was generally ridiculed. Since there are no more castrati today, the absurdity is heightened by having these male roles sung by women. Would not the transposition of soprano roles into the tenor range do less harm to music theater than disguising them as *Hosenrollen* (trouser roles)? Mozart himself was anything but an advocate of castrati, being deeply concerned about theatrical plausibility. In today's opera houses we should do him the honor of not casting these characters as *Hosenrollen*, which in the eighteenth century were tolerated only for subsidiary parts.

19. From today's standpoint we are not sure which is more astounding: that Constanze Mozart embarked on a three-day coach journey so soon after her delivery or that she so unhesitatingly left the newborn in the care of a wet nurse. Her concern for the child was clearly exceeded by her reluctance to be separated from Mozart for three weeks.

20. Helga Lühning has impressively documented how legends about Mozart developed: "The composer 'became sickly and required medication' (Niemetschek, first edition); Jahn explains this as the result of overwork. Niemetschek himself, however, had added in the second edition of his biography (1808): 'On bidding farewell to his circle of friends he became so melancholy that he wept. A premonition of his approaching death appeared to have brought on the melancholia—for he already bore within him the seed of the illness which soon carried him off.' Despite the fact that after his return from Prague Mozart wrote the last part of *Die Zauberflöte*, the Clarinet Concerto, and the greater part of the Requiem, most biographies mention this 'mortal illness' exclusively in connection with *Tito*. Moreover, the illness is overemphasized in a manner that cannot be justified on the strength of Niemetschek's account, as in Hermann Abert's assertion: '*Mozart was already a very sick man when he traveled to Prague for Tito, . . .*' or that of Haas: '*. . . in July [sic!] Mozart was already in a state of psychological exhaustion which made the completion of Die Zauberflöte impossible* [?]. *The next few months were a terrible trial for the mortally ill man,*' etc. A report in the 1791 *Krönungsjournal für Prag*, only lately rediscovered, is probably closer to the truth. There we read regarding *Tito*: 'The music is by the famous Mozart, and does honor to his name even though he was given little time to write it and in addition became ill while completing the final part' "

(Helga Lühning, "Zur Entstehungsgeschichte von Mozarts *Titus*," in *Die Musik-forschung* 27, 1974: 302f.).

21. After Da Ponte's dismissal Mazzolà was engaged for three months as librettist in Vienna. This appointment was criticized by the court: "The engagement of the Dresden court poet Mazzoli [*sic*] is wasteful and unnecessary, because during these few months nothing but older operas are being given and the theater can get along nicely without a librettist" (quoted in Lühning, op. cit., p. 308, n. 39).

22. Quoted in Tomislav Volek, "Über den Ursprung von Mozarts Oper *La clemenza di Tito*," in *Mozart-Jahrbuch* (1959): 284.

23. Ibid.

24. It is entirely possible (and in view of the subject matter, more likely) that the empress shouted the much-quoted phrase "*una porcheria tedesca*" from her box during a performance of *Don Giovanni*. The sources for the remark are so unreliable that this suggestion cannot be rejected out of hand. See also Joseph Heinz Eibl in *Österreichische Musikzeitschrift* 31:329ff.

25. *Dokumente*, p. 524.

26. Viennese performance statistics from 1879 clearly document these shifts. In the preceding 90 years *Tito* had been given just as often as the much maligned (and "adapted") *Così fan tutte* (75 times), while *Figaro* had 331 performances and *Don Giovanni* had 476 at the Hoftheater and a further 180 in suburban theaters (!). *Die Zauberflöte* apparently enjoyed the greatest success, with 354 performances at the Hoftheater and 376 in Viennese suburban theaters. See *Urtheile bedeutender Dichter, Philosophen und Musiker über Mozart*, comp. and ed. Karl Prieger, 2d ed. (Wiesbaden, 1886), p. 10.

27. *Dokumente*, p. 358.

28. *Briefe von Goethes Mutter an ihren Sohn, Christiane und August von Goethe* (Weimar, 1889), pp. 28f. She mentions the "apes" again four months later (p. 45). By today's standards 100 carolins would be the inconceivable sum of roughly $22,000.

29. Quoted in *Josephinische Couriosa oder ganz besondere, theils nicht mehr, theils noch nicht bekannte Persönlichkeiten, Geheimnisse, Details, Actenstücke und Denk-würdigkeiten der Lebens- und Zeitgeschichte Kaiser Josephs II*, ed. Franz Gräffner, 5 vols. (Vienna 1848–50), vol. 3, pp. 182f.

30. All six stanzas appear in *Gedichte und Lieder deutscher Jakobiner*, ed. Hans Werner Engels (Stuttgart, 1971), pp. 101f.

31. Quoted in Emil Karl Blümml, "Ausdeutungen der *Zauberflöte*," *Mozart-Jahrbuch* (1923): 116f., 119f.

32. Franz Xaver Niemetschek, *Ich kannte Mozart: Die einzige Mozart-Biographie von einem Augenzeugen*, ed. Jost Perfahl (reprint, Munich, 1984), pp. 32ff.

33. Letter of October 1, 1826, to the publisher André, *MBA*, vol. 6, p. 515.

34. *Dokumente*, p. 409.

35. Nissen, op. cit., p. 572.

36. Letter to Nissen, April 7, 1825, *MBA*, vol. 4.

37. The recollections of a porter who knew Mozart, written down thirty years after the porter's death and more than sixty years after Mozart's; published in *Dokumente*, pp. 477–79.

38. Letter to Nissen, April 7, 1825, *MBA*, vol. 4.

39. *Dokumente*, p. 460.

40. Being absent from a funeral was apparently not so unusual. Constanze's brother-in-law Joseph Lange lost his first wife in 1779 and on the day of her burial fled with other family members beyond the city gates, where he still felt pursued by the funeral knell. See Lange, *Biographie* (Vienna, 1808), p. 106.

41. *Dokumente*, p. 369.

42. Quoted in *Frankfurter Rundschau*, May 18, 1983.

43. *Dokumente*, p. 380.

44. Niemetschek, op. cit., p. 34.

45. *Dokumente*, p. 452.

46. Quoted in Angermüller, op. cit., part 3/1, p. 338.

47. *Frankfurter Rundschau*, May 18, 1983.

48. Mathilde Ludendorff, *Mozarts Leben und gewaltsamer Tod* (Munich, 1936), p. 146.

49. Ibid., p. 144.

50. Ibid., p. 147. According to Ludendorff, Gotthold Ephraim Lessing was also murdered by lodge brothers because he betrayed Masonic secrets, and she made the same assertion about many other German intellectual heroes. As we can see, the deaths of these prominent figures have been put to all sorts of uses, even to justify nationalist and racist fanaticism.

51. Carl Bär, *Mozart: Krankheit, Tod, Begräbnis*, 2d ed. (Salzburg, 1972), p. 40 (emphasis in the original).

52. Ibid., p. 106 (emphasis in the original). Bär adds: "From the standpoint of today's medical experience, the following objection can be anticipated: an attack of rheumatic fever resulting in death, after an interval of possibly twenty-five years, is improbable; such cases are hardly known." Bär attempts to invalidate this objection, yet oddly enough, he does not refer to Mozart's illnesses of the previous ten years, at least some of which can be conclusively diagnosed as rheumatic conditions. On August 23, 1784, after a sudden change of weather, Mozart contracted an infection that was described thus by Leopold Mozart (with the help of a direct quote from one of Mozart's letters): "My son has been very ill in Vienna. At a performance of Paisiello's new opera he perspired so profusely that his clothes were drenched and in the cold night air he had to try to find his servant who had his overcoat, as in the meantime an order had been given that no servant was to be allowed into the theater by the ordinary entrance. So not only my son but a number of other people caught rheumatic fever, which became septic when not taken in hand at once. My son writes

as follows: 'Four days running at the very same hour I had a fearful attack of colic, which ended each time in violent vomiting. I have therefore to be extremely careful. My doctor is Sigmund Barisani, who since his arrival in Vienna has been almost daily at my rooms. People here praise him very highly. He is very clever too, and you will find that in a short time he will make his way" (September 14, 1784). Bär writes that the usual treatment included emetics, which were apparently administered in this case as well. More ambiguous is a letter in which Mozart described himself as "afflicted with acute headache and stomach cramps" (January 14, 1786). At the beginning of May 1790 he complained of bad "head- and toothaches," which conform exactly to the symptoms of his mortal illness. His susceptibility is also noted in a letter of August 14, 1790: "I could not sleep all night for pain. I must have got overheated yesterday from walking so much and then caught a chill without knowing it." Thus we can assume that there were frequent recurrences of these symptoms, which may indicate rheumatic phases at relatively short intervals.

53. Bär, op. cit., p. 70.

54. Ibid., p. 118.

55. *Vollständige Sammlung aller seit dem glorreichen Regierungsantritt Joseph des Zweyten für die k. k. Erbländer ergangenen höchsten Verordnungen und Gesetze . . .* , 7 vols. (Vienna, 1788–89), no. 496, for 1784.

56. Quoted in Blümml, *Aus Mozarts Freundes- und Familienkreis*, pp. 46f. Anna Maria Schindler was the first wife of Mozart's brother-in-law Joseph Lange; she died in 1779.

57. The funeral of Mozart's sister-in-law Josepha Hofer in 1819 cost 230 florins, although it was by no means in the luxury class (Blümml, ibid.).

58. Bär, op. cit., p. 127ff.

59. Ibid., p. 155.

60. Ibid.

61. Several reusable coffins from the Josephine period have been preserved; one is in display in the Wiener Bestattungsmuseum.

62. *Dokumente*, p. 494. The actual expenditure for Mozart's burial was several times the minimum cost of a simple interment.

63. Nissen, op. cit., p. 576.

64. The last entry before Mozart in the register of deaths at St. Stephen's was one for such a "gratis" burial.

65. No. 9, pp. 90ff., quoted in *Mozarteums-Mitteilungen* (1920), pp. 97ff.

66. Quoted in ibid., pp. 100f.

67. *Dokumente*, Appendix II (*Die Akten des Nachlasses Mozarts*), pp. 500f., 494.

68. *Dokumente*, pp. 375f.

BIBLIOGRAPHY

This bibliography lists only those sources that I have quoted or that deal with important aspects of this book. A more exhaustive list would have been unwieldy, and further literature can easily be found in comprehensive bibliographies.

The following libraries responded generously to my inquiries and requests for material; without their assistance a historical work of this scope would have been impossible: Universitätsbibliothek, Freiburg; Musikwissenschaftliches Seminar der Universität Freiburg; Haus-, Hof- und Staatsarchiv, Vienna; Österreichische Nationalbibliothek, Vienna (and its music and theater collections); Universitätsbibliothek, Vienna; Vienna Stadt- und Landesbibliothek; Vienna Stadt- und Landesarchiv; Staatsbibliothek, West Berlin. I owe a great debt of gratitude to the men and women of these institutions.

UNPUBLISHED SOURCES

Haus-, Hof- und Staatsarchiv, Vienna

VA 40   Letters of Lorenzo Da Ponte
        Files on the Illuminati
VA 41   The lodge Zur neugekrönten Hoffnung and the French Revolution
        Master ritual of the lodge Zu den 3 Säulen in Prague
VA 60   Lodge initiation certificate
        Masonic correspondence
VA 65   Lodge regulations
        Correspondence of provincial lodges and the lodge Zur Wahrheit
VA 68   Certificate of the lodge Zur neugekrönten Hoffnung
        Correspondence, invoices, receipts, membership dues for various lodges
VA 70   Miscellaneous items relating to the lodge Zur Wohltätigkeit
VA 72   Lodge membership lists

VA 74   Lodge membership lists
        Lodge paraphernalia of Baron von Lehrbach
VA 77   Protocol and attendance register for the lodge Zur Wahrheit
VA 78   Financial records for the lodge Zur Wahrheit

Diaries of Count Karl Zinzendorf, 1780–91

GENERAL HISTORY OF MUSIC

Musik in Geschichte und Gegenwart: Allgemeine Enzyklopädie der Musik. Edited by Friedrich Blume. 14 vols. with 2 supplements. Kassel, etc., 1949–79.

Angermüller, Rudolph. "Die entpolitisierte Oper am Wiener und am Esterházyschen Hof." *Das Haydn-Jahrbuch* 10 (Eisenstadt, 1978): 5–22.

Angermüller, Rudolph. *Antonio Salieri: Sein Leben und seine weltlichen Werke unter besonderer Berücksichtigung seiner grossen Opern.* Parts 1, 2/1, and 3. Munich, 1971–74. Schriften zur Musik vols. 16, 17, 19.

Bernhardt, Reinhold. "Aus der Umwelt der Wiener Klassiker: Gottfried van Swieten (1734–1803)." *Der Bär: Jahrbuch von Breitkopf und Haertel* (Leipzig, 1929–30): 74–166.

Biba, Otto. "Grundzüge des Konzertwesens in Wien zu Mozarts Zeit." *Mozart-Jahrbuch* (1978–79): 132–43.

Da Ponte, Lorenzo. *Memoiren des Mozart-Librettisten, galanten Liebhabers und Abenteurers.* Berlin, 1970.

Da Ponte, Lorenzo. *Geschichte meines Lebens: Memoiren eines Venezianers.* Tübingen, 1969.

Eibl, Joseph Heinz. "Ein 'ächter' Bruder. Mozart und Puchberg." *Acta Mozartiana* 26 (1979): 41–46.

Flotzinger, Rudolf, and Gruber, Gernot, eds. *Musikgeschichte Österreichs.* Vol. 2, *Vom Barock zur Gegenwart.* Graz, Vienna, Cologne, 1979.

Griesinger, Georg August. *Biographische Notizen über Joseph Haydn.* Reprint. Leipzig, 1975.

Haas, Robert. Introduction to Ignaz Umlauf, *Die Bergknappen. Denkmäler der Tonkunst in Österreich,* vol. 36.

Hanslick, Eduard. *Geschichte des Konzertwesens in Wien.* 2 vols. Vienna, 1869. Reprint. Farnborough, 1971.

Haydn, Joseph. *Gesammelte Briefe und Aufzeichnungen.* Edited and with commentary by Dénes Bartha using source material from the collection of H. C. Robbins Landon. Kassel, etc., 1965.

Honolka, Kurt. *Papageno: Emanuel Schikaneder, Der Grosse Theatermann der Mozart-Zeit.* Salzburg and Vienna, 1984.

Kelly, Michael. *Reminiscences.* London, 1975.

Kobald, Karl. *Alt-Wiener Misikstätten.* Zürich, Leipzig, Vienna, 1919.

Komorzynski, Egon. *Der Vater der Zauberflöte Emanuel Schikaneder.* Vienna, 1948.

Komorzynski, Egon. *Emanuel Schickaneder: Ein Beitrag zur Geschichte des deutschen Theaters*. Vienna, 1951.

Mahling, Christoph Hellmut. "Herkunft und Sozialstatus des höfischen Orchestermusikers im 18. und frühen 19. Jahrhundert in Deutschland." In *Der Sozialstatus des Berufsmusikers vom 17. bis 19. Jahrhundert: Gesammelte Beiträge*, edited by Walter Salmen for the Gesellschaft für Musikforschung, pp. 103–36. Kassel, etc., 1971.

Meier, Adolf. "Die Pressburger Hofkapelle des Fürstprimas von Ungarn, Fürst Josef von Batthyany, in den Jahren 1776–1784." *Das Haydn-Jahrbuch* 10 (Eisenstadt, 1978): 81–89.

Michtner, Otto. "Der Fall Abbé da Ponte." In *Mitteilungen des Österreichischen Staatsarchivs*, vol. 19, pp. 170–209.

Michtner, Otto. *Das alte Burgtheater als Opernbühne von der Einführung des deutschen Singspiels (1778) bis zum Tod Kaiser Leopold II (1792)*. Akademie der Wissenschaften, Theatergeschichte Österreichs, vol. 3/1. Vienna, Cologne, Graz, 1970.

Morath, Anton. "Die Pflege der Tonkunst durch das Fürstenhaus Schwarzenberg im achtzehnten und zum Beginne des neunzehnten Jahrhunderts." *Das Vaterland: Zeitung für das Österreichische Monarchie* 42, no. 68 (March 10, 1901).

Myslík, Antonín. "Repertoire und Besetzung der Harmoniemusiken an den Höfen Schwarzenberg, Pachta und Clam-Gallas." *Das Haydn-Jahrbuch* 10 (Eisenstadt, 1978): 110–20.

Petzold, Richard. "Die soziale Lage des Musikers im 18. Jahrhundert." In *Der Sozialstatus des Berufsmusikers vom 17. bis 19. Jahrhundert: Gesammelte Beiträge*, edited by Walter Salmen for the Gesellschaft für Musikforschung, pp. 64–82. Kassel, etc., 1971.

Schönfeld, Johann Ferdinand von. *Jahrbuch der Tonkunst von Wien und Prag*. Vienna, 1796. Facsimile reprint with an introduction and index by Otto Biba. Munich and Salzburg, 1976.

Schreiber, Ottmar. *Orchester und Orchester-Praxis in Deutschland zwischen 1780 und 1850*. Dissertation. Berlin, 1938.

Stadtlaender, Chris. *Joseph Haydns Sinfonia Domestica: Eine Dokumentation*. Munich, 1963.

Stekl, Hannes. "Harmoniemusik und 'türkische Banda' des Fürstenhauses Liechtenstein." *Das Haydn-Jahrbuch* 10 (Eisenstadt, 1978): 164–75.

Tank, Ulrich. *Studien zur Esterházyschen Hofmusik von 1620 bis 1790*. Regensburg, 1981. Kölner Beiträge zur Musikforschung vol. 101.

MOZART

"Mozart-Bibliographie (bis 1970)." Compiled by Rudolph Angermüller and Otto Schneider. In *Mozart-Jahrbuch* (1975, supplement).

Mozart-Bibliographie 1971–1975 mit Nachträgen zur Mozart-Bibliographie bis

1970. Compiled by Rudolph Angermüller and Otto Schneider. Kassel, etc., 1978.

Mozart-Bibliographie 1976–1980 mit Nachträgen zur Mozart-Bibliographie bis 1975. Compiled by Rudolph Angermüller and Otto Schneider. Kassel, etc., 1982.

Mozarteums-Mitteilungen. Edited for the Mozarteum by Rudolf Lewicki, 1919ff.

Mozart-Jahrbuch of the Zentralinstitut für Mozartforschung der ISM. Salzburg, 1950ff.

Acta Mozartiana. Augsburg, 1954ff.

Mozart, Wolfgang Amadeus. *Neue Ausgabe sämtlicher Werke*. Edited by the Internationale Stiftung Mozarteum, Salzburg, in cooperation with the Mozart cities Augsburg, Salzburg, and Vienna.

Mozart, Wolfgang Amadeus. *Briefe und Aufzeichnungen*. Complete edition published by the Internationale Stiftung Mozarteum, Salzburg, and edited by Wilhelm Bauer and Otto Erich Deutsch. Vols. 1–4, text; vols. 5–6, commentary prepared by Joseph Heinz Eibl; vol. 7, index compiled by Joseph Heinz Eibl. Kassel, etc., 1962–75. Supplemental commentary prepared by Joseph Heinz Eibl, *Mozart-Jahrbuch* (1976–77): 289–302. Supplemental commentary (2) prepared by Joseph Heinz Eibl, *Mozart-Jahrbuch* (1980–83): 318–52.

Mozart, Wolfgang Amadeus, *Verzeichnis aller meiner Werke*; and Mozart, Leopold, *Verzeichnis der Jugendwerke W. A. Mozarts*. Edited by E. H. Mueller von Askow. Facsimile edition. Vienna and Wiesbaden, 1956.

Mozart und seine Welt in zeitgenössischen Bildern. Edited by Maximilian Zenger and Otto Erich Deutsch. Kassel, etc., 1961. *NAW* vol. 10, supplement 32.

Deutsch, Otto Erich ed. *Mozart: Die Dokumente seines Lebens*. Kassel, etc., 1961. *NAW* vol. 10, supplement 34.

Mozart: Die Dokumente seines Lebens. Addenda und Corrigenda. Kassel, etc., 1978. *NAW* vol. 10, supplement 31/1.

Mozart, Wolfgang Amadeus. *Die Entführung aus dem Serail: Texte, Materialien, Kommentare*. Edited by Attila Csampai and Dietmar Holland. Reinbek, 1983. Rororo 7757.

Mozart, Wolfgang Amadeus. *Die Hochzeit des Figaro: Texte, Materialien, Kommentare*. Edited by Attila Csampai and Dietmar Holland. Reinbek, 1982. Rororo 7667.

Mozart, Wolfgang Amadeus. *Don Giovanni: Texte, Materialien, Kommentare*. Edited by Attila Csampai and Dietmar Holland. Reinbek, 1981. Rororo 7329.

Mozart, Wolfgang Amadeus. *Così fan tutte: Texte, Materialien, Kommentare*. Edited by Attila Csampai and Dietmar Holland. Reinbek, 1984. Rororo 7823.

Mozart, Wolfgang Amadeus. *Die Zauberflöte: Texte, Materialien, Kommentare*. Edited by Attila Csampai and Dietmar Holland. Reinbek, 1982. Rororo 7476.

Köchel, Ludwig von. *Chronologisch-thematisches Verzeichnis sämtlicher Tonwerke Wolfgang Amadé Mozarts*. 7th edition. Prepared by Franz Giegling, Alexander Weinmann, and Gerd Sievers. Wiesbaden, 1965.

Abert, Hermann. *W. A. Mozart: Neubearbeitete und erweiterte Ausgabe von Otto Jahns Mozart*, 2 vols. 9th ed. Leipzig, 1978.

Eibl, Joseph Heinz. *Wolfgang Amadeus Mozart: Chronik eines Lebens*. New ed. Munich, 1977. Dtv 1267.

Einstein, Alfred. *Mozart: Sein Charakter, Sein Werk*. New ed. Frankfurt a. M., 1968. English translation, New York, 1945.

Hildesheimer, Wolfgang. *Mozart*. Frankfurt a. M., 1977. English translation, New York, 1982.

Hutchings, Arthur. *Mozart der Mensch*. Baarn, Netherlands, 1976.

Hutchings, Arthur. *Mozart der Musiker*. Baarn, Netherlands, 1976.

Jahn, Otto. *Mozart*. 2 vols. 2d ed. Leipzig, 1867.

Levey, Michael. *The Life and Death of Mozart*. London, 1971.

Ludendorff, Mathilde. *Mozarts Leben und gewaltsamer Tod*. Munich, 1936.

Niemetschek, Franz Xaver. *Ich kannte Mozart: Die einzige Mozart-Biographie von einem Augenzeugen*. Edited by Jost Perfahl. Facsimile reprint of the first edition, 1798. Munich, 1984.

Nissen, Georg Nikolaus von. *Biographie W. A. Mozart's*. "Nach Originalbriefen, Sammlungen alles über ihn Geschriebenen, mit vielen neuen Beylagen, Steindrücken, Musikblättern und einem Facsimile. Herausgegeben von Constanze, Wittwe von Nissen, früher Wittwe Mozart." Leipzig, 1828. Facsimile reprint. Hildesheim and New York, 1972.

Paumgartner, Bernard. *Mozart*. 5th ed. Zürich and Freiberg, 1957.

Schenk, Erich. *Mozart: Eine Biographie*. New ed. Munich and Mainz, 1977. Goldmann Schott 33102.

Schurig, Arthur. *Wolfgang Amadé Mozart: Sein Leben, seine Persönlichkeit, sein Werk*. 2 vols. 2d ed. Leipzig, 1923.

Schurig, Arthur, ed. *Konstanze Mozart: Briefe, Aufzeichnungen, Dokumente 1782–1842*. "For the Mozarteum, Salzburg, with a biographical essay." Dresden, 1922.

Wegele, Ludwig, *Leopold Mozart: Bild einer Persönlichkeit*. For the Mozartgesellschaft." Augsburg, 1969.

Angermüller, Rudolph. *W. A. Mozarts musikalische Umwelt in Paris (1778): Eine Dokumentation*. Munich and Salzburg, 1982.

Bär, Carl. *Mozart: Krankheit, Tod, Begräbnis*. 2d ed., expanded. Salzburg, 1972. Schriftenreihe der ISM, vol. 1.

Bär, Carl. " 'Er war kein guter Wirth': Eine Studie über Mozarts Verhältnis zum Geld." *Acta Mozartiana* (1978): 30–53.

Blumenthal, Liselotte. "Mozarts englisches Mädchen." *Sitzungsberichte der Sächschen Akademie der Wissenschaften zu Leipzig, Phil.-hist. Klasse* 120, no. 1 (Berlin 1978): 3–29.

Blümml, Emil Karl. *Aus Mozarts Freundes- und Familienkreis*. Vienna, Prague, Leipzig, 1923.

Blümml, Emil Karl. "Ausdeutungen der *Zauberflöte*." *Mozart-Jahrbuch* (1923): 111–46.

Carr, Francis. *Mozart and Constanze*. London, 1983.

Cloeter, Hermine. *Die Grabstätte W. A. Mozarts auf dem St. Marxer Friedhof in Wien.* "For the Vienna Kulturamt, with the collaboration of Leopold Sailer." Vienna, 1941.

Così fan tutte: Beiträge zur Wirkungsgeschichte von Mozarts Oper. Published by the Forschungsinstitut für Musiktheater der Universität Bayreuth. Bayreuth, 1978. Schriften zum Musiktheater vol. 2.

Curl, James Stevens. "Mozart Considered as a Jacobin." *The Music Review* 35 (1974): 131–41.

Deutsch, Otto Erich. *Mozart und die Wiener Logen: Zur Geschichte seiner Freimaurer-Kompositionen.* Vienna, 1932.

Deutsch, Otto Erich. "Lysers Beschreibung des Mozartschen Sterbehauses." *Schweizerische Musikzeitung* 96 (1956): 289–91.

Deutsch, Otto Erich. "Mozart in Zinzendorfs Tagebüchern." *Schweizerische Musikzeitung* 102 (1962): 211–18.

Dürr, Walter. "Zur Dramaturgie des *Titus*: Mozarts Libretto und Metastasio." *Mozart-Jahrbuch* (1978–79): 55–61.

Eibl, Joseph Heinz. " 'Una porcheria tedesca': Zur Uraufführung des *Titus*." *Österreichische Musikzeitung* 31 (1976): 329–34.

Eibl, Joseph Heinz. "Mozarts Umwelt in den Familienbriefen." *Mozart-Jahrbuch* (1978–79): 215–27.

Friedländer, Ernst. "Mozarts Beziehungen zu Berlin." *Mitteilungen für die Mozart-Gemeinde in Berlin*, no. 4 (April 1897).

Giegling, Franz. "Metastasios Oper *La clemenza di Tito* in der Bearbeitung durch Mazzolà." *Mozart-Jahrbuch* (1968–70): 88–94.

Greither, Aloys. *Wolfgang Amadé Mozart: Seine Leidensgeschichte aus Briefen und Dokumenten dargestellt.* Heidelberg, 1958.

Greither, Aloys. "Noch einmal: Woran ist Mozart gestorben?" *Mitteilungen der ISM* 19, no. 3–4 (1971): 25–27.

Gruber, Gernot. *Mozart und die Nachwelt.* Edited by the ISM. Salzburg and Vienna, 1985.

Gruber, Gernot. "Bedeutung und Spontaneität in Mozarts *Zauberflöte*." In *Festschrift Walter Senn zum 70. Geburtstag.* Munich and Salzburg, 1975.

Gugitz, Gustav. "Zu einer Briefstelle Mozarts (Die Affaire Günther-Eskeles." *Mozarteums-Mitteilungen* 1 (1926): 41–49.

Gugitz, Gustav. "Von W. A. Mozarts kuriosen Schülerinnen." *Österreichische Musikzeitschrift* 11 (1956): 261–69.

Hamann, Heinz Wolfgang. "Mozarts Schülerkreis." *Mozart-Jahrbuch* (1962–63): 115–39.

Kerner, Dieter. *Krankheiten grosser Meister.* Stuttgart, 1963.

Kerner, Dieter. "Mozart in Frankfurt und Mainz." *Hessisches Ärzteblatt* 32 no. 12 (1971).

Kraemer, Uwe. "Wer hat Mozart verhungern lassen?" *Musica* (1976): 203–11.

Kunze, Stefan. *Don Giovanni vor Mozart: Die Tradition der Don Giovanni-Opern im italienischen Buffa-Theater des 18. Jahrhunderts.* Munich, 1972. Münchner Universitätsschriften 10.

Leitzmann, Albert, ed. *Wolfgang Amadeus Mozart: Berichte der Zeitgenossen und Briefe.* Leipzig, 1926.

Lühning, Helga. "Zur Entstehungsgeschichte von Mozarts *Titus.*" *Musikforschung* 27 (1974): 300–318. Opposing view by Joseph Heinz Eibl and response by Helga Lühning in vol. 28 (1975): 75–81, 311–14.

Marignano, Nerina Medici di, and Hughes, Rosemary, eds. *A Mozart Pilgrimage. Being the Travel Diaries of Vincent and Mary Novello in the Year 1829.* London, 1955.

Musik-Konzepte 3. Mozart: Ist die "Zauberflöte" ein Machwerk? Contributions by Wolf Rosenberg, Hans Rudolf Zeller, Ulrich Dibelius, Rainer Riehn, and Wolfgang Hildesheimer. Munich, 1978.

Paneth, Ludwig. "Constanze: Eine Ehrenrettung." *Mozart-Jahrbuch* (1959): 266–73.

Prieger, Karl, ed. *Urtheile bedeutender Dichter, Philosophen und Musiker über Mozart. Anschliessend: Hervorragende Musik-Schriftsteller über Mozart—Gedichte.* 2d edition, enlarged. Wiesbaden, 1886.

Puntscher-Rieckmann, Sonja. *Mozart, Ein bürgerlicher Künstler: Studien zu den Libretti "Le nozze di Figaro," "Don Giovanni" und "Così fan tutte."* Vienna, Cologne, Graz, 1982.

Ruf, Wolfgang. *Die Rezeption von Mozarts "Le nozze di Figaro" bei den Zeitgenossen.* Wiesbaden, 1977. Beihefte zum Archiv für Musikwissenschaft 16.

Tyson, Alan. "*La clemenza di Tito* and Its Chronology." *The Musical Times* 116 (1975): 221–27.

Volek, Tomislav. "Über den Ursprung von Mozarts Oper *La clemenza di Tito.*" *Mozart-Jahrbuch* (1959): 274–86.

Wagner, Hans. "Das josefinische Wien und Mozart." *Mozart-Jahrbuch* (1978–79): 1–13.

Walla, Friedrich. "Der Vogelfänger bin ich ja. Die Rolle Papagenos in der *Zauberflöte.*" *Sprachkunst: Beiträge zur Literaturwissenschaft* 8 (1977): 179–90.

VIENNA: CONTEMPORARY SOURCES, PERIODICALS

Briefe des Dichters Johann Baptist von Alxinger. Edited by Gustav Wilhelm. In *Sitzungsberichte der kaiserlichen Akademie der Wissenschaften, Phil.-hist. Classe,* vol. 140, 1899.

Criminal-Process Zalheimb. Josephinische cause célèbre 1786. Mittheilung sämmtlicher hierauf bezüglichen Original-Acten des Wiener Stadt- und des k. k. niederösterr. Appellations-Gerichtes zum ersten Male veröffentlicht . . . Vienna, 1870.

Engels, Hans Werner, ed. *Gedichte und Lieder deutscher Jakobiner.* Stuttgart, 1971. Deutsche revolutionäre Demokraten 1.

Forster, Georg. *Werke: Sämtliche Schriften, Tagebücher, Briefe.* Edited by the Akademie der Wissenschaften der DDR. Vol. 14, *Briefe 1783–87.* Berlin, 1978.

[Gaum, Johann Ferdinand.] *Die Reise des Pabst zum Kaiser.* Vienna, 1782.

Werner, Richard Maria, ed. *Aus dem josefinischen Wien: Geblers und Nicolais Briefwechsel während der Jahre 1771–1786.* Berlin, 1888.

Geusau, Anton von. *Geschichte der Haupt- und Residenzstadt Wien in Österreich.* Part 4. Vienna, 1793.

Gräffer, Franz, ed. *Josephinische Curiosa oder ganz besondere, theils nicht mehr, theils noch nicht bekannte Persönlichkeiten, Geheimnisse, Details, Actenstücke und Denkwürdigkeiten der Lebens- und Zeitgeschichte Kaiser Joseph II.* 5 vols. Vienna, 1848–50.

Gräffer, Franz. *Kleine Wiener Memoiren und Wiener Dosenstücke.* Selected and edited by Anton Schlossar with the collaboration of Gustav Gugitz. 2 vols. Munich, 1918–22. Denkwürdigkeiten aus Alt-Österreich 13–14.

Lange, Joseph. *Biographie.* Vienna, 1808.

Nicolai, Friedrich. *Beschreibung einer Reise durch Deutschland im Jahre 1781: Nebst Bemerkungen über Gelehrsamkeit, Industrie, Religion und Sitten.* 12 vols. Berlin and Stettin, 1783–96.

Payer von Thurn, Rudolf, ed. *Joseph II als Theaterdirektor: Ungedruckte Briefe und Actenstücke aus den Kinderjahren des Burgtheaters.* Vienna and Leipzig, 1920.

Pezzl, Johann. *Skizze von Wien: Ein Kultur- und Sittenbild aus der josefinischen Zeit.* Edited by Gustav Guglitz and Anton Schlossar. Graz, 1923.

Pribram, Alfred Francis, ed. *Materialien zur Geschichte der Preise und Löhne in Österreich.* In collaboration with Rudolf Geyer and Franz Koran. Vienna, 1938.

Pribram, Alfred Francis, ed. *Urkunden und Akten zur Geschichte der Juden in Wien.* Part 1, *Allgemeiner Teil 1526–1847 (1849).* 2 vols. Vienna and Leipzig, 1918.

Richter, Josef. *Die Eipeldauer Briefer 1785–1797.* Selected and edited by Eugen von Pannel. Munich, 1917. Denkwürdigkeiten aus Alt-Österreich 17.

Der Spion in Wien. Nos. 1–3. Vienna, 1784.

Vollständige Sammlung aller seit dem glorreichen Regierungsantritt Joseph des Zweyten für die k. k. Erbländer ergangenen höchsten Verordnungen und Gesetz . . . 7 vols. Vienna, 1788–89.

Wahl und Krönung Leopolds II 1790: Brieftagebuch des Feldschers der kursächsischen Schweizergarde. Edited by Erna Berger and Konrad Bund. Frankfurt a. M., 1981.

Wiener Zeitung, 1781–91.

Wien von Maria Theresia bis zur Franzosenzeit. Selections from the diaries of Count Karl von Zinzendorf, edited and translated from the French by Hans Wagner. Vienna, 1972. Jahresgabe der Wiener Bibliophilen-Gesellschaft zu ihrem 60järigen Bestehen.

EXHIBITION CATALOGUES

Joseph Haydn in seiner Zeit. Exhibition catalogue, Eisenstadt, 1982, presented by the Kulturabteilung des Amtes der Burgenländischen Landesregierung.

Josephinische Pfarrgründungen in Wien. Catalogue of the 92d special exhibition of the Historisches Museum der Stadt Wien, 1985.

Maria Theresia und ihre Zeit. Exhibition catalogue, Vienna, 1980, to commemorate the 200th anniversary of her death.

Österreich zur Zeit Kaiser Josephs II, Mitregent Kaiserin Maria Theresias, Kaiser und Landesfürst. Catalogue of the Niederösterreichische Landesaustellung Stift Melk, 1980.

Wien zur Zeit Joseph Haydns. Catalogue of the 78th special exhibition of the Historisches Museum der Stadt Wien, 1982.

BIOGRAPHICAL SOURCES

Cloeter, Hermine. *Johann Thomas Trattner: Ein Grossunternehmer im Theresianischen Wien.* Vienna, 1952. Wiener Bibliophilen Gesellschaft.

Mitrofanow, Paul von. *Joseph II: Seine politische und kulturelle Tätigkeit.* 2 vols. Vienna and Leipzig, 1910.

Nettl, Paul. *Casanova und seine Zeit.* Esslingen a. N., 1949.

Orel, Alfred. "Gräfin Wilhelmine Thun (Mäzenatentum in Wiens klassischer Zeit)." *Mozart-Jahrbuch* (1954): 89–101.

Padover, Saul K. *Joseph II: Ein Revolutionär auf dem Kaiserthron.* Düsseldorf and Cologne, 1969.

Spiel, Hilde. *Fanny von Arnstein oder die Emanzipation: Ein Frauenleben an der Zeitenwende 1758–1818.* Frankfurt a. M., 1962.

Wandruszka, Adam. *Leopold II, Erzherzog von Österreich, Grossherzog von Toscana, König von Ungarn und Böhmen, Römischer Kaiser.* 2 vols. Vienna and Munich, 1964–65.

Wolf, Adam. *Fürstin Eleonore Liechtenstein 1745–1812: Nach Briefen und Memoiren ihrer Zeit.* Vienna, 1875.

HISTORICAL ACCOUNTS

Blümml, Emil Karl, and Gugitz, Gustav. *Von Leuten und Zeiten im alten Wien.* Vienna and Leipzig, 1922.

Blümml, Emil Karl, and Gugitz, Gustav. *Alt-Wiener Thespiskarren: Die Frühzeit der Wiener Vorstadtbühnen.* Vienna, 1925.

Blümml, Emil Karl, and Gugitz, Gustav. *Alt-Wienerisches: Bilder und Gestalten.* 2 vols. Vienna, Prague, Leipzig, 1921.

Bodi, Leslie. *Tauwetter in Wien: Zur Prosa der österreichischen Aufklärung 1781–1795.* Frankfurt, a. M., 1977.

Bosl, Karl, ed. *Handbuch der Geschichte der böhmischen Länder.* For the Collegium Carolinum. 4 vols., with supplement. Stuttgart, 1974.

Czeike, Felix. *Geschichte der Stadt Wien.* Vienna, etc., 1981.

Czeike, Felix. *Der Graben.* Vienna and Hamburg, 1972. Wiener Geschichtsbücher 10.

Dietrich, Margret, ed. *Das Burgtheater und sein Publikum. Festgabe zur 200-Jahr-Feier der Erhebung des Burgtheaters zum Nationaltheater.* Vienna, 1976. Institut für Publikumsforschung 3, Osterreichische Akademie der Wissenschaften, Phil.-

hist. Klasse, Sitzungsberichte 305. See especially Otto Schindler, "Das Publikum in der josefinischen Ära."

Elias, Norbert. *Die höfische Gesellschaft: Untersuchungen zur Soziologie des Königtums und der höfischen Aristokratie.* Pbk. ed. Frankfurt a. M., 1983.

Gnau, Hermann. *Die Zensur unter Joseph II.* Vienna, 1911.

Hennings, Fred. *Das Josefinische Wien.* Vienna and Munich, 1966.

Hersche, Peter. "Erzbischof Hieronymus Colloredo und der Jansenismus in Salzburg." *Mitteilungen der Gesellschaft für Salzburger Landeskunde* 117 (1977): 231–68.

Jesinger, Alois. *Wiener Lektürekabinette.* Vienna, 1928. Gesellschaft der Bibliophilen.

Kisch, Wilhelm. *Die alten Strassen und Plätze Wiens und ihre historische interessanten Häuser.* 3 vols. Vienna, 1882–95.

Koselleck, Reinhart. *Kritik und Krise: Eine Studie zur Parthenogenese der bürgerlichen Welt.* 3d ed. Frankfurt a. M., 1979.

Lesky, Erna. *Österreichisches Gesundheitswesen im Zeitalter des aufgeklärten Absolutismus.* Vienna, 1959. Österreichische Akademie der Wissenschaften, Phil.-hist. Klasse, historische Kommission, Archiv für österreichische Geschichte, vol. 122, No. 1.

Maass, Ferdinand. *Der Josefinismus: Quellen zu seiner Geschichte in Österreich 1760–1790. Amtliche Berichte aus dem Wiener Haus-, Hof- und Staatsarchiv.* 5 vols., 1951ff.

Mack, Joseph. *Die Reform- und Aufklärungsbestrebungen im Erzstift Salzburg unter Erzbischof Hieronymous Colloredo.* Dissertation. Munich, 1912.

Mayr, Josef Karl. *Wien im Zeitalter Napoleons: Staatsfinanzen, Lebensverhältnisse, Beamte und Militär.* Vienna: Verein für Geschichte der Stadt Wien, 1940.

Osterloh, Karl-Heinz. *Joseph v. Sonnenfels und die österreichische Reformbewegung im Zeitalter des augeklärten Absolutismus.* Lübeck and Hamburg, 1970. Historische Studien 409.

Rommel, Otto. *Die Alt-Wiener Volkskomödie: Ihre Geschichte vom barocken Welttheater bis zum Tode Nestroys.* Vienna, 1952.

Sashegyi, Oskar. *Zensur und Geistesfreiheit unter Joseph II: Beitrag zur Kulturgeschichte der Habsburger Länder.* Budapest, 1958. Studia historica Academiae scientiarum Hungaricae 16.

Schimmer, Karl Eduard. *Alt und Neu Wien: Geschichte der österreichischen Kaiserstadt.* 2 vols. 2d ed. Vienna, 1904.

Schnee, Heinrich. "Die Nobilitierung der ersten Hoffaktoren: Zur Geschichte des Hofjudentums in Deutschland." *Archiv für Kulturgeschichte* 43 (Cologne and Graz, 1961): 62–99.

Schöttel, Josef. *Kirchliche Reformen des Salzburger Erzbischofs Hieronymus von Colloredo im Zeitalter der Aufklärung.* Hirschenhausen, 1939. Südostbayrische Heimatstudien 16.

Schubert, Marieluise. "Wie reagierte Wien auf die französische Revolution?" In

Österreich in Geschichte und Literatur, edited by the Institut für Österreichkunde, vol. 14, no. 10 (1970), pp. 505–22.

Steiner, Gerhard. *Franz Heinrich Ziegenhagen und seine Verhältnislehre: Ein Beitrag zur Geschichte des utopischen Sozialismus in Deutschland.* Berlin, 1962.

Stekl, Hannes. *Österreichs Aristokraten im Vormärz: Herrschaftsstil und Lebensformen der Fürstenhäuser Liechtenstein und Schwarzenberg.* Munich, 1973. Sozial- und wirtschaftshistorische Studien 2.

Tietze, Hans. *Die Juden Wiens: Geschichte, Wirtschaft, Kultur.* Leipzig and Vienna, 1935.

Wachstein, Bernard. "Das Testament der Baronin Eleonore Wetzlar von Plankenstern." *Archiv für jüdische Familienforschung, Kunstgeschichte und Museumswesen* 2–3 (1912–13): 4–9.

Wahlberg, Wilhelm Ernst. *Gesammelte kleinere Schriften und Bruchstücke über Strafrecht, Strafprocess, Gefängniskunde, Literatur und Dogmengeschichte der Rechtslehre in Österreich. Vol. 2, Neuere Praxis und Geschichte der Todesstrafe in Österreich.* Vienna, 1877.

Wangermann, Ernst. *Aufklärung und Staatsbürgerliche Erziehung: Gottfried van Swieten als Reformator des österreichischen Unterrichtswesens 1781–1791.* Munich, 1978.

Wangermann, Ernst. *Von Joseph II zu den Jakobinerprozessen.* Vienna, 1966.

Wehrl, Franz. "Eine Untersuchung der Geistesrichtungen des Klerus in Wien von 1750–1790." *Mitteilungen des österreichischen Staatsarchivs* 20 (Vienna, 1967).

Wolf, Gerson. *Judentaufen in Österreich.* Vienna, 1863.

FREEMASONRY

Österreichischen Freimaurerlogen: Humanität und Toleranz im 18. Jahrhundert. Exhibition catalogue, Österreichisches Freimaurermuseum, Schloss Rosenau.

Zirkel und Winkelmass: 200 Jahre Grosse Landesloge der Freimaurer. Catalogue of the 86th special exhibition of the Historisches Museum der Stadt Wien, 1984.

Abafi (Aigner), Ludwig. *Geschichte der Freimaurerei in Österreich-Ungarn.* 5 vols. Budapest, 1890–99.

Brabée, Gustav. *Sub Rosa. Vertrauliche Mittheilungen aus dem maurerischen Leben unserer Grossväter.* Vienna, 1879.

Dülmen, Richard van. *Der Geheimbund der Illuminaten: Darstellung, Analyse, Dokumentation.* Stuttgart, 1975.

ěhn, Ernst Otto. "Zur Wiederentdeckung des Illuminatenordens: Ergänzende Bemerkungen zu Richard van Dülmens Buch." In *Geheime Gesellschaften,* edited by Peter Christian Ludz. Heidelberg, 1979. Wolfenbütteler Studien zur Aufklärung 5/1.

Hammermayer, Ludwig. *Der Wilhelmsbader Freimaurer-Konvent von 1782: Ein Höhe- und Wendepunkt in der Geschichte der deutschen und eruopäischen Geheimgesellschaften.* Heidelberg, 1980. Wolfenbütteler Studien zur Aufklärung 5/2.

Journal für Freymaurer. Vienna, 1784–87.

Lennhoff, Eugen, and Posner, Oskar. *Internationales Freimaurerlexikon.* Reprint of the 1932 edition. Vienna and Munich, 1980.

Linder, Erich J. *Die königliche Kunst im Bild: Beiträge zur Ikonographie der Freimaurerei.* Graz, 1976.

Ludz, Peter Christian, ed. *Geheime Gesellschaften.* Heidelberg, 1979. Wolfenbütteler Studien zur Aufklärung 5/1.

Nettl, Paul. *Musik und Freimaurerei: Mozart und die königliche Kunst.* Esslingen a. N., 1956.

Reinalter, Helmut, ed. *Freimaurerei und Geheimbünde im 18. Jahrhundert in Mitteleuropa.* Frankfurt a. M., 1983.

Reinalter, Helmut. *Aufgeklärter Absolutismus und Revolution: Zur Geschichte des Jakobinertums und der frühdemokratischen Bestrebungen in der Habsburger Monarchie.* Vienna, Cologne, Graz, 1980. Veröffentlichungen der Kommission für Neuere Geschichte Österreichs 68.

Rosenstrauch-Königsberg, Edith. "Ausstrahlungen des Journals für Freymaurer." In *Beförderer der Aufklärung in Mittel- und Osteuropa: Freimaurer, Gesellschaften, Clubs,* edited by H. Balázs, Ludwig Hammermeyer, Hans Wagner, and Jerzy Wojtowicz. Berlin, 1979.

Rosenstrauch-Königsberg, Edith. *Freimaurerei im josephinischen Wien: Aloys Blumauers Weg vom Jesuiten zum Jakobiner.* Vienna and Stuttgart, 1975. Wiener Arbeiten zur deutschen Literatur 6.

Schmitt, Eberhard. "Elemente einer Theorie der politischen Konspiration im 18. Jahrhundert: Einige typologische Bemerkungen." In *Geheime Gesellschaften,* edited by Peter Christian Ludz. Heidelberg, 1979.

Schott, Otto. *Die Geschichte der Freimaurerei in Wien von den Anfängen bis zum Jahre 1792.* Dissertation (typescript). Vienna, 1939.

Schwarz, Edith. *Die Freimaurerei in Österreich, vor allem in Wien unter Kaiser Franz II 1792–1809.* Dissertation (typescript). Vienna, 1940.

Wagner, Hans. "Die Freimaurerei und die Reformen Kaiser Josephs II." *Quatuor-Coronati-Jahrbuch* no. 14 (1977): 55–73.

Wagner, Hans. "Die politische und Kulturelle Bedeutung der Freimaurerei im 18. Jahrhundert." In *Beförderer der Aufklärung in Mittel- und Osteuropa. Freimaurer, Gesellschaften, Clubs,* edited by H. Balázs et al. Berlin, 1979.

MISCELLANEOUS WORKS

Allgemeines Post- und Reisebuch nebst einer richtigen Anzeige aller in ganz Europa gangbaren Münzsorten, Gewichte und Ellenmasses, samt deren Verhältnis gegen den österreichischen Münz-, Gewicht- und Ellenfuss. 3d ed., revised and enlarged. Vienna, ca. 1785.

Briefe von Goethes Mutter an ihren Sohn, Christiane und August von Goethe. Weimar, 1889. Schriften der Goethe-Gesellschaft 4.

Fengler, Heinz; Gierow, Gerhard; and Willy Unger. *Lexikon der Numismatik,* 2d ed. Berlin, 1977.

Littrow, Carl von, ed. *Meteorologische Beobachtungen an der k. k. Sternwarte in Wien von 1775 bis 1855.* Vol. 1, *1775–1796.* Vienna, 1860.

Mercier, Louis Sébastien. *Mein Bild von Paris.* Frankfurt a. M., 1979.

Meyer J., ed. *Das grosse Conversations-Lexicon für die gebildeten Stände: In Verbindung mit Staatsmännern, Gelehrten, Künstlern und Technikern.* 55 vols. Hildburghausen, 1842–53.

Shaffer, Peter. *Amadeus.* London, 1980.

Wurzbach, Constant von. *Biographisches Lexicon des Kaiserthums Österreich, enthaltend die Lebensskizzen der denkwürdigen Personen, welche 1750 bis 1850 im Kaiserstaate in seinen Kronländern gelebt haben.* 60 vols. Vienna, 1856–91.

ILLUSTRATION CREDITS

p. 273: "Grausame Mordthat so in Wien geschehen . . ." Anonymous. Historisches Museum der Stadt Wien 52.277.

p. 313: [Joseph Richter,] "Warum wird Kaiser Joseph von seinem Volke nicht geliebt?" Vienna, 1787. Bildarchiv der Österreichischen Nationalbibliothek, Vienna.

p. 319: Gottfried Bernhard van Swieten. Copper engraving by Johann Ernst Mansfeld, after a drawing by J. C. Lackner. Porträtarchiv Diepenbroick, Münster.

p. 369: Antonio Salieri. Copper engraving by Johann Neidl, after a drawing by Gandolph Ernst Stainhauser. Porträtarchiv Diepenbroick, Münster.

p. 397: Playbill for the premiere of *Die Zauberflöte*, September 30, 1791, Theater auf der Wieden, Vienna. Historisches Museum der Stadt Wien 9.148.

p. 399: Papageno. Copper engraving by Ignaz Alberti, 1791, from the printed libretto for the premiere of *Die Zauberflöte*. Music collection, Österreichische Nationalbibliothek, Vienna.

p. 427: [Karl Friedrich] H[ensle]r, "Maurerrede auf Mozarts Tod," Vienna, 1792. This is the only copy known to exist. Music Collection, Österreichische Nationalbibliothek, Vienna.

PLATES (BETWEEN 212–213):

Mozart at the piano. Unfinished oil painting by Joseph Lange, presumably 1782–83. Mozart-Museum, Salzburg.

Constanze Mozart, née Weber. Engraving after the painting (1802) by Hans Hansen in the Mozart-Museum, Salzburg. Bildarchiv der Österreichischen Nationalbibliothek, Vienna, NB 523.911 B(RG)F.

Karl Thomas and Franz Xaver Wolfgang Mozart at the ages of fourteen and seven. Oil painting (1798) by Hans Hansen, in the Mozart-Museum, Salzburg. Bildarchiv der Österreichischen Nationalbibliothek, Vienna, 59.389 B.

Leopold Mozart, concertmaster and assistant kapellmeister in Salzburg. Oil painting (1765?) by Pietro Antonio Lorenzoni (?). Mozarteum, Salzburg.

Joseph II at the spinet with two ladies. Anonymous pencil sketch. Bildarchiv der Österreichischen Nationalbibliothek, Vienna, NB 507.273 BR.

Pietro Leopoldino, grand duke of Tuscany, after 1790 Emperor Leopold II. Wax bust by an unknown hand in the Hofburg, Vienna. Bildarchiv der Österreichischen Nationalbibliothek, Vienna, 157.999 B(TR)F.

Emperor Joseph II. Oil painting by Friedrich Heinrich Füger. Initially regent for his mother, Empress Maria Theresa, Joseph ruled alone after 1780. The emperor usually wore bourgeois clothing or a simple military jacket. Most contemporary portraits show him in royal attire, however. In this picture his only symbol of authority is a scepter. Bildarchiv der Österreichischen Nationalbibliothek, Vienna, Pf 36.302 Cv 6514:3.

"Der Spaziergang des Abends am Graben oder der Schnepfen-Strich." Colored engraving by Hieronymus Löschenkohl, 1784. Historisches Museum der Stadt Wien 62.017.

The Michaelerplatz with the Michaelerkirche and Burgtheater. Watercolor drawing by Carl Schütz, 1783. Historisches Museum der Stadt Wien 51.611.

Countess Maria Wilhelmine Thun-Hohenstein, née Countess Ulfeld. Oil painting in the style of Johann Baptist Lampi the Elder. Bildarchiv der Österreichischen Nationalbibliothek, Vienna, 165.568 B, (R)F.

Prince Karl Lichnowsky. Oil painting by an unknown hand. Bildarchiv der Österreichischen Nationalbibliothek, Vienna, NB 502.486 B.

Fanny (Franziska) Arnstein, née Itzig. Mezzotint by Vinzenz Georg Kininger, after a painting by Jean Guérin. Bildarchiv der Österreichischen Nationalbibliothek, Vienna, NB 504. = 97 BR.

Interior view of a lodge. Oil painting by an unknown hand, ca. 1790. According to oral tradition, it depicts the lodge Zur gekrönten Hoffnung in a meeting hall at Schwertgasse 3. Historisches Museum der Stadt Wien 47.927.

Angelo Soliman. Mezzotint by Johann Gottfried Haid, after a drawing by Johann Nepomuk Steiner. Historisches Museum der Stadt Wien 23.766.

Lodge certificate for Ignaz Etzels von Löwenfels, Master in the lodge Zur gekrönten Hoffnung from December 19, 1785. Copper engraving on parchment. Mozart's certificate is lost but presumably had the same design. Historisches Museum der Stadt Wien 42.107.

Lodge apron of Franz Joseph von Bosset, from the lodge Zur gekrönten Hoffnung. Mozart's lodge paraphernalia, which have not survived, were probably similar in appearance. Historisches Museum der Stadt Wien 31.621/1.

Scenes from *Die Zauberflöte*. Colored engravings by Joseph and Peter Schaffer, ca. 1793. It has not been established whether these illustrations represent the first performance at the Theater auf der Wieden. However, there appears to have been little variation in costume and set design among early productions of the opera. Historisches Museum der Stadt Wien 1788(a), 1787(b), 1785(c).

"Ankunft des Hl: Blanchards von seiner 38ten Luftreise zu Stadt Enzersdorf bey Wien d: 6: July 1791." Colored engraving by Hieronymus Löschenkohl. Historisches Museum der Stadt Wien 62.014.

Manuscript page from Mozart's Requiem, K. 626. Music Collection, Österreichische Nationalbibliothek, Vienna, Cod. 17.561 Blatt 87 r, v.

Metropolitankirche zum heiligen Stephan in Vienna. Colored engraving by Carl Schütz, 1792. Historisches Museum der Stadt Wien 64.334.

INDEX

Good Morning, Mr Mandela

Good Morning, Mr Mandela

ZELDA LA GRANGE

VIKING

VIKING
Published by the Penguin Group
Penguin Group (USA) LLC
375 Hudson Street
New York, New York 10014

USA | Canada | UK | Ireland | Australia | New Zealand | India | South Africa | China
penguin.com
A Penguin Random House Company
First published by Viking Penguin, a member of Penguin Group (USA) LLC, 2014
Copyright © 2014 by Zelda la Grange Pty Ltd

ISBN 978-0-525-42828-2
Printed in the United States of America

1   3   5   7   9   10   8   6   4   2

Contents

Contents

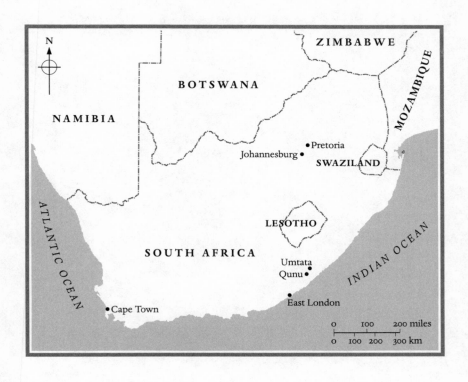

Author's Note

In June 2013 the son of the ANC stalwart Oliver Tambo, Dali Tambo, conducted an interview with President Robert Mugabe of Zimbabwe. Mugabe said: Nelson Mandela is too much of a saint. He has been too good to white people at the expense of blacks in his own country. Some agreed while others protested. To some extent I think the man had a point. It could well have been perceived that way. And yet, in a conversation with Richard Stengel, quoted in *Conversations With Myself*, Madiba himself said a long time ago, 'People will feel I see too much good in people. So it's a criticism I have to put up with and I've tried to adjust to, because whether it is so or not, it is something which I think is profitable. It's a good thing to assume, to act on the basis that . . . others are men of integrity and honour . . . _____ integrity and honour if that is how you

_____ felt responsible for this per-
_____ white people. Indeed he has
_____ eve that he felt proud of how
_____ ften said that if you change
_____ e your duty. He has not only
_____ s. He has done way beyond
_____ eing and perhaps for that he

_____ d Stengel, Madiba said, 'Your
_____ s human beings, not because
_____ ore, once you know that this
_____ this weakness you work with
_____ akness and you try and help
_____ n't want to be frightened by
_____ ain mistakes and he has got

human frailties. I can't allow myself to be influenced by that. And that is why many people criticize me.'

I try not to think 'Why me?', to understand why Nelson Mandela chose me. If I do, I think of these quotes above. In the nineteen years we spent together he learned my weaknesses, he learned my strengths, and he invested in my strengths to make me the person I am today.

I served him for almost twenty years and was his PA until he left us on 5 December 2013. In 2009 I decided to start writing this book to pay tribute to him. I mostly wanted to record my experiences in the hope that others would be changed and influenced by my story too. My book is therefore a tribute to Khulu, as I knew him.

This is not his story. This is my story, and I am content with it. But the reader may be disappointed if they expect me to wash too much dirty laundry in public. I would not disrespect the trust Nelson Mandela had invested in me. That is the biggest honour he could have bestowed on me – to trust me – and I intend to cherish that for the rest of my life. What I decided to write about and what I decided to omit as far as he is concerned is based on that trust. It is therefore not a tell-all book.

It is also not a book of great political insights or a thematic dissection of his life. It's a simple story of my experiences with him. One of the most important lessons I have learned from this great man over the years, reaffirmed by his wife Graça Machel to me later in life, is that you only have one person to account to and that is yourself. You have to go to bed at night with your own thoughts and conscience, and after writing this book I need to feel the comfort of a pillow of a clear conscience. I need to make him proud because as much as it feels that our lives were overshadowed by negativity and turmoil over the last couple of years, there is a beautiful story to be told, and I need to admit that I am part of that story and that it is my duty to tell that story. Above all, I need to know in my heart that if he had to read this book he would be happy with what I told and he would agree with the detail, and spending sixteen of the last nineteen years with him, day in, day out, I know what he would be comfortable with in the public domain and what he would not, and that is what is mine to protect.

The book is therefore a collection of anecdotes, sometimes at my own expense, of a road well travelled. No regrets and only lessons to be learned. I am an emotional billionaire, and if nothing extraordinary happens to me for the rest of my life I will still be content with my memories until the day I die. I have had a rich life. Most people will not experience what I have been witness to, and my story is therefore one of change, of slow metamorphoses of the mind and a belief system to where I am today. The reader has to decide if there is any part he or she can identify with or lessons they can learn from my story. It is not for me to decide.

It would also be incorrect to assume that I was the only one, or a special one, around Madiba. I played a particular role in his life, mostly concerned with his public life. But there are many others, household staff, office staff, security and medical personnel, who played equally important roles in his life and who he was totally dependent upon. Some of them are included in my story but I simply couldn't pay tribute to each and every one of them.

I have tried my best without exception and that is the best I have to give. I hope to contribute to Nelson Mandela's legacy in a small way by sharing the privileges and experiences I have had to anyone open to receiving them. If I change one life by touching another with my story, I have done my duty.

I remain grateful and indebted for ever . . .

Prologue: Zeldina

It was early 2000s. I was in my thirties. I stood outside our office door in Johannesburg, as usual, awaiting the arrival of Nelson Mandela to receive him, escort him into his office and brief him on events for the day. Whenever his car appeared around the corner, my face lit up, no matter how much pressure I was under. The smile that painted my face was one loaded with love and admiration, like one would have when you see your dearest grandparents. His car came to a standstill and the bodyguards emerged. We greeted and briefly exchanged pleasantries before they opened the heavily armed car door for Madiba to step out of the car. Madiba is Nelson Mandela's clan name in South Africa. It is also the term with which people endearingly refer to him. Some call him *Tata*, which means 'Father', but most people refer to him and address him as Madiba. I called him Khulu, an abbreviated version of *Tata um'khulu* which means 'Grandfather'.

While getting out of the car, our eyes met. I exclaimed, 'Good morning Khulu.' He called me Zeldina. He was handed his walking stick to support himself to get out of the car. The stick was made from ivory, a gift from his good friend Douw Steyn. He didn't care much for material things but his walking stick was one of the few items he valued and protected with his life.

'Good morning Zeldina,' he said as he emerged from the car. His face lit up with his usual smile although I detected some reserve. Once the bodyguards had him steady on his feet, they handed him to me. He would support himself on his walking stick and hold onto my arm with his left hand.

'How are you this morning Khulu?' I asked.

'I'm fine Zeldina,' he said but he didn't continue as he usually did, asking after my well-being. That was another sign that something bothered him. As we walked into his office I thought of giving him a few moments to gather his thoughts before I started overloading him with information about the day. Once his office door was closed he opened up:

'You know Zeldina, I had a dream last night.'

I responded with a 'Yes?'

'I dreamt that you left me, that you deserted me . . .' he said.

I was dumbstruck. Me? Zelda la Grange? Abandoning Nelson Mandela? How could he ever conceive me doing something like that? At the time I had been in his service for almost ten years. What would cause him to feel that I would abandon him? To the contrary, because of my early childhood I was the one who feared abandonment. I had to set his mind at ease. I put my left hand on his left hand which was holding onto my right arm and said, 'Khulu, I would never ever do something like that and you should please never think about that ever again. I can give you my assurance that I will never abandon you.' And then added on a lighter note, 'In any event I think you are going to abandon me or chase me away before I can abandon you.'

He looked at me, laughed half heartedly, lifted his eyebrows and then responded: 'I will never do that.'

That was the warmth of our relationship. We needed affirmation from each other. We looked after each other. I have grown to love this man who was once my people's enemy. He resembled fear in our eyes. Growing up in apartheid South Africa as a white Afrikaner, we had spent our lives oppressing the same people that Nelson Mandela represented. He was the voice of the oppressed and the liberation struggle. Less than fifteen years after his release from prison, here I was trying to explain and defend my commitment to the man we once despised.

Apartheid was the system introduced by the white government in South Africa in the 1940s. It advocated for white supremacy and black oppression and was a clear set of legislation providing for the separation and segregation of white and black in South Africa. The laws of apartheid were upheld in churches and schools, on beaches and in restaurants, and any areas where the white minority could feel intimidated by the presence of black people.

Yet I walked next to Nelson Mandela for most of my adult professional life – each of us holding onto the other. I was a young Afrikaner girl whose views and mindset were changed by the greatest statesman of our time. Yet to me, he was more than my moral conscience. I had learned to care for him, because he cared for me. He shaped and changed my thinking because for him to employ a white Afrikaans-speaking young woman as his Personal Assistant was not only unprecedented, it was unheard of.

PART ONE

'If it isn't good, let it die'

1970–1994

I

Childhood

On 29 October 1970 in Boksburg to the east of Johannesburg, South Africa, I was born and not left to die but to make it good, like most babies that are brought into this world.

On the same day, Nelson Mandela was already beginning his ninth year in prison. In prison since 1962, and then convicted for treason after the Rivonia Trial in 1964, he was sentenced to life imprisonment. He and other political prisoners were incarcerated on Robben Island, a desolate island off the coast of Cape Town, for opposing apartheid.

At the time my father worked at a construction company and my mother was a teacher. They were very poor. My only sibling, my brother Anton, was three years old when I was born. Because our parents were white, we were born to legal privilege. That was the way it was in South Africa in 1970. Even though my parents' families shared the same holiday destination every December, my parents only met in Boksburg once my mother was studying to become a teacher and my father was working in the postal service.

My grandfather's family originated from French Huguenots who fled the south of France during the 1680s to escape the persecution of Protestants by the Catholic authorities. The La Grange family originated from a small town called Cabrières in the region of Avignon; a place I discovered and visited twice in the decades after my birth as a result of working for Nelson Mandela.

My father was one of two siblings. Their parents lived in Mosselbay, a coastal town along the picturesque Garden Route in the Cape Province. My grandmother's sister was the first qualified female pharmacist in South Africa and up to this day the Scholtz family own and run a reputable pharmacy in the town of Willow-more in the Eastern Cape. She was therefore quite an impressive woman and someone we automatically looked up to as a result of her unique achievement.

I was also very fond of my dad's father. His name was Anthony Michael but we just called him 'Oupa Mike' (Grandpa Mike). He used to visit us a few times a year and then stay with us for a few weeks. He smoked a pipe and the smell of smoke irritated us. He would sit on one particular chair and constantly wipe his hand on the arm rest. His skin was old and cracked and the tobacco from stuffing his pipe stuck in those cracks. When he left our home the armrest was black, much to my mother's irritation, but nobody ever said he couldn't smoke in the house.

My mother was the eldest of three siblings from the Strydom family. The only famous family with that surname was that of J. G. Strijdom (also sometimes spelt Strydom), the sixth Prime Minister of South Africa who served between 1954 and 1958. He was succeeded by the 'Father of Apartheid', H. F. Verwoerd. When I learned as a child about a Strijdom being Prime Minister, I convinced myself that we were somehow related even though no real connection exists.

My mother's father died in a motorcycle accident when my mother was only twelve years of age. I often asked my mother whether she recalled the night they received the news about her father's death. She has mostly avoided talking about it, but has said that she recalled been woken up by someone knocking on their front door and then hearing my grandmother crying hysterically.

My grandmother had few options about the upbringing of her children. She had a clerical job at the South African Railways and it was financially impossible for her to raise three small children by herself.

She decided to send my mother, being the eldest, to an orphan-age. The children's home was in Cape Town, which is why my mother still detests the city. For her, it stinks of abandonment.

Ma only saw her siblings and my grandmother once a year during the December holidays. Both the La Grange and Strydom families camped in the same area close to Mosselbay, called Hartenbos, during the December holidays, but they never knew about the other's existence.

My mother's childhood memories are limited to suffering, neglect, sadness. The world was suffering the consequences of the Second World War, slowly recovering from the economic recession, and my mother, even as an Afrikaans child in the 1940s in South Africa, felt those consequences through poverty. I greatly admire her for not holding a grudge against my grandmother, whatever the circumstances.

Grandma Tilly, my mother's mother, was part of our everyday life, even though she had given up my mother as a child. She lived close to us and I would often visit her on my way from primary school, as she conveniently lived halfway between our house and the school. Before she moved closer to us, Grandma Tilly lived opposite the Union Buildings. Sitting on the hill overlooking the city of Pretoria, the administrative capital of South Africa, the Union Buildings were built by Herbert Baker and were the seat of the apartheid government. Imposing, monumental and beautiful – for my family, it was like living across from the White House.

On Sundays the La Granges and the Strydoms, my uncle's family, would all visit my gran in her apartment for lunch and then go for a walk on the manicured lawns of the Union Buildings. The Union Buildings represented ultimate authority and we walked up the steps with great respect. My cousins, brother and I would play on the grounds, rolling down the sloping lawn, laughing all the time. We were happy children growing up in apartheid South Africa.

Ours was a typical privileged white family, benefiting from apartheid through good education, access to basic services and a sense of entitlement to the land and its resources. Apartheid was our regime's political solution to enforce segregation and the separation of races, classes and cultures.

Instituted by the Afrikaner leaders in the late 1950s, the then State President, Hendrik Verwoerd, called it 'policy'. 'Our policy is one of good neighbourliness', implying that the Afrikaner cared for all racial groups in South Africa. But the reality was that apartheid was a way of ensuring that Afrikaners benefited from the economy, opportunities and wealth of the country's natural resources, at the expense of others.

By the mid 1970s the apartheid government had created a racist state based on decisions taken in the Union Buildings. Black and white people were separated, not allowed to marry, befriend, have sex together or to live in the same cities. These were the so-called Group Areas Act provisions in South Africa, an attempt to prevent people from freely moving around and living lives within the same boundaries. Black people couldn't ride in the same buses or swim in the same sea as whites. Due to its apartheid policies, South Africa was suspended from participating in the business of the United Nations in 1974, and followed by a resolution passed in 1977 a mandatory arms embargo was imposed against us. However, the United States, Britain and France opposed the expulsion of South Africa from the UN despite several resolutions calling for it.

Even though my country was an international pariah, we kept on playing and laughing at the seat of government. This was because my people were protected. Protected from men like Nelson Mandela. It was people like him – black and determined to overthrow the government, challenging white superiority – who we feared.

Neither of my parents were politicians or worked for the government. But we supported the regime. We were, I suppose, racists. We epitomized the typical Afrikaner middle-class family at the time: law-abiding citizens, cheerleaders for whatever the church and government dictated. Our respect for authority and the ties to the Dutch Reformed Church superseded common sense. Like any other Afrikaans family, we attended church services on Sunday morning without fail and participated in all related activities to exhibit our model citizenry.

So apartheid was in our home. We lived by segregation. It was all acceptable and unquestionable, not only because the Nationalist Party government in power dictated it but also because our church endorsed it.

Black people were anyone who wasn't white. Coloured and Indian people were black in our eyes too. 'Coloured people', now referred to as 'brown' people, originated from different groups, just like the Afrikaners, but some of their forefathers were Qash-skinned. Therefore they were regarded as 'black' in South Africa.

The white Afrikaner has a mixed genealogy that includes Dutch, French, German and British blood. Although unthinkable at the time, it has emerged in modern history and studies that almost all white Afrikaner people have DNA that can be traced to black and brown ancestry in South Africa – facts not all white Afrikaners easily accept.

At the time of apartheid you didn't even contemplate anything but simply did it. I knew that all black people were required to carry a pass book and they had to show their pass books randomly to police that stopped them. I didn't know that they were only allowed to move in areas that their passes allowed them to move in, and if they didn't have a pass for a specific area they would be arrested for transgression of the pass act and thrown into jail, before being deported to their own area. If you had a pass for Johannesburg, you couldn't move in Pretoria – two cities barely thirty miles apart. It was the government's way of controlling black people's movements.

According to our church, we were right. We did the 'right' thing. And yes it was right, as in direction to the right. The utmost conservatism.

Like most white families we had a black live-in domestic worker. Her name was Jogabeth. Reminiscing about those days one cannot help but come to the realization that most white children of my age were brought up by black people. They were not only domestic workers but surrogate mothers. As a child Jogabeth was part of our family to a certain extent, and within limits – apartheid limits. She stayed in a back room. She had a toilet but no bath or shower. She had a separate cup and cutlery and was not allowed to use 'ours'. I cannot recall that my parents ever told her she was not allowed to use anything of ours but she knew and we knew. It was unspoken. Yet, Jogabeth was my lifeline.

Touching a black person was taboo. Apart from the fact that white people were considered superior to black people, we were brought up to believe that they were not as clean as we were, they apparently smelled different and the texture of their hair was different to ours. You would never dream of touching a black person's hair or face. It was just unthinkable. Yet Jogabeth carried me on her back when I was a toddler. Although I never would have touched her hair, her hands, arms and her bosom comforted me whenever I needed it. Because she brought us children up, in our eyes she wasn't as black as other blacks. She posed no threat to us and she served us and therefore she was more acceptable to us than other black people.

I remember on many occasions being bullied by my brother and how Jogabeth had to comfort me after losing the battle. She was my safe house and I knew that, as long as I was in her care, I was protected from my big brother's bullying. And then during such times, I found comfort in her arms, close to her chest.

When I was twelve years old and my father was employed by the South African Breweries, eventually working his way up to become logistics manager, political unrest against apartheid played a role in my life for the first time. The head offices of the SAB were situated in the Poyntons Building in Church Street, Pretoria. On Friday, 20 May 1983 my dad was scheduled to fly to Cape Town to attend to business there. Just before 4 p.m. a bomb blast shook the entire city of Pretoria in its core. The story broke on the news immediately and it was reported that the car bomb exploded right in front of the Poyntons Building.

When news was received my mother called my dad's office, but there was no response. She called the airport to check whether he was on the flight at around 6 p.m. but the airport authorities refused to release information on passengers, as they always do. We couldn't find anyone that could confirm whether my dad was still in the building at the time of the explosion, whether he had safely left by the time of the explosion or whether he possibly walked past or drove out of the parking garage at the time of the explosion. He often attended business luncheons at restaurants in the surrounding areas of his head office and we feared for the worst. It was only at about 9 p.m. that night, when he arrived at his hotel in Cape Town, that he called to inform us that he was safe. It was the longest five hours of my life. We were relieved that he was unharmed. I didn't ask why resistance to apartheid would be so strong, or take such violent forms. The violence only served to strengthen my belief in apartheid, the inherent difference between black and white.

Umkhonto we Sizwe (MK), the opposition African National Congress's military wing, accepted responsibility for the bomb in which 19 people were killed – 8 black people and 11 white people – and more than 217 were injured. The Church Street bomb exploded at the height of rush hour. The two men involved in planning and executing the bombing were also killed, as the bomb was detonated by accident too soon.

Umkhonto we Sizwe, 'Spear of the Nation', was established in 1961 after Nelson Mandela and other founding members of MK decided that violence in South Africa was becoming the only way to respond to the violence exercised by the apartheid government. Since the government resorted to violent means in fighting the ANC and keeping black people oppressed under apartheid laws, MK was the ANC's response to such violence. In Nelson Mandela's speech during the closing moments of the Rivonia Trial in 1964, when he was charged with acts of terrorism and after which he and others were sentenced to life imprisonment, he noted about MK: 'It would be unrealistic and wrong for African leaders to continue preaching peace and non-violence at a time when the government met our peaceful demands with force.'

Having gone to Ethiopia and Morocco in 1962 to receive military training and to secure support for MK, Mr Mandela was prepared to resort to violence. However, I am not sure whether he knew while he was imprisoned what ANC cadres were doing outside and whether those imprisoned were consulted about such acts of violence. In 1983 Oliver Tambo was President of the ANC; Nelson

Mandela was already sixty-five years of age, spending his twentieth year imprisoned, and communication was difficult with prisoners. I subsequently asked him whether he was aware of the Church Street bombing and he said that they had been briefed after the incident.

The ANC knew it needed to force the hand of the racist regime. To do that they would have to turn to violence. The government was not prepared to abolish apartheid or improve the living conditions of black people and they would rather fight the black force with violence. The ANC's response was violence. They did that by targeting strategic installations, crucial to the state. The Poytons Building was strategic because the South African Air Force Headquarters was situated in the same building.

I was generally oblivious to what was happening in the country, the poverty of blacks and the violence, but I knew that we lived in separate cocoons and that we were fighting one another in a bitter battle because we were not able to co-exist. It was pressed upon us instinctively, because of the way we lived, that when approached by a black person, you turned and walked the other way. You didn't make conversation and you feared them. They were not our friends. I was quite happy with my life as it was and knew that we were locking doors and windows from an early age out of fear that black people might attack us at night. It never crossed my mind that we could be harmed by white people too. It was always 'black' people. I didn't ask why they might attack us, or who they were, or what their lives were like. I only knew that they were dangerous.

On Sundays we solemnly prayed in church for the men defending our borders. It was the right thing to do because everybody else did it. Well, all the other whites in my community. I didn't know which border but I knew they were fighting black people. My knowledge was limited to whites protecting the border from infiltration by more black people. How strange that then one didn't ask the question, which black people? Were we protecting our borders from infiltration by more black people or were we protecting our borders from other military forces in the region infiltrating South Africa to support the ANC? You were told just this: we are fighting black communist people. I was brought up to believe that all black people were communists and atheists. Yet on Sundays black people gathered in small groups in open spaces, holding church services. I disregarded seeing that and cannot remember that the contradiction to what I was brought up to believe ever bothered me. As a child it is easy to follow when you grow up in an environment that is safe. Perhaps if I had been oppressed, didn't have access to a decent school, a proper house, electricity and water, I would have asked different questions, and my brain would have developed into being more inquisitive about injustice at an early age. In any case it didn't.

Today I also realize that the community you are brought up in chooses to live in a particular way. The people around you, grown-up adult people, decide what is socially acceptable and what is not. You live that life not realizing that there is a life beyond: issues, policies, world events and tendencies that influence your world. When you live in comfort you don't ask questions, and there was no need for me to question what was happening beyond the walls of our house. No person is born a racist. You become a racist by influences around you. And I had become a racist by the time I was thirteen years old. By that calculation I should never have become Nelson Mandela's longest-serving assistant. But I did.

2

Change

Perhaps something in my childhood suited me to Nelson Mandela.

When I was growing up, my mother often had severe spells of depression where she would simply cry for days or stay in bed and be depressed. We were never neglected but I do remember her sadness. One felt disempowered to do anything about it, not understanding what it was.

My mother is to this day one of the most decent, softly spoken, ladylike people I know. She has never sworn or used foul language in my presence. She has never spoken in a degrading manner to or about anyone, not even people that made her angry or people that harmed her in any way. She has calmness about her and reserves her extreme emotions for her inner self. I also never recall her being overly happy or excited about anything and she is moderate by nature. Her time spent in the orphanage while she was growing up obviously taught her to hide her emotions. It altered her. I recognized that burying of one's self in my years with Nelson Mandela later in life. He too had to suppress his emotions to survive prison.

My dad often got frustrated with Mom's depression and they would end up arguing about it and fighting because my mom would be so passive. My dad is a social person, the more the merrier, while my mother likes her own space and not socializing too much. I inherited that anti-social tendency from my mother. None of us realized just how troubled my mom really was.

One Friday afternoon, after playing at a friend's house, I returned home to an empty house. When I opened the kitchen door I heard mom's car in the garage. I didn't open the door to the garage but merely slipped into the house, lounging around. After a while,

I heard that the car was still in the garage, idling, but I didn't hear her opening the garage door to leave. I decided to go and look what was happening. When I opened the door between the house and the garage I vividly remember my mother resting her head against the window of the car, the car idling; she seemed asleep. I rushed to the car door and tried to open it. It was locked. I then noticed a pipe from the window and traced it to the car's exhaust. Only then did reality hit home. She was trying to commit suicide. I screamed and cried all at once and tried to force the door open.

I was twelve years of age and had little strength to make an impact. I slammed against the window but she didn't react and the rest of the events I cannot remember. I know that I called my grand-mother and my gran arrived quickly because she lived around the corner. I don't know how my mom got out of the car to her bed-room, I don't know at what time Anton, my brother, came home or when the doctor arrived or my mom's best friend came. I don't remember if and who called my dad, who was travelling on busi-ness again. I don't remember where he was and I don't remember how they got hold of him – cellphones were not yet invented at the time. I do remember that this was the last day I smelled anything in my life. And that smell was gas. Doctors say that from the shock my body's ability to smell was shut off, a psychosomatic reaction to trauma.

My mom was admitted to a clinic for people suffering from depres-sion, and stabilized. I was left constantly wondering why she would decide to leave me, just as she had been by her mom; wasn't I good enough? Did she love me enough to live? Was it me and my brother's endless fighting as siblings that drove her to do that? I was never angry at my mother, perhaps rather sad, and I felt abandoned.

Those events in the gas-filled garage in 1982 determined my rela-tionships for ever. I am constantly terrified I will be abandoned. Left alone. So I overcompensate. I sacrifice myself to please people, hop-ing and trying to avoid a situation in which I find myself abandoned. And with the fear of abandonment comes the constant need for affirmation. It is not an ideal recipe for relationships of a romantic kind but it is ideal when you dedicate your life to your job and the world's most iconic statesman. In a strange twist, Nelson Mandela needed someone to devote themselves to him. To help him. He needed someone who was always there. Available to support him and to be depended upon. We complemented each other in a slightly co-dependent way. My need to please fitted with his need for absolute loyalty.

But this was still to come. In 1988 I turned eighteen and completed school. The news was dominated by reports of killings of either policemen or 'cadres', as liberation fighters were referred to. Not a month passed without a bomb blast somewhere in the country. It became such a common occurrence that one later doesn't pay attention to numbers. There was death everywhere. South Africa was on the brink of a civil war. Violence erupted more often than not, and for the middle-class white Afrikaans people perhaps going to war against black people seemed like the only solution.

For me, though, life continued as before. My father had asked me: 'What do you want to study?' I had no idea, but since I was always engaged in cultural activities at school I opted to study acting. He gave me a definite 'No' and said that unless you are Sandra Prinsloo – one of South Africa's most successful and admired actresses – you had no chance at succeeding in the performing arts. It was my life's dream to become an actress. From childhood I remembered role-playing to be a secretary whenever I accompanied my dad to his office at weekends. My father convinced me, like most Afrikaner parents would have done at the time, to opt for a career in which job security took priority over following your passion, and I decided to enrol for a three-year National Diploma as Executive Secretary at the Technicon (now the Tshwane University of Technology) in Pretoria.

In September 1989, almost a year after my eighteenth birthday – the age at which South African citizens become legitimate voters – a general election was held. It excluded black people. No coloured, Indian or black people were allowed to vote under the apartheid laws. In South Africa's last national race-based elections the National Party lost ground and only managed to secure 48 per cent of the vote. The National Party had ruled since 1948. Its policies were based on apartheid, segregation and the promotion of the Afrikaner. People who supported them were known as Nats. Being a stern conservative, even more conservative than the Nats, I voted for the Conservative Party in 1989.

The Nats were beginning to talk about reform: allowing black people to vote, bringing an end to the Group Areas Act and discrimination against people based on the colour of their skin. The Conservative Party opposed any change to apartheid laws and that year they became the official opposition, securing 31 per cent of the white vote. Though the total population at the time was estimated to be in the region of 30 million (there are no official figures available because black people were not counted as citizens), only about 3.1 million voters (all white) were registered, of which just over 1 million voted for the National Party's reform policies.

Unbeknown to anyone, Nelson Mandela had had his first meeting with the then President, P. W. Botha, on 4 July 1989. Mr Botha was known to oppose black majority rule, yet his willingness to meet with Mr Mandela set the tone of concessions to be made. At this point Nelson Mandela was spending his twenty-sixth year in prison. He had become the figurehead of the oppressed in South Africa even though very few people really knew him apart from his cadres. He was becoming the symbol of freedom for the masses in South Africa, even though the pictures that appeared of him were from the 1960s or were sketches of what people imagined he looked like at the time. No one was allowed access to the prison to ever take photographs of the ageing Nelson Mandela.

P. W. Botha abruptly resigned as President in August 1989, a month before the elections, after he felt that the then Minister of Education, F. W. de Klerk, had not consulted with him after a meeting he had with President Kenneth Kaunda from Zambia. Mr Botha felt undermined and resigned; Mr de Klerk was appointed Acting President for the month prior to the elections.

At this time, Nelson Mandela had been moved to Victor Verster Prison in the Paarl, close to Cape Town. He regularly met with President de Klerk and Mr de Klerk announced the release of the first long-serving political prisoners barely a month after becoming President. This was a landmark in South Africa's history: change became inevitable. I knew nothing about the prisoners being released and I can hardly remember that I paid attention to the announcement. These prisoners included Walter Sisulu, Andrew Mlangeni, Raymond Mhlaba and Ahmed Kathrada among others, some of Nelson Mandela's closest friends and colleagues. Who could have imagined that I would later adore some of these prisoners.

On 2 February 1990 President de Klerk announced the unconditional release of Nelson Mandela after being imprisoned for twenty-seven years. February in the north of Pretoria where my family lived is one of the hottest months in our summer. I was swimming in our pool when my father came outside and the fact that someone was watching me distracted my attention. I could see that he had something on his mind. 'Yes Dad . . . ?' I said. He just looked at me and after a few moments of silence he replied, 'Now we are in trouble. The terrorist has been released.' My response was: 'Who's that?' and he replied: 'Nelson Mandela.' I had no idea who it was or what this meant to us. I could sense that he was worried but I continued swimming and left him to ponder about his announcement.

It was only much later after I had joined the Presidency that Mr Mandela told me that Mr de Klerk visited him a few days before the announcement of his release. He unceremoniously told Mr Mandela that he was free to go. Mr Mandela indicated that he couldn't leave immediately and that he needed to afford his people time to allow them to prepare for his release. He asked for an extra few days to allow people on the outside to prepare. If someone told me 'You are free to leave' after twenty-seven years I would ignore courtesy and run out, yet Mr Mandela wanted to stay to allow his people time to prepare. I often asked him whether he wasn't scared that the government could change its mind in those extra days. He looked at me, surprised that I would mistrust people in that way, laughed and then said 'No.'

It was of course only much later that I could comprehend what actually happened in South Africa at that time. Little did I know that Nelson Mandela was already aged seventy-one when he was released. Little did I know that he lost his mother and his son during his incarceration and that he was not allowed to attend their respective funerals at the time. The fact that he was a human being, a person with emotions, didn't cross my mind. All I knew was that we were in trouble, because my dad said so.

By 1992 the white National government called a referendum to decide on the future of apartheid. But, of course, whites only were allowed to vote in the referendum. The apartheid system that had been implemented in 1948 was withering. The white population was asked to express themselves in support or against the reform policies started by President de Klerk. Very few people shared the notion that reform would go further than they anticipated, but it was clear that apartheid was losing its few remaining supporters in the international community.

A total of 2.8 million whites voted in the referendum; 1.9 million were in favour of reform and an election in which non-white South Africans could vote; 875,000 of my compatriots voted against the abolishment of apartheid. I voted 'NO' too. And I was proud of it. This was my contribution, I thought, to ensuring that the country remained governable. There was always this white Afrikaans fear that if the country was run by blacks it would become ungovernable and that they would run the whites into the ocean, take revenge for what whites denied them of for centuries.

Really it was all over by 1990, when Mr Mandela was released. It marked the end of apartheid and the beginning of a country where 'one man one vote' would apply, irrespective of the colour of your skin. But it all kind of passed me by as I was enjoying the life of being a student – the partying and late night studying to catch up on work that fell behind as a result of such partying. I had no involvement or even thought about politics or where South Africa was heading, even though I knew that apartheid had ended and that black people were free to move as they please. At social gatherings we sometimes referred briefly to what was unfolding in South Africa but never with informed detail and all playing on each other's white Afrikaner fears that, indeed, 'we were in trouble'. That was the totality of my understanding of the political situation and I wasn't bothered much.

I do recall driving to my uncle's farm in Ellisras in the north over Easter in April 1993 when we heard the news on the radio that Communist Party leader and chief of staff of the military wing of the ANC, the charismatic Chris Hani, had been killed. For whites in South Africa the communists held the real threat to our safety, security and financial future. Somehow Nelson Mandela was also considered a communist. Because South Africa, or our white world, was dominated by religion and what the church dictated, it was unthinkable that the Communist Party would ever occupy a legitimate space in South Africa. We were a capitalist state in which the whites owned and controlled all the resources.

When I asked my parents later about Chris Hani, I was told that it was a big mistake by whoever initiated his killing because even though Hani was a communist, surely he was a better deal for the white people than the so-called terrorist Mandela. I was confused by my parents' pronouncements because to me anything communist posed a serious threat, and even though Nelson Mandela had not been officially named a member of the Communist Party, surely Chris Hani was more dangerous, being the leader of that party? According to my parents, Chris Hani had exhibited some tolerance towards white people, probably because he hadn't been imprisoned on Robben Island like Nelson Mandela, and therefore they obviously assumed that he didn't have the hatred Mr Mandela supposedly had.

Little did we know, or care, that Mr Mandela had no bitterness.

He had secretly been talking about negotiations with the government from prison, determined to bring about a peaceful transition. As Ahmed Kathrada, one of Madiba's closest friends and a fellow prisoner, said, 'Forgiveness is a choice.' One inherently always expects the worst and we expected Nelson Mandela to live up to our expectations.

It was during these riveting and dangerous political times that I fell in love and got engaged. My aspirations were limited to getting married and having children, like most young Afrikaans women my age. I was only twenty-two years of age but it didn't matter. I had also graduated and I started my first job at the Department of State Expenditure in 1992 as a secretary. A few months into the job I became bored and asked for a more challenging position. I was transferred to the Human Resources division within the same department as an administrative clerk, working in mid-town Pretoria.

Apartheid had ended but life continued unchanged. We didn't feel the end of apartheid in our everyday lives. We still 'lived' apartheid even though politically changes started to emerge prior to the 1994 elections. Violence and unrest continued in far off communities, and we were continuously confronted with the pictures of dead people in rural areas. The violence was no longer only black against white but now also due to tensions between the ANC and Inkatha Freedom Party. The IFP was the ANC's biggest rival at the time.

Then my engagement ended. I was distraught and lost. What I usually do when relationships fail is that I throw myself into my work, completely and utterly, as a way of dealing with pain.

On 10 May 1994 South Africa's first democratically elected black President was inaugurated. I was twenty-three years of age and putting in every extra hour of overtime to build my career in the Human Resources department of the Department of State Expenditure. Even though the day of his swearing in was a public holiday, I was on my way to work to put in extra time. There was hardly any traffic and people avoided the streets out of fear for the outbreak of violence following the inauguration of the ANC government, which was seen as the enemy to all white people, even those whites who voted in favour of reform and for apartheid to end. An ANC government in power meant that the majority of our leadership would change to black people, and that seriously challenged white supremacy. It was pay-back time and we expected black people to settle scores with us whites for centuries of oppression. Military vehicles were visible everywhere in the suburbs and police cars ready to respond on instructions. Still, this didn't affect my life and I found myself safe in the comfort of my office during the inauguration. As long as the police, still from the previous regime, were visible in the streets, surely we were safe. I do recall driving home seeing black people along the street and people smiling, looking happy, cheering and dancing. My thoughts were simple: Yes, you can now do as you please but please don't kill us tonight because we are white.

Prior to the elections some white people collected tinned food and perishables out of fear of civil war, violence and disruption. We expected black people to take over the country and now deprive us of basic services, that they would raid shops and create absolute chaos, sabotaging water and power supply to white suburbs. People stocked up and gathered bottled water, candles, tinned food and whatever would last them and be needed in an emergency. We expected revenge.

But that night nothing happened and we all woke up the next morning, went back to work and to our normal way of life, untouched by the previous day's events and whoever was leading this country. Life continued in a strangely unaffected way. We still had our house, we were still alive and water still came from the tap. Nothing was there to indicate that soon the very foundations of my life, my ignorance, my beliefs, my values were to be shaken up and tested. Little did I know that I would emerge from that paranoid, white cocoon of fear and denial and that the man who would lead me out of that – gently holding my hand – would be Nelson Mandela.

PART TWO

Start of a New Dawn

1994–1999

3

Meeting Mr Mandela

Soon after the elections in 1994 the incoming government needed to recruit new people. My department was tasked to help with the huge project of making the former apartheid government more 'representative', in other words we had to hire more black people. It was the beginning of transformation. South Africa was to be governed for all. It would represent all its people.

Thousands and thousands of people applied. It took us weeks to come up with short-lists for posts advertised. It was clear that there was a great shortage of skilled people but that indeed people in South Africa were desperate for work. A lot of applications couldn't be processed as a result of illiteracy, applicants having been denied a decent education during apartheid. I worked very hard to process these applications. There was no incentive to do so but my nature is such that if given a task I have to complete it in the shortest possible time. I am one of those people who like to clear things off their mental notes and I often work unnecessarily at a pace that is not required. I was looking for a new job, I wanted a new start, away from my broken engagement, but in the meantime I focused all my attention on processing applications.

Then a colleague told me about a typist's job being advertised in an administrative department attached to the newly established President's office. The position would mean being based six months of the year in Pretoria and six months in Cape Town. Whenever Parliament was in session, politicians, their families and support staff lived and worked from Cape Town as our Parliament is housed in Cape Town. Whenever Parliament went in recess, politicians and their families and staff would move back to Pretoria, the administrative capital. It is something I had always dreamt of doing and the fact that the job was on a lower rank than the one I currently occupied didn't matter. What I also found attractive was that the position was advertised for the Minister without Portfolio and I thought that surely someone without a portfolio didn't have a lot of work and it therefore couldn't be too hard to work for him. Later of course I learned that 'without portfolio' simply meant that the minister could be tasked with ad hoc issues and therefore had no fixed portfolio or agenda to attend to.

I soon started discussions within my own department to inform my seniors that I would apply for the job, providing that I could be transferred on the same salary scale if I was successful in the application. They agreed.

The job interview was at the Union Buildings. Not only was I no longer rolling around on the lawn, but a black man was now the most powerful man in South Africa. And he was making sure people like me, conservative Afrikaans white folk, were included in this new government. People were friendly and relaxed and I noticed that there were still a lot of white faces around despite the new ANC government being in power.

During the interview, a black lady entered. She appeared cheerful and flamboyant. Dressed in a colourful satin outfit it was a picture I was not used to – that of a black lady dressed in such style and clearly in something that was more expensive than my mother's most prized outfit. We were rudely interrupted by her during the interview but she exclaimed to my interviewers: 'I need a typist and I don't care if she's black or white but I need her right now.' I smiled and thought: I'm your person. I had no idea what her position was. She briefly exchanged a few words with my two interviewers and then left. My interviewers telephoned me hours after the interview to ask whether I would be interested in a typist position in the actual President's office itself, and it was explained that it would involve working in his personal office. I only had Cape Town in mind, and since they assured me that the job would be on the same terms as the advertised post, I said I was interested.

They told me that the lady that had entered the interview before was the President's private secretary. My understanding was that I was going to work for her, Mary Mxadana, and she looked fairly pleasant. While still working at the Department of State Expenditure I had been tasked to train two junior black officials who had joined our department after the transformation process kicked in. They appeared friendly and I ended up working well with them. Slowly but surely I was starting to see black people a little differently. I was no longer inherently scared of all black people. I was starting to converse with them in normal language, without thinking that they could only understand broken Afrikaans or English. Mary was friendly and she made me feel at ease even though I had my doubts.

I realized that I was going to work in an office that was closer to the political centre of the beliefs I still opposed but I thought it was just a job and I wouldn't have much to do with real politics. I was willing to compromise and by then toyed with the idea that I actually liked the President of the Inkatha Freedom Party, Dr Mangosuthu Buthelezi, the opposition to the ANC. I liked him from seeing him on TV during the election campaign and I thought that since I had changed my mind about him, Nelson Mandela couldn't be that bad either. I was willing to give it a try but was very realistic about the fact that if I didn't like working there, nothing would stop me from leaving.

I can't remember feeling anything except relief when I was called and offered the position. Two weeks after the interview I assumed duty in the President's office as senior ministerial typist.

On 12 October 1994 I walked into the Union Buildings for the first time as an employee of President Mandela's personal office. I had seen pictures of him but knew nothing about him apart from the fact that he spent a long time in prison on Robben Island and that my family regarded him a terrorist. I didn't expect to have any interactions with him or ever see him.

I was well on time and received in reception by another staffer who took me through several glass doors and through security checks to reach what was known as the President's suite. It constituted a few offices along a corridor. She showed me a desk and computer in what looked like a 'pool' office, even though the only other desk was hers. She was an administrator answering the President's private office switchboard and assisting with ad hoc administration.

She explained that the President's personal office consisted of only Mary, herself and Elize Wessels. Elize was from the de Klerk government and used to work for the former First Lady, Marike de Klerk.

I sensed there was a tense atmosphere between the 'old' or white staff and the 'new' or black staff and that people were still marking territory and claiming positions in the new government. It was also clear that the 'old' guard were there to slowly ease the new leadership into power, guiding and teaching them, willing or unwillingly.

It was only much later that Mary arrived at the office. She had a presence about her that could be felt even without noticing her at first. She carried authority and dressed colourfully, which added to her vibrant personality. She entered the office like a whirlwind and hugged me to welcome me to the office. She was extremely friendly and made me feel at ease. Not having worked for a black person before, I was reluctant to let my defences go too soon. There was a superficial trust between black and white people. We still didn't know what to expect of one another. I was prepared to work for her but I held on to my political beliefs, thinking that my practical and financial situation had forced me to be in this office.

It is not necessarily a trait of all Afrikaners but generally speaking we have respect for people of authority or elderly people; whether we agree with their policies or not we were always courteous. If your principles did not allow you to respect a person you would simply ignore that person. I found I respected Mary. She told me about the liberation struggle. I started to be intrigued by the history of my own country. It felt like I had lived on another planet and I was completely unaware of anything she was telling me. Perhaps it was precisely that innocence and ignorance that made her feel at ease with me. She was very warm and friendly towards me and we shared a passion for music. She told me about her choir and brought me a CD to listen to. Her husband was the conductor of the choir and she was one of the founding members. They sang like angels.

Over the next two weeks I was orientated more about the operations around the President. He was nowhere to be seen or heard and I started assuming that I would possibly see him at a distance 'one day', but I did meet a number of people, from Parks Mankahlana, whom I was told spoke on the President's behalf, to Tony Trew, whom I was told helped write all the President's speeches, to the head of our office, referred to as the Director General of the Presidency, Professor Jakes Gerwel. It took me some time to figure out who did what and to remember names.

My main task was to type for Mary and to update the President's programme regularly. She soon taught me how to distribute the programme to the President's security and I was told to ensure that I sent it to both the white and the black commanders of his security team simultaneously. The South African Police Service was going through a transformation process like all government departments and amalgamating the ANC's old military wing, Umkhonto we Sizwe, and Apla from Azapo, another of the old liberation struggle parties, into the old white-dominated police force. Not everything made sense immediately and I would have to send the same fax twice to the same number but mark it for different people's attention. It was clearly a cosmetic merger in the police force and the two sides were very much operating independently, still trying to establish trust. But I'm a person who lives by the book. If instructions are issued, I follow them to the letter, and I did so without questioning or arguing about practicalities.

About two weeks into my time at the Presidency the President was scheduled to be in the office for the first time. By this time Mary had told me a little about the President, what type of person he was and that he was kind but disciplined. Afrikaners grow up with a sense of respect for any authority and before having met him, I had respect for him, purely because he was the President of the country.

He hadn't done anything publicly to prove the contrary and I therefore had no reason to disrespect him.

From my early arrival at the office that morning I could sense an unusual tension within the building but at the same time a kind of excitement. The police guarding our private office were alert and their uniforms neatly pressed, and soon a team of men in dark suits arrived presenting themselves as the advance team of the President's bodyguards. It was then time for the President to arrive and I closed the door leading to my office so as not to disturb anything that might be happening in the corridors. From passing footsteps and ructions I gathered that the President had arrived and he went past my office down the corridor into his office. Guests arrived to see him and were taken to his office without delay. They were all punctual and everything flowed with military precision. I sat quietly in my chair, awaiting instructions from anyone. I had noticed that the bodyguards were all armed and I was tense and cautious not to make any sudden move that could be misinterpreted. It was my first encounter with armed people in close proximity, and it made me nervous.

A few hours later Mary asked me to type something and bring it to her office once I was ready. So I did. I was looking at the piece of paper in front of me when I nearly bumped into President Nelson Mandela as he was exiting Mary's office into the corridor surrounded by bodyguards. He extended his hand first to shake mine; I was confused and not sure whether it was proper for me to greet him. I said, 'Good morning, Mr Mandela.' One doesn't really know what to do at that point except cry. Which I did. It was all too much. I was sobbing. He then spoke to me but I didn't understand him and was completely in shock. I had to say 'Excuse me Mr President' for him to repeat what he had just said to me, and after gathering my thoughts or guts – I'm not sure which – I realized that he addressed me in Afrikaans. My home language.

He was visibly old and appeared kind. I focused on the wrinkles on his face and his warm, sincere smile. He spoke with a caring voice and in a kind manner and asked me my name. I was ready to pull back my hand after shaking his but he held on. I could feel the texture of his hand on mine and I started perspiring. I wasn't sure if I was supposed to hold this black man's hand. I wanted him to let go but he didn't and he asked where I came from and where I worked. I wasn't sure whether to answer in Afrikaans or English and cannot remember which I chose, but we conversed in a mixture of Afrikaans and English. I was completely overtaken by emotion and couldn't continue. I then had a feeling of guilt that swept over me. I felt guilty that this kindly spoken man with gentle eyes and generosity of spirit spoke to me in my own language after 'my people' had sent him to jail for so many years. I instantly regretted voting 'No' in the referendum. How do you correct all of that prejudice in five minutes? Suddenly, I wanted to apologize. I hadn't given any thought to what twenty-seven years of imprisonment would be like, but I knew I was not even twenty-seven years of age. I was a mere twenty-three, about to turn twenty-four and I couldn't comprehend an entire lifetime in prison.

Mr Mandela noticed that I was unable to continue our conversation and still held onto my hand as he put his left hand on my shoulder and tapped it while he said, 'It's OK, calm down, I think you are overreacting.' I was firstly not used to someone being so direct to me to tell me that I'm overreacting and, secondly, I was embarrassed that it was a President telling me this. I calmed down and he was obviously in a hurry so we parted. His last words were 'I am happy to meet you and hope to see you again.' As we parted I thought: Ye, right. How can I be important to a President? After all, it's my people that put him through all that suffering.

I was in shock for the entire day and went home, telling my parents that I met the President today, and what a nice man he appeared to be. He spoke to me in Afrikaans. My parents didn't ask any questions and continued doing whatever they were busy with at the time, unaffected by my announcement. Probably used to me exaggerating a bit, I got the impression that they thought I was lying. I went to sleep puzzled by our encounter, not knowing where my thoughts or feelings were about this gentleman, perceived by my family and community to be a terrorist.

The next day I interrogated Mary about the fact that the President was so fluent in Afrikaans. She explained that he had learned Afrikaans in prison and he did so purposefully to communicate with his warders. It only struck me later that he obviously also charmed the apartheid leaders with his Afrikaans whenever he met them during negotiations. It is quite an amusing experience when events override what your brain expects. The last thing any Afrikaner would expect from Nelson Mandela was that he spoke to you in Afrikaans. It all became clear when he told me much later that, 'When you speak to a man you speak to his head but when you speak to him in his language you speak to his heart.' And that is exactly what he did. I came to understand that by learning the language of the warders he could almost seduce them. Afrikaans, being the language of the oppressor, was a much-hated language at the time and synonymous with the apartheid regime. I later also learned that Afrikaans was imposed as the main language for black education in 1974. This resulted in the Soweto uprising in 1976 in which about 20,000 black students took part, and although official figures estimated that the uprising resulted in 176 deaths it is widely believed that up to 700 students died during the protest. Black people were not accounted for in South Africa in those years and therefore official figures and estimates never correlated as there was no existing official register.

In the weeks that followed I saw the President at a distance on a few occasions as he passed in and out of the office. I concentrated on my typing and supporting Mary and never bothered to be around or be seen when he was in the office. Instead, I befriended the bodyguards, black and white. Some of them were very caring about me and inquisitive about my background. I was never sure whether they were checking on me or not, asking questions out of pure interest or whether it was as part of their job to establish any threat I may pose to the President.

Every time the President passed my office, I ensured that my door was closed so as to avoid having another emotional interaction with him. I literally hid away when I heard him approaching and only saw his back as he was passing the office. I was happy with his presence in the office though, as it brought about some excitement and a list of interesting visitors. I was more intrigued by him than by the visitors and hardly took notice of them, apart from knowing that some of them had names I recognized from the media or magazines.

I do recall the newly crowned Miss South Africa visiting, Baset-sana Makgalamela. I had some practice before she arrived in pronouncing her surname and managed by the time she arrived. She met with the President and we were called by Mary after the meeting to meet Miss South Africa.

Mary announced one afternoon that the President wished to see all his personal staff for lunch at his official residence the next day. Soon after his inauguration he renamed the Presidential house Mahlamba Ndlopfu, meaning 'start of a new dawn'. I thought that was quite appropriate. I was extremely nervous and definitely not ready to eat with any President. I had no idea what cutlery to use first, and one of my colleagues told me to simply watch her and follow her example, which put me at ease. I had also asked my mother the night before what to do about a selection of cutlery and she grabbed her Emsie Schoeman book – a South African lady who was considered the authority on etiquette – and I got a crash-course in table manners.

Arriving at Mahlamba Ndlopfu we were escorted to a sitting room. The President was still in a meeting but our arrival was announced to him. He ended his meeting and joined us in the lounge. He greeted us each by shaking hands and in a relaxing way conversing with us as a group, walking us to the dining room. By now I managed to control myself and I didn't cry. It was a kind gesture from his side to invite his staff to lunch, and looking at my colleagues it crossed my mind that the seven of us at that point were almost representative of all races in South Africa: Mary Mxadana, his private secretary, was black; Morris Chabalala, one of the assistant private secretaries, also black; Elize Wessels, the other

assistant private secretary, white; Alan Pillay, the administrative officer, Indian; Lenois Coetzee, the receptionist, white; Olga Tsoko, the
other receptionist, black; and then me, the most junior in age and
rank, white.

I was told that shortly after his inauguration the President called
all the staff from the old Presidency, people who had served the previous regime, to a meeting, allaying their fears of being fired or
made redundant without discussion or them having a choice in the
matter. He asked people to stay and help build the new government
of national unity but also gave them the option of leaving if they
wished to move on. Staff greatly appreciated the President giving
them a choice. The President's office was now a mixture of black
and white people representing the 'Rainbow nation' he often
referred to in speeches.

I'd noticed, too, that in Tuynhuys, the President's office in Cape
Town situated next to Parliament, the pictures of the old Presidents
and Prime Ministers continued to hang on the walls. Again I'd found
it strange that he wouldn't erase the past, seeing as how these people
had spearheaded the oppression of his people and imprisoned him.
But I was told that President Mandela insisted that those not be
removed. That they were part of South Africa's history, no matter
how unpleasant the memories were.

At the lunch, a round table was set and I quickly chose a chair far
from his to avoid any uncomfortable conversation or difficult questions from him, and I didn't want to take a chair of someone that
wanted to sit next to him. It was 1 p.m. and instead of lunch, one of
the housekeepers entered the room with a small FM black box-type
radio. It looked like an antique and something that was not seen
often being used any longer. It was time for the news and the radio
was switched on and put on the window shelf. While the news was
being read on radio we all looked at one another uncomfortably.
The President listened with concentration, clearly taking seriously
what was being read. I vaguely recall mention about South Africa
acting as a peace-keeping force in Africa, the *Achille Lauro* sinking
off the coast of Somalia and Cindy Crawford and Richard Gere

announcing their separation. I was trying to concentrate on the news but my thoughts wandered about the President, what he felt and thought at that time and, most importantly, how he felt about the three white Afrikaners at his lunch table.

Following the news lunch was served. To the contrary of what I expected, lunch was simple. It consisted of a starter, main course, dessert and coffee. The food was home-cooked, without fanciness, and you knew exactly what you were eating. The President had a glass of wine and even though we were all offered wine I settled for water. During lunch he started to tell us some stories about his years in prison and I had to press my fingernails into the palm of my hand to prevent me from crying again. By the time dessert was served I couldn't control myself any longer and my eyes were filled with tears. I felt *so* sorry for him. He told us about his precious tomato garden in prison and how he cherished his crop. He also explained how they worked in the limestone quarry, and how the reflection of the white rock damaged his eyes, and with his exceptional ability of story-telling he transported our imaginations to South Africa's Alcatraz and his prison cell on Robben Island. I tried to comprehend season upon season in a prison cell, cold cement floors, sharing a bathroom with other inmates, never having privacy, eating at specific times and limited tasteless food for twenty-seven years. It was still too much to comprehend. What struck me was that while he was telling these stories he didn't appear to be sad. To me it sounded like tragedy, yet he recited the stories in a colourful way as opposed to my grim imagination.

Lunch was soon over and back at the office we shared our experience with each other and I was free to express my sympathy. Clearly the President didn't want sympathy. It was something he considered to have been part of history and not to determine the rest of his life. I soon found a quote that expressed it so well: 'It's not important in life what happens to you, but how you handle what happens to you.'

I read later that he had written that it was easier to change others than to change himself, and to this day I often wonder about the struggle within himself as far as it concerned forgiveness and reconciliation, trying to imagine to what extent one has to really work with oneself to change your thinking and your beliefs: to take that decision to forgive, as Ahmed Kathrada told me. But as Madiba said, by deciding to forgive you do not only free the oppressed but you also free the oppressor.

Later that year, a prominent and progressive South African, Dr Johan Heyns, was assassinated and the President called all the generals in charge of the security forces in South Africa to a meeting in his office. Dr Heyns was one of the senior leaders of the Dutch Reformed Church in South Africa. The church was prominent during the apartheid era, justifying it through religion and Dr Heyns was one of the few Afrikaner leaders who criticized apartheid at a time when it was not fashionable to do so. Now it was suspected that a third force was at play, trying to destabilize the country and create tension between black and white at a time when South Africa was still vulnerable. As someone who had walked the Damascus road and showed eagerness to work with the new government, it was believed that Dr Heyns was assassinated by white Afrikaner extremists, the same kind of conservative people I once religiously supported. The conservative Afrikaners did not welcome such gestures of reform. I had slowly started to think about my own beliefs and although I was still a little confused, I had softened up and realized at least that resisting change was neither logical nor justifiable.

As the generals marched past my office to the President's office I couldn't help but feel a sense of pride when I saw them in their uniforms. We Afrikaners are proud people, especially of our generals and people who hold such positions – inherently so, but also because we trust them unconditionally and without prejudice. I felt proud of their presence even though there was tension in the office.

The President also called on General Constand Viljoen, who was the leader of the right-wing party called the Freedom Front and opposed to Mr Mandela on matters ranging from power sharing to land reform. I was extremely proud to meet General Viljoen as he was a pure Boer in every sense of the word (*boer* is Afrikaans for 'farmer'). He was also happy to find a girl in the President's office looking like and epitomizing a real Afrikaner. I imagined it made him feel comfortable seeing someone with the same culture and background in the President's office. The President didn't want to speak to him in his office, probably out of fear for listening devices, and met with him on a couch at the entrance of the ladies' bathroom in our offices across from my office door. When they sat down, the President called me. I was introduced to General Viljoen in Afrikaans and the President smiled warmly as he told General Viljoen that I was a real Afrikaner.

What did President Mandela mean when he said I was a 'real Afrikaner' or *boere-meisie* (farm girl)? Was it because I spoke Afrikaans? Did he sense I came from a conservative family? Or did I simply look like an Afrikaner? Only later I thought that perhaps my weight also played a part in epitomizing a real Afrikaner, something about which I was quite sensitive at the time. The Afrikaners are generally largely built people with a bigger bone structure. Most of them, my family not excluded, love to eat, particularly bread and meat. Did Nelson Mandela think I was really the image of an Afrikaner farm girl?

I went home that night with the same pride to tell my parents that I had met General Viljoen. I still had no interest in politics and only knew that he was there to discuss the death of Dr Johan Heyns. My parents were visibly more impressed by this announcement as General Viljoen was seen to represent the conservative Afrikaners at the time. An intelligence report on the death of Dr Heyns later crossed my desk but I had no interest in reading it, much to my regret in later years.

As the year passed, I started to feel more at home in my new environment, keeping Mary up to date on security, briefing the airforce on the President's movements, working with his staff at the ANC. On Mondays the President spent the entire day at Shell House, as it was known, the ANC head office in Johannesburg (later the name was changed to Luthuli House, after the founding president of the ANC, Albert Luthuli). We were not allowed to interfere with Mondays and in five years, unless we were on travels abroad, the President didn't miss one Monday going to the ANC head offices. We never knew what he did there or who he interacted with, and his party political work was separated from his official duties as President. But he was part and parcel of the ANC, never to be divorced from the party that shaped his life and entire political career and in the execution of his daily tasks as President he honoured the ANC's policies and framework.

Then one day I received a call from Mary to say that the President wanted me to drive to his private house in Houghton, Johannesburg, to help him with some Afrikaans. He was having trouble with his eye following an operation on it and we were told that he would be at home recovering for a few days.

Upon arrival at his Houghton house, I found a few security vehicles parked outside. The President himself was seated in a comfortable chair outside in the garden under a tree. He was wearing sunglasses with his two feet raised on a foot rest. He was wearing sunglasses obviously to protect his recovering eye. We shook hands and greeted warmly. He asked me to take a seat next to him and handed me the *Beeld* newspaper (the Afrikaans daily newspaper in our area). He then instructed me to start reading to him. Panic struck, I think I thought for a moment that I had forgotten how to read.

I struggled until he stopped me and told me to relax. There was humour in his voice and he told me to start from the top and read at a slower pace. It was easier. I then came across the surname Mamoepa in the article. Ronnie Mamoepa was the spokesperson for the ANC at the time. Reading across the surname I pronounced it exactly as it is spelt. The President interrupted me. He corrected my pronunciation to Mamo-epa. I thanked him and continued reading. Coming across the next mention of Ronnie's surname I tried to pass it as quickly as possible but the President interrupted me again and corrected me patiently, prompting me to repeat after him. The third time I realized I had to pay attention and that he was not going to be amused by my lack of trying, so I did and when I crossed the name for the fourth time he congratulated me on my good pronunciation. I felt like I had won an Olympic Gold medal and was almost embarrassed by the fuss he made. I relaxed a little but was still very tense. I also read too fast and he told me a few times to slow down. It was pure tension. He then asked me to explain a term he didn't understand and I read the sentence again and explained the context. After reading a few more articles I was dismissed to return to Pretoria. I remember perspiring like a marathon runner from pure nerves and was happy to be back at home, recovering from another shock interaction.

We returned to business as usual and the next time the President was in the office it was easier to face him. I didn't have any business dealing with him directly but now and then I would walk into him in the corridors or see him passing my office. I was no longer hiding or feeling shy and accepted the fact that if he wanted to get rid of me because I was a white Afrikaner, I would just deal with it when it happened. For the time being it appeared as if I was not going to become a victim of such actions, and although still somewhat sceptical about his feelings towards whites, I took comfort in the fact that he had only shown warmth so far.

I was trying to get an understanding of the political world around me. It wasn't easy and I literally had to do a crash-course in South African history. One of the bodyguards offered to take me and my two best friends, Pieter Moolman and Andries Ellis, to Soweto on a tour. Soweto is a formerly black township on the outskirts of Johannesburg, where the black people were grouped together and restricted to live in, during apartheid. We were nervous and scared but also curious to see what it looked like.

The bodyguard took us to President Mandela's first house in Vilakazi Street, showed us where Archbishop Tutu stayed – in the same street – and the Hector Pieterson museum, and related the stories of the student uprising in 1976. Hector was a child of thirteen years of age participating in the uprising in 1976 when thousands of students marched against Afrikaans being made compulsory as the medium of education for black people. The march was intended to be a peaceful demonstration but turned violent when the police arrived and shot at students to disperse the crowds. Hector was shot, and an iconic image taken of another student carrying him and running from the scene while Hector was dying in his arms became the image the world saw of South Africa under apartheid law. Hector was a hero.

The police officer taking us on the tour showed us some spots that were used as hideouts in Soweto by the ANC and its military wing when they were operating underground, and we were excited to learn but nervous at the same time for being in Soweto. White people didn't easily go into Soweto at the time but I was at ease as he was armed and I knew he would be in trouble if while in the care of a bodyguard of the President something had happened to us in Soweto. We drove around for a while and saw that Soweto was not the township of squatter camps like slums I had imagined it to be. People were building proper houses, some of them mansions, and there was nothing visibly to be afraid of. I later learned that the gentleman who took us on the tour was closely linked to National Intelligence, and I often thought that he was probably only eager to take us on the tour to enable him to dig a little into our lives and assess us on a threat level, as my presence so close to the President warranted.

At the end of 1994 the President went on holiday to Saudi Arabia. I couldn't imagine why anyone would want to go to Saudi Arabia on holiday. I was told the President visited a hospital while he was there, meeting with some South African nurses, and that he had friends there too, but I couldn't comprehend how one has a holiday in a desert like Saudi Arabia.

On the day of the President's return from Saudi, Mary invited me to accompany her to the airport to go and meet him. I was so excited and jumped at the opportunity. By now my attitude towards him had changed. His interactions with me were always pleasant and he was very friendly and warm whenever he spoke to me. I was therefore looking forward to any opportunity to see him. Mary said I had to bring my telephone book in case he wanted to make any calls from the airport, which he then did. By then I had armed myself with a telephone book and any numbers that Mary or the President could need. It was not something she told me to do but I assumed to be effective one had to have certain information at hand at all times, so I started compiling a telephone book with the important numbers Mary frequently used.

Arriving at the airport the President appeared happy to see me and he said that he'd thought about me. Again I thought: Ye right. I'm sure a President has more important things to think about than a typist in his office. Later I realized that he had already probably started working on his strategy to use me as the perfect example of including an Afrikaner in his office and how minorities would react to him doing so. It didn't cross my mind at the time though and although what he said flattered me I did not really believe it.

A huge media contingent awaited the President's arrival at Waterkloof airforce base where the Presidential plane touched down. Just after he greeted me someone took a photo of him and Mary walking towards the VIP arrivals hall at Waterkloof. The photo appeared in the *Sunday Times* newspaper the next day and my dad telephoned the newspaper to have a copy of the original photo sent to him. To my surprise they also took a photo while I greeted the President. It was my most precious possession ever when I received the photo and by now I was noticing some pride in my father, regardless of the fact that he had not met President Mandela but was merely creating an opinion based on the stories I told at home about our few interactions. Nelson Mandela was changing South Africans' views one by one. My dad included.

4

Working for a President

We received the strangest calls and requests sometimes in the President's office. On one occasion a gentleman called to say that he had a parrot that could imitate the President and whether he could please bring the parrot to the office for the President to hear it. I was the lucky person to take the call and I obviously said, 'No Sir, I don't think so.' One day I received a call from an Afrikaans gentleman who said, 'Good morning lady, please give me your pints.' I responded by saying, 'Excuse me Sir.' He said again: 'Your pints, I need your pints please.' I said, 'Sir, I think you have the incorrect number as I don't have a clue what you are talking about.' He then explained that he was calling from a dairy farm and dialled the wrong number: he was looking for the pints of milk our dairy produced for the day. I replied, 'Sir, even if I had the pints I wouldn't know how much a pint is.'

A South African serial killer on the run, Colin Chauke, also called our switchboard and wanted to speak to the President, and the President only, to hand himself over to the police. He wanted the President to help him, probably because he was scared that he might be shot when he handed himself over to the police. Olga was on the switchboard that day and acted swiftly to alert the police from another telephone line. The police arrested Chauke a few hours later and he didn't get to speak to the President. We therefore sometimes dealt with serious matters and on other days you had to keep your sanity in check because of the ludicrous things people would suggest or call about.

Things happened at an enormously fast pace. Especially when the President was around. In his presence things were calm but behind the scenes it was running and organizing at speed. There would be very little time for anything else than work. Somehow Elize based in Cape Town managed much better than us. She had a more balanced life but in Pretoria we raced against time to get through the day. As I have mentioned, Elize had served the former First Lady, Marike de Klerk, and was one of the staff members from the old regime who remained in the dispensation. The rest of us really had no knowledge or skill of having been in a President's office before and a lot was done on trial and error.

The Presidency was focused on implementing the interim constitution and setting up structures to enhance the functioning of the constitution, which was signed into law in 1996. The President himself was very focused on reconciliation and nurturing both black and white people's emotions that were bruised as a result of apartheid.

Apart from typing up the President's schedule and distributing it daily to security, households, airforce and concerned parties, Mary tasked me with a few other mundane things. She would occasionally ask me to bring tea to the President or his guests or even drive her car to be filled with fuel and fetch her dry cleaning. I didn't mind doing anything and whatever was asked. I often dropped off documents at the President's house in Pretoria, received visitors and learned how to deal with any enquiries that came to the President's personal staff. We started operating in a more structured way, where work was divided between the three private secretaries and Alan and I had to deal with most of the administration. Although operating within the larger office as the Department of the Office of the President, the President's personal staff dealt with more of his private matters and day-to-day appointments and movements as well as requests directly related to him or requiring his personal attention, while the Department dealt with policy, cabinet and political issues.

I now knew Professor Jakes Gerwel, the head of the President's office, a little better. Professor Gerwel – or Prof. as we called him – was an academic and anti-apartheid activist since his early life, and was a brown man originating from the Eastern Cape. He was head-hunted from the University of the Western Cape to become the Chief of Staff at the President's office and the Secretary of Cabinet in the first democratically elected government. He was my first introduction to a real intellectual and when I met him for the first time I was a little surprised that a brown man could have so many academic qualifications. Most of his qualifications he obtained *cum laude* and all of them in literature and language. In my ignorant view only white people could be that learned. I was told about all his qualifications before I met him. He was a very likeable person who clearly respected people without prejudice – I had expected to be looked down upon by a person with so many qualifications. Even though it didn't sound right, I was told that he was an Afrikaner too. Again my own prejudices made it difficult to believe that anyone who wasn't white could be an Afrikaner. Prof.'s smile and his hair were his trademarks. His hair was very disorderly and in an afro-type style. It reminded me of Albert Einstein's. Whenever the President was in the office, Prof. Gerwel would frequently pass our offices on his way to see him and always stopped to enquire about our well-being. The president relied heavily on Prof. Gerwel for advice on every detail of his presidency. They had a very close relationship and the President had a lot of admiration for Prof.'s calm and calculated approach not only to matters of national importance but even in dealing with issues in his personal environment.

It was February 1995 and we were all preparing to move to Cape Town for Parliament's first session of the year.

In Cape Town all Parliamentarians lived in a village exclusively built for them called Acasia Park. According to rank and years of service you got allocated either an apartment or a small house, also depending on the size of your family. For us single girls, bachelor apartments with a small kitchen and a bathroom were adequate. I loved the independence and soon made friends with some of my colleagues. Maretha Slabbert was one such person; she worked in the Cabinet Secretariat at the Presidency at the time. Seventeen years later Maretha and I still worked together and she was single-handedly the most important support in my life to date, both professionally and personally.

Come July, Parliament would go into recess and we would all pack up and move back to Pretoria for the rest of the year. It was not something I looked forward to and I was hoping to avoid going back to anything that deprived me of my independence, like living at my parents' home and having to report to anyone. Yet, I looked forward to seeing my friends and sharing my experiences with them, and then of course to certain home comforts such as having your clothes washed and ironed automatically in the course of everyday life and not having to worry about those things. Often at parties my friends would tease me, telling people that I now worked for the 'enemy'. I took it as a joke but as we grew older and more mature we eventually started debating history and politics more seriously. I felt more informed and at least able to converse in an intelligent manner on something I thought I was gathering knowledge about. These debates often ended in heated argument because my perspective on events in South Africa was slowly changing, due to my interaction with the President and the knowledge I had acquired from some of my colleagues.

Mary also spent more time with me and told me about the President's private life; his failed marriage to Winnie Madikizela and about their daughters, Zindzi and Zenani. Apart from official events where the President needed a companion and he would ask Zindzi or Zenani to join him, I rarely saw them, and judging from his diary one realized that the President didn't have much time for a private life. I was also told that he had two surviving children from his first marriage but we never saw them or had any dealings with them.

I had noticed, now, that whenever the President had Afrikaners visiting him, he would call me to deliver documents or ask me to serve tea in his office. I didn't mind as it posed another opportunity to see him. He was removing my defences day by day, chiselling away my prejudices and the layers of apartheid that had grown on me in the same way he chiselled the limestone while he was imprisoned on Robben Island. He would ask with real interest how I was, about my parents, about my well-being. Every time he saw me he would ask something different. Any person that takes an interest in you automatically becomes likeable, no matter what your preconceived ideas about him or her. And then it was done with sincerity in this case so I enjoyed the attention. I had never imagined that I would be of significance for a President to enquire about my well-being.

On one such occasion a documentary was being filmed around the President's day-to-day life. I was instructed to serve tea in his office that day during a meeting attended by Jay Naidoo, Minister without Portfolio in the Presidency, and the man I would have worked for if fate hadn't brought Mary into my interview. I wasn't prepared and didn't feel properly dressed to serve tea in his office that day. I nevertheless served the tea and the President introduced me to Minister Naidoo in Afrikaans. The Minister smiled unconvincingly. I found it hard to be sure whether all former anti-apartheid activists had joined Mr Mandela in the decision to forgive.

When the documentary aired, my parents were taken aback by reports that some friends of theirs had decided to cut ties with them because I served tea to a black man. The entire Afrikaans community was not adapting well to the changes in South Africa. Their interaction and relationships with black people remained on the same level as during apartheid – that of master and servant. Life for most whites continued unchanged, in the same bubble of their materialist comfort as before, and not all white people were actually making a concerted effort to change the country into a non-racial society. Sadly many remain in that bubble even today.

My parents found themselves in an awkward situation. They had no reason to suspect that I wasn't happy at work. They could see that I worked hard and I liked what I was doing, yet it was clear that the community wasn't going to support my endeavours. (Years later the same people wanted to talk to me about having books signed by then retired President Mandela and I took pleasure in arranging this. Whether their views had changed only towards the President, I don't know.)

*

That autumn I got a call from Rochelle, the President's niece who looked after him at home in Johannesburg, to say that he wanted me to accompany him to a United World Colleges event in the Carlton Hotel that night. After the President left his then wife, Winnie Madikizela Mandela, in 1992, his first permanent residence was in a suburb called Houghton and Rochelle moved in with him to look after him, organizing his house and workers but also providing him with some personal support at home. I was in Pretoria at the time of the call and panic struck. I asked my mother what to wear and we selected a simple black skirt and jacket. I was expected to be at the President's house at a certain time and Rochelle said that he wanted me to drive with him. That made me even more nervous. What was I supposed to say or do in the car sitting next to a President? No one prepares you for these things.

I arrived at his house and asked Rochelle what was expected of me. She said I should just go along and when he is supposed to speak I should put the speech where he is supposed to speak from, as well as his reading glasses, make sure he had water to drink, and security would take care of the rest. I was anxious to hear from Rochelle that the President called Mary to inform her that he wanted me to go with him. It made me somewhat uncomfortable that she was not the one instructing me to go with him. That was the totality of Rochelle's briefing.

The President came downstairs and he greeted friendly and invited me to get into the car. The security opened the heavily armoured door and I could barely move it. I didn't want to intrude in the President's space so kept to my corner of the car and sat as close to the door as possible. Tense. On our way to the Carlton Hotel in mid-Johannesburg the President said that I would now meet Queen Noor, the wife of the King of Jordan. I asked him how I was supposed to address her and he smilingly explained, 'No, you see, you call her Your Majesty' because she was a Queen. The President always started his sentences with a 'No' whether the answer was yes or no, and it usually was followed with 'you see'. I paid so much attention to his every word that I couldn't help but notice it.

He had a way of addressing people with the utmost respect, no matter who you were, and even his choice of words conveyed that respect. Starting every sentence with 'No' didn't have any negative connotation. It was just habit and a gentler way of starting off with any sentence.

Arriving at the event people quickly started crowding around the President and the security found it difficult to keep people away from him while at the same time trying to allow him to walk towards the door of the event. At the door he was met by Her Majesty. The President introduced me by saying, 'Your Majesty, this is my secretary Zelda la Grange': a) I wasn't his secretary, and b) I really didn't think she cared. But to my surprise she took interest in me and asked how long I had been working for the President. My answer: almost a year. The fact that I didn't have a long history with him clearly didn't discourage her to show interest in me. She was one of the most beautiful ladies I've ever met and she had the stature of a Queen. She moved with grace and I had to pinch myself not to stare. I had met a Queen!

Little did I know that a greater surprise awaited me inside. The security led us to the main table. I had never experienced such chaos in a crowd before and was trying my best to stay as close as possible to the President. I felt bewildered as people pushed against us, preventing us from moving freely, in addition to the security forming a tight circle around us. Everyone wanted to touch the President or see him close to. As soon as he and the Queen stood behind their chairs in the hall people quietened down and got ready to take their seats. I turned around and asked the security: 'Where am I supposed to go?' I was relying on them to guide me and teach me what to do. They showed me my seat, right next to the Queen. I blushed and felt blood and my heart pumping in every muscle of my body. There was no way, none, zero, absolutely no chance that I had to sit next to a Queen. What would I say? What do I do? I couldn't even remember from my crash course on etiquette what cutlery to use first. Somewhere in the back of my mind I remember overhearing my mom saying 'start from the outside'. OK, that deals with that then.

But still this cannot be happening. I told the security that it was a mistake. In the meantime the President and Queen took their seats and I was confused, nervously trying to get away, at this point being the only one in the room still standing around.

The President looked at me in a way that exclaimed 'Zelda, take your seat.' I looked into his eyes, mine filled with panic as if to say, 'Rescue me; tell me to go away.' But he nodded his head instead to signal sit down. So I sat. The Queen and the President exchanged pleasantries and I had no idea who sat to my other side. The person could have been naked or dead. I wouldn't have noticed. I followed the pattern on the table cloth with my eyes and later put my hand on the table to draw the lines of the pattern with my finger. I was hoping to appear to be relaxed but I was dying inside of tension and nervousness. I knew I was supposed to keep my elbows off the table but I could no longer disguise my ineptness and I thought placing my elbow on the table would ground me a little more. Surely seating me next to a Queen was completely against protocol. Even I knew that.

The Queen turned to me and started talking to me. I smiled and looked past her to the President again with a look in my eyes that said: 'OK Sir, you are supposed to help me here.' I was a bit upset with him as he didn't come to my rescue but only smiled, clearly not noticing my anxiety. The Queen started asking me about the political situation in the country, where I grew up, etc. I cannot remember what I responded but I knew I had to sound like the eternal optimist because I assumed if I was with the President it was expected of one to be positive about the future of South Africa. I didn't really know what I was talking about and I wasn't sure what to think yet: whether I really saw a future for South Africa and where we were heading. My opinion of the new South Africa had not really evolved beyond the fact that I now kind of liked the President.

And then, I was saved by the bell. Proceedings started and after the Queen's speech the President was asked to speak. He was speaking from his seat and a microphone was handed to him. I handed him his speech and glasses and he put his glasses back on the table and started reading his speech. I thought: Why would he need his glasses if he doesn't use them? After completing his speech he handed it back to me and said out loud: 'Thank you darling.' His words were filled with consideration and gratefulness. I wasn't used to anyone calling me 'darling'. Later I realized that it was just an affectionate term he used for many women from time to time. If a woman or a stranger calls me 'darling' I have always felt that there is a derogatory connotation to it. But surely you don't mind Nelson Mandela calling you 'darling'? Blood rushed to my head and I was shy with shock – almost the same feeling as when your mother used to kiss you in public as teenager, somewhat shy over the association and affection. I thought I had done my duty however, and was ready to relax and start eating.

We sat waiting for food for about five minutes and then the President said, 'Zelda, I think it is time for us to leave.' The master of ceremonies announced his departure and off we went. As years passed I also realized that he wasn't fond of eating anywhere. He simply adored his home-cooked food prepared by one of his long-serving Xhosa chefs, Xoliswa or Gloria, and therefore he hardly ever ate at public events.

On the way to the car someone approached with a copy of the President's autobiography, *Long Walk to Freedom*. Security turned him away but the man insisted, reaching the President himself, who couldn't really say no. After he signed the book, he handed it to a security officer and moved to the car. When I looked round the security man had ripped the page with the President's signature out of the book, telling the man that he should not have disobeyed instructions. I went into complete shock. Little did I know that I would become one of the people who had to try and maintain order no matter what it took, although I luckily stopped short of tearing pages out of books.

On the way home, I told the President that I thought it was inappropriate that I sat next to the Queen. He smiled and said, 'Don't worry, it was OK.' That made me even more nervous. The

President wasn't fazed by it at all. At home he invited me in for coffee but I was eager to head back to Pretoria. This was too much to handle. He insisted that security drive with me 'to my house' he said, but outside I convinced them that it wasn't necessary. They were tired and I was definitely not going to have anyone follow me home. When I later accompanied him more regularly he would insist on the security driving with me and we learned to agree only to break our agreement as soon as we left the door.

In the winter of 1995 the President was invited to a town in the Western Cape, Swellendam, a small village-like Afrikaans town along the Garden Route in South Africa, to receive the Freedom of the Town. It was an act of unity for a town that was dominated still by white Afrikaners to offer the President such an honour, and he agreed to accept it. Again, a few days prior to the event, he announced that he wanted me to go with him. He called me to Genadendal the day before, his official residence in Cape Town, and upon arrival asked me to sit down. Genadendal is the name of a small brown Afrikaans community in the rural Western Cape. He adopted the name for his official residence in Cape Town to pay homage to the community of Genadendal, which means something like 'valley of gratitude' when translated directly.

He announced that he wanted to practise his Afrikaans and I had to help him with pronunciation as his entire speech was in Afrikaans. He fired away and unceremoniously started reading. At first I didn't have the heart to correct him but then he would look up every now and again to seek approval. I nodded like a real teacher and hated myself for appearing to be such a supremacist. Although I had been asked to help him, the situation presented was so typical of the apartheid era of a white overseeing what the black man was doing and the black man seeking approval from the white. I also couldn't really understand what he was reading and I had to adjust my concentration level. Then he wanted to re-read the speech for a second time. So I agreed – who wouldn't? – but this time I gathered some courage to add a few corrections. He was becoming more nervous to read and would peek at me over his reading glasses, this time seeking less approval but more affirmation. I nevertheless nodded.

It was my first helicopter ride ever. I was nervous but I watched the President's face and saw that he was at ease in the big military Oryx helicopter. I relaxed. It was being flown by white military pilots and I wondered whether he trusted them. By 1995 very few black pilots had been trained and qualified to be absorbed into the transformed military forces. On our way I thought about his speech and wondered whether he was going to remember the words we'd practised the previous day. I was nervous for him while he appeared relaxed, as if he was on his way to a social gathering of some sort.

Arriving in Swellendam he was received with open arms and insisted on first walking among the ordinary people, and when a little girl came to greet him on stage his face and body language opened up completely. He spoke to her in Afrikaans too and she responded although she was shy. He enjoyed that interaction and I could see that he had a special connection to the child. He delivered his speech and remembered the words I had helped him with. It was perfect. By delivering his entire speech in Afrikaans he reached out to the community's heart and people adored him for that.

Back in the office in Pretoria it was on one of the occasions that I served tea in his office, although he was by himself this time, that he requested me to take a seat at the other side of his desk. I nervously did, not knowing what to expect. The President didn't easily tell you to sit down at his desk. I thought I was in some kind of trouble and tried to remember what stories I told to whom in the last couple of weeks, trying to assess why I was in trouble. He then said, 'No . . . you see, I want you to come to Japan with me.' My first thoughts were: Would that not be considered inappropriate to travel abroad together? and then I thought: Oh no, I'm convinced this is similar to my experience of my first encounter with him; I simply don't understand what he is saying. I think I replied with 'Excuse me Sir?' and he repeated the question while I needed time to process what he was saying. 'I want you to come to Japan with me,' he repeated.

And all I could think of to say was, 'Thank you very much Mr President but I don't have money to go to Japan right now.' He burst out laughing, probably not knowing how to respond to such stupidity.

He saw the surprise on my face to his laughter and he quickly composed himself to repeat the question, this time with a bit of essential detail: 'I want you to travel to Japan as part of my delegation on our state visit.' I had a vague idea that this was work but he continued to say that I should go to the Director General, the Chief of Staff of the Presidency, Prof. Gerwel, who would explain everything to me. I thanked him and left his office. I didn't say a word to Mary and I cannot recall if she was in her office as I passed through to my own office. I returned to my desk to digest what had just happened. I didn't know what to do with the information in my head and who to contact next. The President made it sound so easy to speak to Prof. Gerwel but he was, after all, the head of our office and it was not as simple as walking through his door and demanding answers. So I decided to leave it there and not speak to anyone about this again and forget that it had ever happened. I was convinced it was just a mistake.

A few days later Prof. Gerwel passed our office on his way to the President and greeted us as usual. He approached me at my desk and told me that he had spoken to the President and that he had mentioned to him that I should be included in the delegation. I was nervous. He pointed me to the Department of Foreign Affairs to have a passport issued and told me who to speak to, to make arrangements. He also told me that we would be joined by another young lady from the Western Cape. Her name was Melissa Brink. The President encountered a debate with her in the Western Cape at a public meeting with the brown community, during which he was impressed by her inquisitiveness and the way she challenged the ANC to provide her with the education that her parents believed would be provided if they voted the ANC into power. In her view, progress was too slow and she had the courage to challenge the President when she had the opportunity. He liked the fact that such a youngster was so serious about her education to have the guts to question the President over it.

I had no idea why I was invited to go on this trip and no one else knew either. What I really thought was a bonus was that I wasn't expected to pay for anything but rather received an extra allowance for travelling abroad. When I heard the amount I would be paid I was alarmed as it sounded like a danger pay of some sort. I think I drove the officials at Foreign Affairs crazy with all my questions – clearly a sign of my inexperience. I also had a sense of guilt towards Mary. I didn't know whose duty it was to inform her that I would be accompanying the delegation on this trip or what my role would be and I felt uncomfortable being in a space where she was uncertain about my role too; after all, I was working more for her than for the President.

The day arrived for me to depart with the advance team for Japan. I don't think I've ever been so excited in my entire life. Armed with my diplomatic passport, newly sewn clothes and manners recited from my mother, I departed on my first ever trip abroad. Before that day, I had never left the borders of South Africa and my first trip overseas being to Japan was almost like a fantasy.

Upon arrival in Tokyo we were met by officials from the Embassy and driven to the Osaka Palace Hotel. I could sense that all the officials were as puzzled with my presence as I was. Mary arrived a day later and things were tense between us. People were careful not to offend me because they knew my presence was the result of a direct instruction from the President. I was trying to figure out who did what on a state visit but it was not easy. We were surrounded by security and protocol officials and I soon took a liking to a gentleman by the name of Johan Nieman from Foreign Affairs. Johan guided me and explained things in great detail. He was also the first person to say: 'So how did you get to be put on the trip and what is your role?' I explained that I was merely the typist and I had no idea what my role was, but he comforted me with the fact that the President personally invited Melissa and I and therefore we should not be intimidated by anything or anyone. That made me feel a little better.

In my conversations with colleagues on the trip I got a sense of why we were there: for the South African government to strengthen its economic ties with Japan. We were accompanied by a few ministers and it became apparent what is expected of such office bearers during state visits. I was slowly developing a sense of politics.

President Mandela was to meet the Japanese Emperor. Upon arrival at the Emperor's palace we were told to stand in a receiving line. The most senior officials, the ministers, closest to the President and then in order of seniority down the line to the most junior. Of course Melissa and I were right at the end.

It was the first time it dawned on me why Melissa and I indeed accompanied the delegation on the trip. Melissa was introduced as a coloured, mixed-race young lady and I was introduced as an Afrikaner. I looked at my colleagues and realized that our delegation was completely 'representative', and I was happy to be part of that. The President wanted all the races represented in his team. He was determined to show the world that just as he preached reconciliation to the South African public, it was something he felt so strongly about that he wanted to apply that methodological thinking also in his own office, and commit to bringing about unity in South Africa even in his closest environment.

When the President got to me he introduced me to the Emperor by saying, 'This is Zelda la Grange, she is my secretary and a real Afrikaner *boere-meisie*.' I wasn't sure the Emperor knew what an 'Afrikaner *boere-meisie*' was and he appeared puzzled, but courteously smiled while he shook my hand.

I also soon discovered that I could speak to the President in Afrikaans whenever I didn't know what to do and that he would calmly direct me on the right protocol. He was being briefed by protocol officials and whenever he saw me hesitating, he would speak to me in Afrikaans and direct me. When the President had rest periods we didn't move from the guest house. Other delegates went out shopping and sightseeing but I was too scared to move. What if the President called me and I wasn't there? It was inconceivable. At the state banquet I sat at a good distance from the President but I could see and watch his every move.

★

Life for ordinary South Africans still hadn't changed much since President Mandela's inauguration in 1994, although there was a sense of optimism. What one saw of the President on TV was that he always greeted people respectfully and without prejudice. The public liked that. Our economy stabilized and investors started having confidence in the new South Africa. However, a watershed moment in President Mandela's Presidency approached in 1995 and an opportunity to show the world that South Africa would survive; that we were healthy and well.

The Rugby World Cup was being played in South Africa. Rugby was still very much considered a white man's sport in South Africa, even though I later discovered that black people, especially in the Eastern Cape, had played rugby for decades, but because of apartheid they were never allowed to participate in the sport publicly, or to be active spectators. Rugby is something most white Afrikaner people religiously follow and support, but the teams and attendance of public matches during apartheid were restricted for whites only. Prior to the World Cup the selectors included a brown Afrikaans-speaking young man in the national team (the Springboks) by name of Chester Williams.

The President met the Springboks before the start of the tournament at their training camp in the Western Cape, and on the day of the opening match in Newlands he was there to cheer them. When Chester (or Chessie as I later fondly addressed him) entered the field the crowd went crazy cheering him along. Chester was scoring points during matches and for that, white people started supporting his selection.

I never knew that the President even knew the rules of rugby but apparently he did – probably understanding more about the game than I did. He sat next to the Managing Director of SA Rugby, Dr Louis Luyt, as well as the Prime Minister of Australia, as the Springboks were playing the Australian team, the Wallabys, in this opening match. The President was in good spirits and took a bet with the Prime Minister that whoever won that day would win the tournament, and the loser would send the other a case of wine as both countries had reputable industries. South Africa won the match and we went right through to the historic day of the final in Johannesburg. (After our victory, the wine arrived from Australia and it was donated to a charity for fundraising purposes.)

I heard Mary calling around a few days before the final asking for a Springbok jersey, but didn't know why or for who. Then the day before the match, when we said our goodbyes at the office, she told me that the President would enter the field on the day of the final wearing a Springbok jersey. I thought that was quite original but didn't make more of it.

Mary gave me two tickets to the final match and I invited my dad to accompany me. We were well on time at the stadium and the crowd was excited and the vibe explosive. Shortly before kick-off the announcement came: 'Ladies and Gentlemen, please welcome the President of the Republic of South Africa, Mr Nelson Mandela' and he entered surrounded by bodyguards and rugby officials. The crowd cheered but when they caught sight of him in his green and gold jersey people started chiming 'Nelson Nelson Nelson'. At first I thought it was disrespectful to call him by first name but then when I looked around me people didn't seem to think about that but like one man they stood up and started screaming, whistling and shouting with excitement to see the black President in a Springbok jersey and cap. People felt a sense of pride irrespective of their political convictions. He greeted both teams and the National Anthems were sung.

It was a tense match and my dad and I jumped up and down with excitement like old buddies. Then in the extra time Joel Stransky kicked a drop goal which led South Africa to victory. The crowd exploded. People were hugging and kissing strangers, some even crying with joy. For a few hours our past didn't matter; we went colour blind and people embraced the opportunity to celebrate as South Africans. South Africa was excluded from the first two Rugby World Cups in 1987 and 1991 because of apartheid and was only allowed to participate in the international sporting arena after our first democratic elections. It was our first participation and we won the tournament.

It remains one of the best strategic moves of Nelson Mandela's Presidency in uniting the country to wear that jersey that day. The world saw South Africa as a united nation. He embraced what was considered the 'white man's sport' and by taking that leap into their most emotional territory he reached way beyond the borders of race and touched the people's hearts. He was proud of the Springboks but he was also proud of every citizen in the country, for them and with them. He would often refer to that day when saying that sport had the ability to unite people way beyond borders of division, and in a humble way I think he underplayed his own genius on that day.

The President soon invited the Springbok team for lunch after their victory and from there his close association with rugby started. He was fond of Francois Pienaar who captained the Springboks, but as proud of all the other players that led us to be not only a victorious team but a victorious nation. For years to follow the President would be very supportive of rugby until he got criticized for supporting it too much and not paying enough attention to other sports. There was always a juggling act to maintain. As much as he had to nurture the rugby players in the beginning he then had to learn to create a healthy distance.

Later, in 1998, the former President of the South African Rugby Union, Dr Louis Luyt, took President Mandela to court to contest a Commission of Inquiry that the President had established into the affairs of South African rugby. Luyt contested the President's constitutional right to appoint such a body to investigate rugby for alleged racism and nepotism, the SA Rugby Union being an independent private body. Luyt was described in the *Sunday Times* of 16 August 1998 as 'the nearest thing to a rugby war lord and the man fans loved to hate'. The now late Steve Tshwete was the Minister of Sport and Recreation at the time and he was concerned about the President's insistence to defend himself in court. The President's lawyers and advisors offered to represent him but he refused.

Judge William de Villiers was presiding over the case and on 19 March 1998, when the President walked into court, he walked to the prosecuting lawyers first and shook hands with each and every one of them, including Dr Luyt. He then greeted his own team and took his seat. I was angry on the first day at him and thought that if these people had the audacity to question the President, why should he give them any attention or even be friendly with them? When I raised the incident with the President during tea time he taught me a lesson I would never forget: 'Remember, the way you approach a person will determine how that person reacts to you.' If you start off by disarming your enemy the battle is halfway won. The prosecutors were indeed caught off guard by this gesture but they quickly recovered when they launched their attack. The other thing he said was never to allow your enemy to determine the grounds for battle. If they wanted the courtroom to be the battlefield, we had to neutralize them by showing them that it was not a personal matter, but by being friendly we have moved the battle to a psychological advantage. I heard and believed what he had said but to me it was very personal and ugly.

They eventually called him to the stand and he insisted on standing while being questioned, regardless of the Judge inviting him to sit down. The prosecutor would ask him questions in different ways and then the President would answer by saying, 'My Lord, I believe Mr Maritz has already asked that question and I responded.' The Judge would ask the prosecutor to continue and again the President would respond by saying he had already answered the question and that he felt his intelligence was being undermined if the prosecutor put the same question three times in a row in a different manner. It was tense in the courtroom as the President was getting angry. The trained lawyer within the President bloomed. He was shining in court even though I felt they were being unreasonable.

During lunch we would let his food be brought from Mahlamba

Ndlopfu and he would sit quietly in a chamber eating. He was think-ing and reflecting and strategizing for the next session. In the afternoon he was back on the stand. I had to pinch myself several times to keep quiet as I was disgusted by the prosecuting team. On more than one occasion I wanted to offer my remarks too. I gasped a few times at the way they tried to ridicule the President. How times had changed! Dr Luyt was a pure Afrikaner. Now I was siding with the President. Not because I worked for him but because I believed in what he stood for and his right as President to ask for this inquiry to be established. After proceedings had closed I made no secret of my feelings and told the President. He was calm and col-lected as ever, tired but not emotionally affected by proceedings like I was.

The government and therefore President Mandela lost the case but then appealed. The outcome was overturned much later by the Appeals Court but by that time the Commission of Inquiry had lost its relevance and never resumed its work.

While still recovering from the bruises of our defeat in court, we were preparing for the state visit of President Jacques Chirac of France to South Africa. A massive state banquet was being planned in Johannesburg. The President called me and told me to ensure through our Protocol department that Dr Luyt as well as his legal team be invited to the banquet. I agreed but when I put down the phone I thought: Over my dead body. I will deliberately just forget about it. Why would we invite people who belittled the President the way they did? He had not an ounce of bitterness in him towards white people despite apartheid, yet they wanted to so badly prove him wrong, not in private but in public. How could I be party to inviting them to enjoy a banquet which clearly every person in South Africa wanted to attend? So I neglected my task and I didn't tell the Protocol section about the President's request. The next day he specifically called me to ask: 'Did you invite Dr Luyt and his legal team?' And I said, 'No Khulu, not yet.' I also didn't reveal my plan to conveniently, deliberately forget about it. But the next day and the day after he reminded me again. And I realized he was not going to forget and that if he looked for them at the dinner, which he then did, I was going to be in an enormous amount of trouble if we hadn't invited them. He wanted to greet them and I was shocked. Despite all that had happened, he was his charming self and greeted them like old friends. My ego's most expensive lesson: that is how you deal with the enemy.

Travelling with a President

In 1996 the President asked me to accompany him again, this time on his state visit to France. I was excited having the opportunity to visit France, obviously, because of my ancestral history. The only difference this time was that I was the only secretary to accompany him and it was therefore my first fully fledged working state visit. In Paris a lady visited him and I was suspicious about her presence. She arrived at the guest house with our Ambassador to France, Barbara Masekela. Barbara escorted her straight to the President's suite in the guest house. The President's suite had a dining room, its own lounge and ample space befitting for a President. But Barbara soon left, without the visitor, and the door to the President's suite was closed. I knew that was never allowed – that a door be closed when he was alone with a female. I rushed up to Parks Mankahlana, the Presidential spokesperson, and with panic in my voice announced that the door was closed and the lady was still inside. Parks told me it was Mrs Graça Machel, the widow of the late President Samora Machel from Mozambique. What crossed my mind first was: Oh hell, I don't know all this history, and then: Well, they've closed the door and I may be in trouble about it.

It was one of the very few occasions that Parks was irritated with me and told me 'leave it'. So I did.

Before we left for a public reception, the President called me and formally introduced me to Mrs Machel. And he said something I remembered and tried to adhere to for years to follow: 'This is Aunt Graça Machel. She is my friend. We are going to this event now and I want you to stay with her at all times. You are not allowed to lose sight of her at any time and I need you to take care of her.' That made me nervous because I didn't know how I was supposed to look after both of them at this event. Somehow I managed.

After we returned to South Africa it was leaked to the media that Mrs Machel and the President were in a relationship. I was shocked at first when I saw it in the Sunday papers, fearing that someone might think that I leaked it to the media, but Parks later told me it was deliberately leaked.

On Wednesday, 12 February 1997 a debate followed in Parliament after the President's State of the Nation address a few days before. The debate was about racism and minority groups accusing the government of the aforementioned. The President said during his debate:

> May I challenge each and every one of those honourable members to come out with me now, not to fight [laughter] but to show them evidence which will disprove all their propaganda. However before I refer to that, I was asked the same question that has been raised by my friend here, F. W. de Klerk: 'Why are you applying racism in reverse and letting our people down, punishing the Afrikaners?'
>
> I said, 'Very well. Can you give me some statistics? How many Afrikaners have been dismissed? When? Who replaced them?' He said: 'I do not have the facts with me.' I said: 'I am very surprised that a professor should put a question like that to the President of the country without facts.' I said I would give him time and asked how long he needed before he could supply me with that evidence. That was the last time I saw him [laughter].
>
> I want to say that whilst we are empowering those who have been discriminated against, we are acting sensitively to the people who were there before we took over. Just outside this Chamber is Superintendent Riaan Smuts, who comes from the apartheid regime. I have retained him. I have two white secretaries from the old regime, typical *boeremeisies* [laughter]. They are Elize Wessels from Kakamas and Zelda la Grange from George. Those honourable members can go through my staff.

I laughed when I heard of this. Elize was never from Kakamas and well, I've never been from George, although for years later Madiba still believed I was from George. My grandparents and father were from that region and because I told him that we often go there he accepted that I was from George, which is a well-known sizeable town in that area. It worked for him so I left it at that. Years later Mrs Machel corrected him one day and then the story disappeared. He appeared disappointed in his own story.

After this debate I was approached by a journalist from an Afrikaans women's magazine in South Africa called *Rooi Rose* (Red Roses). They wanted to do a feature about a white female bodyguard and wanted to include me as one of the white ladies around the President. At first I said no, but it came to the President's attention that I had been asked and did not want to participate, and he called me into his office and instructed me to do it. He told me he wanted me to participate when asked. I was part of his Government of National Unity, and he would not succeed if he preached to the world something he was not operating in his close environment. By now I understood what the President wanted with me. It was becoming more than a job for me. I was becoming dependent emotionally on him, while he afforded me the opportunities of a lifetime. I was not skilled for everything he asked me to do, but he wanted to ensure that a white, young Afrikaner, who epitomized the community, remained close to him.

I looked forward to every opportunity to spend time with the President. He was kind and always interested about my well-being. That made me even more committed to support his efforts and I made an effort to ensure that I was diligent in every possible way. But the fact that he would contact me directly and involve me in his affairs caused some tension in the office. I tried to remain in Cape Town as much as possible, even during the recess in Parliament, for the sake of peace, though I was promoted to acting assistant private secretary in March 1997.

My parents were intrigued by my commitment and change of heart towards the President. They sensed that I adored my new boss and when I spoke of him it was with fondness. My dad appeared sceptical but my mother embraced and encouraged the loyalty I was expressing. I didn't discuss work much at home but they saw that I was completely focused and dedicated to my job. They hardly ever saw me and when they did, I slept most of the time. Whenever I wasn't at work, or with the President, I slept. I no longer went out with friends and I alienated myself from the social scene, for reasons both intentional and unintentional. I wanted to avoid being constantly quizzed about my job. Having very little free time I wanted to isolate myself in that short space of time to digest whatever was happening at work, to internalize and process and plan, but also to provide myself with the space to accommodate the changes that were happening within me. When I now look back over those nineteen years the days are all faded into one large chunk of life. It was at such a pace that I find it difficult to remember individual or isolated incidents. There was little time to ever digest and even though I was proud, grateful and totally committed, my work absorbed my entire life.

I was embracing the new South Africa through serving the President. I was changing from within and in general felt more tolerant and respectful towards people despite the differences of the colour of our skin, our cultural or political beliefs and the texture of our hair. It was something my friends and some family found difficult to comprehend because they had not been exposed to the same diversities that I had been exposed to. We were not accustomed to interracial relationships in South Africa, whether platonic, romantic or professional of nature. We still operated and lived separated in our clusters of comfort. It was starting to be problematic having conversations with friends and family as I was growing to accept and embrace the diversity of people. I often walked away from conversations with friends thinking that some of the black and brown people I worked with were much more intelligent than most people we as white friends knew, yet some of my friends maintained their position of superiority over anyone who was not white. I had grown intolerant of people who didn't open themselves for change, but at the same time I realized I was privileged because of my closeness to the President and exposure to non-racialism.

People often ask me: 'Did you keep notes of your experiences?' And I think to myself: With what time and energy was I suppose to do that? They say: 'You must have been to the most spectacular places', and I think: Can't remember. Then they say: 'You don't have kids and aren't married', and to this day I calmly smile and respond appropriately but think: Where and when could you imagine that could have happened in the last nineteen years? Your being becomes consumed by the job and you wake up worrying and stressing about what lies ahead, not contemplating anything else that would resemble 'normality.'

It was around this time that my relationship with the President took a step forward. Even though I was in Cape Town most of the time, I knew that he was negotiating with Laurent Kabila and the incumbent President of what was then known as Zaire, now known as the Democratic Republic of the Congo. In addition to attending to the duties of a President that included dealing with domestic affairs, keeping opposition politicians at bay, debating changes of legislation and so on, the President would fly off to Zaire in the morning, be back at night and the next day have an incoming state visit to attend to. He did his duties without ever cancelling or failing his obligations, yet he was determined too that it was not only South Africa that had to benefit from our democracy. Africa had to succeed as a continent too and he was devoted to bringing about a regeneration of the continent at the same time.

The DRC is a country rich in resources on the west coast of Africa. But the country and its people were impoverished as a result of greed – that of the ruler and dictator for more than twenty years, President Mobutu Sese Seko – and an ongoing civil war in the region. The President's intention was to get Laurent Kabila and Mobutu to meet on neutral ground and for them to start negotiations to enable Mobutu to step down in a dignified manner and hand over power to Kabila to effectively run the country on new terms to benefit its people, hoping that a free, fair and democratic election would follow. Kabila was threatening to overthrow the government and take over by violent means, and to ensure stability in the region it was in the best interest of all concerned that a peaceful transition be negotiated. President Mobutu, who was sixty-six at the time and suffering from prostate cancer, said he would never bow to Kabila, but international pressure was increasing.

To prepare for this meeting a South African navy ship, the SAS *Outeniqua*, was sent to anchor in international waters off the coast of Zaire to provide that neutral ground for the affected parties to meet. For days the media was dominated by reports that Mobutu refused to meet Kabila on the ship. Once they had both agreed to meet, the President flew off to Pointe Noire in Zaire with the Presidential plane, the Falcon 900, to attend and facilitate the meeting. He was scheduled to return late the same night.

My duties at that stage included the tasking of the Presidential plane: to provide airforce staff with details of departure and arrival times, passengers on board, food to be consumed during return flights and return times. Meticulous detail. In turn, they would provide me with flight times and from there an arrival time at each side could be determined and the programme for the day could be negotiated. The President specifically didn't take a secretary with him on that particular trip due to the sensitivities of the talks and the fact that there were only men on board the SAS *Outeniqua*. He probably also had a premonition that things would not go according to plan. They arrived in Pointe Noire and were taken by helicopter to the vessel. And there he started preparing himself for the meeting.

I was usually in constant contact with the pilots of the plane so as to establish what time they departed and to enable me then to provide an expected arrival time back in South Africa to all parties concerned.

On that night it didn't happen. No one contacted me and I contacted our pilots to enquire about their plans. They informed me that they were still waiting for word from the President but that it was already 9 p.m. and they didn't have hope of him returning that night. Then luckily the President called me and told me that neither Kabila nor Mobutu had arrived for the negotiations, but he'd sent word to them through our embassy that he was waiting. The President had a way of instructing his peers to do things in which they felt obliged to adhere to. And he was waiting for the two to respond. He told me that he was going to spend the night on the vessel and wait for them to arrive the following day, but if they didn't arrive the next day he was going to return. I remember asking him whether I should not help to call them from this side and he laughed but said it wasn't necessary.

He then asked me to inform Mrs Machel, which I did. I called the Director General of our office, Prof. Gerwel, every time I received an update, and then also the Minister of Foreign Affairs and the Minister of the Defence Force. To me, they all had to be informed that our President was stuck out on one of the navy's ships on the open seas. It was just common sense. I had no training in dealing with matters of this gravity but did what I thought would be expected of me. The President also asked me to call him back and give Mrs Machel's response. I called back and said that she sends all her love and hopes that he is OK and sleeps well. When I called to the only satellite phone in the vessel, a young man answered and I had to try to convince him why it was necessary for this Afrikaans woman to speak to the President. They found it suspicious.

The pilots were accommodated in either a hotel or they slept in the plane, I don't know, but they were informed that there was no flight back that night. The next morning I called again. This time to inform the President that the plane crew didn't take personal items to stay overnight and they had to return to South Africa to go and regroup or to send up a relief crew. They were also working against time as aviation regulations didn't make provision for them to be on standby for that long and soon they would not be allowed to fly, and there would be no relief crew to return the President home.

I called again, and again the young man answered the phone and we started being acquainted. I then asked him to call the President, which he did, and the President came down the stairs to take the call. 'Yes darling?' he responded. By then I had started calling the President 'Khulu', the abbreviated version of the Xhosa word for Grandpa. It was only in formal situations where protocol was required where we would call him Mr President. Everyone else called him either Madiba, or 'Tata' (Father) or President Mandela. I had asked Parks for a word that would help me be at ease with him a bit more and he suggested 'Khulu'.

I explained the situation but then said something stupid, again. 'Can we send you some toiletries and clothes at least?' His response was, 'That would be very thoughtful of you but also send me newspapers.' Always newspapers. He used to read all five daily newspapers in his region every day, including those in Afrikaans. He often said that the Afrikaans papers reported in a much more accurate way than the English papers and I guess he meant it is because Afrikaans is such a descriptive and expressive language.

We sent his toiletries and newspapers back with the plane that returned almost immediately after it dropped off its crew, refuelled, and took on fresh crew and food for the return flight. The fresh crew knew somehow that it may still be a day or two before they returned so they took their own personal items too.

The President never carried telephone numbers with him, but by now he knew my number by heart from constantly calling me (which is also why the cellphone company Vodacom always allocated me some simple numbers to make it easy for the President to remember the number whenever I had to change it). So while he was on the ship he kept calling me to call people, ask questions and then to call him back with responses. Two days later Mobutu arrived. It appeared that he and Kabila were willing to negotiate a peaceful settlement, but a fortnight later the Zairean army informed Mobutu that they could no longer protect him. He fled the country and Kabila declared himself head of state and suspended the country's constitution.

Upon his return to Cape Town, the President made a point of calling me into his office to commend me for the support while he was on the SAS *Outeniqua*. I felt proud of keeping things going during that time, of course with his guidance. Though I was puzzled he could think it would have been any different. It was thoughtful of him though. It was the moment, perhaps, that it was clear that he relied on me, and clear that I would always be there.

One day Mary sent me to fetch dry cleaning for her. I'm not the type of person who minds doing anything for anyone as long as it remains within the law. It is probably as a result of my Calvinistic upbringing: we serve, we obey, and we are humble to anyone in a more senior position than us. We basically do what we get told.

I was on my way out of the office when the President was on his way in, and our paths crossed. By now we had established a good working relationship and we were comfortable with one another. He asked me where I was heading and I told him that I was running an errand for Mary. He was furious. 'How can you do that?' I responded that I didn't mind at all. He insisted that it wasn't proper and I ended up begging him to let it go, like one would do with your father to save a sibling from being disciplined, and realized that I shouldn't have told him. I was really surprised that this angered him. The President liked strong women but Mary was perhaps too strong. He never liked people telling him what to do. I discovered he wanted to be given input but in a consultative manner rather than being prescribed, which one can understand of a person that had been imprisoned for twenty-seven years, following the authorities' schedule of when to eat, sleep, exercise and put the lights out – it was his way of winning back the little freedom he had, by at least feeling in control of his own life.

He called me to his house shortly after this and by now I was driving to Houghton myself – as long as I didn't have to go anywhere else in Johannesburg, I was fine to drive between Pretoria and Houghton, not being familiar with Johannesburg and its surroundings. This time when I arrived, he handed me some letters to prepare for him but then asked me to sit in his lounge and told me one of the most valuable things ever: 'There is no room for cowards here. If you are going to be a coward you are not going to last here for very long. I cannot always defend you so you need to defend yourself by doing what is right.' It was only when I drove home that I realized he was referring to the incident in the office that week and that he expected me not to simply take instructions but to question them. These words will remain with me for the rest of my life, and in later years, when he was indeed no longer able to defend me, they gave me strength in whatever battles I was facing.

And so on the President's insistence I had to be considered too when it came to international travel. Since the secretaries took turns to accompany him I now had to be added for consideration. Soon I was tasked to accompany him to India and Bangladesh, and then to England in the summer of 1997.

The President went to Oxford and I was overwhelmed by the beauty of the town and the real English countryside. Prince Charles attended the event at Jesus College at Oxford. This was after his divorce from Princess Diana had been announced and we were all a bit wary. The President however was his charming self and despite all the bad press about the Royals he was extremely courteous and respectful towards Prince Charles. The President didn't judge people.

Earlier that year Princess Diana paid a visit to Angola and South Africa. The President was hugely impressed by her gesture of visiting HIV/AIDS-infected patients in Angola and sitting on their beds while conversing with them. She was helping to destroy the stigma attached to people suffering from AIDS and he said, 'For a Princess to sit on AIDS patients' beds goes to show that people have nothing to fear but that we have to care for people with AIDS.' On the day that Princess Diana visited him at Genadendal, the official residence in Cape Town, the President arrived in his lounge with his slippers on. He had forgotten to put on his shoes and humbly apologized to Princess Diana once the entire room realized he had asked for his shoes to be brought from his room. The Princess wasn't fazed at all.

The President had no trouble laughing at himself and sharing such small embarrassing moments with others.

I was increasingly struggling to marry my past and the present. I was a daughter of apartheid, yet I was supporting and serving the same man my Afrikaner compatriots warned me against. I was guided and taught so much by Parks Mankahlana, the Presidential spokesperson, and Tony Trew, the director of communications in our office, and one day I had the courage to go and tell them that I needed to speak to someone to try and come to peace with myself about the way we lived when I grew up under apartheid laws, and the fact that I was so ignorant. They suggested I go and speak to the Reverend Beyers Naudé. I also met Ronnie Kasrils, who served in President Mandela's Cabinet and who had been an early leader in MK, the group that was responsible for the Church Street bombing in 1983, when we couldn't trace my father for some hours. I had these struggles within myself, not knowing what was right and wrong. Rev. Naudé started his career as a Dutch Reformed priest but later left the church when he spoke out against apartheid and was put under house arrest for several years as a result. Yet he had no bitterness. I knew a bit about him but it was limited to that he was seen as a 'sell-out' by many white people. Parks and Tony arranged for me to have tea with 'Oom Bey' (Uncle Bey) as he was fondly known.

I drove nervously on my own to Johannesburg to go and see him. I was met by his wife upon arrival and joined him in his sitting room. It felt similar to being received by my own grandparents – with love and hospitality, even though the Naudés had never met me and didn't know much about me. I told him my story and we conversed for about two hours about life in general and religion, and he emphasized to me that I should not put so much pressure on myself by wanting to take responsibility for everyone around me and what apartheid did, and that I should come to peace with the fact that this journey is probably part of my own awakening. We prayed before I left and I felt emotional. I was so grateful to God for the enormous opportunities in my life and all my blessings, yet it was the same God in my eyes that allowed apartheid to happen and Nelson Mandela to be locked up in a prison cell for twenty-seven years. My journey of discovery included questions about the role of organized religion, coming to the conclusion that my relationship with God is a personal issue for which only I can account within myself and to Him one day. Indeed, this journey has led me to some strange beliefs and I would argue with my mother about the creation of institutions by man but then claimed as if God created these.

Sometimes Mrs Machel accompanied us on visits abroad and sometimes she simply was too busy with her own work. By now she was becoming a prominent part of the President's life and the President often boasted about the important work she was doing. She would often attend official functions but also spend time with him in private. I knew it made the President happy when she was around so I was fiercely protective over their private space and moments too.

Mrs Machel and I had a cautious relationship at first. The President had many duties to fulfil and targets he wanted to achieve, and in addition the world wanted him to be everywhere at the same time. His objectives were mainly focused on reconciliation and education but also bringing about stability in South Africa in a unified manner to ensure a favourable climate for the country to grow economically. I was often caught in the middle of having to ensure that he was satisfied with the pace at which he was working but then also setting enough time aside to be a husband.

I had to work many years to establish a solid working relationship with Mrs Machel. I didn't expect her to like me. It was my government and my people that brought down the plane in which her husband, Samora Machel, was killed in 1986. In later years, when we became much closer, I would often ask her and her children to recite the details around the events of his death. It was very hurtful but by arguing the events I think she also perhaps saw that I had a certain understanding for their pain and loss, something they appreciated. (Following Madiba's passing I also had the opportunity to see Samora Jnr's two boys, Samora III and Malick, for the first time in about ten years, and the resemblance to their grandfather was striking.)

The Machels are warm, hospitable, caring people and despite challenges we faced in the beginning we are close now. I have always been close to Mrs Machel's children. They say life takes a little time and a lot of relationship and indeed it took Mrs Machel and I a long time to build the relationship we have today, but we did with effort from both sides and I cannot imagine my life without her influence and the stability she brings about in my small world. I also admit that any two people work on a relationship and I had as much blame to take for the more difficult times as I wanted to give her.

At first I thought Mrs Machel was just asserting her position as wife in the President's life and it felt as if her expectations of us were too high. But then one noticed how she made the President smile. She awakened his senses again. She allowed him to live. She made him dance and see the beauty in flowers, appreciate good music and see the wonder in every sunset and every sunrise. On many of our travels she insisted that we all watch the sunset together, something he missed for so many years, being locked in a cell before sunset. She brought about a different appreciation of life for him again and made him love life more than I thought he was capable of. If you truly love someone, like I loved Nelson Mandela, you want what is best for him and you want him to be happy. And when he was with her and he lived again, despite the confines of their schedules and the pressure of their work, he was truly happy. Slowly I came to the realization that she was not there to assert her space; she was there to make him happy and we had an even better boss because of her. There was no single bigger gift to Nelson Mandela's life than what Graça Machel brought about with her presence.

This is in stark contrast to the presence of Winnie Mandela in my life – I didn't meet her until much later and never saw her during Madiba's Presidency. She seemed to have little presence in the President's life after they separated. He never spoke about her and I didn't ask. No one tells you but you assume it's not something you ever raise. As time passed he spoke more openly in confidence about these events in his life. However, sometimes he seemed sad and I often wondered about the silent pain he was going through.

When I came to the President's house I often found him sitting alone at the breakfast or dinner table. He usually had lunch at his official residences whether in Cape Town or Pretoria. One couldn't help but feel the loneliness whenever you entered his Houghton home while he was having a meal by himself. It was only when Mrs Machel became part of his life that this changed. It was as if light entered the sombre household, the curtains were opened and the entire house was filled with life.

When one sat down with him, he started telling his stories. Stories about prison and the years that he grew up in the Transkei. Meals were times for him to 'reflect' and relax. I loved listening to his story-telling as I've always loved my own imagination and it was easy for me to picture what he was telling me and virtually be transported to the scene he was describing. He often told me about Justice, the boy he grew up with and who was his best friend. Justice was more than a friend, he was the 'brother' Madiba never had. They ran away together when they both suddenly found out they were being set up for arranged marriages by the Regent who brought Madiba up, like people usually do in the countryside and in accordance to their tradition at the time. Madiba and Justice fled the Transkei to Johannesburg where his life was shaped into politics. He spoke fondly of Justice but sadly Justice passed away while Madiba was still imprisoned. As a result of too much drinking, Madiba said.

I often thought about Justice. If there is one person I wished to be alive to be part of our lives it was Justice. I wanted him to know what happened to his friend and I wanted him to know what one could become despite their humble beginnings. I wanted to turn back time and warn him to stop drinking, to tell him that he would be reunited with his friend some day, and I wanted him to witness and share in the life of his best friend. I knew he would have been invited to the Inauguration if he was alive at the time and

I imagined his joy and excitement over his best friend taking the oath. I think, however, once Madiba was imprisoned Justice perhaps gave up hope of ever breaking the cycle of poverty in his family and resorted to drinking.

His wistful remembrances of his boyhood in Qunu and his adolescence in Mqekezweni with Justice seemed to take up a lot of Madiba's quiet time. It was like he travelled there – to those old, simple days – to get peace, to get a sense of himself. Over and over again, I would find him remembering his childhood. Those experiences seemed not only to shape him as a man and define his values, I think his memories of his childhood became an escape – it was also a survival mechanism he probably used in prison. Those experiences – of herding cattle, of stick fighting, of roaming the hills of the Eastern Cape, listening to village elders, of stealing out of beehives and finding gooseberries – became like movies in his head that he could access when the realities of prison or being President just got too much. He replayed those images, those pastoral scenes, in his head and retold the stories so often that many of us who heard his whispered remembrances can recite them word for word. But those are not my stories, they are his.

When Madiba left prison, everyone had grown up and grown away. It seemed it was difficult for him to open up emotionally. Prison had taught him how to hide his feelings. I saw him try with his grandchildren but he was a reserved disciplinarian, which often did not go down well with the young ones. He yearned for his children while imprisoned and he wanted to have a part of such pleasures. But it wasn't easy.

I would often go to the President's house in Johannesburg as he hardly ever slept at the official residence in Pretoria, Mahlamba Ndlopfu. Four of his grandchildren were living with him at the time. They were the four sons of Makgatho, the President's only living son at the time from his marriage to his first wife, Evelyn. Mandla, the eldest grandchild, was in the last years of high school; Ndaba, the second born, was a teenager and then the two younger boys, Mbuso and Andile, were still small toddlers. They were adorable and loving.

Their father lived somewhere in Soweto but the President enjoyed having them around. They were effectively raised by the house-keeper, Xoliswa – who they referred to as Mama – and then Rochelle, the President's niece, until she left. At the time they provided liveli-ness to the house in Houghton and some sense of family.

In the early years I often found myself alone, other staff being in Pretoria, in the President's office in Cape Town. I was handling the President's personal office switchboard when I was called by recep-tion one day at the entrance of the building. The police on duty at the entrance informed me that I had visitors who wanted access to the President's office. This warranted me to get up and go to reception myself as no one was allowed access to the President's office. Upon arriving I was introduced to someone from NI (National Intelligence, even though I didn't make the connection immediately). I found it strange that two men randomly showed up at reception and told me that they needed to 'sweep' the President's office. I had no idea what they were referring to and told them, completely innocently, that we had cleaners in the office who swept the office daily, thank you very much.

I remained speechless in reception until the police working at the entrance told me that they were National Intelligence officers and that they used the term 'sweep' to mean looking for listening devices that could have been planted in the office by other parties. I felt extremely embarrassed and allowed them access. For years to come security would tease me over this. I took it in my stride. It was all part of this new world opening up to me, totally foreign to my past.

That summer I was also asked to accompany the President on a two-day rest to Bali, followed by a state visit to Indonesia and Thai-land on which Mrs Machel accompanied us. It was now generally accepted that even though I was still the senior ministerial typist, I would accompany the Presidential party on visits abroad and perform the duties of secretary. In those years I was too scared to enjoy anything and I didn't enjoy the waters of the swimming pool or the sea. I was determined to stay in my room for whenever the

President may call on me. And he did. He got used to the fact that I was always there and I started sleeping when he did, eating when he did and following his routine to ensure that I was always available in my room whenever he called.

Part of our duties included making sure that he got served food at the right time, his clothes were unpacked and packed whenever Mrs Machel was not around, and things around him were the way he preferred them to be. In his programme we also had to find time for him to have massages every second day, and press clippings had to be sent from South Africa every day in the absence of newspapers. I made sure those arrived before breakfast and took every effort to ensure that things were exactly the way he wanted them. No matter which time zone we were in, the poor staff at the office had to work shifts to prepare news clippings and send them in time. Even after computers and the internet dominated our lives, he insisted that the clippings be exactly that – newspapers cut out, photocopied and faxed to us no matter where we were. I tried my best to introduce alternatives, also to lighten the burden on the staff back in South Africa, but he wouldn't have anything but the originals as they appeared in the particular font in the newspapers.

The President was always very uncomfortable if left alone with massage therapists. Either security or I had to be in the room with him at all times when these therapists were around. It was extremely frustrating to me as I am not a person that can sit still for an hour. It was way before we had BlackBerries or smart phones and there was literally nothing to do to pass the time. On several occasions I tried to get security to take my place but he would then usually call me back when he noticed I wasn't there or called upon me and I didn't answer. I did it probably more than a hundred times and he called me back more than a hundred times over the years, until I explained to him one day that I really cannot sit still for that long and he accepted the fact that one of his security people would be with him, which also made a little more sense practically. An hour to me meant falling behind on work or things to be arranged. In any event I thought, how was I ever going to be of any use in an emergency?

It was better for a bodyguard to be there from a security point of view. It also gave me at least an hour to do some other things, email the office, go through programmes or return phone calls.

The President had this enormous ability to break things down to the simplest method of reason and argument. He always told us that Oliver Tambo, another liberation struggle hero and former President of the ANC, never wanted to have massages and he was convinced that if Oliver had done, he would still be alive. What he meant was that he thought that Uncle Oliver, who died of a stroke, would have dealt better with the stress and pressure if he had learned to relax by ensuring that he took care of his physical well-being through massage or physiotherapy. The President had a unique way of relating stories and he would use the exact same words and phrases whenever he repeated a story. They were precious. And the conviction with which he conveyed this started worrying me so much that I also later imagined that it was necessary for me to have massages when I became too stressed.

From Bali we went to Indonesia, to the capital Jakarta on a state visit. I didn't see much of Jakarta and all we experienced was heat and humidity, but while he was there the President had a special meeting. It was done secretly. He only agreed to pay a state visit to Indonesia if he would be offered the opportunity to meet with Xanama Gusmão. The Indonesians delayed, probably thinking that the President wouldn't insist, but he did. One night Gusmão, the leader of the resistance movement of East Timor, was snuck in via the emergency staircase of the Presidential guest house. Gusmão was considered the equivalent of the political prisoner Madiba represented while imprisoned. His hands were cuffed. I found the visit exciting and wondered how Madiba dealt with it. After all it was only seven years before that he had been that very same prisoner.

Gusmão looked well under the circumstances and was friendly. He was alone with the President and Prof. Gerwel and others for a while before he was taken back to prison. It was agreed that he would be allowed to visit South Africa a few weeks later where he would feel free to talk. President Suharto agreed and a few weeks later we received him in South Africa. It was less exciting as he now no longer had handcuffs or seemed like a prisoner in normal clothes. Years later he visited the retired Madiba in Johannesburg to thank him for the negotiations and only then was I reminded about events of that night. He was by then freed and the legitimate President of an independent East Timor. It is believed that Madiba's intervention put Suharto under pressure to release Gusmão.

Wherever there was conflict around the world, people would ask for the President's intervention to negotiate a peaceful settlement. He often declined to intervene in the domestic affairs of other countries because he said we did not have enough knowledge about the intricacies of the problems they faced. Yet the political will to help where it was possible or where he thought we had a chance to succeed made him do otherwise.

From Indonesia we went to Bangkok. We stayed in a lavish hotel and I came to the realization that I was becoming an expert on hotels worldwide. However, even though I could recite their room service menus I didn't see much of any cities. My experiences were limited to the extent of the President's sightseeing experiences. We were not there on holiday but to work. The President only asked to do sightseeing on a few occasions but usually limited it to the main tourist attractions and if there was anything he had read about before that could be of interest to him. Generally there was no time for sightseeing as his schedule was packed with meetings and then time blocked off for much needed rest. He was seventy-nine years of age and he needed rest at any given opportunity.

Despite spending every waking hour helping to make the President's day faultless, I was unfortunately not a paragon of diplomacy. In Thailand, we were sitting at an official lunch hosted by Prime Minister Chuan Leekpai and by now advance protocol teams doing planning knew that the President liked to have eye contact with his secretaries at the table so that when he called for them or needed them, he could just look at us and we would know. Seats were therefore arranged accordingly. I could see his face but it luckily wasn't too close for him to witness what happened next.

I had a long-sleeved blouse on and the sleeves were wide. The first course was served and breadrolls were served on our side plates. I reached out for the butter on the table in front of me and I didn't realize that my sleeve caught the breadroll on my plate, and as I picked up the container of butter to bring it closer to my plate the breadroll touched my elbow, where it had now rolled down my sleeve. Not realizing what had happened I reacted with shock and thought something had crawled into my sleeve. I was already nervous from not knowing what I was eating and this didn't help. I quickly jerked my arm back to get whatever was crawling up my sleeve out, and the breadroll flew over the table to the middle, where it landed. Silence followed in my immediate surroundings. Luckily the Thai people are extremely friendly and hospitable. They laughed it off and the gentleman next to me said it meant good luck. My first thought was that it seemed everything in this country meant good luck no matter how unfortunate it appeared to us foreigners. I took his best wishes and quietly reached for another breadroll, swallowing my own embarrassment with each piece of bread.

The President was travelling non-stop and working relentlessly. When he was at home, he would take time to address union organizations like the National Union of Mineworkers, the National Union of Metal Workers of South Africa and the National Education, Health and Allied Workers' Union. He was always balancing, always ensuring that he was not seen to discriminate in any way and applying his fair mind to every situation possible. He was driven to lay the foundation for a prosperous future for South Africa but back in July 1996 he announced publicly that he would only serve as President for one term of five years. He honestly believed that younger people could achieve more than him, and by announcing that he would only serve one term he had hoped that other heads of state would follow suit and not be tempted to become hungry for power and serve for endless terms, becoming dictators.

At every public event he called upon the police on duty afterwards to greet them, or if there was a choir that performed he wanted to shake hands with each and every one of its members. He would also always spot children in a crowd and call upon them to come to the front so he could greet them. In the beginning I thought it was just something he occasionally felt up to, but then when I realized that he did so without fail at every event, I would start making plans for this to happen at all events once I got there. It was his way of acknowledging the small people.

However, he could become harsh with people who he didn't feel were loyal to him. He would give, give and give and then if there was the slightest indication that he felt someone was not behind him 120 per cent then he would abruptly cut ties. He inspired loyalty but then he expected you to be faithful. This happened with Mary Mxadana. The working relationship between Mary and the President was increasingly tense. Mary was friendly with the President's ex-wife, Winnie Madikizela Mandela, and that unsettled him. He asked for her to be transferred to a diplomatic position in the Department of Foreign Affairs. Mary left gracefully. Very sadly a few years later she passed away after a hernia operation. I was really sad when I saw her in hospital and I will always be grateful for the role she played in my life.

The President would spend his Christmas holiday with his grandsons in Qunu, the village where he grew up. It is in the Province of the Eastern Cape of South Africa and about 30 km south-west of a town called Mthatha in what was formerly known as the Transkei. By then, his niece Rochelle, who had looked after him, had left the house to further her studies in America, and the President relied on me to take care of some issues Rochelle had done before. One of them was organizing a Christmas party on his farm in Qunu on Christmas Day for the children of the village. Well, that is what it was supposed to be.

He made a list of a few people to be called and asked them all for donations of sweets, toys and other simple Christmas treats. The first year I was involved it was 2,000 of everything. I took responsibility for orchestrating the collection of the goods and making sure that they arrived in Qunu a few days before Christmas. I realized we needed bags, so bags were bought, and I involved the children from the community, and even our security, to help pack parcels for the 2,000 children expected to come to the President's house on Christmas Day. I set up a proper production line in one of the facilities around his house and we packed parcels for days ahead of Christmas, sometimes losing encouragement when so overwhelmed by 2,000 of everything. One only knows what 2,000 constitutes when you've packed and handled 2,000 parcels. When the President told me that for many children from the region this was the only day they had a proper meal or received something for Christmas, I didn't believe him at first. But when Christmas arrived, truth was put to the President's words. Thousands of children descended on Qunu.

The majority of black people in South Africa lived and still live in severe poverty. It was going to take a very long time for economic transformation to be implemented and to affect the lives of rural communities in a beneficial way. Things have somewhat changed now but not nearly as fast as we had hoped for, and people in rural South Africa are angry and disappointed for not having benefited from democracy yet. And as the crowd descended on Qunu I realized that the people in these communities had not tasted the fruits of our newly achieved freedom. When I asked where they came from the President said that some of them started walking the previous night to be in time. When I arrived on the farm from town on Christmas Day at around 7 a.m., which I thought was a reasonable time, children had already lined up along the fence of his farm all the way up the hill – about a kilometre. I couldn't believe what I saw. We prepared to hand out parcels and the children would then be taken to the yard at the back of the house where they were fed. The very friendly Mr Bread, a bakery in Qunu, would take care of preparing food for the elders and VIPs from the region, together with Madiba's eldest grandson, Mandla.

Soon the children started streaming through the gates. The President sat outside for most of the day, greeting children as they moved along and got handed their parcels before they went to eat. Shaking hands with each and every one of them, one by one, and conversing with them briefly. Being the disciplined, organized person that the President was, he appreciated my military precision for order in the way things were handled. Children filed past in single line and got handed a bag of surprises from the helpers, after which they were guided to the lunch area. I made sure we didn't overlook anyone and they all had the opportunity to shake hands with him for the time he was seated outside.

Since many of them had never been accustomed to the belief of Father Christmas because of the remote areas in which they lived, this was their fantasy and what their entire worlds revolved around – seeing President Mandela and receiving gifts from him. When a company donated frizbees for all the parcels you would soon see thousands of frizbees flying around and people dodging them everywhere. The next time there might be balls, and balls would be heading for targets such as your head. We assume all children know what a ball or a frizbee is, until you see how children in rural South Africa live and you understand that they do not recognize something we take for granted. One year someone wanted to donate plastic play guns and we had to decline as we didn't want to promote violence with our message of goodwill. The children were not entirely sure whether they were happier about the parcel or shaking hands with the President. It was precious to see. And then the evidence of the President's comments about their only meal. The proof was there. I saw children infected with diseases without names. Underfed, deformed, mistreated, neglected. I could finally relate to what he described. Somehow when you see the innocence and gratitude in their eyes you manage to look past appearance.

Some of them had never seen white people before, and one child rubbed my arm to see whether the 'white' of my skin gives off in some way. I adored picking up the little ones, although the white of my skin sometimes scared them. It was so ironic – years earlier I had conformed to the racist approach that it was inappropriate to touch a black person because we inherently feared them. Some of the children were scared of me and the few other white bodyguards. We must have been aliens to them. On more than one occasion I had a child 'bound by my hip' for the entire day . . . probably encouraged by curiosity to see whether I returned to a different planet afterwards.

When you spend a day like Christmas in such a poverty-stricken area one is truly and honourably thankful for your own privileges, and an event like this brings a different meaning to Christmas. It was the first Christmas I celebrated without my parents, without presents and the focus on 'what I'm receiving for Christmas'; the focus changed to what can I give and do and that in itself brings so much more fulfilment and meaning to Christmas. We had lunch with Madiba following the children's party and some of his grandchildren and elders from the area visited.

The following year we realized that preparing for 2,000 children was not going to be sufficient. We increased to asking for donations for 5,000. This time around the President left everything to me. I consulted him about decisions and asked advice on certain matters but by now people knew about his initiative and it wasn't difficult to find sponsorship. Again in December we prepared a few days before Christmas but this time for 5,000. We still didn't have enough gifts and food. The following year we increased to 10,000 until we ended with 20,000. Again, packing 20,000 parcels is no joke. Yet the children of the area and some of the grandchildren participated in the preparations and somehow we managed. The last year of our private party we ended up packing for two weeks around the clock prior to Christmas. And all I repeated to encourage people helping was 'remember, for some children this is the only opportunity during the year to get a decent meal and a gift bag . . . this is the *only* gift they get for Christmas', reciting the President's exact words. Not that the children in the village were used to much more but it made the bodyguards participate in my task at hand.

In the last year, Oprah Winfrey asked to participate following our visit to Chicago and the President telling her what we did in Qunu over Christmas. I think they prepared for 25,000 children in

Qunu and she also distributed around another 25,000 to other rural schools across South Africa. But she did it properly. Children received clothes and school stationery in addition to sweets and a very nutritious meal. We underestimated the size of the crowd and how widely it was advertised that both Oprah and the President would be there and we ended up avoiding a stampede. Some mothers travelled with children from as far as the Free State, hundreds of kilometres. Buses of children were offloaded and security was insufficient. It was then decided that, after closely escaping tragedy, the Christmas party would be taken over by the Nelson Mandela Children's Fund and decentralized to regions.

At the time he initiated the annual Christmas parties in Qunu, the President then also initiated visits, close to the end of the year, to pre-primary schools in both Johannesburg and Cape Town. He loved interacting with children. Again the first year he instructed his niece to handle matters, and when she left for the USA I inherited the job. The President was teaching me valuable lessons on how to ask for donations and support for people in desperate need of resources when you yourself cannot afford to buy them something. In return for sponsors donating sweets and goods for him to hand out during his visit, they would get to spend an entire day with him while he was handing these out, as well as exposure on television and in newspapers. The plan was simple but worked like a bomb. We would then invite a media contingent to follow us on the day when we visited the crèches, and the media representatives got to spend a day with their beloved President too, while giving the sponsors the exposure that the President promised. At the end of the day the media and sponsors were invited to a lunch at our offices or a nearby hotel where the President thanked them for their support. News spread and people were eager to help in the years to follow.

On a few occasions politicians tried to hijack or interfere with his arrangements, upon which he made it clear that the initiative should not be limited to any one political party but that the parents and teachers of these children should be respected for their political views too. I always had to make sure that the selection of schools was

100 per cent representative. If we visited five schools it had to be two black, one Indian, one brown and one white school. As schools got more integrated after transformation in South Africa it became quite a challenge and we had to visit the schools in advance to make sure that we had the correct denomination of each race group covered. We also had to be careful not to visit a predominantly Xhosa school – Xhosa being the ethnic group to which the President belongs. He was extremely sensitive about matters of this nature and it became a blueprint in my mind that if we did something for one group, we had to do something for another. He never wanted to be seen to be prejudiced or accused of favouritism, and it was as if he was determined to remain the figurehead of nation-building, regardless of efforts from people to tag him to a specific group, race, religion, class, whatever.

I have no idea why I ended up carrying the responsibility of the Christmas parties or pre-primary school visits and why he didn't hand it to his Children's Fund that he had established even before I joined him. Although I benefited emotionally from taking on this task, being introduced to a new meaning of Christmas, I had more than enough work pressure and challenges to deal with. I was happy when it was decentralized to the Children's Fund.

At the same time the President initiated his schools and clinics building project. He managed to persuade business, both locally and internationally, to build schools and clinics in the most remote countryside in South Africa. More than a hundred schools were erected through this initiative and more than fifty clinics. President Mandela was never the greatest administrator but his intentions and strategy were faultless.

At first government didn't pay much attention to these new structures being erected. The process was simple. The President would speak to a particular chief, the person from the traditional leadership in a particular rural area in charge of his community. The chief would plead for a school. The President would read of excellent financial results of companies in newspapers and then task me to start looking for the CEO or managing director or owner of the company. He would then invite them to have breakfast or lunch with him. Who would say no to being invited by the President? Towards the end of the project business people teased among one another that if the President invited you for breakfast, it could be the most expensive breakfast of your life. Only on two occasions did people promise to build structures that they never fulfilled. It was impossible for government to provide services at the pace at which the public expected them to, and the President did what he could to speed up the process by involving the private sector to support these efforts, education and health care being his priorities. He always said that education is the only weapon with which one can fight poverty.

First we would arrange for the business representatives to fly with us to these rural areas to be shown where the school or clinic had to be built and to be introduced to the community leaders who had to oversee the project. We spent hours and hours travelling to remote areas. Once the project was completed, we would return with the businessmen to the area and the President would personally open the school or clinic.

In the advanced stages of the project, and by the change of government in 1999, it was discovered that many of these structures were left abandoned. Government was not providing the teachers, equipment, nurses or facilities and infrastructure to support the initiative. While one can appreciate their challenges it was a pity that there was no co-ordination in time for them to be able to provide the backup to ensure the efficient running of these institutions. The President was also sometimes to blame as he too gave in to requests from traditional leaders too easily, without any proper investigation into whether a school or clinic was really planned in the right area. In later years the Nelson Mandela Institute for Education and Rural Development partnered with the University of Fort Hare in the Eastern Cape to support some of these schools the President initiated.

Sadly the education system in South Africa, and specifically in the rural areas, tends to fail its learners. To date, this is one of the biggest challenges South Africa faces, the education of our children.

The teaching profession is one of the worst paid professions in South Africa and as a result it has stopped attracting people with a passion for the job. Teachers can simply no longer afford to support their own families and in rural areas the infrastructure fails in supporting teachers in terms of providing them with the right tools and textbooks. Because of the remoteness of the location of some of these schools they hardly receive support from the national education department and it is at the same time difficult for the department to exercise discipline.

On each visit where a rural school or clinic was built, the media was invited to accompany the President as well. The exposure for any company associated with this project on prime-time news, with the President, was worth the money they had to fork out. Many of them still continue to support some of the schools and clinics they erected originally and shared in his passion about education for our youth.

In 1998 President Bill Clinton faced the biggest challenge of his political career. The scandal over the relationship with Monica Lewinsky threatened his political career and was making world headlines. In the middle of the fallout he was scheduled to be in South Africa on a state visit. When in trouble, one cannot ask for a better friend than Nelson Mandela. The President was never going to condone what had happened, but he had a way to put things in perspective of one's humanity. You would still feel guilty, but he made you feel safe and in a gentle way persuaded you to take responsibility without feeling humiliated. Observing this over time I realized how my thinking had changed and how I assessed things I would feel very opinionated about before. President Mandela was never scared to admit his own mistakes and then almost jump at the opportunity of apologizing and then to move on. He consistently told people whenever they wanted to sing his praises that 'a saint is a sinner who keeps on trying'.

That doesn't imply that he ever justified something that was without integrity or honesty but he inherently believed that people always had the best intentions and that they stumbled occasionally, as all human beings do. What was important to him, and became clear to me, was that those who faltered, sinned or stumbled didn't feel alienated because they made mistakes. He was honest about their mistakes but assured them in a way that he acknowledged their humaneness while making it clear that honesty to admit one's mistakes was far more important to the event in forgiving yourself and moving on. President Mandela welcomed President Clinton with open arms, admitted the personal difficulties he was facing with regard to the Lewinsky saga, but reassured President Clinton that he still respected him and had faith in his ability to lead.

On 27 March 1998 a banquet was hosted in honour of President Clinton's visit to South Africa. By now the secretaries were all taking equal turns in attending events and supporting the President. I was surprised to be asked to work during the state banquet held at Vergelegen, a wine farm in the prestigious wine lands close to Cape Town. It was a rare historical event and everybody wanted to work that night. Vergelegen is a forty-five minute drive from Genadendal, the President's official residence, so to avoid traffic and save time security decided it would be better for us to take a helicopter to Vergelegen.

I was never good (and still am not) at dressing up. I am most comfortable in my favourite jeans, flip flops and a shirt or t-shirt. However, I realized for this banquet I had to really make an effort. This was, after all, the state event for what was considered the most powerful nation in the world. I had a black long dress made for the event, nothing extravagant, and decided on shoes with a bit of a heel, not too high though, as we are usually on our feet all night.

Our military helicopters were rough and soldier-like. I could always imagine us being on our way to combat whenever we were in the helicopter. The Oryx is a solid military machine, considered one of the best helicopters manufactured in the world, with space for sixteen passengers in full armour. By now I loved flying in our helicopters. I loved the sound of them and especially when the pilots manoeuvred it a bit; always being fond of a bit of adventure.

We landed at Vergelegen and the steel steps to disembark were put in place as soon as the rotorblades stopped. According to protocol, the President always enters a plane last and disembarks first. Then if Mrs Machel accompanied us or he had an official partner, that person would follow, and then whoever could manage to get to the door first. The security detail usually jumped out of the helicopter as it was low. The President disembarked and Mrs Machel followed. As the President started climbing down the stairs he started talking to me and asked me a question as he reached the ground. The question probably dealt with something about the programme or President Clinton's arrival time. He was about to turn round to make eye contact and get my response when I came flying down the stairs and landed on both my knees behind him. It turned out that my long dress got stuck over the railing of the steel steps and prevented me from stepping down further. Everyone around me started laughing, except the President and Mrs Machel. It must have been the funniest sight people ever saw. It's one thing falling, then another dressed in evening wear, but it surely is a sight when doing all of that out of a helicopter. The President was still trying to make eye contact with me on his level but found me on the ground behind him. He commanded 'Help her up, help her up' and was very concerned about my well-being. 'Did you spoil your dress?' he asked and I did a quick check, but all seemed to be OK.

People had great difficulty composing themselves. As President Clinton was also expected to arrive by helicopter, the entire area was filled with secret service agents. They were hiding in bushes everywhere and it looked like a sudden wind blew through the estate as the people in bushes started laughing at my entrance. The President was the only one that seemed troubled by my tumbling down and the rest of the people all laughed and had great difficulty to get themselves to be serious again. I composed myself and we moved to the house where we were going to await President Clinton's arrival.

President Mandela was given a seat in the house adjacent to the marquee where the banquet was to be hosted, to await the arrival

of President Clinton so they would enter the banquet simultaneously. I remained outside to try and gather information about his
expected arrival time to enable me to give feedback to the President. Vergelegen is a private wine farm and the house beautifully
decorated in Cape Dutch style. While waiting outside I met one of
South Africa's best comedians, Pieter-Dirk Uys. He was getting
ready for his performance at the banquet and I was distracted from
earlier events. The President loved his satirical performances and he
usually didn't spare anyone in his comic interpretations of South
Africa's politicians. Upon stepping back into the house where the
President was waiting I didn't see a brick placed in front of a door to
keep it from being blown closed by the wind and tripped over it as I
entered the building. This time I didn't fall but rather found myself
much faster in front of the President than expected. He just said:
'Oh no darling, rather get a chair and come and sit down.' I was
very embarrassed and obviously more nervous than ever when I
handed the President his speech at the podium when he was
expected to speak later that night. I prayed as I walked up the stairs
to the podium that another disaster wouldn't strike. It didn't and the
rest of the evening was uneventful.

I was now often looked to by both the President and Mrs Machel.
We were having great difficulties marrying their diaries. We had to
find time for them to be together but it was not easy. Mrs Machel
continued her work in Mozambique and across the world, mainly
advocating for children's rights, and she was travelling a lot. I was
often in trouble for not finding time for her and the President to
spend together, but it was a nearly impossible task. They both
worked at a pace, almost racing against time. The President would
want a hundred things done in a week and when we managed to fit
in everything, Mrs Machel's schedule was packed. Often the President would agree to arrangements and then the day before the
entire diary would change, not because of Mrs Machel but he would
also have pressing priorities or simply change his mind about something. We were running out of excuses why we had to cancel

arrangements at short notice and we always feared that people might suspect health problems being the cause.

In those days, if the President had as much as a common cold South Africa's currency, the rand, would plummet at the news of any rumours about the President's health – the world fearing that South Africans would be dumped in chaos and burn the country to the ground. The President was the symbol of stability to all South Africans, black and white, and the world knew it. Using his health or 'not feeling well' as an excuse was therefore never even contemplated unless it was the absolute truth. He was almost becoming a super-being in the public's eyes. If he wanted to take a rest, public speculation about his health would start.

Early in 1998 the President was scheduled to do a fundraiser for the Nelson Mandela Children's Fund. The Children's Fund was established by him in 1995 to help children, especially orphans affected by the AIDS crisis. In addition to donating his prize money from the Nobel Peace Prize to establish the fund, he also annually donated a third of his salary towards the fund and set out on a fundraising drive for it when time allowed. On this particular occasion he was scheduled to host some top international celebrities and models and they would then embark on a trip to launch the newly refurbished Blue Train – South Africa's luxury passenger train – after which he would do a trip on the *QE2*. People could pay thousands of dollars to join him and Mrs Machel, proceeds that would obviously benefit the Children's Fund and so the journey was sold out.

It was also during these events when the much-disputed diamonds were given to Naomi Campbell by then President Charles Taylor of Liberia. Naomi was a supporter of the Children's Fund right from its inception and was one of the first international donors to the fund.

During the trial of Charles Taylor at the International Criminal Court that recalled events of the fundraiser, I was interested in the order of events. No one asked any of the South African security officials at the time who the bodyguards were that knocked on

Naomi's door in the Presidential guest house and handed her the 'bag of stones'. If they were South African bodyguards, they would have opened the bag before handing it to her. No one, not even a President, got to deliver a gift on official premises without the gift being opened and searched. If anyone asked security they could well have verified how many stones were inside and it would be on record whoever entered the house that night. A South African police officer is required to keep what they refer to as a pocket book. In there they write every day whatever they do and they account for every minute, precisely, for in the event of court procedures they could refer back to the pocket books. I doubt the South African police would have allowed two Liberian bodyguards unaccompanied into the Presidential guest house, and the answers are therefore somewhere on record in South Africa. We knew nothing of the gift, but Naomi said that she handed the bag of diamonds to the CEO of the Children's Fund, although he was later found not guilty of possessing uncut diamonds.

We embarked on the *QE2*. It was a lovely experience although the vessel was clearly equipped for elderly people. It was grand and old-school. People dressed up to go and have dinner every night but to me it looked like they were going to church. There were no parties for young people but rather ballroom dancing. It was sweet though to see elderly people dancing and still so in love. The President and Mrs Machel didn't go dancing though, but enjoyed being on the *QE2*. They attended only an introduction and a dinner on the ship and the rest of the time they finally had some privacy and quality time together away from the pressures on the 'mainland'.

After the *QE2* trip I fell ill, for the second time in four years. I just couldn't maintain the pace. The President was driven by many factors, one being that his retirement from public office was less than a year away and he wanted to capitalize on being in a position to fast-track the changes he had hoped for, for his Presidency. The doctors said it was a repeat of a myocarditis infection I had sustained after our state visit to Japan in 1995 and that I was just exhausted. I was put on sick leave at home for four weeks and after about a week

I got a call from the bodyguards to tell me that the President wanted to visit me at my little house in the government village, Acasia Park. I didn't think it was appropriate for a President to come to my little simple one-bedroom house, and I called him to try and persuade him that I was fine and would report back for work soon and that it wasn't necessary to visit me. He insisted and soon arrived with the most beautiful basket of flowers I have ever received.

While visiting and encouraging me to regain strength he also very innocently said, 'You know only weak people get sick.' I thought he was going to show a bit more sympathy. He had believed all his life that you are very much in control of your own body, and in the process of healing your mind had to be stronger than the medicines applied. You also had to have the determination to get better.

No matter how difficult things became, how much pressure we were under or how tired I was, seeing his face and his smile lighting up the room was a highlight every day of my life. I later couldn't help but smile whenever I saw him. When you work closely with someone you inevitably start reading the other person's emotions and moods. Yet still in the most difficult times the smile was never far from my face, sometimes just reserved to my heart.

So I continued to work at a relentless pace, though the stress and fatigue were overwhelming at times. Once Madiba read me an article that appeared in a newspaper about a study on people who carried more weight around the hips and buttocks and that it was found that they deal with stress better. The first time he read it I took the point and said: 'You see Khulu, that's why I still deal with all the stress, because my hips and my bum are big.' He laughed out loud and then read the article to me for a second time. I didn't find it funny. He was teasing but I was able to stop him.

He was always very attentive to people's weight and health. He would often ask a lady whether she was pregnant even if she had just picked up a few kilograms around the waist. Sometimes he would request a private discussion with a visitor and then lecture them on their weight. I have lost count of the number of times he would point out someone's big tummy and then tell them, 'You have to reduce.' Some people find it offensive to have their weight discussed but it is extremely embarrassing when Nelson Mandela tells you 'you have to reduce', implying you have to reduce your food intake or reduce your weight. We tried to avoid these discussions at all costs and whenever he said he wanted to have a 'private discussion' with people we would try and tell him that he shouldn't do it and it was not appropriate. He would laugh and find it very funny that we would try to spare people from having to go through that with him. And then sometimes people insisted that they have their private discussion with him because they thought he was going to reveal confidential secrets and they would insist on having the private time with him, only to leave a few minutes later feeling not so fulfilled.

On one occasion I was waiting for his arrival at a public event; when he disembarked from the car he asked whether I had been there for long waiting for him. I said, 'Yes indeed.' And his response out loud was: 'I can see because you look hungry.' I wasn't. Always concerned about my security and always concerned about whether I had eaten or not.

One time I was on a diet and I declined to eat the food that was offered at the table prepared for him but rather stuck to my salad, and he questioned me and said I wasn't eating enough. I spoke to him openly and said that I was trying to lose weight. He then said that my weight didn't matter because I moved quickly. What he meant was that even though I was overweight it didn't affect the pace at which I walked or moved. He had such a funny way with food and body weight. When you didn't eat he encouraged you to eat more, but when you took a second serving he would watch your plate with disapproval. I've always been sensitive about my weight but somehow not with him. When I complained about my weight he just said, sweetly, 'But you are dignified.'

That June the President had lunch at Mahlamba Ndlopfu with Wolfie Kodesh. The President told me that he had stayed with Mr Kodesh before he was incarcerated and I was very impressed when I learned that Mr Kodesh had actually hidden Madiba for a while in his apartment in Johannesburg in 1961. The President used to exercise early in the morning and he would jog on the spot in Mr Kodesh's apartment for ten or twenty minutes a day. Despite the warm friendship that I witnessed between the two when they were reunited, I couldn't help but imagine the annoyance of having a person jogging on the spot in your flat at 5 in the morning. Altogether their tolerance of one another, these liberation fighters, distinguished them to be a special breed. I admired their patience and tenacity.

I had once seen the seriousness with which the President exercised early in the morning in a hotel room. I had to control myself not to yell, 'Khulu, you are going to injure yourself' as he did his exercises. He was tall and trim but you underestimated his strength unless you saw him exercising. He resembled a boxer training and did every movement with conviction and determination. Whenever one asked him what exercise he was doing, he would freely offer advice, and on more than one occasion while we travelled abroad I had to find a medicine ball for him to roll on. He said I should try it as it makes your stomach flat. At times, his exercise routine would be frenzied. So much so that Rory Steyn, his bodyguard, and I would find it hysterically funny. We would have to hide our giggles while Madiba exercised manically in some luxury hotel somewhere. I may not have been to all the touristy things in cities across the world but I can advise anyone on the hotels with the best room service menus, and where to find a medicine ball.

By now Virginia Engel was the head secretary of our office, after Mary had left. The President still knew my cellphone number by heart and simply kept on calling me for each and every thing, which sometimes put me in great difficulty having to report all his calls to Virginia. He would call me at night and tell me what medicine he wanted to be delivered the following day, or sometimes he would call me to remind him of something the following day. It is never a nice feeling to feel undermined by anyone and although I was really committed to my job, and adored the President, I am sure it was difficult for anyone not to feel undermined by these events.

During those years I tried to keep away from him as much as possible. I believed that the closer you get to the fire, the easier it is to get burned. I didn't want to impose myself upon him and tried to create a healthy distance and to avoid a situation where he ever felt cramped by my presence. In later years it became more difficult as he would become uncertain whenever I wasn't close in a professional situation. He knew I knew exactly what he wanted and how he wanted things to pan out around him so that he could comfortably deal with them. He wanted to know exactly what to expect from each moment or meeting and he trusted completely that I would ensure that order prevailed around him and that his needs would be my most important focus. Because they were. But officially at this point, I was simply one of the President's assistant private secretaries.

Another of my colleagues was Morris Chabalala. Morris was one of the sweetest people I ever met. He was softly spoken and had a very kind and humble demeanor. In a certain way the President was very old-school, not easily accepting the fact that a man could be his secretary too. It was not that Morris did anything wrong, but the President just felt different about women in particular positions. The President never discriminated but would simply move focus to the women. It was the same situation with pilots. As soon as female pilots were trained in the airforce they started flying his plane or helicopter, and even though he never expressed reservations he was a bit more alert knowing there was a woman behind the wheel. We would always tease him about being discriminatory but he admitted that it was just something one had to get used to. He was very conscious of these stereotypes and he never showed his reservation publicly, but if you knew him you could sense his uneasiness. As much as he was for equality he admitted that he had to work harder at changing his own perceptions first.

Once Morris had to deal with a particular diplomatic incident. It involved the Spanish and Portuguese embassies. Morris was supposed to hand-deliver a letter to the Spanish Embassy that contained information that South Africa would in future recognize the Western Sahara as an independent country. Unfortunately he mistakenly and totally unintentionally delivered the letter to the Portuguese Embassy and not the Spanish. The Ambassador didn't report the incorrect delivery but opened and sat on the note for days before the President discovered that the letter he had sent to the Spanish Embassy had never been received. Morris figured it out himself that he had delivered it to the wrong embassy and called Professor Gerwel, who reported it to the President. The Spanish were livid.

The mistake caused a diplomatic incident and the President expelled the Portuguese Ambassador instantaneously from South Africa, for holding on to the note and not reporting its delivery. It was unethical to sit on information of national importance without alerting the government and could have potentially resulted in a very serious international diplomatic crisis. The President then felt he had to take action within his office as well, to demonstrate both the seriousness and fairness in dealing with the issue, and Morris got transferred, ironically as it may seem, to the Foreign Affairs Department. I pleaded with Prof. Gerwel and the President to give Morris another chance but the President was adamant that he had to take action, and once the President decided something not even something the scale of a military invasion could change his mind. I checked on Morris on a few occasions and he seemed to be happy in his new job, despite the turmoil and hurt his departure caused.

This incident, no matter how upsetting we found it, was a very clear indication of how President Mandela performed as a diplomat. Even though there may be nothing diplomatic about it. In a matter of days, the public had forgotten about the incident. He was swift with a response, both publicly and in private, took decisive action and the matter was resolved. Recently in South Africa, by way of contrast, it was found that friends of our current President, Jacob Zuma, were allowed to land at the military airforce base in Pretoria without proper authorization. The family that landed there had planned a lavish family wedding at the Sun City resort outside Pretoria. Despite the availability of commercial international and private airports in the region they landed at the military base and were escorted to the wedding venue in official police vehicles. Politically very little was done about this case.

As the year progressed, so did the President's travels. He was working hard to show the world that South Africa was a healthy country. So we travelled to Burkina Faso. It was an African Union meeting attended by all heads of state. In the first few years it was interesting to watch and be part of these large gatherings of heads of state around the world but it becomes your worst nightmare because of all the time wasted waiting around while protocol is being observed.

Accommodation was newly built in Burkino Faso, but apart from providing for food for the heads of state we were very much left to our own devices to find something to eat even though we were housed in these newly built guest houses. It was usually chaos at meetings of this sort and everything took hours. Other heads of state all argued for private audiences with President Mandela. Sometimes he agreed and sometimes he wanted to avoid too many individual meetings. Presidents were expected to arrive at the plenary in alphabetical order, either by name or the name of their country, as seniority was always a point of dispute – some heads of state had been in power for ever, originally by election but then by means of dictatorship. For some reason my father gave me a huge consignment of biltong (beef jerky) to take along on the trip and that became our staple food, together with fresh bread that we went to buy along the road from an informal stall. A former French colony, the French influence remained in Burkino Faso and we bought hot baguettes off the street stall, filled them with biltong and for two and a half days the security guards and I lived off that shipment of dried meat.

In comparison to other delegations, ours was always the smallest. It usually consisted of a secretary, a doctor, two close protection bodyguards and then between three and five bodyguards who arrived in advance, plus at most two people from Protocol: one from the Presidency and one from Foreign Affairs. Ministers got added when they were required for certain bilateral talks but we never exceeded fifteen to twenty people in our entire delegation on our biggest visits, and that was only by exception and to countries with which South Africa had very close trade relations. Other heads of state travelled with delegations of twenty plus people and the Americans were the biggest with delegations of over two hundred, but they also had the money for it. Our President showed through his actions that we had other priorities and wastage was not going to be tolerated. While one appreciated that it also mounted the pressure on us as individuals to multitask.

Because of the President's advanced age – he was seventy-nine by now – he also liked continuity and he didn't like too many unfamiliar faces around him. Whenever there was a new member of staff on the delegation he would ask behind closed doors: 'Who is that person? What does he/she do?' And you would know that he spent time thinking about costs and productivity too. He often asked about costs involved, whether we were travelling locally or abroad. 'How much does the hotel cost where you are staying? Who is paying for it?' Regardless of your answer one knew that he was concerned about expenditure.

Following the visit to Burkino Faso we went to the United Kingdom and stayed at a house in the countryside belonging to the Roode family. They had a very large food company in South Africa. It was my first time in the English countryside and I loved it. After a few days' official visit in London, we went to Wales.

We paid a courtesy call on the Queen in Buckingham Palace and I was struck by the warm friendship forged between the President and the Queen. 'Oh Elizabeth' he would say when he greeted her and she would respond 'Hello Nelson'. Being a dog lover myself, I was intrigued to find the corgis' food bowls at the side entrance we used to Buckingham Palace.

After Wales we went to Italy for a state visit. We also paid a state visit to the Vatican. The President had a private conversation with the Pope, after which they called our delegation inside. The

President always insisted on introducing his entire delegation to the head of state and it was the same with the Pope. We each got introduced and the Pope, already frail at the time, shook hands, blessed us and gave us a rosary. I had no idea what a rosary was and thought it was some sort of Catholic necklace. I called my mother that night and told her I thought the Pope could see the sins in my eyes when he looked at me. Although some of my colleagues felt the same experience my mother laughed it off.

While at an official state lunch in Italy, one of the ministers choked on a prawn. He started by coughing and then suddenly silence descended on the table as he dropped off his chair. Luckily for President Mandela his doctor was at the official ceremony. Because we travelled with such a small delegation he always insisted that all his staff be included. Our doctor was able to literally save the minister's life at the table.

Later he also insisted on inviting the Presidential plane's aircrew to banquets even if it meant he had to request the head of state/ government himself to allow them to attend. He never treated any of his staff as just the hired help.

It was also on this trip that I was introduced to Yusuf Surtee, whose father used to be the President's tailor before he went to jail. Their family business continued supplying the President with suits and his famous patterned shirts. Yusuf brought a famous Italian gentleman, Stefano Ricci, representing the famous Brioni brand, to greet the President. As much as I resembled the typical *boere-meisie* Stefano was the typical Italian: jovial, lively and generous. He would always send the President the most beautiful clothing and one could always feel the love and care that went into the selection of clothes. Whenever Stefano sent clothes via Yusuf, Yusuf's shops would adjust whatever needed to be changed if needs be. Both Yusuf and Stefano had exceptionally good taste.

The President's eightieth birthday approached. A massive party was being planned by the ANC, the Mandela family together with Suzanne Weil, a business partner of the Mandela daughters, for the night of the President's actual birthday, 18 July. The President's entire personal staff were invited to the glamorous event at Gallagher estate in Johannesburg, together with the cream of the crop of the South African social scene as well as people like Naomi Campbell, Michael Jackson, Quincy Jones and Stevie Wonder, to name but a few.

Earlier in the week speculation started doing the rounds that the President and Mrs Machel were going to get married on the 18th. I thought about it and decided that it was not true. Nothing out of the ordinary happened in our environment for me to believe that there was any truth to the speculation. Parks Mankahlana, the spokesperson for the President, was repeatedly asked: 'Are they getting married?' And Parks would at first say he wasn't sure, then he vaguely denied it, and finally he said that there was definitely no marriage. I called Josina (Mrs Machel's daughter) earlier in the week to ask if she knew anything. She didn't and we just laughed it off. Josina stayed with the President at his official residence in Cape Town during his Presidency while she was studying at university there. We therefore spent a lot of time together and became close friends. I said to her: 'Zina, if you are lying to me you know I am going to have to kill you.' Jokingly. We were excited about the birthday but we really didn't know. On Saturday 18 July I woke up to newspaper headlines that read: THEY ARE GETTING MARRIED. I just smiled. I was, among a few others, asked to go and work at the Houghton residence later that day. I thought they were probably expecting family for the birthday celebrations and therefore needed extra hands.

The President and I were used to speaking on the phone. He would give me tasks or I would call him with messages or questions. We were on the phone all the time, much to the irritation of many people. He got to know my voice and could easily hear me, whereas with others he had difficulty hearing them clearly over the phone. So on his eightieth birthday I decided to call him in the morning to wish him happiness for his birthday. I would never call or disturb him if I didn't have a very good reason to discuss business, but on this day I thought that it was such a special birthday that I had to call, despite knowing that I would see him later in the afternoon at his residence.

The President and Mrs Machel spent the Friday night at Mahlamba Ndlopfu, the President's official residence in Pretoria, something which didn't often happen as they preferred to stay in Johannesburg. The household staff transferred me to him and I said: 'Good morning Khulu' and started singing 'Happy Birthday' to him. After the last note I said: 'I hope this day, today, is the most beautiful day of your entire life.' I could hear his amusement and he knew that I was fishing for information. He just said: 'Thank you darling, it definitely will be,' and then I knew, *they were getting married*. I felt like a jack in the box. I couldn't contain my excitement but I didn't want to say a word to anyone. I spent the entire day trying to figure out where/when/how. I then recalled the President asking me to call on a jeweller to see him at Mahlamba Ndlopfu a few weeks before; when the jeweller arrived they went outside and sat under a tree for their discussion. I thought it was someone the President knew from before and didn't pay attention. I felt that they were surely going to get married at the official banquet since they would have all their friends and family there but I was too scared to speculate.

They had a lunch at the Presidential guest house where the family was gathered. Staff were not invited. We proceeded to the Houghton house and arriving there it was clear that the media was not going to let go of the story. There were media everywhere, some trying to jump the walls and some climbing into trees from the adjacent plots. The security people had their hands full. We went inside and things were somewhat sombre and quiet. We stayed in the back and started putting out cups and whatever was needed for a tea later on. Soon the President and Mrs Machel arrived, followed by a few other guests. Again I didn't want to intrude and stayed as far away from them as possible. Then, like a veldt fire, news spread through the house: 'There is a wedding here in a few minutes.'

Things were simple and beautiful. Only a few people attended and really people closest to them: Archbishop Desmond Tutu, Thabo and Zanele Mbeki, Prince Bandar bin Sultan of Saudi Arabia, Yusuf Surtee, George Bizos, Ahmed Kathrada and the Sisulus, to name a few. And in true Madiba style there was complete representation of all the religious denominations in South Africa. Although they were married by the Methodist Bishop Mvume Dandala, all other religions had some role to play. It was very respectful and stylish. We saw Mrs Machel coming down the stairs by herself, gracefully, almost like her name says: Graça. Most of us couldn't control our emotions, and peeking from an adjacent room we couldn't help but wipe our tears. It was so beautiful and the President deserved to be happy at last.

That evening was every bit of the celebration it should have been. When Madiba finally took to the stage to say a few words on his birthday, his first words were to roaring applause when he said: 'My wife and I . . .' The country was celebrating with and for them.

It was a great evening and wonderful celebrations. I continuously had to check myself as if to pinch myself. Was all this real? I had never dreamt that I would ever be at the eightieth birthday and wedding celebrations of Nelson Mandela. The short journey with him at the time had already changed me so much. Luckily we were too busy and under too much pressure for me to ever sit and become complacent or conceited about where I found myself at any given point.

On 10–12 September 1998, a SADC (Southern African Development Community) meeting was held in Mauritius. Member states included countries from Southern Africa and the meeting was chaired by South Africa at this particular time (heads of state assumed the chairmanship on a rotating basis). When the President and Mrs Machel arrived in Mauritius a few days before the meeting, there was already word that Lesotho, a tiny kingdom surrounded by South Africa, was on the brink of a coup. We were regularly in contact with Prime Minister Mosisili and King Letsie III of Lesotho and even though I didn't understand why, I knew that they were facing difficulties. Both the President and Deputy President Mbeki were out of the country at the time and Minister Mangosuthu Buthelezi was Acting President of South Africa.

After President Mandela's inauguration, the National Party had joined the newly elected ANC government and that tenure of co-operative rule was known as the Government of National Unity. But by this time the Government of National Unity had been dissolved following the National Party's departure from the government. The Inkatha Freedom Party (IFP) was therefore the biggest opposition party in Parliament and appointing the leader of the IFP, Minister Buthelezi, as Acting President while both the President and his Deputy were abroad was a gesture of trust on the ANC's side.

I remember the President being bitterly tired and upset with events back home in which around 134 people were reportedly killed as a result of South Africa's invasion of Lesotho, in what is referred to today as the biggest mistake during Mr Mandela's Presidency. The President was literally on the phone throughout the night consulting with Minister Buthelezi and the Lesotho government.

It was no fun being in Mauritius for the first time. Instead of swimming in the beautiful waters of the Indian Ocean we attended to official engagements from banquets and meetings to a visit to the Botanical Gardens. I wanted to swim rather than stare at a rare flower that only bloomed once every seventy-five years. We were also tired and disturbed by events back at home.

The following day the SADC meeting convened. The meeting was scheduled to start at 10 a.m. but President Mugabe from Zimbabwe entered the room more than an hour late. President Mandela didn't like chairing meetings and would usually open a meeting and then hand over to someone else to ensure the rules were observed. No one ever questioned this peculiar arrangement, and he would only occasionally comment on proceedings or nod to add his approval to process. While President Mugabe entered another head of state was busy addressing the meeting. President Mandela interrupted him and asked him to stop his address. This was unusual for him and the atmosphere grew tense as silence descended in the big hall; it was one of the few occasions that President Mandela interrupted someone while he was speaking.

President Mandela waited for President Mugabe to be seated and then launched into an off-the-cuff speech of about twenty minutes about being disrespectful and wasting other people's time, and that 'some heads of state' considered themselves more important and therefore thought it was acceptable to arrive late. He didn't mention President Mugabe's name once, but we all knew. He subsequently used words that never left me: 'Because you hold a particular position, doesn't mean that you are more important than anyone else. Your time is not more valuable than anybody else's time. If you are late you show that you have no respect for another person's time and therefore no respect for other people because you consider yourself to be more important than others.'

After President Mandela finished his speech President Mugabe allowed proceedings to continue for a while and then quietly left as unnoticed as he could. That was the last time I ever saw any kind of interaction between them and there was no contact again that I am aware of, except exchanging courtesies whenever they shared a stage at an all-Africa event.

President Mandela often related the story that before South Africa's democracy Zimbabwe was considered the star of the continent, but then when South Africa became a democracy they said the sun came out and the star disappeared. I was of the opinion that was one of the reasons why President Mugabe felt bitterness towards South Africa's efforts on the continent. More recently in an interview, President Mugabe paid back by commenting on President Mandela being too much of a saint and pleasing white people at the expense of black people. President Mandela was no longer able to defend himself due to his age at that point, and I thought that Mugabe had waited for a very long time to seek revenge through public humiliation. His comment clearly lacked understanding of the South African situation and that had it not been for the focus on reconciliation at the time, our country would have gone up in flames, ending up much like the state in which Zimbabwe is today.

The President was scheduled to pay a state visit to Saudi Arabia and I was asked to accompany him. John Reinders, the Chief of Protocol in the Presidency and I, together with some security members, set off to Riyadh a few days in advance. I had received correspondence from the South African Embassy in Saudi and staff offered to 'rent' an *abaya* for me – the 'cloak' Muslim women wear to cover themselves. Since I didn't know what they were talking about, I agreed to that.

Upon arrival in Riyadh it was clear that this country, culture and religion was very different to any place I had imagined. I was handed my *abaya* at the airport and told to cover up immediately and every time I appeared in public. On our way to the Presidential guest house I was given a crash-course in the Islamic faith and Muslim culture. I was stunned to learn of all the rules that applied mainly to women only. I didn't take most of it seriously until I spoke to some of the officials later that night, who told me that they still had public executions in Riyadh for people committing 'religious crimes'. Being a bit of a deliberate rebel I decided to test the boundaries of this belief system on me as a 'Westerner'.

First we went out to a night market. As I jumped into the first available limo with an open door I heard a lot of people starting to argue around the car in Arabic. Apparently the argument was over who was allowed to travel with me and who not. As an unmarried woman, one is not allowed to travel in the car with any man who is not a relative. Especially and definitely *not* a married man. So I drove by myself.

The custom is that shops only open around 10 a.m. and at noon every day everything closes as they all go to the mosques to pray. At 1 p.m. they open again and around the hour some shops close for people to go and pray again. You could find yourself in the front of a queue to pay for something in a store and be chased out of the shop when the sirens for prayer time start. It was therefore better to go to a night market where things would be open until late and praying wouldn't interrupt shopping as much as it did during the day.

In my briefing I was also told to watch out for the Mattawa, the religious military police. They were there to police people observing the Muslim culture. They walk around, dressed in uniforms similar to that of the ordinary police but they carry sticks with them dipped in red paint, I was told. If they catch someone not observing the culture they hit you with the stick on your ankles and the red paint sticks. If you are caught a second time, they arrest you. And who knows what then. I was once reprimanded in the market with a 'cover up, cover up' but quickly ran away before they could mark me with the paint and didn't see the paint myself. There were so many beautiful carpets to see and things to buy that it distracts you from focusing on the things around you, and I appreciated with what ease we lived back in South Africa. I nevertheless enjoyed the experience, so different from what was familiar to me. One was not allowed to visit Saudi as a tourist at the time and the visa process was thoroughly controlled and checked by the Saudi authorities. I therefore considered it a privilege and unique experience to be able to visit Saudi.

We had our first meeting scheduled with the chief of protocol the night before President Mandela's arrival in the country. It is definitely not one of the easiest countries to work in, particularly being a female. We waited for days to confirm a time with their chief of protocol to discuss a programme of some sort. The only response one would get is: 'wait'. So you wait. You can't go anywhere and you sit around for hours waiting for word from the officials.

The meeting was scheduled in the Presidential Palace where President Mandela was going to stay. At first the gentleman dressed in his traditional Arab garb seemed friendly. I avoided eye contact as I had been told. The Saudi chief of protocol started the meeting with the usual exchange of courtesies and how honoured they were to receive President Mandela, etc. We felt honoured. But I wanted him to stop and get to details of the programme. It was late and I was tired. By midnight, however, we were no closer to any details on the programme. By that time President Mandela's plane had already left South Africa.

John Reinders would put a question to the chief of protocol and he would pick up the phone and converse in Arabic with someone on the other end. He would end the call and move to the next question. After two hours of this I had enough. John decided to go outside for a smoke break and I followed. We discussed what was happening inside and I told him that when we returned to the office I think I had to take over. Which I did. John was completely capable of negotiating by himself but we had run out of options in our approach, trying to get answers. I completely disregarded custom and looked the man straight in the eyes. I said: 'Sir, President Mandela is on his way here right now. In a plane. It is the first time in my life that I've heard of a state visit without a programme while the head of state is already on his way. The President expects us to know what will happen to him when he arrives but at this stage you are not helping us.'

The chief tried to avoid eye contact and picked up the phone again. He then excused himself and John and I started laughing. It was really ridiculous. When he returned thirty minutes later I lost it. It was well after 1 a.m. I slammed my fist on the table and said: 'Sir, if you do not give us any details now, right now, we will instruct the President's plane to turn around as we cannot expect our President to arrive in a foreign country without a programme for his visit.' I felt that he undermined our responsibilities to the President and he was simply not willing to share information. The man was clearly disgusted by me. Women just don't talk to men like that in that country. 'Madam,' he said to me, 'please calm down.' That is the second worst thing you can say to me. I said, 'I will not calm down unless you give us details now.'

He picked up the phone and clearly, without me having to understand a word, told the person on the other line to rush to the office. John calmly said to me in Afrikaans: 'I think they got the point.' Not long after two other gentlemen arrived and we moved to a bigger meeting room. A programme was laid out, and although times were not completely confirmed at least there was an indication of what was expected of the President.

The next morning I noticed that none of the staff in the palace spoke to me any longer. I assumed it was because of my behaviour the previous night. I didn't give a damn. About three hours prior to the President's arrival and an hour before we left to go to the airport, the entire palace came to standstill by the announcement of a prince arriving. Everyone rushed to the front door and formed a receiving line. We didn't know who to expect and I was told it could be one of 2,000 princes. Much to my surprise it was Prince Bandar, President Mandela's close friend, who was serving as Saudi Ambassador in the United States at the time. Clearly he was respected by everyone in the Palace.

When he entered he greeted by nodding his head and walked right up to me and kissed me. 'Oh hello Zelda.' I noticed from the corner of my eye how people's faces around me dropped. I was the only woman in their company, unmarried, and here a prince kisses me. 'How are you Zelda? Welcome,' he said and we exchanged some pleasantries. He walked me to a sitting room where he asked me about the President's arrival, programme etc. When he left, I was treated like a princess.

The Saudis are extremely hospitable people. They don't spare any trouble to ensure that one feels comfortable – that is, once you behave. They are generally friendly as long as you observe their culture and respect their beliefs. Madiba was accompanied by a few female ministers but we learned that even they were not allowed to attend the state banquet or meeting with the King. All the women subsequently went to a private dinner at a businessman's house. The state banquet that the President and his fellow men attended only started at midnight and they were only back at the Presidential guest house after 2 a.m. The next morning we were all tired, but despite our exhaustion the President had his breakfast at exactly 7 a.m. as usual. He was an eighty-year-old at that stage yet his enthusiasm and spirit was that of a young man.

When we departed the next day I was fed up with the rules and regulations and I wanted to be home in my own environment. As we checked in at the airport to board our commercial flights back home, the security men got stopped and their luggage was searched. They usually carried firearms with proper licences they obtained from the hosting government and security equipment like radios and their own metal detectors that they needed to perform their duties. Yet they got stopped, searched, and had to take every little piece of equipment apart. I made no secret of my disgust at Saudi bureaucracy. For goodness' sake, we were leaving the country not entering it! Why did it matter to them what we took back home!

Strangely, in the years to follow I became fond of Riyadh. We returned on a few occasions. Once you know a place and you know what to expect and what not to resist it becomes easier. I liked the food and I knew then how to approach things . . . with calmness and a *lot* of patience. I guess one also matures and becomes more patient with age. In all the Arab countries we visited I learned that their governments rarely provided a lot of detail in advance. It was a question of hurry up and wait . . .

6

Running to Keep Up

The President visited a schools and clinic project in the Northern Cape on 19 February 1999. It was a Friday afternoon and I was working in Cape Town at the time. Virginia accompanied the President on his visit on that particular day. As I had befriended the commander of the Presidential Protection Unit in Cape Town, Hein Bezuidenhout, we decided to have a drink in their canteen to end the week and avoid peak-hour traffic when going home. These were the days before news spread as fast as it does now; not everyone had a cellphone and people were not connected on the internet to get news updates continuously.

As I prepared to join Hein in the canteen I received a call from former President P. W. Botha on my mobile; he wanted to speak to the President to tell him that Schalk Visagie had been shot. 'Lady, I want to talk to Mr Mandela right now.' He spoke to me in Afrikaans but he was obviously angry and irritated. He never called him President Mandela, but always Mr Mandela. It was as if he couldn't make the leap to having complete unconditional respect for Mr Mandela as a President. I told him that the *President* was in mid-air and I could hear that he didn't quite believe me. He ended the conversation without saying goodbye. Schalk was Mr Botha's son-in-law. He was a policeman and the President liked him as he was progressive in his thinking and clearly had some influence over his wife, Rozanne. Rozanne was very conservative and earlier the President had tried to get them to persuade her father to appear in front of the Truth and Reconciliation Commission, established in 1995.

On 11 February 1998, eight years after the President's release from jail, he invited Rozanne and Schalk Visagie, Rozanne's sister Elsa and her husband to join him for dinner. The President asked me to arrange the dinner and I was somewhat uncomfortable calling on Rozanne Botha, knowing very well how the family felt about Nelson Mandela. It took me some hours to respond to the President's request. A request by the President for someone to have a meal with him was usually greatly appreciated and welcomed by those invited. I knew in this instance it might be different. It was clearly not a great deal for Rozanne to be invited by the President to have dinner, but I realized that they were still filled with anger and regret because their father was driven until his back was against the wall to surrender power at the end of apartheid and to hand over to President F. W. de Klerk, who would later call the first democratic elections in South Africa.

The President met with them over dinner to try and lobby them to persuade their father to appear in front of the Truth and Reconciliation Commission, a body set up by President Mandela's administration to allow people the opportunity to apply for amnesty for deeds they may have committed during the apartheid years. If perpetrators came clean and presented the truth on injustices they may have been party to, they could apply for amnesty. This was to give people on both sides of apartheid the opportunity to first of all make peace with themselves, but also for families who lost loved ones and who still had unanswered questions to get closure. People wanted answers and thousands of people in South Africa wanted closure surrounding the deaths or mysterious disappearances of loved ones. It was not a matter that needed closure by any one side only. South Africa needed to heal as a nation and it was only going to be possible if all parties decided to participate in the TRC hearings. The Botha family couldn't agree unanimously on the matter – Rozanne was especially fiercely opposed to it out of fear that her father could be prosecuted or humiliated – and former President Botha went to his grave years later with many answers that could have provided solace to many people.

I knew that the President would be concerned for Schalk so I tried to reach him, but was told that they had just taken off from the venue they had visited. They were en route back to Pretoria. News quickly broke of the incident and I could sense tension in the air. I thought therefore that I had to inform the President as on many occasions I'd learned something like this could snowball into a much bigger political issue if one procrastinated. I called the control tower of the South African airforce in Pretoria to contact the pilots and ask them to inform the President that Schalk Visagie had been shot. My idea was to tell him once he landed in Pretoria that Mr Botha was livid and insisted on speaking to him.

Hein and I had our first drink. I told him what had happened and he called some of his colleagues in the police force to try and get more information. Schalk was previously part of a gang-related investigation unit in the police and from the information the police had at the time they suspected that it was possibly an act of revenge from a gang after he brought some of its members to book.

Then I received a call from the airforce to inform me that the President decided to turn his plane around mid-air and proceed to Cape Town. He'd instructed them to let me know and said that I would know what to do. Hein and I got into action. It was like gears falling into position as everyone started calling whoever had to be informed of the President's expected arrival in Cape Town. We decided to proceed to the airport ourselves. It was Friday afternoon and the traffic was moving at snail speed. Hein managed to organize half a convoy and an advance team to go to the hospital, which was not far from the airport. We were both very tense. We took our jobs extremely seriously and this was one of those occasions where that mattered. The President landed and while we drove to the hospital I briefed him.

Upon arrival at the hospital Rozanne appeared, obviously still in shock. Schalk was still in theatre being stabilized and the President called Rozanne and other family members into a private meeting room. Mr P. W. Botha wasn't there as he lived in a town called 'Wilderness' at the time, about five hours' travel from Cape Town. The President expressed his sympathy and offered support to the family in a genuinely sympathetic way. We called Mr Botha too and the President expressed his sympathy and sadness over the matter. Mr Botha was brief but told the President that he had warned him that crime in the country was getting out of hand and that the President had to really step up and take this to task. I couldn't hear the entire conversation but the President seemed calm while I could hear Mr Botha raising his voice on the other side. Then as we left, Rozanne accompanied us to the exit and told the President, waving her finger at him as her father was known for doing: 'Mandela, if something happens to Schalk tonight it will be on your conscience. It will haunt you for the rest of your life.' She was obviously in shock and I cannot imagine her fear at that point, but I thought she was completely out of line and disrespectful.

I was always very offended when someone didn't call him Mr or President but just addressed him using his first name or surname. In a way it was derogatory. And it was an Afrikaner thing to address people with respect (or then with the lack thereof if you didn't have respect for them). I turned to her and said: 'That's enough, Rozanne. We have to leave . . .' and we left. As we walked outside the President took my hand but he was quiet. I was visibly upset, and thinking back to that day I realize how much the world had changed for me by then. Here was the black President holding my hand to comfort me while we were leaving behind my people in distress. He was genuinely concerned for Schalk but I think he didn't take easy to all the emotions being flung around. Schalk did survive and we didn't hear from him again.

Like the country, I had moved a long way from the time of P. W. Botha and apartheid. Many people in South Africa, especially the black youth, feel that Madiba's attempts to reconcile and unify our country were over-credited. They are of the opinion that the moments when South Africa was unified were limited to sporting events when the country briefly appeared to be in celebration mode. According to them, those were superficial moments that did not last. I understand how they feel, although such thinking in my opinion is also prejudice. We have not made the progress in economic transformation which we had hoped for and generally people are frustrated and angry. Some young people even go as far as saying that Madiba sold out to the whites, because he did not force transformation fast enough. Yet, what South Africa needed at the time was healing and to present a consolidated front to the world to gain the confidence of international investors. Madiba was like true north on a compass: we all know where we are supposed to go but he knew that we had to take a slightly different approach to achieve stability first.

Some angry young people feel that things have not changed, but the advantage of my age is that I can attest to the change I have seen and experienced. I am a product of that change.

The end of an era was approaching. In May 1999 the second democratic elections were planned in South Africa. President Mandela repeatedly indicated throughout his term that he would only stay for one term of office, after which he would hand over the reins. He did so mainly hoping that others would follow suit but also because I think he was eager to have a bit of freedom himself. In 1997 Deputy President Mbeki was elected President of the ANC and voted their Presidential candidate for the elections in 1999. President Mandela symbolically handed over power to the Deputy President two years into his term. He was adamant that Deputy President Mbeki was at the helm and that his own role was purely ceremonial. It wasn't that easy though. While the day-to-day running of the country was largely left to Deputy President Mbeki, President Mandela was still lawfully the executive head of state and there were certain obligations he couldn't give up.

We hardly had anything personally to do with Deputy President Mbeki and very seldom saw him in the buildings we shared. President Mandela would often call him to report events to him or even to ask for his advice. Being the considerate human being that he was, he never wanted to be seen to make anyone feel inferior to him. On the occasions that we did see the Deputy President their interactions were limited to formal exchanges, and I personally got the idea that the Deputy President felt that the President didn't always do the right thing. That was my personal impression from a distance. I also learned that Deputy President Mbeki's father, who was imprisoned with President Mandela, wanted a more senior role in government after his release but only became a Member of Parliament and that was apparently the cause of uneasiness. I never dwelled on it though. Mrs Zanele Mbeki was always friendly and stately but quiet.

I was literally surviving day by day. The President was depending on me even more than before, and even though a new private secretary had been appointed it still didn't prevent the President from calling me day and night. He would sometimes call me at 2 a.m. and ask me to remind him to do something the following morning. It was not that he was more considerate for those with families but he knew that I didn't mind him calling on me.

It is widely documented that there were differences within the ANC about who would succeed President Mandela. Cyril Ramaphosa and Thabo Mbeki were the contestants. Senior ANC members were divided on the matter. From the first time I met Mr Ramaphosa I liked him. Mr Mbeki was distant and appeared dismissive towards me. Regardless of my lack of knowledge about the ANC I was always trying to uphold the ANC's good intentions in public. I often wondered whether the President regretted supporting Mr Mbeki's nomination as President of the ANC or his successor at a time after his retirement when the government really treated him badly, but soon learned that the President considered regret as the most useless emotion and there was no use in asking 'what if'.

President Mandela was always forthright in that he didn't run the country but that the Deputy President did most of the work. President Mandela's role was that of nation-builder and he passed with distinction. To this day I think history has provided us with the right leader at the right time, or South Africa could have easily gone up in flames. I often compare our democracy with the growing process of a child. Up to the age of five you simply have to feed the child, care for it and love it. That is what President Mandela did best. From five to fifteen years you have to start educating the child and shape it into a personality, and that is exactly what President Mbeki did. With distinction. Now we are in the teenager phase and we experience the growing problems in our country similar to that of any adolescent. And as with an adolescent we can no longer blame our youth and we have to start acting responsibly.

In the first few months of 1999 the President worked at a pace that would see any younger head of state crawling on all fours. He was campaigning for the ANC, building schools and clinics, attending to official obligations and in between finding time and insisting on fetching and dropping his wife at the airport, attending to his children's and grandchildren's issues and then also embarking on saying 'goodbye' or taking leave of structures, people, business, institutions and even foreign countries before his retirement. Or should I say from the outset, his first attempt at retirement? The President's private secretary, Virginia Engel, had a health condition and she was off sick for an extended period of time, so most of the travelling and work load came down on me. But I was ready to take on whatever was needed to see the President through the last couple of months of his term. Change is inevitable and I was ready to drive myself past the finish line, probably for the first time in my life at full speed. I often sat in planes and helicopters trying to comprehend what had happened to me. A certain sadness would then fill my heart. I hadn't fully experienced what had happened because I was so obsessed with doing more than what was expected of me, always over-delivering, that I probably missed some valuable opportunities to get a deeper understanding of what was historically happening around me.

On 1 April 1999 the President took representatives of McDonald's, Datatec and Nokia to the Eastern Cape, visiting three different areas where he wanted these respective companies to build schools and clinics in the communities of Bizana, Mbongweni and Baziya, very remote communities in the rural Transkei. The President never had a McDonald's hamburger. He just never ate fast food and he didn't know what a hamburger was. It is not something he was brought up with and his distance from society also meant that he missed out on many things that evolved around us. We take it that everybody should know what a hamburger is. During his speech in the community where he introduced McDonald's the name slipped his mind and he referred to them as 'the people who make these sandwiches'. I thoroughly enjoyed that reference and so did the representatives from McDonald's. It also provided much laughter to the community. There were these moments, some of them which seem so distant to me now, when you completely forgot that this was Nelson Mandela.

The President had no problem calling together competitors to work together. In his schools and clinics project he would easily call together rivals, like the two cellular phone operators at the time or both BMW and Mercedes-Benz. When I once asked him about it he said that when people are competing to do good, it inspires them to do even better. It made perfect sense although I thought it was only Nelson Mandela that could get some rivals to sit together sometimes. It was entertaining to watch how companies would almost compete to showcase what they were able or willing to do.

President Mandela made sure he left not necessarily the best but the biggest for last. His last state visit was scheduled for April 1999 and would include Russia, Hungary, Pakistan and then China. He was hoping to strengthen ties with these countries prior to his departure from public office and to pave the way for a solid relationship to trade on in future. He also wanted to thank both Russia and China for their support during the apartheid years by honouring them with a state visit.

On 28 April 1999 we arrived in Moscow with all the fanfare, bells and whistles one could expect. President Boris Yeltsin was our host. We stayed in the Kremlin and I still consider it one of my most awkward experiences. I always felt like I was being watched, even alone in my room, although I was probably just imagining so. Passages were as wide as highways and people behaved like machine-like robots. Emotions were rarely expressed and everything appeared to have been rehearsed a thousand times. It all unnerved me but, being a disciplinarian myself, I kind of liked it. Language was a big problem. It was difficult asking for food to the President's liking and then when it came to our own food it was even worse. Rich food and vodka for breakfast. The only way I could get an egg for breakfast was to imitate a chicken several times. Saying 'cluck cluck' in the Kremlin while flapping your imaginary wings is never very graceful.

We visited the burial sites of J. B. Marks and Moses Kotane, former ANC leaders and communists who were instrumental in shaping the President's life. We laid a wreath and spent a few minutes of silence around their grave sites.

Next we visited the mausoleum on the Red Square where Lenin's body was exhibited. One of the little pleasures of travelling with the President was that they would close down the mausoleum for our visit so we could do so in private without interference from the tourists around the site. On the few occasions that we actually did sight-seeing we avoided having to stand in queues to buy tickets or get access to places. Protocol officers briefed us before descending into the grave site: No talking, no eating or drinking and under any circumstances, no photographs. We quietly went down the steps until we saw Lenin's mummified body. No one uttered a word.

What we had forgotten was that the President's hearing was already not good, and when the Russian protocol officer briefed us the President in all likelihood didn't hear the instructions. We were all quiet, almost admiring the body of the dead Communist leader. It was kind of spooky. And then, without any warning, the President with his booming loud voice said: 'So, how long has he been lying here?' The protocol officer was shocked beyond belief and looked at us for explanation or order, I don't know which. No one responded, out of pure shock, and the President repeated the question to even more chaos. Zenani, his daughter who accompanied us on the visit, then said to him, 'Daddy, you are not allowed to talk,' and he whispered back but loud enough for anyone to hear: 'Oh OK, I'm sorry.'

We also went to watch the world-renowned ballet *Swan Lake* at the Bolshoi. I was very impressed to be able to say that I stayed in the Kremlin, saw Lenin and watched *Swan Lake* at the Bolshoi. The fact that I walked that history with Nelson Mandela added to my delight. And for an Afrikaner this was something quite out of the ordinary, having spent so much time during my childhood praying for the abolishment of communism in these countries. Indeed times had changed.

The ballet was every bit of what I had imagined it would be. The dancing, decor, music, everything was brilliant. I sat right behind the President because he always wanted to know where I was in case he needed something. I touched his shoulder before the show started and told him I was right behind him in case he wanted water or anything.

Russians have a custom that they add 'ina' behind a man's surname to identify the wife of that person. Therefore Yeltsin's wife would be called Yeltsina. Just before the visit, I am told there was a discussion about my name in Maputo. The names that run in the Machel family, like Gracina, Josina and so on, sparked the discussion and apparently the President decided there that my name had to be changed to Zeldina. In Russia, with the occurrence of 'ina' at the end of these surnames, he was reminded of this discussion in Maputo and so he kept calling me Zeldina. We all found it very amusing. Needless to say, the name stuck and he called me Zeldina right up to the end, as every other person now does. I am reminded of him every time.

The President never realized the loudness of his voice and how recognizable it was. Between two of the ballet items he turned his head towards me and in the silence of the moment after the audience had stopped applauding he said, 'Zeldina, you and I should be doing that,' and pointed to the stage and ballerinas. We all burst out laughing and luckily I think only the South Africans and the few people in the audience from other countries but Russia could understand. It was hilarious and for minutes later we all laughed out loud. Luckily our laughter was drowned in the music but he enjoyed his own joke and kept on smiling for a long time.

It is also the only time I saw the President drinking any strong spirits, such as vodka. He was a stern believer that you should do what is possible not to offend the host, so he did exactly what was required of him. At the night of the state banquet he was heavily in conversation with President Yeltsin. President Yeltsin was a dramatic talker and, not knowing what they were discussing, it looked like they were arguing. In between they took a few vodka shots although President Mandela was only sipping his, and then without announcement President Yeltsin jumped up and left the room. He left President Mandela at the table for about fifteen minutes and it made me nervous as I thought they really had had a fight and he had left. He returned later to say that he had a call from President Clinton which he had to take, and apologized during his speech. Back in the Kremlin I told the President about my worries and he laughed at my assumptions that he would have an altercation with President Yeltsin. He did however raise the issue of Lenin's burial with Yeltsin, telling him it was time for Lenin to go to his grave. President Yeltsin was adamant that Lenin should stay in Red Square. President Mandela disagreed with him. But they remained on good terms.

From Russia we went to Hungary. I think the President was excited to end his term in office and therefore the visit was relaxed and enjoyable. Our protocol officer in Hungary told us about twenty times that Budapest, the capital, is actually two separate cities, Buda and Pest, divided by a river. We ended up teasing one another about it, repeatedly asking everybody around us: 'Did you know that Budapest is actually two different cities?' Even the President checked a few times whether we knew it was two different cities and we enjoyed him participating in our teasing. His sense of humour never failed.

From Budapest we went to Pakistan for a two-day state visit and then continued on to Beijing in China. If you thought that you had a problem in Russia with food and the language barrier, China was worse. We were told that two days before our visit all factory activity was stopped to clear the air of pollution. Whether that was really honestly the truth I don't know, but I probably wanted to believe it. Again I noticed in Beijing that everything worked like a machine. Emotions were far off and people were rehearsed in their responses. Some of the delegation went to see the Great Wall of China but I didn't feel that it was wise to leave the President alone for that long, especially in a country where hardly anyone spoke English and he definitely didn't speak or understand a word of Mandarin. Our colleagues returned, exhausted, and I was a little sad that I didn't see the Wall but decided that everything was worth the sacrifice.

Returning to South Africa we were gearing up to take our leave from the Presidency after the elections. Luciano Pavarotti was hosting a concert in Pretoria and the President and Mrs Machel attended the concert. It was very emotional for us all and almost announced in a stately way the beginning of the end of the term. The President was looking forward to his retirement. Little did I know that he was looking forward to doing less of what he had to do and doing more of what he wanted to do.

On 14 May the Presidency hosted a farewell for its entire staff attended by the President. It was a wonderful event and a party for us all. Once the President left the function we danced until late at night, saying our goodbyes. By now we had fostered great friendships and we were celebrating a successful term and great achievements. In any normal office environment you become friends with people, but in a Presidency it is as if you know there is a shelf life to the particular structure's existence and when the sell-by date approaches you become sentimental and emotional, even if it feels to you at the time that the term was dominated by challenges. You don't even necessarily like everyone but you foster bonds with people probably because you are forced into a situation of this highly stressed environment and you learn to co-exist for the benefit of the success of the legacy of that term. We had a fairly small office in comparison to the other Presidencies that followed. We were effective and although we had made our fair share of mistakes, we had done a good job in supporting the President's focus on reconciliation and building national unity.

We were campaigning for the elections day and night and travelling around the country non-stop in the weeks leading up to the vote. I was tired and emotionally depleted from pure exhaustion. The President repeated the same speech, off the cuff, over and over again to such an extent that I could anticipate exactly what he would say next. It is that last stretch when you see the finish line and you decide to give it your everything until you cross that line. He was there; I was about two laps behind him. People would often say: 'If the President can operate at that speed, why are you tired?' What people didn't consider is that the support staff didn't have their own support staff. No one bought the bread in my house, no one did the washing or drove me from point A to point B. You had to invent ways to deal with the ordinary course of life in between while dealing with the rest of the President's life on his behalf. I wouldn't say it was easier on him, and he was more than twice my age, but one underestimates the stress the most mundane things can cause in your life if you continuously work at such speed as we did.

On 19 May, His Royal Highness Crown Prince Abdullah bin Abdulaziz Al Saud from Saudi Arabia arrived in South Africa for a farewell visit. His plane was set to arrive at around 7 p.m. By 11 p.m. I was still at the airport awaiting him. The President asked me to be at the airport to ensure that things went smoothly. We waited and waited and I was irritable by the time the plane touched down. We still had a dinner to attend and I kept phoning the President to update him on the Saudis' arrival time. Even though he was tired he was willing to wait until the Crown Prince arrived and willing to attend a dinner at whatever hour. By midnight the Crown Prince had arrived at the Presidency in Pretoria with his entourage of fifty-plus and the dinner commenced. One of my colleagues, Lizanne van Oudshoorn from Protocol, was on duty too that night. When the President stood up to start his speech at the dinner, I asked Lizanne to stand in for me as I was at breaking point. It was close to 2 a.m. and having heard the President's campaign speech four times earlier that day I realized that I was too tired to listen to it for the fifth time. Regardless of the fact that he must have been tired, he was optimistic about the elections and the future of South Africa, sounding ever so energetic whenever he spoke about the prospects of the new South Africa. The President wasn't fazed about the time and he enjoyed the Crown Prince's visit.

On 2 June 1999 the second democratic elections were held in South Africa. President Mandela went to the polling station close to his house and cast his vote. It was always intriguing to watch. When the President wasn't doing anything impressive or spectacular, there was no audience. When he went about everyday life, few people were interested. But the day he voted, the strangest people showed up wanting to accompany him to the polling station. Few people actually took the time and trouble to take interest in what was challenging for him. It was clear that self-interest was going to become an agenda for many people even way beyond his retirement. After his vote the media asked him: 'Who did you vote for, Mr President?' and he responded: 'For myself.' I thought that was funny although people could have misinterpreted it.

Before the elections President Mandela called me into his office one day. He asked me to sit down and I knew that something serious was to follow. He hardly ever asked me so formally to sit down. But a formal request like this was different and his tone was serious. 'Zeldina, I want you to retire with me.' My response was: 'Well Khulu, I'm a bit young to retire but if you mean you want me to keep working for you, of course I will.' He just laughed. After five years he knew me better than anyone else. He had seen me grow up in a way and thinking back at earlier days he must have laughed when he was by himself about my ignorance and stupidity. But he recognized my tenacity and commitment.

Even though our lives were so different, I realized that there is a chance this person will not abandon me. Nelson Mandela didn't leave me behind. He took me with him. It was obviously one of the greatest, if not the greatest honour of my life, being chosen by Madiba to serve him beyond his retirement.

Every retiring President in South Africa is afforded some rights in retirement. One of these is keeping a full-time secretary on the payroll of the President's office but then using his/her services exclusively. It also included a telephone line, some administrative support such as a fax machine, etc., but that was the basics apart from security and official car transport within South Africa. Days before his retirement we started packing up our personal belongings at our offices in the Union Buildings.

On 11 June the President presented the last set of credentials to incoming ambassadors. I watched him really enjoying it for this last time. I was always surprised at his memory when it came to remembering the names of heads of state.

On 13 June the 'Brother Leader', Colonel Gaddafi of Libya, visited the President to bid farewell. Since the early 1990s the President had been involved in the process related to the court case that dealt with the Lockerbie plane incident in which 270 people were killed. First Mr Mandela asked President George Bush, Snr, in the early 1990s to agree that the trial be held in a neutral country. President Bush agreed to the suggestions from Mr Mandela but the British Prime Minister, John Major, refused. Then when Tony Blair became Prime Minister he put the request to him and they agreed that the case would be heard under Scottish law in The Hague in the Netherlands. A long process followed, during which the President negotiated with Gaddafi to have the two suspects delivered to The Hague, and finally Prince Bandar from Saudi and Prof. Jakes Gerwel succeeded in persuading the Brother Leader to deliver the two suspects for trial.

Later, in 2002, we visited Barlinnie Prison in Scotland where the Libyan Abdelbaset al-Megrahi was serving a minimum twenty-seven-year sentence following that trial. Al-Megrahi was unhappy with his conditions and sent word through Gaddafi that he wanted to speak to Madiba. There was little Gaddafi could do himself, as he was still considered an enemy by the West despite keeping his promise of delivering the suspects of the Lockerbie bombing and compensating the families of the victims who died in the plane crash. Yes, compensation could never bring back a life, but Gaddafi had delivered his promise yet still the West did not suspend all sanctions as they had promised. There was nothing Madiba could do to convince the West to suspend the sanctions. He had great appreciation for Gaddafi acting reliably and was willing to look into al-Megrahi's situation when asked to do so.

As we entered the prison surrounded by Scottish prison officials the mood was sombre. We entered al-Megrahi's cell, which consisted of a living area, a bathroom and kitchen. Comparing that to Madiba's old cell on Robben Island I thought al-Megrahi had something more like a suite. He was obviously touched to receive Madiba and we conversed with him for a long time. He produced evidence that he thought was not taken into consideration in court and he complained that it was very difficult for him to practise his Islamic faith, since he was in solitary confinement and was not able to worship with others. Madiba listened carefully and with sympathy but clearly he was not going to argue for the case to be re-opened. Afterwards, Madiba addressed a huge press conference, during which he pleaded for al-Megrahi to be moved to another prison in a Muslim country. (Al-Megrahi was later moved to Greenock jail out of solitary confinement and later released as he was terminally ill. He passed away in 2012 at the age of sixty in Tripoli.)

Prince Bandar and Prof. Gerwel were both awarded the Order of Good Hope, South Africa's highest honour, for their success in bringing about the trial in The Hague. The President had a close relationship with Gaddafi as a result of these negotiations and Gaddafi had to know that he could trust Madiba before he would co-operate. I also suspected that Madiba was entertained by the fact that the Brother Leader publicly expressed his fearlessness of the West. The West had not supported President Mandela during the time of apartheid, in general maintaining their links with the apartheid regime as a bulwark against communism. It was therefore an emotional day for Gaddafi when he came to bid farewell to President Mandela from his Presidency.

We only saw him on a few occasions after President Mandela's retirement and the last time, during President Zuma's inauguration, I made a point to ask whether he didn't want to pay a courtesy call upon Madiba. I never received a response and Madiba was shocked when he was killed in 2011. No person deserves to die without dignity. I will never condone what he did to his own people but in my view he was always good to us and to Madiba and he earned respect in our eyes for that and always delivering his promises during those negotiations. Madiba was loyal to those in whom he invested friendship and the Brother Leader was one of them. He never omitted to point out the mistakes he thought Gaddafi made, but they maintained mutual respect even while expressing their differences at times. Another of Madiba's great lessons: you can have a vast difference of opinion with someone but that never justifies disrespect.

We travelled to Cape Town for the swearing in of the new President and Parliament and to prepare for the inauguration of President Mbeki in Pretoria on 16 June. Attending the inauguration at the Union Buildings it was the first time that I saw any kind of interaction between Mrs Machel and Mrs Winnie Madikizela Mandela.

Up to that point I had only seen Mrs Mandela at a distance on a few occasions. We had no contact with her of any kind. It was one of those unspoken rules that when you work for the President you don't ask questions about his relationships with his family or his former wives. Apart from the four grandchildren who lived with the President we only occasionally saw Zindzi and Zenani, the two daughters from that marriage. When I saw the look in their eyes when Mrs Mandela and Mrs Machel passed each other in the crowd at the inauguration it scared me. There was no relationship between the two women and I could never imagine them being friendly.

I have learned over the years to have appreciation for Mrs Winnie Mandela. I was angry at her when I learned that she maintained physical distance from Madiba following his release, yet her affair with Dali Mpofu was widely talked about. It must have hurt him. Yet Mrs Machel was the one to bring me around to accepting and appreciating the fact that if it had not been for Mrs Mandela, Madiba may have given up hope over the long years in prison. Apart from the fact that she was mother to two of his children, she represented hope for him and she must have been the person he dreamt about at night; the person he longed to touch and to be with. I grew a sense of understanding for her and also how lonely she must have become without him. It is only once we really experience loneliness ourselves that we can fully comprehend its darkness, and as I matured awareness of these things in life often occupied my mind.

On the day of the inauguration of President Mbeki we woke up as usual and prepared for the ceremony. We attended the ceremony, after which President Mandela returned to his office in the Union Buildings to collect his personal belongings. The office was deserted because it was a public holiday. As I entered the glass doors where I first entered his office five years earlier I quietly started sobbing. He held Mrs Machel's hand as we walked down the passage to his office. I walked a few yards ahead of them and the only sound to announce their arrival was the familiar sound of the security door opening in front of them as they approached and automatically closing behind them. Our offices leading to his were already empty. I left them alone in his office as they went through his drawers and bathroom to clear the limited items he had left in the office. I later took them a small box in which we packed his things and he saw that I was crying. He looked at me and said: 'Zeldina, you are over-reacting.' He said those same words back in 1994 when we first met; he said them under different circumstances and I was crying at that time for exactly the opposite reasons. In 1994 I was crying because of guilt and fear of what lay ahead; now I was crying because it was all over. Little did I know what really lay ahead . . .

PART THREE

Gatekeeper to the Most Famous Man in the World

1999–2008

7

Travel and Conflict

We had made plans to set up office in the President's old house in Houghton. By now he had moved to a new house following his marriage with Mrs Machel in 1998. His old house was a large double-storey house that, despite being his home for over five years, was run down and not well decorated. It was empty though and I knew it would be a good place to set up the office because it was close to his new residence too. I also asked Madiba if I could stay there while I found a place to live in Johannesburg.

At first he wanted me to come and stay on his premises but I turned down the offer, knowing too well that I needed the distance and that it would not be welcomed by all of his family. I arranged for my furniture arriving from Cape Town to be delivered at the old house in Houghton.

I started cleaning the only bedroom upstairs that was liveable – Madiba's old bedroom, which was painted in the ugliest shade of blue one can imagine. I don't think such things ever bothered him. Everything was blue and even though I loved blue it was too blue. It was a modest room, definitely not befitting for a President, and I was happy that Mrs Machel's presence in his life had both enlightened his life but also introduced him to a few more materialistic pleasures, like a bigger room and a dignified space to live in to appreciate the sunlight through your bedroom window, and a room that welcomes you as opposed to depressing you. Still in comparison to the luxuries others with similar positions enjoy, his remained modest.

I called the Ministry of Public Works and asked them to send an official to look at obtaining furniture for Madiba's office, in accordance with government policy. They agreed. They also agreed to speed up the installation of a telephone and fax machine as soon as possible.

In the days to follow I unpacked and settled and started what would effectively be known as our post-Presidential office – the Nelson Mandela Foundation, from where he would continue his public service. Prof. Gerwal drafted an outline of what the office had to focus on and the Foundation's trust deed provided for him to further his ambitions to build schools and clinics, fight the AIDS epidemic, provide a space for dialogue and a physical building to host his writings and memorabilia. Chaos ensued and soon the entire world was looking for President Mandela, trying and pushing to get him to attend to their causes. I didn't know how we were going to pay for them but I had to hire help as I simply couldn't manage by myself. Prof. Gerwal visited regularly and asked one of our former colleagues, Loïs Dippenaar, to help put order in the chaos. One after the other I convinced Lydia Baylis, Maretha Slabbert and Jackie Maggot to join our office temporarily, although the arrangement ended up lasting for many years.

They would sometimes leave me in the afternoon behind my desk when they went home and find me there the next morning. Some nights I didn't sleep and simply read letters and typed responses throughout the night to be faxed the next morning. My argument was, the quicker we were able to respond, the less people were going to call to follow up on requests, so I was trying to bring down the volume of telephone calls so the pressure would be less. Many times I wanted to give up and leave but I never could. On many occasions I wondered what drove a person to make him/her pick up the telephone or a pen to contact Nelson Mandela. It was all just too much and I was at the brim of my frustration levels, more or less something that had become the norm.

I would only go upstairs and shower at around 7 a.m. in the morning before the other staff arrived back at work, and then continued the day without any sleep. After about three days in a row I would crash for an entire day and then start again.

Soon Madiba started coming into the office more regularly, and in the first few days of conducting appointments in his post-Presidential office he reminded visitors who referred to him as 'President' that he was now retired and no longer wanted to be called 'President'. He wanted to be called either Madiba or Mr Mandela.

Since I called him Khulu, there was adjustment for me only in the way I spoke of him and not to him. I now had to learn to speak of Madiba or Mr Mandela and not the President when I spoke of him. He would often ask people when they called him Mr President, 'Where were you when I retired?' so word spread and it eventually stopped. He also didn't want to be awarded titles like Honourable, etc. He was content with Mr Mandela or Madiba and told people on endless occasions: 'Just call me Madiba.' He said a title doesn't change the person that you are, and that was his way of telling us that he didn't have to be given titles – even though by the last count he had been awarded 1,177 tributes, of which 697 were awards of some kind and over 120 were honorary doctorates. When people wanted to address him using the honorary doctorate titles he was fast to explain to them that he didn't study for any of those doctorates and that they were merely honorary titles.

In late 1999 I received a letter from the Presidency promoting me to the post of Assistant Director in the Office of the President. Even though I was still seconded to Madiba, the higher rank could be allocated as a result of the availability of posts within the structures of the Presidency.

It was clear that the Foundation was going to need funding. To run the office we started off by borrowing money with the only surety being the words from Madiba and Prof. Gerwel that 'We will repay it as soon as possible, please don't charge us interest.' Madiba was still an icon to the world, but unlike in other countries former Presidents do not receive funding from the government to allow the person to continue his public life. Yet in our case, the world had the same expectations of him regardless of his official position.

It was clear that Madiba, too, expected things to continue as before. He woke up the morning of his retirement as if nothing had changed. He was as determined as before to bring about change in

South Africa, to reform society until it was free from discrimination of any kind. He called to issue a few instructions and when I dropped the call I panicked, not knowing how I would manage to arrange all the things he had expected of me. He did the same with Professor Gerwel, who jokingly told Madiba that he no longer worked for him. Prof. Gerwel was going to serve as Chair of the board of the Nelson Mandela Foundation and even though I was still employed by the state I had no idea how to make things happen without any infrastructure. Yet, Madiba knew how to drive me beyond my limits. I did not recognize or trust that I had the ability to continue with business as usual despite our entire infrastructure disintegrating overnight. He did. He patiently guided me and I am fortunate to have learned from such a great mentor and teacher.

Even so, in August 1999 Madiba said that he was tired and they needed a holiday. That was a challenge. Where do we go? How do we get there? It suddenly dawned on me that we had lost the luxury of the private plane and that it would cost us over R1 million (today about US$100,000) to travel to the US in a private plane. We didn't have that kind of money and Madiba would never agree to such expenditure on a holiday. He and Mrs Machel had been invited to the Bahamas by Tony O'Reilly, former owner of Heinz and at the time the owner of Independent News and Media, and his wife Chryss to stay at their house in Nassau. They would take care of us once we got there but I had no idea how we would get there. I was panicking.

Madiba couldn't go in a small plane as he needed proper sleep and he needed to be able to stand up straight without having to bend his injured knee, and to be able to use ablution facilities on a plane. He had a problem with his knee as a result of a Robben Island injury and as he aged it got worse. He had difficulty climbing stairs and couldn't manage more than just a few steps at a time.

I called Tokyo Sexwale, one of South Africa's richest businessmen and an old comrade of Madiba's and whom I knew had connections to people with private planes. He put me on to a few people but none of them could help us. I asked all the wealthy people in South Africa with private planes, the Oppenheimers, the

Ruperts and even called up Michael Jackson abroad to ask if we could borrow his plane. None of the planes were available as they were all chartered out or being used by their owners at the time. The only solution in the end was using a commercial scheduled flight. I don't know how we did it, but we managed. As time went by we perfected the art of commercial travelling with Madiba. As long as first class provided a proper flat bed for him to sleep in and the airport had the facilities of a passenger assistance unit that could elevate him to the level of the plane, avoiding the climbing of any steps, we could fly commercially. We just had to keep passengers and crew at bay and avoid him having to sign menus and other items throughout the flight. It was a nightmare at first.

So we set off to the Bahamas on holiday, our first holiday in five years. Madiba, Mrs Machel, Josina Machel (Mrs Machel's daughter), me, security and a doctor. We were all nervous but it all worked out well. We transferred in Atlanta and went on to Nassau. One had to find a way of both accommodating Madiba's needs but also taking facilities at airports and their supporting staff capabilities into account. It was negotiating and compromising all the time. At every airport, disembarking after long flights, people wanted to take photographs with him or ask for autographs. After a sixteen-hour flight an eighty-one-year-old just shouldn't be asked to have photo-graphs taken or sign autographs. He needed space to breathe and to regain strength at every opportunity, and although one didn't want to be nasty to people I would go to great lengths to explain that he was elderly and needed space and shouldn't be bothered with auto-graphs. In most instances people understood although the die-hards always persisted.

After the Bahamas trip we travelled the world trying to raise funds for the newly established Nelson Mandela Foundation. In Germany Madiba met with the Chancellor of the time Gerhard Schröder to ask for support for our Foundation. From Germany we went to Tunis to see President Ben Ali to also ask him for support. He had the most beautiful palace decorated in the finest mosaics.

From Tunis we went to Tripoli to visit the Brother Leader Gaddafi and ask for his support for the Foundation. The leaders from the West turned a blind eye to Madiba's association with Gaddafi. It was always entertaining to see the Brother Leader. One waited for days and days to receive word from him and then suddenly everyone had to jump and move to where he was hiding, sometimes in the desert, always fearing surprise attacks by the West in retaliation of the Lockerbie bombing. On this particular visit he invited us to dinner, and during our audience with him in the afternoon he asked what he could have prepared for us that night. By then I had been with Madiba when he had seen the Brother Leader on a few occasions and your face becomes familiar. He treated me with great respect and made me feel at home.

Earlier in the afternoon Madiba and I had a discussion about camel meat as we drove past camels and, when asked by the Brother Leader what we wanted for dinner, Madiba felt it was appropriate to ask for camel meat. 'Of course,' the Brother Leader responded. (He never wanted to be called President as he felt it was an invention by the Westerners which he refused to accept. To the end, we referred to him as the Brother Leader.) The camel meat tasted exactly like lamb. I was later told that they had to slaughter baby camels as the meat became tough the older the camel grew. I was not going to encourage the slaughter of baby animals so I never wanted to eat camel again. But it was a rare occasion that a head of state would ask Madiba what he wanted for dinner and I quite liked that Gaddafi was so considerate. Conversations were limited to pleasantries and a general view on whatever was happening in the world at the time. They always dwelled back to Lockerbie and the Brother Leader's unhappiness with the West for not delivering on its promises to lift all sanctions. And whenever Madiba travelled to the US, it would be a point of discussion there too.

Back home we were soon in the swing of things and attending to business as usual. We would attend a South African Chamber of

Business and National African Chamber of Commerce dinner the one day, and the next take the Afrikaans Trade Institute to rebuild a school in Qunu. Prof. Gerwel remained our anchor and adviser on everything we agreed to. He remained central to our decision-making process. We were also attending farewell functions, although it wasn't clear where we were going because business was continuing as usual. One such function was the welcoming ceremony hosted by the Qunu community and King Dalindyebo, the King of the Thembus of which Madiba was a clan member. They were hoping that Madiba would return to Qunu in retirement but we realized that even there he would never retire fully, as people would constantly approach him with their problems, considering him as the solver of all their tribulations no matter how mundane – from arguing about someone who stole his neighbour's chicken to serious traditional affairs and differences between the respective clans. Madiba was never overly traditional but he respected the tradition and culture of his clan.

We would welcome visits by groups of children from the organization Reach for a Dream when terminally ill children expressed their last wish as being to meet Madiba, have luncheons and dinners with old friends and comrades, fundraise for schools and clinics and even for the Bushbucks soccer team, the regional team that represented the area where Madiba came from. They weren't doing too well in the soccer league but he nevertheless felt obliged to help them because they were his 'home team'. He would see families of late warders, attend his grandchildren's graduation ceremonies, and in between try and find time to spend with Mrs Machel. He could fly to Botswana to receive an honorary doctorate and back at home that evening have dinner with Helen Suzman, his long-time supporter and friend from the Progressive Federal Party, now sadly departed. The pace was never a consideration to him. He wanted to continue doing as much as possible and squeeze a twenty-six-hour programme into a twenty-four-hour day.

A month later we were on our way abroad again. While we had the full support of a Foreign Affairs department before and the backing of diplomatic services, I now had to deal with negotiations from programmes to VIP rooms at airports to courtesy cars from foreign governments to accommodation needs etc., all by myself, in addition to asking for meetings with presidents, heads of state and people of importance. While at home in Johannesburg I started preparing for the next trip abroad. I also think Madiba just loved travelling, so he accepted invitations for no good enough reason and invented visits because he was determined to fundraise for the Foundation now. He looked for opportunity in everything.

If I ever thought of saying 'I'm sending someone else with you', the suggestion would be met with hostility. Not because of favouritism but only because he trusted that I would know what to do in any situation he would find himself in. I was not scared to tell a minister or a senior official when to stop as I could read his face and the unspoken gestures became easy to read. I constantly had to fend off media requests while abroad and my defence mechanisms were in overdrive. I was playing the role of that actress I'd wanted to become; doing things I could never do for anyone else but the position and the person in question required it.

Madiba called Prof. and told him about his intentions to visit the Middle East. They had discussed this for a while and strategized about the countries to be visited and what agenda to push for. As much as Madiba was our true north, Prof. was Madiba's true north politically and when it came to planning any strategy. Madiba admired Prof.'s intellect and insight apart from the fact that he considered and treated Prof. more like a son.

Our first stop was in Iran. I covered myself out of respect for the Muslim culture and kept my distance as far as possible. We then set off to dinner at the residence of President Khatami. As we entered his residence, a complete palace as one would expect, I fended off some photographers who used flashes while photographing Madiba. It is a known fact worldwide that Madiba's eyes were sensitive as a result of the bright reflection in the quarry where he'd had to dig out limestone on Robben Island for most of the eighteen years of imprisonment on the island. When his eyes were exposed to too much flash light they became red and teary to the extent where he had to wear sunglasses, even indoors and at night. We were all very protective over his eyes and therefore knew to fight off any photographers, with authority. So, of course, I assumed that position even though I was the only woman in sight, fending off the photographers.

President Khatami saw me fighting off the photographers but after Madiba entered his residence I kept to the back of the delegation so as to not offend anyone sensitive to the presence of women and left them to go upstairs alone for dinner. There were no other females present in President Khatami's residence. After about ten minutes at table and our food being served already, I got called by a panic-struck butler to follow him upstairs to where the President and Madiba were seated. I thought Madiba had purely called me as he usually would to introduce me, which he did, but then he said that President Khatami insisted that I sat at their table. I was extremely uncomfortable and didn't know how to behave; it was similar to how I felt being seated next to Queen Noor in 1995. The only difference was we were the only three people in the room this time and I was exposed to the scrutiny of two politicians: a serving and a former president.

President Khatami kept on asking me questions about my upbringing and the Afrikaans culture, almost as if Madiba wasn't even there. I kept on referring questions back to Madiba but Madiba was determined to let me answer and he peacefully enjoyed his meal, just nodding occasionally giving his approval to what I was saying, or then saying, 'Zeldina, what do you think?' To try and stop the enquiry launched at me, I thought of saying, 'Well, I actually just don't think anything,' but that was impossible to conceive. That must have been the least Madiba spoke during any dinner ever.

I remember from our state visit to France in 1995 I was intrigued that presidents could discuss the prices of import and export items, limited to oranges and bananas, and how many Boeings South Africa was willing to order from France, but here in Iran the entire conversation was limited to the Afrikaans culture. Madiba thoroughly enjoyed the grilling I was getting and only now and then would he come to my rescue with a supportive smile. For years after he would remind people of my importance, of course jokingly, teasing me by reciting this story, telling people that the President of Iran insisted on inviting me to his table, and I would respond by saying that Madiba merely wanted to enjoy his food and therefore put me on the spot that night. Such was the teasing and joking with Madiba; always a story and a moment to remember.

I had to ensure, when drafting programmes for visits like these, that we were seen to do the politically correct thing. We would have to include a wreath-laying ceremony at the memorial site of the late Ayatollah Khomeini. As a youngster I remember a prayer for the people 'behind the iron curtain' and when asked what the iron curtain was, reference was made to the people who lived under the oppression of the Ayatollah Khomeini or the communist regimes. Now I was arranging wreath-laying ceremonies at the Ayatollah's grave. Then we would visit former President, Ayatollah Rafsanjani, as well as His Eminence Ayatollah Ali Khamenei, the Supreme Leader of Iran. As I was the only female at all these events the Supreme Leader noticed me amid a full room of photographers taking pictures of the two eminent people sitting together. The Ayatollah asked out loud: 'Who is that young lady at the back?' Madiba, knowing that I was the only woman in the room, answered excitedly, knowing that he would embarrass me and of course without even looking at me, 'Oh that's Zeldina. My secretary.'

I wanted Madiba to make eye contact with me so I could signal him with my eyes 'don't call me, please'. But he also knew when to ignore me because he knew I would be signalling to please not embarrass me. He avoided eye contact. I felt out of place but took the Ayatollah's instructions to sit next to Madiba, closer, where he could see me. Somehow my presence amused these people and they were intrigued by me, possibly not knowing what to make of a white lady being with the famous black freedom fighter.

I didn't bother about who I considered to be politically right or wrong in any discussion or who seemed progressive in their ideals; I was purely concerned and obsessed with the next five minutes, followed by the next twenty-four hours of Madiba's life, making sure that everything was organized for him in a way that would make life easier for him. Although my general understanding of the world improved I didn't have the space to absorb or understand the intricacies of these countries we visited.

From Iran we went to Damascus in Syria where we met the elderly President Assad. This was only a few years before he passed away. We also met his son who was an impressive young man at the time. The young President Assad clearly also overstayed his welcome and right now he is being challenged by rebels in his own country to force him to step down from the Presidency. Madiba would often say, when referring to people who served in such positions for too long, that 'leaders got drunk with power', and often when a head of state is being challenged like this, I think of those words, whether they apply to his situation or not.

From Syria we flew to Israel, via Jordan. Due to the strains between Syria and Israel we were not allowed to leave Syria and fly straight into Israel. Whenever I shared my frustrations with Madiba about these political difficulties we faced, trying to do the right thing, he would always say to me: 'No Zeldina, you see they just make life interesting', trying to encourage me to bear up. But sadly, in that moment, they were not so interesting to me.

Upon arrival in Israel we were rushed to our cars like sheep through a crush pen by Israeli police. They nearly left me and Charles (the doctor) behind. I was irritated by the way they handled us and this was one of the many times I had to try and justify my position and why the doctor and I had to be close to Madiba in such a way that they didn't think it was only because we simply wanted to be close to him. That was the challenge of travelling without a delegation, just me and the doctor and security. You had to fight your way open on the spot. There was never any back-up plan and your only concern was for Madiba: you thought of yourself and the rest when you were already in the situation. I am not a confrontational person in my private life but in situations like these I became another person, playing the actress I'd wanted to be trying to defend us all.

We stayed at the King David Hotel, and on the first night I ordered meat for Madiba's dinner and salad with cheese for myself from room service. Shortly after I put in the order a butler rang my door-bell. 'Madam,' he told me, 'we wanted to come and explain to you that this is a Kosher hotel and that you cannot have cheese and meat in the same room. You are not allowed.' I really didn't have the cap-acity to argue about food too. I lost the battle and sat with Madiba during dinner and then went to my room to have my cheese salad. The next morning we visited the grave of Yitzhak Rabin, the person who was believed could have negotiated a settlement between Israel and Palestine had it not been for his assassination. From there we visited President Weizman and then Prime Minister Ehud Barak. I liked President Weizman. Prime Minister Barak appeared some-what intolerant of Madiba and I didn't enjoy their interaction.

We walked on the Via Dolorosa in the Old City of Jerusalem. It was touching for me as a Christian when I was told that Jesus carried the cross along this road. They made a huge fuss over Madiba walk-ing the Via Dolorosa and hardly allowed him enough space to comfortably walk on the cobbles. We were all nervous as he could trip on the cobbles with his problematic knee and then injure it badly. He was already unstable on his feet. I touched the ancient cobbles and then asked our guide once again, 'So you mean that Jesus walked on these exact cobbles?' 'No,' he responded. There are apparently around seventeen storeys of building on top of the original road, but this is more or less the road he followed. I was very disappointed.

We then went to the Holocaust museum. One leaves it feeling traumatized and deeply disturbed. As we exited the museum a microphone was pushed in front of Madiba's face and his impres-sions of the museum were asked for, despite me explaining to journalists outside that he was not prepared to answer questions. He never liked to be pushed into a corner and he was irritated by any surprise factors. His response was simple: 'This is a tragedy that happened to the Jewish nation, but one should never lose sight of the fact that this burden is carried by the German people too. The current generation of Germans suffer to rid the stigma they have had to carry as a result of these events for which they themselves cannot be held accountable at this time and age.' These comments were not appreciated by the Israelis. I sensed some hostility and I was uneasy. (When we arrived back home Madiba had received several letters of complaint from Jewish friends from as far as America about these comments.)

We had a meeting the next day with the President and Prime Minister. They discussed politics and Madiba stuck to his guns around a solution to the Middle Eastern conflict. These conditions had to be adhered to by both parties before any settlement could be reached: 1. Israel had to acknowledge Palestine as an independent country. 2. Palestine had to acknowledge Israel within its clearly defined borders. 3. Parties had to identify a mediator that would be trusted by both. Madiba repeated this over and over again but it fell on deaf ears. There was no chemistry between Madiba and Ehud Barak or the Minister of Foreign Affairs, David Levy. President Weizman was older, however, and a bit more lenient and less aggressive in his response to these suggestions.

From Israel we went to Palestine and met with Yassar Arafat, whom we had encounters with on a number of previous occasions. He was very respectful towards Madiba but by now I was getting irritated by people's general feeling of victimization in the region. Everyone was a victim and I decided that that was half of the problem in the region for me. People should start feeling pride and dignity regardless of the past. The Palestinians were as unreasonable in their approach in solving the Middle Eastern conflict as were the Israelis.

While Madiba explained to me that the current conflict was started back in 1967 during the Six Day War (when Israel captured and occupied the Golan Heights, West Bank and Gaza Strip) I could clearly see myself that it had escalated to levels to which we won't see solutions in our generation. To me it visually presented a worse picture than apartheid. Families living 500 metres apart have not been able to visit one another in over thirty years, separated by barbed wire. Wherever there was a blade of green grass it was declared Israeli ground and protected by heavily armed guards. Wherever there was nothing, it was declared Palestinian ground. I found it difficult to understand but, with credit to the Israelis, it was clearly beyond a reasonable fight. The Palestinians lack the leadership to come to a resolve. They tried to compare their situation with that of South Africa but people were generally being extremely unreasonable in their thinking.

Madiba was scheduled to address the Palestinian parliament on the day before our departure. Prof. Gerwel edited the speech back in South Africa and emailed the new version to me. I didn't have time to read it and somehow a virus of some sort crept into the computer program. The last sentence of the speech ended with a mathematical formula. Madiba also didn't read the final edits and as a result he read out the maths at the end of the speech. It was in letters and, although I cannot remember the exact words, it was something like: 'For every two equals four minus seven times eight. I thank you.' We were all puzzled but after his speech the entire Palestinian parliament rose to their feet in resounding applause. The speech was translated simultaneously and either the translator didn't translate the maths formula or translated it into something profound. We were all surprised by the occurrence of this virus but amused by the fact that no one picked up on it. Prof. and I had many laughs about this incident for years to follow. The right thing would have been for us to proofread the speech prior to Madiba delivering it, but that was one of the disadvantages of travelling with a non-existent delegation and working at the pace and pressure we were subjected to.

From the Middle East, we travelled to Washington to meet with President Clinton. He was still in office and it was the first time I entered the White House. President Clinton was his charming self to Madiba, respectful and relaxed. He listened to Madiba's assessment of the Middle East and generally agreed with his suggestions. He was determined to try and help find a solution to the conflict. In our minds President Clinton was the right person to spearhead a peace process there as he had the trust of both parties. Or so we thought.

On the night of our stay in Washington we stayed in the Watergate Hotel. I felt weird as it was the Watergate scandal that saw the end of the Nixon era and I also believed that Monica Lewinsky, the woman who gambled with the future of the Clinton administration, also stayed in the Watergate apartments.

We had dinner with Madiba's old friend Morgan Freeman and the next day we set off to Dallas in Texas with Prince Bandar. The Prince had bought the Dallas Cowboys football team and we attended a real American football game with him. What an experience, but it was a chaotic day to say the least and it felt like every American in the stadium wanted to shake hands with Madiba. The following day Prince Bandar took us to a proper Texan café where we had tacos and tortillas, something Madiba had never eaten before and I am sure if questioned about it afterwards he would not have remembered what it was. It was very strange to him. What we ate and such traditions never appealed to him like they appealed to me. He liked his simple Xhosa home-cooked food. He was more interested in Prince Bandar's company and conversing with him, discussing the world's problems and probably on a few occasions successfully concluding how to bring about world peace.

From there we travelled to Atlanta to do a CNN interview, and from Atlanta we travelled to Houston to address the university. Our schedule was tight but Madiba loved every minute of it. He would never agree on doing something if he didn't feel up to it, and if there was an open space in his diary he had to find a cause to fill it. Security was tight on this visit because of Prince Bandar's involvement and this was probably the closest I ever came to assaulting a bodyguard. As we arrived at the university the car in which the doctor and I were travelling got cut off by security guards. We tried to tell our driver to insist on passing through the same entrance as Madiba's car, but he adhered to the traffic police instructions. As a result, Charles and I had to get out of the car and start making our way to Madiba. It was about a 600-metre walk. While we didn't mind the distance we did mind Madiba disappearing somewhere where we were not able to find him again.

Charles had his heavy medical bags to carry and I had my flaming temper and we walked at a fast pace. As we approached the building we could see that Madiba had already entered with Prince Bandar.

A bald-headed, massive American bodyguard stopped us; we told him that we needed access as we were part of Mr Mandela's delegation. He point blank refused. He didn't give an explanation nor was prepared to listen to an argument; he just said 'no'. Charles kept me calm and said wisely that eventually Madiba would look for us. As if he knew, the next minute Madiba appeared in the door again. He had come outside to look for us – something very unusual for a person of his stature. Ironically, the black man came to look for his two white servants, to rescue us. We could see him standing on the steps and he could see us, but the bodyguard was facing us and refused to turn his back on us to see for himself that Nelson Mandela was standing on the steps of the building calling us.

I was tempted to plant a flat open hand on his bald head when Prince Bandar's bodyguard, Neigfh, came running towards us to 'rescue' us. Due to previous interactions with Prince Bandar we knew Neigfh and he was an extremely kind gentleman. I turned round to the bodyguard and said: 'Are you happy now? Did it take Nelson Mandela to come outside to come and fetch us? You can bloody well hear we don't have an American accent. You can see the doctor has medical equipment . . .' I guess looking back at events today, he was just doing his job and I was being unreasonable, but sometimes people are just not open to persuasion or then even attempting to find out whether there may be any truth to your story.

People would always comment on the unlikely event of Madiba appointing a white fiery Afrikaner as his assistant, and Prof. would say, 'She has a good healthy mind', and Madiba would add, 'with logic and simplicity'.

I was feeling responsible for Madiba's well-being and I got the sense that he knew it, always enquiring where we were and looking out for us. Our presence made him feel secure in a way as he knew we would deflect any surprises or challenges. It was a professional co-dependency. We equally felt insecure not knowing where the other one was.

Because of all our travels together Charles and I had become close friends and, being the same age, we could relate well during our experiences in this world unknown to anyone else. Like many of the other doctors Charles deeply cared for Madiba too but people would jokingly refer to him as my slave. Madiba only once or twice fell ill during all our travels abroad and Charles was therefore on stand-by most of the time, not having much to do himself. We worked well together as a team and I would often ask him to do small things, like help to fetch laundry, or search for a newspaper or check up on a room service order for Madiba, wrapping a gift, finding a printer, etc., and from there his title as my slave was born. We had much teasing about it.

I sometimes didn't have time to unpack myself, or as soon as I sat down to make a telephone call back home there would be a foreign protocol person or hotel staff knocking at my door – President Mandela this and President Mandela that. I was the only point of contact in our delegation, for everything, and Charles sometimes had to man my door to enable me to just finish one thing at a time. The pressure was relentless. It sometimes felt like I was going crazy not being able to deal with the pressure but then people like Charles eased the pressure by helping with the mundane issues. He was the only other semi-permanent fixture to our team. Doctors rotated to travel with us too, but because of our hectic travel schedule not all of them wanted to sacrifice their medical day-to-day practices to accompany us. Our security teams also rotated and it was not often that the same team accompanied us on consecutive trips abroad. And when you spend that much time with someone it starts feeling like family.

We were very tired when we returned to South Africa but had the luxury of Prince Bandar's plane in which we all had proper beds to sleep on. It was always a big spoil to be hosted by him as he spared no expense to ensure that we had the best food and service possible. He was a gracious host, very tolerant of Madiba's age, and he had great respect for Madiba as a person, something which I in turn appreciated and valued.

Returning home, Madiba called a few influential Jewish people, such as Elie Wiesel, in the United States, warning them about the risks they were facing in that prominent American Jewish leaders were clearly agitating for America to take sides with Israel. Hoping then to bring about peace in the region was not going to happen as long as the mediator clearly took sides.

We heard that President Mbeki was not happy with Madiba's visit to the Middle East. Our visit there interfered with the South African government's diplomatic agenda. It is one of those situations where you are doomed if you do and doomed if you don't. Madiba wanted to try to help along the Middle East peace process and was continually asked to lend a hand, but in the end it seemed that sensitivities with the South African government prevailed. Thinking back it was also not the right thing to do for him to jump on a plane and try and resolve the Middle East war. Prof. Gerwel had to intervene, like on so many occasions, to neutralize the situation. It was clear that the external pressures from people were going to cause a lot of conflict for us in South Africa but ultimately Madiba's loyalty to his friends is what caused us to be in such situations.

On 6 November 1999 Nelson Mandela nearly died. Along with his team.

We were in Postmasburg, a small town in the Northern Cape. It was mid-summer and it was extremely hot. Gauteng (where Johannesburg and Pretoria are found) has a summer rainfall and the area is known for its intense thunderstorms in the midsummer afternoons. Despite trying to finish our work on the ground early, we took off later than we would have liked. We were travelling to Waterkloof, the military airforce base in Pretoria, on a King Air, a twin-propeller light aircraft. It was an ongoing battle to try and persuade the government to allow Madiba to use jet aircraft and they were running out of aircraft due to the busy schedules of President Mbeki and his deputy. Madiba was no longer priority but on this particular day a bigger plane could not be used because of the length of the landing strip in Postmasburg.

About thirty minutes before landing back in Pretoria the pilot turned around and called me to the cockpit. He told me that both

Waterkloof and Johannesburg International airports had been closed as a result of thunderstorms and that we might have to go and land elsewhere. I relayed the message to Madiba. He sat calmly, strapped in his seat watching the every move of the pilots. Soon we started hitting turbulence and the atmosphere in the plane was becoming tense. From where I was seated I could both see Madiba's face and hear the pilots' communication. It was growing urgent as the pilot was informing the control tower that we were not able to circle for much longer since we were running out of fuel and that they were being forced to decide where to land. All neighbouring airports were closed. As we dived through the clouds the turbulence was getting worse and at intervals the pilot had to let go of the steering column of the plane completely to allow the plane to be guided by turbulence. It was terrifying.

Madiba had a frown fixed on his forehead and was pouting his lips in dissatisfaction and Wayne Hendricks, one of the bodyguards, made a few jokes to try and ease the tension. At first he was funny but then I started getting angry at him out of panic. Wayne always had a charming and funny way to ease tension with his sense of humour and under the circumstances, even though he failed dismally, it was nice that he tried.

Madiba didn't say a word. One of Madiba's grandsons, who was also on the plane, looked half-sick when we hit an air pocket which threw the plane a few metres down. The contents of my handbag flew across the plane and we were holding on for dear life. The grandson's cellphone flew from the top pocket of his shirt across the plane and Wayne caught it mid-air in the front like bodyguards do. I could hear the pilots panicking but they were determined to try and land the aircraft at Waterkloof. Emergency services were being called on standby at the airport and by now tears were streaming down my face uncontrollably. I was crying reprehensively. Wayne was comforting me, trying to tell me that we were going to be OK but I couldn't see us emerging from this alive. At last we landed. The pilots were perspiring as they brought the plane to a standstill on the ground. Madiba put his hand on my shoulder and said: 'Don't worry Zeldina, we are safe now.' We disembarked, got into our cars and proceeded to Houghton.

I immediately left to go home but as I drove around the block I got a call from Xoliswa, Madiba's long-serving chef at the house, saying that Madiba wanted me to return to have coffee with him. I returned and he called me into the lounge. His grandson was still sitting with him. Madiba made me sit down and he could see I was visibly still in shock. He said: 'Zeldina, today was a terrible experience. But we should forget about it as soon as possible and the best thing for us would be to get on to a plane again as quickly as possible.' He was comparing it to like falling off a bike. The best you can do is to get back on again as soon as possible. He continued: 'I never want to fly in a small aircraft like that again and I never want to travel with any of my grandchildren again.' What he implied was that it was too risky for him to fly in a propeller aircraft and if anything ever happened to him he didn't want to risk his grandchildren's lives as well. From that day we refused for him to travel in propeller aircraft again. It created a lot of trouble for us with the airforce as they did not have a large fleet of jet-engine aircraft and they often had to charter. It contributed to the strained atmosphere between us and the Presidency but it was not something I was willing to compromise on after this experience.

Years later we were also in a helicopter incident. Madiba travelled to a rural area in the Transkei on one of our schools and clinics building visits and on our way there the pilots had expressed their concern over something in the engine overheating. They were convinced though that they would be able to fix it once they landed and they were not overly concerned. They thought they had managed to fix it but we were nervous before our return. We told our security on the ground about our concern, and as soon as we took off again after the event they left by road for the direction of Mthatha, where we were heading. About fifteen minutes into the flight oil sprayed all over the outside of the windows. We could no longer see through the window and you could clearly see it was oil spill, which obviously created a fire hazard. The pilots told us that we had to land and they slowly manoeuvered the Oryx helicopter to the ground.

They landed in a piece of open velt and, since the entire region was rural, there were no houses or people in sight. While we landed I called the security men on their way to the airport to tell them that we had had to do an emergency landing. We didn't land too far from the road and if they approached us they would see us in the velt. They arrived about twenty minutes later, but before they arrived I was concerned about our presence in the region, with the community not knowing why a military helicopter with heavily armed bodyguards outside it had landed in the middle of nowhere. The pilots tried to find the problem but they were unable to fix it. We subsequently got into the cars and drove to Mthatha where our flight back to Johannesburg departed from. Madiba was inclined to think that there may have been deliberate sabotage involved but I managed to convince him otherwise.

Huge parties were being planned around the world for the turning of the millennium and South Africa was bracing itself for the same celebrations. By now tension appeared to be growing between Madiba and President Mbeki. We heard rumours that the President seemed to be of the opinion that Madiba was conducting himself like a head of state. Madiba was doing what he always did – responding to ad hoc requests and trying to please everyone possible. Even though we sometimes disagreed with such decisions, he was the captain of his fate, the master of his soul (as he recited the poem 'Invictus' from his prison years) and he wanted to continue what pleased his soul. It was very difficult to focus on what we had hoped his post-Presidential office and its focus would be. Then there was always the feeling of entitlement from people across the world. They felt entitled to him in a way because some of them supported the struggle against apartheid and they expected him to do certain things, and he would eagerly oblige also feeling the need to repay dues. Secretly I think he also just loved travelling, and having been incarcerated for such a long time I do think that it was normal for him to want to travel and almost make up for lost time. The result of these influences, whatever its purpose was, is what constantly guided his actions and landed him in trouble from time to time.

I was not sure how deep the so-called rift was between Madiba and the President and how much it was imagined in other people's minds. For example, in November 1999 Madiba received a call from President Mbeki asking him to lead negotiations in the war-stricken Burundi. Personally I thought that Madiba couldn't take on more work but he agreed. Because of Madiba's intervention in Zaire (now known as the Democratic Republic of the Congo) during his Presidency, I assumed that President Mbeki thought it would be easier for Madiba to try and broker peace against the backdrop of what happened in the DRC. President Mbeki's agenda was also to try to bring about peace in Africa, as it would have economic advantages for South Africa. I also felt that it was perhaps a way for the government to keep Madiba occupied elsewhere and that giving him such a task would fully occupy him and distract him from being tempted or persuaded to interfere as he had done in the Middle East, or in what was going on at home for that matter.

I felt somewhat for President Mbeki. He was expected to fill the shoes of an icon in history. Yet I also believed that the ANC was responsible for creating this icon, identifying him as the symbol of freedom for the oppressed and it was wrong for ANC people to now feel that Madiba was behaving out of line. Publicly Madiba remained firm, saying that South Africa had never had a better President or Prime Minister in its history than President Mbeki. Sometimes I thought that President Mbeki probably felt that Madiba was patronizing him but Madiba believed in what he was saying, and years later his vision in this regard became apparent. Our country has never been economically as stable as after the Mbeki Presidency, and as a result we were completely shielded from the worldwide economic meltdown of the late 2000s.

There was never any ill intent or deliberateness in anything

Madiba did and therefore no reason in my mind why people would feel that Madiba was upstaging the President. It was these prophets of doom's own insecurities that showed. Whether it was really the President himself or his staff that were responsible for this perception I will never know. Madiba would often ask to speak to the President and was told that the call would be returned and it never happened. I felt people were becoming intolerant of the elderly Madiba. We would ask for appointments and were told the President was too busy. What the ANC should have done was to set out an agenda for Madiba but I understand it was difficult precisely because Madiba had such a strong will and determination to do what pleased his heart.

Alan Pillay, who was the administrative officer in our office during Madiba's Presidency, was one of President Mbeki's private secretaries and unless Alan acted as go-between, communication was extremely difficult between the two. Somehow when Alan helped, things happened and worked out fine without politicking.

It was difficult to manage that publicly though. Madiba was making a concerted effort to make sure that he spoke well of the President. Whenever Madiba and the President were together I had the task to ensure that Madiba showed the necessary respect by following protocol and ensuring that we were not seen to undermine protocol and the President in any way. It was difficult because people and the public would still give Madiba the standing ovation, the loudest welcome, and make a big fuss about him.

The President and Madiba were scheduled to be together on Robben Island for the turn of the millennium. At first a verbal invitation was extended and when we heard that the President would be there, we declined, precisely because we feared that Madiba's presence would put the President in a difficult position. We then received a call from the Presidency confirming that the President wanted Madiba to be there. Madiba refused again. We had to convince him by telling him that all his old comrades would be there, and it would be necessary for him to go to see them as there would be a live broadcast worldwide. He eventually agreed.

It was a beautiful evening on Robben Island and I remember chasing people back into the tent to try and force them to show some respect for the President, and not follow us as we were preparing to leave, deserting the tent to follow us while President Mbeki was still inside. I was becoming increasingly unpopular no matter what I did. While I was trying to be loyal to Madiba, I assumed the duty that he had to appear respectful towards the President, but the public and people made it difficult. I would also have to do it in a way not to make Madiba feel inadequate in any way but that he still got afforded the respect he deserved. Every little action therefore turned into a complex situation of thinking about scenarios and analysing everything that got proposed, and it took a lot of energy and emotional capabilities to please everyone and do the right thing. But then you have to stand firm and do whatever the person who employs you expects of you and take criticism and politics on the chin. I had to learn not to be a coward.

People would often write to Madiba to ask him to intervene in matters that were clearly the jurisdiction of a President. And then when I corrected them and referred them to the President's office I was often blamed for overprotecting Madiba and/or controlling him. I was called his 'minder' and I joked to say yes I don't mind. Yet Madiba himself didn't want to be involved in many things. He wanted to continue raising funds for his charities, to build his schools and clinics, but also to have the freedom to speak out on issues for which he was well known – issues of morality and human rights. People insisted on Madiba's attention and personal intervention and it was a lost battle no matter what one did.

Madiba was well known to be an outstanding fundraiser. He raised millions of dollars for the ANC following the unbanning of the party in the 1990s. Now he was focusing on his charitable causes. The ruler of Dubai had agreed to support his Foundation but due to interference from a South African diplomat in Dubai this particular effort was fruitless. We were only able to speculate as to the reason for the interference and on whose behalf the diplomat acted.

Madiba often boasted about his fundraising abilities. He said as long as it was for a good cause it was easy. Relentless in his approach, and because he never asked for money for himself, it was easy for him to put pressure on someone by arguing the importance of the cause. At first I couldn't figure out how it was so easy for him but after seeing him in action I understood that if you believed in the cause you fundraised for, it comes naturally.

Something which has puzzled me over the years is a story Madiba often repeated and went to great effort to report to President Mbeki and other ANC officials. Madiba was never a great administrator and he genuinely trusted people until the contrary became apparent. It would amaze me how he recited his fundraising efforts and the simplicity with which he considered the process. During his fundraising days for the ANC the moneys would simply be handed from one official to the next and he never mistrusted anyone in the process.

It was an arrangement I thought sounded practical and made sense. Madiba would receive the money, hand it to Tom Nkobi, the Treasurer General of the ANC at the time, to have the moneys deposited. (In our fundraising he refused to receive money personally and would insist that it be deposited or given directly to the Foundation or the Children's Fund, whichever he was trying to help at that stage.) Madiba was removed from society for twenty-seven years and he knew very little about banking or investments. I would then ask Madiba, while he told the story, whether anyone ever kept a record of the money. I was not suspicious of anyone but found it surprising that Madiba himself did not know how much money he really raised.

There was no doubt in his mind that the money reached its final destination, but then he would add that Tom Nkobi later suddenly died of unknown causes. I don't know how this related to the fundraising but it puzzled me and I would lie awake many nights trying to imagine what had happened. Madiba told us how he was sent from pillar to post when he tried to find a reason for Tom's sudden illness and that when he managed to visit him in Durban he was not left alone with him. Madiba said there was an 'awkward fellow' present, the Indian male nurse who was looking after Tom. Tom lived in Johannesburg, yet when he got ill he was sent to Durban, whereas we are supposed to have some of the world's best medical practitioners in Johannesburg.

In recent years, when the South African businessman Schabir Shaik was charged with corruption and fraud I simply noted the coincidence that his company was called Nkobi Holdings. Madiba, however, was concerned about then Deputy President Jacob Zuma's friendship with Schabir Shaik. Call it a sixth sense, I don't know. Part of Shaik's fraud charges were that he wrote off more than US$150,000 of loans made to Jacob Zuma. In South Africa, the donor of money to a private individual is liable to pay tax if annually that amount exceeds about US$10,000. It was argued that these amounts were paid to Jacob Zuma to influence the outcome of tenders around a controversial South African arms contract to supply the government with world-class artillery.

Shaik was found guilty of corruption and in the court proceedings the judge said that a 'corrupt relationship between Jacob Zuma and Schabir Shaik' had been found.

Madiba went to great lengths to try and discuss this with several ANC officials and on more than three or four occasions we were running around after officials trying to find time for Madiba to raise this matter and ask that it be looked into. No one ever got back to him and I was slowly introduced to the hypocrisy of politics. They would sit in front of him, listen to him and sometimes even agree with him, but then as soon as we left the matter disappeared. On tens of hundreds of occasions I heard him saying to crowds and in speeches that people must guard against only doing what serves their best interests but remain loyal to the cause and to their conscience. More and more even today, you see the hypocrisy that he warned against. As if he could see it coming. Some people have lost the passion for the party, the purpose of the cause: representing the people. It has become a selfish, self-righteous war in South African politics where self-interest is the only agenda, and that has become the cancer of corruption.

We visited Arusha in Tanzania for the first time as part of Madiba's negotiations in the Burundi peace process. After Arusha we went to New York. It was my first trip to New York too. We stayed in the Waldorf Astoria Hotel and I remember being impressed by the size of the room, although we were guests of the late US Ambassador to the UN, Richard Holbrooke, and didn't stay in the ordinary part of the hotel. My experience of New York was limited to having a proper Waldorf Salad in the Waldorf hotel and visiting the UN. As we had no protocol or media liaison people around us – it was just me – I became even more adamant not to leave the hotel, in case anything happened or Madiba needed me during my absence.

Madiba was interested in engaging with Ambassador Holbrooke to help us raise funds but also to discuss the issues he touched on during his visit to Israel and Palestine the year before, as well as briefing him about Burundi. During our visit Ambassador Holbrooke hosted a reception in his apartment. It was the first time I met Whoopi Goldberg, whom I was told by Madiba did a lot to oppose apartheid during his incarceration. She made a powerful speech during the well-publicized 'Free Mandela Concert' at Wembley Stadium in England in 1988.

I fondly recall meeting Robert De Niro for the first time too. He brought Grace, his wife, and his lovely sons to meet Madiba. Madiba was completely at ease but one of the boys didn't want anything to do with him. Over the years I've come to the conclusion that Madiba has almost been turned into a fantasy character as a result of media exposure. Children do not know how to react towards him and then usually they don't react the way parents expect them to. It's similar to children's reactions when they are confronted with Santa Claus or someone dressed in a Disney character suit. Robert pulled his son to the side and said: 'You will regret this for the rest of your life . . . now behave.' The little boy of about seven years of age had little understanding of that statement and both Madiba and I were amused by Robert's efforts to get his son to react in a way that would be valuable to him in future. The child just refused to co-operate.

It was impressive to visit the United Nations, a body for which Madiba had great respect. We met with Kofi Annan, the then Secretary-General, and I couldn't help but feel the aura of respect between the two men.

Madiba was scheduled to have an interview with Larry King on CNN. In my negotiations with the producers I asked them countless times to provide us with a set of questions or topics to be discussed as Madiba wanted to be prepared for the interview. They refused and said that Larry never provides such material before an interview. I let it go. Not one of the best interviews Madiba had ever done and it was to Larry's detriment. Madiba closed down and his answers were short and to the point, very unlike him as the warmth of character got lost. He answered the questions he was asked but he didn't really engage. It was clear that the producers were more interested in adding Madiba to Larry's interview CV than getting really good content had he been prepared for the interview. It was a very different experience when Madiba appeared with Oprah. She was warm and friendly and supportive of his work and her team had no problem providing topics beforehand; as a result Madiba responded better.

People always asked very similar questions of Madiba, whether they met him for interviews or extended interactions at functions. They would usually ask him one of a few things and his responses would be standard, sometimes adapted to fit the circumstances during the interview but usually more or less the same: to 'What do you consider the characteristics of a good leader?' he would respond, 'A person who serves his people' and elaborate on that. To 'Do you have no bitterness or regret after spending so much time in prison?' he would respond: 'Regret is the most useless of emotions because you cannot change anything. I made the choices I did because they pleased my soul at the time.' They then frequently asked, 'How would you like to be remembered?' and he would say without hesitation: 'One would leave that to other people to decide how they want to remember you.' I found that funny. He could have said 'a humanitarian', 'a person that served his people', or whatever, but he simply wanted to leave it to others to decide and not be dictating history.

When he passed away in 2013 I noticed how many people had stories to tell about Madiba – some of them so unbelievable and sometimes a bit out of character that made them hard to truly believe for those who knew Madiba well. Yet, at that point I was reminded of his wish that people should be left the freedom to remember him as they wanted and I specifically made a point in an interview, when asked about it, to say that people should be left to do exactly that. Whether their memories were good or bad or even fictional, it really is about what happens in the heart when you hear his name, providing that such stories do not betray his legacy.

We also visited the estate of George Soros, as Madiba asked him for a donation for the Foundation. Sadly nothing happened and we returned to New York empty handed. I heard later that Mr Soros wasn't completely clear on the strategic direction of the Foundation, hence his hesitation to support it financially, which I thought was fair. The Foundation tried to cater for Madiba's changing agenda. First it was schools and clinics and his post-Presidential office, then the latter remained but its focus shifted to AIDS and education, and later dialogue was added too. It was confusing to the public.

We often found ourselves (me, the doctor and security) waiting for Madiba in these palaces, grand hotels and houses we only ever before saw in movies. On the first few occasions you admire other people's success in life and I think then you are envious, but later a house becomes a house and you don't even notice any longer. The grandeur loses its charm. The only concerns I had was that there should be no stairs to where Madiba was supposed to go, as he had difficulty climbing them, and that he should never be left alone where he could be caught in any situation where he felt compromised and we were not close enough for him to call on us when necessary. I usually settled him in at the meeting and then started monitoring the watch. He never wanted to stay longer than thirty or forty minutes anywhere and usually got to the point of his discussion pretty fast. After thirty minutes, if I was not inside the meeting (which I usually tried to avoid to be able to do other things while waiting outside), I would go in to remind him to watch the time. He would then jokingly tell his hosts, 'No, you see, this is my boss and I have to listen to her otherwise I would lose my job', and people would look at me with strange expressions, from 'oh that's funny' to 'oh yes the whites were the apartheid regime so I'm sure they still do that', totally confused with such remarks. I usually laughed at his comments to try and ease the tension one felt in the room as not everyone got his sense of humour immediately. So whether it was funny or not, I forced a laugh to try and show people that it was just a joke. If he was still there twenty minutes after my first announcement, I would then remind him again and he would without fail get up and announce that it was time for him to leave.

He expected to be 'rescued' sometimes as well. In some meetings he would call me to ask 'how much time do we have?' and that would be an indication to me that I should watch the time and not allow things to drag on for too long. Time was therefore always a matter of great contestation between other people and myself. Not to Madiba, but to outsiders who felt he should or could stay longer or that he was being disrespectful. To try and please so many people one needed a thirty-six-hour day and it was simply impossible. He was, however, never someone who would do anything against his will. He was a born leader and the person who wanted to remain in charge even when he made others feel that their input was of vital importance to his decision-making process. He had an excessive need for discipline but then also a very very strong will that bordered on hard-headedness sometimes.

*

On 28 April 2000 we visited Bujumbura in Burundi. It is one of the most beautiful cities in Africa, surrounded by trees and beautiful landscapes. Sadly the roads and infrastructure have been damaged by the civil war and clearly much had to be done to repair not only the infrastructure but also faith by potential foreign investors. It was tense in the area and although the Burundian people were very happy to receive Madiba, one had to be very careful not to be aligned to any one party involved in the negotiations. We travelled right into the war zone where Madiba addressed refugees and gave them the one thing people needed: hope.

On 3 May we paid a one-day visit to London in order to appear in the royal court in London, following Madiba's appointment as a Queen's Counsel by his friend Queen Elizabeth. We really tried to convince him not to travel to London for one day but he insisted. He wanted to honour his warm friendship with the Queen. I think he was one of very few people who called her by her first name and she seemed to be amused by it. I was entertained by these inter-actions. When he was questioned one day by Mrs Machel and told that it was not proper to call the Queen by her first name, he responded: 'But she calls me Nelson.' On one occasion when he saw her he said, 'Oh Elizabeth, you've lost weight!' Not something everybody gets to tell the Queen of England.

We travelled like businessmen who often go to Europe for one day. It was however difficult as Madiba was growing old and the logistics weren't as straightforward or simple as hopping onto a plane for a one-day visit overseas. We could only stay for one day as we were scheduled to attend a farewell dinner for Madiba's close friend Dr Mamphela Ramphele at the University of Cape Town the next evening. She had been appointed to the World Bank and was leaving Cape Town. She was the first medical doctor to attend to his health after he was released from prison and she referred him to some of the best cardiologists in South Africa at the time.

Life also continues to happen even when you are this busy. Madiba's good friend and colleague Dr Ismail Meer passed away and we flew to Durban to go and pay our respects to the Meer family. I noticed that more and more of his friends were passing away and he clearly noticed it too, which must be unsettling for any elderly person. He knew so many people and frequently we found ourselves attending funerals over consecutive weekends. Still it was also something that was expected of him and little consideration was given to what impact it must have on an elderly person to be attending funerals almost weekly.

In May 2000 we travelled to Monaco upon the request of South African billionaire businessman Johann Rupert. Johann provided a private plane to fly Madiba to Monaco where he attended the first ever Laureus Sports Awards. We also met with the now late Prince Rainier and young Prince Albert. It was the first time we met the singer Bono, who was introduced by Naomi Campbell. I had to take time to explain to Madiba who Bono was, that he boycotted South Africa with his music during apartheid and that he was a musical legend to my generation. I was sad to leave Monaco, being a Grand Prix fan, as it was only a day before the qualifying rounds in Monaco. We could hear the Formula 1 cars being tested in the streets and I left feeling disappointed that I came so close to attending a Grand Prix, but I simply couldn't stay.

Then in late 2000 Madiba was invited to visit Australia to attend the 'What Makes a Champion?' conference. He was also scheduled to receive honorary doctorates from the University of Sydney and the University of Technology. Whenever we had to prepare for an honorary doctorate we had to send his measurements in advance for the particular university to prepare his academic robes, including his head measurements. Whenever I would ask to take his measurements he was tolerant but he was eager to get it done sooner than later. He was not the most patient person when it came to fiddling over him. He would agree but urge me to be quick.

By now I had changed so much and I was comfortable around him. He had managed to destroy all my prejudices about black people. I had a deep sense of caring for him like one would care for your own elderly grandparents. Whenever I didn't see him for a day or two, I would kiss him when I saw him again as we greeted. Later it became every day even if I saw him consecutive days. How much I had changed! I started missing him whenever a day passed that we didn't work. He often held onto me when he walked or took my hand when climbing up or down stairs. I could touch his hair without thinking anything of it, trying to push down on disorderly hair whenever the wind or a hat rumpled it. I had come such a long way and felt angry about the prejudices we were brought up with.

Madiba was always well groomed and took great care in making sure that his skin was well moisturized, and I remember how I sometimes had to struggle during his Presidency to get a particular lotion that was not available on the South African market at the time – simple Palmer's Body Lotion that he used while he was imprisoned. I think the company may have stopped manufacturing it in South Africa for a while and we had to ask people in the United States to buy it in bulk and send it to us in South Africa. The same with the eye drops he preferred: Refresh Plus, the blue and white box. He was just so meticulous about certain things.

In Australia he was scheduled to have meetings with Prime Minister John Howard as well as the famous and rich Packer family, concerning a donors' internet portal to raise funds for the Nelson Mandela Children's Fund and Foundation. His meeting with the Prime Minister was merely a courtesy call. The attempt to persuade the Packer family to donate to his charities was one of the efforts that never realized a donation and I don't know why.

The flight to Australia was tiring but the captain of our commercial plane offered Madiba the crew rest room for him to be able to have a flat bed to sleep on. I thought it was very kind and we were extremely grateful.

Arriving in Sydney we settled in, and after adjusting to the time difference we took Madiba to Sydney's famous zoo. We were allowed to feed giraffes, hold baby kangaroos and koala and watched dingos being fed. I am convinced that we would not have had these privileges if we were not in the company of Nelson Mandela. We toured past the Opera House on a boat and went to have lunch at Prime Minister Howard's residence. I liked him. He was really a kind man and without any pretence. They debated the Aborigines' issues and Madiba was under pressure to speak out against the government for their treatment of the Aborigines. Madiba maintained what he had said for a long time – that he would listen to the grievances of people but that he would not interfere in the domestic affairs of another country. While he acknowledged and respected them he refused to be drawn into any controversy. It was shortly before the Sydney Olympics and we visited the South African team in the Olympic village, where Madiba addressed them and wished them well.

From Sydney we went on to Canberra where we were hosted by the Governor-General, the equivalent of a head of state. We stayed in his beautiful guest house where one could see the kangaroos through the window while having breakfast in the dining room. On these occasions and while we shared meals Madiba would recite all the knowledge he had about a particular topic. On kangaroos he gave me a long lesson about their pouches and he freely offered knowledge until I asked a question that he didn't know the answer to. That was usually the end of that particular conversation. He didn't like me asking difficult questions.

We also visited Melbourne and it became clear to me that unless one experiences another country by moving around with the ordinary people, it would always be difficult to figure out why so many South Africans move to Australia to start a new life there. Staying in government guest houses and being hosted by them never gives you a real sense of life in another country.

Back at home the pressure was on the increase. Madiba was more in demand than ever before. He was becoming the saviour of everything and everybody. Whenever people didn't get satisfactory responses from government they would turn to him. He was seen as the person who could intervene in anything and resolve any problems anyone had. People elevated him to a saint-like status and he would remind them: 'A saint is a sinner who keeps on trying.' I loved that saying.

Often people wrote to him from pure frustration when they didn't get solutions from government. We could never interfere with service delivery or matters that could be seen to tread on government territory. We had no desire and we had no time, and sometimes it was really a blessing in disguise to be able to say 'we simply can't'. One had to understand though, that when a person turned to Nelson Mandela it was almost in a last desperate attempt – no matter how frustrated we as administrators became with the endless paperwork involved. Even people writing to him from prison had to be given the dignity and consideration they deserved of a response, even if it was just an acknowledgement of their existence. Something I didn't ever want on my conscience was a person committing suicide or something happening to someone as a result of our ignorance: if we didn't respond to a letter or simply ignored it.

Being a public figure and making that choice to be in public like Madiba, one has an obligation to the public. It drove my colleagues insane that I would insist on acknowledging people's correspondence even if we couldn't help or weren't interested. Floods of letters were being received from people who needed schools, clinics, medicine, financial assistance, scholarships and every kind of help imaginable. Sometimes it was as simple as: 'Dear Mr Mandela, Can you please buy me a bike.' Madiba was, according to the writer of every letter, their only hope, whether it was poverty, education, social issues, disputes, he was still their President and President to the world.

How we agreed upon things came down ultimately to what he essentially felt like doing. He was, however, never able to turn offers down personally as he never wanted to disappoint people, and if someone had to do that, it was me. I often relied on Professor Gerwel to give us guidance and input but things were pretty much left to Madiba himself to decide. But often Madiba would be convinced to do something by someone who saw him at a meeting and talked him into taking another trip. Madiba was equally to blame. He could say no, but secretly I think he just loved travelling. It was bordering on the ridiculous, though. We were all exhausted. No other person of Madiba's age followed such a gruelling travelling schedule loaded with formal engagements as he did. Yet he would never complain about being tired and always look for another opportunity to travel or do more. His duties were never going to come to an end.

Apart from the Burundi peace process and the schools and clinics project (as well as trying to please the entire world), Madiba was also depended upon by leaders from the rural area he came from. So he received a call from the head of the Pondos, King Thandizulu Sigcau, one day. The call was short and to the point: 'I want you to arrange two bursaries for my daughters to study in the United States', and that was the end of the conversation. There were no other words in that conversation and Madiba, the subject, knew what to do. So he arranged the two scholarships through Coca-Cola. His relationship with the Pondo King was strange and I had great difficulty trying to understand and comprehend traditional affairs. Whenever we travelled to Qunu over Christmas, King Thandizulu would appear with a sheep as a present to Madiba for Christmas. This gesture meant a lot to Madiba.

The King's daughters successfully completed their studies in the United States and they really made us all proud. They've become role models in their own right and didn't waste the opportunities they got, but grasped them and worked hard. Sadly the King passed away in 2013 while Madiba was hospitalized and we were unable to reach out to them in time to pay our respects. I nevertheless maintained contact with them.

In 2000 I turned thirty. It was an emotional time for me and I felt as if my youth was over. Silly as one can be at that age. Madiba made fun of me, understandably, and teased me. He would repeatedly ask how old I was supposed to turn in October with a broad smile on his face, and I would respond every time saying thirty!! He would laugh and say, 'Oh no, you are still very young.' He would deliberately pretend to forget just for the sake of teasing me. I didn't feel young and every time he asked I would be upset. He knew that but he loved teasing me, though there was no cruel intent from his side. He would also always ask: 'How many boyfriends do you have now?' And I would come up with any number. Sometimes he would ask when arriving in the office whether I had called all my boyfriends and I would play along and say I couldn't get hold of one or two of them but the rest were all taken care of. My responses in playing along created great laughs on both sides. He had standard questions to all the female staff and teased people in different ways. His humour never failed.

I reflected on matters over the years and decided that even today, in my forties, I am emotionally immature as a result of the stress and pressure of the years. It was a young age for me to have experienced the things I did and absorb the pressures I did. I never had a normal relationship after I started working for Madiba: I was working all the time and when I didn't work I was resting. I never got in touch with mainstream youth apart from my colleagues but I was also never in the same place for long enough to even maintain stable platonic friendships. As a result, I still lack the emotional capability to deal with very ordinary things. But I was becoming good at understanding politics, how the world operated, taking care of Madiba, and perfecting the art of dealing with logistics and arrangements around the most famous person on earth, and that was my only concern at the time. Still I would never exchange the experience and opportunity of working for Nelson Mandela for any other privileges.

Again, we got called by former President P. W. Botha. He seemed insistent on holding Nelson Mandela personally responsible for his grudges and grievances with modern South Africa. Many people who have not accepted the new South Africa do that. Whenever something goes wrong, it is put on Madiba's shoulders. People inherently want a scapegoat or someone to say 'I told you so' to when something doesn't go their way. For whites to have surrendered power they were always going to be over-critical of a black government, and when things no longer pleased them it would be blamed on the fact that blacks were inefficient and unable to run the country as they insisted they could. Some people just love complaining, they make a life of it. There is a difference between really being concerned about service delivery and incompetence and just complaining for the sake of it. It is just part of human nature but the racial issue complicated matters.

One day I received such a call from Mr Botha's residence and was told that the former President wanted to speak to Madiba. I returned the call and connected them. I was never Mr Botha's biggest cheerleader and because he didn't address Madiba in a respectful manner to my liking I was always on the back foot when he called. Whenever someone referred to Madiba as 'Mandela' or 'Nelson' my neck hair raised. Yet Madiba was always overly friendly and courteous to Mr Botha. I was reminded of a well-known statement Madiba made saying that it is easier to change others than it is to change yourself. I had to work on my perceptions about Mr Botha. Madiba truly and honestly didn't hold grudges. He had, as a result, no reason to be anything but friendly with his former enemies.

They spoke briefly, after which Madiba asked me to get the Minister of Police. He told me that Mr Botha had complained about the number of bodyguards he was given while he (Madiba) and former President de Klerk received a full contingent of security personnel, yet they were all former presidents. To me, the older you became the less the threat level against you, and the less you moved in public the less security you needed; I also didn't see how this was Madiba's problem. I nevertheless did as I was told.

We called the Minister and Madiba asked him to look into the matter. Madiba had also promised Mr Botha that I would call him back in a few days and give him a progress report. Two days later Mr Botha called again: *Juffrou* [Miss], when am I supposed to get a report from Mandela?' Not 'how are you?' or anything, just that. I deliberately over-emphasized titles in my response, saying: '*Mister* Botha, *Mister* Mandela has spoken to the Minister and we are awaiting feedback. I am sure that *Mister* Mandela will respond to you as soon as we have a response from the Minister.' He insisted that I remind Madiba to talk to 'them', implying the government. It was a common occurrence among white South Africans to talk of 'them' and 'us'. 'Us' referred to white South Africans and 'them' or 'they' referred to black people more specifically. The more tolerant I became of certain things such as people's diversity and allowing them to believe what they want without the urge to force my opinion on matters, the more intolerant I was growing to the use of language that demonstrated lack of respect from my own people.

In the old South Africa people used the 'k-word' (*kaffir*) to refer to black people. It is a derogatory term and now considered hate-speech in our new constitution. Strangely, in my immediate surroundings or whenever I was in their presence family and friends who sometimes used the 'k-word' stopped doing so or avoided it whenever I was around. If they did use it I would reprimand them and possibly avoid seeing them again. It is something that became unbearable to me. And not only the use of that word but also people's generalizations and judgements when it came to black people. Those generalizations were baseless and unjustifiable and I often found myself in heated debates with whites about issues around respect. I would point out the same to black people on social media whenever they used derogatory terms towards whites too, but it could easily get out of hand as I, being white, would cause a furore for trying to reprimand black people, which distracted from the initial argument.

I told Mr Botha that Madiba had spoken to the Minister but he ended the call with 'tell him I'm waiting'. Dropping the phone I thought: I don't think so. There was really no need for me to report this to Madiba and agitate him. I knew that he was waiting to hear from the Minister and that the Minister would act on it. Two days later Mr Botha called with the same questions and orders. I told Madiba this time and asked whether he could speak to Mr Botha to calm him down; perhaps he then would stop calling me. Madiba said no. I couldn't believe what I heard and laughed at his response. I thought at first he was joking with me. It was not that he was not willing to help either Mr Botha or myself but he didn't want to talk to him again. End of story. And I knew when Madiba felt like that about something or someone, there was no use in trying to convince him otherwise. He didn't often respond like this, so when he did you knew it was the end of the movie. I don't know whether the matter was resolved but we didn't hear from Mr Botha again. I left the matter at that and really couldn't care about how many security guards he had. It was as if he intended to say to Madiba, 'I started the negotiations around you being freed and the ANC being unbanned and now I don't even have enough security guards.' Mr Botha wanted to hold Madiba responsible too. Well, approach determines attitude.

Increasingly, we were working on peace missions around the world. In March 2001 we travelled to Seoul to talk to the Prime Minister of South Korea about the idea of a Peace Park connecting North and South Korea. The Peace Parks Foundation negotiates and establishes conservation areas that stretch over national borders, creating an area to restore ecological communities. Madiba was the Patron of the Peace Parks Foundation, headed by Prince Bernhard of the Netherlands and Dr Anton Rupert. Prince Bernhard and Dr Rupert had been friends for centuries and together they established the World Wide Fund for Nature Conservation with great success, followed by the Peace Parks Foundation. On our visit to South Korea President Kim Dae-jung was receptive of the idea but clearly expressed his disbelief that North Korea would come to the party. Our requests to meet with the Chairman of the National Defence Commission of North Korea, the supreme position of power held by Kim Jong-il at the time, fell on deaf ears and we never received a response.

The public probably thought that Madiba would be welcomed anywhere in the world. Well, no. North Korea was one such place. No interest whatsoever. We tried to avoid situations where we felt there was a chance of failure but because of Prince Bernhard's and Dr Rupert's involvement in this particular case Madiba wanted to try at least. We sat around in South Korea for a few days, and when we realized that the North Koreans were ignoring us we simply returned home. Strangely, being so far away from home and not attending to official business gave us a bit of a break from the craziness back at home. On this particular visit I was again asked to be in Madiba's room when the masseuse came to his room for treatments. As usual I tried to give that task to one of the security men, until I noticed that the masseuse was blind. Even though I had told Madiba in Afrikaans that she was blind he was alert all the time during the massage as opposed to being relaxed. I feared that at some point he was going to tell her to stop and I just couldn't control myself from laughing out loud. It's not that I didn't have respect for her or her disability but more about Madiba, who appeared so tense in the situation. She was, contrary to what I expected, exceptionally professional. They say if you are born without one of your senses some of the others overdevelop and I got to see that. It was clear that she was an excellent masseuse and had 'healing hands'.

Madiba had this strange habit of keeping his watch on local South African time no matter where in the world we were travelling. We had to wake up at the strangest hours in order for him not to adjust his body clock to time difference too much so that he would not suffer from jet-lag when we returned home. And then, wherever we were in the world, in whatever time zone, we had to call Mrs Machel wherever she was in the morning and in the evening. I remember being in Seoul and not finding Mrs Machel immediately and Madiba insisting on staying awake until we did. It was one of those precious things he insisted on, being a husband. She had to be called in the morning before she had breakfast and in the evening before she went to sleep. 'How are you Mum, how was your day?' he would say. Upon which I would leave the room to give them a few minutes of privacy before resuming our programme or getting on with business. It would also give me the opportunity to then tell Mum what we were up to during the day.

We were then invited for Madiba to receive the German Media Prize in Baden-Baden and to be flown to Germany courtesy of Mercedes-Benz. By now I had appointed an assistant, Marianne Mudziwa, and Maretha was filling the gaps where necessary. They relieved me of much of the admin pressure. The staff in the office were still relying on me for guidance in terms of responses to people who wrote to Madiba. Since we didn't have a protocol or media section, all liaison where it concerned Madiba personally was pretty much left to me. So were the media enquiries. Madiba and Prof. Gerwel were my only guides. I would sometimes call Madiba twenty times a day to ask his advice on things whenever he didn't come to the office. He patiently answered me and told me how to do things, how to respond and where to find answers if he couldn't give them to me, and then always consult Prof. Gerwel.

He would explain his strategy to me, how he thought it best to approach a particular issue he wanted to raise or what his plans were to achieve an end goal in the greatest detail, and I was expected to ensure that we stuck to whatever strategy he decided upon. And when he spoke, you listened. I always made notes of things he said, of crucial keywords. I would often repeat something to him after he had said it but then he would correct me or go into more detail if it was necessary or he suspected that I misunderstood. Semantics subsequently became a passion to me. It is not easy for someone whose first language is not English to speak it fluently and I realized I had to be extremely careful of what and how I said things. Sometimes I got it right, sometimes I didn't, but Madiba was patient and he never pointed out mistakes but would find a subtle way to explain things to me differently. 'No, you see . . .' followed by the explanation. Most of the time though I managed to get it right. I couldn't afford to be a liability to him.

The trip to Baden-Baden was approaching in March 2001 and, having a full travelling schedule ahead, I had to focus my attention on organizing the upcoming trip, liaising to ensure that travel, accommodation, planes, trains and automobiles were all organized to not only befit Nelson Mandela but also to his best comfort. The pressure was increasing and for two nights prior to departure I worked right through the night, preparing for the visit and trying to avoid a situation where I left the office behind with a backlog of correspondence.

As flights from South Africa to Europe leave early evening we departed for Germany on a Thursday evening. I usually sat next to Madiba in the plane if the seat beside him could not be left open to afford him more space or Mrs Machel didn't accompany us, and on this night the Lufthansa flight was full so my seat was next to his. I would usually settle him in once we got on board the plane, making sure he didn't want anything to eat or drink, and then prepared his bed for the night in the best possible way in a first-class cabin after take off. Generally airlines were great in having specific food on board for him and making sure we had enough pillows and blankets for him to be comfortable. After helping him to settle in I strapped myself in my seat for take off and promptly fell fast asleep, only waking up the next morning as we landed. I had slept right through the night and I deserted Madiba. I hadn't even brushed my teeth or washed my face, something I never neglected no matter what.

I was angry at myself and questioned the security staff about his comfort through the night. The crew took care of him together with security and he was fine, but it was inexcusable to me as I failed in my task. I felt guilty for days after.

I noticed when I woke up I was covered with a blanket and had a pillow behind my head. When I asked the security who had covered me they said Madiba did. The poor man. Here I was supposed to take care of him but he was taking care of me instead. Madiba was worried that I was not getting enough sleep and he would complain to Prof. Gerwel often that I was working too hard – however it didn't make Madiba stop calling me or slow down either.

I remember on another occasion on a British Airways flight waking up during the night because of movement around me. Madiba went to the bathroom in the middle of the night, under the watchful eye of security. I lay awake waiting for him to return to his seat to see if he needed anything and when he passed me on his way back to his seat, he stopped and covered my feet with a blanket. These moments touched the most inner part of my heart. I couldn't remember as a child being tucked in by my parents, yet here the man we all had feared in the late 1980s (when we became aware of his existence) was covering my feet, worried about my well-being. Sometimes when I was tired I would silently weep, appreciating how much this man cared for me. It felt like no one else loved me as much as Madiba did. He treated me like I was part of his people, caring for me like you would for your own. And my history made it almost impossible to accept that I deserved any of this care and love.

There was never really any down time and we spent hours together each day. When we travelled without Mrs Machel or one of the daughters he didn't want to be alone during meal times and I would therefore often have to sit with him. I wanted to give him space but he would insist on me returning shortly after I left him anytime.

I enjoyed sitting with him at meals while we travelled, listening to his stories but also hearing his views on so many things. He remained adamant that the biggest challenge that faced 'our people' was education and the rationale behind his belief made perfect sense. I understood all the challenges the government faced, not having been in power before and having to deal with the financial challenges involved in reworking the financial system and replenishing the funds that were used to keep apartheid going. Few people realized that the apartheid regime borrowed money from the state pension funds to support apartheid and now that a new government was in power no one knew where the money would come from to rebuild those pension funds. It was not something that was revealed to the ANC before they came into power and now they had not only to deliver on their promises to the people but also find the funds to replenish pension funds.

I valued these explanations from Madiba. Simple and to the point and in terms I could understand. It changed my way of thinking and soon I would defend the ANC in debates with my friends. I started withdrawing from my more conservative Afrikaans friends as few of them understood the new political reasoning.

Madiba was everybody's hero. Black people hailed him for bringing them freedom, and whites simply because he wore a Springbok shirt to the Rugby World Cup final in 1995. He achieved his goal to unite the country, but it didn't bring relief to the poorest of the poor. While he was acceptable to most white people there were still 'pockets of racism' as he described it. And sadly South Africa is still dismally failing its youth. For example, in 2012 some schools in the impoverished Limpopo Province to the north of the country did not receive textbooks for their pupils from the government for an entire academic year, despite being ordered to by the courts as a result of action taken by a non-governmental organization. They just didn't deliver them to the schools and the books were found in a warehouse. It was precisely during these travels and conversations that I got so much of an understanding about politics, its mechanics and how the ANC operated.

From Baden-Baden we travelled to India, where Madiba received the Gandhi Peace Prize. We also visited Kerala, a province in India. We were taken from Delhi by helicopter to Kerala and although it gave us a picturesque view of India's landscape I was not completely convinced that we were safe aboard the huge helicopter they transported us in. (I would often invent stories in my mind about tragic headlines whenever I didn't feel safe. It was stupid but one cannot help but contemplate these things when you travel that much in so many foreign countries, sometimes facing challenging situations. You can't ever tell your host that you feel unsafe.) It was visibly old and bigger than some planes we had flown in before, yet in the back of my mind I knew that the Indian government wouldn't risk Madiba's life while in their country and that made me feel safer.

The Indian people were hospitable and they adored Madiba. If there is one thing Madiba and I shared a love for it was eating biryani, an Indian dish made from rice, spices, meat, chicken or fish.

Madiba had loved it before he went to prison, enjoying it with his Indian friends. It is one of the things he greatly missed while being imprisoned, not having the food that he enjoyed. And in India we were looking forward to having Indian meals and had biryani or samosas at every possible occasion. I never knew what biryani was until he suggested I try it. After that, I could comprehend his fondness for it.

On a visit to Ireland in April 2001, while being hosted by Tony and Chryss O'Reilly after being invited to address an event for the Independent Newspaper group, news broke about South Africa's cricket captain, Hansie Cronje, being embroiled in match fixing. Being the Chairman of the Independent Newspaper group at the time and a great sports man himself, Dr O'Reilly debated this matter with us. Both Madiba and I were adamant that these were merely allegations and that we were convinced that there was no truth in them, but Dr O'Reilly doubted Hansie's innocence. We called Hansie to wish him strength. In the days to follow Hansie Cronje, who was everybody's hero in South Africa, was disgraced when he admitted to the match fixing.

The following year, on 1 June 2002, I was with Madiba at Shambala, the house built by businessman Douw Steyn on a game farm in the north where Madiba intended to write his memoirs, when I received a call in the early morning from the media, asking for comments on the rumour that Hansie had been killed in a plane crash. I started panicking. I had received a voicemail message from Hansie the week before congratulating me on my birthday, and I still wanted to call him to tell him he was light years away from my real birthday date which is only at the end of October. But I hadn't. We were friends and I couldn't believe what I heard.

A few hours later, confirmation was received. I went to tell Madiba of the news and I was very sad when I broke it to him. Hansie was a kind, gentle human being and yes, he'd made mistakes but at some point we all do. The last time Madiba saw Hansie was a few months before, after Hansie had admitted to match fixing and was banned from the sport for life. He was a broken man. At the time

My brother Anton and me.

Proof that riding a motorbike is in my
blood: my grandmother Betty la Grange
(on the right) on her motorbike in
the 1940s.

My early childhood (early 1970s),
dreaming of becoming an actress.

Greeting Madiba at the military airport
upon his arrival back from holiday in
Saudi Arabia, 1994. To his left, behind
him, is Mary Mxadana, his Private
Secretary at the time.

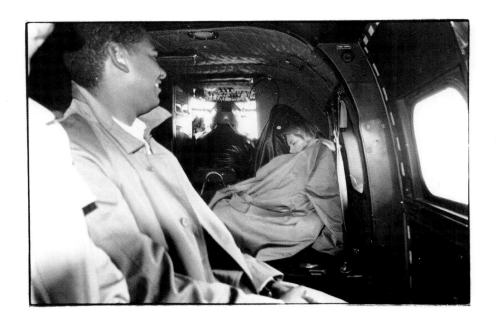

Desperate measures: I mastered the art
of sleeping anywhere, here covered
with Madiba's raincoat, on board an
Oryx military helicopter flying off to
a school-building project in rural South
Africa. To the left is Linga Moonsamy,
one of the bodyguards.

I learn to dress up. (1): in my designer *abaya* on the stairs of the government guest house in Riyadh, Saudi Arabia, late 1990's.

I learn to dress up. (2): Early 2000s in Iran with one of Madiba's bodyguards, Anton Calitz; (*bottom*) Madiba's last state visit abroad as President, standing in the Bolshoi theatre in Moscow with my colleague Priscilla Naidoo, 1999.

Assisting Madiba out of a meeting
with his good friend President Bill
Clinton, at the Waldorf Astoria
Hotel, New York, mid 2000s.

Meeting Pope John Paul II at the
Vatican during Madiba's state visit.

A silhouette of Madiba on board our
presidential plane, the Falcon 900, 1998/9.

(*top*) Adjusting Madiba's hearing aids at an event at the Nelson Mandela Foundation. (*bottom*) Seeing Madiba off outside the office after his day at work.

Christmas in Qunu, with Madiba
and Mum in the early 2000s.

During the launch of the 46664 campaign
in Cape Town, 2003, Bono and The Edge
visit Madiba at his house in Cape Town.

Keeping Madiba busy in the office while
we wait for the mould of his hand to set.
The cast of his hand was sold at his
ninetieth birthday celebration in London.

Photo taken in 2008 while I was busy
explaining to Madiba how a cast would
be made of his hand. The hand that
changed my entire being.

we went to Fancourt, a hotel resort with an adjacent estate, for a few days' rest and Madiba asked Hansie to visit him as Hansie had a house on the estate too. He sat him down and told him: 'Boy, you made a big mistake. Now you have to man-up and face the consequences. It doesn't mean we won't forgive you. You have admitted to your mistake, now move on.' Hansie was just getting back on his feet again when he died on that cold winter's morning. I was also taught that no matter what mistakes a person makes, you yourself cannot expect to be forgiven if you are not willing to forgive. It reminded me of a piece Madiba wrote in prison that was later published in the book *Conversations With Myself*. He wrote: '*Don't* run away from your problems; *face* them! Because *if you don't deal* with them, they will *always* be with you.'

It was a very sad winter's day as I also received a call from my father to inform me that his nephew Ettienne, whom I had been very fond of, had been in a motorbike accident in Cape Town. He was returning DVDs his children had rented and took a quick trip with his motorbike. He hit an oncoming car. A week later Ettienne died in hospital. It was a sad time and I didn't understand why two such young lives had to end so tragically. All my senses were over-reacting and I felt extremely alone that night in that big house. Madiba was never an overly emotional person and it was therefore difficult to lay my sadness out in front of him. He would go quiet and that was his way of dealing with things. I wanted to give vent to my emotions but it sometimes felt reprehensible. I felt very lonely.

Back at home, the normal day of business included time with family and business people. Madiba always had a cause to fundraise for. If it wasn't a young AIDS sufferer, it was a youngster who performed well at school but struggled to find a bursary, or even relief for areas hit by severe floods. Madiba also insisted on staying in touch with ordinary people and so he went to have lunch at the residence of the family that owns and runs a major dry-cleaning business in Johannesburg. They had been handling his dry cleaning for years, and despite the fact that he insisted on paying for it he felt compelled to have a meal with the family who had looked after his clothes with so much care.

To me it is still one of Madiba's greatest virtues: his attention to people that not anyone of his stature would usually pay attention to. He recognized and really respected the small people. No one was treated as a servant.

He also didn't want to be removed from his old colleagues and people of his age group. He would ask to have lunch with the musicians and stars from his generation, like Ken Gampu, Miriam Makeba, Hugh Masekela, Dorothy Masuka and Dolly Rathebe, and after the lunch he would decide to raise 'cars' for the women who struggled financially to make a living with their singing. These women all used their music to convey political messages during the struggle years and Madiba felt that he owed them a gesture that would show appreciation. He felt responsible for everyone around him: his family, his colleagues, his staff and in this case even the people that supported the anti-apartheid movement while he was imprisoned. He found inspiration through their art while being imprisoned and felt a great deal of gratitude towards them. We would then phone all the major car companies in South Africa and convince them to donate cars to these struggle heroes.

A little boy of about eight years of age wrote to Madiba one day, in quite a formal tone, asking for an appointment. His only reason for wanting to meet with Madiba was to discuss matters relating to South Africa. The letter was formal and amused us as he also said that his parents didn't think he stood a chance in being granted an appointment with Nelson Mandela. I showed the letter to Madiba and we agreed to grant him the appointment. He visited Madiba and he was as formal in his interaction with Madiba as he was in his letter. 'No, there was no particular reason for my asking for an appointment with you, Sir; I simply wanted to meet with you.' Madiba was entertained by the young man's honesty about the matter and it gave us great joy to experience such moments that really made him happy to be in contact with ordinary people without any agenda, just wanting to meet him because they were intrigued by him.

Madiba also had the needs of his grandchildren to cater for. Whenever we left for an overseas trip the boys (the three youngest of his eldest son), Ndaba, Mbuso and Andile, would give me a shopping list of the things they wanted their grandfather to bring them like all children do when their parents go abroad. He then sometimes sent me out on the streets of wherever we were to try to find things I had never heard of before myself. Not having my own children it was quite difficult to even distinguish between animated characters, let alone computer games. When Sony introduced PlayStation, we had to call the Japanese Ambassador to ask him to ship a PlayStation to South Africa as the children could simply not wait for it to be released here. One of the very few privileges of the children having Nelson Mandela as their grandfather was that they would always be the first to have the latest games and gadgets, before many of their peers.

During a visit in Cape Town he was again going from pillar to post trying to oblige with expectations, and after recording a TV interview he felt dizzy and nearly fainted. As he was generally always well these spells whenever he wasn't feeling well created great concern. Despite that he continued and only the next day, after visiting an area in the Klein Karoo where a school had to be built, did he agree to visit a doctor when we returned to Cape Town. He was stubborn and insisted on going to the school and not cancel it to see a doctor first. The cardiologist examined him and couldn't find anything alarming. It was pure exhaustion.

Madiba was scheduled to leave for London that night. We protested and begged him not to go, but he insisted. He said he was fine and he didn't want to alarm anyone by cancelling the visit. We left for London and then went on to visit Morocco (where we saw the King and asked for a donation for the Foundation) and then to visit Sharjah, an emirate within the United Arab Emirates and the cultural capital of the UAE. There we found the same diplomat who was involved in our previous visit to Dubai (when we had failed to secure a promised donation from the Ruler). Before we landed I made sure that the Embassy received our message that we wouldn't need any diplomatic support and that diplomats were not required to accompany us during the visit. Yet when we landed that same man was there.

Madiba was beyond angry at him but somehow he left it to me to deal with. By now I could read his facial expressions. He was blunt and unfriendly. The diplomat sat around in Madiba's lounge when we arrived at the hotel. I entered and told Madiba that it was time for him to retire for the day. I told the diplomat that he was free to leave and he announced that he would still stay for a while. He also asked for the programme for the following days. I got irritated and in front of Madiba told him that I had sent a message that while we appreciated he had a responsibility, we would call him if we needed any assistance. Madiba's eyes went big and years later he would still tease me over the matter and warn people that if they didn't listen to me, I would deal with them. I really wasn't that stern but he enjoyed it that I had the courage to set someone straight like that. However, I also think he was only too grateful that I did it rather than him having to do so.

In May Madiba visited a urologist, Dr Gus Gecelter, accompanied by Mrs Machel. He was taken to Parklane Clinic in Johannesburg the following day where some tests were administered, but he didn't say anything and I didn't want to interfere or question him over his private matters. I knew from previous experience that if there was anything to share, he would do so.

In June 2001 the head of Coca-Cola in South Africa invited Madiba to address the Coca-Cola group of Africa on a cruise the company undertook through the Mediterranean. By this time the company had built a school in rural South Africa and helped with other donations for projects whenever he called upon them. Madiba felt obliged to respond. I didn't complain about a trip on a luxury yacht for five days and it also meant we would be away from the pressures in Johannesburg, the endless requests via telephone and faxes being received and considered daily. At least we would have five nights to sleep in one place and on a ship where no one could find us.

When I read some of the guests' names to Madiba, including the world-famous boxer Sugar Ray Leonard, he became excited. He used to box in his youth and still enjoyed the sport and would often quote Muhammad Ali or Sonny Liston. His favourite quote from Ali was 'move like a butterfly, sting like a bee'. I would ask him what he meant and Madiba would explain in great detail how important it was to be light on your feet in the boxing ring, and that Ali's punch stung like a bee. 'Painful,' he would say, pulling a face while he said it to make me understand that it must have been really painful if Ali hit someone. He loved talking about all the boxers, some of them names I had never heard before.

The trip on the cruise was pure bliss. The hospitality outstanding. The captain of the ship told me to 'drink as much champagne as you can, in fact bath in it if you can because you'll never find another ship with so much champagne on board'. We couldn't really drink too much however, as we had to be 'on standby' for Madiba twenty-four hours a day. Madiba was expected to attend two events while on the ship and to make a speech at one of them, encouraging loyalty and dedication from the employees and congratulating them on the company's achievements in Africa while he inspired them to continue having the goodwill of the previously disadvantaged at the top of their agenda.

However, Charles, the travelling doctor, and I decided to join the festivities. When Madiba retired to bed at night we sneaked out to go and join the party on the deck. We couldn't go far because we were stuck on a ship and the security men knew where to find us at all times, so we had a bit of freedom to move around on the vessel. Unlike any of the trips we had been on before. One morning we were the last ones dancing and got back to our respective cabins just in time to prepare to join Madiba for breakfast. Charles had no obligation to be with Madiba during breakfast, but I did. I could hardly keep my eyes open and suffered the entire day. We were cruising and I took Madiba outside to enjoy the view of the beautiful coastline while he sat and read his newspapers, now and then staring across the ocean to the endless horizon. I sat next to him, snoozing on and off from time to time. After five days on the ship Madiba became uneasy and we all started to get 'cabin fever'. It was time to return to the fast-paced life.

We were scheduled to stop over in Barcelona on our way back to South Africa in support of an initiative for the Nelson Mandela Children's Fund called Frock and Roll. This was a concert and fashion show organized by Naomi Campbell and Bono. The rest of U2 were present too, and while performing their hit 'One' Madiba was scheduled to enter. I felt so proud that Nelson Mandela belonged to our country. The crowd first went completely crazy when Bono took the stage and we could hear and see their reaction from the wings until Madiba was prompted to walk on. The crowd erupted with joy to see him. It was not announced that he would be there and he caught the public by surprise. Bono introduced Madiba and it took some minutes for the crowd to quieten down to allow him to speak.

Upon embarking the plane for our departure back to South Africa, Madiba sat down and stared in front of him for a while. He then leaned towards me and said: 'Zeldina, this Bono chap, it seems to me he is quite popular.' I couldn't help but laugh out loud and told Madiba that Bono was one of the world's music heroes and that he had a following that few other musicians could reach for. Madiba seemed interested in this 'Bono chap' and he looked impressed that a young man was so popular among young people. It was the first time he witnessed his following.

8

Working with World Leaders

Although Madiba appeared healthy and strong, he was not. In July 2001 he was diagnosed with prostate cancer. One afternoon after having his lunch at home, he called me to his house and I could hear that there was seriousness in his voice. I had forgotten about the medical tests a few weeks earlier. I rushed over and found him in his usual comfy chair reading papers with his greeting smile as usual. He said: 'Zeldina, sit down.' Which I did. And then he said, 'Now you know we've been for tests the last couple of weeks. I don't want you to be alarmed but we have prostate cancer.' The way he delivered the news made me want to laugh and cry, all at once. By now he knew me so well and knew that I would never say anything disrespecting him, but he also knew my sense of humour. I replied: 'Khulu, oh no. I am so incredibly sorry to hear that but I am sure you are going to have the best treatment possible . . .' He smiled and was appreciative, and then I said, '. . . but I have to tell you *we* cannot have prostate cancer.' He laughed and then explained the treatment to follow. It was so considerate of him to share his condition with me before he went public with it, and it really showed me that he knew how much I cared for him.

He could never speak in singular terms or in the first person. He could never speak of 'me' or 'I'. It was part of the humble man that he was and everything included everyone around him. It was also part of the collectiveness of the ANC which was imprinted upon him while incarcerated. He was determined that the cancer was merely a little stumbling block that *we* would overcome in no time. He instructed me to call a press conference where he and

Dr Mike Plit, his physician, would explain the situation and treatment to follow. He always insisted on being extremely open about his health or any medical condition. The next day he started with radiotherapy which continued daily for six weeks. By the second or third week he was losing strength and I was extremely worried about him. I stopped going to the oncology centre with him and Mrs Machel, as it was hard for me to see. She was there every step of the way and they grounded themselves in Johannesburg to slow down the pace and give him time to recover from the treatment. He was OK but stressed from going to the clinic every day.

People prayed and sent good wishes daily. We were inundated with well wishers and that posed its own challenges. The heading of the daily newspaper in Johannesburg, *The Star*, read on 24 July 2001, MANDELA HAS CANCER. LOW GRADE PROSTATE MALIGNANCY SHOULDN'T SHORTEN LIFE SPAN, and it didn't. I am convinced today that the butterfly effect had a lot to do with his healing. All the prayers and good wishes, the positive thoughts from the public and the complete outpouring of love, in addition to God's grace, of course, is what healed him. Although we didn't travel he insisted that his schedule continue as usual during his six weeks of radiation therapy. He would have appointments in the morning and only go to the clinic early afternoon. After about four weeks we had to simply lighten his work burden as he was becoming tired and worn out, no matter how much he wanted to push forward. He had no particular focus at work and his appointments were really to ensure that he didn't feel isolated while receiving treatment.

Madiba and Mrs Machel needed a holiday after the treatment was completed. The question was, where do we take him? It felt like there was nowhere in South Africa, and in fact nowhere in the world (barring North Korea), where they could have peace and quiet. But we did find a solution. Madiba and Mrs Machel were invited by El-italia, Italy's communication network, to visit Rome and Venice for a holiday the previous year and we decided to accept the offer. They didn't have any expectations from Madiba and Mrs Machel but purely offered time to come and enjoy Italy. It worked out perfectly. Madiba got to see the Coliseum as they managed to close the entire site for a private tour for him. I was grateful for that because by then I realized that he was merely a prisoner in another life again. He couldn't do the ordinary things we take for granted because he attracted too much attention in public. It was logistically impossible for him to move around without crowds following and people wanting to get close to him, take a picture, touch him, talk to him. While he didn't mind attracting crowds it sometimes became too much.

He was not doing the ordinary things of life and the ordinary pleasures were limited for him. He spent so many years almost chained down by the determination of his own cause and working towards a better life for others, I wondered at what point he himself would stop and do something for himself. His was indeed a life of service. He did whatever he could always to the benefit of others. He was, however, happy when Mrs Machel was with him and that, at times, was enough for him. With her in our company we did many things that Madiba would never agree to if we were by ourselves. She managed to convince him to try the local cuisine and do touristy, normal things, such as take a tour through Venice on a boat. It was precious to see him trying his very best to be like a tourist. Our hosts were gracious and very respectful of Madiba's privacy.

Soon afterwards we visited Los Angeles, where Madiba had hoped to raise some funds for the Foundation. Hollywood, it turned out, either wasn't that generous at the time or not prepared for our visit. The only support we did get was from the people who were known to have supported the anti-apartheid struggle. Again I didn't leave the hotel in fear that Madiba might need me and I missed really seeing Los Angeles. But our hotel rooms were beautiful. Sadly, some of the people who made huge promises to Madiba never fulfilled them.

★

On 11 September 2001 I was attending a course in Cape Town. Proceedings took longer than anticipated and when I arrived back at my parents' house, where I was visiting, my dad told me that two planes had flown into the World Trade Center in New York. I watched the report on CNN and immediately called Madiba, as he was not accustomed to watching news during the day and unless he was in the car he no longer listened to the news on the radio over lunch. He was shocked and I took the opportunity to ask him for a message, as I knew the media was going to start calling for comments. (Whenever anything of any significance happened in the world, the media would call us instantaneously, wanting a comment, advice or an opinion from him about something.) And soon they did, and I relayed his words conveying condolences to the American people. We heard through staff that this angered President Mbeki who felt Madiba was too quick in releasing a statement. The Presidency felt the right thing would have been for us to wait until the President had issued a statement.

While I understood their concerns, I felt that Madiba never issued statements or spoke on behalf of the country but as a humanitarian. Why couldn't he express his sadness and sympathy? Again I will never know if it was really President Mbeki's concern or that of his staff.

The benefit of our small team was that we could respond to situations immediately. I was not paid extra to deal with the media all hours of the day or night but it became part of my job to be Madiba's spokesperson in addition to being his personal secretary and managing his office. The advantage was that I had two calls to make to react to anything. First to Madiba to ask what he wanted to say, and secondly to Prof. Gerwel to get his opinion on the matter. We were not tied up in bureaucracy because we were such a small team and it worked well.

Even though the media knew I was a rookie they tolerated me and respected me. But Madiba would jokingly tell them sometimes when they still wanted to pose a question after we had ended a press briefing: 'You'd better listen to her, she is my boss.' At one stage I called a Professor of Communication at one of the local universities. I asked for some guidance in dealing with the media and he spent some time with me giving me rules to follow and protocols to apply. The most important were: don't let the media own you or control the territory you are responsible for. Always make sure your territory is clearly defined in which you control them.

I took these lessons to heart. However, to many people I seemed like a bitch: I have been described as a lioness, a witch and a Rottweiler dog. Being the gatekeeper to the most famous man in the world meant I just had to be tough and brusque sometimes. Few realized the challenges I had in trying to deal with the world's media in addition to the other ordinary tasks I had. However, I befriended many people in the media and we built a common trust. I learned from mistakes others made around me and I tried to steer clear of those pitfalls. The effort and stress that goes into counting every word you say has its price. It's exhausting. But the most important advice anyone ever gave me was, *never lie to the media*. There are literally a million ways to deal with any situation and Madiba was the best teacher in tutoring me to see those ways, but lying was never an option.

We were scheduled to pay a visit to the United States to attend a special session at the United Nations late in September 2001. At first we thought that the meeting would be cancelled as a result of 9/11 but they pressed ahead. Cleaning operations were still under way as we visited Ground Zero. It was very touching and very moving. It was just a few weeks after the actual incident and there was a haze above the area. It was as if I could feel the souls of those thousands of people still drifting in the air. The workers all stopped when they saw Madiba and started applauding him. Only once we stood at Ground Zero did the enormity of the tragedy sink in. Madiba was visibly shocked and disturbed by what he saw. We conversed with Mayor Giuliani for a while and he explained the clean-up operations.

Following our visit to New York, we tried to get in touch with President Bush but he never returned our call. We realized he was facing huge challenges. I called the Situation Room at the White

House and asked to schedule a time for Mr Mandela to speak with the President. One also had to reveal the topic of such a conversation. I explained that we were in the US and Madiba simply wanted to offer his support for the challenges the President was facing. Whether the President simply didn't want to speak to him or whether the person in the Situation Room decided for him, we will never know.

We were still taking part in the negotiations in Arusha in Tanzania on Burundi. Judge Bomani, the administrative head of the negotiating process, then brought some of the rival parties to South Africa where Madiba met with them in Johannesburg to listen to their sides of the conflict. Many of the rebels had never travelled to South Africa before and they were obviously impressed and excited to be in Johannesburg. It was clear that they were nowhere near a peace deal though. The peace negotiations continued for two years. Over the following two years we would travel to Arusha, a town close to the foot of Kilimanjaro in Tanzania where the peace talks were situated. It was necessary for the parties to meet on neutral grounds. Madiba was extremely tough on all parties in the negotiations. Our visits were kept short as facilities in Arusha were limited. He would sit in meetings for hours and hours, negotiating but also forcefully reprimanding all parties. Sometimes Prof. Gerwel and I became nervous and embarrassed as Madiba would be very hard on some people. He was, however, never disrespectful and despite his tenacity and determination the various parties simply didn't give ground.

We visited Bujumbura in Burundi only on a few occasions, but while we were there one could hear the gunshots in the distance of ongoing fighting in the mountains. In the book *Conversations With Myself*, Madiba wrote: 'Leadership falls into 2 categories a) Those who are inconsistent, who[se] actions cannot be predicted, who agree today on a [matter] and repudiate it the following day. b) Those who are consistent, who have a sense of honour, a vision.' It was clear to me that if these leaders were consistent in their pursuit for a peaceful solution in their country, if they consistently showed their commitment to driving the process towards a settlement, he would have had more patience with them as it is a leadership style he could then respect.

Often President Mkapa of Tanzania and Presidents Museveni of Uganda and Moi of Kenya, the neighbouring states, would attend joint meetings with us in Arusha. They all referred to Madiba as 'Mzi' – which I gather means 'great one'. People were friendly and hospitable but it was a process that took way too much of Madiba's energy, and I personally felt he could have made a bigger difference by spending that energy in our own country, assisting the government to fast-track delivery of services to the masses, something which now became critical to the people who voted the ANC into power. But it seemed the Mbeki government didn't want him to help; they saw it as meddling.

After two years of negotiations in Tanzania, Madiba called on former President Clinton, President Chirac of France and others to support the signing of an interim peace agreement by all parties involved in Burundi with President Buyoya as an interim head of state. Personally I didn't think they would sign the deal but Madiba sat night after night, sometimes until three in the morning, talking to the parties involved and convincing them that they couldn't disrespect the President of the United States of America by not signing the deal. He said it would be a very bad reflection on them as leaders and a sign that they were not serious about peace.

Thinking back it was actually funny that he used the title of the President of the United States to convince them in this way. Their reasons for not signing were not reasonable and he had exhausted all other avenues by then, trying to convince them that peace was the only solution. There was a budget for the peace process and each participant received a daily allowance, food and accommodation while in Arusha negotiating. For many rebels who lived and fought their battles from the bush in Burundi it obviously paid to be involved in such peace talks as they could then collect money to support their battles. They therefore dragged out the talks as long as possible and sometimes stayed for two or three weeks while we only went for three days at most. The people in the negotiations, leaders of rival groups, were all highly educated, many of them educated in Europe, and there was no way that they couldn't comprehend the advantages of a peace deal. But like in all similar circumstances they were not necessarily willing to surrender their personal power base for the sake of their country's future. Madiba would remind them continuously that that alone was a sign of a lack of leadership qualities, and even though it sometimes felt as if he rarely stopped short of insulting them, no progress was made.

President Buyoya was an impressive charming intelligent gentleman, apart from the white socks that he wore. On 18 April 2001 some rebels invaded a radio station in Bujumbura and news spread across the globe that it was the start of a coup. Madiba was somewhere and couldn't be reached for several hours. I couldn't get hold of Prof. Gerwel and Judge Bomani's phone was switched off too. Media started calling our office and wanted confirmation about the coup. At first I was sarcastic about it and asked the first caller whether he/she thought I would know about a coup sitting in my office in Johannesburg. I then decided to call President Buyoya as he was the only one I had a number for and who would be able to confirm such a rumour or not. I spoke to him and he was as friendly as always and happy to hear from 'Mzi's' office. 'Oh Miss Zelda, I am happy to hear from you, how is Mzi?' he asked. He explained that it was simply some rebels who'd taken over a radio station and I told him what the international news bulletins were reporting. I urged him to issue a statement to dispel the rumours and from our side we were able to confirm that there was no coup. I clearly remember that I had had plans for that evening to socialize but spent the entire evening fielding media calls. As soon as Madiba became available I briefed him. He laughed at all the unnecessary commotion of which he was completely unaware.

Dr Percy Yutar requested to see Madiba one day. Percy Yutar was the state's lawyer in the trial that sent Madiba to life-long imprisonment. He was in financial difficulty and wanted Madiba to assist him to sell the Rivonia Trial documents. They had seen each other once since that time, while Madiba was President, when he invited Dr Yutar to lunch at the official Presidential residence in Pretoria. He explained that he had tried to convince the government to buy the documents from him, but we refused to help too. I couldn't quite comprehend how he ended up having these documents in his possession but thought he probably owned them because it was the case in which he appeared. Luckily the documents were later bought, by the Oppenheimers and Douw Steyn, and most of them are now in the National Archives.

When Madiba asked to see Yutar for the first time after his release, in the 1990s, I felt sorry for Yutar, knowing that he had to live with himself after all of that but now it somehow disgusted me that this man sent Madiba to life imprisonment, had a wonderful free life himself, and then he still wanted Madiba to help him to sell the exact documents that sent him to prison. Those documents belonged to the government; how did he manage to take them to his personal archive after he retired? It just didn't sit well with me and I decided even before Madiba declined to help with the sale of the documents that I would not be party to that deal on principle.

On 2 November 2001 Douw opened the house on his game reserve in the Limpopo Province called Shambala that he had built for Madiba as a retreat. Shambala is the Tibetan word for 'heaven on earth'. Douw Steyn's generosity didn't stop the time he housed Madiba for six months after he left Soweto in the early 1990s after he'd separated from Mrs Winnie Mandela. On one occasion Douw invited Madiba and Mrs Machel to his farm Shambala in the Waterberg. It was a relaxed luncheon that was planned with just Douw, his wife Carolyn and his staff on the farm. When Madiba and Mrs Machel returned they told me that Douw had offered to build a house on the farm for Madiba and Mrs Machel's use, where they could relax and go to as no one would be able to disturb them there because of the privacy of the farm. Madiba and Mum (as we started calling Mrs Machel, imitating Madiba) knew not to refuse the offer as Douw didn't take lightly to being refused. In no time he built the most beautiful house on the farm, before even completing his own.

In many ways Douw Steyn reminded me of Jay Gatsby. He would always host short-notice, over-the-top lavish parties at one of his residences. Madiba only attended a few of these but he always valued spending time with Douw and was most entertained by the lavish lifestyles of the rich and famous. Douw would tell Madiba about his extravagant deals and it would intrigue Madiba that one person could have so much wealth. After his release Madiba was introduced to Douw by members of the ANC. When Madiba left Soweto in the mid-90s, separating from his wife Mrs Winnie Madikizela Mandela, Douw housed Madiba for six months and it is there that Madiba completed his memoirs, *Long Walk to Freedom*, and regularly met with ANC officials to work on an interim constitution for South Africa. That residence belonging to Douw was later converted to the Saxon hotel.

Finally there was a space where we could hide. Even though Madiba loved people and being with people it was difficult in the city to find time for peace and quiet, time to think. He was confronted by requests in the city from many people he eagerly wanted to please, but if there was a place where people would have difficulty to find him, we could create the space where he could think and perhaps write. Shambala is a good distance from Johannesburg and we all agreed that few people would actually go through the trouble of travelling there to visit Madiba. He would visit this house on a few occasions and instructed us to clear his diary for a few weeks at a time to spend time there.

The launch of the house at Shambala coincided with a visit of the Miss World contestants to South Africa and Douw hosted them on the farm at the same time. Madiba had made a point before to always meet the Miss South Africa winner after she was crowned every year. Then one year he indicated that he wanted to meet a Miss World who was visiting South Africa but at that stage he had not yet met the reigning Miss South Africa. I warned him he couldn't meet Miss World and not Miss South Africa because we'd be in trouble for not paying attention to our own people first, and he agreed to meet the Miss South Africa first. Then he repeated the story of how well I advised him. I would have rather preferred to be known as someone who advised him about preventing a major world war, but he was very impressed about my good advice about Miss World vs Miss South Africa. Friends and associates of Madiba complained that he spent too much time with beauty queens and that it negatively impacted on his image. Just one of the struggles we had to face. He admired beauty and these seemingly frivolous interactions were purely because he enjoyed being in the company of these beautiful women, who of course all adored Nelson Mandela.

Early in November 2001 we visited Brussels where we spoke to Prime Minister Verhofstadt about the settlement being reached in Burundi and how the European Union could support the country – on 1 November we had travelled to Bujumbura for the swearing in ceremony of the new interim government. I felt that the peace deal was somewhat forced but if Madiba hadn't insisted on it they would still be negotiating. He was relieved that it was over. A South African peace-keeping force is present in Burundi to this day.

In December we proceeded to Tripoli to visit the Brother Leader, after which we set off to the US to attend a fundraiser for the Mosaic Foundation, a foundation run by the wife of Prince Bandar. We also visited Maryland as well as delivering a report to the United Nations on Burundi. We then proceeded to Toronto and Ottawa where Madiba was bestowed with Canada's highest honour by Prime Minister Jean Chrétien. We were tired after a very long year and Madiba's age was not on our side. Yet his urgency to make a difference didn't diminish. He wanted to continue to spread the good news of a new South Africa to the world. He wanted to encourage foreigners to maintain confidence in our country and to invest. And in between, he wanted to maintain relationships with his friends.

Before travelling to Tripoli we had again visited Saudi, Oman, Bahrain and Kuwait to fundraise for the Foundation. I liked Oman and Bahrain and the King of Bahrain was very hospitable, as was the Emir of Oman. In Kuwait something strange happened. We've all taken bath soaps or toiletries in our own bathrooms when travelling to luxury hotels. In this particular guest house Madiba's bathroom was stocked with a very expensive brand of soaps, aftershave, body-wash, etc. While we were at an appointment away from the guest house, someone, presumably a bodyguard as they were the only ones who remained behind, decided to help himself to some of these toiletries in Madiba's bathroom. Little did he know that Madiba had taken note of every item in his bathroom before we left. Upon our return he noticed that something was missing and he called all the security detail to stand parade. He also called me and told me to come in as 'witness'. The lawyer in Madiba was holding court. I wanted to hide my face in embarrassment on behalf of the bodyguards.

He questioned them and gave 'the villain' the opportunity to replace the item or else he would report him to the Minister of Police when we returned home, or else he would have all of them fired if the 'villain' didn't come forward. He wanted me to call the Minister there and then from Kuwait to report the case, but I thought it was better that we left it until our return to South Africa (and pretended that I couldn't get hold of the Minister immediately). Madiba was very serious. The next morning the item was replaced and he forgot about it, as he promised he would. He didn't mind you taking the toiletries from your own bathroom, but not from his. And when we left, he didn't want to take any of the items in his bathroom with him; he left it all untouched and unopened. He never wanted to take advantage of our hosts and he expected everyone to behave that way.

On another occasion elsewhere someone nabbed cutlery from our host and when he was caught by his senior I knew I had to deal with the matter with the utmost discretion, as Madiba would not tolerate such things. I decided that we had to deal with it internally rather than call on the 'lawyer' to become the 'prosecutor'. Because teams rotated, people never knew what happened to others while we were on trips abroad and therefore this particular team had no experience with the 'prosecutor'. I insisted in this case that the guy be disciplined within his force structures upon our return home even though we returned the cutlery to its owner before we left. The one thing Madiba was totally intolerant about was dishonesty. Whether it involved a bar of soap or a political agenda.

To me, Madiba was a kind, generous soul but principled and disciplined in every sense of the word. I don't know whether it is as a result of my Calvinist upbringing or my sensitive personality and having grown up in a house where the only violence experienced was that of my father's loud voice, but I get scared whenever someone raises his/her voice. I avoid confrontation of a personal nature and rather become quiet and withdraw myself completely. It is not that I fear confrontation as such, but I get nervous whenever other people raise their voices. It was the same when Madiba raised his voice. He had a loud voice by nature but increasing the pitch just a little made me nervous. It wasn't as if he had raging outbursts and I only heard him raising his voice on a few occasions during the years I worked with him. It was usually only in situations that really angered him, like when someone betrayed him or was dishonest or over a personal matter. I would cringe for the other person's sake and then as soon as the person left, I would try and defuse the tension. Those close to Madiba knew when he got angry. But he would never take out his anger on others then. He would become quiet too and disturbed.

During the latter part of his Presidency, when I often found myself 'manning' the office in Pretoria by myself, I would often call his bodyguard Rory Steyn, whenever he was on duty, to give me an assessment of the President's overall mood before he arrived at the office. The bodyguards would drive the President from his home in Houghton to the office in Pretoria and Rory would be one of the people who would know whether the President was serious, in a humorous mood, or if his mind was elsewhere occupied. Rory's assessments helped me to ease into the day with the President without making inappropriate comments or an overly friendly greeting when he didn't feel up to it.

★

By these accounts of all our travels it sounds as if the Nelson Mandela Foundation raised millions but in fact we didn't. It was clearly easier for Madiba to fundraise for the ANC, a liberation movement, than for a foundation. The Foundation was not well established, or rather, its direction was constantly changing, and I think people hesitated to donate, not knowing whether it was merely a family foundation or a NGO implementing projects.

In early 2002 I ran into someone from the Protocol section at the President's office. I was told by this particular person that paintings and photos in which Madiba appeared had been removed from the display area at the Spier wine estate in the Western Cape, in preparation of a visit there by President Mbeki. I had no reason not to believe this person and it was confirmed when it appeared in the local *Mail* and *Guardian* newspaper a week later. It put validity to my point that it was not necessarily President Mbeki who fostered the particular feelings towards Madiba but that it was aggravated by actions like these from staff. Surely it must have been an embarrassment to President Mbeki to read something like this in the newspapers. It is so petty and there is no way that I could believe that the President would instruct his staff to remove any items that bear relation to Nelson Mandela.

In March 2002 Madiba gave me a task. He wanted me to organize a gala dinner for struggle veterans, similar to what he did during his Presidency when he hosted wives of struggle veterans by inviting them for tea at Mahlamba Ndlopfu. Even though they no longer shared the focus of a liberation struggle he felt it was necessary for them to be honoured and that he was not seen to have forgotten them even though his life had moved on beyond the struggle. Only this time, it had to be around 1,500 guests. We quickly fundraised and set up a task team for the event.

The memories of this event and the difficulties we faced in organizing it will remain with me for the rest of my life. It was worth every effort though when one witnessed how old people's faces lit up when they saw friends and colleagues they hadn't seen in many years, often not knowing if people they were close to in the struggle were still alive. Most of them still lived in poor circumstances without basic services despite their history in the liberation struggle. I somehow also felt angry for them and did what I could to ensure that at least once they were paid tribute to in a festive way.

It was impossible to make everyone happy. Simply, Madiba was never keen on staying anywhere too long. He wanted to keep moving and I think an urgency drove him to do as much as possible before he got too old to move around. He was attending at least five to seven public events per week at the time and every event was the same story. There was no reason for him to sit at an event for two hours to listen to endless speeches. I recall him once bringing a priest's prayer to a rude halt when he asked the Master of Ceremonies to go and stop the priest from continuing to pray. When I asked him about it afterwards he said that he didn't have a problem with praying but that it was not necessary for the priest to try and convert us all with one such long prayer. He was right. The prayer was not limited to blessing or opening the ceremony but was longer than a sermon!

There was a fine line between appearing to be disrespectful and allowing the programme to reach its functionality. In February 2003 Mathatha Tsedu wrote an editorial in the *Sunday Times* criticizing us for not allowing Madiba to remain longer at an opening of a school. Mathatha wrote: 'It was very embarrassing, and many people here say because Mandela's life is run by some white woman, when he attends black events he is always in a hurry. "We understand that when he attends white events he stays longer," an organiser told me.' He continued:

> I know Zelda la Grange, Mandela's personal assistant, and believe she would not snub occasions simply because they were black. The question must be asked whether Mandela's office is managing his diary correctly to ensure that he not only attends fleetingly to issues and events but stays long enough not to be seen to be just passing through.

Easier said than done. Madiba was the one who would look at a draft programme before we attended events and tell me where to insist they cut the programme, and then it was up to me to make sure I got him out of an event, usually about thirty minutes after arrival. Yes it was 'fleetingly passing through', but he wanted to fleetingly pass through irrespective of race, the nature of the event, or where it was.

The reality was that the fact that I was white was never going to be overlooked by many people. Race was still an issue and many people have not come to terms with the fact that that we are all South Africans, irrespective of colour. The damage done by apartheid was underestimated and it manifested in ways that whenever no other excuse could be found for a problem, race was the easiest issue to blame. I had learned from Madiba that two things would destroy the validity of your argument immediately if you used them: race and insults. When your argument is based on principle there is no reason for you to grapple with issues of race or try and insult your opponent. Stick to the principle, and if you can't it means you don't have an argument.

(In 2008 I was awarded one of the ten Women of the Year awards by *City Press* and *Rapport*, two Sunday newspapers in South Africa. Mathatha was the Editor-in-Chief of *City Press* then and I appreciated the gesture regardless of our earlier differences. I'm sure he did not argue for this award personally but it must have passed by his desk and he could have objected to it if he'd wanted.)

There were two things Madiba was completely intolerant of as far as events were concerned: a briefing and a waiting room. He argued if we could be on time, everyone could, and he refused on many occasions to go to waiting or holding rooms. He would enter the events and by his presence force proceedings to start whether people were ready or not.

In April 2002 South Africa had its first space traveller, Mark Shuttleworth. Mark was well known in the country for his invention of an internet banking security software program which he sold for billions abroad. He was South Africa's youngest billionaire and, of course, he got tasked to build a school too. Mark visited us on a few occasions and it was agreed that he would call Madiba on my cellphone once he was in space. It was very exciting. We all watched him flying off into space but on the next day we went on with life, and while his trip dominated the news we had to continue with business as usual.

The agreement was that Mark would call on a particular day and I of course forgot to make a note of it. My cellphone rang and the number was disguised as 'private number'. Usually I don't answer those but I did as Madiba was next door in the office and he heard the phone ringing. On the other end of the line the person said: 'Hello, is that Zelda?' It sounded like a call from America and I was irritated as I hated people disturbing me during the day on my cellphone to tell me about their long proposals or to have lengthy discussions while I was attending to Madiba. I said: 'Yes, can I help you?' The person said: 'I'm calling from the ISS.' I thought: What is the ISS? Again, now slightly irritated, I asked the man how I could help him. He repeated, 'It's Mark from the ISS.' I thought it could be some organization and tried to think quickly so as to not sound stupid. His last attempt was: 'Zelda, it's Mark, I'm calling from space.' Oh my word. The penny dropped and I said: 'Oh *Mark*, how *are* you . . . ? Just hold on for Madiba.'

I rushed into Madiba's office and he too didn't know at first what I was trying to tell him when I said 'It's Mark, Mark Shuttleworth, he's calling from space.' It was funny at the time though and later when Mark returned he came to visit to tell us about his experiences and he enjoyed our story. We were very proud of him.

It was about this time that Madiba announced on one of his visits to Qunu that he wanted trees to be planted on his farm, big full-grown trees to protect the view of his house from the road, the N2 highway that ran past his farm. He tasked me with this and I didn't have a clue where to start searching for someone who could do this. I called my dad and asked him whether he knew who one contacts for something like this and he said that he would make a few calls and get back to me. Comprehending my sense of urgency about everything in life he soon called back and said he would try and help me to find someone. Then a day later he called to say that he managed to get a quote from someone to do the job and he would forward it to us. It was way too expensive and I reported back to him. He said he would try to find a solution. Being a daddy's girl I always expected my dad to find solutions for all my problems. And so he did. He called back to offer to go and do it himself.

I was hesitant and sceptical about this. I asked him to put his proposal in writing and I gave it to Madiba. Madiba was receptive of the idea and asked to speak to my dad. By this time they had already met and Madiba liked my father's unpretentious attitude, and because of Madiba's influence in my life my dad's attitude had changed towards him. I then made it very clear to Madiba that I did not wish to be involved in these dealings at all and that my dad had to report to his lawyer, Ismail Ayob, who was responsible for all payments. Madiba understood my concern that I didn't want to be blamed by anyone for nepotism.

Exactly as I expected my dad put his heart and soul into the project and soon the trees were planted. To the end Madiba always asked after my parents and specifically about my father's well-being. My father didn't charge Madiba for the work he had done, but only for procurement of the trees, groundwork and the labour he had to bring in from elsewhere. Madiba was extremely appreciative. We teased my dad and said: 'You see, times have changed . . . here you are, the old conservative, planting trees in a black man's garden!' and we would all laugh about it. My dad was extremely proud of his job and always asked me to report about the trees whenever I visited Qunu. My parents were so appreciative of the opportunities Madiba had granted me that it changed them and softened their hearts too. Those interactions, Madiba's genuine appreciation and the respect with which he dealt with my father, changed my father for ever.

We returned to New York in February of 2002 to attend the launch of the Tribeca Film Festival established by Jane Rosenthal and Robert

De Niro. Following the attack on the Twin Towers in Lower Manhattan, Wall Street was desperate to rebuild its reputation as a safe environment in the city. We were also invited to a cocktail function in City Hall hosted by the new Mayor, Michael Bloomberg. We loathed going to cocktail parties or stand-up informal events with Madiba. People would just overwhelm him completely and, in addition, it was useless talking to him in such circumstances. His hearing aids would cut out all sound completely once too many people talked around him or the surroundings were too noisy.

We entered the room where about 200 people were gathered. There was no one to meet us and we started making our way through the crowd until we came across some children in the room. Madiba immediately started conversing with them as all chidren attracted him like a magnet. He had to bend down to hear them properly and I was trying my best to repeat what they were saying so that he could respond to them appropriately. While bending down a man approached him from the back and pulled on his shirt to try and draw his attention. I thought: What on earth . . . ? He continued and I turned to him and said, 'Excuse me Sir, but what are you doing pulling on Mr Mandela's shirt? He is busy with the children.' He looked around as if to try and get help from someone and then said to me, 'I want Mr Mandela to greet these people, they are my friends.' My blood rose and I said: 'Well, can you give him a chance to finish with the children please?' He then said, kind of tongue in cheek, 'Do you know me?' and I abruptly responded: 'No I don't, but please just stop doing that.' A third person appeared and whispered in my ear, 'It's Mayor Bloomberg, he is the host of the function.' You could bowl me over with surprise. I apologized but nevertheless told him to please not pull on Mr Mandela's shirt as he was already unstable on his feet, and that he would turn around once he had finished with the kids. The Mayor didn't like me but I had no choice.

As we moved through the room a little later I saw another familiar face, that of British actor Hugh Grant. Everyone in the room wanted their picture taken with Madiba and soon chaos ensured.

Hugh Grant didn't ask to meet Mr Mandela but he smiled and from the look on his face I could gather that he was obviously excited to see him. Hugh moved in right next to Madiba and while still holding his own camera turned it around to take a picture while he was standing next to Madiba. A selfie as we have now named it. I then said, 'Excuse me Mr Grant, I am Mr Mandela's assistant. Can I please help you take a photo?' I had become the ex officio official photographer as I always had to take the pictures people wanted and became an expert on how people's cameras work. I didn't mind if the time and place was right for it. He was grateful. I didn't explain to Madiba who exactly he was.

On 16 February 2003 Mathatha Tsedu wrote another editorial, this time attacking the Treatment Action Campaign for using Madiba's face on a t-shirt. The TAC was in the forefront of pushing government to give the poor access to anti-retroviral AIDS drugs, something that Madiba was supporting and prepared to fight for publicly. At that point South Africa was fast becoming the country with the highest incidence of AIDS in the world. The government did not give people free access to AIDS drugs. Madiba tried to meet with the now late Minister of Health, Dr Manto Tshabalala-Msimang, on several occasions to discuss this issue and he was upset and disgusted that she had paid so little attention to the matter. South Africa was becoming the laughing stock of the world because of its AIDS policy and behind the scenes Madiba was trying to fight the battle on behalf of faceless and nameless people. He didn't mind the TAC using his face and again Mathatha attacked Madiba's office for not conducting itself in the right way by protecting Madiba's image from 'abuse like this', as he put it. I was starting to feel rebellious about many issues, this being one of them. Abuse to me consisted in the fact that people without a voice and platform didn't have access to drugs and were dying by the millions. By not providing treatment the government was denying people their human rights.

We were extremely frustrated by the lack of response from the government on Madiba's calls to meet with them and to discuss the issue of HIV drugs. On one occasion, Minister Msimang only met Madiba for thirty minutes and then she told him that she had to leave as she had an appointment for a dress fitting.

The denialism reached right to the top. President Mbeki said that he had never seen a person with AIDS, yet Madiba helped countless people to get access to AIDS drugs – people who then recovered and led some quality lives. The President also denied that there was a relation between HIV and AIDS. We helped a young lady who was on her last legs when she came to see Madiba to ask for help. She couldn't eat by herself. He had her admitted to hospital and when the drugs she took created side effects another cocktail was prescribed. She was later discharged and today she is happily married with children and leads a normal life. Because of both local public and international pressure, and also pressure from people like President Clinton, government now provides anti-retroviral drugs and South Africa's AIDS incidence rates are lower than before.

On the evening of 5 May 2003 I received a call from someone who told me that Madiba's best friend, Walter Sisulu, had just passed away. They were imprisoned together but had been friends since they were young. I immediately called Kgalema Motlanthe, whom I respected and liked, to ask him to confirm it. Kgalema was the Secretary General of the ANC at the time. He didn't know about it either but another source soon confirmed it. It was already late at night and Madiba was asleep but I knew he would want to know immediately if anything happened to Uncle Walter. Mrs Machel was in her home village in Mozambique and couldn't be reached and so I drove to Madiba's house. I entered and told the household staff why I was there. I knew that this was not the kind of thing that one did over the telephone as this would be a great shock to him. I went up to his bedroom and for the first time I was scared to wake him up. I often woke him when we travelled but this was different.

I first touched the duvet around his feet and said, 'Khulu, Khulu, I need to speak to you, please wake up.' The second time around

I touched the duvet close to his shoulder and he woke up. All he said was 'Yes Zeldina?' as if he expected me to ask him something. I said: 'I'm very sorry to be the one to have to tell you this but Uncle Walter passed away.' He either didn't hear me at first or he was in shock. I repeated myself. With one hand he reached for his hairline on his forehead and exclaimed: 'Good God.' It took him some time to sit up straight. I decided to sit at the foot of his bed for a while to make sure he was OK and repeated that I was very sorry to be the carrier of such bad news and told him what I had heard. I also told him that I thought he would want to know and he responded: 'Yes, yes of course.'

We agreed that he would go to the Sisulu residence very early the next morning and he asked me to wake him in the early hours. It was hard for Madiba too to see the sadness of Aunt Albertina, Uncle Walter's wife. He had known these people his entire life and they were part of him. He had so much respect for Uncle Walter and always commented on his admiration for Uncle Walter's humility and simplicity, and also for his outstanding leadership and always being willing to lead from behind and to push others forward. Silently I thought that was exactly it. Uncle Walter must have pushed Madiba to the front those years they were imprisoned. Madiba often told stories about their interaction and how often they discussed things. It was indeed a sad day for everyone. South Africa lost one of its biggest heroes.

It was becoming time for Madiba to slow down. He simply could not keep up his schedule and continue to respond to every request that was put to him by friends, colleagues and associates. He would divide his time between Johannesburg, Qunu and Maputo and then spend some quiet time at Shambala whenever he wanted to write. The house at Shambala also presented the opportunity for him to entertain high profile visitors who couldn't go to a normal game farm, as Shambala was completely private.

A few prominent artists suggested that Madiba's prison number be used to start an AIDS campaign. It would be called 46664. Madiba

had always felt strongly against his face, image or name being commercialized, whether it was for charity or commercial purposes.
The artists therefore came up with this idea of using his prison
number to help raise funds for the AIDS campaign. They proposed
launching the brand at a big concert to be held in Cape Town, all of
them of course offering to perform free of charge. While some of
the singers were rehearsing in Cape Town the CEO of the Foundation decided that Madiba should speak to the artists to thank them
for their tireless dedication in their efforts to support a cause close
to his heart.

We were at Shambala at the time. A telephone call was scheduled
when the singers would all be together so that Madiba could speak
to them. I typed out their names, for instance 'Brian May – Queen'
and 'Dave Stewart – Eurythmics', after briefing Madiba. I tried to
explain to him who everyone was and gave him the piece of paper
in order for him to remember the names. Brian May was first on the
line. I stood beside him to point to the piece of paper who he was
talking to. When Brian answered he said, 'Hallo Madiba, how are
you?' Madiba politely said, 'Hi Brian, I'm well thank you and how
are you?' Brian responded to say he was well and that they were
excited to be part of this event. Madiba acknowledged and then
asked: 'How is the Queen?' He then spoke to Dave Stewart and
asked him 'How is the Eurythmics?' He had no idea that these were
bands. He'd lost track of technology during his imprisonment and
it was hard to explain to him even what a CD was, let alone musicians and bands that were familiar to us – I'd overloaded him with
the wrong information. It was precious to watch such innocence
but the intention behind it was pure.

Earlier that year Madiba turned eighty-five. I was tasked by the
CEO of the Foundation to organize a celebration for Madiba's
birthday. I fundraised for the event and over 1,200 guests were
invited to the black-tie event. Associates of Madiba from all over the
world were invited – supporters, friends, politicians, royalty, etc. I
guessed that I would be in the middle of the firing line when people
started taking the guest list apart. I invited from gardeners to

royalty to ensure that the group was fully representative. I worked day and night and my task was simple: we needed to ensure that Madiba was celebrated *during* his lifetime. When we walked to the elevator on the night of the event for Madiba to depart, close to midnight, Mrs Machel said: 'Well done Zeldina, Madiba was really honoured tonight.' Those words stuck by me despite all the flak I had to endure. People were complaining that Madiba was being 'poppified' – being made a pop star – because many celebrities attended the event, but no one paid attention to the gardeners, drivers and security who attended the event as guests, clearly because they were not considered famous or important enough to receive attention from the media. In addition, when we wanted help from the international community the celebrities were always called upon to give time and effort for free.

Madiba liked parties. He had gone over the guest list several times and approved of every person that was there. Some family members were angry as they were not seated around the main table, yet there were royalty and heads of state present. I subsequently wasn't invited to Madiba's ninetieth birthday at his farm in Qunu, and when Mrs Machel insisted that I be there, I was deliberately seated at a children's table right at the back of the tent. Not that I had hoped to be at the main table but it was a clear sign of some of the family's value of me in their father's life, and an indication of what was to be expected. I never discussed my problems with Madiba because I felt he had enough to worry about. That day, perhaps, I should have spoken to him.

On 7 November Madiba travelled to Shambala where we organized for him to spend the weekend with ex-Robben Islanders and ex-colleagues. A smaller group this time and people who were close to him during the struggle years. It remains one of my best memories, to see them all interacting, enjoying and reminiscing about old times. They all enjoyed visiting Shambala and we made sure they were well treated and spoilt. I loved listening to their stories and teasing one another. These were the men that drove the struggle, planned sabotage and actions to try and bring the apartheid government to its senses. They'd spent a lifetime in prison and now they were all elderly men, enjoying their senior years, free at last. It was a proper reunion and everyone tried to outdo each other's stories. One of those exceptionally precious occasions.

We had come such a long way in South Africa. Here I was enjoying time with ex-Robben Islanders, while at the time I was growing up I'd considered it a good thing that they were imprisoned. I became fond of many of them, such as Ahmed Kathrada, Eddie Daniels, Mac Maharaj and Andrew Mlangeni. These were the people we had to thank as they'd kept Madiba's spirit alive in prison. And I often wondered if they ever lost hope during their time in prison or whether they ever had imagined that they would be there that day, on a private game farm, enjoying reminiscing with Madiba.

9

Holidays and Friends

By now we were spending weeks without end at Shambala. Madiba often invited people to come and visit him on the farm and we had to be mindful to not allow Shambala to become just another venue for people to flock to where he would soon feel overwhelmed by visitors. On one such occasion he invited Zwelinzima Vavi and Blade Nzimande, the President of the Council of South African Trade Unions and General Secretary of the South African Communist Party respectively. Madiba enjoyed lunch with them after which he asked me to accompany them on a game drive, which I did. Shambala hosts the Big Five game animals and one could easily see four of the Big Five, including lion and elephant in a short game drive. I liked Blade and Zweli as they had always treated me with respect and dignity despite all the whispering about my white presence in Madiba's life. They never considered me as just the hired help. By now the SACP and Cosatu were in a tripartite alliance with the ANC. Zweli and Blade enjoyed the game drive and at one point I turned to them and said, 'You are not allowed to enjoy this, are you?' They laughed and I continued: 'Communists and socialists are not allowed to enjoy capitalism, so if you're enjoying it, just don't show it!'

Towards the end of 2003 Madiba received a visit from Sol Kerzner, the hotel tycoon from South Africa. In the past, people usually knew South Africa for two things: Nelson Mandela and Sun City. Sol built Sun City to much controversy in the mid 1980s, as the property is situated in what was then known as Bophuthatswana, one of South Africa's 'homelands', run by President Mangope. Mangope was perceived to be supportive of the apartheid government in the

1980s. After his release Madiba called Sol and convinced him to show support for rebuilding South Africa, which Sol was happy to help with. Eventually Sol sold his stake in Sun City and started Kerzner International abroad. He told Madiba about their resort in Mauritius and extended an invitation to Madiba for a holiday. We made arrangements for Madiba, Mrs Machel and some of the grandchildren to go.

It was like arriving in Paradise. Sol had booked a private villa for Madiba and Mrs Machel at the One & Only Le Saint Géran Hotel in Mauritius while the rest of us were accommodated in the hotel adjacent to the villa. Of course Sol knew that Madiba and Mum came with an entourage; no President or former President travels without. One also had to be careful not to make people feel, no matter how wealthy they were, that they were being exploited. They offered to pay for me and the doctor, in addition to the grand-children that Madiba chose to accompany us. What I always greatly appreciated about my boss was that he was very aware not to over-play someone's hospitality. So despite them paying for us, we didn't clean out the mini-bar or make international calls on the telephone, but rather dealt with the hospitality with the greatest respect.

I had now been working for Madiba for ten years and I had never seen him enjoying a holiday this much. He had private time with his wife and grandchildren and we all enjoyed meals like a big extended family. For the first time there was no rush. And it was difficult to get used to. Mum had to remind us constantly to relax and that we were on holiday. We watched performances by Mauritian dancers and it is one of the only two occasions that I remember Madiba dan-cing with Mum. He also jokingly insisted that we do the pata pata. 'Pata Pata' is a song by the legendary late South African singer Mir-iam Makeba, co-written by another legend, Dorothy Masuka. The song was released in 1957, before Madiba's imprisonment, and it reached the Billboard Hot 100 in 1967 in the US when Madiba was already imprisoned. The Xhosa song means 'touch-touch' and while singing it you are supposed to show how you 'touch-touch' your dancing partner. One of the bodyguards, Sydney Nkonoane, showed me how to dance the pata pata, much to Madiba's amusement. He was so fond of the song that I could well imagine him dancing to it back in the 1950s.

Security and I would exercise in the mornings while Mum did her walking, have a late breakfast and then swim and be in the sun for the rest of the day around Madiba. He would sit in the shade on the lawn overlooking the sea and wave at tourists walking by 'half naked' as he described them – people in swimming costumes. He enjoyed having us all around all the time. We were so busy back at home that one hardly ever got time to really appreciate the time spent together and here we were looking forward to actually having meals together.

The only connection to home was of course the news clippings. Every morning, before he woke up, I had to ensure that staff at the office in Johannesburg selected news clippings from the papers and faxed them to us. He wasn't interested much in the international publications that one found at a resort of this nature but insisted on news from home. Well, and we couldn't wait for him to finish with the clippings so that we could all catch up on the news too. The suffering staff back at the Foundation offices had to be in the office at all hours to prepare the clippings to be sent to us wherever we were.

After a few days Madiba announced that he wanted to go into the water. We were hesitant as we were not sure whether he would be able to stand in the water. He was having difficulties walking and was using a walking stick. Security took him down the terrace to the water and he sat on a chair in the water allowing the waves to break over his feet. The pure joy on his face touched my heart in a way that is difficult to describe. How could something so ordinary, something we take for granted, bring such pleasure to a human being?

We then discovered that Madiba hadn't swum in the sea for over forty years. The last time he had been in the ocean was when he removed seaweed from the water while on Robben Island, but that was manual labour under the watchful eye of prison guards and in the cold Atlantic Ocean, and at the same time he slipped on the rocks and injured his knee for ever. This was so different. Mum helped him to experience the simple things again, like family meals, sunshine and appreciating the beauty of life in flowers, landscapes and music – things that just seemed to pass him by after his release.

Madiba was getting tired of his busy schedule and wanted to spend more time at Shambala, writing. He started saying that he wanted to 'retire' and I reminded him that he was retired. We discussed it with Prof. Gerwel and called a press conference to announce he was retiring from retirement. Madiba addressed a press conference on 1 June 2004 where he said: 'Don't call me, I'll call you.' Well, they never stopped calling. The public pressure continued for him to honour their events, to open their projects or intervene in any situation where people felt they had reached a dead-end. Everybody saw themselves as the exception, the one for whom Madiba should step out of retirement. Madiba made everyone feel special and people therefore always felt that they had a special relationship with him. The same people who complained that he was too busy or was seen doing too much of this or that were then the ones for which he sometimes had to make the exception. You sometimes feel like going crazy in that environment. Many of the people who claimed they had special relationships with him did, but it is precisely this that made it difficult for him to retire until the age where he was simply no longer able to do anything physically.

The ANC came calling too. The next election was approaching and the ANC came to announce to Madiba that they were in financial difficulty. Big business was reluctant to be seen to support any one political party and so Madiba roped in former President F. W. de Klerk too. The two former enemies jointly set off on the streets to fundraise for both the New National Party (the former National Party) and the ANC. I had to make appointments for them with the CEOs and together they went cap in hand asking for financial assistance for the parties they had once led. Of course any company enjoyed having both Madiba and Mr de Klerk in their offices and the fundraising attempt was successful.

In March 2004 Charlize Theron became the first South African to be awarded an Oscar at the Academy Awards in Los Angeles, for her role in the movie *Monster*, and soon she was back to visit her country of origin. Madiba was in Maputo but he agreed to return to be in Johannesburg to meet with Ms Theron. The media was in a frenzy. We ordered *koeksisters*, an Afrikaner delicacy that Charlize mentioned she was hoping to eat while in South Africa. Madiba offered her *koeksisters* and although she took one, she never ate it. She announced her intention to start an AIDS charity but I wasn't sure how informed she was of the intricacies of the disease. They appeared in front of the media following their meeting and she told Madiba in the presence of the world media how much she loved him. Women always loved Madiba as he was charming and generous in paying compliments. A real charmer.

It couldn't have been pleasant for Mrs Machel to hear people declaring their undying love to Madiba and him charming them; however, she never complained. I recall an incident in the Presidency at some stage when it became too much and all female staff kissed him whenever they greeted him. Female staff were then asked not to kiss the President in public. It was funny. Everyone just adored Madiba but it was becoming a liability for him to be seen being kissed by women every day wherever he moved.

About a year later we were looking for Charlize to ask her to record a message in support of Madiba's 46664 AIDS awareness campaign. First we struggled to get hold of her and when we eventually did, we were told by her publicist that she was busy filming and unable to record a twenty-second promo. I insisted that she could find five minutes to do this but I was told that it was not possible. We were offended because on the occasion she visited South Africa Madiba flew from another city to meet her in Johannesburg. Only when she heard about it personally did she intervene.

Sometimes staff can cause considerable damage to your reputation and relationships, as we'd learned.

One of the ministers Madiba had appointed in his Cabinet, the Minister of Intelligence, Joe Nhlanhla, had had two strokes and was bedridden. Kgalema Motlanthe, the Secretary General of the ANC at the time, reported to Madiba that Joe was not well. We visited him in hospital and were told that he didn't have the financial means to be taken to a hospice. Madiba mobilized business to start a fund for Joe Nhlanhla and soon he was moved to a high-care centre. I was sad to hear of his death but I was saddened that the responsibility of these things kept coming back to Madiba, as if he was for ever expected to pay down on a refund for what people had done for him in the past. At times, the requests were relentless, and it seemed everybody wanted him to personally bail them out of whatever financial mess they found themselves in.

On 24 March 2004 we set out on another visit to Saudi Arabia. Sometimes it was for fundraising, sometimes just to honour a request from the Saudis. I now had my own *abaya* and was quite comfortable wearing it and moving around in Riyadh. After my previous experience, I knew I had to tone down my frustrations with the Saudis. I grew to enjoy our Saudi trips because I knew exactly what to expect, I knew what to do and not to do and was happy to follow their rules because I no longer had unrealistic expectations. I still had difficulty communicating with some of the officials as they wouldn't take instructions easily from women, but while I was with Madiba they obliged.

We were scheduled to meet with the King and as usual I was told that I was not allowed to accompany Madiba as no women are ever allowed to meet the King. Madiba insisted and, surprisingly, the messenger returned to say that I would indeed be allowed to accompany him. The appointment time arrived and we set off to the King's palace. Upon arrival Madiba did what he usually did whenever he was scared that I would go astray. As soon as he exited from the car he stopped and asked, 'Where is my secretary?' The men would run around looking for the secretary and then rush me to him. I sometimes deliberately remained in the car for a few seconds longer because I knew I would not be able to fight my way through the security on my own and unless Madiba called me I would get stuck. As we entered the palace, surrounded by a mass of people, he took my hand. I was uncomfortable as I knew it was unheard of for me to be there and then, secondly, it was not proper for an unmarried woman to be seen to have any physical contact with a man. But he didn't let go of my hand and he knew the rules very well.

We were escorted to the waiting room where we sat until the King called for Madiba. Again Madiba took my hand and we entered the King's chambers. He greeted the King and left me standing behind him. I wanted to turn around and run, but I didn't. I just felt so uncomfortable. Madiba then turned around and said, 'Your Majesty, this is my secretary and granddaughter, Zelda la Grange.' I knew I was not supposed to make eye contact with the King either and I didn't. I bowed my head and smiled although I knew not to curtsy. Madiba was very intolerant of people being submissive in situations like these. But I was really scared. The only thing that went through my mind was: The King can see I'm not black; I can't be your granddaughter. The King extended his hand to shake my hand and I saw Madiba nodding his head in approval of me sticking my arm out. So I did. The King held my hand and I could feel sweat dripping down my back.

The King was visibly old but he seemed friendly. He was talking to us through a translator and welcomed me. I wanted him to let go of my hand but he didn't. He asked me how I was and Madiba interrupted and told him that just before I left Johannesburg on our way to Saudi I was involved in a smash and grab robbery incident in my car, where thugs stole my handbag from the front seat. I was indeed very upset when we boarded the plane the previous night – my life was in the handbag that was stolen and for the first time I boarded a flight without even so much as a cellphone. However, right there I was more concerned about my defiance of the Saudi culture just being in the same room as the King. Madiba told him that I was still in shock and the King expressed his sympathy. He eventually let go of my hand and we were all seated to have tea with him. The King no longer often received visitors as he was old and ill. Nevertheless we had a brief chat to him before we departed. He was clearly very fond of Madiba and appreciated the courtesy call.

Madiba had also asked to meet with the Crown Prince and in the afternoon we set off to meet him. Clearly he was already ruling Saudi Arabia and he was more serious and pressurized for time. His office and environment were a bit more reformed and we had no trouble with my attendance. We had a few days to spare in Saudi and Madiba had an idea for us to visit Medina and Mecca, the place of pilgrimage where Muslims travel to annually to pay their respects. We had everything arranged when I was told that I was not going to be allowed to travel with Madiba as I was not Muslim. My response to the officials was, 'But Madiba is not Muslim either!' They were stunned. They thought he was Muslim. It never ceased to amaze me about Madiba – that he could associate and relate so well with people that they started believing he was 'one of them'.

We ended up going to neither Medina nor Mecca. From Saudi we were set to visit Tunis and then Iran. In Tunis Madiba was supposed to attend an African Infrastructure Fund board meeting and in Iran he was scheduled to receive the highest honour of that country from President Khatami. In Tunis Madiba was tired and he didn't attend the board meeting but only a short reception. Cyril Ramaphosa accompanied us and he explained that Madiba was tired and unable to attend the board meeting. It was the first time I saw him simply being tired and not wanting to do anything. For me it was a big crisis. I didn't know how we would explain that to people. Luckily Cyril did all the explaining and I didn't have to take the blame. I also called Prof. Gerwel and both he and Cyril spoke with one voice: 'If he doesn't want to do it, he shouldn't. He is entitled to be tired.' Then Madiba announced that he no longer wanted to go to Iran but he wanted to return home. He had never cancelled an international trip before nor had he simply not felt up to travelling.

We informed the Iranian government and they were clearly very disappointed. He wanted to spend time at home with his wife and not to have a life dictated by a schedule. I had expected these signs much sooner than they appeared, but gave him the freedom to decide when enough was eventually enough; however, it still came as a surprise.

When we were back in South Africa, Madiba decided that he had to send a gift to both the King and the Crown Prince of Saudi Arabia to thank them for all their hospitality over the years. He asked me for suggestions. The Saudis are so rich this was a huge challenge. I suggested that we perhaps send them each two springbok and two oryx antelopes. I had done my research and knew they would survive in the Saudi environs. What kind of presents do you give to people who have everything their hearts desire? I learned that they both loved their animals and therefore the antelope would be a welcome gift. Madiba agreed.

We asked the farm manager at Shambala at the time, Dries Krog, to assist us. The animals had to go into quarantine before leaving and it took weeks to organize all the necessary paperwork and export permits. People often asked me over the years what exactly my job entailed. I didn't know where to start but would say, 'I can type, answer telephones, call press conferences and export springbok and oryx to Saudi Arabia.'

Back at home we attended another ANC rally prior to the elections but by now Madiba had lost the appetite to actively campaign. They would have ANC National Executive meetings during which people would voice their unhappiness about his alleged disrespect for the President. These people were never willing to confront Madiba directly and he had to hear of these discussions from other attendees.

South Africa was bidding for the 2010 FIFA World Cup. Madiba was informed about the initiative but we saw our role being minor if anything because it was the role of the head of state to drive these initiatives. In late April 2004 Tokyo Sexwale, former premier of

Gauteng Province and then running a multibillion-rand business empire, visited Madiba in his capacity as one of the members of the bid committee. Tokyo announced that they wanted Madiba to go to Trinidad and Tobago to help in the lobbying. Madiba was tired and he didn't feel like travelling. At first he said no. Tokyo didn't let go and two nights later we were on our way to Trinidad and Tobago. We were unable, as his advisers, to maintain the consistency of implementing his decisions. The public was confused about who held the structure of power around him. I declined to accept that responsibility on many occasions, and as much as I tried to execute his wishes, the decision-making really depended on a lot of external influences as well as decisions by Madiba, Prof. and the CEO of the Foundation. Ultimately Madiba had to decide to do anything, and once he had agreed or been convinced it was difficult to persuade him otherwise; the same would apply to his refusal to do anything. He would just become stubborn.

I insisted that this visit be downscaled and that the programme be minimized. The reason for the visit was to convince members of FIFA who resided in Trinidad and the region to vote for South Africa's bid. We flew in a comfortable plane but Madiba was used to complete silence when he slept. The configuration of the plane was of such a nature that one had to walk past him while he was sleeping to get to the toilets. He didn't sleep well and that worried me. Tokyo tried his best to ensure everybody's comfort but when we landed I looked through the aeroplane window and saw that the government had put out a full guard of honour for Madiba's arrival, when we had asked them not to. It was not practical to expect Madiba to perform any ceremonial duties after such a long flight. When I noticed the guard of honour Tokyo and I had words and I asked him to step in. He himself could see that Madiba was tired so he called Jack Warner, the FIFA member in Trinidad who obviously wielded power in that country, on board the plane to meet us. We were told that the guard of honour was simply a receiving line and that Madiba would be free to depart from the airport immediately.

The entire visit was a battle. Merely two weeks after our visit to

Trinidad we travelled to Zurich where South Africa was awarded the bid to host the 2010 World Cup tournament. I suppose it was worth it. After Zurich we went to Douw Steyn's estate in the countryside in England where we could take a breather for a few days.

I cannot recall what year it was but during one of our visits to London we paid a courtesy call to Prime Minister Tony Blair, as we did on many occasions. I loved going to 10 Downing Street, especially after it featured in the 2003 movie *Love Actually*. When Hugh Grant was dancing as Prime Minister in one of the rooms in Downing Street I smiled, having been in that room myself before. Not dancing though. But on this particular occasion we hurriedly got ready for the appointment at Downing Street. Prime Minister Blair was always warm towards Madiba and we returned to the Dorchester Hotel where we stayed, satisfied with the meeting.

It was autumn and the sun rose later and set earlier. Added to that was the usual cloudiness outside. When I stepped out of the car upon our arrival back at the Dorchester I noticed that I was wearing two different shoes. You idiot, I thought. I was too ashamed of myself to point out my mistake to anyone, but later confided in the doctor with us and we laughed at my stupidity. I always stayed in a particular room in the Dorchester whenever I was there with Madiba, kindly arranged by a South African ex-pat, Nigel Badminton, who had become a close friend due to all our visits there. This room had a small dressing room, but it was more a corner than a room. There was no natural light and I had to rely on artificial light. I was in such a rush when we left, trying to gather everyone and to make sure Madiba was ready to leave, that I didn't notice that I had put on two different shoes. The two pairs I had were more or less the same style with similar heels and therefore I didn't feel the difference when I was walking. The one was black though and the other dark brown. It is to this day probably the most stupendously ignorant thing I've ever done. You try and reverse such an action a thousand times or try to remember if anyone in Downing Street might have noticed.

From London we set off to Spain where Madiba and Mrs Machel attended the wedding of the son of King Juan Carlos and Queen Sofia of Spain. This was nothing short of a fairytale. Mostly royalty from other countries attended and hardly any other politicians were invited to all parts of the celebrations. We would tease Madiba about it and he would remind us that indeed he was born into royalty too. To us it may only be considered Xhosa royalty but still it was royalty and he loved being reminded that he was a prince.

On 24 May 2004 we received a visit by the renowned boxing promoter Don King. He was a controversial character but this was another occasion on which we were told that Madiba had to do it. Of course, being a boxer himself, Madiba didn't object. I was in my office when the receptionist called to say 'King is here'. I'd forgotten for a moment that we were expecting him and responded: 'The King of what?' We all laughed and indeed it was King, the King of boxing. There were many of these moments that lightened the days and kept us sane in a way.

As expected, after a brief rest (and despite his retirement) Madiba decided that he wanted to attend the International AIDS Conference in Thailand. He was hoping to continue the fight even in retirement and to leave a strong message behind. This was shortly before his eighty-sixth birthday. On our way back from Thailand I wrote a piece for the *Sunday Independent*, a message for his birthday. On the Sunday of his birthday the article appeared on the front page reading: 'Khulu, my wish for your 86th birthday is time – Zelda'. I truly wished for him to have time for himself, time with his wife and time to reflect. But as soon as things became too quiet, he would initiate things again. Soon the retirement status changed to 'to allow him to choose to do what he wants' and off we went again. I sensed that it was a struggle within himself between staying at home and being isolated from the world. We came to the conclusion that he would just never stop and as soon as he sent out signs that he was available again, the usual suspects saw their way in to approaching him again.

I felt as though some of the family and their associates

disapproved of my presence in his life. For some it seemed personal and for others it seemed to me as though they were uncomfortable with him depending on a white woman. I felt caught between my duty to Madiba and the perception that I was a public burden to him. If I tried to make myself scarce, he would call me and sometimes become irritated that I wasn't at my post. He was becoming more and more dependent on me for very simple reasons: he was old; he needed someone there when he entered a meeting because he needed to be reminded of what to expect or what was about to happen. His memory wasn't as good as it had been. I felt stressed and he saw it.

Madiba would sit me down and give me a lecture about the fact that I worked for him, that I had to do as he told me and that I shouldn't allow people to distract me. Thinking back now, I should have told a few people back then, when he was still able to defend me, that they had to voice their complaints directly to him, but I never wanted to burden him with my personal battles. I had to face the fact that a young white Afrikaner woman caring for him was always going to be an unlikely and unpopular situation. Yet I was determined to never abandon him for as long as he wanted me. He told me about such disgruntled visitors on a few occasions, explaining how they challenged him for appointing a white Afrikaner woman. The first time he told me, he was cautious about the way in which he conveyed it, but after a few occasions both of us would laugh whenever he repeated it.

Xoliswa, Madiba's long-time chef, and I spoke a lot over the phone, as she was usually working whenever I had to be connected to Madiba on the telephone. We came to the conclusion that everybody wanted our jobs, but few people were prepared to put in the hours and effort.

Back in early 2003 I had noticed Madiba was disturbed about something. He spent days being reserved and withdrawn. Madiba told me that his only surviving son Makgatho had been to the house to tell him that he had AIDS. I was devastated by the news but I assured Madiba that I would do whatever to support him.

When Makgatho was admitted to hospital in December 2004 I went with Madiba to the hospital on the first afternoon. There we found Makgatho already in the High Care Unit. Madiba went inside and insisted that I walk with him. We only saw Makgatho occasionally and he really only became part of Madiba's life in later years. I was fond of him even though my dealings with him were limited. He was always very courteous and respectful in his dealings with me and helpful whenever I asked him to help with something around Madiba or attend an event on his father's behalf. I didn't know why children from his first marriage were absent from Madiba's life at that stage but I did see how Mrs Machel tried to bring the family together. She constantly tried to broker peace between the different parts of the family and insisted that all his children become part of his life. It wasn't easy for her because some of his children felt bitterness towards him. I was an employee and never interfered with the family matters, and never lost sight of the fact that I was an employee.

I was sad to see Makgatho in hospital. He couldn't talk but Madiba spoke to him, and just before we left I bent down and whispered to him: 'Hi Makgatho, this is Zelda. Remember, we love you very much and be strong.' I had seen a person with AIDS recovering before and I was hoping that he would too. Before we left Makgatho's sister Makaziwe entered. I was asking the nurse what Makgatho's temperature was so as to try and give Madiba some kind of comfort or something and Makaziwe told me: 'Leave my brother's medical records alone. It's got nothing to do with you.' I was desperate to tell her I had known for two years that her brother had AIDS and I had never done anything to harm him or talk about his condition. I wasn't about to start; my asking was purely to try and hopefully give Madiba some comfort.

I was on holiday over December in Paternoster, a small coastal town on the west coast of South Africa, when Meme, Madiba's housekeeper, told me that it was better to return as things were turning for the worse. I knew we had to assist with support to the household if that was the case and so I cut my holiday short and returned home. While I was driving home, Makgatho passed away and I never saw him again after that one visit. I was never asked to stay away but you just know when your presence is not wanted. I informed Mrs Machel that I was back at home but I waited two days before I went to Madiba's house to pay my respects. When Mrs Machel asked why I hadn't come before I said that I was mindful of people hurting and mourning and that I didn't want to add to the burden or be an irritation to them. She was irritated with my assumptions but understood how I felt. Makgatho was the father of Mandla, Ndaba, Mbuso and Andile. I hurt for these children as they were part of our everyday life and I felt like I grew up with them. Those years they mostly treated me like a sister and we had a close bond.

I tried to stay away from the family as it mourned but I did try to help with logistics. It was a very sad funeral and my heart broke for Madiba. In African tradition the body is brought back home for a night vigil before the burial the next day. The person 'sleeps' in his/ her bedroom for the last night and the next morning a prayer service is held in the foyer or entrance hall of the house where the body is displayed for the last time before the burial commences. Madiba insisted that I be there and take part in saying our last farewells. Mrs Machel was next to Madiba and held his hand in a tight grip throughout the ceremony. I had only once before seen someone who was dead, when my grandmother from my father's side passed away while I was still a child. That memory haunted me for many years. Makgatho looked peaceful though, being back home. It must have been one of the saddest times with Madiba, seeing him burying his son. Mrs Machel held his hand tightly throughout the proceedings.

In the early 2000s Madiba called on Douw Steyn and asked him to think of methods to generate an extra income. Madiba was receiving only a pension as former President but not nearly enough to maintain his residences and the needs of his extended family. I got a sense that he felt responsible for providing for everyone around him – his continuing desire to support people – and whenever someone needed something, they would turn to Madiba. Even during prison years, letters now published in the book *Conversations With Myself* point to the fact that Madiba was always the provider.

At the time Madiba's lawyer was Ismail Ayob, who used to handle all his finances. Madiba never handled any money himself and would simply request any of his lawyers to deal with financial matters on his behalf. Life had evolved while Madiba was imprisoned and he didn't know how to operate the technology around banking in the modern world.

Madiba had the ability to trust people unconditionally. I got to know of Ismail Ayob early in the Presidency and whenever Madiba needed something that cost money, Ismail would be called. Ismail took his responsibilities very seriously. He also dealt with all Madiba's intellectual property and the use of his image. Whenever someone promised Madiba money for whatever project they agreed upon, the money would need to be in the bank first before the door was opened for discussions. Madiba never handled such matters personally and, from my experience, half the time he didn't know what Ismail was negotiating on his behalf, but Ismail was tenacious when it came to dealing with Madiba's financial matters.

Whenever anyone wanted money, Madiba would send them to Ismail. But he would call Ismail first and instruct him how to handle the matter. On many occasions Ismail would question the expenditure intently. That irritated people and in my experience no one ended up having a good relationship with him. And sooner rather than later everybody said: 'Ismail must go.' But he didn't. Madiba was also a very loyal person so despite what others' opinions may have been Madiba was steadfast in his loyalty towards Ismail.

Another of Madiba's lawyers was George Bizos, who had been a lawyer for Madiba for decades, since before his imprisonment; he was even part of the team that represented him at the Rivonia Trial.

He was someone who commanded authority as a result of his legal experience and knowledge. He was also one of the few people who shared a very special friendship with Madiba and someone of whom Madiba was extremely fond.

Douw Steyn came back to Madiba after Madiba's request with an idea to generate some income to support his family. However the idea involved a commercialization of his image to some extent. The proposal was circulated to the lawyers, who were all vehemently opposed to it. It would create enormous difficulty in trying to stop illegitimate commercialization of his image in future, and therefore Douw's idea was declined. His intentions were nevertheless good. We had always been consistent in maintaining Madiba's wishes not to allow his image or name to ever be commercialized, something he tasked the Nelson Mandela Foundation with after his Presidency.

We were offered money over the years for many things but there were a few unwritten rules no one was ever going to compromise on, no matter what amount was put on the table.

There were just certain things Madiba was never willing to compromise on. Jeopardizing his relationship with the Queen was one, association with tobacco and alcohol another, and never selling his time. On one occasion a famous alcohol brand offered us US$2 million. They wanted nothing in return from Madiba, but alcohol and the association with Nelson Mandela as a humanitarian didn't fit and we declined. Once we were offered money from the South African Breweries as a donation and Ismail declined that too.

In Paris we were offered US$5 million from a well-known luxury brand for Madiba to do an advertisement for them. I liked the people but I knew that we could never commercialize his name. And so we never sold Madiba's time either. People wanted to pay to meet him, we declined and sometimes they met him but we refused to take the money nevertheless. To me the rationale was that if you didn't believe in the legacy of Nelson Mandela and only wanted to pay if you could benefit from the human himself, it meant that your intentions were not pure. We have indeed lost millions over the years but we succeeded in avoiding commercial exploit-ation or association with anything that didn't relate to the legacy of Nelson Mandela. Or at least we tried and mostly succeeded. That doesn't mean we liked people less who produced alcohol or people that made such advances. People are sometimes oblivious and it is in no way a reflection on their integrity. Most celebrities worldwide, and even world leaders, lend their images to advertising or contribute auction items by putting a lunch or dinner or a rare experience with them up for sale. It's a good way of making money, but not for someone with the moral responsibilities of Nelson Mandela.

Here, though, it was for personal benefit, to support some of his extended family, and it was more complicated. Ismail came to Madiba a few days after the proposal from Douw was declined with a counter-proposal. Madiba would create artworks that were repro-duced from drawings he was guided to do, sign them all and then they would be sold. As Madiba became older he kept reminding those around him that he had a large family to provide for, which indicated to us that there was urgency to the matter. He fundraised for an education trust as he was adamant that his grandchildren should all be well educated. There was nothing sinister about it; people understood that he'd been imprisoned for a long time and felt that he had to support his family somehow to compensate for his absence.

Ismail's proposal was accepted and soon he entered a deal with businessman Ross Calder on Madiba's behalf and they brought an artist to Madiba's house who helped him to colour in some draw-ings and do some charcoal sketches. The initiative was based on another project done by world icons who did similar amateur-like art and it ended up being very profitable for them. The first phase was completed and then reproduced and Madiba then started col-ouring and again those were reproduced. The next phase was for him to sign thousands of these prints. And so I was left with sched-uling the signing sessions. Every few days Madiba would sit for an hour or two signing these sketches. Hundreds or perhaps even thousands of them. I don't know. As Madiba fully trusted Ismail I was not present at all these signing sessions. Sometimes they were done at home and sometimes they were done at the office. No one kept a record and there was no reason to question the conviction with which this project was being run. After all, as Madiba was always quick to point out, never question a person's integrity until you have valid reason to do so. Moreover, I found Ismail in Madiba's service back in 1994. I never questioned their relationship or Ismail's authority because they had a history, and as I so often got pointed out to me, I didn't.

In April 2005 an article appeared in the *Noseweek*, an investigative magazine, with the title CIVIL WAR IN MADIBALAND. The author wrote:

> In order to understand the civil war that is breaking out in Mandela-land, it is useful to imagine a medieval monarchy when the King is nearing the end. The family, and factions within the family, are agitating for position in the aftermath. The court is rampant with whispers and plots.

At the centre of this 'civil war' was the issue of who controlled Madiba's future income and, more importantly, the licence that trademarked his name and image. Madiba wanted objective people such as his lawyers Bizos, Bally Chuene and Wim Trengove, not his family, in control of his estate. More so, he was disappointed at Ismail's conduct. Someone planted a seed within Madiba's mind that Ismail should report on progress, and when he started questioning Ismail and asking about the project, in my opinion the relationship started deteriorating. Madiba made a turn-around on his decision about the project. He instructed George Bizos and others to halt the project. Papers were served on Ismail and Calder's company and an order was obtained to stop the sale of the artworks. This caused anger among those who profited from the project and war ensued.

In the latest legal battle in 2013, two of Madiba's daughters – Makaziwe and Zenani – and Ismail served papers on Bally Chuene, arguing that his appointment and those of Advocate George Bizos and Tokyo Sexwale to the trust controlling the proceeds from the artworks were not legitimate. The case was withdrawn in September 2013.

We were often, now, at Shambala. Shambala not only created the perfect setting for him to write but also much needed peace and quiet time. Madiba often said that he missed prison. I was troubled and surprised by this. He then went on to explain that in prison he had time to read and time to think and I comprehended what he meant. He would insist on going to Shambala for weeks at a time as he was eager to complete his memoirs. It was a long and tedious task. He would write every page in longhand, finish about five pages for me to type and once I'd typed them he would make factual corrections. Then, instead of giving me the typed page with his corrections on to execute the corrections, he would insist on rewriting the entire page in longhand. I suggested sitting with him with my laptop to type as he spoke. He refused. He didn't like technology and he wanted to be able to put pen on paper. I even suggested that he simply spoke into a recorder and I could type from there, but to that he also said: 'No, you know, I wouldn't like that.' We also appointed a researcher but Madiba was simply not up to writing.

Extracts from the manuscript are published in *Conversations With Myself* and hopefully soon the unpublished parts will be used in a sequel to *Long Walk to Freedom*, this time dealing with his Presidential years only.

The reality of the matter was that we were slowly but surely putting on the brakes. Even so, in May 2005 Madiba went on his last visit to the United States. Our first stop was in New York. There a fundraiser was organized by the former chairman of Goldman Sachs and Madiba was scheduled to attend a dinner. Mrs Machel couldn't join us in New York and Madiba was grumpy as he was becoming uncomfortable when she was not around. Madiba took his usual nap on the afternoon of the event and when I went to wake him to get ready for the dinner he announced that he was not feeling well. My heart came to a standstill. We called the doctor. The doctor couldn't find any sign of serious illness and it was probably pure exhaustion. We agreed that we would bring the main donors to the room for him to greet but that he didn't have to go to the dinner. We were all nervous at people's reactions when he decided to cancel something.

The sponsors were very understanding though, and I wish all people were so accommodating. The next day Madiba was fighting fit. He got up for his meeting with President Clinton and was happy to see him as usual. It was also a day closer to Mrs Machel joining us and that always cheered him up. Two nights later we went to a dinner hosted by Sol Kerzner and Robert De Niro and organized by Jerry Inzerillo in Tribeca. It was a lovely dinner attended by a lot of good friends but also celebrities from the music and entertainment industry – half of whom I didn't know myself. They swamped his table to greet him and we had to be firm to keep people away from the table; I had to 'instruct' Madiba to focus on eating his food to keep up his stamina. Madiba didn't have the faintest idea who many of the celebrities were. Some of the names and faces he recognized from reading about them in newspapers but most of them were strangers to him. I think this may have been quite a shock to them as he didn't always react when meeting some of them for the first time as their fans usually did. It was entertainment in itself to watch. They were flocking his table. When we walked out one of the gentlemen we stopped to greet was Richard Gere. I looked at Madiba as he was introduced to him and wondered whether he knew how many women across the world would literally do anything to be in his shoes at that moment. He was completely oblivious, but as he introduced me I think he could see that I was dumbstruck.

It reminded me of another occasion when we travelled to Ireland in support of the Special Olympics. As we were about to enter an elevator I saw a man rushing around the corner to try and catch it too. He wasn't aware who was inside. When I looked a second time, it was Pierce Brosnan. I whispered to Madiba, 'The man about to enter the lift is a famous actor. He plays 007 in the James Bond movies.' I should have stopped just after 'famous actor' but was overtaken by surprise myself that he moved without any entourage. And of course as he entered the lift Madiba was still asking, 'He plays who?' I didn't respond and instead said, 'Khulu, you remember the famous actor Pierce Brosnan?' And Madiba said, 'Oh yes, of course, pleased to meet you.' I was relieved when the elevator stopped on our floor and we could get out. Mr Brosnan eloquently greeted us.

A similar incident happened when Brad Pitt visited South Africa in support of the Mineseeker project, an initiative started by Richard Branson to fund the detection and destruction of landmines in previously war-stricken areas. Nelson Mandela's life revolved around politics, not entertainment, and apart from the few movies they were shown in prison he literally didn't have time to visit the cinema and there was nothing relaxed about his life that would allow him to for instance watch a DVD. He ate, slept and lived for politics and his humanitarian efforts. I tried to explain to Madiba who Brad Pitt was but it was difficult. When they finally met the next day Madiba asked (as he usually did) whether Brad had a business card with him. Of course Brad didn't. Madiba asked: 'So what do you do?' I luckily had explained to Brad that he had to understand that Madiba was not aware of developments in Hollywood and the film industry in general. And Brad was every bit gracious in his response and said: 'I try acting for a living.' I added, 'And he is very modest because he is one of the best actors in the world.' Brad didn't make a fuss nor was he surprised or embarrassed in any way. He was a true gentleman.

The night before his visit I got called by a mutual friend who was with the Mineseeker project. He said that Brad wanted me to join them for dinner. At first I declined. I told a colleague of mine and she enquired after my 'sanity' and asked who on earth declines to have dinner with Brad Pitt? Well I do. Although I appreciated the fact that the dinner was meant to give him an overview of South Africa and what to expect when meeting Madiba, I had had enough of dinners and evenings out talking about my boss. As much as I loved Madiba, I didn't want to feel that I had to entertain people with him. I had to reconsider this invitation though, and I was happy I did. Brad was an exceptionally pleasant, humble person and we shared a love for motorbikes; we even discovered that we drove the same motorbike at the time. He wasn't only interested in hearing about Madiba but in really interacting with people who could give him a sense of South Africa and its future.

Our American trip continued after the New York party. This time President George W. Bush did return our call and Madiba went to Washington to meet him. For the first time, we stayed in George-town at the Four Seasons and the hotel used the pseudonym Mr and Mrs Smith for Madiba and Mrs Machel. I thought that was quite ironic. In South Africa the Smith surname is considered a white sur-name; it was shortly after the release of the movie *Mr and Mrs Smith* about a spy duo who fall in love, played by Angelina Jolie and Brad Pitt. There were always these moments that provided much humour to the most stressful situations. Having my sense of humour also helped because I could quietly laugh at things to keep me sane.

While in DC, Madiba addressed the Congressional Black Cau-cus. We couldn't greet any of the attendees as it was a huge group of people and we were mindful of pleasing some and offending others. Back at the hotel after Madiba's address to the Black Caucus, I heard that Barack Obama, who was a senator at the time, hadn't attended the caucus as he didn't agree with their views on a spe-cific issue. There was also a request from Senator Hillary Clinton to see Madiba and due to our relationship with the Clintons over the years, and knowing that it was more a social call than politics or business, we agreed, despite the fact that Madiba was exhausted by now after a busy programme in New York. The long-distance travel was just too much for him this time too. He still had to visit

President Bush and we had to save any reserve energy he had. We also got a message that Senator Obama wanted to have an opportunity to greet Madiba. John Samuel, our CEO at the time, Prof. Gerwel and I unanimously said no to that request. Madiba was just too tired.

We were told by a long-time American friend of Madiba's, Frank Ferrari, that it would be just a handshake and that Senator Obama could be the first black American President in future, and quietly I thought: Ye right. We eventually agreed to the meeting in which they greeted and exchanged pleasantries. He was overly respectful to the elderly Madiba and it also struck me how he paid attention to everyone, from the door man to the 'secretary'. Something very similar to the character of Nelson Mandela. The small people mattered, which speaks of the greatness of any man. Madiba didn't even get out of his chair to greet him as he was simply too tired. I cannot recall who took the picture of Madiba and the Senator but a picture showing Madiba seated was taken with only Senator Obama's silhouette showing as he bent to shake hands with Madiba.

This was the first time we would see President Bush after Madiba had pronounced that America was wrong to invade Iraq and that Prime Minister Tony Blair was merely acting as a Minister of Foreign Affairs for America. Ouch! He also said that President Bush didn't respect the wishes of the UN because Kofi Annan was black. Double ouch!! Madiba had a number of issues to discuss with President Bush and the plan was that they would appear jointly in front of the media following their meeting to show their 'agreement to disagree' to the rest of the world but that they were friendly again after all that had happened. Madiba often said that one should never be scared to hide your differences but that you should always remember that they are differences and that it doesn't determine the rest of any relationship. In the same way he had differences in opinion with Gaddafi but never snubbed him as a result of those differences.

I was worried Madiba was too tired and just too fragile for a meeting of this nature. So I made a note for him with pointers for the discussion. We entered the White House as we had done before and proceeded to the Oval Office. In the waiting room we were met by an intern who tried to make silly small talk with Madiba. My face usually shows my emotions and he quickly got the message. The President was available immediately and the meeting started. I appreciated their punctuality. At first I thought that he was friendly but when Madiba repeated himself the third time I could see that President Bush was getting impatient. Madiba didn't stick to the pointers and dwelled on conversation and then when he returned to the pointers he would repeat something he had already said. I was getting nervous as I could see President Bush had little understanding of the limitations of his old age. Before Madiba could finish, President Bush said, 'Well Mr President' – meaning Madiba – 'it's time for us to go and see the media.' Madiba wouldn't stop as he was not finished. The President interrupted him and repeated his request. I was disturbed.

To me it appeared as if President Bush was more interested in appearing in front of the media than in listening to what Madiba was trying to say. To his credit President Bush agreed to increase aid to Africa, but that didn't change my mind about my experiences that day. I felt disempowered and I felt sorry for Madiba as I couldn't do anything to support him more in those circumstances. But he carried himself with pride, even realizing himself that he was starting to be forgetful and that his mind often wandered. He would often say, 'you know I am almost one hundred years now, I forget things', and my heart would go out to him, sometimes just squeezing his hand or touching his shoulder to try and show him some comfort, that we understood and that we were there to support him even as he became forgetful.

I lived on the West Rand in Johannesburg at the time, about 21 kilometres from Houghton where our office and Madiba's residence was. In normal traffic it took me about forty minutes to get to Houghton or back. In peak-hour traffic it took me about two hours.

It was killing me. In addition Madiba would call me for anything. On a Saturday morning while I was working in the garden Madiba would call and ask: 'Zeldina, are you busy?' Of course I would never say I was busy and would ask, 'How can I help Khulu?' He would then convince me that it was not something he could discuss over the telephone and could I come over to his house. So I cleaned up, dressed up and went to his house in Houghton. When I got there, nine out of ten times he couldn't remember why he had called me.

I tried to get him to write down whatever was on his mind at the time so he could remember when I got there, but he wouldn't do that. Then I tried to convince him to tell one of the household staff what it was about so I could remind him when I got there, but he wouldn't do that either. I had to make another plan. I had to start looking for a new home closer to him. I had bought my first motor-bike at the time and my father convinced me to grow up, sell my toys and invest in property. So I bought a house much closer to the office and Madiba's residence.

But really I simply could no longer maintain the pace at which we were working and travelling in addition to taking care of 'Zelda'. The administration was overwhelming and being every day absent from the office, attending events with Madiba, created an administrative backlog for me. Happily the Foundation's CEO approved the appointment of three assistants to help me. They were angels sent from heaven. The extra hands helped and I managed to delegate some of the duties so that I could find head space to strategize about everything around Madiba, from media communication to time management. But nothing ever happened according to plan. Madiba wanted to know from me what was expected of him every second of the day. And yet no matter how much I planned and paid attention to detail it was never flawless. I am told I am a slave driver myself and not an easy person to work with. I am a perfectionist and my expectations from others are sometimes too high. As Madiba got older I became more pedantic about detail around him, but at the same time strangely I grew more patient with others.

And sometimes Madiba was difficult. If I didn't pay him enough attention or didn't attend enough events to his liking, he would find a reason why I should do something myself and not delegate it. And then I would be caught up between the staff, trying to spare their feelings and protecting them from feeling that they were being shunned. I was no longer the shy scared white girl and he was very used to my obsessive-compulsive behaviour and perfectionist ways. They suited him. He would tolerate a lot of tardiness from other people but not from me.

In October 2005 we set off to Kenya for two weeks to spend time with Mrs Machel as she was working on the African Peer Review Mechanism in Nairobi. It was probably the longest two weeks of my life. At home I had a friend packing up my house and in Kenya all I wanted to do was go home. Madiba was talking less but even so he had never been the kind of person who can be unoccupied for long periods of time. He was frustrated too but it was a catch-22 situation. He wanted to be with his wife but he didn't want to be stuck in one place.

We first stayed in a hotel in Nairobi, beautifully surrounded by lush green trees but these blocked the sunlight coming into his room. As Madiba could not freely move around without being over-whelmed by people, we stayed indoors most of the time. After a few days, we decided to move to a golf estate where at least we had some sunlight and he could sit outside. There was, however, little else to do apart from reading the news clippings from home and receiving a few visitors. Across from the room where Madiba stayed was a lake, surrounded by trees and bushes. My imagination runs wild when there is nothing to do and I imagined that the lake looked like Loch Ness. It was quite an eerie and strange lake. I told Madiba that I thought it was Loch Ness and told him about the Scottish myth about the monster in the lake. A few days later I referred to the lake as Loch Ness when Mrs Machel was home for lunch, and she told me to stop as I was scaring Madiba. Me? Scaring Madiba? We laughed.

With the help of my friend I moved home as soon as I got back to South Africa. I then decided that it was time for some normality and since I've always been a dog person, I decided to get two Boston terrier puppies. They were called Winston and Roxy. I had decided much earlier that I would never have dogs with mediocre names. They had to represent famous political figures. Winston looked every bit like Winston Churchill and only needed the cigar to be picture perfect. Roxy was a powder-puff girl and had no resemblance to any political characters. In hindsight I could have called her Christina after Christina Onassis or Madeleine after Madeleine Albright rather than Roxy, but Roxy suited her too. Soon they were my children and since Madiba was no longer eager to travel it was easier for me to give my pets the attention they needed.

Madiba spent even more time in Maputo but gave up on his writing. At home he still wanted to meet with interesting people and after the South African Idols competition he would read about it in the newspaper and announce that he wanted to meet the youngsters, and we would arrange it. Then a policeman got shot eleven times while on duty and miraculously survived. Madiba read about it in the paper and he wanted to see him. Some days he would say that he wanted to meet people and when they arrived he simply wasn't up to interacting with strangers. It became more difficult to predict what he wanted and it was clear that more patience and understanding was what was required from us. It is a natural process, part of ageing. You change your mind more frequently as the years progress and we get older.

From this time, everything started to calm down. Madiba was in Maputo with his wife most of the time and would only come to South Africa when he had important engagements to attend. Mrs Machel had to continue with her work. Being the dynamic person that she is, she had to keep her work going and we spent most of the time at home and subsequently became bored. In my personal opinion, one of the characteristics that Madiba found attractive in Mrs Machel was the fact that she was dynamic and passionate; that she had the determination and commitment to bring about change not only in Mozambique but also across Africa and in effect to change the world. She was ambitious and while he wanted to spend time with her, he never expected her to give up what and who she was. She had a passion for children and improving the lives of her own people in Mozambique. She received the Nansen Medal from the UN in 1995 in recognition of her work with refugee children and she was determined to continue pursuing that agenda, to be a voice for the voiceless, something Madiba appreciated and admired and often boasted about when she was not around.

In January 2006 we set off to Mauritius again at the invitation of Sol Kerzner. This time we made sure that Madiba's schedule was clear and he could stay for ten days as opposed to one week. It was as enjoyable as the first time. As usual, Jerry Inzerillo from Kerzner International made sure that all our needs were taken care of as requested by Sol Kerzner. The same manager, Mauro Governato, was in charge of the property and he left no stone unturned to make sure Madiba had the time of his life. We enjoyed complete privacy and he returned to South Africa rejuvenated and ready for another year.

I met a young Mauritian trainer in the gym, Prakash Ramsurrun, who claimed that he was a trained biokineticist and when he asked about Madiba visiting the gym I told him that Madiba could no longer walk freely without assistance or his walking stick. Prakash challenged me and said that if he could do some stretching exercises with Madiba he guaranteed me that with some resistance training he would be able to walk again. I was usually very irritated when people made suggestions like these. Madiba had medical doctors around him at all times. In my own frustration I thought people underestimated our care for him. Didn't they think that we had looked into things already by the time they approached us? The doctors didn't want to listen to these suggestions, so I had to. And I had to invent the excuses why it wouldn't work or wouldn't happen.

I discussed Prakash's suggestion back at the villa with Madiba and Mum and they agreed that he could come round to show some stretching exercises. The next morning Prakash started with his training. Of course, he had to do the stretching on me first for Madiba to approve of what would happen to him next; I was the guinea pig. Before we knew it Madiba took to the programme and he was co-operating with Prakash. Upon our departure Madiba was walking, unassisted, without his walking stick. He looked radiant and I wrote a note to thank Sol for the hospitality afterwards, stating that his generosity 'added years to Madiba's life' because I really believed it did. We brought Prakash to South Africa to train our masseuse but it needed determination and tenacity to keep Madiba going – not something Madiba was always open to. So a few months later, he was back on the walking stick.

Returning home Madiba spent more time in his lounge, and one day announced that it was time to get rid of some colonial art that was hanging there. Mrs Machel asked me to source African art and I had bought some similar art the previous year for my new house of individual Xhosa women. I went back to the shop and asked for the owner to come and show some African art to Madiba. At first he was happy with a painting depicting three Xhosa women. It was colourful and bright, and then two weeks later he decided that he was not happy with it and said: 'No, you see, this cannot be correct. This painting only shows women, there has to be a man too.' A man had to be added. The painting was returned to the artist, who added a Xhosa man to the image. I realized that Madiba's mind was programmed to be completely representative and balanced in any and every way. It was no longer a conscious decision but part of the fibre of the person and a response that came naturally. There had to be space for everyone and everything had to be perfectly balanced.

When you witness this every day, you become a little like that yourself. Your entire being changes being around someone like Madiba. Indeed as they say, be kind to every person you meet

because we don't know their battles. I've learned to appreciate
strangers more, to thank a person properly and to try and be respectful, always keeping in mind that the way you approach a person will
determine how that person treats you – one of the great lessons
from Madiba. Through watching him over the years I've come to
realize the truth in the saying 'people will forget what you said, but
they will never forget how you made them feel.' And even just
greeting someone in a friendly and respectful manner has shown
me the truth around this.

President Clinton visited South Africa regularly. In 2007 he agreed
to participate in a fundraiser which would benefit the Foundation.
This was one of those occasions on which I called on some of
the friends of ours to support a fundraiser like this. And they did.
President Clinton donated some memorabilia to be auctioned and
so did the Foundation. We raised a whopping R18 million (US$1.7 mil-
lion) in one night only, with less than a hundred people in attendance.
Unprecedented in South Africa. The money was added to the
endowment fund for the Foundation to ensure its sustainability.

Sadly, to date the Nelson Mandela Foundation is the only one of
the three Mandela charities that has not been able to reach its
endowment. We often had to share proceeds with the other charities whose area of focus, children and scholarships, are things that
easily attract goodwill. I was never paid an extra salary for
fundraising. It was never part of my job description to arrange
events or fundraisers, but it was what I expected of myself. I so
believed in the necessity for us to preserve Madiba's legacy, for
people and generations to come to be able to learn from the man,
even after he was gone, that I wanted to leave no stone unturned to
make sure everything was a success. Yet it is sad that I then got asked
by some of his family: 'Why does a secretary get to do this and
that . . . ?' I am unable to answer them and guess the best answer is,
because no one else did it. I remain eternally grateful to people who
answered my calls, who supported when I asked them, and for the
friendships and relationships built over the years.

During a visit of President Clinton to the Foundation the day before the fundraiser he made a very moving speech in which he said about Madiba:

> I regret very much, more than I can say, but I was never in a position like Robert Kennedy to speak out against or do anything to help my friend [Madiba] when he was suffering all those long years. But he did live, and I believe God ordained it for a reason, and now in the grace and beauty of his later years, he doesn't even have to say anything for us to know that you look better, you feel better and you live better if you think our common humanity is more important than our interesting differences.

It was moving and touching in every possible way and to me one of the best speeches President Clinton had ever made in our presence.

We also started to befriend Gordon Brown and his staff. We knew him as a British politician but he was very passionate about Africa as Chancellor in the UK and worked hard at pushing governments as best he could to meet the Millennium Goals. He was preparing to take over from Prime Minister Tony Blair, who was suffering politically as a result of the UK's involvement in Iraq. Gordon was a very humble person and Madiba was fond of him. The ANC was an ally of the British Labour Party but not as long as it supported violence or war. Gordon had ideals to withdraw from Iraq, but in the same way President Obama inherited a very complicated situation from President Bush, Gordon inherited equal challenges from Tony Blair. Tony was charming and I was close to his office staff too, but it was as if the private and public persona didn't marry: in private talks I liked him and his ideas but politically when in public he pronounced decisions that contradicted that person. Gordon epitomized a generous giant to me. He also visited Mozambique where he launched an education project with Madiba and Mrs Machel.

A few years later, Shaun Johnson, the Chief Executive of the Mandela Rhodes Foundation, wanted Madiba to meet with David Cameron on one of our visits to London. He was the leader of the opposition Tory Party in Britain at the time. Shaun also said that David could be the next Prime Minister. This time I knew not to say out loud even though I thought: Ye right, as if in my lifetime a Conservative will become the Prime Minister in Britain again – similar to my reaction when I was told that Barack Obama could become the first black President in the United States. But both did, and so I'm glad we agreed to meet with David Cameron at the time too.

Still, Madiba sent conflicting messages to us all about his 'retired' status. One example was the launch of the Elders, a global group of leaders and opinion makers who jointly speak out on matters relating to peace and human rights. The idea had come about in the early 2000s during a lunch at entrepreneur Richard Branson's home in London. The musician Peter Gabriel and Richard Branson suggested the idea, an organization of elderly statespeople to give guidance in terms of the world's ongoing struggle to find justice and peace. Although a brilliant initiative Madiba was already too old and tired to participate in something like this actively but he was adamant that he wanted to support it. It was agreed from the start that he would launch it and then resign immediately as a result of his retirement. In principle he gave his consent that the initiative be launched with his support, taking in mind that the formation of the entity would provide much-needed advice on issues globally from an independent group of influential and respected people.

The more things changed, the more they stayed the same. At times Madiba would be at home for a few days and then announce that he wanted to go to a shop to buy a pen. I would then offer to go and buy the pen as I knew exactly which pens he preferred writing with – normal Bic plastic ballpoint pens. When I offered to go and buy the pen, he would resist and say that I would buy the wrong pen, and I would know that he simply wanted to be among people and it was the perfect excuse to have to go to a shopping mall. It was the security men's and my worst nightmare. We had great difficulty trying to get him in and out of shopping malls and one couldn't trick him by taking him to a stationery shop with an entrance from the street. It had to be a shopping mall. He would return with his simple pens.

On one occasion he went to Sandton City, a big shopping mall on the outskirts of Johannesburg. He was determined to buy a pen and the security detail took him to the Mont Blanc store, somehow not knowing that a Bic pen would have been totally adequate. I wasn't with him at the time. He selected the pen and when he was about to pay he realized that he didn't have any money on him and that none of the security had the amount, even if they added up all the cash they had together, to pay for the pen. Of course not. The police in South Africa are some of the lowest paid people in our country, yet they are expected to 'protect and serve'.

Nevertheless, Madiba never really carried money with him and only occasionally he would ask for cash from whomever, but then he would forget when he had given it out to grandchildren and as a result his wallet was always empty. The only permanent fixture in his wallet was a business card of Mrs Machel inside. It was sweet. I then got a frantic call from the security saying that Madiba said I should please pay for the pen. I asked to speak to the shop owner to make arrangements but the gentleman then said he would call me back later and send me an invoice.

Montblanc belongs to the Rupert family. They have been friends with Madiba for many years, first the father, Dr Anton Rupert, and later the son, Johann Rupert, who now runs the dynasty of some of the most successful luxury brands in the world, such as Cartier, Montblanc, Van Cleef & Arpels, etc. There was no way Madiba would have remembered or known that Montblanc belongs to the Ruperts and it was an honest intention by the security to find him a good pen when they took him there, thinking that he would have the money on him to pay for it. Of course Johann was not going to allow Madiba to pay for the pen and the word came back that the pen was a present. Madiba didn't want to accept it but eventually he had no choice and Johann won the battle. Until he got ill Madiba wore the pen in his pocket, referring to it as a Presidential Pen. It was a fountain pen that regularly had to be refilled with ink and it usually didn't have ink in so we tried to avoid using the pen purely because it would start a process of finding ink and refilling it, and then it would not write immediately and so whatever had to be signed was usually a mess.

Madiba had very few personal things that he was religiously holy about. His two pens, his wristwatch, his empty wallet, his ivory walking stick and the holder for his reading glasses, as well as his hearing aids. The most important, of course, was his wedding ring which he wore without fail whether he was indoors or outdoors, working or resting. These items had to be neatly placed beside his bed every night and they were the first items he looked for when he woke up. Whenever we flew overseas in commercial planes, he would give his wallet to me to keep until we arrived. He thought it was safer with me than with him. Yet I was usually just a few seats away from him, not any safer or unsafer than he was. And then it was always empty. On one occasion the household packed something in his suitcase as opposed to his hand luggage and he insisted on having it with him during the flight. It took some convincing for the captain of the aircraft to allow me and security to go down into the hold to look for our luggage to search for the item, as he would not rest without it. He was meticulous about certain things and these were some of them.

The other thing that was considered holy was his newspapers. One was not allowed to read his papers before he got to read them. He didn't like newspapers that had been opened. You had to remove the advertisement brochures inside without opening the papers. He would point-blank refuse to take a newspaper that had been opened before. And no matter what one did, you could never offer to refold them when he had finished reading them. He insisted on doing it himself, whether the Queen or the Lord was waiting for him. He took his time in folding newspapers and knee blankets with the greatest precision. I came to the conclusion that these were the proof of a person living in isolation for twenty-seven years and there was no reason or need for us to try and change that. Clearly he had time to be as meticulous but then it becomes so entrenched that it becomes part of one's daily life. I often removed his shoes for him and then helped him to put his feet on a footrest. And woe betide me if the shoes were not put neatly next to him where he could see them. Don't think you could hide them under a chair or put them down loosely. You would soon be called back and asked to correct them. It was part of the disciplined person he was. 'Zeldina, just come and correct this,' he would say, calling me back to put down the shoes where he could see them, precisely next to each other facing the same direction.

On many occasions Madiba would announce that he wanted to go to a bookshop. He had more books than many libraries owned and I would then try my luck by asking what he was looking for, as I could go and buy it for him to avoid us being overwhelmed in public. He would then either say he wanted to go and look for a specific book, and I knew not to ask for the title, or he would be completely honest and say he just wanted to go and look at books. But he meant he wanted to see people too. Soon the bookstore would be in complete disarray. People didn't know why they originally wanted to come to the bookstore themselves, while I was trying to get him to focus on titles and sections in the store so we could leave as soon as possible. People overwhelmed him completely and we often feared that people would eventually kill him out of kindness.

He would sometimes page through a book and if the print was too small, even though the book was interesting, he would leave it behind. On more than one occasion did we ask Naspers, one of the biggest publishing holding companies in South Africa, to reprint a book for him in a bigger font. They were only too happy to oblige. And of course Madiba always left with a few books he got for free, but he usually insisted on paying and being treated like a normal paying customer or he would threaten the managers to never return if he was not allowed to pay. Other people would just accept anything for free, wherever they could get it from. Not Nelson Mandela. He insisted on paying and only occasionally accepted freebies. Sometimes he would buy one book and sometimes we would leave with boxes of books. Many of them I'm sure never got read to a second page.

He loved South African authors and biographies. One of his favourite books was a poetry book by an Afrikaans poet, C. Louis Leipoldt (1880–1947). He subsequently visited Leipoldt's grave in the Western Cape in 1999 as he always loved his writings. And on some occasions he bought a book by Antjie Krog, the famous South African writer who wrote *Country of My Skull*, and I tried to reassure him he already had two copies at home, which I knew he did, but he insisted and it was pointless arguing. He even got angry at me once when I said we already had the book, so we bought the fourth or fifth copy at the time.

He would also announce sometimes that he needed a dictionary. After we bought a few dictionaries on different occasions I realized that one of the most stupid things I could do was to tell him that we had already bought a dictionary, just a few weeks ago. The dictionary was only an excuse to go to a bookstore and I think I may have bought twenty big print Oxford dictionaries with him. Even in foreign countries he would sometimes announce that he needed a dictionary, and we would set off to find the closest bookstore to our hotel, buy the dictionary and bring it home without a page being turned in it ever. He just couldn't say 'I want to be among people' or 'I want to see the city'. I think he thought it would appear vain if he did that so he'd rather settle for using a bookstore or needing a pen as a good excuse. It is one of the disadvantages of being such a famous person. He could never do things we just take for granted but only once that freedom is removed from you do you know what it is to appreciate it.

Strangely the Afrikaans section in bookstores always attracted him. He refers to his love for the writings of the Afrikaans writer Langenhoven in *Conversations With Myself*:

> Well, firstly he wrote very simply. And secondly, he was a very humorous writer, and of course part of his writing was to free the Afrikaner from the desire to imitate the English. His idea was to instil national pride amongst the Afrikaners and so I liked him very much.

I clung on to these words, trying to instil pride among the young Afrikaners for who and what they are. It was important to him that one remains an individual and embrace your history and ancestry and I often recited these words when I found myself in conversations with young Afrikaners.

We also went to a bookshop in Pretoria once, in the area close to the University of Pretoria right in the middle of the student area. We were on our way from his grandson's graduation ceremony when the convoy came to a complete standstill. I jumped out of my car (as I usually drove along in my own car) to ask the security why they were stopping. The answer was simple. We are going into the bookstore. We paged through a few books and then he stopped at the shelf where material on foreign languages was displayed. You could buy tapes and books to help you to learn a different language at the time. And so we bought the set to learn Portuguese. As Madiba spent a lot of time in Mozambique he wanted to learn the language and he wanted to understand what Portuguese was spoken whenever he was in Maputo. He made me promise not to tell Mrs Machel that he was going to try and learn Portuguese as he wanted to surprise her by learning her language, a very romantic gesture. I don't think the packet ever got opened and I don't know what happened to the DIY kit but we only managed 'morning', 'thank you' and 'please' in Portuguese.

On 14 November 2006 Madiba was heading to the Saxon Hotel where he was meeting Morgan Freeman for lunch. We drove in the convoy as usual and I drove my car at the back following the convoy, as I usually did. We were late. I always had a battle to get people away from Madiba in order for him not to be late for anything as I knew how much importance he paid to punctuality. This was one of those events and we were nervously trying to get out of the traffic to still have him arrive in time for lunch. It was blue lights and sirens everywhere trying to get through the stationary traffic.

At a traffic intersection where we had to turn right (keeping in mind that we drive on the left side of the road in South Africa) we were entering a crossing at the traffic light and the police closed the intersection as usual by blocking off traffic with one of their vehicles to allow the main car and back up to smoothly enter and exit the crossing, even though the traffic light may be red for oncoming traffic. So they did exactly that and we started entering the crossing. A gentleman in a sports car came speeding down the road with earphones in his ears and obviously did not hear the sirens or notice what was happening in front of him. He drove full speed right into the security car that was blocking the intersection. Everything seemed to happen in slow motion. I could see the X5 BMW lifting into the air from the impact. The convoy stopped for a few seconds and it was really the first time I saw the Presidential Protection Unit in full operation. They were exceptionally good.

The security guards in the car that was hit by the sports car got out, grabbed their firearms and bundled into other cars, including mine, for us to get Madiba away from the scene as quickly as possible. We left the damaged car and two of the bodyguards behind and proceeded straight to the hotel. Madiba was looking in another direction at the time of the accident and he didn't hear the impact as his car is heavily armoured and therefore soundproof to some extent. The security dropped Madiba at the hotel and then rushed back to help their colleagues. I called a friend whose office was right across from the scene of the accident. She sent some of her staff outside to help our guys. Madiba had lunch with Morgan as if nothing happened. Lori, Morgan's business partner, who was with him, said we all looked visibly shocked when we arrived except for Madiba. This was reasonably typical of life with Madiba. Very little affected him because wherever he was layers and layers of protection absorbed the pressure of everyday life around him.

It was the year that the movie *Last King of Scotland* appeared on the movie circuit and, running out of ideas how to keep him occupied without him having to work, I asked Madiba whether he wanted to go and see the movie as it related to history he knew so well. Nu Metro booked out the entire cinema for Madiba and arranged a private screening at a time convenient to him, helping us of course to get into a back entrance to the cinema. When someone offered him popcorn he said: 'No I've had enough of that in my life, it is now the turn of the young people like them [pointing at me and security] to have that.' I doubt Madiba was ever introduced to popcorn, but since he had never 'snacked' in his life he was not eager to do so now. He thoroughly enjoyed the movie and when I told him that Forest Whitaker, who played Idi Amin in the movie, was visiting South Africa, he was eager to meet him. On two other occasions he also went to the movies, once to see *Fahrenheit 9/11* – the Michael Moore movie – and once to see *The Queen*. During the screening of the latter he turned to me a few times and whispered when he saw Helen Mirren on the screen: 'By the way, that is the Queen, right?' It was precious to see someone like Madiba enjoying a movie, something he was not used to but something we take for granted.

I remember when South African film director Gavin Hood won an Oscar for the film *Tsotsi* featuring South African actors Terry Pheto and Presley Chweneyagae. The three came to visit Madiba at his residence in Cape Town after returning from Los Angeles and we were extremely proud of them. This was only the second time South Africans had won an Oscar (following Charlize Theron) and it dominated the news for days. Madiba was so excited about holding an Oscar that he jokingly asked them whether they would not consider giving it to him. There was complete confusion on Gavin Hood's face. Of course you would even give your Oscar to Nelson Mandela. Or not.

Early in 2007 Prince Albert of Monaco offered to host a fundraiser for the Foundation together with his own Foundation later in the year in Monaco, providing that Madiba attended. Madiba was tired of travelling and only wanted to stay home and spend time with Mrs Machel. However when royalty invited him, he was more eager to agree. Occasionally he would suggest we travel somewhere but then he would forget and we knew that he wasn't too keen or else he would remember. I was tasked by Achmat Dangor, our CEO at the time, to work with a colleague and the Royal office in Monaco on the event.

I would travel to Monaco every month. We had meetings with the office of Prince Albert but it soon became clear that they had, like any administration, their own power struggles. It was one of the most difficult tasks to negotiate.

I contacted every person I knew with a little money to their name to sell tables to them for the event. I emailed people I'd met over the years to tell them about the auction items that would go on sale and that we hoped they would support us, and they did. At the end most of Madiba's friends from over the years showed up. It took me nine months of intense communication with people worldwide to persuade them to support the initiative and to travel to Monaco at their own expense to come and support an auction. It was a successful fundraiser. It all paid off and I was proud of what we had achieved. The Foundation raised a considerable amount of money, building a much-needed endowment to ensure its sustainability into the future yet still not enough to feel secure.

I fell ill during one of my visits to Monaco and ended up being admitted to hospital for X-rays. I thought I had pneumonia. Apart from the fact that no one could understand a word of English, which made a simple procedure like examining a patient almost impossible, the hospital was not great. As soon as I could stand up straight, I took a plane to London where two of my ex-colleagues, a doctor and bodyguard, lived and I had to rely on them for help. The irony was that here I was, thinking that I was dying and the only people to help me were ex-colleagues. There was no other support structure in my life than those who worked with me, and I realized how isolated I had become from life in general.

Before travelling to Monaco Madiba and Mrs Machel stopped in London to unveil a statue of Madiba at Parliament Square. In between organizing Monaco I also had to regularly meet with Wendy Woods, wife of the late Donald Woods, both anti-apartheid activists, with regards to arrangements around the unveiling. Wendy was heading the organizing committee together with Richard

Attenborough. I adored him and loved meeting with him. It was a historical event and one of the few occasions Madiba could be convinced to unveil a statue of himself. He was never in favour of things being named after him, statues being erected and him being honoured everywhere. He constantly reminded us that there were other struggle heroes too who had to be recognized and honoured. And then if he agreed to a statue like this one, he would not be in favour of unveiling it himself out of fear that he may appear conceited.

We had a close relationship with the Browns and their staff and it was always pleasant to visit them. Even though Gordon Brown would be present at the unveiling of the statue a few days later it was appropriate for us to pay a courtesy call to him before meeting him at the unveiling ceremony. On 28 August 2008, before entering 10 Downing Street I briefed Madiba about the press awaiting our arrival and that we had agreed with the Prime Minister's office that there would be a short photo opportunity with the media when the PM met Madiba and Mrs Machel. Madiba was becoming very forgetful and even admitted so himself, in public. He needed constant reminders of what was expected of him and minute-by-minute warnings of what he had to do next. But then there were always these moments of complete clarity when he would surprise us all with his sharp sense of humour, totally aware of what he was doing and getting up to.

I had told him that he would not be expected to answer any questions from the press upon his arrival in Downing Street but he could simply say that he was happy to be there and to meet with Gordon Brown. When we entered the two exchanged pleasantries and Madiba turned to the media and jokingly said: 'My wife and I are proud and happy to be here because as you know, this was one of our rulers, but we overthrew them. We are on equal basis now.' Everybody started laughing. Everybody except me that is. I was shocked and didn't know how the media would perceive such a statement. Madiba had a very good sense of humour and this was his way of emphasizing that we had moved away from colonialism.

We tried to be careful not to allow situations to occur where he could feel overwhelmed and it increased the stress and tension. I no longer felt worried whenever I had to deliver his speech to the podium. My insecurities now revolved around him. Was he going to be OK? Could he handle the pressure? But every time he walked onto a stage and stood behind a podium, the old Madiba was back and he was as strong as ever. It was hard for us younger people to witness the ageing process, and also not always knowing how to deal with it. You had to adapt and adjust things all the time, thinking, planning, providing for every possible scenario just to make sure that he would be OK and that every possible eventuality could be catered for. Over the years making simple appointments for others with him changed from 'Yes for sure it's confirmed' to 'Let's confirm closer to the time' to 'It's difficult to predict any day right now' to 'It's simply no longer possible'. It had its own metamorphoses and ageing timeline to it.

After the successful fundraiser in Monaco we also went to Paris. President Sarkozy came to the airport to meet us, and Madiba was touched by his kind gesture and repeated for years to follow that it was extremely courteous of a serving head of state to come all the way to the airport to meet a former President. It was the first time we had visited the Ritz Hotel since the death of Princess Diana. Being who I am, I secretly asked the manager to show me the route she'd walked and recite the exact events and steps from that night. I was not trying to investigate the matter but trying to comprehend what that night must have been like.

I was aware that many of those I loved were growing older. Madiba turned eighty-nine in 2007. I made sure we never forgot other people's birthdays, or when someone was ill we would send flowers and sometimes just enquire about their well-being without wanting something from them. It was my simplistic way of investing in relationships and to me it didn't make sense (and it was rude) only to call on people whenever you wanted something from them. I recently read: 'Life takes a little time and a lot of relationship' and that captures it all.

I think people often wondered what I was busy with at the Foundation as it was difficult to measure outcome apart from specific fundraising initiatives I was tasked with. I was maintaining relationships. I attended luncheons, breakfasts and had more coffee than was good for any human being to show our appreciation and interest in people genuinely, whether they gave us money or not. Sometimes I felt overwhelmed by people, not being a people person generally speaking. But I showed interest nevertheless and it was always genuine and with the best intention. I made sure they all got Christmas cards or good wishes for Ramadan or Jewish festivities. As Madiba got older he could no longer do these personally and then the Foundation could no longer afford to print thousands of cards. I nevertheless tried to maintain these small gestures. After all, Madiba taught me the most important thing any person can give you is his/her time. He wrote in a letter to his daughter Zindzi, dated 1 March 1981, while he was imprisoned and published in *Conversations With Myself*:

> Often as I walk up and down the tiny cell, or as I lie on my bed, the mind wanders far and wide, recalling this episode and that mistake. Among these is the thought whether in my best days outside prison I showed sufficient appreciation for the love and kindness of many of those who befriended and even helped me when I was poor and struggling.

What I read from it was that it was of vital importance to him to be courteous and grateful at all times, as we never know whether we will have the opportunity to thank people or pay respect whenever they have been good to you.

It was also my father's seventieth birthday that year and my mother's seventieth the following year. We decided to all go on a family holiday and my brother, his partner and I decided to share my parents' costs. They hadn't been to Mauritius since the late 1970s and we'd hardly had time for a family holiday so we set off to Sugar Beach resort in Mauritius. While on holiday my brother's partner, Rick, received a call from his parents who were looking after all our dogs. I think there were about ten dogs on their smallholding outside Pretoria. I remember him taking the call and getting up from the table. He returned and I went to fetch food from the buffet. Upon returning things were sombre at the table and I asked after my dogs and they said everything was fine. My brother is a strange person though. He seemed irritable with me and I could sense something was wrong. On the night we got home I rushed off to the smallholding to fetch the dogs. As I parked my car, I realized my dad was already there, having rushed from the airport to arrive at the smallholding before I could. He walked towards me, took my hand and said: 'Zelda, Roxy is dead.' My baby. My poor baby was dead. She was in season when we left and the bitches were all kept in a small area where a fight broke out and the rest of the dogs formed a pack and killed the weakest.

It was one of the saddest days of my life. I regretted every minute I didn't spend with her and I wanted to blame my work for not spending enough time with her. How could I have children if I couldn't even find the time to spend with dogs? This was my child or the closest thing to a child I ever had and I felt that I had failed her.

I had to sit for a long time and decide that these are choices I had made in life. There is no one to blame but myself but I cannot use the word 'blame' when there had been so many privileges and opportunities. I cried and mourned and didn't go to work for three days over the death of Roxy. It was five days before 46664 was hosting a concert in Johannesburg. I couldn't pull myself together and it was the worst thing that had happened to me until then. It took me at least a year to get over her death and to this day she has her proud place in my house.

Roxy had had a litter the year before and I'd sold off her puppies (and two had died while very small). They all got names, proper politicians' names, before they left me, including Indira, named after Indira Gandhi, the third Prime Minister of India who was assassinated in 1984. However, in the April after Roxy died the people who'd bought Indira called me up to say that they would have to put her down as she was not adapting well and they were worried about their child. They wanted to tell me if I found another home for her they would be willing to give her to another owner but otherwise they would put her down. I had her delivered to my house the same day and apart from her father Winston, she is now the love of my life. Having Boston terriers is therapeutic for me. They have seen me through the most difficult times. They are the ones I miss when I travel and they are the ones that I think of when at work during the day. I like to joke and say that at least I don't have to pay school fees for my 'children', so their school fees can be spent on my motorbike riding!

10

The Biggest Fundraiser of My Life

Madiba was turning ninety and I was thirty-eight. I never had imagined that he would turn ninety or that I would still be with him at the age of thirty-eight. Yet it felt like time passed so quickly. I was starting to realize and comprehend the full value of my privileges and experiences. And, more than ever, I was willing to contribute whatever it took to ensure that his ninetieth was the biggest fundraiser in our organization's history in his honour.

Madiba was no longer keen to leave the country to go on holiday. Like every year in January, the house in Houghton had to be closed for a few weeks to enable the staff to go on leave. The staff would also serve Madiba in Qunu, which meant that going to Qunu was not an option. Mrs Machel asked me to look at a few other options and I contacted a good friend, Jabu Mabuza, who is the Chairman of Tsogo Sun in South Africa to ask for advice. We decided on Noetzie where a few old castles are built on the shore, not easily accessible for the public. The castles are surrounded by the Knysna forest and Madiba loved sitting outside looking at the forest. Long after that holiday he would ask me sometimes: 'By the way, Zeldina, you took us to the Knysna forest, right?' 'Yes Khulu,' I would say, although he didn't mean that I really took them but rather that I made the arrangements.

Early in the year we received a call from a former Minister of Foreign Affairs during the apartheid years, Mr Pik Botha, indicating that Professor Stephen Hawking was scheduled to visit South Africa and that he wanted to meet Madiba. Mr Botha had contact with Prof. Hawking through a university in South Africa he was involved with. In the year 2000 Mr Botha had left the old National Party and joined the ANC, much to the public's amusement. Madiba of course welcomed such a move in favour of the ANC, whatever the motives may have been. At first we said no to the meeting and then we were talked into reversing that decision, as was the case on so many occasions.

We agreed with Mr Botha about a protocol for the meeting. Madiba was no longer able to deal with any surprises in meetings. He was becoming old fast and he needed clear direction and guidance. Mr Botha was accompanied by Professor Block, a gentleman from the University of Johannesburg who was famous for physics and his distribution of pieces of 'moon rock', a piece of which he'd given to Madiba years before.

It was amazing to experience Prof. Hawking but it took some concentration to get a ninety-year-old who knew very little about technology to communicate with the Professor, as he was talking through a computer. Mr Botha, not knowing the circumstances of Madiba's difficulty in communicating, kept interfering, and at some point I felt my face going red as I told him: 'Mr Botha, please stop. We cannot all try to tell Madiba how to do this. Let him figure this out himself as I have explained to him.' It was often the problem with people. They either thought Madiba was completely unintelligent or different people in the room thought they had to tell him how to do something, because of his age, which didn't help the situation at all. Madiba's hearing aids would soon cut out all the voices in the room trying to tell him what to do and he would appear confused.

When you tried to tell people not to interfere they took it personally or thought you were being territorial, yet they themselves had no experience dealing with a ninety-year-old trying to conduct a professional life. The meeting with Prof. Hawking was therefore not a great conversation, and to crown it all, despite agreeing that they would not throw any surprises at Madiba during the meeting, books and messages appeared that Prof. Block and Mr Botha wanted Madiba to sign, personalize and inscribe. I was furious. It was clear that they had no respect for the protocol they had signed and agreed to prior to the meeting.

Surprises threw Madiba, and he would then look at one with helplessness in his eyes and one would be left to explain or argue with visitors. By now Madiba knew me well enough and I didn't pretend to be anyone I am not. We instituted some protocols. We also had had enough of people approaching us with a particular request and then, once they sat in front of him, presenting a totally different agenda. People knew he found it hard to say 'no' to them. Soon, when the protocols became known to people, some tried to argue that it was like the behaviour of the Gestapo. What do you do? We insisted as we were left with no options. People kept on pushing their luck.

It was also in June 2008 that we learned of the sudden illness of John Reinders, the Chief of Protocol during Madiba's Presidency. Madiba liked John a lot and was grateful for his service. John was already in a coma in a hospital in Bloemfontein by the time we visited him. An outcry followed in our inner circle about Madiba travelling to Bloemfontein to see a white man in hospital. It is not something anyone would ever dare to confront Madiba with personally but I wasn't spared the backlash. I never managed to send people to him to lay such complaints but simply absorbed them and walked away. By now I had the skin of a baby rhino and even though it hurt to think that Madiba was to be deprived of visiting people he liked, it was now becoming like water off a duck's back to me.

I made a point of responding to newspaper articles that dealt with race issues to remind people of what Madiba so often repeated, that if we continued to judge people by the colour of their skin, chances are that we have a long way to go building the rainbow nation we all dreamt of. And he was right. I was getting sick of being labelled according to the colour of my skin too. I'm a South African and that is all that mattered.

46664, headed by Tim Massey, was organizing a massive ninetieth-birthday concert in London's Hyde Park in July. Again we relied on friends and relationships and started preparing them to budget for a ninetieth celebration fundraiser. Tim and I proposed a fundraising dinner to be held together with the concert.

Although it was often tiresome and tedious to arrange an event for Madiba in a foreign country I made sure that a South African element was always present, even when it came to the detail of the food served. The guest list was another problem. Everyone and his mother wanted to be there but we only had limited space.

Tables were sold in tiers and we filled up a massive marquee that was erected in Hyde Park. People always wanted to be invited to these dinners but they didn't always want to pay. You just get to live with it. Some people will never see the common sense that the more free seats you give away, the less your chances of fundraising, and having a hundred free guests as opposed to twenty free guests increases your overheads and the fundraising becomes less successful. Some people, having done little to nothing to fundraise or support any of Madiba's work, always wanted to be on the free-seat list. And at some point you just have to put your foot down because your professional reputation is on the line and the success or failure of the fundraiser will come back to haunt you.

Together with a friend who I knew from her time in the White House, Sara Latham, and the Nelson Mandela Children's Fund in the UK we put together a guest list to ensure that it would be a profitable event. The event was sold out and we included some of Madiba's friends, family and fellow struggle veterans to ensure representation. In the days leading to his arrival London was buzzing and I couldn't believe that Madiba's birthday was around the corner and in London there was so much excitement, even among ordinary people.

It was while preparing the logistics for the trip that we got caught in the middle of another power battle. President Mbeki was still

President in South Africa and politically it was an uncertain time for many. In 2005 President Mbeki and the ANC 'released' Deputy President Jacob Zuma from all his duties, following a ruling by the Durban High Court which found a corrupt relationship between Schabir Shaik and Jacob Zuma. In 2006 a family friend of Zuma's laid a rape charge against him, while Zuma argued that they had consensual sex. Zuma was cleared of the charge at the end of the trial and it was widely speculated that the Mbeki administration was waging a political war to prevent Zuma from ousting Mbeki at the four-yearly ANC national conference in 2007. Indeed, in December 2007 President Mbeki was unseated by Jacob Zuma, who was elected ANC President.

The leadership struggle manifested itself on all levels of society. You were either a Mbeki or a Zuma person. As much as the nation was united following Madiba's Presidency there were clear divisions deeply rooted in every level of society. Once Zuma was the President of the ANC the ANC also 'recalled' President Mbeki as President of South Africa in a very humiliating way, arguing that he no longer served the interests of the party and its people. The Deputy President at the time, Kgalema Motlanthe, was appointed Acting President until the next national elections, when Jacob Zuma was elected the country's President.

The Nelson Mandela Foundation was non-political. And Madiba himself had detached himself from politics. With his retirement he stopped going to ANC meetings and announced that although he was never going to part with the ANC and that he would always remain a loyal member, the running of the party was up to the younger generation. However, people willingly perceived us to be anti-Mbeki and therefore Zuma loyalists. It was in the middle of this power struggle, preparing for Madiba's visit to London, that we informed the South African High Commission in London about our intention to visit.

Three days before our arrival for Madiba's ninetieth-birthday celebrations in London I received a call from the South African High

Commission logistics office, indicating that they would not extend the usual courtesy of allowing Madiba to move through the VIP room at Heathrow domestic arrivals and they would not pay the few hundred pounds it cost. I exploded: 'What? Are you serious? For the past nine years you allowed him, organized, paid for the use of the VIP room because he is a former head of state of South Africa and now you expect him to what? Walk through the terminal building like a normal passenger?' I even wrote an email sarcastically pointing out that had it not been for Nelson Mandela many of us wouldn't have jobs. I was bordering on being ridiculous but I was beyond anger.

I declared my 'fight' to our CEO and Chairman as I was willing to do whatever it took to stand by my principles. I have never burdened Madiba with my problems or challenges, and in this particular case I also thought that it would hurt and upset him to learn about this matter. It cost a few hundred pounds to pay for the VIP lounge. I was in principle not going to allow the Foundation to pay for it. This sudden change of decision that a former head of state of South Africa was no longer allowed the courtesy of the support of the foreign mission to move through a VIP room had to be changed at Cabinet level as far as I was concerned. It was not a decision to be taken by an office bearer. They simply didn't give in and told me because it was not an official visit tasked by the South African government they couldn't pay. Yet they had paid on many other occasions when there was nothing official to the visit.

People assumed that Madiba was aligned with Jacob Zuma in the ANC's power struggle and therefore did things that would be seen to carry the approval of President Mbeki. Mr Mbeki would never have been so petty himself to decide to withdraw a privilege like this to a former President, and it was evident that this incident was a manifestation of that divide among South Africans, of either being a Mbeki person or a Zuma person. (I eventually called Prime Minister Gordon Brown's office and asked them to arrange for the use of the lounge from their side, which they did.)

★

The event was a massive success. We raised over R105 million (around £7.5 million at the current exchange rate) clean profit and to date it was the most successful fundraiser of any of the Mandela charities. The money was split between the Nelson Mandela Children's Fund, the Mandela Rhodes Foundation and the Nelson Mandela Foundation to further their respective mandates. My favourite auction item was a cast replica of Madiba's hand bought by Sol Kerzner for £2.9 million, making Sol the biggest donor of any of the Mandela charities at that point.

Madiba was almost intrigued by other people's wealth and fame. Yet that was never the consideration with which he dealt with people. He just found it fascinating that someone could be as rich as a Bill Gates or Sol Kerzner. He would often boast about the wealth of his friends in South Africa – Patrice Motsepe, Tokyo Sexwale, Douw Steyn, the Ruperts and the Oppenheimers to name but a few. They were all good to him and whenever he called on them to support his charities, build a school or clinic or support a cause he was arguing for they willingly did so. Yet it was critical to him that even when he didn't call upon them, they were always treated with the utmost respect and courtesy. He wrote in a letter to Zenani Mandela, quoted in the book *Conversations With Myself*, 'But the habit of attending to small things and of appreciating small courtesies is one of the important marks of a good person.' And so we never forgot a birthday or an anniversary and we made sure he spent time with people even when there was nothing to be asked of them, as these were part of the 'small things'. To honour Madiba, you have to honour his relationships with people.

Madiba insisted on staying longer than expected at the fundraising event and when he eventually went to bed I escorted him back to the hotel to enable Mrs Machel to remain at the event a little longer, so it didn't appear that they both deserted the main table at once. Afterwards I returned to the event, which certainly was one of the highlights of my career. I didn't want accolades or awards but I so desperately wanted Madiba to feel honoured and celebrated in a proper way while he could still enjoy it, and that night I felt we had achieved that. Driving back to the event from the hotel my heart was filled with pride and joy that he was able to witness just how much people revered him. Famous people and celebrity friends of Madiba all helped us to attract big donors and they were the people who travelled at their own cost, gave their time at no expense to honour Madiba and help us draw attention to his causes. Yes, they also benefited from the association, but one hand washes the other.

The concert the next evening was an equal success although the travelling was taking its toll on Madiba. He was tired. The usual scramble ensued for people to go up to Madiba and greet him. I watched from a distance as I could see there was going to be a fight about who got to greet him and who not. I felt incredibly sorry for him as I felt he really wanted to just enjoy the music and performances by South African, African and international artists, all performing for his birthday. I remember us watching a performance of a South African band named Mafikizolo in Tromsø, Norway, and how he enjoyed seeing them playing for him on an international stage. After all, this time it was his birthday.

Before Madiba went on stage I was approached by a tiny woman whom I didn't immediately recognize as Emma Bunton, the former Spice Girl singer. Emma was one of the celebrities making announcements or statements during the concert. Emma told one of the stage directors that she insisted on giving Madiba her present personally, either before or when he walked on stage. It was a huge box. I couldn't imagine that she would herself accept a huge box with a present inside from someone and carry it around all night. In addition I was also still p-ed off with the Spice Girls after I had learned that they had boasted about stealing toilet paper from Madiba's official residence while they visited him when he was President. So I had a preconceived opinion about her already. I didn't allow her to hand him the gift as he needed his hands to be free at all times.

As she walked on stage I could clearly see that she was upset and I told our security to keep a close eye on her as she was forcing her way to Madiba while many other, African artists were being pushed to the back. She may be a perfectly innocent lady, but in those circumstances you straighten your spine and tell off even celebrities if necessary. Part of my duty was to be proactive and to try and ensure that situations got resolved before they actually happened. I knew that Madiba would want the African artists present to take a prominent role around him while on stage and I wanted to make sure that he didn't get upset if the contrary happened. As Madiba walked onto the stage the crowd erupted. Some people cried and the noise was deafening. I was overwhelmed with excitement and joy for him.

Pressure was mounting on Madiba from the media and the public to speak out on the gross neglect of human rights in Zimbabwe under President Mugabe. We had been withstanding pressure from around the world for Madiba to make some kind of pronouncement because of the previous incidents where he was criticized for working independently from government because they felt his actions could interfere with diplomatic process. However, at the end his simple line was: 'Nearer to home we have seen the outbreak of violence against fellow Africans in our own country and the tragic failure of leadership in our neighbouring Zimbabwe.' And saying less meant more and not saying certain things meant saying others. The press around the world grabbed this and it headlined the news for a couple of days.

The following day Madiba also met with some old colleagues of his, all people who were in the Rivonia Trial with him back in the 1960s. It was more than forty years since the trial that sent Madiba to life imprisonment and he had not seen some of them since that time. He could vividly remember all of them and enjoyed spending time with them. Here they were having tea in the Dorchester Hotel in London while they last saw each other as prisoners in cells awaiting trial over forty years ago. Back at home the Foundation also arranged a private celebration for him with his former political colleagues from the Rivonia Trial and fellow ex-prisoners who were still alive and lived in South Africa. It was moving to watch these people interacting and I wished that I could have talked with some of them for hours, asking so many questions. The conversations were dominated by 'Have you seen so-and-so again?' 'Whatever happened to so-and-so?'

His ninetieth-birthday celebrations in London were the perfect ending to his international appearances. Twenty years earlier his seventieth birthday was celebrated at Wembley Stadium in England, viewed by more than 600 million people worldwide. The concert was named 'Free Mandela' and two years later he was a free man. Even though these celebrations were smaller it was a befitting way to end our travels, him being present where they celebrated his life. After that, we never went abroad again. He was becoming too old to travel.

Madiba sometimes called me from home to say that he was about to take the elevator down to the ground floor in his house. He was scared of being stuck in the elevator and I needed to call him in ten minutes to make sure that he was not stuck. At the time I thought it was funny but I now become sad when I think of it. Being there and answering those calls made me love the man even more, perhaps the fact that he depended upon me, yet it is exactly that admiration and love that caused so much animosity.

These calls also reminded me how much he had aged. Just a few years before, if he was stuck in an elevator he would be the person making everyone feel safe. Years earlier it had happened in Kampala with the Deputy President of Uganda. Of course, in addition to the people that needed to accompany him, everyone would try and fit into an elevator with Madiba. It made me very claustrophobic so I took the stairs. And as the devil may have it, he was stuck that day. For twenty minutes we stood outside on the ground floor waiting for technicians to come to their rescue. Emerging from the elevator eventually the Deputy President was in a panic and somewhat embarrassed, but Madiba had kept everyone entertained with his humour.

Mrs Machel taught me that I was to be true to myself and to always remember that the only thing that matters is my relationship with Madiba, that I cannot be held accountable for other people's relationships with him, and when I do something I must listen to my inner voice because it will always tell me what is right and wrong. If I was concerned about something or something troubled me, there was probably a reason for my feelings and I should go with what made me feel safest. Mrs Machel and I have not had an easy relationship over the years. I have been very sensitive to the fact that a young woman spent all this time with her husband, a white woman told them when to get up and when to relax, and it couldn't have been easy to have people around you all the time. But despite that she is the one person who shows appreciation and respect and affords me dignity. I salute her ten thousand times for keeping her cool and teaching me the things she did.

Around his ninetieth birthday we also made sure Madiba enjoyed meals with many of his old colleagues and comrades, staff and friends in smaller groups. He also received a set of stamps from the national post office printed as a limited series commemorating his birthday. The stamps featured two of my favourite pictures of Madiba.

He had lunch with his former ANC ladies, Barbara Masekela, Jessie Duarte and Frene Ginwala, then with the artists from his generation – Dorothy Masuka, Miriam Makeba, Abigail Kubeka and Thandi Klaasen – and he attended an ANC rally in his honour on 2 August, during which attendees all enjoyed celebrating with him. The government also wanted to host a concert for the people but due to only last minute advertising the concert wasn't well attended. The June 16 Foundation was also allowed to hand over a statue to Madiba (16 June being Youth Day in South Africa, commemorating the start of the Soweto uprising in 1976). It was a beautiful statue of Hector Pieterson and I felt touched when Madiba received it. One of the board members made some remarks towards me about how grateful they were that I had taken care of Madiba, and I deeply appreciated this coming from an organization like theirs, established to remind the public about events that led to that fateful day in 1976. We had come a long way in this country. I was an Afrikaner and here they were thanking me.

It was around the same time when Madiba had the dream one night that I had resigned to take another job, and very seriously told me the next morning in the office that he dreamt that I'd deserted him. Me? Zelda la Grange? I reassured him that I would never, ever do that. I overcame my insecurities and was determined to serve him until the day one of us passed away.

PART FOUR

What Next?

2009–2013

11

Staying Until the End

It was January again and the house in Houghton needed to be closed to enable the staff to go on holiday. We had no idea of where to take Madiba. It was difficult to take him to a hotel and we either had to find a big-enough room where he could be indoors all day or a private place where he could move outdoors without being in public. Challenging! And so the idea came up of taking him to Sun City. It is merely a thirty-minute flight from Johannesburg and he wasn't keen on going too far.

First I received a call from one of his daughters complaining, 'How can you take Madiba there?' As if the decision had been mine. I referred it to Mrs Machel. Only once his daughter understood that the Presidential suite was being offered to him free of charge, and that the three-room suite was big enough for him not to feel isolated in and that he could sit outside out of the public eye, did she settle.

In Sun City on one of the mornings Mrs Machel and I had agreed to go walking for exercise. My cellphone rang at 7 a.m. and I thought she was going to postpone our exercise. I thought it was strange that she didn't call my hotel room, but as I answered my cellphone I smiled as I was preparing for her to say that she would sleep in. She didn't. She just said: 'Zelda come quickly, bring the doctor.' I ran down the corridor as fast as I could. I knocked on the doctor's door and yelled at him 'Harold come quickly.' He was dressed and without me explaining anything he grabbed his bag and we ran off to the suite grabbing one of our bodyguards too almost in mid-flight. Madiba had slipped and fallen on the bathroom floor and hit his head against something. It wasn't serious but a head wound bleeds excessively. We helped and the doctor immediately did all tests needed, cleaned the wound and reported to Dr Plit, the physician in Johannesburg. When Madiba was finally on the bed with the doctor treating him, he saw me moving in and out of his room and his face lit up and he said, 'Oh Zeldina, you are here.' If ever I had thought to leave, that was the day I decided to stay until the end.

Unconsciously my body went into shock. I have never had such a big fright in my entire life and my shoulder and neck went into spasm. It took me three weeks of treatment of every kind possible to get rid of it – massages, acupuncture, medication, nothing helped. Mrs Machel was in trouble too. The family was furious and wanted to blame her for taking Madiba to Sun City and for his falling. He could have slipped anywhere and that is just the way it was. Old people fall. Period.

Madiba was no longer talkative every day; he was becoming more reserved. Whenever he was at the office – occasions that became few and far between – he would sit quietly by himself, thinking and only really converse on days that he felt strong and talkative. I always had to make sure that someone sat with him, whether he just read papers or wanted to be quiet in his chair. He did love interacting with all the colleagues at the Foundation and whenever new staff joined I made a point of introducing them. I also made sure every-one greeted him whenever he visited the office so that he could feel a sense of belonging. He had standard jokes for some of the staff. To Maretha, when she was pregnant with her first child, he would repeatedly ask, 'How many babies are you expecting?' because she is of small frame and carried large during her pregnancy. To Vimla, Mrs Machel's assistant, he would say, 'You appear to have grown taller,' because Vimla is short.

On a few occasions he would catch me by surprise when he said: 'Oh Zeldina, we have been together for a long time, haven't we?' And I would smile at his peculiar choice of words. What he meant was that we had been working together for a long time. If you work for someone for that long, you no longer need a detailed explanation for everything they say and you are familiar with intent. I would respond: 'Yes, Khulu, we have. We've now worked together for fifteen or sixteen years', and my answer would be met by a surprised 'Gee whiz'. I never asked why he was so surprised about the years we'd worked together, if he had expected me to leave earlier or whether he was surprised that time had gone by so fast.

Over the years we had built a close relationship with Morgan Freeman and his business partner Lori McCreary. We occasionally saw them during trips when we were abroad or whenever they visited South Africa. In Monaco they attended our fundraising event and told us that Clint Eastwood had agreed to direct the movie they were planning to make about the 1995 Rugby World Cup in South Africa. It was to be called *Invictus*, named after the poem Madiba recited in prison, which ends 'I am the master of my fate: / I am the captain of my soul'. Teams of people from Hollywood visited South Africa in preparation of the film and I would often meet with them to direct them to people who could assist or help with logistics. They also asked if I would be willing to assist them in Morgan's interpretation of Madiba's character. I read the script and agreed to help. I wanted as much as them for the movie to be a success even though I did not play a prominent role in Madiba's office in 1995.

After asking for help from the Presidency at the Union Buildings the pre-production team was allowed to do a site inspection. The Foundation also supported them with research and I gave them legitimate examples of letterheads and access cards and drew plans of the layout of the office. I knew they would get it right, but I didn't realize that when Hollywood recreates, they do it perfectly. When I walked onto the set on the first day, I walked into a replica of Madiba's first house in Houghton. I was finding my way through the crew and stood behind a half-open door until they could give me the green light to enter the set. Then, unannounced, I heard Madiba in the room next door. My instinctive thought: What is he doing here? and then I realized that it was Morgan doing a scene of Madiba sitting in the lounge of his house. It was scary to hear as he sounded *exactly* like Madiba. Over the years we all commented that the older Morgan grew the more he started looking like Madiba.

I only stayed for the day on the set and helped with small things that I picked up around the house or in Morgan's interpretation of 'Madiba's role' that could be improved. Morgan was the perfect Madiba and for someone who knows Madiba fairly well it was the closest to him that we've seen portrayed in a movie. The only thing I could really help Morgan with was some small mannerisms which he quickly picked up. He was crossing his legs too often or using his hands too expressively.

It was exciting but soon the day was over and I had to return to Johannesburg. I could only take a day's leave but soon when more scenes around Madiba or bodyguards were being shot, I took more leave and joined the crew, trying to assist them and pointing out whenever I thought something could be done differently to make it even more authentic.

During Madiba's ninetieth-birthday celebrations we had asked people, friends, ordinary people to send messages of congratulations to Madiba which we would put in a book for him to keep, together with the pictures to remind him of the celebrations in Hyde Park. One such note was a letter from Bono. He wrote: 'Happy Birthday Madiba. I am working to make July 18th a public holiday in every country that acknowledges that the struggle of Nelson Mandela is not over until every individual who yearns for freedom has the chance to grasp it. I believe your birthday should be an occasion around the globe to honour those who still struggle.' Tim Massey and I looked at the note and smiled. There was much more to this than what met the eye. How do we achieve this? We toyed a bit with the idea, and after consulting Fink Haysom, Madiba's legal adviser during his Presidency who now worked at the United Nations, the Foundation and 46664 decided to ask the South African Ambassador to the UN to put forward a proposal to the UN to declare 18 July International Nelson Mandela Day.

The UN unanimously accepted the proposal and the resolution

was passed. Our Ambassador to the UN, Baso Sangqu, was out-standing in lobbying with his fellow ambassadors to gain their support. We were extremely proud when we were told that the resolution had been accepted and although 18 July was not to be a public holiday, it was declared a day of service for people to make a difference worldwide in their own environments. Even though Bono refused to take credit for the idea I often remind him that his sometimes crazy ideas make the world a better place and this was the perfect example.

We held another 46664 fundraiser in New York to raise money for the Foundation, but it was difficult. We were trying to raise money during a world economic recession and it was our first attempt at fundraising without Madiba being present. People were not keen to be seen to be ostentatious during a financial crisis, not even for char-ity, and again most people who attended were the people who we always relied on. The fundraiser wasn't a big success but we had prepared ourselves for that. The good part about it was that a boy-friend at the time accompanied me for the first time abroad, at our own expense of course. For the first time in sixteen years I had someone to turn to at night when the work was finished.

The loneliest part of my job over the years had been the nights alone in hotels across the world. I had had the odd boyfriend, rela-tionship or fling over the years but no one really understood my environment. There was also the constant thought and occurrence of people befriending me for the wrong reasons, whether it was to get a book signed, to benefit from my contacts or to meet interest-ing people. After a few disappointments I started behaving like a modern version of a recluse. Hence I was always alone. There was no one to call and no one to say goodnight to, so you tend to turn to your job and become even more focused and almost emotionally reliant on what the job offers you to compensate for that loneliness. I think at some point it became less complicating to share my life with someone. I didn't have to find excuses to work or be so dedi-cated, and although the freedom allowed me to grow as a person,

I had missed the sharing and caring from a soulmate. This time it was different.

For year end the plan was that Madiba would spend a few days in Shambala for him and Mrs Machel to rest, and to give the staff at the Houghton house the opportunity to take leave. It was becoming clear towards the end of our stay in Shambala that Madiba was getting older much faster than we anticipated and his strength was deteriorating.

Madiba no longer moved easily by himself. Something was bothering him. Near the end of the trip he awoke one morning in a bad mood. He refused to eat and wanted to leave the farm immediately. 'Mum,' he said to Mrs Machel, 'we have a crisis.' Mum and I questioned him about the crisis but he wouldn't tell us what it was. And then he would start again: 'Mum, can you not see the crisis?' Madiba insisted he leave immediately. He usually flew to Shambala by military helicopter. The drive to Johannesburg was too far for him. It was the holidays and finding pilots to act on such short notice was difficult. Douw Steyn, the owner of Shambala, was on the farm too and Mum asked him to help find a helicopter.

In the meantime some of the security called Makaziwe, Madiba's eldest daughter, in Johannesburg to report that Madiba insisted on leaving immediately. Makaziwe called Mum and instructed her: 'Release my father now . . . release my father.' I could hear it all on the phone standing next to Mrs Machel. I cringed. We were trying to ascertain what the crisis was that Madiba was referring to. We were also waiting for Douw to help organize a helicopter. The next minute the security pulled up in their convoy, loaded Madiba in the car and started driving him back to Johannesburg. Panic struck. Never before had the security abandoned or left Mrs Machel behind. Madiba was not registering clearly what was happening. Mrs Machel, a former First Lady of South Africa and the wife of Madiba, was left stranded at Shambala without any security or transport. Between Josina (her daughter) and me we had to figure out how to get her home.

In the meantime Douw had managed to organize a helicopter and he was chasing the convoy from mid-air. Not knowing how the South African Police Force operated, he instructed the helicopter to land on the highway – not realizing that the helicopter would probably be shot at by the bodyguards. The farm manager, Tinus Nel, sped behind the convoy trying to catch it to communicate Douw's plans to them and only when the convoy stopped at the KFC drive-through in a nearby town, to apparently buy KFC for Madiba for lunch, did he manage to catch them. The helicopter was diverted and Douw was asked to fly to Johannesburg to meet Madiba there.

When Madiba left Shambala he was furious, but none of us understood what the furore was about. All he repeated was that there was a crisis. Little did we know that Madiba had had a vision of the years that lay ahead for him. That of ill-health and suffering. He knew his body was changing but he was unable to tell us what he felt.

I had been angry on many occasions over the previous sixteen years but at some point laughter at the irony takes over from anger. Some of us had spent those many previous years looking out for Madiba, caring for him, making sure that he ate the right food at the right time, that he was treated with dignity and that things happened according to his wishes, and then suddenly the situation changes, and you are on the outside looking in. I had never imagined that anyone would take Madiba to a drive-through KFC, but suddenly that was happening.

He arrived home while we were still trying to pack up in Shambala and rush Mrs Machel to Johannesburg. Shortly after Madiba's arrival, Douw arrived at the Houghton house too and then Makaziwe arrived. Madiba was deeply disturbed, and still not able to verbalize his frustration. But he chased everyone except Douw out of the house. 'Get out!' he said. 'Get out!' and they left. Madiba said he didn't want anyone interfering with his business.

At times like these when Madiba got angry I honestly feared for his health. He got so angry that I sometimes thought he was close to having a stroke. A day or so passed and Madiba calmed down again, and they soon left for Qunu where they had planned to spend Christmas.

Early in 2010 we were approached by the organizers of the *Top Gear* show in South Africa and asked whether the Foundation would consider partnering with them and in turn they would then make us the beneficiaries of their fundraiser. The request went, like all requests, past our committee, consisting of the CEO, Chairman and some senior staff members, and finally we asked Madiba whether he would be interested in meeting them. Upon running down their credentials he agreed. The organizers, contrary to what was subsequently reported in the media, asked whether Jeremy Clarkson and his team could pay a courtesy call to Madiba. Seeing that *Top Gear* is the most viewed TV show on earth we agreed, under condition that the Foundation would be featured somehow as it provided a platform to introduce the Centre of Memory's work, hoping to secure Madiba's legacy into the future, to the world. All parties agreed. On the night of the fundraiser around 800,000 rand was raised and we were happy. Despite promises of Clarkson and James May attending the event, they were nowhere to be seen. I had hoped to meet them to get a sense of them as they were paying their courtesy call to Madiba the following day. Personally I had always been a fan of *Top Gear*.

On the same day as the fundraiser, Neil Armstrong, the first man to walk on the moon, in 1969, visited Madiba. Madiba was imprisoned in 1969 but he remembered the prison warders telling them about it as they had no access to newspapers or a radio at the time, and of course no television. As opposed to many other meetings at the time, Madiba found it very curious and captivating to engage with Mr Armstrong. Mr Armstrong had been a recluse most of his life and we didn't know much about him. I was inquisitive about the reality of his life after such an extraordinary experience and he was eager to share his experiences with us. I was fascinated and almost in awe of him and asked him the strangest questions once Madiba ran out of questions himself.

Madiba found it most intriguing. Neil Armstrong was a gentle soul and one could sense in his character that he had a different understanding of life having gone through such an experience. He was also elderly, and it was easy for Madiba to relate to him. This has to be one of my top ten moments with Madiba, seeing the two of them conversing as elderly men, exchanging their most awkward life experiences.

I knew that Jeremy Clarkson was humorous but I thought he had tact. As he walked into Madiba's office the next day he asked Madiba if he had ever had a lap dance. I thought it completely inappropriate for him to ask something like that to an elderly statesman and Madiba looked at me as if he expected me to answer. I turned to Madiba and said: 'You don't have to answer that, Khulu.' I looked at Jeremy and I was on guard. He could see that I thought it was a stupid question to put to a ninety-one-year-old.

They took their seats and I reminded Madiba who they were, obviously explaining that they had the most popular show on TV and recited the number of viewers worldwide and elaborated a bit. He listened and took note and entertained what they said. They handed him their books and he paged through them. He didn't feel like conversation and appeared a bit withdrawn.

The first problem, which I was not aware of at the time, was that Clarkson thought Madiba had asked to see them and Madiba thought they had asked to see him. Jeremy then asked Madiba whether he often came to the office and Madiba said no, it was his first day in the office for the year. Yet I knew that it was reported in the papers that he had met Eddie Izzard and Armstrong the previous day. I corrected him as I usually did and said: 'No Khulu, remember you were here yesterday. You met Neil Armstrong, remember he was so interesting as he told us about his trip to the moon.' Madiba responded and said: 'Oh yes that's correct, now I remember.' Looking at Clarkson and May he had little else to say to them and jokingly asked, 'Have you ever been to the moon?' He was trying to crack a joke and if Jeremy could make jokes out of line, surely Madiba could make a joke too?

Yet later, Clarkson wrote an article in which he very inappropriately said that Madiba mistook him for Neil Armstrong, which was definitely not the case. He may not have known who Clarkson was, but he definitely didn't confuse him for someone else. Theirs was an underestimation of Madiba's intelligence because he was old. In my view, there was no respect.

Added to that, the organizers met with us a few days later and told us that the close to 800,000 rand we thought was raised during the fundraiser, and which was reported to have been raised for the Nelson Mandela Foundation, was not entirely all ours. They still had to offset the costs of the dinner and event and then we would be left with about half the money. I was furious. In terms of governance it created difficulties for us. It subsequently all appeared in the *Mail* and *Guardian* newspapers in South Africa and I came across as an utter bitch towards the organizers, but I didn't mind a bit. I was just sick and tired of, as it seemed to me, people taking advantage of Madiba and us and people pussy-footing around issues rather than saying it straight. The Foundation did accept the money but we had to follow up with each of the buyers separately. It created hassle and was far away from what we believed the arrangement to be. Coupled with what I felt was utter disrespect for the Foundation, it was a difficult pill to swallow. People later asked how we could have allowed Clarkson to meet with Madiba, but we followed due process and the matter was discussed with all Madiba's advisers and at the time, like in many other cases, what was presented on paper – and more specifically the opportunity to showcase the work of the Foundation to an international audience – appeared advantageous. It was not all about the money but about the promise of giving much needed exposure to the work of trying to preserve Nelson Mandela's legacy. And so you learn . . .

In 2010 South Africa hosted the FIFA World Cup. Madiba was only visiting the office occasionally. He was starting to show signs of his age. We were not surprised but the public was. He was more forgetful and sometimes he didn't feel like seeing people or getting up.

Other days he would not want to be isolated and he would ask to see people. Most days he wanted to spend time at home resting. Soon we were overwhelmed by artists, visitors, tourists and every head of state present in South Africa for the World Cup all wanting to pay a courtesy call on Madiba. It was impossible for him to grant all these appointments and we decided to close his diary in fear that he may be too exhausted by the time of the opening ceremony, which he was meant to attend.

And then there was FIFA. We joked that we felt invaded by this world body and I decided that FIFA was not a worldwide football organization but a country by itself. But they were particularly accommodating as far as the planning around Madiba's attendance at the opening ceremony. Generally people in South Africa felt that the World Cup cost the country too much money as we had to invest a lot on the infrastructure to deal with the number of visitors. The majority of people in South Africa still lived in poverty even though it was sixteen years since the ANC took power. Delivery of basic services was slow due to the frequent and diverse challenges faced by a developing country, and even while we were promised good returns on social responsibility projects from FIFA for hosting the World Cup soccer there was little proof of that at the time, or since.

I thought I enjoyed a generally good relationship with FIFA officials, regardless of friction sometimes over them wanting to overburden Madiba. I attended many meetings in preparation of the opening ceremony where all involved parties would be present. Afterwards I would put Madiba's needs to the executive and they changed and adapted plans to work for him. Of course they were desperate to have him appear and 'endorse' the opening of the tournament but I also wanted to believe that they honestly cared enough to really accommodate all his needs. I was extremely open to Danny Jordaan, who was the CEO of the Local Organizing Committee in South Africa, and FIFA executives about the need to avoid exploiting Madiba and about the difficulties involved in him attending a function like this in the middle of winter.

All presidents and deputy presidents in South Africa have a team of medical staff that move with them. This privilege was also extended to Madiba whenever we travelled abroad, even past his retirement from public office. As his age progressed the team became more prominent, and by the time he was ninety-two they accompanied us even to all local events. After one of the briefing meetings to prepare for the opening ceremony Jérôme Valcke, the CEO of FIFA, called me aside and told me that he had received a call from the Surgeon General, responsible for Madiba's health care. However, it wasn't the Surgeon General that had called but General Dabula, the Surgeon General's second-in-command and the person overseeing the medical care of all the former presidents. Until that point we mostly saw General Dabula whenever an important visitor came around to see Madiba.

Jérôme told me that he had received instructions from General Dabula that he (Dabula) was the only one to decide anything about Madiba's movements. His decision was that upon arrival Madiba would go to SAFA House, the office building close to the stadium which housed the South African Football Association. Madiba would be taken to a holding room in Chairman Irvin Khoza's office, and then when the time came for him to go onto the field he would be taken to a golf cart and driven about a kilometre to the entrance of the stadium.

To me, it just didn't make sense in practical terms. Why would you drive an elderly person – in mid-winter – that far in an open golf cart? It was two days before the opening match that Jérôme received these instructions. I could see that he was puzzled. I had been working with them for years prior to the World Cup and now he received a call from someone he had never spoken to or seen before just two days before it began. Luckily, the Head of the Presidential Protection Unit, Brigadier Dladla, was also present during the meeting that had just adjourned. I called him and asked Jérôme to repeat the story, which he did. Brigadier Dladla would have none of it. Security had always decided on the means of transport and Madiba's movements, in accordance to the programme we developed.

I was stunned by this interference and the odd logic of their choices. Luckily, the matter was put to rest after Brigadier Dladla called General Dabula. But it was evident that there was a battle over authority. The medical staff under General Dabula felt, now, that they were the ultimate authority, while the security staff under Brigadier Dladla viewed themselves equally. Madiba's office had a long working relationship with his security teams and a respect and deep sense of understanding for our respective fields of expertise. It felt as though there was an attempt to undermine the authority of the Foundation and Madiba's office: the older he became and the less able to express his own wishes, the more people were going to move in and get him to do what they wanted him to do, serving their interests rather than his, although they might have seen these as the interests of the country. I was caught in the middle and I found it hard.

Sadly on the evening of the opening concert of the FIFA World Cup, prior to the day of the official opening of the tournament, Madiba's beloved great-granddaughter Zenani was tragically killed in a car accident. I woke up the next morning to a message from the Presidency asking whether the rumours were true. I checked and indeed it was the case. I was numbed with shock. Zenani was the sweetest, most loving child imaginable.

Hearing of Zenani Jnr's death I immediately assumed that Madiba would not be able to attend the opening ceremony. Yet I was receiving confusing reports. Mrs Machel had left the house to go and support the family and I couldn't reach her immediately. When she called she said that the family had met and decided Madiba should not go. Barely thirty minutes later I received a call from the household telling me that Madiba was definitely going. When I asked how this had come about I was told that some of the staff at the house went to convince Madiba to make a short appearance. I called again to check who was at the house and it seemed that between the medical staff and security they had convinced Madiba that the world was waiting to see him. Indeed the

world was and they were playing the guilt card, but they were looking for a way to go to the opening ceremony themselves and by
convincing Madiba to go, they would get in clearly at the expense of
him and his family during such a challenging time for them. I was
spitting fire. I reported this to Mrs Machel again and when she arrived
home she resolved the issue. Until minutes before the opening ceremony people were trying to change plans to get Madiba to go.

It was becoming clear that the struggle for authority over what
Madiba got to do and what he didn't was going to be a tough battle.
Madiba didn't go but appropriately attended a vigil with the family.
The battle for authority was exhausting. The medical staff clearly
had the desire to assert their authority in Madiba's life. Those who
have served Madiba for years were steadily being sidelined. Little
did I know what lay ahead. At the time I felt for Madiba. I imagined
him feeling like an antelope hit by a vehicle, confused, being pushed
around by people and no longer being able to have a clear sense of
reason himself.

Despite this sad day for us all, the country exploded with excitement as the first match kicked off at Soccer City. Again South Africa
was a united nation. Sport brought us all together and after a successful opening match people dispelled fears of failure. There were
tourists everywhere and business was blooming. Flags of each
country hung everywhere and people draped their cars and houses
with the flag of the country they supported.

Zenani's funeral was the week after the opening game. Two
weeks later, while I attended a match with the Clintons, my grandmother also sadly passed away. I had two sad funerals during the
World Cup and it left me with mixed emotions; I found it difficult to
be swept away by the national celebrations. Mrs Machel and Josina
attended my grandmother's funeral in Pretoria. My family was
extremely touched and grateful. Never ever had I expected that they
would take the time and make the effort to drive that far to support
me or my family. She was the last of my grandparents and regardless of the fact that I felt a bit bitter about her putting my mother
through the trauma of having to go into an orphanage, I was

nevertheless very, very sad about her passing. My wonderful mother didn't have grudges and was very close to my grandmother. She was with Grandma right to the end.

Mrs Machel comes through at the most surprising times and she has a motherly instinct to know when one needs her support. It made me think about support for her. Madiba was getting older and it was becoming difficult for her too, to see her husband ageing. She is not a machine and she needs support as well. She has been there for me at times when I was heartbroken about boyfriends that left me, or when life was simply getting too much. More so than any other person.

Madiba's entire being was based on respect. Respect for your friends, respect for the enemy, for those poorer than you, those worse dressed and those less educated, and even those who harmed you or those who made mistakes. But also for those more powerful, those wealthier and smarter than you. There was not one day that I felt that Madiba disrespected me because I was a lesser person than him, knew less, earned less, knew so little about life and sometimes, yes, well, was so stupid. Not one day. Not *one* occasion. Mrs Machel is the one person who made Madiba truly happy and just for that she deserved respect if there was ever any doubt that she earned or demanded it. She deserved it.

In May I decided that I had to do something for Mandela Day. After toying with an idea with a colleague, Sello Hatang, I decided to organize a ride with a group of motorbike riders. The idea would be for a representative group to ride between Johannesburg and Cape Town (approximately 1,400 km) to advocate for Mandela Day. Along the way we would stop at charity projects where we could offer sixty-seven minutes to support the charity. Mandela Day is an ethos we can all subscribe to in honour of Madiba. It is a day of service and Madiba, having spent sixty-seven years fighting social injustice, asks only sixty-seven minutes of your time. The idea was also to demonstrate to people that if we all do just that, we can change the world for the better.

Between the pressures of the World Cup I was also looking after business people who visited South Africa for the tournament as well as organizing the bike trip. I had started a business the year before specifically catering for VIPs' logistical needs whenever they travelled to South Africa. My role at the office was slowly diminishing and I had to keep busy, which made me decide to start the business. During the World Cup I took on a few such high profile clients and my time and energy was thinly spread amongst all my responsibilities.

The day after the tournament ended, our bike trip departed from the Foundation in the cold of mid-winter. It was enjoyable and a great success, and seeing that Morgan Freeman and his business associate Lori McCreary were in South Africa for the World Cup, they too accompanied us on the bike trip. The trip was successful and we got coverage for Mandela Day countrywide, and on international networks worldwide. And, most importantly, we touched thousands of lives. It is something I hoped to continue into the future. The entire group felt good at the end of the ride. We felt like we really made a difference to people's lives.

On the Thursday before the final of the tournament, Madiba indicated that he definitely wanted to attend the closing match or at least make an appearance, as he'd been unable to attend the opening match due to the death of Zenani Jnr. I informed all parties about his wishes. We had to put all mechanisms in place again for an appearance.

On the Sunday of the closing match we finally had all arrangements in place for Madiba to go onto the pitch at the closing ceremony to at least wave to the crowd. He was excited but it was winter and we knew to make his appearance as short as possible. Upon our arrival at the stadium, General Dabula and the entire Defence Force top brass were there waiting for Madiba. I couldn't see why as they were all line managers and were not going to deal with any situation, if anything happened, themselves. While the security team had prepared a particular golf cart for Madiba the medical team had prepared another. The power struggle started. General Dabula insisted that he accompany Madiba on the golf cart to take the 50-metre drive onto the pitch. The security didn't agree but kept quiet. That arrangement would also mean that there wouldn't be space on the golf cart for Mrs Machel. I wouldn't hear of this and a huge altercation broke out. All the staff were young and fit enough to walk next to the golf cart, if there was any need for them to. In any event, if anything ever happened to a VIP in public you would not deal with the matter there but would rather take him/her to a safe place. Why would Mrs Machel's seat need to be compromised for medical staff? They would have to shoot me to give in on that one. There was just no common sense in this proposal at all. By the time Madiba arrived it had still not been resolved.

The security and I insisted and I could sense the resentment from General Dabula. He wanted to have a final say but we would not make Madiba's life practically difficult to give in to his ways. As Madiba's name was announced the golf cart drove onto the pitch. Of course the cart was surrounded by security and a horde of medical staff. Even the top brass of the Defence Force medical fraternity. I stayed in the tunnel and witnessed the circus from a distance. The noise the crowd made became deafening when they noticed Madiba. He smiled and waved. He had his furry Russian hat on and was dressed in his favourite warm coat, scarf and gloves. Mum sat next to him and they both waved at the crowd. Madiba was happy. It was a befitting ending to his career in public. It was indeed the last time he ever appeared formally at a public event.

Towards the end of 2010 Madiba returned to Shambala to allow his household staff time off. Since Madiba no longer travelled and seldom went anywhere the staff at home were working round the clock. They were stretched to their limits and seriously needed a break. From Shambala they went to Qunu for family Christmas and I spent Christmas with my family.

When I arrived in Cape Town in late December 2010 to be with Madiba and Mum over New Year, I was deeply concerned when I saw Madiba again. He had lost weight since I saw him two weeks before and he was extremely uncomfortable and edgy. When I left for the holiday he had great difficulty walking. I did, as usual, express concern about my boss to the medical staff and they just said to me, 'Madiba is fine.' It was clearly none of my business how my boss was doing.

Mrs Machel was concerned too but it was becoming clear that medical staff were now acting on instructions from certain Mandela family members and that introduced different priorities to those Mrs Machel felt were important for her husband. Sky News later reported that Madiba had bedsores. The Cape Town medics who acted independently were concerned and stressed.

Rodney, a paramedic in Cape Town, and I decided to go and do some shopping to buy medical equipment to make him more comfortable. The nurses and medical staff who accompanied him from Pretoria seemed uninterested in his condition and discomfort. The secretary, so often blamed for inefficiency, was now in cahoots with the Cape Town medics to investigate every possible way to attend to Madiba's medical needs. The mere fact that I am not in a mental institution right now remains a wonder to me. Situations like these made me feel like I was going insane.

My first question was, if his care was in the hands of the government, why didn't they provide these basics? Surely when a person becomes elderly his needs change and it was common sense that one had to continuously adapt the situation to make him as comfortable as possible. I once read in Madiba's *Conversations With Myself* what he had said during a conversation with editor Richard Stengel: 'I moved in circles where common sense and practical experience were important, and where high academic qualifications were not necessarily decisive.' And yes, indeed, I have come to precisely that realization. There were certain instances where the common sense my dad had taught me became more decisive than my lack of degrees and academic qualification.

As days progressed things were deteriorating fast. The situation was reported to those in charge of Madiba's care in Pretoria, General Dabula and Surgeon General Ramlakan. It was clear that Madiba needed a specialist to examine his knee.

In the meantime we realized that Madiba would not be able to return to Johannesburg on 11 January as was originally planned. He had great difficulty walking and we acquired a wheelchair to move him. It would not fit into the current elevator in the Johannesburg residence and it was necessary to replace the elevator with a larger model. That meant that the company installing it would have to enlarge the shaft for the bigger machine. Meme Kgagare, Madiba's Household Manager, and I contacted the company responsible for the installation of the original elevator and made arrangements for them to start work as soon as possible. Meme would keep us posted every day on the progress made in rebuilding the shaft. This would take time and we therefore needed to remain in Cape Town a little longer than expected. By then we were looking at a week's extension of our stay in Cape Town. The odd visitor came to see Madiba but as for the rest of the time an uncomfortable silence descended on the house.

On Wednesday, 13 January 2011, a specialist in orthopaedic surgery at 2 Military Hospital was ordered to come and examine Madiba. He entered the living room while Prof. Gerwel and I were with Madiba. He examined Madiba's knee and Madiba protested from the pain. The doctor requested the medics to take Madiba to the bedroom for a proper examination. He looked shocked when he appeared from the room. He said to us that he would be in touch but that he was concerned that there may be underlying problems that could be the cause of the deterioration we witnessed in Madiba in the past few weeks.

Mrs Machel was in Mozambique on this particular day as she had to prepare her family for her son paying *labola* (paying the price to marry a woman in African tradition). Mrs Machel's family hardly ever depended on her for time and attention but these were among the few occasions that her own children needed her presence in Mozambique. By now, General Dabula was in Cape Town too. The doctor briefed him and expressed his shock over the general care of Mr Mandela as a patient. He appealed to us to admit Madiba to the local Military Hospital in Cape Town – immediately. I indicated that Mrs Machel would return that night and that it was not a decision I could take, and that we would have to wait for her unless they insisted that it was an emergency.

General Dabula said he was more concerned that Madiba was homesick. He suggested that we fly in one of the housekeepers from Johannesburg. I told him that household affairs and the way staff work rosters were determined were not medical matters nor my business, and that in my opinion Madiba had been homesick for almost two years. Anyone who spent enough time with Madiba knew that if he was in Johannesburg, he wanted to be in Qunu, if he was in Qunu he wanted to be in Johannesburg. If he was in Cape Town he wanted to be in Qunu or Johannesburg. It is just the way old people are. I advised that we leave household affairs to Mrs Machel and that he focus on the medical issues. I felt he was upset with me but I saw his actions as another symptom of disregard for Mrs Machel. There was always politics at the house, like there is in any working environment.

Mrs Machel arrived back late on the 14th but I had texted her to say that General Dabula and the specialist who had examined Madiba wanted to see her the next morning, and she agreed to meet at 11.00. By then I had learned that General Dabula had decided not to include the specialist who had examined Madiba but rather to bring in a third doctor, a physician by training. She had not seen Madiba before, yet she was asked to brief Mrs Machel despite never having examined the patient they were discussing.

After our gym session on Friday morning I walked Mrs Machel to her car. I told her that the specialist who had examined Madiba suspected some underlying problem which resulted in Madiba's rapid deterioration, and that they were going to suggest that Madiba be admitted to hospital that afternoon. I was increasingly becoming worried about her too. The constant stress of dealing with family politics put a strain on her and I feared that if she was caught by such a shock announcement that her husband had to be hospitalized she might end up having a stroke. We couldn't live without her being Mum and being there for Madiba. The doctors arrived at the house at 10.30, and after the discussion preparations were made and Madiba was taken to 2 Military Hospital to be admitted for a series of tests. More and more tests were done, including X-rays and scans.

I had often been told by some of the Mandela family members to stay out of Madiba's personal life, but I was extremely frustrated, as any layman could see that things were not being dealt with in the best possible way, and the constant need for the medical team to consider the internal family politics above the interest of the patient was clear. The doctors were also pertinently instructed by some of the Mandelas not to discuss any medical issues around Madiba with me. It was clear that me pointing out certain things was starting to irritate them.

Things went generally well in hospital but Madiba was uneasy as he had never liked hospitals. He didn't want to be there and he protested. On Saturday morning at about 6 a.m. I received a call from Madiba's long-serving loyal bodyguard and driver, Mike Maponya, who had been Madiba's driver since his release from prison. My heart came to a standstill. Mike didn't often call me and it was too early to receive an unimportant call from him. You expect the worst. Madiba wanted me to come to the hospital immediately. I still had to get dressed and make myself presentable and as a result I only arrived a little later. Madiba was furious at me. 'Zeldina, you, you of all people deserted me and left me here.' He had not spent a night in hospital in years and he detested it. Mike tried to diffuse the situation by telling Madiba that Mum was about to arrive at the hospital herself, as she was. I explained that the people were there to take care of him and to examine him to make sure he was OK but he wouldn't take any of it. Luckily Mrs Machel arrived soon and that calmed him down. It was difficult to see him as uneasy as that and I disappeared from the room as soon as I could find an opportunity. I couldn't bear seeing him not being well and so frustrated. The doctors were busy with him all the time and had several closed door discussions. I was relieved because I knew they were now paying full attention to him and he was in specialists' hands, which is all I really cared for.

General Dabula was nowhere to be seen and the GP on duty with Madiba was off sick with tonsillitis. It was of great concern to me that two of the key role players concerned with Madiba's health were absent. Mrs Machel informed Madiba's three daughters of their father's hospitalization and I informed Prof. Gerwel. I told Prof. that I was not alerting anyone at the Foundation as it was critical that we kept this under tight wraps or else we would be overwhelmed at the hospital by media and the public.

The Minister of Defence at the time, Lindiwe Sisulu, paid a visit to Madiba on Saturday night at hospital. She is the daughter of Madiba's late friends Walter and Albertina Sisulu and also a cousin of Makaziwe Mandela. In South Africa, the Ministry of Defence is responsible for the healthcare of heads of state and former heads of state. I wasn't there but Mrs Machel was and the Minister was also concerned about Madiba's well-being. Late on Saturday night rumours started doing the rounds in the media that Madiba had passed away. The government wanted to issue a statement to say that Madiba was admitted to the military hospital in Cape Town for tests, but I advised against disclosing his whereabouts to give him privacy. They wanted to stop rumours from running that he had passed on.

In the meantime the Foundation contacted me to ask whether there was any substance to the rumours of Madiba's passing. I said: 'Madiba is alive, but please speak to Prof. for any other info.' I didn't want to be the one to give out information as I knew what could happen and I was often blamed for leaks to the media. We had already suspected that our phones were being monitored as confidential discussions somehow appeared to leak for inexplicable reasons. In instances like these it is better for senior officials to discuss the process. A statement was subsequently issued that read that Madiba was on holiday with his wife and there was no substance to the rumours that he had passed on. I advised the Presidency that such a statement had been issued and they decided not to issue their statement.

On Sunday Madiba was discharged after all the specialists saw him for the last examination. We arrived home around 1 p.m. to find the GP who had been off work because of tonsillitis at Madiba's house in Cape Town. I wondered to myself, couldn't she have gone to the hospital that morning to receive discharge instructions from the specialists if she was now well enough to come to Madiba's house? But if she was sick, surely it was not the best thing to be around Madiba? Aren't old people – especially in a vulnerable state of health – more susceptible to infections?

On Monday and Tuesday Madiba was showing progress. The medication was obviously starting to work. On Thursday morning I was eager to hear from the Doctor on duty how Madiba was but I was told by medical and security staff that the Doctor was not at work. When I asked where she was I was told that she had gone shopping. For me, this was too to much. How could shopping be a priority three days after Nelson Mandela had been discharged from hospital if you are the doctor? I was stepping way out of line to think that I could question the doctor for not being at work and soon I was reported to the family.

Mrs Machel left for the traditional wedding of her son, Malenga, in Maputo. She was told Madiba was OK and it was safe for her to leave, although we agreed that we would be in constant contact with one another to update her on progress.

On Saturday Madiba's daughter Zenani was scheduled to arrive in Cape Town; Mrs Machel had asked her to come and be with her father while she attended the wedding in Mozambique. She arrived at the house around 10 a.m. and her father was not out of bed yet.

The specialists were going to see Madiba at 11.00. Zenani, Shirley the housekeeper and I ended up chatting in the kitchen and lost track of the time. Sometime after 11.00 I enquired about the specialists and was told that they could not come to the house by themselves but were awaiting orders, like in any military bureaucracy, to be fetched from the hospital and brought to the house. When I called them and asked whether they couldn't drive themselves, I was told they were not allowed. I thought to myself: What if there was an emergency? Do we wait for Pretoria to issue orders for specialists in Cape Town to be fetched from the hospital because they are not allowed to drive there themselves?

I was stressed and beyond anxious about Madiba's health and went to see Prof. Gerwel at his office in Cape Town to tell him that the situation was turning for the worse and that we needed intervention. Because of all the politics within the medical team and family there was no way that anyone could make all parties agree to something. Prof. was my point of call on anything and everything. Madiba hardly ever took decisions without consulting or sound-boarding it to Prof. Prof. was Madiba's point of balance in a way. He knew exactly how to find mutually acceptable ground between what Madiba wanted to be done and what had to be done. I was one of the few people who could always get hold of Prof. irrespective of the time of day or night. He was engaged on many fronts but he knew that we depended on him with our lives. He also knew that whenever an emergency occurred he would be my first port of call. He offered to speak to the Minister of Defence, and they arranged to meet on Monday after Mrs Machel had returned from Maputo.

On Sunday when Mrs Machel returned, Madiba's situation had deteriorated further. Madiba didn't want to lose sight of any of us and insisted that someone stay with him all the time. He was pale and weak. He was seriously ill. I was prepared to say goodbye but not without giving this fight my last shot to ensure that everything in our power was done to guarantee that he was in the best possible hands.

On Monday morning one of the specialists was dismissed because of disagreements over the best course of action with Madiba's care. Another specialist was flown from 1 Military Hospital in Pretoria to join the team. He examined Madiba and had some serious concerns. There was no way that we could fly home with Madiba in his current state. He advised that Madiba be taken to 2 Military Hospital again for a chest X-ray. I suspected that Madiba had pneumonia. Most deaths among old people are the result of septicaemia or pneumonia. In the meantime Mrs Machel, Minister Sisulu and Prof. Gerwel met and Mrs Machel provided details of the past weeks. Prof. Gerwel was as concerned as she and I about Madiba's health and care. Mrs Machel felt hopeless and undermined. Because I'd raised concerns and because the specialists were also all white, I felt that it also became a racial issue. There was no way out unless Prof., Mrs Machel and the Minister intervened.

The Minister explored the possibility of replacing the entire team, but Mrs Machel felt that they would (figuratively speaking) crucify her if she dared interfere with appointees endorsed by the family. It was clear to us all that, no matter who appointed who, Nelson Mandela was supposed to get expert attention and medical support. The Minister offered to put together an international team of specialists but Mrs Machel also guarded against something that could be seen as a vote of no confidence in our own medical practitioners in South Africa. She was right. We have some of the best medical specialists in the world.

By Tuesday the specialist from 1 Military Hospital had informed us that we would be going home on Wednesday. An ambulance plane was ordered from Pretoria to collect Madiba, equipped with emergency medical facilities to transport him home. I was informed by Maretha, my colleague who now dealt with logistics, that the plane could only accommodate four or five passengers due to the extra equipment on board, but that a second plane was chartered to transport the extra medical and security staff back to Pretoria.

On Tuesday morning I was sitting at the breakfast table with Mrs Machel and Ndaba, Madiba's grandson, who had arrived the previous day to look after his grandfather, when I briefed them both about the space in the plane so we could determine who got home on which plane. Ndaba said that he insisted that he be on the plane with Madiba as a family member had to be with him. Mrs Machel said that they would sort out spaces once they got to the plane in the morning, but that the doctors should get priority. I felt deeply hurt for her because what Ndaba was saying was that she was not family. It's not the big things that hurt me, but these mundane things. And then of course how it would have hurt Madiba if he'd heard how his wife was being treated. I had already made plans to fly commercially as I knew too well not to get in the way. Mrs Machel asked whether I didn't want to reconsider and fly with the back-up plane but I declined, saying that it was better that there was extra space for whoever wanted it and I needn't get in the way too.

I sat with Madiba at some point with my legs crossed and he touched my leg almost to feel whether I was really there. Tears shot to my eyes and I had to get up to not show him how upset I was. He was no longer conversing and one could see he was terribly weak. I didn't know why he was not hospitalized but was told that we were flying to Johannesburg the following day where there would be a full team of medical specialists that could attend to him.

On Wednesday morning I arrived early at the house. Madiba was at the breakfast table and being attended to. I had coffee and something to eat and then decided to make my way to the airport for my flight back home. I greeted, starting with Mrs Machel, and after greeting Madiba I quickly turned around and walked out so that no one could see that I was crying. I thought I had said my final goodbyes. He was coughing non-stop.

I was anxious at the airport and called the security to tell me once Madiba's plane was in the air. The decision and agreement with the doctors was that Madiba would be taken home once he arrived in Pretoria, upon which Dr Mike Plit, Madiba's private physician for over twenty years, would come and examine him. Madiba literally trusted Dr Plit with his life. Whenever Madiba didn't want to eat, a loss of appetite that occurs with age, we would tell him that Dr Plit insisted that he ate three meals a day. And Dr Plit did. He would then oblige. The thought of Dr Plit being in Johannesburg, waiting to care for him, was therefore a consolation if there could be any in such circumstances.

My plane was delayed and Madiba's took off before I could board my commercial flight. I was tired and emotional and kept my sunglasses on, like a proper wannabe celebrity, to disguise my red-wept eyes. Rumours about his health had quietened down in the public and media and I didn't want to fuel any speculation if anyone I knew came across me with my red eyes.

I had completely withdrawn from my friends and didn't want to see anyone. I didn't want them to sense how upset I was because they would figure out things themselves. They knew too well that my entire world revolved around Madiba and seeing him like that couldn't compare with the worst heartbreak I had ever suffered. I didn't respond to texts and/or calls from friends and just withheld myself from society completely. I was lonely too, as I couldn't share my stress and pain with anyone. I reported to Prof. Gerwel every day and kept him informed but apart from that I couldn't speak to anyone. No one told me but I knew what was best for me and the situation, and that was to withdraw completely.

Usually I find it very easy to sleep on planes or in anything that moves. I had mastered the art of a power nap. However on the flight back to Johannesburg I couldn't close an eye. I was wide awake and aware of everything that happened around me, even though I was exhausted. Upon landing in Johannesburg I didn't switch my phone on at first. I jumped on the Gautrain to make my way to Sandton where my brother would fetch me and take me home. I was anxious to not speak to anyone on the phone in public as I expected to hear the worst.

The first call I received once I arrived in Sandton was from our CEO Achmat. He asked whether I knew where Madiba was and I said that I hoped he was home already as they had left Cape Town before me. He then said they had received calls that Madiba had been taken to Millpark Hospital, a private hospital on the outskirts of Johannesburg. I called the security and they told me that they were arriving at Millpark. I called Achmat back and confirmed what the security had told me. By the time we spoke, a statement had already been issued by the foundation in consultation with the family stating that Madiba had been taken to Millpark for routine tests. I reported this to Prof. Gerwel and raised my concern over the statement being issued. I worried about referring to routine tests.

I went home and was glad to see my dogs and to be with my brother and my long-serving colleague and rock Maretha. I left a little later to go to the hospital. When I arrived doctors were busy with Madiba and I could only see him through a sliding door. I waved at him and he waved back and somehow I knew that he was OK, even though he still looked very weak. He had pneumonia, or respiratory infection as they described it, in addition to the bedsores and inflammation in his knee. All these combined were toxic to his body.

Another two days passed with on and off visits at the hospital. By the second day we discovered a secret route in and out of the hospital so that the media couldn't use me as a 'barometer', as the family put it, for Madiba's well-being. The media started watching my every move, and I appeared in the newspaper with Josina laughing over something stupid between us and it was interpreted that 'Madiba was fine' because we laughed. By Friday afternoon he was going to be discharged and he was already showing improvement. In the meantime I was supporting the housekeeping staff to get the house ready for Madiba to return. A huge press conference followed at the hospital, during which time Madiba was taken home. The security cleverly created this decoy and by the time the media thought Madiba was about to leave, he was safely at home already.

On the Saturday after his discharge a story was being prepared for the Sunday papers that there was tension between the Foundation and family and that government had to intervene, and that was, according to speculation, the reason why no one issued a statement following Madiba's hospitalization after the first statement by the Foundation. That was not the case. There had always been tension between Madiba's staff and certain factions of the family but it was not worsened by the situation. Nor would it be correct to say 'the family', implying the entire family.

As Madiba became weaker over the years, certain family members saw the opportunity to tell his Foundation and staff what they thought we had to do and how we had to do it. If Madiba was strong enough he wouldn't allow it. He guided his staff and guarded us against many things over the years and his weakness presented an opportunity for some family members to step in and start controlling matters to their advantage.

Soon Madiba was much better, but it was taking time for him to recover completely. During his prolonged illness we were running into problems paying accounts and keeping the households running. As no one held signatory over any of Madiba's accounts, an alternative arrangement had to be made. A family feud ensued while trying to make arrangements.

The fight over who controlled Madiba's money continued and got messier as time progressed.

Over the years the bank had always called me to verify transactions on Madiba's account. Because he was a high-profile person and they couldn't speak to him directly, they called me whenever there was a deposit, withdrawal or transfer being made to merely verify the movement in his account and that it was really him requesting the activity. The bank required, with the new power of attorney which now placed Mrs Machel and two of the Mandela daughters in control, a letter to be signed from Madiba that they could still call me to verify such transactions. I prepared all the documents and delivered them to Mrs Machel before I left for New York, where I was scheduled to travel to speak to the Clinton Foundation about another fundraiser for the Nelson Mandela Foundation, and to Tribeca about a joint venture on Mandela Day. I had never been a signatory on any of Madiba's accounts but was merely responsible for the administration, Mrs Machel didn't want to take control. I hated these calls from the bank to verify any movement in his account as it was just an irritation. The Foundation appointed a bookkeeper years ago to isolate me from having any powers over any of his moneys. I preferred it that way. Perhaps we subconsciously knew what awaited us all.

While I was in New York Makaziwe came to the office early on the Monday morning looking for me. She couldn't find me and asked Achmat where I was. He told her that I was in New York and she asked who had given me permission to travel. Achmat as CEO said he had and that I was there on official business for the Foundation. She then asked why it was necessary for a secretary to travel to New York and I don't know what he responded. She questioned why a secretary had to verify transactions when they, the Mandelas, signed documents on Madiba's account. I have learned to know that sometimes it's better to not raise your opinion about something, as the situation speaks for itself.

By now Mrs Machel had lost all her privacy in her own house. One appreciated that Madiba needed round-the-clock medical care but her privacy was just never a consideration. Imagine living in your own house where you couldn't walk from your bedroom to your kitchen with a dressing gown on. Where you can never leave your room without being properly dressed as there are always strangers in your house. Never letting your guard down, and eyes and ears to every move you make.

Another of the great lessons that I learned from both Madiba and Prof. Gerwel is that you sometimes have to allow things to happen and simply be a spectator. Bitterness will make you sick. During his imprisonment they were forced to work in the limestone quarry. Chipping away for no reason. Bitterness is the same. You reduce your own character with such a mindless exercise of cultivating bitterness. You have to allow for things to play out the way they are intended to. Not every situation can be changed by us.

I often during my career wanted to respond to things immediately, but over time and with age I have learned that you must just allow things to take their course. Watching Madiba over the years hiding his disbelief in people, he in a way sometimes, in my opinion, allowed them to create their own fortune or misfortune. Patience is everything.

12

Saying Goodbye

A few months after his first long hospitalization, it was decided to move Madiba to Qunu. He often asked about people he grew up with or deceased family members. Qunu is a remote area in the Eastern Cape and since it is the place where Madiba got sick the previous December, we met the instruction with scepticism. At home in Johannesburg he was close to medical attention, close friends popped in from time to time and some family occasionally visited. One could call on people like Ahmed Kathrada and George Bizos to pop in to visit him but in Qunu that would be difficult. We didn't know what to expect in Qunu. The family insisted and there was no way that Mrs Machel could object. Madiba was emotionally stable wherever she was, whether that was in Qunu or Johannesburg.

I started travelling to Qunu weekly, through the support of the Nelson Mandela Foundation, or every second week at least. Madiba stopped being talkative but he wanted company. Hardly anyone visited him and Mrs Machel was the only one apart from the medical staff and household staff that he had around him. Qunu is remote and it was difficult to travel there. One had to set an entire day aside to travel there and back and it would mean getting up at 3 a.m. and arriving back home at 8 p.m. if you only went for the day. It was probably not easy for everyone to travel there but Qunu became quiet and isolated.

It was announced at the Foundation that the organization was about to restructure to focus more on its core work. I understood and supported the fact that the Foundation had to become a Centre of

Memory, similar to a Presidential Library, to preserve his legacy. Madiba supported the setting up of a Centre of Memory, and the conversion of the Foundation in to a non-governmental organization specializing in memory and dialogue work. He launched the project in 2004, and during the years thereafter made donations of private papers, gifts and awards to the Nelson Mandela Foundation for the Centre's permanent archival collections. However I didn't agree that Madiba's office had to be closed. While Madiba was alive people wanted to remain connected with him even though it was not personally possible for him to reciprocate. His friends and associates, people who all had relationships with him, wanted to feel acknowledged. By closing Madiba's office that would become impossible. But it was expected that we should close his office and transfer relationships to people who did not have the institutional memory our office had. It was envisaged that his friends would be treated as part of the process which I felt would lack acknowledging their respective individual relationships.

Prof. Gerwel and Mrs Machel protested and said that Madiba deserved to have an office and a Personal Assistant to the day he died. Prof. Gerwel, who was Chairman of the Foundation, said that Madiba handpicked me and that he would refuse to sign off on me being made completely redundant when Madiba made that choice when he was in a position to choose the people around him. Madiba's office was closed and we were all made redundant, although I was reinstated on a part-time basis. But I was undermined and sidelined to such an extent that my position really became a ceremonial job. Both Maretha and Thoko, the other two staff members, with equally long service histories with Madiba, were told to go. I had luckily never been in it for the money, and I had been rewarded in ways money can never buy, and decided that I would remain committed to Madiba and Mrs Machel even if I was not paid anything. Loyalty and dedication can't be bought or paid to go away. I had also made a promise to myself and to him that I would never desert him until indeed the last day.

*

By the start of 2012 Madiba was permanently living in Qunu. I would travel there every week for a day or two to spend time with him. On 28 February 2012 I worked my last day as a full-time employee for Nelson Mandela. I didn't expect the next day to be any different but it was. I suddenly felt empty and without purpose. I know Madiba wouldn't have allowed it, but he was no longer making decisions or able to voice his wishes. In fact, he seemed to be slowly distancing himself from us. He was visibly old, needed permanent care and was no longer the jovial man we knew.

I was informed by the Foundation's CEO that my rank had to be changed from Executive Personal Assistant to Personal Assistant. In eighteen years I had gone from Typist to Assistant Private Secretary to Private Secretary to Manager and Spokesperson for his office and now finally back to Personal Assistant. It was actually laughable that love, care, loyalty and trust could take you on that roller-coaster ride.

I never had any aspirations to become anything other than whatever served his best interests, and I was not fazed by these latest attempts to marginalize me. You see, if Nelson Mandela believes in you, handpicks you and defends you until he is no longer able to do so, despite even criticism from the party that moulded him, little else should distract you in life. I never used these events to defend myself but allowed things to happen as they were probably supposed to happen. I never referred to the fact that I was chosen as I thought that it could be interpreted that I am conceited, but I always believed that there would come a time when I had to defend myself and on that day I would rationally think differently about things.

It is, I believe, one of the least attractive characteristics of us Afrikaners: we are brought up believing that we deserve nothing, we are nothing and we can accomplish nothing. Well, those who have achieved did so sterlingly and managed to raise themselves beyond these mental limitations. I really had to work hard at accepting the fact that I was chosen by Madiba to be anything. The upside is that you never ponder about these things and that probably prevents you from becoming absorbed with self-importance. I am the first to admit that I am nothing, was nothing, without Madiba gracing and blessing my life.

The poison within the family was leaking out everywhere. Many of his family had never wanted me around, and they were now getting their chance. But I still refused to abandon him. They didn't want me to fly down to Qunu every week to see him and I heard them asking our CEO 'What does she do there?' Even if I had to find a sponsor to fly me to Qunu every week for me to see him, I was willing to look for that. It was just Mrs Machel, household and medical staff there. He was lonely. President Zuma passed through from time to time and so did a few very close friends who went through the trouble to make the tedious trip to Qunu, but more and more he became isolated from the rest of the world. Whenever someone important visited, there would, however, be a sudden influx of interested parties. And from time to time we called on people like Ahmed Kathrada and other old friends to visit for the day, and one could see how they lifted his spirit whenever they came around.

Madiba always appeared very happy to see me. There was very little conversation but whenever Mrs Machel was around he enjoyed watching us converse and exchanging stories. He needed life around him. He needed people to touch him, care for him and create a sense of normality around him, so that he would not feel left behind. Some days the totality of our conversation would be: 'Oh Zeldina, you are here. How are your parents?' and I would tease him and say, 'Are you not going to ask how I am, Khulu?' and his shoulders would shrug with laughter. He would drowse off and wake up only to reach out to your hand. He did so with most visitors.

It was decided that the house in Qunu needed refurbishment and Madiba returned to Johannesburg for a while. Weeks quickly passed and it was easier to visit him more often. On a particular Friday afternoon Mrs Machel and I spoke about the son of Queen Beatrix of the Netherlands who had been seriously injured after a skiing accident. Mrs Machel tried to reach the Dutch royal family to convey our support. We had been close to them and therefore felt personally affected by the news.

That Friday night I went to bed thinking of the family in suffering. I sometimes put my phone on silent when I go to bed and the next morning I slept in for a little while. When I woke and picked up my phone I noticed that something was wrong. I had seven missed calls and sixteen messages. We were no longer working and there was no reason for the amount of communication in normal circumstances. The first message I opened was from Robyn Curnow, a journalist friend: 'Madiba is in hospital.' I responded: 'What, are you serious, how do you know?' She then told me it had been all over the news. I traced things back and discovered that indeed he was in hospital. I knew nothing. No one had told me. I contacted Josina and she confirmed it. She didn't know any details either. I then texted Mrs Machel to ask whether they were OK. I told her not to give me any detail of where or when but simply to tell me whether they were OK, as I didn't want to be blamed if it leaked. She gave me a brief overview about what was happening.

I don't know of any person alive who has been treated with the amount of disrespect that people have shown towards Mrs Machel. Politics within the family about his funeral took place for years before his death. In April 2005 the first article about funeral arrangements and a special committee dealing with such eventualities appeared in the *Noseweek* magazine. Mrs Machel and some of the children had refused to be party to arrangements about Madiba's funeral. He was still in fairly good health and it was unthinkable to be planning someone's funeral while the person was still happily alive, still being cared for by his wife. It is only much later in 2013 when the Minister of Defence Nosiviwe Nqakula empathetically reeled Mrs Machel in that she was consulted about certain arrangements and briefed about what had been planned. I do know that Mrs Machel had to put up a fight to get my name added to the funeral list. I made a promise to *him* though. I was going to be there right to the end, even if it meant I had to stand at a fence outside his farm in Qunu when they laid him to rest. Unbeknown to me, that would be close to the truth.

It is true what Madiba referred to sometimes . . . to test a man's character, give him power. Once people have power they will always reveal themselves.

Every time Madiba was admitted to hospital we held our breath. I knew by now that I had to seclude myself when he was hospital-ized. I became a hermit at such times, not speaking to anyone, not answering my phone or even having conversations with my parents. I would not speak to anyone but Prof. Gerwel, Mrs Machel and Josina. They understood that if I was ever seen to break trust or leak information, I would simply be refused access to Madiba for the rest of my life because then the family would have reason to get rid of me. I was not going to give them that pleasure and I kept my dis-tance and relied on updates from Mrs Machel. I was also becoming worried about her. She had a huge burden to deal with. The family was as divided as ever while she was worried sick about her hus-band's wellbeing.

At work pressure finally subsided from the public and apart from a few people who could not comprehend that Madiba would ever stop being actively involved, correspondence and requests became less. There was always that one request or proposal that someone thought had to be the exception to the rule and people would find reasons beyond logic why Nelson Mandela was the only one to sup-port their ventures, or at least lend his association to endorse their efforts. I had realized over the years that if you continuously do negative things in your job, like saying no to people, it inevitably has a very negative impact on your psyche. You tend to become cynical by nature and it takes constant effort to pull yourself back from that negativity. With fewer requests and the negativity that came with them it was easier to find balance in life. I was opening myself to the next phase of my life.

People often ask me whether I don't regret not getting married or having children. It would be selfish and extremely ungrateful to use 'regret' when describing my life. I gained so much being with Madiba but I suppose I gave him my youth, and perhaps I gave him my future too. But I will never blame him for it – ultimately, I made that choice. Was it sacrifice? Or not? I don't feel burdened or sad that I might have lost oppportunities. I gained so much. I gained myself. I am completely content with the life that I have.

My part-time status and compromised income meant that I had to generate a salary and find something to challenge me again. I still had limited responsibility to Madiba and was adamant that I was not going to take another full-time job unless I was financially forced to do so. I was determined that I wanted to remain available to Madiba and Mrs Machel whenever they needed me, and I needed to make myself useful, but it was impossible and illogical to think that you could find another part-time job and be available to some-one else when there was a need for it.

It is the weirdest experience though. From being on a constant adrenalin rush for about eighteen years to a complete shutdown of that adrenalin overnight is not a joke. One needs to find purpose. It was hard. Certain factions within the family still wanted me out. On the first day of the 'rest of my life', 1 March 2012, I had a tattoo engraved around my left pulse to be reminded what I had discovered about myself along this journey. 'Pursue your passion.' As long as I did that, I knew I would be happy for the rest of my life. My passion is to serve and I find fulfilment when I serve people. I had the words tattooed in French because I also wanted to remind myself for the rest of my life about what Madiba had said: 'Find your roots', and since my family is of French descent I wanted the words in French.

The first few months of my new life were difficult. I still went to the office from time to time to do some administration and then went to see Madiba occasionally. It was announced that he would return to Qunu once they had renovated the house there. So soon I was back in my routine of travelling to Qunu weekly or every second week. Sometimes Madiba was talkative, sometimes he wasn't. Sometimes Mrs Machel and I would debate for the entire day about whatever was happening in the world and South Africa, the politics in the ANC, and world events like the Arab Spring and developments in other African countries, and occasionally Madiba would just smile at us with approval of the liveliness around him. We would sit in the lounge and converse, with Madiba suddenly pointing out to me that my handbag was on the floor and that I needed to pick it up. He was always there and totally aware of things happening around him. Sometimes I would call Prof. for Madiba just to say hello to him over the telephone. It always lit up Madiba's face whenever he heard Prof.'s voice. 'Oh Jakes,' he would say. 'I am happy to speak to you.' While sitting with him Madiba often drifted off into a nap in his favourite chair but then would suddenly wake up to check that we were still there. And once one thinks your privileges come to an end, there's sometimes even more. I had the most precious and valuable times there with them then.

Whenever Mum wasn't there, he would repeatedly ask: 'Where is Mum? When is she returning?' and then you had to recite the day of the week and exactly when she would be back. Mrs Machel and I would sometimes pass each other in mid-air – she would be off to Johannesburg for the day and I would visit Qunu – and by the end of the day it felt like Madiba asked one about two hundred times: 'Where is Mum?' He was totally reliant on her presence and unsettled whenever she was not around.

People were busy and hardly anyone visited. It was really a schlep to get there, in addition to the fact that Madiba didn't feel like seeing people every day so it was not always easy to invite even his closest friends for social visits. We stopped scheduling visits by people who weren't very familiar to him, but of course later realized that whenever we were not there occasionally some of the family would take advantage of our absence and take strangers to see Madiba. The Foundation then had to defend Madiba again when photos or reports of such visits appeared in the media. People would say: 'But if so and so got to see him, why can't I?' and the battles would start all over again, with us trying to diplomatically tell them that we didn't approve of the visits as we had been instructed that visitors would not be allowed any longer. On some occasions the Foundation declined a particular request for him to endorse or sign something, or even see certain people, and then would learn afterwards that the request had been agreed by someone in the family and they had allowed whatever to happen when Mrs Machel or I wasn't there. Some people started to take advantage of this when they realized that he no longer had the ability to argue or stand by his principles. Business people would call us to ask about strange requests they'd received from Madiba personally.

Madiba no longer really talked a lot so it was awkward to take people to him who didn't know him. There would be uncomfortable silences during visits.

By now I had moved from the neighbourhood I had so loved in Johannesburg because I could simply not afford to live there any longer. I was now staying on the outskirts of Johannesburg, which made travelling to and from the city a daily challenge. I wasn't bound to office hours but I had to watch my finances. I also started missing the friends and closeness I shared with people from my neighbourhood and I had to stop myself getting depressed. I felt neglected by the Foundation and removed from my friends and I realized that I had not built a steady support structure for myself over the years. Generally people were also getting on with their lives and I really had to struggle to find my feet again and pull myself together. I also lacked the courage to share my fears with many of my friends, probably also because I knew people perceived me to be a strong person and I had to keep up appearances. I also missed politics and having inside information about everything that happened in our country.

Prof. Gerwel hadn't seen or spent time with Madiba in many months and we decided that we had to make a special trip for him to go and visit Madiba. In August 2012 Prof. and I agreed on a date and I met him in East London, from where I drove him the 260 km to Qunu to see Madiba. We had a very special day and both Madiba and Prof. enjoyed seeing each other. They had a few good laughs and when I left to take Prof. back to East London that afternoon it crossed my mind that this was really an exceptionally enjoyable day for Madiba.

I loved Prof. but I think Madiba loved him even more. Mrs Machel also hardly ever saw Prof. and enjoyed spending time with him. We left agreeing that Prof. would start writing about Madiba's Presidency. Prof. and I drove back to East London and laughed about the years in the Presidency, the many things that had happened, the stressful times, and we both agreed that if we had known what lay ahead we would probably have made different choices when we were not so emotionally attached to Madiba. The three hours back to East London took us on a journey through memories of eighteen years, and when we said our goodbyes at the airport I knew Prof. was happy and pleased about the day he had spent with Madiba. He sent a text message later that evening when he got home, thanking me that I'd insisted he made time in his busy schedule to be with Madiba. He was engaged on so many fronts, served on countless boards and was involved in so many things but I was happy that I forced him to take a day out to travel so far to see Madiba.

When a few months later I received the news that Prof. had died, I was sleeping in my bed in the Holiday Inn in Umtata, about 40 km away from Qunu. When Madiba was told by Mum of Prof.'s passing the sadness and sense of loss was visible in his eyes and he went completely quiet for hours. It is difficult to tell how a person of that age will react to such news and Mrs Machel had to ensure that her timing was impeccable so as to soften the blow of such a shock. She was scheduled to travel to Johannesburg for the day but subsequently cancelled her travels to be with Madiba, uncertain how he would digest such shock and sadness.

It is difficult to try and put value to Prof. Gerwel's role in the previous eighteen years of our lives. Take whatever you believe anyone could mean to you and multiply it by 100. That's more or less it. Prof. had a way of dealing with things in the most unconventional ways. When we all tended to grapple with a particular issue he would be the one to come up with the most balanced solution that would make everyone feel that they were winners, even though they were actually compromising in a way, as Koos Bekker, the CEO of Naspers, put it at his funeral. He was definitely not a push-over and people easily respected him. He would watch things silently from a distance and then make one pronouncement to steer the issue in a totally new direction and thereby assist you to come up with your own solutions. He listened to every word I ever said to him, no matter how mundane or how much complaining I did, and if I was wrong he was the one person to honestly and openly but respectfully point it out to me.

During Madiba's Presidency Prof. used to travel with us a lot and he was very involved in our everyday lives. After retirement from government that involvement diminished but Prof. was always just a phone call away. I could call him from anywhere in the world to ask his advice on any matter. And he would be my first point of contact whether it was a major incident or something really stupid or funny that happened. We gossiped and joked, but then when it came to serious matters he was a leading father-figure to me. He loved his Afrikaans and we would have very open, honest conversations and, in joking, then sometimes use very expressive Afrikaans sayings that made us both laugh. He was a person who related to anyone in any situation and he role-played perfectly. He could guide a conversation with a foreign head of state and the next minute address the most junior office staff and make them feel like their interaction was more enjoyable than that of the more important people.

On the day of Prof.'s memorial, Chief Justice Arthur Chaskalson also passed away. He was appointed by Madiba as the head of the Constitutional Court in South Africa, the most senior judicial position in the country. Minutes before we entered the memorial, I received a message from the Judge's son to tell me his dad had died. One of our favourite ministers, Trevor Manuel, was presiding as programme director during Prof.'s memorial and I told him about the Judge's passing. So before proceedings started we also observed a minute of silence for Judge Chaskalson. Two key figures in our lives that passed on in one week. It was too much to bear. I was heartbroken: the one person I expected to be by our side right to the end was Prof. I was also angry, in a way, that he wouldn't be there the day we buried Madiba. But such is life. Whenever Madiba spoke about mortality or people started discussing his, I realized that any of us could go before him. And Prof. leaving us was proof of it.

A few months before, the security personnel with Madiba, Mrs Machel and some household staff noticed that two new people had joined the medical team looking after Madiba. Mum, security, some of the household staff and I wondered if they could possibly be intelligence agents. The permanent medical team looking after Madiba didn't know them either. I sent a message to President Zuma's office to ask whether they were aware of this arrangement. I received a response that they would look into the matter and get back to me. I heard nothing. So I sent another message, this time adding 'this situation could potentially cause a huge embarrassment to government as this is clearly infringing on Madiba and his family's privacy and dignity.'

I immediately received a response that the matter was reported to the Minister of Intelligence and that I could expect a response from him soon. And so I did. Minister Siyabonga Cwele called me minutes later to enquire about the situation and again about an hour later informing me that the staff did not belong to National Intelligence but that he would still discuss the matter with the Surgeon General to assess whether the military approved of such placement. I repeated to the Minister what I said in the text to the Presidency. I never heard from the Minister again, but three weeks later these two characters disappeared and then reappeared a few weeks later despite our enquiry. We could never figure out their mission. I was disgusted at how I understood state resources were being used and there is little else that angered me as much. Influences were at play that allowed people to abuse state resources for their own benefit. We had a terrible problem with corruption within government – probably the biggest threat to our democracy – and this was a clear example of a corrupt government that allows this kind of interference in their business.

Kgalema Motlanthe was our Deputy President at the time. His relationship with Madiba dated back many years in the ANC. Madiba was very fond of Kgalema and he hadn't seen him for some time. A visit was arranged to Qunu on Friday, 7 December. On Thursday I was made aware of Kgalema's intention to visit. I was happy to hear that but had no intention myself to get onto another plane that week. Then suddenly Kgalema's office called to say that the visit was cancelled from our side. Meme, the housekeeper, told me that Madiba was not having a good day but in order to control wild speculation she had asked the Deputy President's office to cancel the visit from their side. But now the Deputy President wanted to know from me what the reason was for cancelling the visit. The ANC's national conference was planned to start in a week from that day. We all had our suspicions whether there was any political interference about the cancellation of his visit. I called back to say that it was really just that Madiba was not having a good day. It was an awkward situation. Yet, by now, we were used to Madiba just not feeling up to seeing people on some days and he would prefer to stay in bed. We really assumed it was one of those days.

On Saturday, 8 December I was in a radio studio when Achmat Dangor called. By now I had agreed to co-present a Saturday lifestyle show on a local radio station. I couldn't take the call and called him back as soon as the show ended. He said that there was speculation about Madiba's health and that the Sunday papers were trying to put a reason to the cancellation of Kgalema's visit. I called Meme and she assured me again that Madiba was fine. I could actually hear him talk in the background while on the phone to her and I called Achmat back to tell him that. The phone didn't stop ringing.

Two hours later it was on the news. Madiba had been admitted to hospital in Pretoria for a routine medical check-up. And again my response was 'What?' I sent Mrs Machel a text: 'Mum are you OK? I hear Madiba is in hospital.' She didn't read or respond to the message at first. We suspected that our phones and conversations were being monitored. In South Africa, if you pose a threat to the stability of the country, or you plan an act of terrorism, your phone could be tapped. We did neither of these but we wondered if government officials including medics were under instructions from some of the family to report Mrs Machel's every move to them. I later got a call from Meme explaining that they had been told by the medical team not to tell anyone what was happening, but indeed that Madiba had been taken to Pretoria to a hospital. I didn't understand this. Why did they have to rush him so secretively to Pretoria?

Again we started holding our breath. This was just unbelievable. I am not superstitious at all but couldn't help thinking that Prof. may have gone first to prepare for Madiba, and my own thoughts scared me. Soon Mrs Machel told me what was going on and I could hear that she was under tremendous pressure. She was stressed, worried and concerned. It was clear that I had to wait for the storm to pass before I could try to go and see him. Eventually Josina and I went off to see him a few days later. I was anxious and didn't want to make the same mistake as I'd done with Prof. – by the time I managed to visit Prof. in hospital in Cape Town before he passed away he was already unconscious and I didn't want a repeat of that. Madiba recognized me and briefly interacted with me and that calmed me down. I just needed him to say 'Oh Zeldina' and I would be fine. I relied, like everyone in the world, on him being well. We spent some time with Mum and then we left.

The public were anxious about events as the government failed to issue regular statements to update them on his progress. By now we had been told that the government would handle all communication around his well-being and I had no desire or wish to interfere with that task. I knew too well how difficult it was to deal with things around Madiba – something very few people wanted to ever give me credit for – and now it was their turn and I was happy about that while I dealt with my own emotions.

I was deeply troubled about Madiba's illness and as with any ninety-four-year-old his condition changed every day. One day it was good, the next day it was not so good. I soon packed my things and left to go to my parents for the holiday. I couldn't take it any more and I was unable to visit him.

While on holiday Mrs Machel sent me a message one day to say that Madiba was doing better and that he had started calling one of the white nurses 'Zeldina', and that she thought he missed me. There was nothing I could do. As much as I wanted to be there, I also had to be with my parents for Christmas. I could no longer see Madiba regularly or just pop in, and I silently hoped that he didn't think I really neglected him. My parents were also getting old and I was starting to realize that they too were not going to be around for ever. I had neglected them for years as a result of my job, more than seven years not spending Christmas with them while I was organizing children's Christmas parties in Qunu; it was time to correct that and spend time with them.

When I arrived back from visiting my parents at the coast over Christmas Madiba was discharged from hospital and settling in back at home. I resumed my, now limited, duties at the Foundation and tried to keep busy as much as possible. Some days I really got depressed, staying in bed the entire day. It was not healthy. As much as I wanted to see Madiba I was mindful also that certain staff members in the household texted or called Makaziwe to report to her whenever I was in the house to visit him. I was waiting for them to tell me that I wasn't welcome.

It was time for the first screening of the documentary *Miracle Rising*, in London. It was a powerful story of South Africa's transition between 1990 and 1994. Although questions were asked of the interviewees about Madiba's role in the transitional period, the focus was very much on Cyril Ramaphosa and Roelf Meyer, who led the negotiations for a peaceful settlement between the ANC and the National Party at the Convention for a Democratic South Africa (Codesa). The production company flew me to London for the screening at end January as part of the production team. I hadn't travelled in a while and was excited to leave the country. The screening was well received and I was proud to have been involved when I saw the final product. I enjoyed seeing people I had lost contact with or no longer regularly had dealings with since we stopped travelling. I wasn't overly impressed with all the celebrities who were interviewed in the documentary but understood that for it to appeal to the broader public the celebs were the selling factor. I liked contributing to history in this way as I could comprehend the difficulties we faced at the time. The documentary was also aired in South Africa and was well received.

On 14 February 2013, the Paralympic athlete Oscar Pistorius shot and killed his model-girlfriend Reeva Steenkamp when he allegedly mistook her for an intruder. The country went into a complete state of shock. One of our heroes had fallen, and with him our hope, and everything the new South Africa embodied, the miracle, somehow stumbled. I don't know why it mattered so much, but we all felt a sense of loss that Valentine's Day. People, especially South Africans, always wanted a hero. Madiba was every man's hero and so was Oscar for overcoming his disability and putting South Africa on the map. People idolized him. Madiba always warned against people idolizing others, including him, too much. He knew too well that one could easily fall. We'd put Oscar on a pedestal so high that the fall was greater than we could have anticipated.

In *Conversations With Myself*, Madiba wrote in a letter to Winnie Mandela on 9 December 1979:

> We are told that a saint is a sinner who keeps on trying to be clean. One may be a villain for ¾ of his life and be canonized because he lived a holy life for the remaining ¼ of that life. In real life we deal, not with gods, but with ordinary humans like ourselves: men and women who are full of contradictions, who are stable and fickle, strong and weak, famous and infamous, people in whose bloodstream the muckworm battles daily with potent pesticides.

He believed that there was good and bad in every human being and made me change my thinking about people whenever something like this happened. I realized again how much Madiba had changed my thinking and perceptions about things we consider straightforward.

On 9 March 2013 Madiba was back in hospital. I was told by Mrs Machel that it wasn't serious but for a simple medical procedure. Again it was a reminder of just how vulnerable he was. Every time he got admitted to hospital, I was reminded that my time with him was becoming limited.

On 22 March after his discharge I tried to visit Madiba three times. The first time I arrived at his house, Makaziwe was there. She had made it clear in a previous discussion about me that I was not welcome to see her father. I no longer had work to do there. I was adamant that she was not to determine that and decided that I would try and avoid her but that I would not stay away just because it pleased her. Mum had to defend me once again, arguing that she was willing to defend Madiba's decisions whether they liked it or not, and that she was going to see that his wishes were fulfilled until the day he passed on. She told them that my presence from time to time provided him with emotional stability and when I heard that she said that I quietly thought: Yes, *my* emotional stability too, selfish as it may seem. I couldn't help but feel that one gets chewed and then spat out when people no longer see a use for you. I know too well how Madiba would feel about that, but it is not my place to try and judge how or what he may have felt at this stage. I was torn between fighting and leaving things to play out, and the latter seems to be the lesson I'll take with me.

The second time, at around 3 p.m., when I wanted to visit again, Makaziwe was still there. By now Mrs Machel had left for her office. I decided to return home and agreed with Mrs Machel to return at 6 p.m. I hadn't seen Madiba in two weeks and planned to spend time with my family for the days to follow and was therefore eager to see Madiba before I left. At 6 p.m. when I went back to the house Makaziwe had gone. Mrs Machel was seeing someone when I arrived and because I also had business to discuss with her, I agreed to wait until she had finished.

It seemed to me that, as usual, the household staff that sided with Makaziwe texted or called her to tell her that I was there. Soon she arrived again. Mysteriously the staff disappeared as I was waiting in the kitchen. Makaziwe entered and closed the door behind her. She said: 'Oh I've been wanting to talk to you about something for some time. There are rumours going around that you are working on a documentary film with the History Channel entitled "Mandela: The Last Years". I wanted to say to you that since you are one of the people Tata trusted most, it would be highly unethical of you to do something like that.'

What surprised me was that she admitted for the first time in her life that I had any role to play in her father's life. She had probably heard about the *Miracle Rising* documentary, which did not focus on Madiba at all, and confused the two issues but I was not bothered to correct her. My commitment was to her father and my trust relationship is with him. I am committed to protecting his dignity and integrity and that of his wife but my commitment does not go beyond that. People may then argue, why am I talking about it now? But I feel this is different. I am not infringing his dignity. This is not an account of his medical state or how illness and suffering affected him. There are many things that I will never talk or write about. My relationship was with Madiba. Not with the family or anyone else.

As the conversation was heating up Mrs Machel called for me. Saved by the bell, I thought, or I may have said things I would later regret. I briefly saw her and left without seeing Madiba as Makaziwe had gone upstairs to be with her father and I knew she would chase me out. I was deeply disappointed about not seeing him but angry enough to realize that it would not be the best time for me to persist trying to do so. The next week I returned and managed to see him. His face lit up when he saw me and he exclaimed: 'Oh Zeldina, you are here.' 'Yes Khulu I am, how are you?' He just gave me a thumbs-up and then said: 'How are your parents?' I was so incredibly touched. He no longer spoke much and this was again the extent of our entire conversation that day, but he had it in him to ask about my parents. How inexplicably had this man changed my life, my thinking and, most importantly, my heart! I sat with him for a while holding his hand and when he dozed off I left.

A few days later news broke of Zenani and Makaziwe challenging the appointment of Madiba's long-time friend George Bizos, his lawyer Bally Chuene and Comrade Minister Tokyo Sexwale to a trust that managed the sale of artworks from the 'hands and art' project. Madiba appointed these trustees to oversee matters on his behalf. This was going to be an ugly fight. I was deeply disturbed by the news and thought (or was under the impression) that the matter had been resolved a few months before. As these private matters never concerned me I didn't bother enquiring about them often. Insults and counter-allegations followed in the media, each party feeding information to their own sources and lashing out in the most disrespectful way towards one of Madiba's oldest friends, Advocate Bizos. What effectively happened was that Zenani and Makaziwe were challenging their father's decisions. They knew very well that he was no longer able to defend himself or his decisions and it was the time for them to challenge these as they knew no one could rely on Madiba's evidence any longer.

I was not going to enter into their private business now but agreed with the trustees' lawyer that if and when called upon I would support their defence. My resolution was easy. If Madiba wanted to appoint any of his children in charge of his affairs, he would have done so when he was able to. And I was willing to defend his decisions with the facts at hand. The same applied to appointing staff and people in charge of his charities, and his lawyers could vouch for that.

Later it emerged in the lawyer's defending affidavit that indeed Zenani Dlamini and Makaziwe Mandela were acting against their father's wishes. The lawyer produced proof of minutes from meetings that we all remembered too well when Madiba made his wishes very clear. The case was then withdrawn.

I had to remind myself that this was not my battle to fight. I had to focus on ensuring that Mrs Machel had the support she needed and that I gave Madiba the occasional hug and smile and held his hand. I often found Zoleka, one of Madiba's grandchildren, with him whenever I visited during this time. She was the mother of Zenani Jnr, who was killed in the car accident in 2010 just prior to the FIFA World Cup opening. Zoleka wasn't threatened by my presence and was comfortable with me sitting with her grandfather. She had really made an effort to spend time with him almost every day and I could see that he enjoyed it.

On 27 March 2013 Madiba was admitted to hospital again. He had pneumonia again. A few days before I had visited him in the house and recall one of the housekeepers having a terrible flu while I was there. As I left I shook my head in disbelief. And here he was back in hospital with pneumonia. At that age he was much more susceptible to germs. Yet in his own household people were working even though they were sick. If they were sick, why where they still there? One just has to know when to give up. Not because you want to, but because you have to.

And once again the world held its breath. These were the most difficult times I had ever experienced. I've grown to realize that it is good that one never knows what lies ahead because you would easily give up at an early stage. Whatever I had thought were the worst experiences, these were, by far, the most stressful times of anxiety and uncertainty. I was desperate to go to the hospital but realized that I had to stay away as long as Makaziwe was there. I wanted to spare Madiba an altercation and I was simply willing to take the lead from Mrs Machel and Josina as to when I could visit. On the day that they agreed, Josina drove me in. We noticed the media camping outside the hospital and were fearful that they caught us both on camera. Like in 2011, if we were to appear in the media together I was afraid that I would experience what I felt to be outrage from some of the family. When we left, we agreed that I would hide on the back seat to avoid anyone seeing me. As much as we were tense and stressed about Madiba, we had some relief laughing about my lying down on the seat. I felt like I was a Cold War spy being driven from East Berlin to West Berlin. Madiba stayed in hospital for eleven nights and was then moved back to Johannesburg.

Once he recovered satisfactorily, Mrs Machel and I planned to have some of his old colleagues and friends visit occasionally. Weeks before, the ANC executive asked to pay a visit to Madiba. On the day I contacted them to come for the visit, they had some crisis to attend to and asked to postpone. I responded telling them to please tell us when they were ready as we would encourage them to visit. But then Madiba fell ill again and some weeks passed without either party following up on the matter.

By early 2013 Dr Mamphela Ramphele announced that she was establishing a new political party with the aim of contesting the general elections to be held in 2014. The only sizeable opposition to the ruling ANC party is the Democratic Alliance, a party largely still seen as dominated by white people even though they are much more liberal than the old Nationalist Party. Dr Ramphele is a well-respected academic in South Africa, a former activist against apartheid and a leading businesswoman. She is also a trustee of the Nelson Mandela Foundation since its inception. Her announcement was welcomed by a lot of people, but the party, Agang, seemed to lose momentum fast. Dr Ramphele was the first person to advise Madiba on health matters after his release in 1990. She introduced him to the cardiologist who treated him for many years until the Defence Force medical team took over his care from private special-ists. Dr Ramphele was therefore an old friend to Madiba and a good friend to Mrs Machel. She paid a visit to Mrs Machel on a particular day when Madiba was well enough to sit downstairs in his lounge. She saw him and was disturbed about his deterioration as she hadn't seen him in a very long time. Her visit was brief but she then mis-takenly announced in a radio interview that she had seen him.

A week before, the Democratic Alliance had launched its election campaign entitled 'Know your DA'. Part of the campaign was to inform the public of the DA's policy and in doing so they used a pic-ture of their founder, the late Mrs Helen Suzman, where she walked with Madiba, him embracing her. This made the ANC nervous and they lashed out at the DA for using an image of Madiba in their election campaign. The DA's campaign as well as Dr Ramphele's visit made the ANC unnecessarily nervous. No one had ever con-tested the fact that Madiba was part and parcel of the ANC and that it was a lifelong commitment, yet these interactions made the ANC somehow feel challenged over their 'ownership' of Madiba.

The Reverend Jesse Jackson was in South Africa to receive a national award from President Zuma for his contribution to the liberation struggle of South Africa. Rev. Jackson wanted to see Madiba and someone from the Presidency contacted me, telling me that the President wanted him to ask me about a possible visit to Madiba. Madiba was really not well enough to receive visitors and especially not people he was not very familiar with. I explained to the gentleman from the Presidency that a visit was not possible and he responded that he understood and would convey the sentiments to the President and Rev. Jackson.

One of the people who was on our list to visit Madiba as soon as he was well enough was Deputy President Kgalema Motlanthe, who had been trying and asking to see Madiba for months. He had contested the Presidency of the ANC at their national conference in December 2012 and had lost. He was sidelined by the party and it was clear that his challenge to President Zuma was not well received by all. Madiba was very fond of Kgalema and Mrs Machel and I discussed a possible visit. On the Friday night I contacted Kgalema's assistant to say that we would try something the following week, providing that Madiba was well enough. I told him not to repeat our conversation to anyone.

Since my contract had been changed by the Foundation and I only worked part time for them, there were certain days I didn't go to Johannesburg, when I didn't have work to do on that particular day or when I decided to work from home. On that Monday I was busy with something else and on my motorbike for most of the day. I didn't follow what was happening on Twitter and was pretty much off line most of the day.

While I was away, the ANC had come calling. What was strange was that they had insisted the visit be filmed – as a sort of 'proof of life' that Madiba was 'well'. The ploy backfired – Madiba did not look well or happy with the visit.

Upon returning to Johannesburg in the evening I checked Twitter and noticed total outrage from the public over video material about Madiba that appeared on the news that night. I didn't know anything. I found it on YouTube and was disgusted by what I saw. Madiba was clearly not happy. There was total chaos in his lounge and because it was a visit by the President and senior members of the ANC, flash photography was allowed – something that every South African knew was prohibited because of the sensitivity of Madiba's eyes. In the footage Madiba appeared withdrawn because he was overwhelmed. It was clear to me from what I witnessed that there was no control. Even the medical staff responsible for his health, General Dabula and Surgeon General Ramlakan, were themselves taking photos rather than protecting Madiba's eyes and looking out for his well-being. I was disturbed. Was this what it all had come to? It was like a zoo and Madiba was the caged animal that the tourists all fawned over. He looked helpless. Mrs Machel was attending meetings at the Foundation, literally two minutes from the house, and she was not even informed of the visit.

They didn't tell me about the visit at the house, probably because they knew that I would not tolerate such drama. People detested me for keeping order and telling them what to do around Madiba and it was clear why. If I wasn't there, this is what they did. A war broke out on Twitter and journalists asked where I was. I had to literally sit on my hands to stop myself from replying. The next day when I arrived at the Foundation the then CEO, Achmat Dangor, commented with disgust over the footage, and I said: 'Well this is what they all wanted, isn't it?' Isn't this why people argued so fiercely that Madiba no longer needed a secretary? If I had still been there, I wouldn't have allowed him to go in front of the media looking so weak and vulnerable. I wasn't the only one who was upset. The public and family were outraged with the ANC.

In the weeks to follow it got easier for me to see Madiba. The family eased their 'watch' over him and I could visit him more freely. I never knew on any day if that was going to be the last time I ever saw him.

★

On 8 June 2013 he was back in hospital and the Presidency announced that his condition was serious but stable. It was a recurring lung infection. We were filled with anxiety. We realized that it was on a knife's edge this time. Two days after his admittance I sneaked back into the hospital early one morning on the back seat of Josina's car. He was clearly very sick and weak but opened his eyes and managed a smile.

It was only then that I was told about events of the night of his admission. Someone, either medical or security personnel, decided to take him to hospital in an unmarked military medical vehicle to avoid suspicion from the public. My first question: 'Who in the public is watching him at 3 a.m. in the morning?' Halfway to the hospital in Pretoria the unmarked vehicle broke down. Forty minutes later help arrived. At first I thought this was a joke. How can Nelson Mandela, gravely sick, be stuck along a highway in the middle of winter for forty minutes at three in the morning? How is this possible? It was good that I had not been told earlier. I think it would have pushed me over the edge. I had been disabled in every possible way. Disarmed. I had no influence or power to question these matters any longer. And I felt I had neglected Madiba and Mrs Machel. My heart bled for them. How scared Madiba must have been! How scared Mrs Machel must have been, helpless, stressed! When I saw her she was clearly traumatized. How do things come to this? How does this happen to Nelson Mandela, the world's most revered person alive? And the fact that he was still alive was clearly only a miracle.

Soon the media set up camp outside the hospital. Journalists were flying in from all over the world. Millions of dollars were spent on outside broadcast vans as people around the world watched with bated breath. However, inside, the fighter was slowly making his way back. Some people in public argued that it was time for us to 'let him go'. 'Stop praying for his recovery,' some said. What they had missed was that the hard-headed freedom fighter was going to decide for himself when enough was eventually enough. I worked twelve-plus hours per day responding to people from across the world and at home who wanted answers and confirmation of what the President had said – he was critical but stable. I simply confirmed exactly what the President had said and was vague in my responses but people were anxious. Josina and I had long conversations and we anchored one another. I was mindful that, if one didn't help to ease the anxiety, the anxiety would soon rub off on the family and eventually Madiba would feel it too.

During one of her visits to the hospital, Madiba's daughter Zindzi asked Josina whether I had been there. Zindzi explained by saying that she thought I should be given the opportunity to visit her father, upon which Josina said I had been there a few days before. Zindzi replied: 'Then I can rest.' I was very touched when I heard that. Someone other than the Machels was looking out for me and I was grateful. The day after my visit security at the hospital had been tightened. Josina and I laughed when I told her I had thought that the extra security was probably because I'd sneaked in on the back seat of her car. I then told her I had convinced myself that not everything was about me. Amid the anxiety these unbelievable things at least made us laugh. It was later reported in the news that the tightened security was to keep journalists out. I was happy it wasn't about me.

The last time I saw Madiba alive was on 11 July 2013, the night before I departed on my annual Bikers for Mandela Day ride across the country, doing my bit for Mandela Day. I entered the hospital with Malenga Machel, Mrs Machel's son. We used a back entrance so we would not be spotted by the media. Madiba was still very sick. I gave Malenga a chance to spend some time with Madiba and his mother alone, and they then called me in. Madiba could still open his eyes and show emotion but then drifted off quickly. I was shivering standing next to his bed, shocked to see him in the state that he was in. I couldn't see his hands. I wanted to touch his hand but I couldn't find it. I was helpless, numb. Mrs Machel told him I was there but his eyes remained closed. She then nodded at me that it was OK to start speaking to him.

I knew I had to sound cheerful and not sad and said, 'Hello,

Khulu. It's Zeldina. I am here to see you . . .' and there it was. He opened his eyes, followed by the biggest brightest smile and he looked at me and fixed his eyes upon me. 'How are you Khulu? You look well,' although he didn't. 'I miss you, Khulu,' I said and he kept on smiling. Mum and Malenga were making fun of me, joking that Madiba had not afforded others that smile but to me he did. Then he drifted off again and closed his eyes. I stood there for a few minutes and Mum and Malenga went to the side of the room and Mum said I could talk to him if I wanted to. I said what needed to be said, again. I composed myself and told him that I was leaving on my bike trip the following day, reminded him about his comment about my bike trip the first year back in 2010, when he'd said: 'Why did you do that?' and I responded: 'For you, Khulu.' I was on my way for him again. I was very sad that night to leave but the smile was all I needed to keep me going. I didn't expect that to be the last time I saw him.

Upon my return to Johannesburg after the bike trip I tried to go on a few occasions. But every time I asked Mum there was something that prevented me from going. I went back twice, seeing Mum on other business, but I couldn't see him.

On 15 June an article had appeared on the front page of the *Saturday Star*, repeated in the Afrikaans Sunday paper *Rapport* the following day. Shaun van Heerden, a trusted bodyguard and friend for more than ten years, had snapped. He had been suspended for a second time following allegations from the Surgeon General that he had leaked information to the media about Madiba's whereabouts when he was hospitalized. In the article he referred to the incident at the Soccer World Cup in 2010 and the Defence Force medical staff ruling our world with an iron fist. I felt very sorry for Shaun. He was the one that helped me to see Madiba whenever I was at the house and Mrs Machel wasn't there to get me through the red tape being placed by the family to keep me out. I didn't know how I would cope without Shaun.

A few days later the story about the ambulance that broke down as Madiba was transported to hospital made world headlines after it leaked to the media. Newspapers described Mrs Machel as being 'frantic' during these events. The next day Makaziwe entered the hospital calling Mrs Machel 'Ms Frantic'. Mum was hurt and emotionally brutalized and Josina and I constantly tried to keep her strong by supporting her. Josina often went to support her mother whenever I couldn't. I missed Prof. He would have been there for us, he would have guided us, and his death left a void that is so difficult to explain.

In the week prior to Madiba's hospitalization I'd received word from a good friend who worked at the South African Breweries that they'd managed to track down our old family housekeeper, Jogabeth. She had been on my mind for years and on occasion I'd tried to find her but then abandoned the search when I hit a brick wall. But her husband was on a pension from the SAB and, just by my providing his name and a bit about his location back in the 1980s, they'd managed to find them for me. I immediately texted my mother and brother and we all called Jogabeth and Esau one night. We were overwhelmed with happiness to be reconnected. We planned to have a get-together but then Madiba fell ill and we had to postpone. My heart was filled with joy and my eyes filled with tears when Jogabeth said: 'All these years I have seen you on TV and thought "my Zellie has grown up" but how was I going to contact her again?' I was touched by her feeling of belonging. I hope to meet her soon, to reconnect and to see if there is anything I can do for them to help them in their old age. There was a time she gave up her life for me. It is time to return the favour.

And Madiba never ceased to amaze us. Even through the extended period of his illness he gave us and the world the time to prepare for a life without him. It took its toll on everyone. People were emotionally depleted. I would often dream about him at night. Sometimes good dreams and sometimes nightmares. I woke up every morning and realized with a shock that he was still ill. I would nervously reach for my cellphone to check if there had been any news or messages about him during the night. I was constantly worrying about him. During brief moments one continued with life as normal but then reality jerked me back to this state of limbo we were all in. I started feeling useless and worthless. My job was no longer a full-time occupation and time was treating me like a ship in the perfect storm at sea. Emotional ups and downs every day, frustrated and hurt by my inability to see him or to reach out to him. My dreams became vivid and in the morning I had to convince myself that it was only a dream. They occurred more frequently as I prepared myself to take the final step away from him.

What worried me most and kept me awake was whether during this prolonged illness there was ever a moment when he was conscious enough to think: Why hasn't Zeldina been here? I cringe when I think about the fact that it may have crossed his mind that in the end I had perhaps left him as I promised I would never do. Did he think that I had neglected or abandoned him? And now, nineteen years later, I was longing to put my white hand on his dark skin; to touch the skin I was brought up to believe was not as good as mine. Yet it was that dark skin that gave my life significance. My entire being at the age of forty-three yearned to touch that hand once more, to feel the ripples around his knuckles, to see his smile lighting up the room when I say: 'Don't worry Khulu, I did not desert you.'

13

Tot weersiens Khulu!

There is a scene in the movie *Long Walk to Freedom* where the character of Nelson Mandela slowly walks up a hill in Qunu. His back is towards the camera, as he walks away. The light is gentle, his familiar gait meandering up a gentle slope. I knew it wasn't him. It was Idris Elba, a British actor, but the image was so powerful, so evocative, so gutwrenching that I burst into tears in the cinema. The tears came and came, over and over and in a way I have never experienced before. They just pumped from my eyes uncontrollably and streamed down my cheeks. It didn't help that I tried to stop it. That night when I first saw *Long Walk to Freedom* at its premiere in South Africa I also cried myself to sleep, something I had never done in forty-three years. It was like a pre-mourning. I knew Madiba had almost gone. That he was in pain. But this re-enactment of his life pierced through all that and reminded me about him so much.

Madiba never got to see the movie. It was released in November 2013 when he was near the end. It was a story he had given his blessing to almost two decades earlier. The producer, Anant Singh, bought the rights to Madiba's life story and it had taken twenty years for it to come to the big screen, just in time for us to be reminded of his story.

Besides reminding us of Madiba's sacrifices, the movie also reminded me of a younger, fitter Nelson Mandela. His body was so broken, so damaged and deteriorated now but in the movie he was strong, robust, vibrant. He loved to dance, not that shuffle of his later years when his knees had given out, but the jazzy bop of the 1950s. Madiba used to tell us how he went dancing in Sophiatown and through the movie I could now visualize such stories. We would often sit during lunch or dinner on foreign travels, often just the two of us, and he would eagerly offer the details of his early life and he had the perfect audience in me. I had never had a problem allowing my imagination to run with a story and I would question him about his looks, his posture, his dress code, whether he charmed girls and what the dancing was like. He was amused by my directness and I often asked: 'Did women just fall over their feet to dance with you?' and he would laugh in a somewhat shy way and boast with a 'Yes of course!', upon which I would burst out laughing.

I had stopped seeing Madiba a few months before. Mrs Machel called me to the house one day to have tea, after Madiba had been discharged, although he was still considered critical but stable. She said that she knew how much I loved Madiba and that she didn't think it was advisable for me to see his deterioration knowing how I felt about him. At first I had suspected that the family told her to tell me that I was no longer able to see him, but after thinking about it I was happy that it happened. I didn't want to see him in a power-less state. I didn't want to lose control over my emotions in his presence. It was only after his death that I learned that indeed I had been banned from seeing him.

I was constantly battling in my mind, trying to understand why he didn't let go and whether he was able to let go himself. It haunts you. It eats you daily, piece by piece, not knowing and not under-standing what was happening to him.

At times I wondered, like many South Africans, whether he was being kept alive artificially. But Mrs Machel and Josina told me there was a still a spark there, that he occasionally held someone's hand or managed to open his eyes. But by November even that didn't happen. He was slipping away, despite an overwhelming effort by the doctors to keep him alive.

His doctors thought it was amazing that he had such strength even when he was so weak. I often wondered – was he now becom-ing afraid of dying? He was often flippant about death, saying things like 'when you're gone your body is dead'. People raised the issues around his ancestors not having called upon him yet and I wondered whether he was aware of these issues. He was respectful of tradition but not overly obsessed with it.

As the days passed, I was permanently on standby, anxious, waiting for an update on his health. You start living in a permanent state of limbo. I communicated with Mrs Machel and Josina by text and messaging because we were worried. Sometimes I met them trying to resume duties as normal and I would not often ask too many questions but just 'Is he OK?', 'Mum, do you think he is free of pain?' or 'Mum, do you think he is aware of what is happening?' I was also trying to be one less person asking after him and, rather, showing my support to him, through supporting her. He had after all told me the first day I met her in Paris back in 1996 that I had to look after her and not lose sight of her at any given point. I was still doing just that.

And then the message that I knew was inevitable. On 3 December Mum and Josina told me that Madiba's condition was deteriorating. This seemed like the beginning of the end.

I saw Josina on Thursday, 5 December at the Foundation. She looked exhausted.

Early evening on Thursday, 5 December Josina phoned me with instructions from Mrs Machel. I had to inform some of Madiba's closest friends that things were turning for the worse. It was so hard. So brutally frank. It took me hours to get hold of everyone on my list. They included people like Archbishop Emeritus Desmond Tutu, Ahmed Kathrada, Thabo Mbeki, George Bizos and others close to Madiba but who were outside government structures and who would not normally be informed in such instances. I was strong when I started making the calls but their reaction, a mixture of pain, shock and disbelief destroyed the strong spirit with which I started off. After each call I composed myself and repeated Madiba's quote: 'It always seems impossible until it is done', and I would call the next person.

Later in the evening two helicopters flew dangerously low over my house. As I lived halfway between Pretoria, the base where military helicopters were stationed, and Johannesburg, where Madiba's house was, the helicopters had to fly over the area where I lived. Was the military preparing for the worst? Or had it happened? If it was the military it meant that it had happened. There were two issues to consider: firstly they probably became involved at that point from a protocol point of view, and secondly I thought that they perhaps feared the much speculated *uhuru* or 'night of the long knives' when, it was said, blacks would kill whites the night after Madiba died. It was only the extremists that participated in this kind of talk and I knew by now that South Africa was stronger and more capable as a nation of dealing with what we all feared, black and white: Madiba's death.

And then it was done. I just knew he was gone. I didn't have to ask. I was numb for a few minutes and then I jumped up from my chair at the kitchen table thinking it would stop me from becoming hysterical. I went outside and sat quietly alone in the hot summer night just thinking, praying and trying to internalize what had just happened. I was alone at home and my first instinct was that I had to pray, light candles and then get to bed as soon as possible. I knew what lay ahead. My phone started going crazy. I didn't answer anyone and rumours were running. About two hours later I started receiving messages from as far away as Los Angeles: 'Is Madiba OK?' I knew that if I answered one message then it would spread like a velt fire. I also did not want to lie.

My phone didn't stop ringing and I decided to put it on silent, took two sleeping pills and went to bed. I knew that the President had to make an official announcement but I had no idea when that would be done. I told the CEO of the Nelson Mandela Foundation, Sello Hatang, that I needed to meet him at the office at 6 a.m. the following morning. He agreed and off I went to bed.

I sent a message to my brother and his partner Rick, asking them to collect my dogs early the next morning. I said: 'Please don't ask any questions, just fetch Winston and Indira as early as possible.' They would need to be cared for and I knew I would not be at home much over the next couple of days.

On 6 December 2013 I awoke just after 4 a.m. I had twenty-eight missed calls and literally hundreds of emails, texts and messages already. I showered and when I went downstairs to have coffee I sat reading through some of the messages. The world had woken me to my worst nightmare. Madiba was gone. The President made the announcement during the midnight hours and to this day I have not seen the footage of the announcement.

I called my parents before 6 a.m. They had both heard already. They sleep with the radio on in their room and when the usual music on the radio was interrupted by an announcement by the President my dad woke my mom to tell her. My dad, the man who warned me about the terrorist's release back in 1990, wept like a child for Madiba and spent the entire night watching events unfold on TV. When I heard the sadness of their voices over the telephone I broke down for the first time.

I rushed to the office and found some of my colleagues there already. Everybody was emotional but we composed ourselves, like soldiers moving into total operational mode, knowing that we had to get work done right away in preparation for the next few days. Condolence books had to be bought, statements prepared and we needed to create the space for the public to mourn Madiba's passing too. The staff were brilliant and under the leadership of Sello they had created such a space in no time. I also called one of my friends, Minèe, to our office and asked her to supervise my phones and start responding to people. I needed help to contain the activity on my phones. The media started hunting me for comment or a response of some sort and Minèe had to keep the pressure at bay while I tried to figure out what to do next. To try and cage in the media pressure I decided to issue a statement. As I sat in front of my computer words and tears started flowing at the same time.

The Nelson Mandela Foundation agreed to issue my statement. I wrote:

> I often battled with the relentless pressure. But then I looked at him who carried himself with such grace and energy. I never left. I never could. Nelson Mandela did not demand loyalty, but he inspired profound and unwavering loyalty from everybody whose life he touched. And now, as we grieve the departure of Madiba, I am

slowly coming to terms with the fact that I will never see him again. But heroes never die. As sad as it makes me that I will never walk into a room again and see his generous infectious smile or hear him say 'Oh Zeldina, you are here', I have come to terms with the fact that Madiba's legacy is not dependent on his presence. His legacy will not only live on in everything that has been named after him, the books, the images, the movies. It will live on in how we feel when we hear his name, the respect and love, the unity he inspired in us as a country but particularly how we relate to one another . . . I will cherish every smile, the pleasant but also the difficult times and especially my barefoot moments . . . *Tot weersiens Khulu* [until we meet again grandpa]!! Will love you every day for the rest of my life.

The reality of it all hit home as I typed the last sentence. I was saying goodbye. Was this really happening? I had never, ever imagined that I would be sitting at my desk typing these words and it felt as if I was saying goodbye from another stratosphere. Minee was receiving calls and responding to messages on my behalf. People reached out to me from a personal perspective because it was known to them in particular how much he meant to me, but then others also called because I was their link to Madiba. They didn't know how or where to express the sadness over their loss. I first had to figure out what needed to be done before I could start thinking about my own feelings.

For some time I had worked with Mrs Machel and Josina to compile lists for this eventuality. They included people who had served Madiba, people who had been with him during the Rivonia and Treason Trial, friends, the heads and trustees of all his charities, supporters and those we always called upon when Madiba needed something – not only for his charities but also sometimes to get a job for one of his grandchildren or to help a child with something specifically. The lists had been updated several times but the last one was updated in June 2013 when Madiba was hospitalized. The lists were then submitted to Makaziwe and Ndileka Mandela, Madiba's eldest grandchild. They were the only two family members involved in funeral arrangements and they had been planning the funeral for the past eight years.

The state originally had a plan to have the funeral at the Union Buildings, the centre of power in South Africa and the place where all other state funerals were held in history. Although Madiba wanted to be buried in Qunu he didn't specify that he wanted a state funeral in Qunu. He was a simple man with modest needs, somehow underestimating his importance to the world.

This funeral was going to be about maintaining power over the Mandela legacy and roles within the Mandela family.

I felt gratitude to those who remembered me and the small role I had played in Madiba's life. Archbishop Desmond Tutu mentioned me during a very moving sermon he gave at St George's Cathedral in Cape Town. But as a humble reminder of how we are all forgettable, replaceable, he forgot my surname and called me Zelda van Graan repeatedly. He was becoming old too. Fragile and upset at the passing of the man he respected. Amid the sadness people were texting and tweeting me saying that if they were me, they would just change their surname now to Van Graan. It was funny but I couldn't laugh at the time.

I was also incredibly touched by Defence Minister Nqakula's statement about me, thanking me for my years of service. She said that she didn't ever think I had time to have a boyfriend and although I didn't want people to talk about it she was right, and it was the first time someone said it in public. There was a time I couldn't be with a man for twenty minutes without Madiba calling on me to do something. I never got angry. He was my number one. When I occasionally had a fling or a dysfunctional relationship I could never give it my full commitment. My job was everything and I didn't mind it. It was my choice. Her thanking me made me even more emotional. I had never expected to be thanked by anyone. Madiba thanked me. That was enough to me and my blessings having been chosen to serve him were beyond any expectations I had from life. But for someone from the ANC to thank me really ripped my heart apart. I didn't care for Madiba just because I cared for him. I knew millions of others cared for him too and I tried to serve his interests best to ensure that those relationships with others could be honoured.

My Twitter and Facebook accounts, text and emails were suddennly flooded with people thanking me. It was all too overwhelming and simply too many to answer. I am a person for detail and a left-brain thinker and at first I thought I would thank each and every one personally, but as time passed my cellphone constantly froze on me as a result of traffic and I simply didn't get the time to do what I wanted. What made it worse was that the people pouring out their gratitude to me had all suffered the same loss. They all had their own emotions to deal with yet they thought of me. I was deeply touched.

We now had to figure out how the people on those Madiba 'friends lists' got accredited. Sello, the now-CEO of the NMF tried from his side to get info too, while staff worked around the clock putting out fires of disorganization from people who wanted confirmation of arrangements. Sello as CEO couldn't get any detail and neither could his staff. People were calling asking for details about the memorial service to be held at the FNB Stadium in Soweto on Tuesday, 10 December. I couldn't answer anyone as I didn't have information and it was not forthcoming. In addition to the Madiba 'friends list', as we called it, the Machel family was suddenly told that they would only be allowed five accreditations and Mrs Machel would count as the first. So she plus four other Machels would be allowed accreditation at her own husband's funeral. It is so ridiculous that you actually couldn't help but laugh out loud at this.

In the few days to follow before the memorial many of us hardly slept, trying to make sense of arrangements and trying to get information. To say it was chaotic would be an understatement. A combination of bad planning and state secrecy, it seemed surprisingly badly managed for an event that had been inevitable. I had travelled with Madiba across the world, attending functions where there were sometimes hundreds of heads of state present. Arrangements at such big events were always a little haphazard yet I had never experienced such chaos. No one person could give you all relevant information and plans were changed every few minutes. Even those in charge didn't know the answers to anything, it seemed.

On Sunday night, after much fighting and crossfire of words between myself, the government's protocol people and the family, we were saved by a senior ANC official. She came to our rescue when she managed to get the accreditations for the Machel family and delivered them to the Saxon Hotel where Josina and I were meeting.

It was becoming farcical. If we could barely get Nelson Mandela's widow and her children accredited to attend his memorial service, it was becoming downright impossible to get anyone else officially accredited.

In the meantime the advance teams for President Obama and President Clinton had arrived and were trying to get details from everyone – me included. Tempers were flaring as everyone felt the pressure and frustration of the disorganization. I repeatedly asked why they had been planning for eight years and now no one could give us any answers. We appeared unprofessional and caught off guard. We received assurance that we would get the Madiba 'friends lists' accreditation the next day.

Early Monday morning we started calling around. By 2 p.m. one of our friends, Basetsana Khumalo, went to the ANC head office to collect accreditation for the 'friends lists', but then we realized that only half the people on the list had been accredited. The memorial was the next day. There was no way people from abroad would take the risk to fly to South Africa for the memorial or funeral if they did not know for sure whether they would be accredited. No invitations were sent and Madiba's friends were expected to go to the stadium on a first-come-first-served basis to get access and then be seated with the crowds of public people attending the memorial. That included people like Archbishop Tutu.

In the midst of all of this, just when it seemed things couldn't get worse, I remembered an appointment I had scheduled the previous week. Root canal. The pain in my tooth was shadowed by the pain of my heartbreak. A friend, Marli, collected me and took me to the dental surgeon. I couldn't manage to drive and answer the stream of phone calls and queries at the same time. Marli answered my phone during the root canal procedure and then asked me questions while I was lying open mouthed in the surgeon's chair, close to being strapped down by the dentist as illustrated in cartoons. I would write the response to Marli on a piece of paper, nearly illegibly, but she managed to give directions for the hour and a half I was in the chair. The surgeon soon realized that he was not going to complete the job and asked me to return the following week for the rest of the work. He realized I was under pressure and he was exceptionally patient. He managed to stop the pain and off we went.

With a mouth full of cotton wool and enough painkillers to numb my brain as well as my mouth (I did ask him to inject me with more than the allowed quantity of local anaesthetics to try and calm my nerves as well, although he declined), I tried to convey to people that I still didn't have any information. I tried to remain optimistic. But as soon as I managed to answer everyone, the first person on the list would start asking for an update again. I was bordering on a nervous breakdown and couldn't bear the pressure.

At times Josina, Basetsana and I all yelled at one another, then we cried hysterically and then we would pick up the pieces and try to find order again. We knew our outbursts were safe with one another no matter what the nature. George Cohen, the manager at the Saxon Hotel who had become a good friend, as well as the owners, the Steyn family, insisted that I stay at the hotel during the funeral time. George wanted to support me and tried to do so in every possible way. I lived some distance out of Johannesburg and by offering for me to stay in the city he already alleviated some pressure.

As some of Madiba's friends also stayed at the Saxon Hotel it made it easier, not having to communicate with them all in different venues but from within the hotel. Whenever I got one piece of information, no matter how mundane, I would share it with George and he would disseminate it to the friends who were staying in the hotel and even beyond to those he had contact with. The staff at the Foundation were busy with their own arrangements at the office to create a public space for mourning and George and the hotel staff helped me to take calls, they sent drivers around to try and help us get information, and in addition George force-fed me. On more than one occasion he found me sobbing, a mixture of pain and frustration, and he would calm me and help think of ways to find solutions. To me Madiba's friends all felt they were important in his life and their requests for information or detail were legitimate and my inability to help anyone seemed unprofessional and uncaring.

On Monday night the Minister of Defence called to say I had to travel to the Union Buildings in Pretoria to sort out the accreditation of the 'friends lists'. She suggested this to be the only solution at such a late hour. By now I had texted and called every possible person I thought could help us. By 7 p.m. on Monday night, we didn't even know yet what time the proceedings were to start the next day.

It wasn't just us. The media were also unable to plan. The government was working on a 'need to know' basis – slowly giving out information tidbit by tidbit.

In the meantime Madiba was being embalmed at 1 Military Hospital in Pretoria. From my friend Robyn Curnow, who had been briefed by the family for years, I learned that he was being 'escorted' to the afterlife by the elders of the Thembu tribe. They would talk to him, explaining the process of what was going on day by day. Madiba detested red tape and bureaucracy and I couldn't but wonder what his response would be if he had been told about our frustration.

My friend who took me to the dental surgeon drove me to the Union Buildings, accompanied by Sara Latham, the advance for President Clinton and an old friend too. She was sent to South Africa by the Clintons personally to also support me in whatever way possible. Half way to the Union Buildings Basetsana called us to say that they were not printing accreditations at the Union Buildings and that we had to return to Johannesburg, so we did. We were told that we would receive the remaining accreditations by 10 p.m. At 10.30 I called again and Josina and I were told that we would receive word by 1 a.m. Tuesday morning. At 1 a.m. we were told 3 a.m. So, we didn't go to sleep; 3 a.m. arrived and 3 a.m. passed without any word. We were still waiting. By 5 a.m. we started calling around. People like the business tycoon Johann Rupert had flown from Cape Town to attend the memorial, but his accreditation too was not delivered. At 6 a.m. I delivered two accreditation cards at the gate of his house, cards with names on that weren't known to him or his wife. There was no other way I could help him. Johann got on his plane and returned to Cape Town.

Johann was one of the people Madiba always called upon whenever he needed financial help for a project. Madiba's relationship with the family dated back to negotiations in the early 1990s after Madiba's release, yet here this man could not go to Madiba's memorial despite the fact that Madiba considered him as one of his sons.

In addition, none of the Nelson Mandela charities, their respective CEOs or trustees had been accredited. Their names all appeared on the list that was submitted on several occasions over the previous two years. Long-serving staff members who played critical roles in Madiba's life were omitted from accreditation.

At 8 a.m., after sleeping for only forty-five minutes, I arrived at our offices from where the Machel family was going to depart. I profusely apologized to Prof. Ndebele, the Chairman of our Foundation, and to Sello our CEO and I was deeply disappointed, hurt and embarrassed that they had not been catered for. Had my name not been submitted by Mrs Machel as part of her family list, I would not have been accredited. It seemed like chunks of Madiba's past were being whitewashed or ignored. The people he personally appointed, the legacy institutions he established were being marginalized in an act of pettiness.

Advocate George Bizos, one of Madiba's oldest friends and the lawyer whose relationship with Madiba dated back to the Rivonia

Trial, arrived at the office too, as his name was submitted as family too. I helped him onto the bus and asked Lori, my friend from Los Angeles and Morgan Freeman's business partner, to remain with him at all times. Arriving at the stadium it was chaos. It rained continuously and an unrelenting storm passed over Johannesburg. Some people said this was lucky and that the gods were welcoming Madiba. He would have thought that was nonsense. The rain further complicated an already difficult and chaotic situation. Someone recently said that Madiba didn't like too much of a fuss being made over him and that the rain was probably his way of ensuring that not too much of a fuss was being made.

We were sent from pillar to post between suites. Up and down we walked with the elderly Advocate Bizos. At one point I tried to assist Archbishop Tutu, Kofi Annan and the Elders as they were manhandled by police at one of the doors to a suite. It felt so disrespectful to me.

When Bono, Sol Kerzner, Charlize Theron and Douw Steyn's wife and children arrived they were also blocked access to any of the suites. A protocol officer literally chased them away and directed them to 'any open suite' along a long corridor. I escorted them and simply took them to the closest empty suite, where there was no catering and only orange plastic chairs to sit on. At least they had privacy there. What made it worse was that the suite was situated behind a screen to the back of the stage where they could hardly see anything. I told them that I would return to fetch them once I had made arrangements for them to enter somewhere more dignified but that they needed to stay in the suite for now as I did not want them to be manhandled by police or protocol people. The only words that repeated in my mind were: 'to honour Madiba, you have to honour his relationships'. If it was the last thing I would do for him, I would try to honour the relationships he had nurtured.

After fighting, more crying, yelling and losing my temper, Jessie Duarte, the Deputy Chair of the ANC, came to my rescue. I had told her what had happened and she entered the argument with the protocol officials and police at the door to the Ministerial suite to allow Madiba's friends access to a decent suite. She shared my frustration and thought it was unacceptable that people were treated with such disdain. She allocated a protocol person and one of our friends went off to fetch them.

Madiba detested events where endless speeches were made. He detested people singing his praises for hours and hours. He argued that once someone has said something good about you, it was enough. It was hardly the celebration of his life we had hoped for. It was not a public holiday and the 90,000-capacity stadium was not even half-full. It was embarrassing. People had to take time off from work to attend the memorial, and being right before the Christmas holidays many probably simply could not take leave to attend the memorial service.

Josina and Malenga Machel, Mrs Machel's two children and Madiba's two stepchildren, had not been catered for either. They were with us, and the rest of the Machel family, in the Ministerial suite. Halfway through the programme someone came to announce to them that there was provision for them on the field with the rest of the family, but we stopped them from humiliating themselves and walking onto the field as an 'afterthought'. Madiba had spent more time with these two young people than with many of his own blood. They made him smile, yet they were treated with what struck me as the utmost disrespect.

President Clinton called me to the Presidential suite because he, Secretary Hillary and Chelsea wanted to greet me. JD, the President's PA, fetched me and when I saw them I nearly collapsed. It was like seeing your parents and family. I have spent many hours with them over the past nineteen years and they had appreciation for how much I loved Madiba and I knew how much he loved them. They shared the pain we were all feeling. They really deeply loved him, over and above professional admiration. Seeing them made me realize that the loss was theirs too. It was irrelevant how much time you spent with Madiba. Your relationship with him depended on how you felt about him in your heart, and the Clintons understood that.

President Obama had what we described as a Martin Luther King moment and delivered a speech that will go down in history as one of his best. Too many speeches were made though, and it was not the celebration of Madiba's life we had hoped for. It took hours and hours for the speeches to be completed, with very little singing and dancing or musical items – something Madiba would have preferred. It just exposed how badly some people really knew Madiba that they could get it so wrong.

Very embarrassingly, President Zuma was booed by his own compatriots every time his name was mentioned or his face appeared on one of the big screens in the stadium. I was not in the least surprised. It was the same disrespect towards the President that Jacob Zuma had not condemned during his rape trial some years before, when ill-disciplined ANC youth started burning t-shirts emblazoned with the face of the then President Thabo Mbeki, that now manifested itself in a different time and in a different form. It was like a relationship in which abuse occurs. Once you allow it to happen you can never go back over the line that was crossed. It was allowed back then, so why would it not be allowed now? I was embarrassed not only for President Zuma but for South Africa as a whole.

On Tuesday night after the memorial we went to the Houghton house to see Mrs Machel, and President Clinton and his family departed South Africa soon after that. Sol Kerzner, one of the people who always brought a smile to Madiba's face, also left, and the astute businessman had a sadness in his eyes too. Even if Sol or the Clintons hadn't called, I sometimes in the last years told Madiba that they had, and it always brought about a smile whenever I saw that Madiba's mood needed a lift. They visited as often as they could and whenever their business brought them to South Africa, and President Clinton, without fail, always made sure that he combined his other visits to Africa with a visit to South Africa over Madiba's birthday period.

Before I went to sleep I tried to make arrangements for Bono, Naomi Campbell and the Steyn family to go and pay their respects at the Union Buildings the next morning, where Madiba was lying in state. Madiba liked Bono as he used his profile as a celebrity to support good causes. In turn we could always call on Bono to perform at concerts and events to benefit Madiba's charities, without charging an appearance fee or travel expenses. Naomi was the first celebrity to support the Nelson Mandela Children's Fund publicly, and she got christened the first of Madiba's honorary granddaughters. And after Madiba left his Soweto house on his separation from Winnie Madikizela Mandela, the Steyn family housed Madiba for six months and he completed the writing of *Long Walk to Freedom* in their house and where the interim constitution was prepared by the ANC. They entertained Madiba's friends and comrades and provided a space for him to spend time with his son Makgatho's children. These people all deserved their rightful place in Madiba's life and now they had not been catered for to pay their last respects at the Union Buildings while Madiba was lying in state.

Bridgette Radebe, the wife of our Minister of Justice Jeff Radebe, offered to come round to the Saxon Hotel to help us get to the Union Buildings the next morning. Roads were all cordoned off and unless your car was accredited you were expected to go and stand in a queue for hours to take public transport to the Union Buildings. At 6 a.m. on Wednesday morning Bridgette called to say that Jeff would be there at 8 a.m. I waited until 7 a.m. and then asked George, the manager at the Saxon, to wake Naomi, Bono and the Steyns. At 8 a.m. Bridgette called to say that Jeff had been called to another ceremony and that he would not be able to help us. Panic struck again. How was I supposed to get these people to the Union Buildings? Surely the government couldn't expect these VIPs to go and stand in a queue for five or six hours with the public to pay their last respects to Madiba?

I felt impotent. I had always been able to fix things, to open doors, but one by one they were closing. It didn't help to contemplate how this would have angered Madiba. You simply square up and deal with it and find another way around.

While I was having a telephone conversation at the Saxon,

former President F. W. de Klerk, who was also staying at the hotel, overheard me. Mr de Klerk was the President in 1990 when Madiba was released from prison. Madiba liked him and spoke of him with great respect and I shared that respect. After I finished the call he said: 'Zelda, speak to Norman, my security, and see if you can work out something with him to help you.' And at 9.15 we all left in convoy with former President de Klerk and his wife Elita. The irony in this was just too much for me. Here the man who represented apartheid to so many was, in a way, rescuing Madiba once again. It was just too much to handle and it is something I so badly wanted to tell Madiba about. It wouldn't have surprised him though that Mr de Klerk came to our rescue. He truly believed that despite their political differences from time to time, Mr de Klerk was a reasonable and good human being.

Arriving at the Presidential guest house, the celebrities were allowed in but I was shut out together with the Steyns. When Minister Jeff Radebe and wife Bridgette arrived they had to escort me inside and I had to figure out a plan to get the Steyns inside. Eventually we managed to get all our guests transported to the Union Buildings where Madiba was lying in state.

As we walked down the steps of the Union Buildings a calmness came over me. I had to be ready to say goodbye to Madiba. I had to get the words right in my head. I didn't plan to say anything out loud but he would hear me. He always knew what I thought before I could even say it. And when I sometimes told him something or raised something with him he would say, 'You know, Zeldina, it's strange that you mention it, I was just thinking about that now.' It won't be different this time, I decided.

A few steps from the coffin I realized that it was going to be too difficult. I hadn't seen him in a few months. I had already started missing him. Naomi was walking behind me and she then froze. She was scared and again tears streamed from my eyes. I was hysterical and as much as I wanted to help her, I couldn't help myself. I was holding on to Bridgette Radebe's hand but she then let me go and took Naomi's hand. I wanted her to help Naomi too. The next moment Olivia Machel, Samora Machel's daughter and Mrs Machel's stepdaughter, took my left hand and Bono took my right hand with his wife Ali on the other side and it was our turn to approach the coffin.

I was as composed as I could be until my eyes met those of Mandla Mandela, Madiba's grandson, standing guard next to his grandfather's coffin. My heart shattered. A physical pain I cannot describe to anyone but I am sure has been felt by many people. I so badly wanted to walk to Mandla to give him a hug but I couldn't. Mandla was like my little brother.

Bono and Olivia led me to the coffin and there was Madiba. Lifeless. Dead. Cold. Khulu was gone. The first thing I noticed was the scar on the side of his neck where they obviously inserted a tube. Probably a tube from the many that had given him life the last six months. Now there was nothing, nothing left but the scar. The hole was closed but when you work with someone for so long you eventually even know each other's scars. I knew every little mark on his face and this one in his neck was new. Then I noticed that he was a dark grey colour and next I noticed that his chest was completely flat. As flat as the top of a table. It upset me to see him like that but I knew that I only had a minute to say goodbye. Bono took charge and said a prayer, and although it was beautiful I couldn't breathe and suppress my gasping. He thanked God for blessing us with Madiba and asked Him to be with Madiba and with us while we put sense to life after Madiba. Bono led us away and I felt like turning around and running back. I still wanted to say, something. We always have something more to say, don't we? But life has taught me that we will often more regret the things we didn't say than the things we said and I had made sure in the last few years that I told Madiba how much I loved him and appreciated him. I never wanted to regret not saying it, and walking away I knew that it was the one thing he knew about me as he was lying there.

Bono and Olivia held my hands and I cannot remember climbing the stairs up the Union Buildings, probably doing so for the last time. On the journey back to the Presidential guest house, no one said a word. By now I had stopped trying to control my tears, they were just cascading from my eyes. I felt like I couldn't breathe and I wanted to be alone, by myself, but I had others to think about.

Back at the Saxon we had lunch and I was very sad to let Bono and his wife Ali go. I have also become close to their staff over the years and they have become close friends. They have all become somewhat of a spiritual pillar and Bono is a bit of a preacher man. He has a very deep understanding of life and throughout Madiba's prolonged illness he often sent messages of encouragement, never asking for anything or for information but sending a string of beautiful words. I remembered the saying 'we're all just here walking each other home', and it calmed me a little; I was exhausted from the tension and emotions of the day. In a way I also felt that Madiba's friends were all a special breed of people. He attracted a certain kind of person and I know it would have pleased him that they were there looking out for me. 'That's good, Zeldina,' he would say.

The ad hoc lack of planning continued and I had to make a decision on how to survive the next few days. There had been brief moments of breaking down but there hadn't been time to sit and think, to internalize the reality of Madiba's passing. I did not have time to think about myself or fully come to terms with the event. Also, not having seen Madiba for a couple of months made it almost unbelievable to think he was really gone. I'd got used to the fact that he was home, and waking up every morning with the first thought crossing my mind that he was critically ill. You never knew how any day would end but you never expect the end either.

My challenge now was to get Alfre Woodard, Oprah, Gayle King, Stedman Graham, Forest Whitaker and Richard Branson accredited for the funeral in Qunu. It was planned at Madiba's home village for Sunday 15 December 2013. They had all travelled from the US to be there but I was not sure whether we would succeed in getting them accredited. They were below the status of heads of state yet they were above a ministerial level. There was no level catering for their needs.

They had to be treated like the public, with the rest of the masses. I would not have any of that. The bizarre and unnecessary difficulties of an event that had been planned for eight years continued.

Arriving at Madiba's house to deliver something to Mrs Machel I was told by the uniformed police on duty that I could not enter the premises as my accreditation to the house had expired. It was not a person I had seen before and she refused me access. However, next to her one of Madiba's bodyguards was seated. He didn't try to help and kept quiet. I went into the guard house and tried to call the kitchen staff to ask them to verify that I was expected at the house. I couldn't get through on the phone. I asked the bodyguard how long he had worked for Madiba and he responded eight years. I told him that I was called to the house by Mum and asked whether he did not think his behaviour by not helping me to get in was unaccept-able. He responded by saying he was not on duty and simply keeping the lady in uniform company. My last response to him was: 'How do you think Madiba would react if he heard you now? Having served him, you should know. I don't have to answer for you. You really ought to be proud of yourself.' I called Mum on her cell-phone, of course again in tears, and she sent her bodyguards to come and collect me at the gate.

Arriving in the house I was told that I needed photo accredit-ation. I went to the room in the back of the garden where accreditation was done by state protocol officials and told them that Mrs Machel, as she had, had asked me to come for accreditation. They refused to accredit me and said my name was not on the list and that Makaziwe and Ndileka were the only ones that could give permission for me to be accredited. I left and went to Mrs Machel again to tell her that I was leaving and would not be staying for the prayer service she'd invited me to. I was disgusted that it was left to the mourning widow to intervene to get us accredited. She instructed Makaziwe's husband, Isaac, to accompany me to the room again to try to get me accredited. Despite him telling them that he was Makaziwe's husband and then saying that it was a 'special request from Mrs Machel' they refused. It was only after a long argument that they agreed. I thought it somewhat strange that Isaac put this to them as a special request from Mrs Machel.

I went to greet Mrs Machel and left. She wanted me to stay for the prayer service but I was too upset. I assured her that I would be around if she needed any assistance. She still relied on me for some of the administrative issues that I had performed while Madiba was alive: paying accounts or making transfers as instructed by them. I think the irony of it all intensified my own emotional feelings. The family was fast to call me to ask whether a transfer to them had been made, but felt that I wasn't good enough to be treated like a human being or afforded just the courtesy of a basic greeting when they passed me, let alone accredited with just a little dignity.

I still had the Oprah/Branson/Whitaker obstacle of accreditation to overcome and left the house.

The next few hours were spent on doing exactly that. I emailed everyone, called, sent text messages to people to ask them to accommodate Madiba's friends, and the same state protocol people told even the Director General of the Presidency that they did not take instructions from him. It appeared that some sections of government were at loggerheads with other members of government. I felt that it was nothing about honouring Madiba or giving him the dignity he deserved but all about asserting power and settling scores. But on the other hand, no one really knew who was in charge. One couldn't help but wonder whether it was just eight years of bad planning, wasting money on foreign travel to consult with other countries about events of this magnitude, or whether it was a deliberate attempt to exclude from Madiba's funeral people who were not aligned with the right people. Surely if you have eight years to plan, you get it right. It was distasteful to listen to and it deeply pained me that people who loved Madiba dearly were to be treated like that. They insisted that Oprah and others came to the accreditation room at the Houghton house to be accredited. I communicated this to everyone.

Sadly I heard that the accreditation was only done after Oprah,

Forest, Gayle and others had had to pose for countless photos with the protocol people. It was revolting. I could not imagine that Madiba would have agreed to this type of treatment of his friends. I would never, ever, have subjected Madiba to this kind of treatment, yet here his friends were expected to pose for photos with fans in order to smooth their way through accreditation. In nineteen years of serving Madiba I had never, not once, asked any of his guests for photos with them. I had never asked Madiba to take a photo with me. Photos were taken in the course of working with him or he would sometimes ask me to join him when a picture with guests was taken and only on a few occasions some of his friends asked that I be included in a photo. But that was precisely one of the reasons why I lasted with him for so long. I never allowed familiarity or opportunity for photographs to distract from how he wanted me to behave. At one point he asked whether it was the case that I didn't want to have my photograph taken with him and I laughed it off and had to assure him that was not the case. This behaviour by them now was totally unacceptable to me.

I eventually arrived in the Eastern Cape on the Friday, together with Josina, some of her family and friends, via the private plane organized by Faizal and Malaika Motlekar. When we landed in Umtata I noticed how lush and green the hills were. It had been raining heavily and still continued to rain, which is something that would have really pleased Madiba and I so wish he could have seen it. He was happy when the soils of his soul were adequately watered and became fertile for grazing and farming. In an interview with Robyn Curnow from CNN, one of his grandsons told the story of how he and Madiba were sitting in the living room of his Qunu house and Madiba urged Mbuso, his young grandson, to go and run naked in the rain. Madiba said that's what he used to do when he was young. He loved life unconditionally despite what life handed him time and time again. Just imagine eighty years ago – a young Nelson Mandela frolicking in these same hills. Naked, unencumbered by the past and unknowing about his future. Perhaps the rain was a fitting way for him to come home.

349

Driving from the airport I was reminded how I made him smile whenever we were in Qunu and I greeted him by his circumcision name: 'Ahhh Dalibhunga!' The Afrikaans girl was greeting him in his Xhosa name; he was entertained by that and it usually brought about the biggest smile on his face.

We passed a few cattle and I reminisced about his adoration for his cattle. We used to drive on his farm, going out to see the cows and bulls and secretly I think he would have loved to have been a big cattle farmer. He often told me that a man's wealth in their tradition was measured by the number of cattle he had. He had between thirty and sixty cattle at any given point and I would respond: 'Oh Khulu so you are very rich!' and he would laugh.

His easy accessibility, his natural affinity with people was what I remembered. My main role during my years with him was to be his protector – the shield – the person who had to protect him from being smothered with love by others. His openness seemed at odds with the closed nature of the funeral arrangements. It confused me, it saddened me and it even embarrassed me.

The world's media had descended on Qunu. I was reminded how fond Madiba was of journalists and seeing them made me think that he would really be impressed to see so many of them in Qunu and how boastful he would be about his little village to them. He used to call them often, whenever a journalist wrote an article about him that was critical in nature. He would invite them to a meal and at first they assumed they were in trouble for being critical of him. But they soon learned after arrival at his house for a meal that he merely wanted to engage with them to get an understanding of their criticism. The journalists would often leave not having changed their minds, but Madiba didn't attempt to change their minds. He would have an informed opinion after having engaged with them, and even though he occasionally changed an opinion by offering correct information, they never parted feeling hostile. Seeing so many familiar faces in Qunu made me think of many such occasions and how he courted them with his charm. He loved sharing information with the media and appreciated the fact that they had a job to do.

This set-up was so different – the media being kept away and information withheld as a show of where power resided.

On Sunday we woke up at 4 a.m. to get ready for the funeral. I tried to manoeuvre a plan to get George Bizos to the house so that he didn't have to get into a bus. He is old and struggles to walk. He is frail. Ironically again, one of Madiba's ex-bodyguards, Piet Erwee, helped us to get him there, fighting us through the roadblocks and police checkpoints, without any accreditation himself but paying his last dues to Madiba. Piet was employed by Rory Steyn, his ex-police commander and one of Madiba's close confidant bodyguards from his Presidential days. Rory now has a very successful security company and his story is another of how you become successful as long as you serve your passion in life.

Arriving in Qunu it was only proper that George Bizos would go to the house and greet the family. We entered through the kitchen door as they locked the front door and refused us access. Makazi-we's daughter was standing on the inside shouting that the door would not be opened for anyone no matter who. I led Advocate Bizos and his son through the kitchen door at the back and through the dining room. Makaziwe passed and barely greeted us. As Madiba became more frail it was clear that they didn't approve of his choices. Not in staff and not in friends. And such was George Bizos. Maka-ziwe had challenged his appointment as trustee to one of Madiba's trusts earlier in the year and a public mud-slinging followed in which Makaziwe's daughter insulted and belittled Advocate Bizos. None of us were welcomed in the house.

We greeted her in a civilized manner and she walked into the kitchen. In the kitchen I could see her making a determined turn around and she stormed back into the dining room. 'Zelda we don't want you people here. Now that Uncle George is here, he can stay but we don't want you people here.' I responded by saying: 'I am happy to oblige Makaziwe if someone could just give us direction of what to do with people like Uncle George.' She repeated her instructions: 'We don't want you people in the house.' Isaac was watching and I turned around and left. Uncle George and his son walked past her and went into the lounge where others gathered.

Shortly after us Tokyo Sexwale, an ex-colleague of Madiba's from Robben Island who had served in Madiba's government, arrived and he was also shown the door. Tokyo's appointment by Madiba as trustee on the same trust that George Bizos served was also questioned by Makaziwe; he too was aligned with the wrong side of the family. These people were appointed by Madiba to serve on his trusts for a very good reason. When he became ill and unable to speak for himself the family started challenging his decisions and it was clear that once he was gone, they were going to do that on all fronts. It was also clear that if you were friends or aligned with anyone outside Makaziwe or Ndileka's camp you were not welcome in the house. I was not the only one to be chased out.

I found it difficult and emotionally challenging to reconcile his last years and what we had experienced for sixteen-odd years with what was happening now. To say it was in complete contrast would be putting it mildly.

Qunu is a valley-like community sunk between the majestic mountains in the Eastern Cape. Madiba's farm itself is small but in comparison to that of his neighbours quite lavish. Although the house he and Mrs Machel built in the early 2000s is in stark contrast to the living standards of the surrounding area it is modest in comparison to those of people of similar or close stature. The huge dome erected for his funeral first shocked me. It wasn't just a big tent but a dome, probably the size of a small aircraft hanger. I heard that the dome had been stored away for years to have it ready when the 'life event' occurred. It had been bought from Germany, I learned, and thought that it was probably only Madiba's funeral that could get away with something like that being bought from Europe; the unions would have argued that it could have been a perfect job-creation opportunity to have it made in South Africa. Many years ago we had bought t-shirts in bulk from the East for one of Madiba's campaigns and got a good lashing from the media and public for not supporting the South African textile industry. I guess the funeral was different. From the house to the dome was probably a good 1.5 km. The road that connected the house to the dome was a simple gravel road. To take either the front road or the back road towards the dome one got a pretty good sense of the size of the property and you saw the cows Madiba was so proud of.

I started making my way up to the dome where the funeral was to take place and simply kept Madiba in my thoughts and heart. He would not have approved of the fact that I had been asked to leave the house. He would not have approved of the ostentatiousness of this huge dome on his farm. A few years ago when he was able to take decisions and voice them himself he insisted I be in the house with them for the final ceremony when Makgatho passed away. Now I was being excluded because he could no longer insist on my presence. On occasion Madiba chased people out of the house, as recently as in December 2009 and regardless that I joined in trying to convince him to be more lenient to them; his voice had been silenced.

In these trying times, I had to remember some of Madiba's greatest lessons . . . my relationship was with him and no one can ever remove that from me. People die, relationships don't die and my relationship with Madiba will never die.

Arriving at the dome – where more people were gathering, shepherded in buses from Umtata, almost an hour's drive away – I heard that Oprah's bus had not been allowed onto the premises. We had had great difficulty obtaining landing rights for her plane in Umtata as only heads of state's planes were allowed to land there. It was understandable – until I heard that exceptions had been made already for other planes to land there too. The bus she took from the Umtata airport was not accredited to enter the farm and she was offloaded at the main house. She had to walk up to the dome on the dusty roads, past the cows. Rory, Madiba's ex-bodyguard, managed to get a minister's car to transport her and her delegation the rest of the way to the dome. She had visited Qunu twice before and the last time she joined us and hosted a Christmas children's party for more than 25,000 children in the village and surrounding area. Madiba had also asked her to build a school once, as part of his school-building project, and she established the Oprah Winfrey Academy close to Johannesburg. One of a kind in private schools in South Africa. Madiba had great appreciation for her and her support for underprivileged children in South Africa. He was also entertained by her wealth and repeatedly told people about her generosity to buy all the attendees at her show cars. He would end the sentence with: 'can you imagine that?'

While Oprah, Stedman, Forest and Gayle were making their way to the dome, I tried to find seats for Advocate Bizos, Richard Branson and others. Whenever someone arrived at the door that I knew I ushered them to an area where Bridgette Radebe and her brother Patrice kept open seats for Madiba's friends.

Mum was still in the main house, getting ready to accompany Madiba up to the dome and his final resting place. I could see on footage the day before that she was brutally exhausted. They were preparing Madiba for his final journey up the hill on his beloved farm in Qunu.

Once I had managed to seat all the guests I felt responsible for I couldn't find a seat myself, unless I was prepared to go and sit among the military people who were part of the proceedings. I was too ashamed because I was so emotional so I left and found a spot on the grass outside to sit close to Robyn Curnow, my friend who was reporting for CNN from inside the premises. From there I could hear the proceedings on a SABC speaker and see visuals on a close-by screen attached to the back of a satellite truck. The hearse arrived – with Madiba's coffin on the back of a gun carriage, draped in the South African flag. There was more irony. I was outside and even though I felt shut out, there were very few people left outside and it strangely provided another almost personal opportunity to say goodbye. When the military procession moved past, I couldn't breathe from the sobbing. At first I saw Mandla in the front of the military vehicle, still guarding his grandfather, and after Madiba passed Mum's car followed and I could see her through the window. I so badly wanted to hold her to give her comfort, but also for her to hold me. Madiba was afforded full military honours for his funeral, which meant that all or any ceremony and protocol from the military applied to his burial.

A furore about Archbishop Desmond Tutu's attendance at the funeral played off in the media 48 hours before the event. He was shunned as no proper arrangements were communicated to him. When he arrived at the dome with Trevor Manuel I could see his own pain and sadness. I hugged him for as long as time allowed. I wanted to console him but I also wanted consolation from him. Madiba was so fond of him.

A stranger, a black man, saw me shivering from pain and walked up to me, put his arms around me and said 'Zelda don't worry *sisi* [sister], it will get better.' I felt like collapsing in his arms but I knew that I had to compose myself and thanked him with a hug. Weeks after I tried to recall this man's face, tried to remember who it was and whether I could trace him again. I wanted to thank him again for doing that. It wasn't just a hug and trying to console me. He genuinely cared. It touched my inner core when strangers, black people reached out to me in this way. How far we had come!

The service started and the stage was beautifully decorated with ninety-five big candles, one for each of Madiba's years. I should have been able to just pay my respects and pray. But I was worried about admin again – and particularly about how we would get Oprah and her delegation back to the house. Rich and famous and people I've never seen or heard of in nineteen years were given accreditation to the burial site. Only 400 of the 4,000 guests were accredited to go to the burial site. I was shown what the accreditation cards looked like but I was not given one.

Ahmed Kathrada, Madiba's long-time friend from prison, delivered the most moving speech during the ceremony. He paid tribute to Madiba and said Madiba had joined the ANC A-team in heaven. He was so emotional and it was sad to see him like that. Kathy, as we fondly refer to him, had been friends with Madiba since before his imprisonment. They spent eighteen years together on Robben Island in addition to the time in Pollsmoor after being moved from the island.

Soon the ceremony was over – speech after speech. Some of the speakers were touching while others wanted to make sure they basked for the last time in Madiba's bright light. The only thing that really reminded me of Madiba was the song sung by children. 'Roli-hlahla Mandela' is a song written to Madiba, and Mrs Machel asked Mbongeni Ngema, a prominent South African artist, to record the song with children the week prior to the funeral. Madiba's infectious smile was vivid in my mind when I heard it. I could so well imagine his liveliness at the sound of these voices. But that was all gone now. This and the 95 candles in the dome depicting Madiba's life were the only requests from Madiba's widow that were adhered to.

While waiting for the proceedings to come to an end I read the obituary in great detail. None of the Mandela legacy institutions that Madiba personally created were mentioned in any obituary, tribute or vote of thanks. As if they never existed.

People started making their way to the burial site. People walked past me, many of Madiba's friends and of course all the family. Some of Madiba's friends asked whether I was not going to the site and I told them that I had not been accredited. Some of Madiba's friends wanted me to put up a fight to get access. I knew that I had said my goodbyes. My relationship with Madiba was not defined by whether I stood next to his grave or not. It was way, way more than that. Rory Steyn, who was looking after Oprah during the funeral, joined me and Robyn outside. Robyn, Rory and I, three white South Africans whose lives had been changed by Madiba's leadership and personal love, stood together and watched the proceedings on the screen. My relationship with Madiba was not about being at his side at key moments in his life. It was defined in the ordinary moments I spent with him. Rory, Robyn and I held each other and knew this was a moment in history where we were on the frontlines. Saying goodbye in person to a great man in our respective ways, our Khulu, our Tata and our Madiba.

We were standing watching the proceedings on the screen and when the twenty-one-gun salutes were fired it sounded like a barrage of tears into the sky. And the fly-past, helicopters with South

African flags flying in unison, low over the hills of Qunu, followed by the fighter jets. The sound of those machines shuddered through my body. It finally sank in. It was over. I burst into loud tears, sobbing on Robyn's shoulder while Rory was holding both of us, consoling us while we shivered from pain. The tears cascaded down my face again. Robyn was not on air at the time and she was just being my friend, but unknown to both of us, her microphone was still connected live. My gasping sobs were heard on CNN across the world as pictures of his last journey were aired. Robyn says the studio in Atlanta shouted in her earpiece, 'The microphone is hot!' She knew my tearful breakdown had been broadcast to millions of people. I didn't. At the same time she felt the dilemma of letting me go. She knew she couldn't let go of me and held on even tighter, consoling me. A few minutes later she stepped back to the camera and described the scene around her and mentioned the powerful sense of departure and sadness, her eyes clearly red from crying with us. She described how I, Madiba's longtime assistant, had burst into tears, explaining to all those listening who had been the person crying. It was only two weeks later that she told me what had happened and what she had reported. I didn't feel betrayed. I needed my two friends Rory and Robyn to hold my heart together from falling apart. I felt I wanted to share my pain with the world and unknown to me I had, but at the same time I have never felt so lonely. I was haunted by loss and the emptiness made me convulse.

They were still busy at the gravesite when I started making my way back to Madiba's house. I had to get home. First to the hotel and then I was determined to get back to Johannesburg as fast as possible. I couldn't take any more and I needed to be home, alone with my dogs. I'd walked halfway down to the house when one of Madiba's bodyguards, Sam, gave me lift in a golf cart. I cannot imagine what I looked like but as we drove past familiar faces, people who had served Madiba in different capacities noticed me on the back of the cart, stopped the cart and had a few words. I felt like a bag of washed out clothes. I had no energy left in my body and I no longer controlled any of my emotions. Old ANC colleagues of Madiba's who were all sidelined or withheld from going to the burial site stopped me to chat. I was tempted to go into the house to have a last look at the empty yellow chair in Madiba's lounge but I was rushing to find transport and decided that today was not a good day to expose myself to more sorrow. I knew I would be back soon.

By the time I left, I had managed to arrange transport for Oprah and her delegation from the dome back to the house where they would find their bus. Richard Branson was sorted and I left transport behind for Advocate Bizos. There was nothing else I could fix. I had made sure everyone was OK and it was time to let go. I left for the hotel and got into bed with my funeral clothes still on. I was depleted in every possible way. I slept for two hours and when I woke I learned that my dearest colleague, Yase, had managed to change my flight to enable me to return to Johannesburg the same night. He just grasped that I wanted silence and solitude and pulled out all stops to change my flight. And so I drove the 260 km in rain to East London where I got the plane back to Johannesburg. I got home after 1 a.m. and it took me some time to fall asleep.

The next few days were spent on paying accounts. The funeral was merely ten days before Christmas and suppliers had to pay staff before the holidays.

I had the rest of my root canal work done, attended Douw Steyn's sixty-first birthday dinner, which was somewhat of a sombre affair as he was also ill at the time, and had some other physical problems attended to that manifested themselves as a result of all the stress of the previous week. In June I thought I had sustained an injury during a gym session at around the same time Madiba was hospitalized. I constantly had a pain in my hip and sometimes it crossed over down into my knee. No matter how I stretched or how many painkillers I took, I couldn't get rid of the pain. On 19 December I woke up in the morning thinking that I had become paralysed. Both my legs were numb. I could feel the same pain in my hip as before but my upper legs were both numb. I called a physio friend back from holiday to help me as I was desperate. After much treatment she managed to get rid of all the spasms I had been walking around with since June. As was the case over the years, whenever Madiba suffered physical distress, the stress and worry that caused me also manifested itself physically in my body.

Finally on Friday, 20 December I made my way back to Umtata. I wanted to go and say my last goodbye and pay my respects at Madiba's gravesite. In the days prior to this trip I had wondered much about the meaning of life, about mortality, and even though we did not discuss it much, as he considered it a very personal matter, what Madiba really believed about life and death. We tried to shelter Mrs Machel from as much as possible over the preceding two weeks but she knew I hadn't been there when he was buried. I was not the only one who wasn't allowed at the burial. Meme, the housekeeper, and Betty, one of the household assistants, had also been pulled out of a row and were prevented from going to the grave, or even being in the foyer of Madiba's house when the casket Arrived from Johannesburg, yet they too had been loyally serving him for years.

The hills of Qunu were back to the slow pace of life. The dome had been removed and sprinklers watered the newly planted grass where the dome was previously erected. The cows and goats were roaming freely as before, unaffected by the change in life. I went straight to the farm to greet Mrs Machel. This would be the first time I had seen her since the Thursday before the burial.

I wanted to know specifics from her about his burial. Did he go in one of his favourite shirts? She said he didn't. It wasn't one of his favourites. He went with some of his personal items, some of the few things that were so dear to him. I asked about his walking stick. An ivory stick he got from Douw Steyn made from the tusks of a bull elephant that had died on Douw's farm Shambala, where Douw had built a house for Madiba to use to write the sequel of *Long Walk to Freedom*. Sadly but not surprisingly I was told that the stick had not been found. I took time with Mum talking about the stick, tracking its journey to the house in Qunu and then to Houghton where we last saw it. Neither of us had the energy or the emotional strength to start looking for the stick and I put her mind to rest that the stick will eventually one day surface, and hopefully one of us will still be alive. Or someone will read this and discover it perhaps. It is clearly marked 'To Madiba, from Douw Steyn' and one of its kind. A solid white ivory walking stick. Madiba should have left with it.

Driving back after 10 p.m. from Qunu to Umtata that night, the most beautiful moon rose over the hills of Umtata. The brightest orange moon I had ever seen. It dawned upon me that here this white Afrikaner girl was driving from Qunu to Umtata all by herself. Madiba would have insisted that security accompany me, being concerned for my safety. Thinking about that made me smile. But I kept my eye on the moon and realized that he had removed all fear from me. I had finally grown up. Almost twenty years ago I wouldn't have dreamt of driving this road by myself at night. But the Transkei, as it was formerly known, gets under your skin. The place becomes part of you. I was fearful of so much twenty years ago – of life, of black people, of this black man and the future of South Africa – and now I was no longer persuaded or influenced by mainstream thinking or fears. I was my own person. Madiba had given me peace and freedom too. He had freed me from the shackles of my own fears. He not only liberated the black man but the white man too. I felt light, free and thankful that my teacher was Nelson Mandela. As much as I grieved for him, I had gained so much and I spoke to him in the car on my way back to Umtata, keeping my eye on the bright moon.

We ended up going to the grave on Sunday morning. We were scheduled to leave around midday. Shortly after 8 a.m. Mum, Josina, Meme, Betty and a few other workers, security and I drove up to the burial site. We had ordered fresh flowers the previous day and we started cleaning the graves of Madiba and his three children. We were quiet and the mood was solemn. The tombstones all had the family crest on them, that which had become familiar to me through its appearance on the House of Mandela wines. We removed the old flowers, bunches of white flowers that had been laid on his coffin and placed around the tombstone, orchids and roses. Now scattered in the wind and damaged by the sun. We replaced the flowers with fresh ones, after which Mum called us together and she asked Meme to pray. Meme said a beautiful prayer and I was shuddering as we were holding hands during it. Meme prayed in Sotho as well, during which my thoughts went off to Afrikaans prayers and my mind wandered, trying to send a message to Madiba. I thanked him again and told him like so many other times how much I appreciated him but that, most importantly, he should remember that I love him.

Shortly after noon it was wheels up from the Umtata airport. It was the longest fifty-five-minute flight from Umtata to Johannesburg of our lives. It was all over. Final. And the next chapter would be harder. I knew that a battle was brewing over the will and Madiba's estate and control over his legacy. It was like they say, a sign of the times. I knew that it was also time for me to start moving away. My duty was done. The last days and months reminded me of the story of Tolstoy. Ironically there were a lot of similarities to the life of that great Russian writer whose work Madiba also loved so much. How crowds gathered before his death, but also the contest for control over his legacy and his estate.

I was seated closest to the door in the small aircraft, facing the back of the plane. It was much better and more convenient than a commercial plane but we all felt somehow exposed, naked, as there was nowhere to hide our emotions. I could feel Mum's pain as I watched her breaking down in tears when our plane slowly made its way through the thick clouds. And eventually we all just broke down, crying in our seats. Me, Mum, Josina, Celina – Mrs Machel's sister-in-law – Betty and Cordier the bodyguard. No one spoke during the flight.

Mum is normally so stoic, so strong. But breaking through the clouds, flying away from him, leaving him alone we all shared a sense of abandoning him, deserting him. The only thing we never wanted him to feel and the one thing I promised him I would never do. But what do we do now? He is home and heroes never die. He will be present in those beautiful hills for ever and I now know he will be even more powerful in death than he was in life.

His image, his legacy must be protected.

I don't know what I will do for the rest of my life. His prolonged illness had forced me to grow up. It has taught me some of the most valuable lessons of life and showed me what not to expect of people. Madiba did not only unify a country once again even through his illness and in death, but he taught us more than we ever bargained for. I will allow life to take its course with me and I now know that I will always be at the place where I am supposed to be at any given point in time. I have no plans other than annually honouring him through Bikers for Mandela Day. Maybe I will find another job and perhaps I will find a man to spend time with, one who knows and will respect that a piece of my heart has already been taken . . . given to an old black man who was once my people's enemy and is now lying, like an ancient King, deep in the soil of South Africa's golden hills of Qunu.

We will see him in every sunset and every sunrise. We must keep looking for him. He will look after us if we remember his lessons.

And slowly we climbed above the clouds, reaching the sunshine and the warm light of the African sun shining through the windows of the plane, eventually heating up our faces and drying away the tears. Whatever happens now, I know we did our best.

Tot weersiens Khulu! Until we meet again.

To be continued . . .

Acknowledgements

I need a separate book to thank all the people who have contributed to or played a role in my life over the last forty-three years. I may forget many names here and in that case I apologize in advance. In a very strange way, even the people who I felt hurt by played a role in shaping me. Every person that crossed my path blessed me irrespective of the role they played in my life.

I pay tribute to people who have suffered and sacrificed paving the way for me to have the freedoms that I now enjoy in this beautiful country of ours.

'I am because you are.' I thank my parents Des and Yvonne la Grange. I love you more than you will ever comprehend. I don't show it often and indeed I am strange being, but I hope you know how much I appreciate your unconditional love and support. You laid the foundation for discipline, principle, the morals and values I cling to today. Commitment, loyalty and determination I inherited from you. I know what it is to love because of you. To my brother Anton and his partner Rick Venter, my second brother, thank you for always being there, and if no one else could be trusted, you stood firm. Thank you for the encouragement, unwavering support and taking care of me. You are my rock.

To the rest of my family, the La Grange's and Strydoms thank you.

To Maretha Slabbert, my long-serving and -suffering colleague, thank you for sticking it out with me. We shared the best times but also the worst. I will love you for ever.

To my long-time friend Jennifer Preller, for your support and motherhood. I remain grateful to have a friend care for me the way you do. Thank you for pushing me beyond what I thought were my limits and for constantly adjusting my attitude and making me strong.

The godparents to my dogs, Johrne and Alet van Huyssteen, I cannot imagine life without you. You lived in my house at one stage more than I did. Thanks for being there at the drop of a hat to care for my house, my dogs and for me and sometimes picking up the pieces. I cannot wait for us to sit on the porch of the old age home together.

To the friend that kept my mind sane and clear Dr Ralf Brummerhof. Thank you for being there to count on, day or night, and even the knee jerk exercises.

To Robyn Curnow and Kim Norgaard and their children Freya and Hella, thank you for an instant family and an enormously privileged and trusted friendship we share.

To Douw and Carolyn Steyn, thank you for loving me and caring the way you do.

For guidance, protection and invaluable wisdom, thank you my pact: Minee Hendricks, Marli Hoffman, Ann-Lee Murray, Lori McCreary, Anele Mdoda, Sara Latham, Dianne Broodryk.

To some very special friends, some associates and a special breed of people thank you for blessing my life in one way or another with your kindness, support or even just consideration: Constant and Hane Visser, Rian van Heerden, Gareth Cliff, Doug Band, Jon Davidson, Justin Cooper, Matt McKenna, Marius van Vuuren, Ian Douglas, Lucy Matthew, Catriona Garde, Rory Steyn, Elaine Saloner, Roddy Quinn, Kim Mari, Basetsana Khumalo, Johanna Mukoki, Rebs Mogoba, Mashadi Motlana, De Villiers Pienaar, Wayne Hendricks, Henk Opperman, Adriaan and Cecile Basson, George Ludeke, Waldimar Pelser, Pauli Massyn, George Cohen, Jonathan Butt, Matthew and Tracy Barnes, Dan Ntsala, Dot Field, Greg Coetzee, Rob and Amanda Flemming, Libby Moore, Jovita Machel, Patricia Machel, Lisa Halliday, Cora Forsmann, Tracy Davenport, Silvia Viljoen, Attie van Wyk, Artem and Sayora

Gregorian, Huma Abedin, Sonja and Coetzee Zietsman, Hannah Richert, Deon Broodryk, Driki van Zyl, Hein and Helmien Bezuidenhout, Deon and Yzelle Stone, Angie Khumalo, Gretchen de Smit, Tinus and Chelyn Nel, Annie Laughton, Adrian Brink, Beverly Loxton, Jean Oelwang, Pieter de Waal and Janice Ferrante, Darren Scott, Donne Nicoll, John Carlin, Thato and Thabiso Sikwane, Niel and Andrea Viljoen, TJ, Louis, Tanya and Liz Steyn, Arpad Busson, Rina Broomberg, Ami Desai, Bryan and Jenine Habana, John and Roxy Smith, Schalk and Michelle Burger, Ryk Neethling, Tim and Clare Massey, Jerry and Prudence Inzerillo, Marilyn Karstaedt, Barbara Hogan, Jabu Mabuza, Graham Wood, Alan Knott-Craig, Mthobi Tyamzashe, Norman Adami, Don and Liz Gips, Rob and Lawri Brozin, Kevin Wilson, Dan Moyana, Karlheinz Koegel, Andrew Mlangeni, Olivia Machel, Frank Guistra, Susan Kriegler, Jogabeth and Esau Shilaluke, Oprah, Gayle King, Richard Friedland, HRH King Willem Alexander and HRH Queen Maxima, Former President Thabo and Mrs Zanele Mbeki, Former President F W de Klerk and Elita de Klerk, Deputy President Kgalema Motlanthe, Judge Themba Sangoni, Khanyi Dhlomo, Unathi Msengane, Shiela Sisulu, Faizal and Malaika Motlekar, Jonathan and Jennifer Oppenheimer, Nicky Oppenheimer, Gavin Koppel, Tommy Erasmus, Bongi Mkhabela, Charles Priebatch, the Kunene brothers, Cyril Ramaphosa, David Rockefeller, Leon Vermaak, Benny Gool, Roger Friedman, Mac Maharaj, Archbishop Thabo Mokgoba, Anant and Vaneshree Singh, Bishop Malusi Mpulwana, Robyn Farrell, Dr Mike Plit, Prince Bandar, Jolene Chait, Alfre Woodard, Roderick Spencer, Yusuf Surtee, Sharon Stone, Arki Busson, Charlize Theron, Advocate Thuli Madonsela, Zwelinzima Vavi, Nigel Badminton, Mauro Governato, Ben King, Whitey Basson, Wendy Luhabe, Bernard Krige, Vincent Maphai, Koos Bekker, Fred Phaswana, Ton Vosloo, Chris Liebenberg, Jeff and Bridgette Radebe, Roshann Paris, Joel Johnson, Amy Weinblum, Esmare Weideman, Denese Palm, Ayanda Dlodlo, Minister Nosiviwe Nqakula, Mayor David Dinkins, Forest and Keisha Whitaker, Prof. Jonathan

Jansen, Zindzi Mandela, Zoleka Mandela, Chief Zwelivelile Mandela, Chief Ngangomhlaba Matanzima, Bantu Holomisa, Patekile Holomisa, Zolani Mkiva, Phoebe Gerwel, Jessie Gerwel, Joseph Kruger. Zondwa Mandela, Mbuso Mandela, Andile Mandela, Zinhle Mandela, Luvuyo Mandela and Nandi Mandela.

To Archbishop Desmond Tutu, Ahmed Kathrada, President Clinton, Secretary Hillary Clinton, Chelsea Clinton, Bono, Ali, Sol and Andrea Kerzner, Naomi Campbell, Richard Branson, Peter Gabriel, Morgan Freeman, Peggy Dulany and their respective staff thank you for the love and support. My life had been blessed beyond measure having had the privilege to know you.

To Johann and Gaynor Rupert, thank you for loving and caring.

Frederick and Natasha Mostert, thank you for believing in me, inspiring me and the many many hours of legal consultation, support, guidance but also a privileged friendship.

Jeremy Gauntlett, thank you for your expert advice, support and consultation.

Bally Chuene, Michael Katz and Wim Trengove, Uncle George Bizos and family thank you for your support over the years and always making time and effort with me.

To Sacha and Christa Held, for allowing me to work on the book at their house in Mauritius, thank you.

To all my colleagues from the Presidency and the Nelson Mandela Foundation, some of whom I have lost contact with, thank you for your patience and tolerance. Special thanks to those I have worked closely with or over long periods of time: Lois Dippenaar, Virginia Engel, Alan Pillay, Vimla Naidoo, Elize Wessels, Morris Chabalala, Meshack Mochele, Joel Netshitenzhe, Tony Trew, Fink Haysom, Fanie Pretorius, William Smith, Gerrit Wissing, Marieta van Rensburg, Hayley Lyners, Pam Barron, Shaun Johnson, Heather Henriques, Lydia Baylis, Jackie Maggot, Meme Kgagare, Betty Dima, Xoliswa Ndoyiya, Gloria Nocanda, Yase Godlo, John Samuel, Achmat Dangor, Marianne Mudziwa, Denise Pillay, Shereen

Petersen, Buyi Sishuba, Thoko Mavuso, Gloria Jafta, Maeline Engelbrecht, Ruth Rensburg, Lee Davies, Tania Arrison, Elaine McKay, Marie Vos, Dudu Buthelezi, Jo Ditabo, Makano Morojelo, Merlyn van Voore, Mothomang Diaho, Ethel Arendze, Sandy Pillay, Ella Govender, Shirley Naidoo and anyone else I may have forgotten.

Thank you Prof Njabulo Ndebele, Chairman of the Nelson Mandela Foundation and the CEO of the Nelson Mandela Foundation, Sello Hatang, for your leadership and wisdom.

Special thanks to Verne Harris from the Centre of Memory at the Nelson Mandela Foundation for helping with factual correctness of this book and for your cameraderie.

All members of the Presidential Protection Unit and the South African Airforce who I worked closely with and that served with diligence, thank you.

The passionate and professional medical staff from the SANDF and private hospitals that cared for Madiba and Mum, thank you.

The staff of the 1st for Women Insurance Trust and Beeld Children's fund.

In memorium: My grandparents on both sides of the family, thank you. Special people who have passed on: Chief Justice Arthur Chaskalson, Oom Beyers Naude, Sean Chabalala, Mary Mxadana, John Reinders, Parks Mankahlana, Eric Molobi, Aggrey Klaaste, Dullah Omar, Marinus Daling, Miriam Makeba, Steve Tshwete, Uncle Raymond Mhlaba, Kader Asmal, Aunt Adelaide Tambo, Uncle Walter and Aunt Albertina Sisulu, Makgatho Mandela, Zenani Mandela Jnr.

Thank you my Prof., Jakes Gerwel. I still miss you every day. You enriched my life both professionally and personally in ways beyond comprehension and I am the most fortunate and blessed to have worked so closely with you. I will pay tribute to you with deep appreciation for the role you played in Madiba, Mum and my life, for the rest of my days.

Acknowledgements

My expert agent Jonny Geller, Kirsten Foster, Anna Davis and the team at Curtis Brown, thank you.

Helen Conford, Penelope Vogler, Richard Duguid, Rebecca Lee, Casiana Ionita and the team at Penguin, with deep appreciation for your enthusiasm and support. Also to Stephen Johnson, Frederik de Jager, Ellen van Schalkwyk and all at Penguin South Africa. And to Clare Ferraro, Wendy Wolf and all at Penguin US.

To all my friends in the media, too many to mention, thank you for your patience and understanding and even for our differences in opinion some times. Thank you for showing me how to grow a back bone.

To everyone who took my call when you no longer had to . . . THANK YOU!

To the unfamiliar face of the black man who comforted me at Madiba's funeral. If I don't get to thank you in person, this is it.

To everyone who spared me a smile, a hug or a word of encouragement over 19 years, I salute you with gratitude.

To Mrs Graça Machel, my second Mum and her children, Josina, Malenga and Samora, thank you for accepting me as your family and for caring for me like I am your own. I love you with the same unconditional love that Madiba taught us. I will remain forever indepted to you with love, care and appreciation and I will keep my promise to Madiba, but also willfully so, to care for you for as long as I live.

Lastly, but most importantly, thank you Khulu!